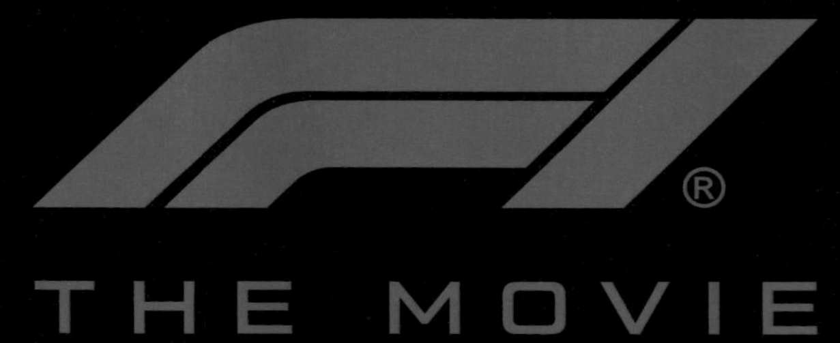
THE MOVIE

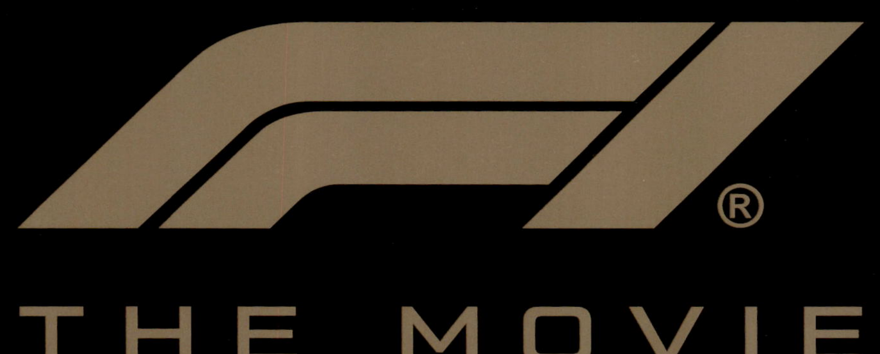

THE MOVIE

WRITTEN BY MARK SALISBURY

F1 FEATURES BY CHRIS MEDLAND

SET PHOTOGRAPHY BY SCOTT GARFIELD

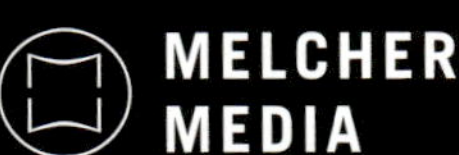

TABLE OF CONTENTS

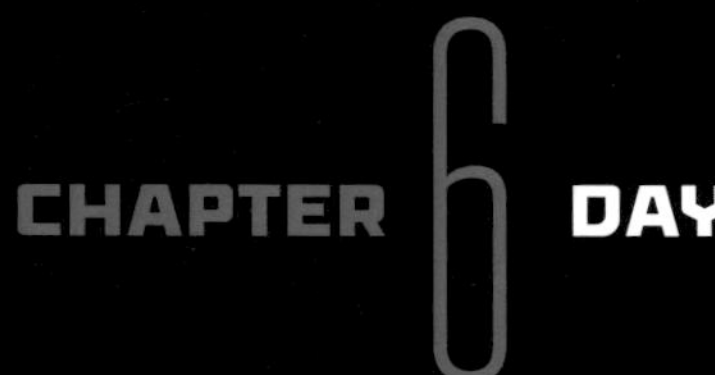

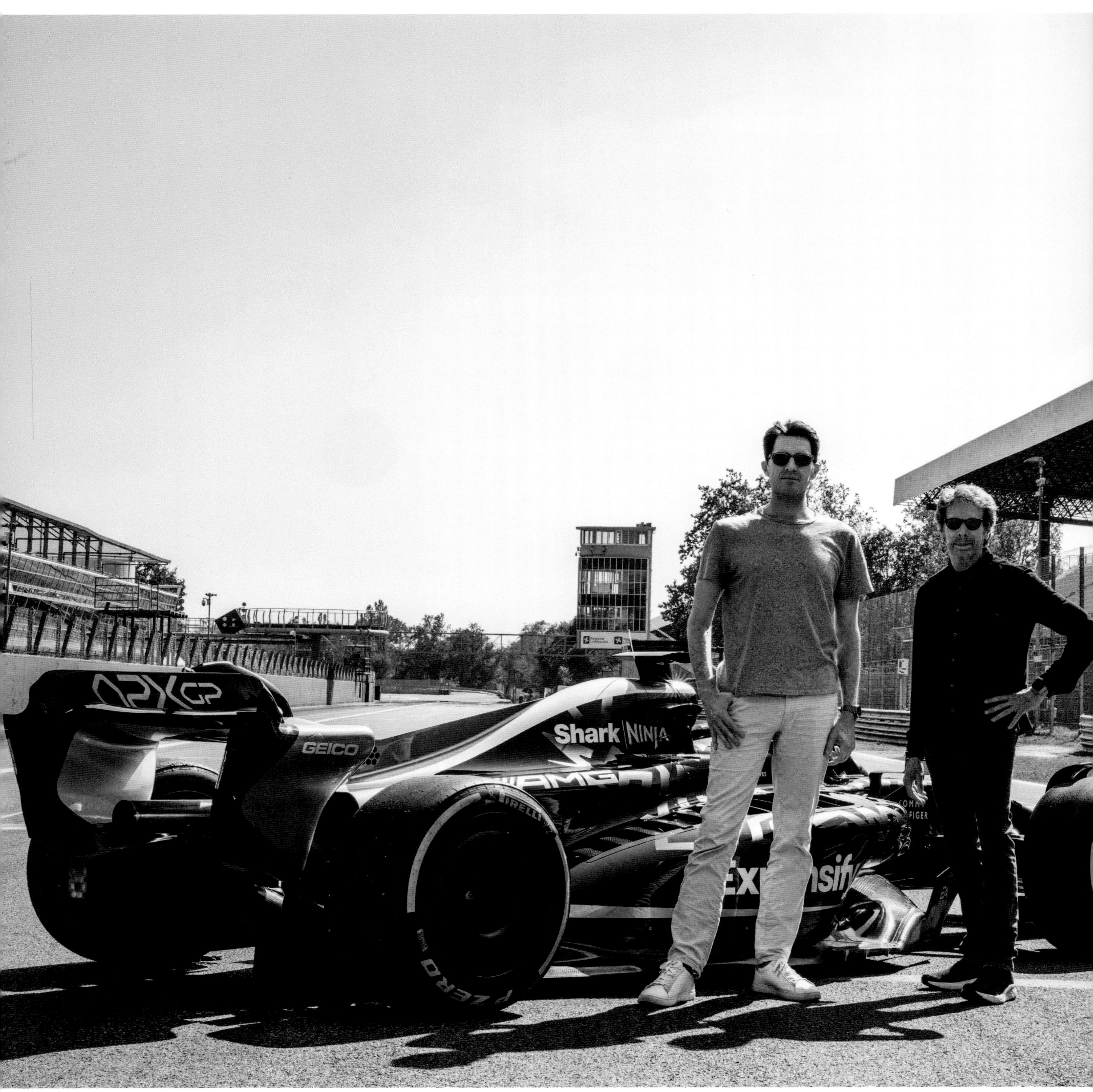
GEICO
Shark NINJA

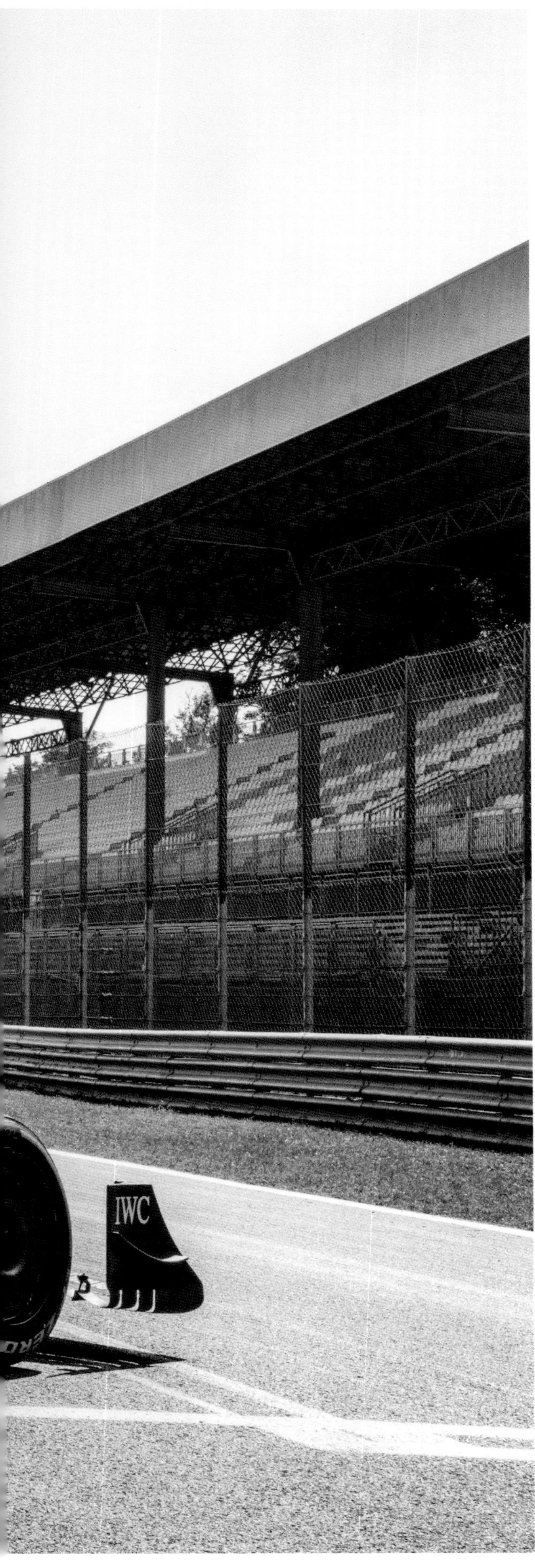

I've always wanted to make a racing movie. I came close a couple of times, as this book details, but nothing stuck. Looking back, I'm glad they didn't happen, because if any of those other films had come off, I wouldn't have made *F1*.

Formula One is the pinnacle of motorsport and I wanted to create a movie that warranted that. Not only that, I wanted to make the most authentic and realistic racing movie ever. One that put the viewer behind the wheel of a Formula One car as it accelerates around a racetrack at 200 miles per hour. I think we've succeeded, but I'll let the audience be the judge of that.

It takes an army to make a movie. And many thousands of people helped make *F1* a reality; a vast majority of whom are listed in the credits, but many who are not. My thanks go to the cast and crew of *F1*, to all the Formula One teams, drivers, team principals, mechanics, and marshals, to everyone at F1 Racing, the FIA, and NASCAR, as well as to the crowds at every race we filmed at.

But I'd like to single out a handful without whom *F1* wouldn't have been possible. Those five are Jerry Bruckheimer, Lewis Hamilton, Brad Pitt, Stefano Domenicali, and Toto Wolff, all of whom went above and beyond to help will this movie into existence. It's been a wild and fun ride. We made it for you. I hope you enjoy it.

Joseph Kosinski
Director/Producer

I love movies. They have been my life for more than fifty years, and during that time I've worked with some of the most talented filmmakers in front of and behind the camera.

When Joe pitched the idea for *F1* to me and we met with Lewis Hamilton for the first time, I knew we were onto a winner. Joe has an amazing sense of storytelling and is unparalleled in how he weaves characters and themes together. He did it with *Top Gun: Maverick* and that movie took over the country. And so, he was the perfect person to tell this F1 story. Alongside Claudio Miranda, our incredible cinematographer, Joe and I were determined to produce the most spectacular, exciting, and realistic car movie ever made, with visuals that get you in your stomach.

F1 took three years to make, and we all put everything into it, to bring you the best moviegoing experience possible. Brad, Joe, and I love making movies, and we love entertaining people. I think the result speaks for itself. We're all extremely proud of it. *F1* is emotional, authentic, and thrilling. Buckle up.

Jerry Bruckheimer
Producer

1 START YOUR ENGINES

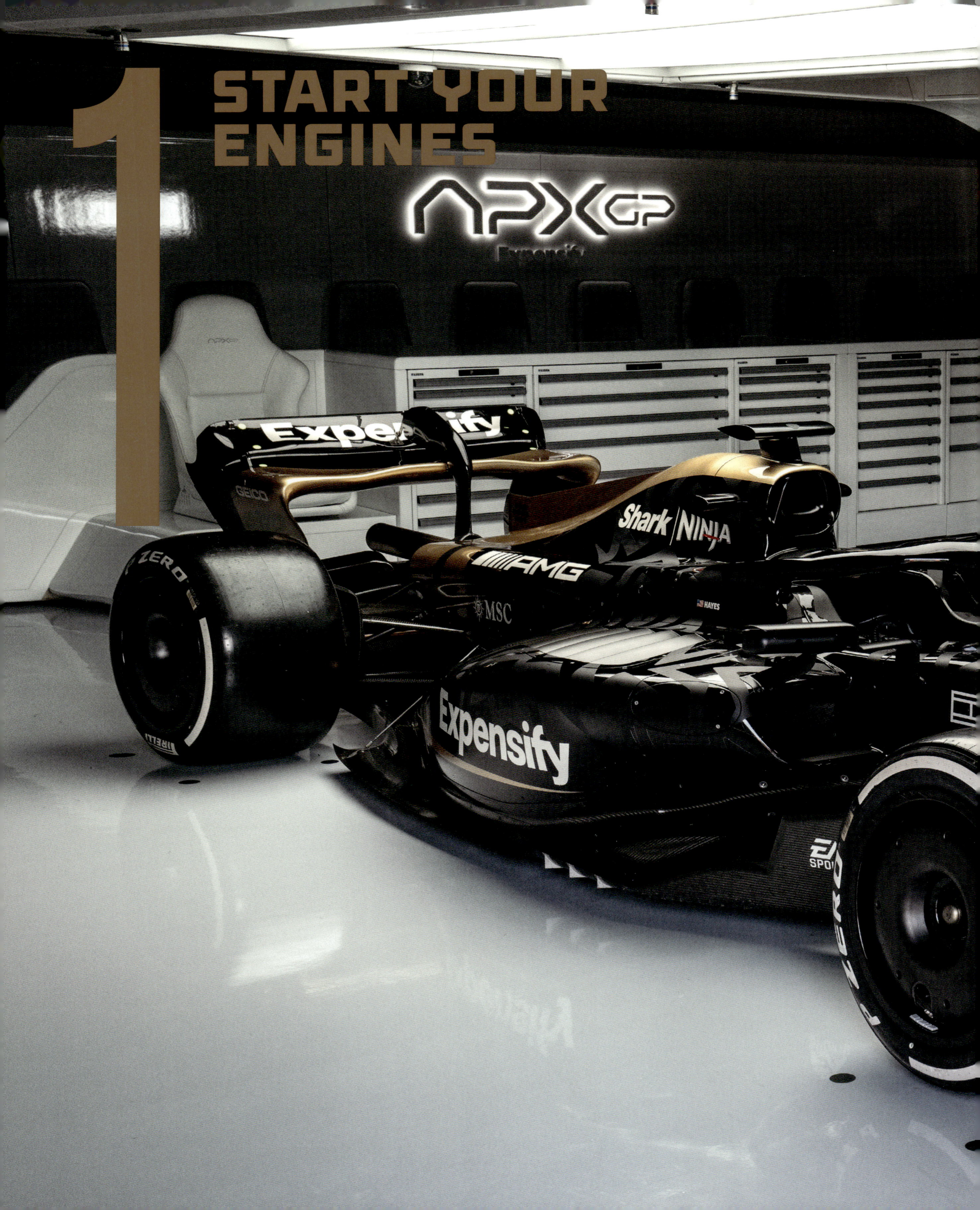

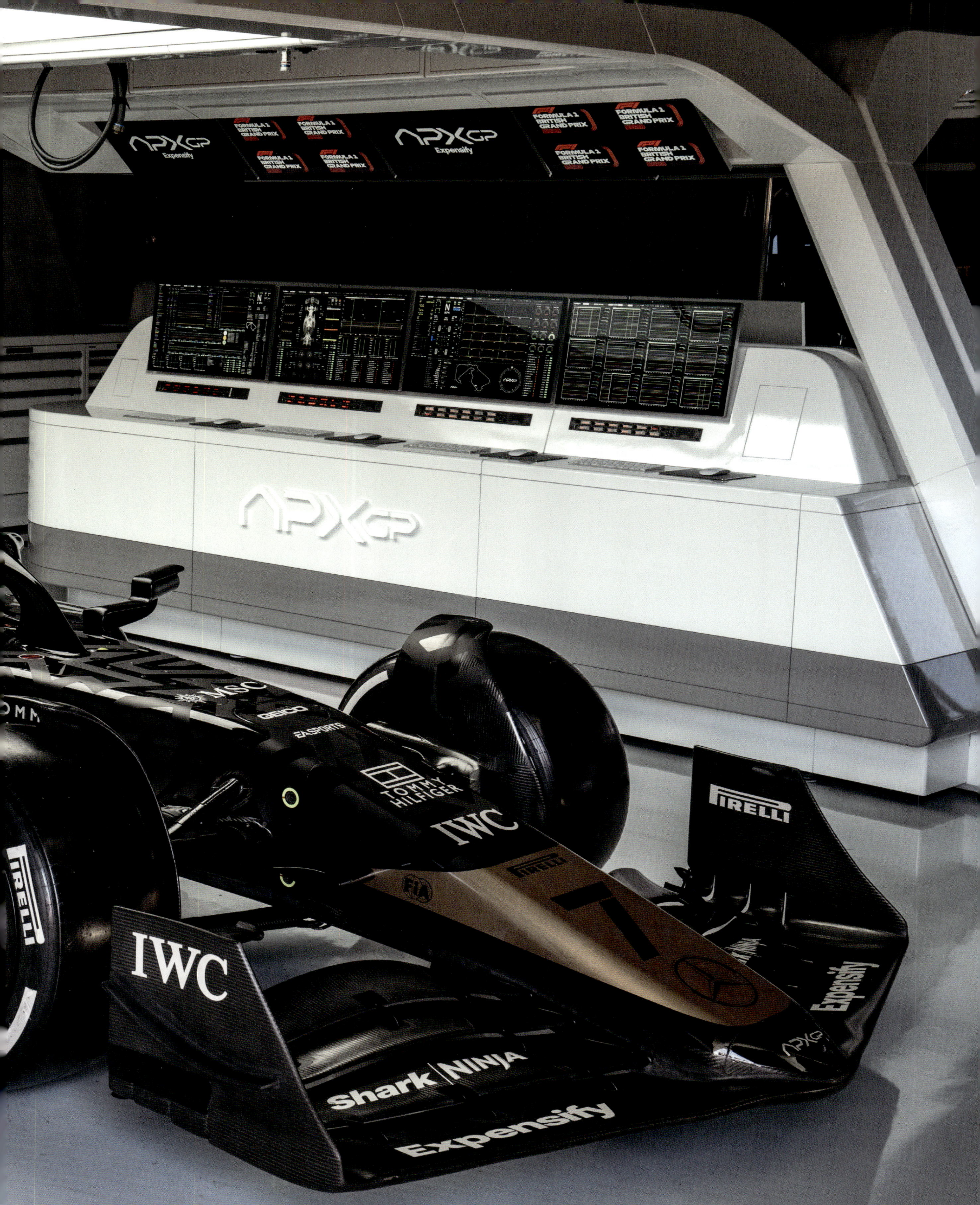

APXGP
Expensify
FORMULA 1 BRITISH GRAND PRIX
MSC
GEICO
EA SPORTS
TOMMY HILFIGER
IWC
PIRELLI
IWC
PIRELLI
Expensify
Shark NINJA
Expensify

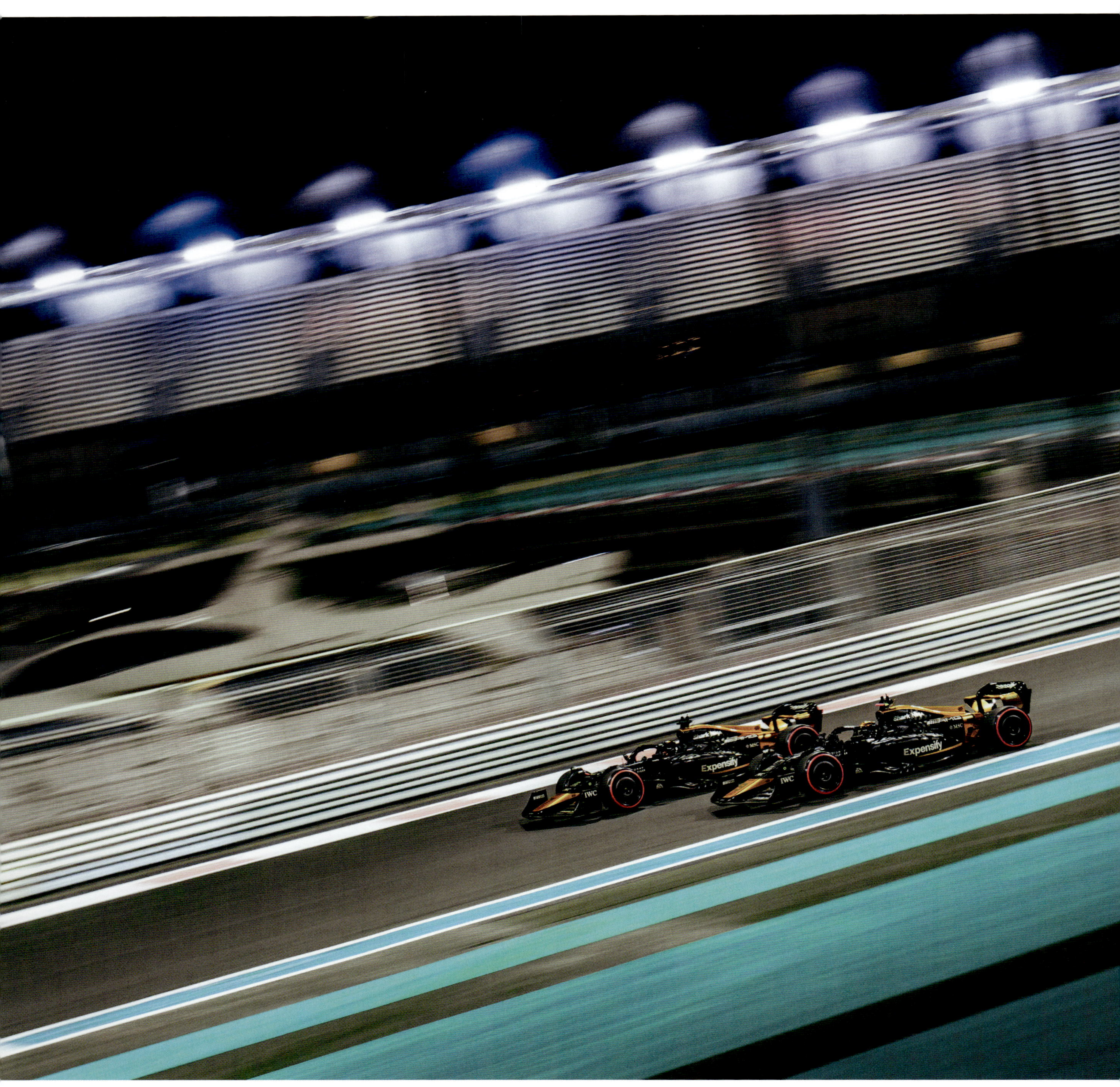

Above: Three APXGP cars built for the *F1* film speed down a track.

Right: Movies like *Grand Prix* (1966), *Le Mans* (1970), and *Days of Thunder* (1990) brought the next level of realism to racing films.

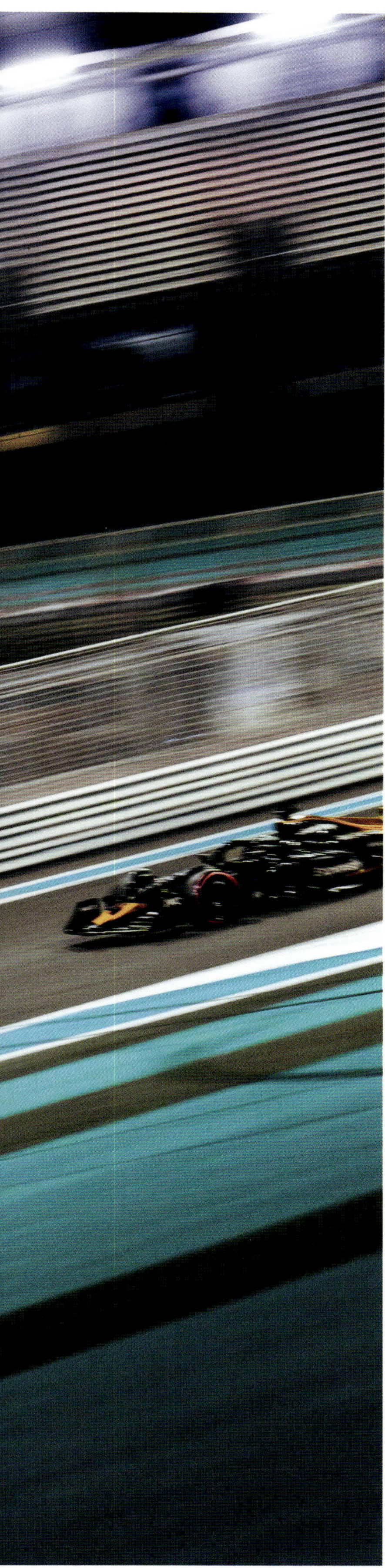

Fast cars and the movies have always gone hand in hand, dating back to the early days of the silent era, when filmmakers first trained their hand-cranked cameras at cars as they roared around racetracks, beginning with the 1913 comedy short *The Speed Kings*. As the decades whizzed by, and cars and camera technology improved, so did the quality of filmed, on-track action. *Burning Up*, released in 1930, was the first racing movie with sound; *The Crowd Roars*, set at the legendary Indianapolis Motor Speedway, saw James Cagney take part in the Indy 500. The film employed real-life drivers and was remade first in French in 1932 as *La Foule Hurle*, and again in 1939 as *Indianapolis Speedway*.

But racing movies reached a new level of excellence and realism with 1966's *Grand Prix* and 1970's *Le Mans*, both of which filmed at real races with cameras (and sometimes cameramen) strapped onto the cars. Directed by John Frankenheimer and set against the backdrop of the 1966 Formula One season, *Grand Prix* starred James Garner and Yves Montand as rival racers vying for the drivers' world title, with cameos from real life champions Graham Hill and Juan Manuel Fangio. Frankenheimer used large format Super Panavision cameras mounted to modified race cars to capture the drivers as they thundered around various circuits, including Monaco, Spa-Francorchamps, Zandvoort, Brands Hatch, and Monza.

Le Mans was a fictional drama shot in semidocumentary style on location in Le Mans in 1970 and during that season's 24-hour endurance race. Steve McQueen, who turned down *Grand Prix*, played a driver with the Gulf-Porsche team, risking life and machine in the ultimate test of speed, skill, and stamina. Despite little plot and even less dialogue, *Le Mans* was a visceral thrill ride, with its high-octane action and immersive race sequences, and, together with *Grand Prix*, set the benchmark for racing films for years to come. Indeed, in the four decades following, only a handful of movies—Tony Scott's NASCAR-set *Days of Thunder*, Ron Howard's *Rush*, and James Mangold's *Ford v Ferrari*—came close to capturing the adrenaline rush of real wheel-to-wheel racing.

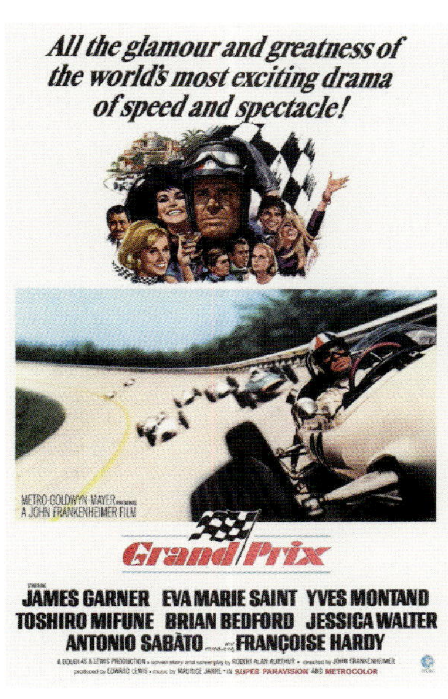

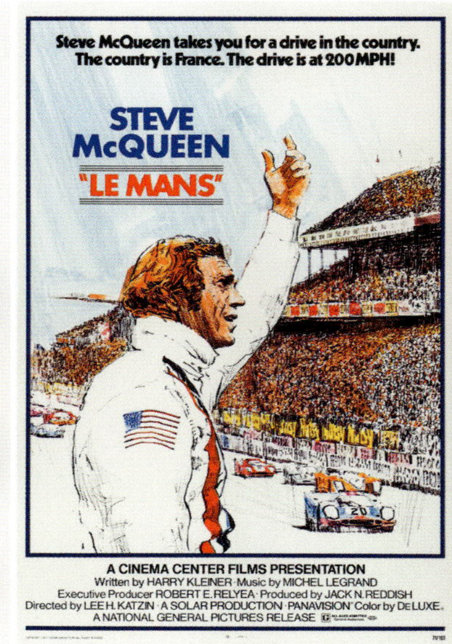

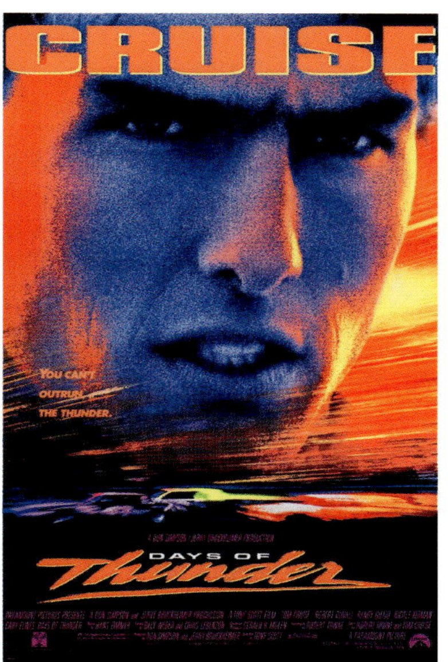

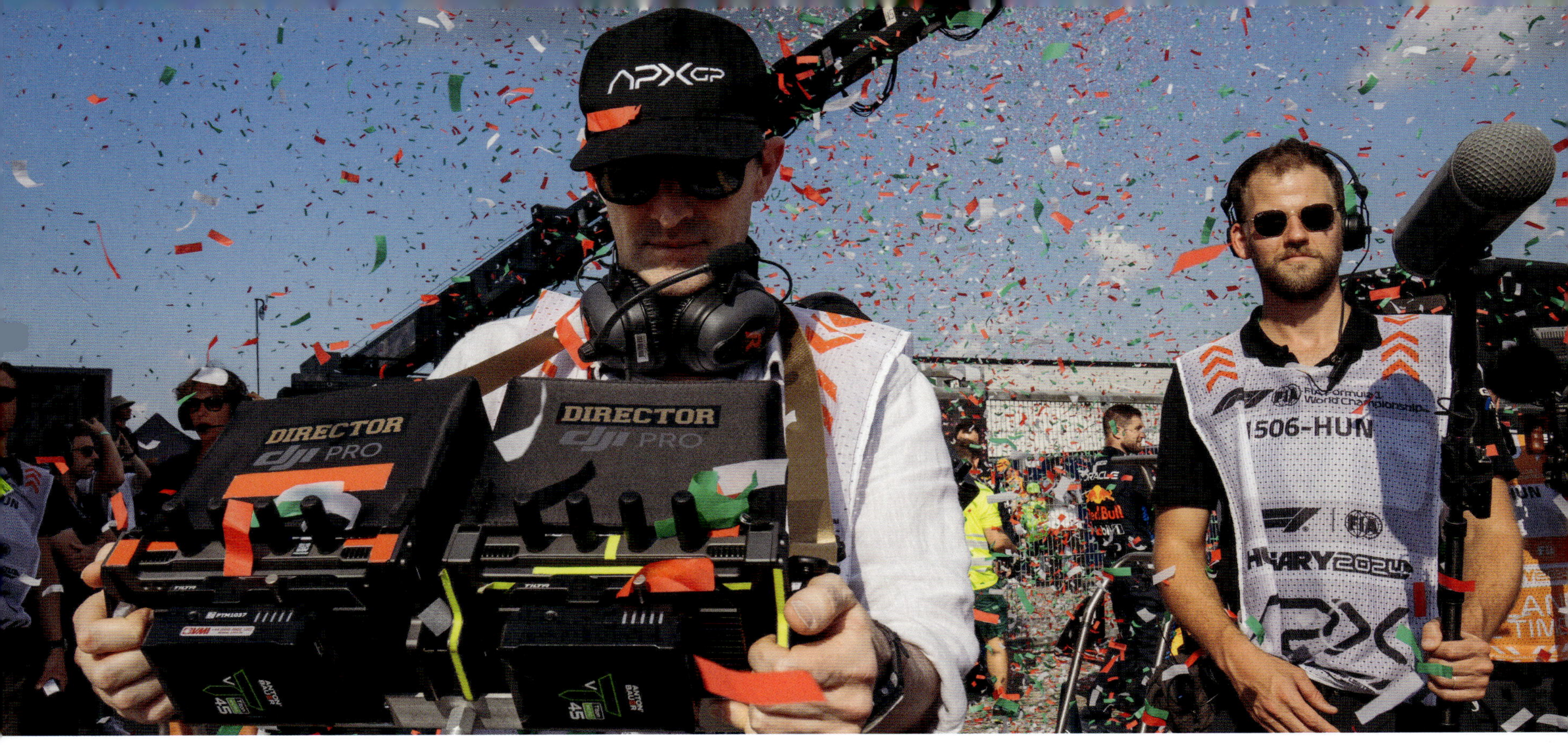

Growing up in Marshalltown, Iowa, in the eighties, future film director Joseph Kosinski was a fan of fast cars—if not Formula One itself. "F1 wasn't on television when I was a kid. For whatever reason, it never penetrated the U.S. the way it did in other countries. But I was a fan of the idea of it, and the notion of car racing."

As a teenager, Kosinski built and raced his own radio-controlled cars and planes and dreamed of one day designing racing cars as a career. "I was very interested in racing from a design and engineering point of view rather than a sports point of view. I went to school thinking I was either going to be a car designer or an aerospace engineer. Then I got diverted into architecture because [it offered] the creativity I was looking for. But there's a version of me that could have easily been an engineer at Mercedes."

After earning a degree in mechanical engineering at Stanford and a master's in architecture from Columbia, Kosinski relocated to Hollywood, where he turned to directing. He initially made a name for himself with a series of inventive shorts and commercials for Nike, Lexus, Saab, Nissan, and Sony, as well as video game spots for *Halo 3*, *Assassin's Creed*, and his award-winning Mad World ad for *Gears of War*, before he segued into features with 2010's *Tron: Legacy*, the belated sequel to Disney's groundbreaking 1982 computer-generated adventure, *Tron*. Set largely inside a computer

"I was very interested in racing from a design and engineering point of view."

JOSEPH KOSINSKI

Top Left: Joseph Kosinski reviews racing footage taken during the 2024 Hungarian Grand Prix.

Top Right: Joseph Kosinski and camera operator Lukasz Bielan get up close to the action on the track using a telephoto lens.

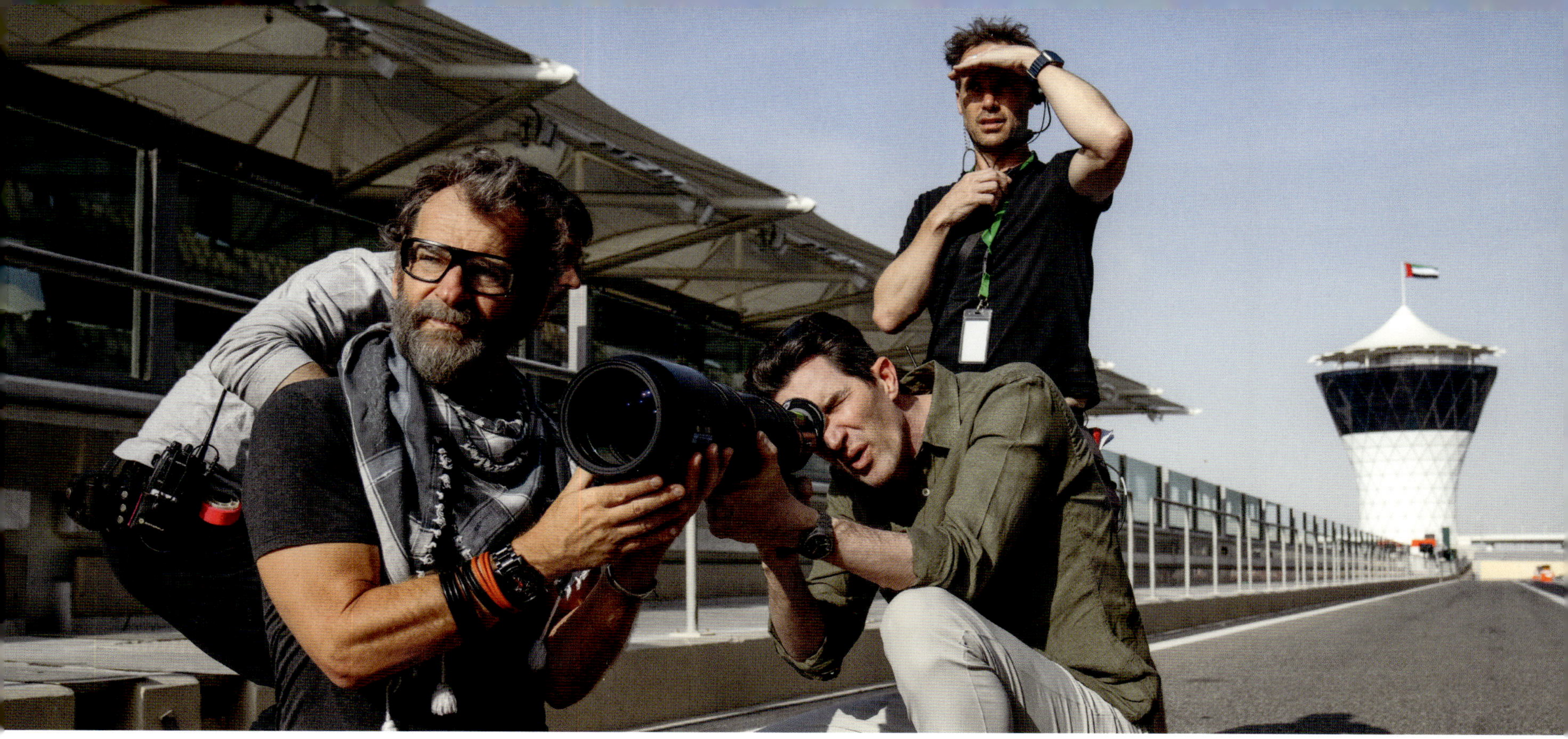

game, *Tron: Legacy* was lauded for its dazzling visuals and innovative effects and established Kosinski as a talent to watch. He followed it up with sci-fi thriller *Oblivion*, starring Tom Cruise, based on an unpublished graphic novel he had created.

Both *Tron: Legacy* and *Oblivion* featured exhilarating chase sequences, and Kosinski continued to incorporate high-speed pursuits—involving either cars, planes, or boats—into all of his subsequent features. But what Kosinski really wanted to do was direct a racing film. To that end, in 2015, he spent nine months developing *Go Like Hell*, an adaptation of A.J. Baime's nonfiction book *Go Like Hell: Ford, Ferrari, and Their Battle for Speed and Glory at Le Mans*, which centered on the Ford Motor Company's plan to build a race car, the GT40 Mk II, to take on the mighty Scuderia Ferrari at Le Mans. The film had Tom Cruise attached to play designer Carroll Shelby and Brad Pitt as driver Ken Miles.

"I did a lot of research on the cars and how we were going to shoot it," explains Kosinski. "We even did a script readthrough with Brad at Tom's house." But then Fox, the studio behind the project, balked at the proposed budget and shut down the film. "It was just too expensive for what they wanted to spend on a period car racing movie at that point, so it didn't come together, unfortunately. Or, maybe, fortunately, because I don't know if I would have ended up doing a Formula One film if I had done that." There was another upside to the whole experience. "That was my introduction to Brad," says Kosinski.

Go Like Hell would eventually become *Ford v Ferrari*, aka *Le Mans '66*, starring Christian Bale and Matt Damon as Miles and Shelby. By then, Kosinski had moved on to other projects, briefly developing *Gran Turismo*—which centered on the true story of a teenage gamer who became a racing driver—before signing on to direct the long-in-the-works sequel to Tony Scott's 1986 blockbuster *Top Gun*, which had made a star out of Tom Cruise. *Top Gun: Maverick* would see Cruise reprise his role as cocksure naval pilot Pete "Maverick" Mitchell, this time as a world-weary flier tasked with training the next generation of fighter pilots for a deadly mission behind enemy lines.

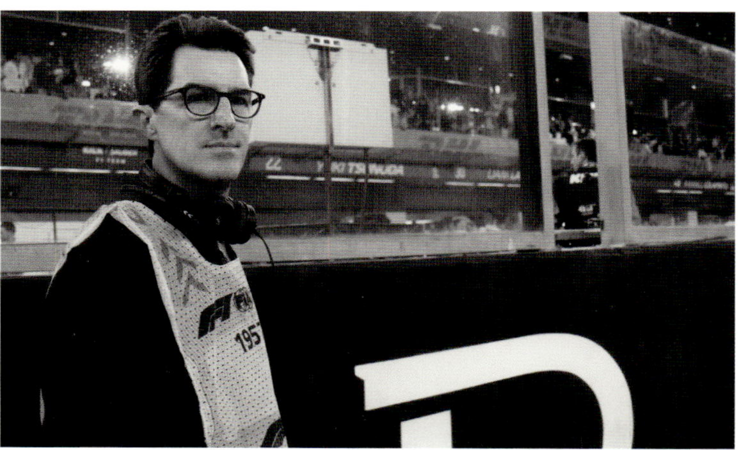

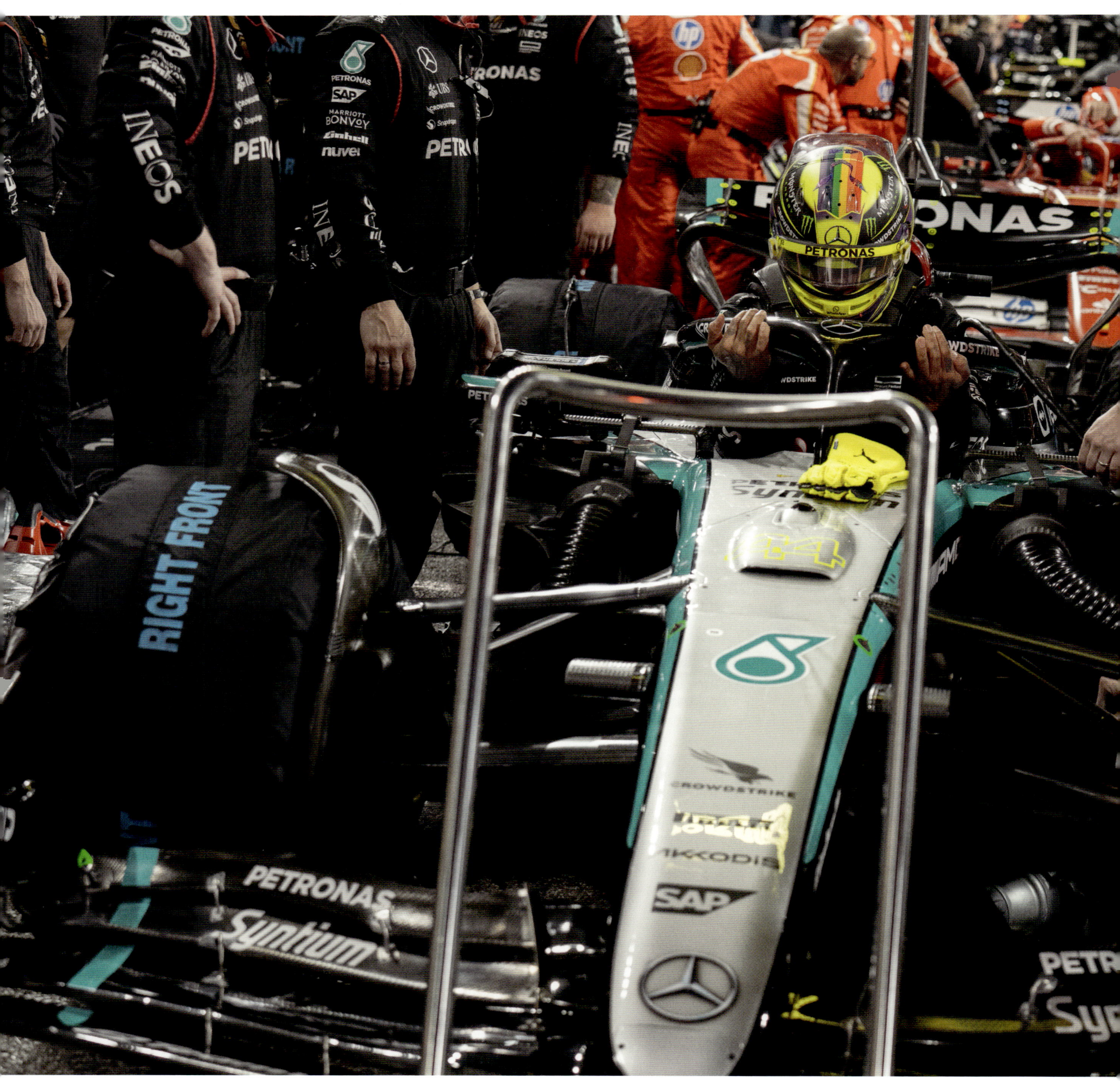

Above: Lewis Hamilton raring to go in his Mercedes-AMG Formula One car.

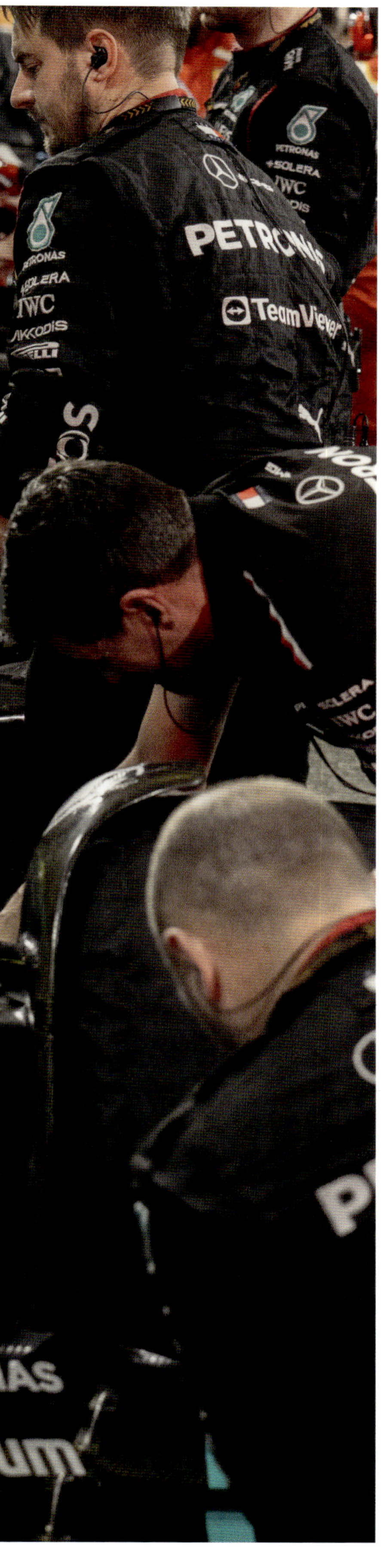

Unlike in the original movie, Kosinski and Cruise were determined to film all of Maverick's aerial scenes for real, training the cast to fly in F-18 fighter jets at high speeds and capturing the action using an array of small digital cameras that could be mounted inside the cockpit. During the casting process, Cruise, who was also a producer, mentioned to Kosinski that Sir Lewis Hamilton, the seven-time Formula One world champion, who then drove for the Mercedes-AMG Petronas F1 Team, was interested in auditioning for a part and asked if it would be okay if he gave Hamilton his email.

A few days later, Hamilton messaged. "He said, 'I'm very interested in filmmaking, and I'd love to throw my hat in the ring for one of the pilot roles,'" recalls Kosinski, who sent Hamilton a few pages of the script featuring the character of "Fanboy" for him to audition. Given that the two men were on opposite sides of the Atlantic, Kosinski outlined the audition process for Hamilton. "I said he would need to put himself on tape reading the scenes, then send them back. Then I might give him some notes, and maybe he would have to do them again." Kosinski also explained that the film's shoot would be "intense" and would likely span nine months to a year. At the time, Hamilton was embroiled in a fierce battle with Ferrari's Sebastian Vettel for the Formula One World Championship and realized he wouldn't be able to devote the time that Kosinski and the movie required of him. "Lewis wrote back and said, 'If I can't commit 100 percent to this, I probably shouldn't be doing it. But thank you,'" recalls Kosinski. "I was struck by how humble he was in his communication and his interest in everything related to the filmmaking process."

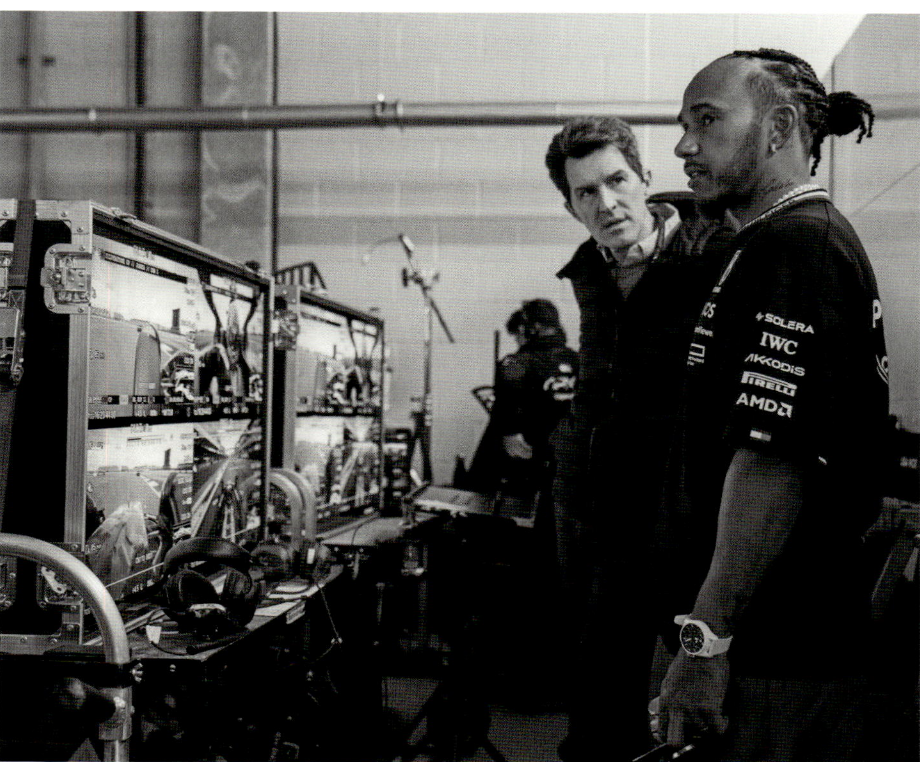

Left: Seven-time Formula One World Drivers' Championship winner Lewis Hamilton, who signed on as executive producer for the film, worked closely with Joseph Kosinski to ensure the authenticity of racing scenes.

As Hamilton returned his attention to the track, Kosinski and Cruise began filming *Top Gun: Maverick*, completing the movie in mid-2019 for a planned May 2020 release. But when the Covid pandemic hit, the film sat on the shelf for two years, as the filmmakers refused to allow the movie to be sold to a streaming service and held out for a theatrical release; the film eventually opened in cinemas worldwide in May 2022.

The move paid off handsomely, as *Top Gun: Maverick* earned stellar reviews, six Academy Award nominations, and $1.5 billion at the global box office, making it Cruise's highest-grossing film, as well as the biggest film in the forty-year career of its legendary producer Jerry Bruckheimer, whose long list of credits includes the original *Top Gun* and NASCAR action-drama *Days of Thunder*.

That was all to come, but in autumn of 2021, Kosinski, like most people, was stuck at home in Los Angeles, waiting for the pandemic to run its course. One night after his family was asleep, he started watching Netflix's Formula One documentary series, *F1: Drive to Survive*, and was hooked. Offering an insider's look at the 2019 season, *Drive to Survive* devoted as much time to the personalities—the drivers, team bosses, et al.—as it did to the racing. Kosinski wasn't alone in his fascination; the series proved a gateway to the sport to millions of new fans, especially in the United States, a territory the sport's owners, Liberty Media, had ambitious plans for, including new races in Las Vegas and Miami.

What struck Kosinski most about the first season of *Drive to Survive*, however, was how it focused on the last-placed teams and lesser-known drivers rather than those at the sharp end of the grid. "They didn't focus on Lewis and Max [Verstappen]; they focused on Alex Albon, who was an up-and-coming driver in a lower team." Kosinski, who had been toying with the idea of making a movie set in the world of Formula One for a while, realized this underdog approach might be an interesting way in. "Not talking about the front-running teams, but one struggling at the bottom, who pull this 'Hail Mary' move by hiring a driver that nobody wanted or had been lost to history and forgotten about, someone who never reached their potential, who was supposed to be the next great thing but had an accident, then pairing him with a rookie driver."

He decided to email Hamilton about it. "This was a year or two after I'd last spoken to him. I said, 'I'd like to create a movie in the world of Formula One and for it to be the most authentic racing film ever made, and I can't imagine a better partner than someone who lives it every single day like you. And since you're interested in film, how would you like to produce it with me?'" Within the week, Kosinski heard back that Hamilton was interested in discussing the idea further and wanted to meet when he was in Los Angeles next.

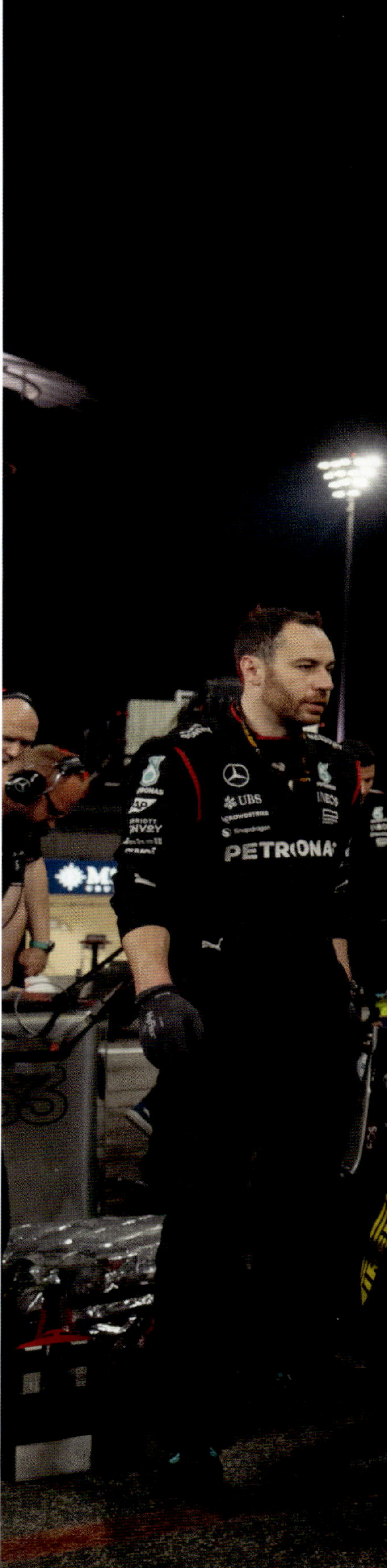

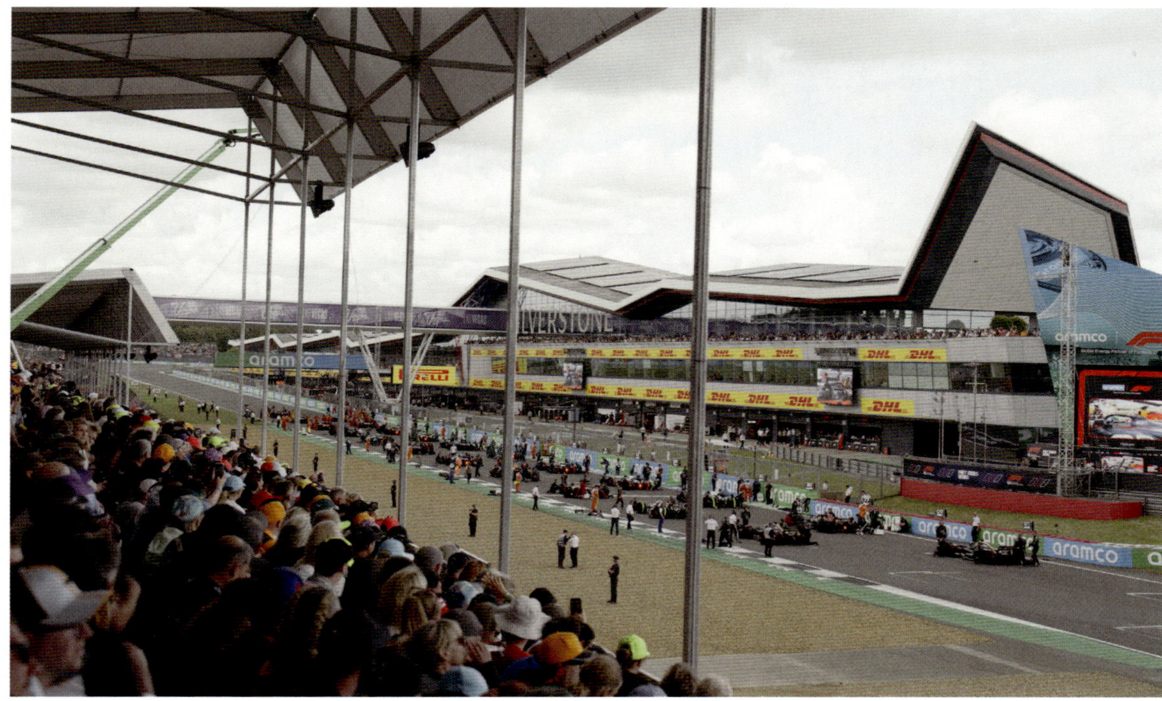

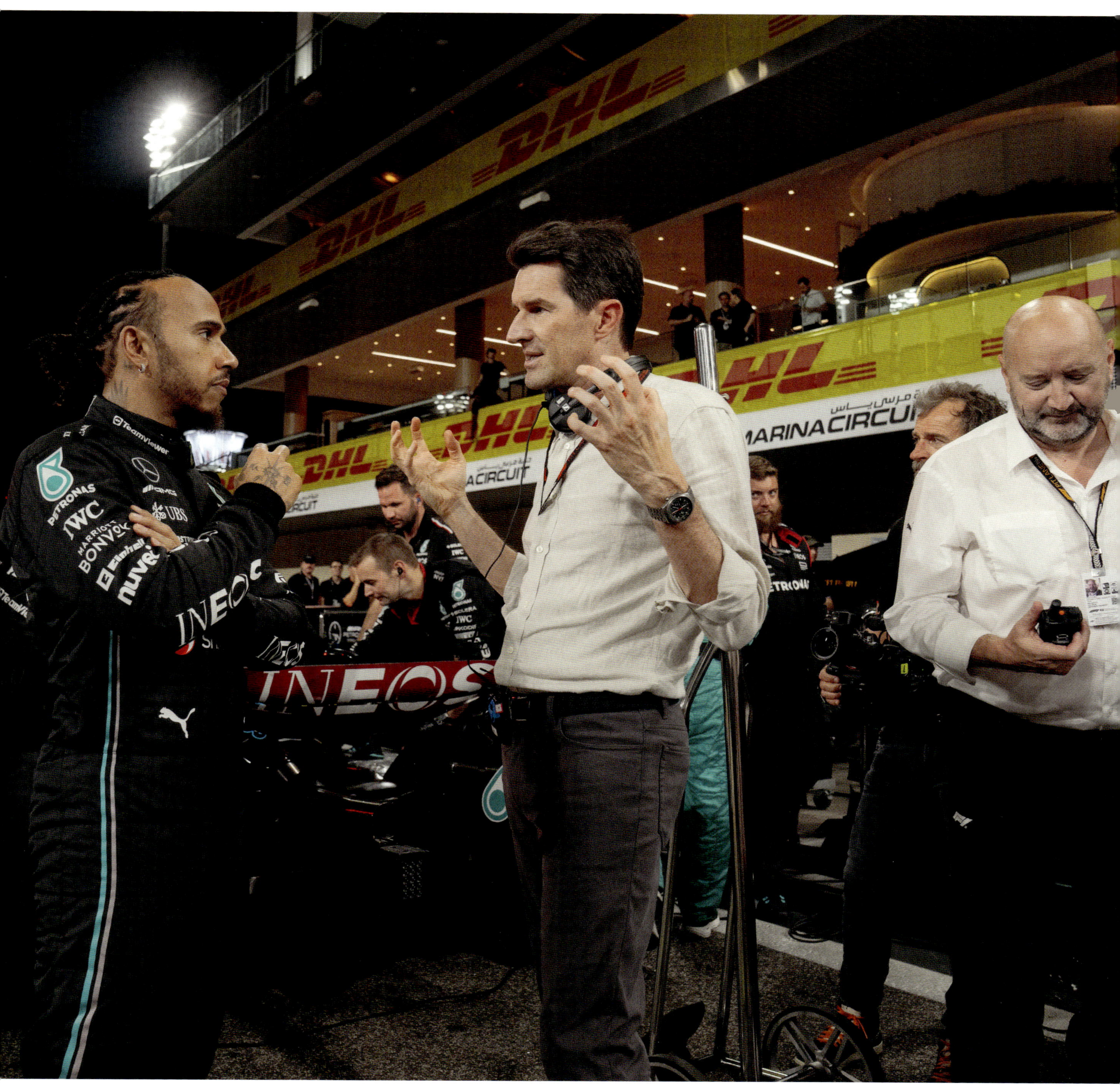

Left: All the Formula One drivers take their places on the starting grid for the British Grand Prix with the two APXGP cars at the back.

Above: Lewis Hamilton and Joseph Kosinski discuss an upcoming shot during the Abu Dhabi Grand Prix.

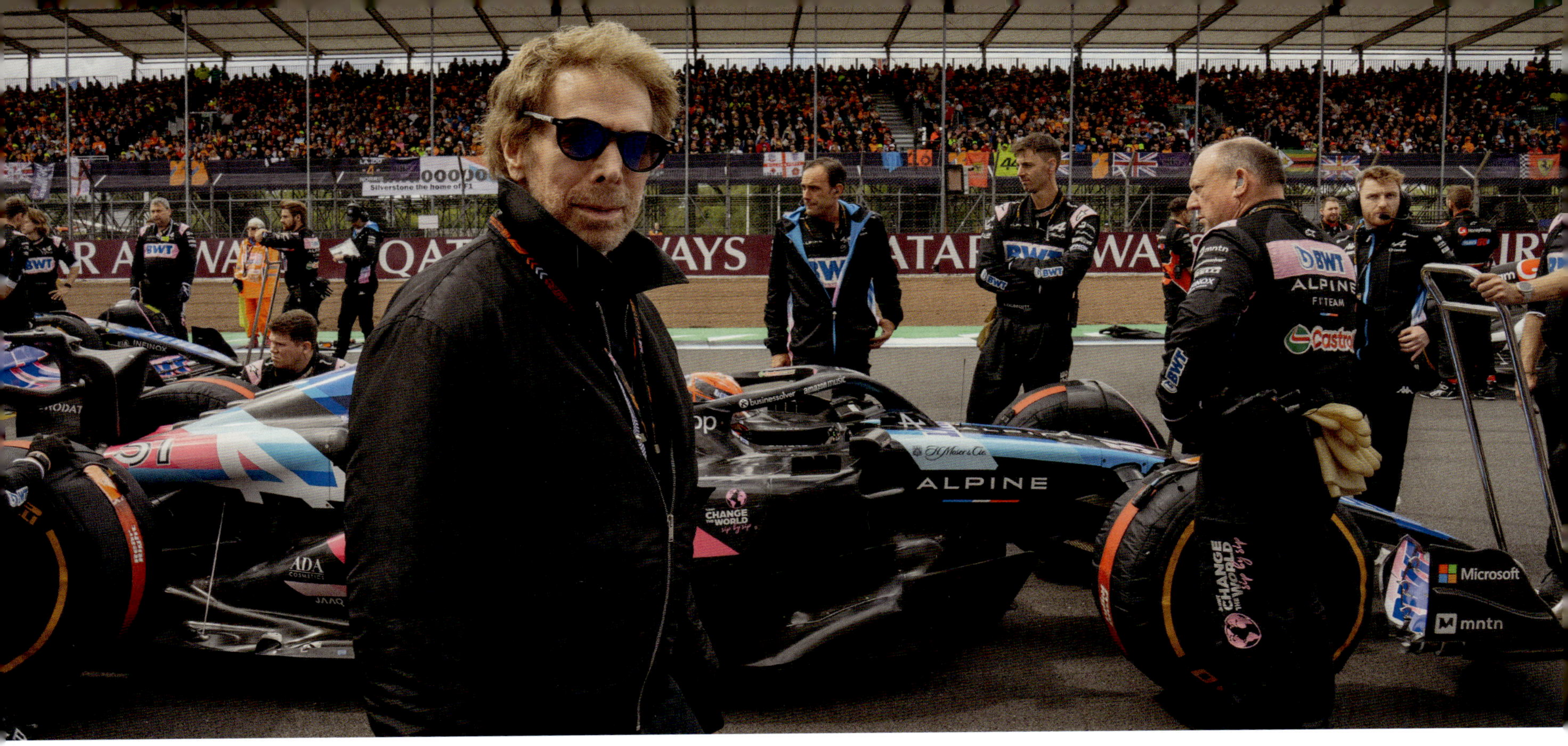

Meanwhile, Kosinski began talking to his agents at CAA to build a team around him to bring his idea to life. "They asked, 'Who would you want to partner with? Of any producer you've worked with, who would you want to do this with?' Instantly, I thought of Jerry [Bruckheimer], having just done *Top Gun: Maverick* with him. I mean, he's a legend," says Kosinski. "And I thought, *I'm going to be dealing with Formula One. I'm going to be dealing with a studio. I'm going to need a giant movie star at the center of this. Who better to have as your partner than a producer who's been working at that level for forty years.* I asked Jerry if he would be interested, and he said, 'Absolutely.'"

Oscar-nominated for *Top Gun: Maverick*, Bruckheimer started in advertising straight out of college, before moving into filmmaking in the late 1970s, producing *American Gigolo* for Paul Schrader and *Thief* for Michael Mann among others. In the early 1980s, Bruckheimer joined forces with former Paramount head of production Don Simpson and together they produced four of the biggest box office hits of the decade, beginning with *Flashdance* in 1983, directed by Adrian Lyne. *Flashdance* was quickly followed by *Beverly Hills Cop*, which made Eddie Murphy a superstar, *Top Gun*, which did the same for its star Tom Cruise, and *Beverly Hills Cop II*, the latter two from British commercials director Tony Scott.

Known as the masters of high-concept, action-packed, popcorn entertainment, Simpson

> "I've made a career out of giving you inside looks into a world you'll never be a part of."
>
> JERRY BRUCKHEIMER

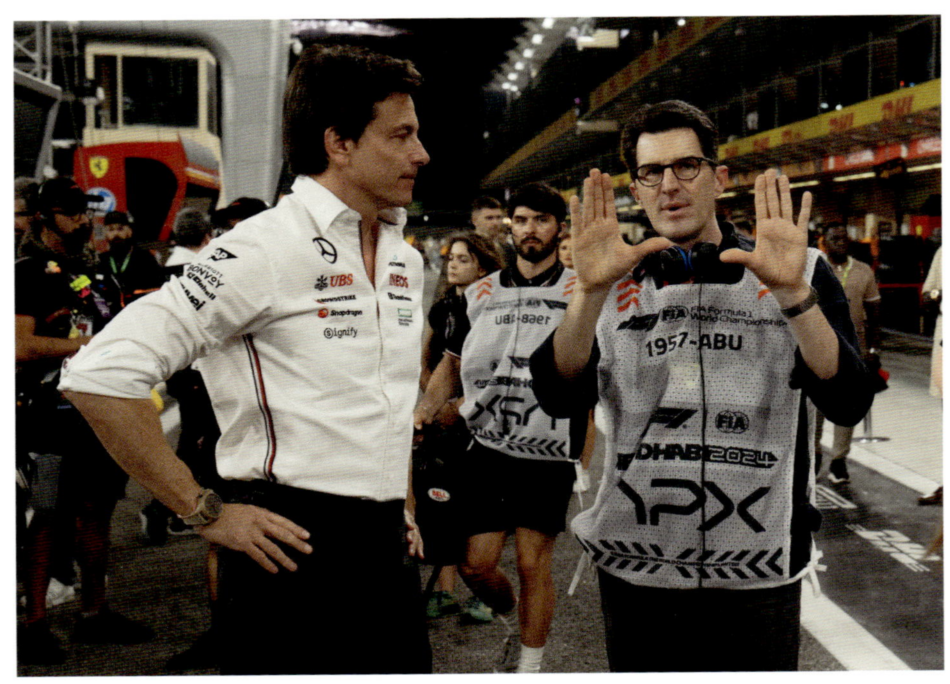

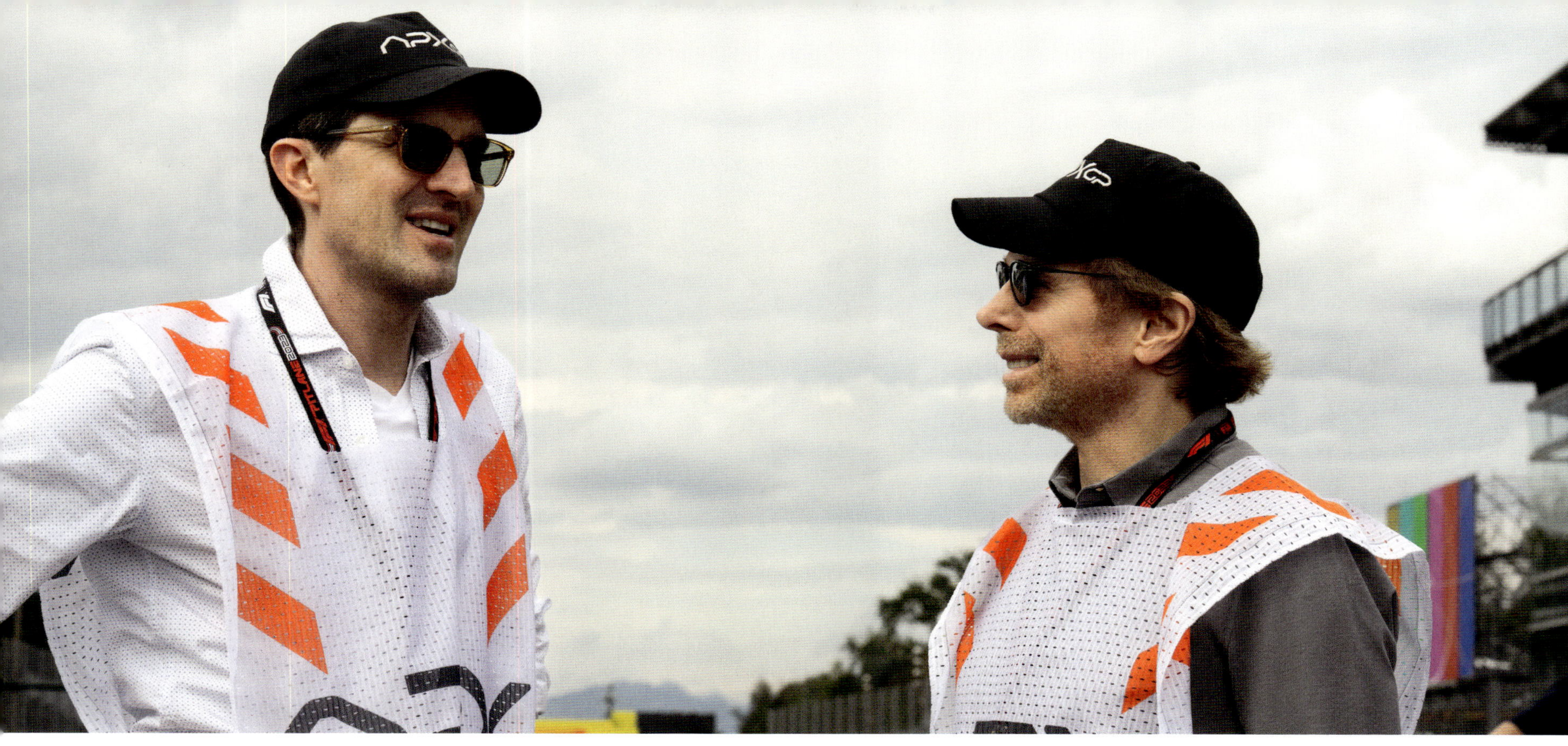

Top Left: Producer Jerry Bruckheimer poses in front of the BWT Alpine F1 Team as they get ready to race.

Top Right: Joseph Kosinski and Jerry Bruckheimer first collaborated on the blockbuster *Top Gun: Maverick*.

Bottom Left: Joseph Kosinski confers with Toto Wolff, CEO and co-owner of the Mercedes-AMG Petronas F1 Team.

and Bruckheimer helped reshape Hollywood filmmaking in the 1980s by reformulating the look and sound of movies, thanks to a winning combination of commercial instincts, marketing acumen, killer soundtracks, and their decision to hire visually stylish directors. The pair also produced Tony Scott's *Days of Thunder*, again starring Cruise, a high-speed car movie set against the backdrop of real NASCAR races, including Daytona, with thrilling, pulse-pounding on-track action; and a film that paved the way for Bruckheimer to be the perfect producer for Kosinski's Formula One film decades later.

Following Simpson's untimely death in 1996, Bruckheimer struck out on his own, continuing to craft hit after hit, for both the big and small screens, including *Crimson Tide*, *Dangerous Minds, Black Hawk Down,* as well as the *Bad Boys, Pirates of the Caribbean*, and *CSI* franchises.

"I've made a career out of giving you inside looks into a world you'll never be a part of," says Bruckheimer. "We did it with *CSI*. We did it with *Top Gun*. We did it with *Black Hawk Down*. All these things give you a view, not from 1,000, 10,000 feet, but by putting you right in the driver's seat, like we did with *Maverick*. So, when Joe called with the idea of making a movie set in the world of Formula One, I thought it was perfect timing. *Drive to Survive* was a hit. The expansion of the sport into America was underway, and he had Lewis Hamilton, who was already a big star, attached."

Kosinski and Bruckheimer met Hamilton for lunch in Los Angeles shortly after. "I pitched him the basic bones of the story, the themes, this unexpected pairing of two drivers on the last-place team," says Kosinski. "Lewis loved the idea from the start and invited us to the Austin Grand Prix, which was a week or two later." Hamilton joined the project as a producer and introduced Kosinski, Bruckheimer, and Chad Oman, president of Jerry Bruckheimer Films, to Toto Wolff, team principal, CEO, and co-owner of the Mercedes-AMG Petronas F1 Team, who would become a major benefactor as well as an executive producer. "For me, having watched *Drive to Survive*, Toto was a rock star," says Oman. "He is just so cool and calm."

The trip to Austin proved to be an eye-opening experience. "I said to Jerry after that, 'I thought walking onto the deck of an aircraft carrier and watching two F-18s launch would be the coolest thing I'd ever seen in my life. Until I walked into the Mercedes garage and stood behind the car when Lewis dropped in, and they started it up and it pulled out of the garage,'" admits Kosinski. "That scene is in the movie, when you see Sonny get in the car for the first time, start the car, and peel out of the garage from behind, that was essentially what I witnessed. That first trip blew my mind. The technology on display was beyond anything I'd seen on *Top Gun*. This was totally different. And that got me excited."

"Sitting in the Mercedes garage was clearly cinematic and exhilarating. The pinnacle of technology combined with something visceral, with the point of views of the different engineers and data crunchers of how the car should feel and react based on a hundred thousand data points collected from the simulator. But what it really comes down to is, is the driver confident and can the driver turn that into performance?"

From that point on, Kosinski was engaged in a "research mission, absorbing everything, learning everything" to craft the most authentic, realistic, and immersive racing movie ever made. "Everything I was seeing, I was recording with my brain. It's what I did for *Top Gun*. I immersed myself in the world to figure out what's the most interesting story. I asked myself, 'How do I make the story as authentic as possible? How do I capture this world in a way people haven't seen before?'"

One way was to build upon the technology he'd employed on *Top Gun: Maverick*, to film his actors behind the wheel of Formula One cars as they drove at speeds of up to 180 miles per hour. "Part of it was taking everything I had learned and developed on *Top Gun* and taking it to the next level," he explains. "The cameras are much smaller and lighter, but, more importantly, we could operate and move them as we're shooting the scene, which we couldn't do on *Top Gun*. Now we've got the ability to pan the cameras left and right, to connect the characters to the action in a more dynamic way, to show our actors are driving these cars on a track and show the viewer what it's like to be in a race. Typically, in a racing movie, you cut from an exterior of a car to a close-up of an actor. I wanted to pan from the action straight to the actor's face."

Kosinski's other big ambition was to film at real tracks, during the actual Grand Prix, as well as shoot dramatic scenes in the paddock and pit lane, and on the grid during race weekends, much as *Le Mans* and *Grand Prix* had done. "But doing it to an extent far beyond what they did. How do I do that today? How do I do that in this world that's so much bigger and more complex? For every project, there must be something new to get me excited. Beyond the story, those challenges were very exciting."

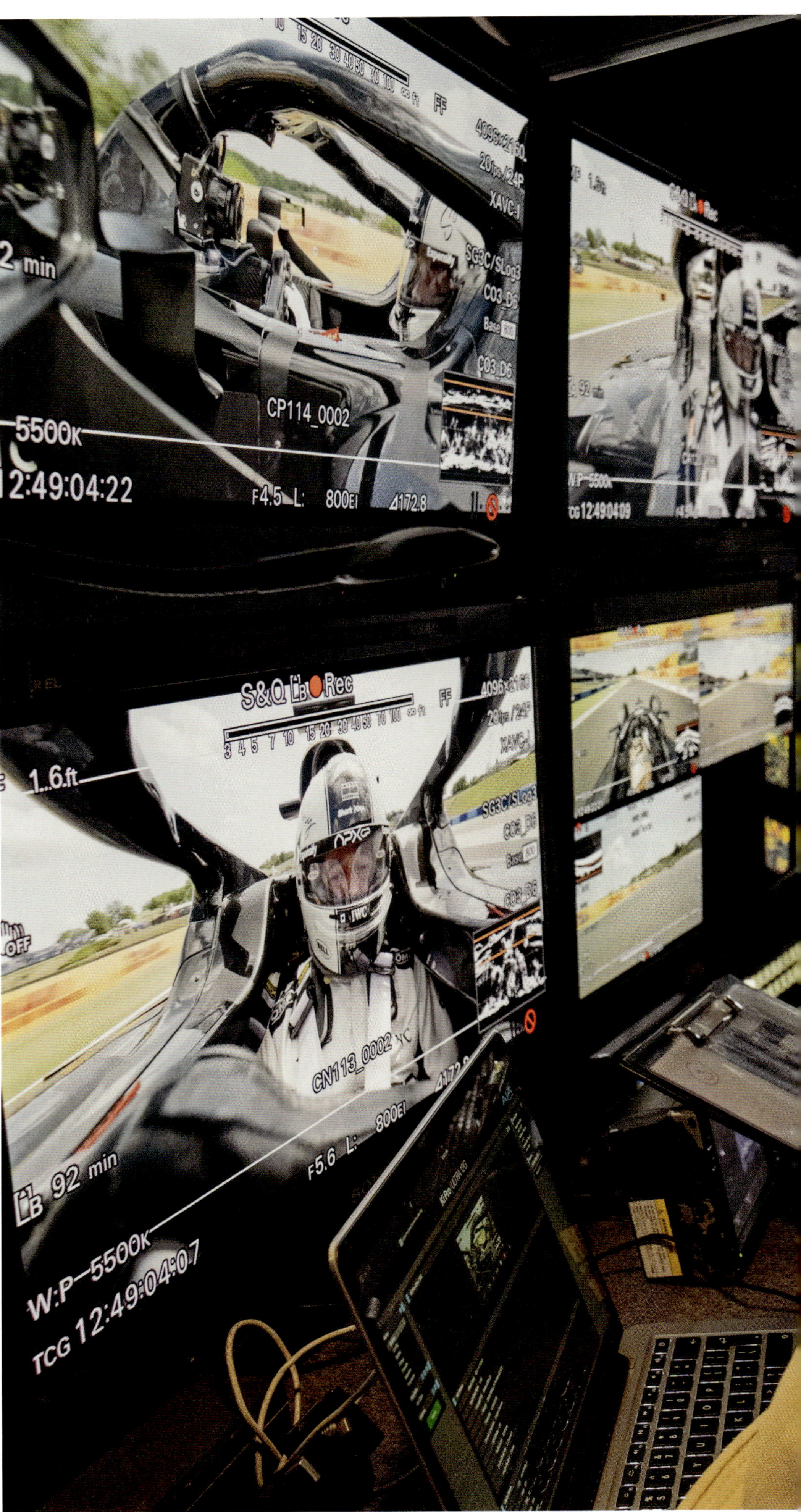

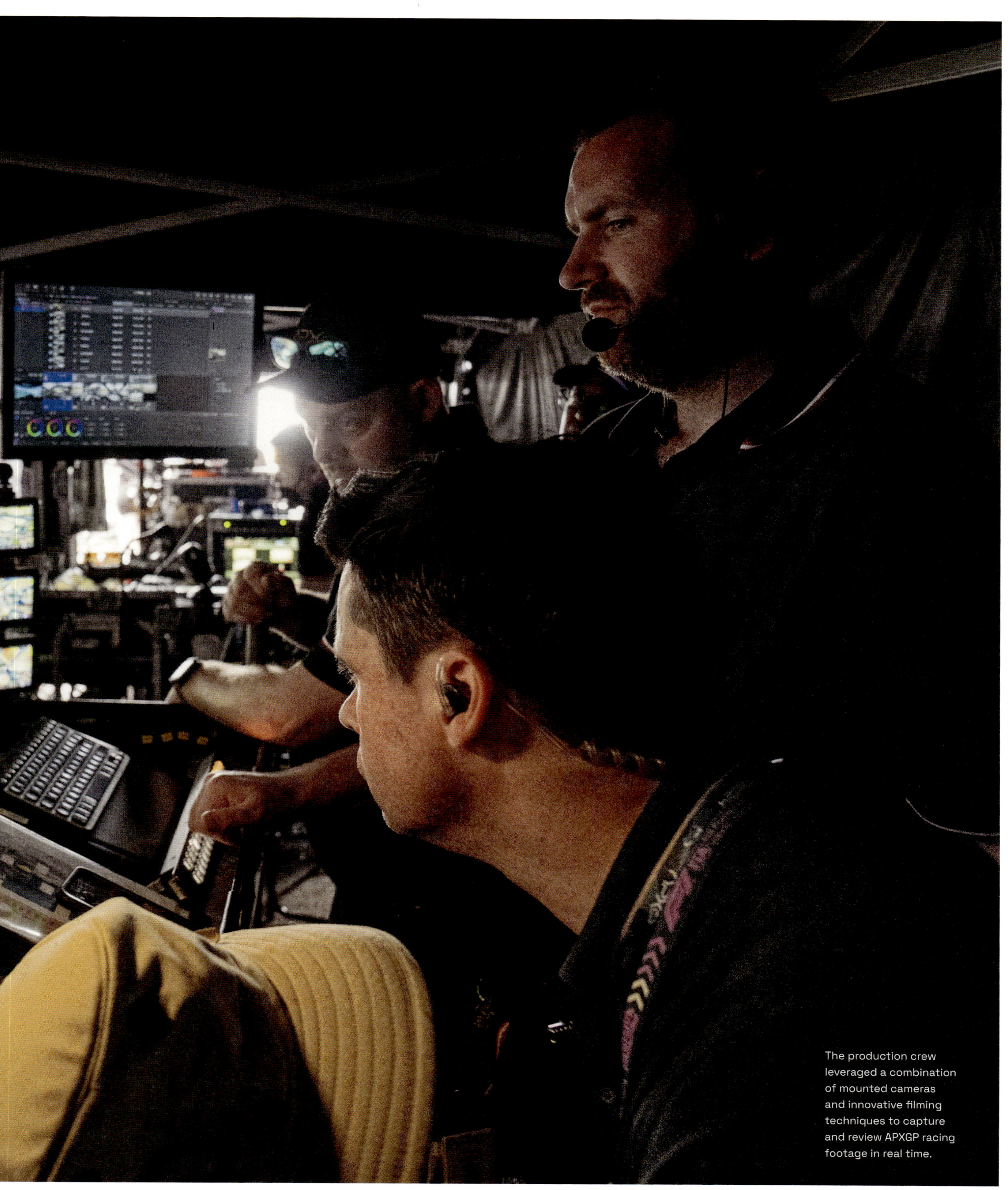

The production crew leveraged a combination of mounted cameras and innovative filming techniques to capture and review APXGP racing footage in real time.

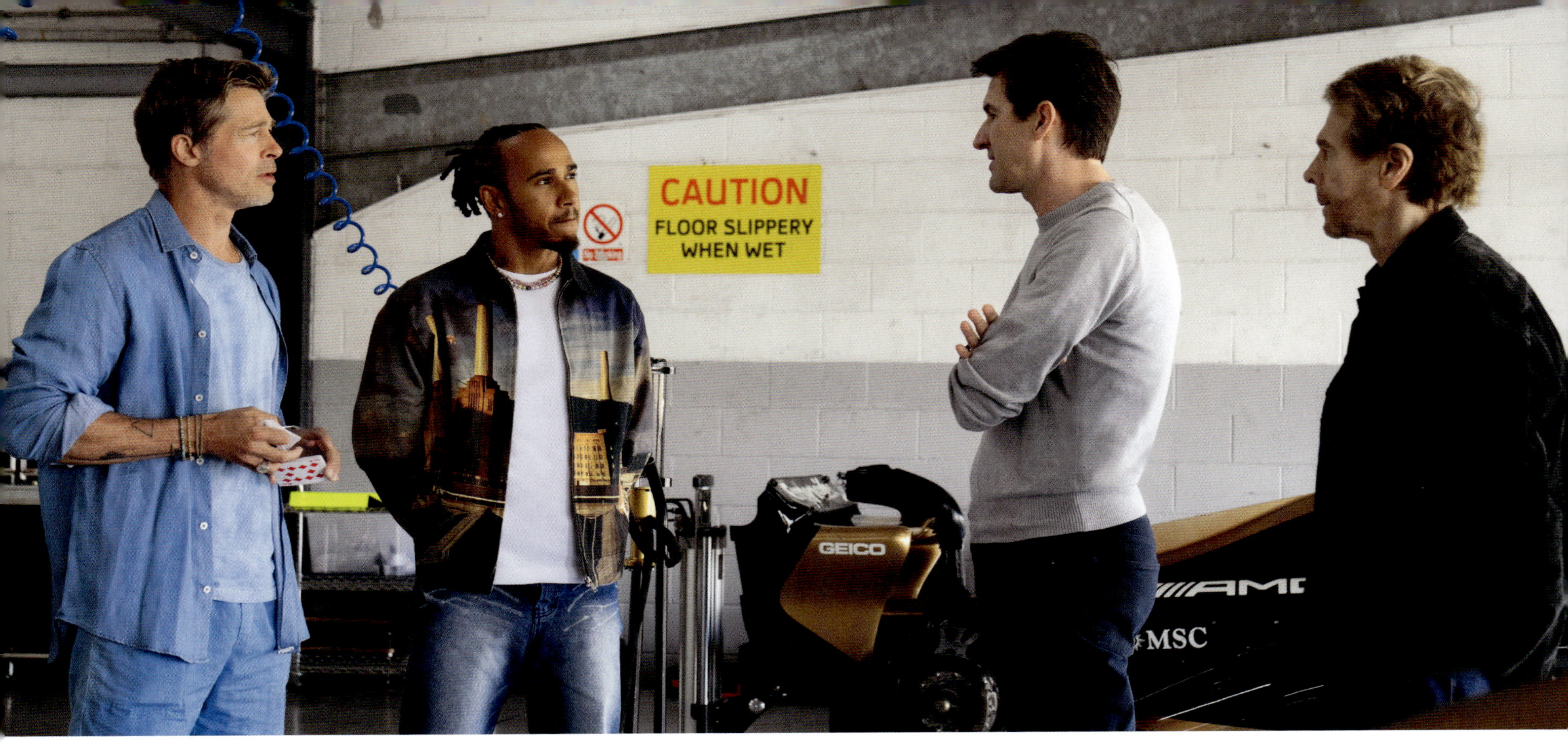

> "I've been trying to get a race film made for decades, and for one reason or another, they've always collapsed."
>
> BRAD PITT

Top Left: Brad Pitt, Lewis Hamilton, Joseph Kosinski, and Jerry Bruckheimer in deep conversation next to the APXGP race car.

Top Right: Brad Pitt, who plays Sonny Hayes, also joined the team as a producer.

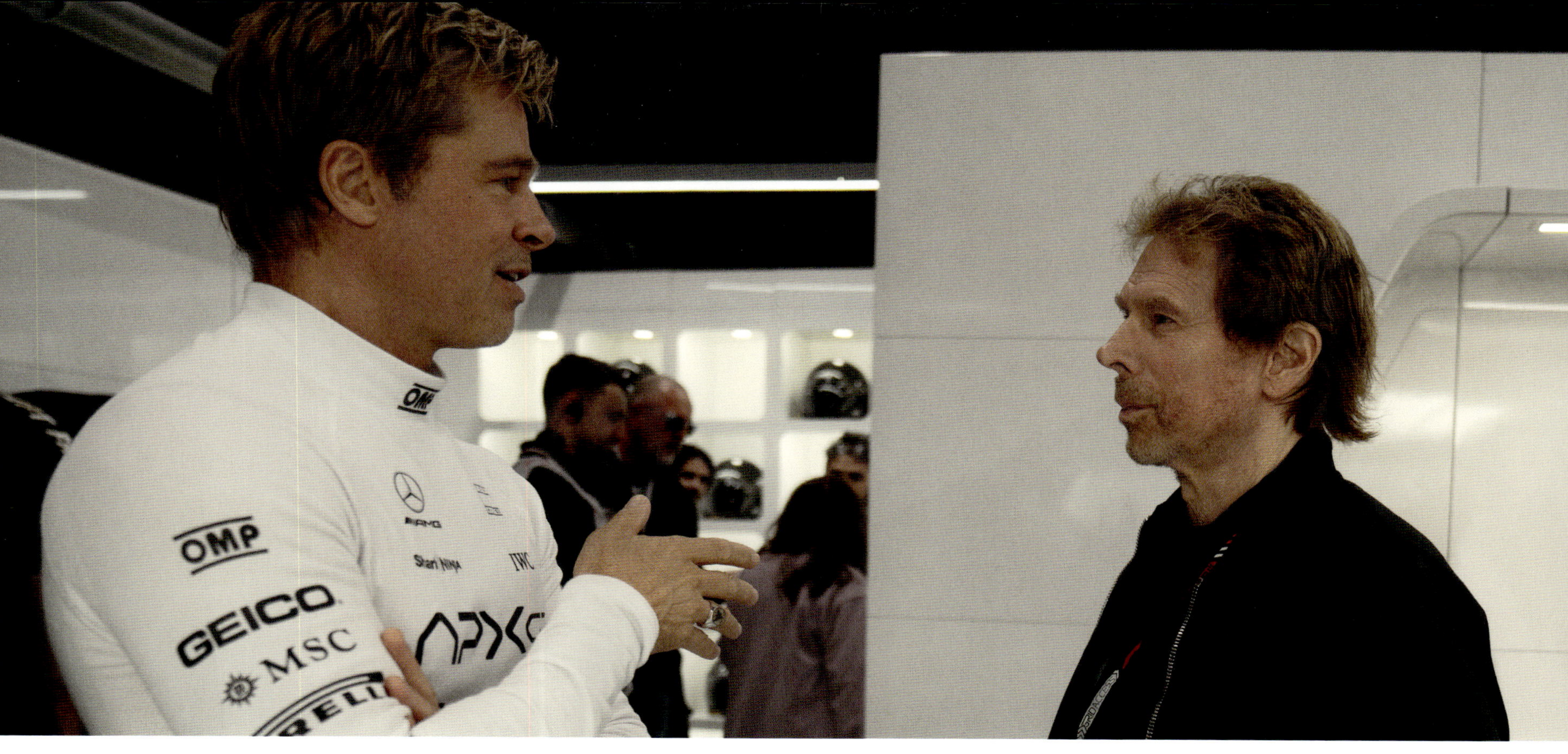

By October 2021, Kosinski had Hamilton, Bruckheimer, and Mercedes on board, but he knew any film set in the world of Formula One would be costly and complex to make and would therefore require a giant movie star at its center. Having worked with Brad Pitt on *Go Like Hell*, Kosinski felt the star of *Seven*, *Fight Club*, *Ocean's Eleven*, *Moneyball*, and *Once Upon a Time . . . in Hollywood* was not only big enough to assuage the concerns of any studio interested in financing the film, but would be perfect to play Sonny Hayes, the veteran driver drafted in to save his friend's ailing Formula One team.

"I knew he had this passion for motorsport from the few months we developed *Go Like Hell* together, and I knew it was on his bucket list of movies he always wanted to make," says Kosinski, who had his agent reach out to Pitt's. "Brad came over to my house, and I spent an hour taking him through the bones of the story. I had a poster, a long-lens image of an F1 car cresting a hill, I had some photography. I had some images of where we find Sonny Hayes at the opening of the movie, in a very different world than Formula One. And I had a basic story. The most important thing is story. Story is always going to be key when you're pitching to an actor at that level. They want to know who this character is and what's the emotional throughline of the film. That's what's going to hook them. Driving the car for real was a bonus."

By the end of that hour, Pitt was in. "I've been trying to get a race film made for decades, and for one reason or another, they've always collapsed," Pitt says. "*Go Like Hell* was one. Even MotoGP and bike racing. Many different forms. And it just never happened. So, when Joe called and talked about this new approach, how we were going to integrate ourselves into the season and drive the cars ourselves, I was glad the others [had] failed."

"He's a race fan. He's an amazing actor. And we were lucky to get him," says Bruckheimer of Pitt. "He doesn't do that many movies. And it just so happened he's always wanted to do a race one. He's a great storyteller too. He loves movies, and he added an enormous amount of story wisdom and character wisdom to Sonny. He came up with so many things that we incorporated in the movie."

Pitt, who won the Best Supporting Actor Oscar for *Once Upon a Time . . . in Hollywood* and the Best Motion Picture Oscar for producing *12 Years a Slave*, also joined as producer alongside his partners at Plan B Entertainment, Jeremy Kleiner and Dede Gardner. "At that point," says Kosinski, "I felt I had a pretty good package in terms of building a project that I knew was going to be undeniable. Then we needed a writer."

Ehren Kruger was one of the writers on *Top Gun: Maverick*, earning a Best Adapted Screenplay Oscar nomination, and he and Kosinski had almost worked together when the latter was developing *Grand Turismo*. "I knew Ehren had the sense of story and emotion, but also the brain to handle the amount of information that an authentic Formula One movie should have in it," says Kosinski. "You're talking strategy, engineering; all that has to be part of it."

Kruger was familiar with Formula One but wasn't "a religious fan, where I'd watch week-to-week, like I do now," he notes. "But the thing I grabbed onto, that made me say 'There's a movie here' was the notion that in Formula One, your teammate is your greatest enemy in many respects. You are working toward the same goal but are rivals while you're doing it. There've been lots of racing pictures, but Joe and I didn't feel that dynamic had been truly explored and suggested an opportunity for a character conflict-based movie. I said, 'This is the core of the movie. Whatever happens in the races, whoever these characters are, we'll figure it out.'

"Part of the challenge was to be as authentic and real as we can for die-hard Formula One fans but also give new fans an entree into that world," Kruger continues. "The other thing Joe wanted was to be as authentic as possible, to entertain people and give them reversals and surprises, although the logistics of Formula One couldn't be less than real."

In December 2021, Kosinski, Kruger, Bruckheimer, and Oman pitched their idea to nine Hollywood studios over the course of two days in a series of one-hour Zoom meetings. "It was a very good pitch, it was very emotional," says Oman. "We had Brad. We had the promise of *Maverick*. And it felt like you could see the movie with the pitch."

The reaction was overwhelmingly positive. "Everyone wanted to buy it," recalls Bruckheimer. They opted for Apple Original Films, with Warner Brothers enlisted to distribute the movie worldwide. For Kosinski, having his film—then called *Apex*; the title *F1* wouldn't officially be announced until July 2024—released at the cinema was non-negotiable. "This movie is made for the big screen."

Below: Brad Pitt and Joseph Kosinski share a laugh between takes.

Right: By the time the film was being pitched, Brad Pitt was already on board to play Sonny Hayes.

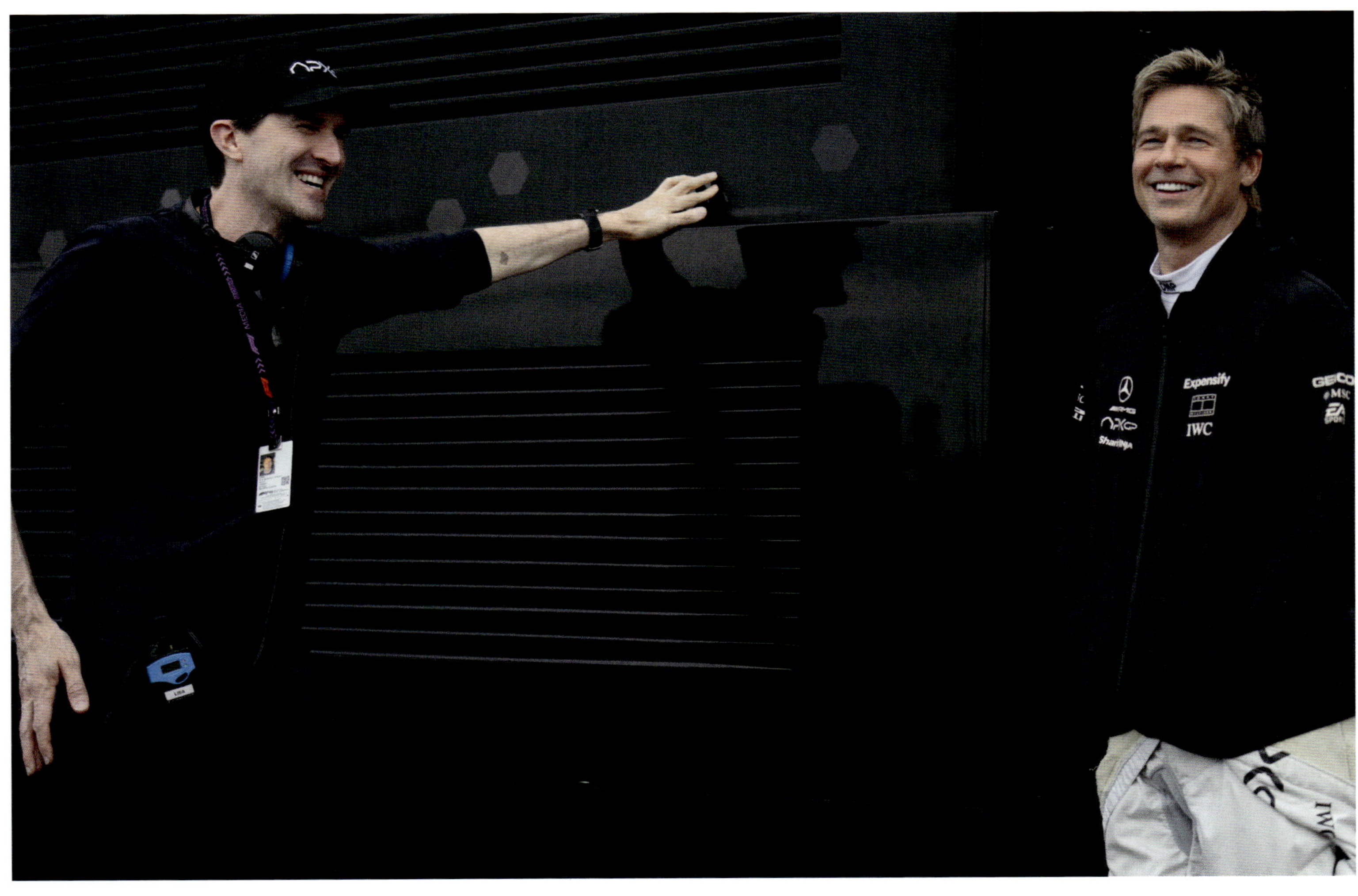

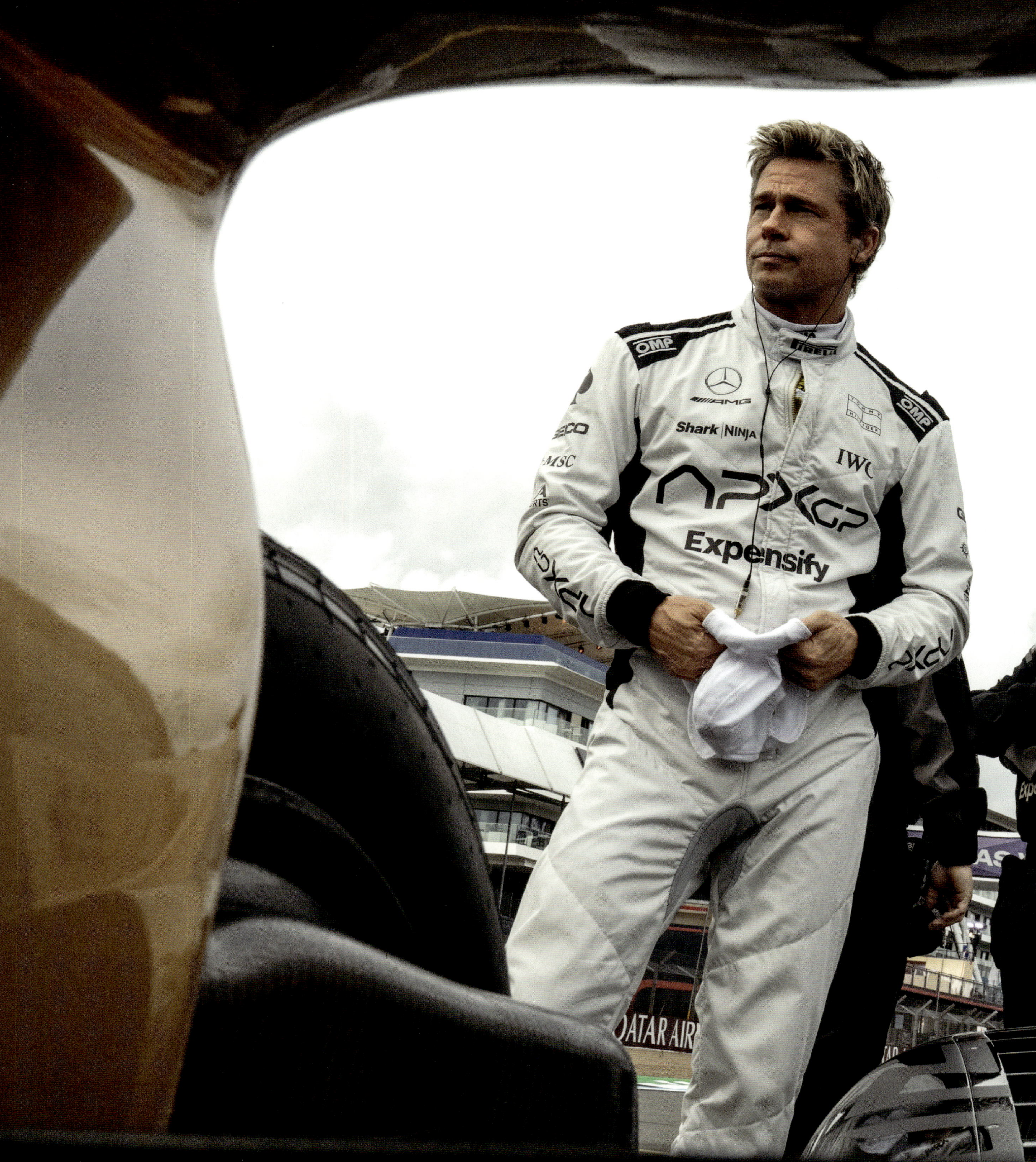
OMP
AMG
Shark NINJA
SECO
MSC
IWC
OMP
Expensify

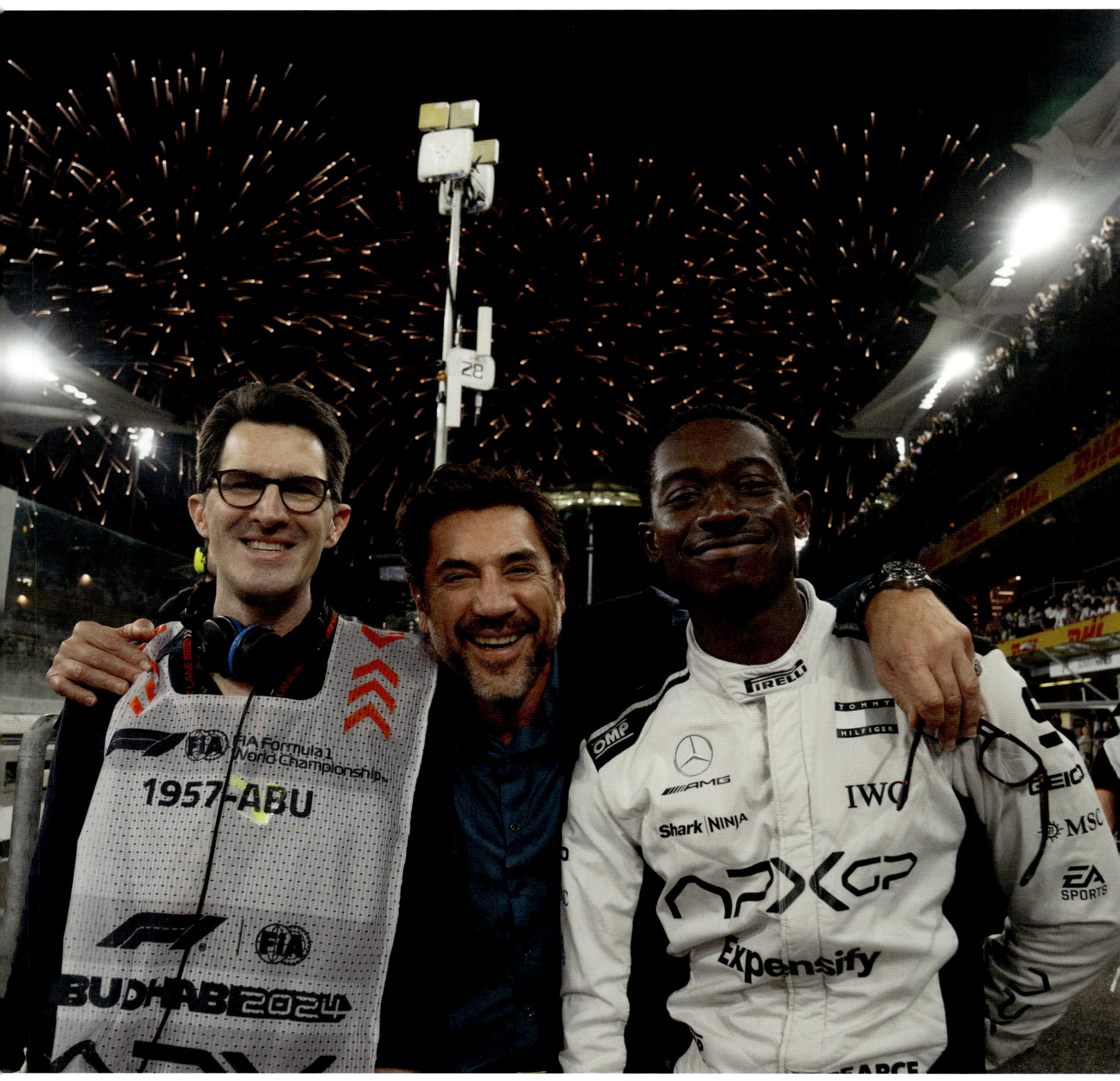
28
FIA Formula 1 World Championship
1957-ABU
FIA
PIRELLI
TOMMY HILFIGER
OMP
AMG
IWC
Shark NINJA
MSC
APXGP
EA SPORTS
Expensify

Left: Damson Idris joined the cast to play Joshua Pearce, a racing rookie, alongside Joseph Kosinski and Javier Bardem, who plays Ruben Cervantes, the owner of APXGP.

Bottom Right: A POV shot of the Silverstone racetrack.

In early 2022, Kruger joined Kosinski on a research trip to Silverstone, home of the British Grand Prix, to watch preseason testing with Mercedes, before spending a week at the team's factory in the U.K., speaking with engineers and aerodynamicists as well as pitching the story to Hamilton and Wolff. It was during that meeting that Kruger realized he had much to learn about Formula One after he mentioned a scene in which Hayes jumps into Pearce's car and takes it for a spin. "Lewis and Toto immediately said, 'Whoa. Wait a minute. You do know the seats in F1 cars are molded specifically to the driver's body. He could not just get in. You do know that, right?' And I said, 'I know that *now*. And we will not do that.'"

The following month, Kruger visited the Bahrain Grand Prix as a guest of Mercedes, hanging out in the team garage with his notebook, sitting in on strategy meetings with Hamilton, his teammate George Russell, and their engineers, absorbing every detail during the four-day race weekend. "That was the first time I'd been to an F1 race, and I got to talk to lots of people about the technical nuts and bolts of what happens during practice, during qualifying, during the race," says Kruger. "To have that experience, in the garage, in the room with engineers as the race was going on, was fascinating. It was like spending time at NASA. It blew my mind. Then I went into a slight panic, thinking, *How am I going to get all this experience on the page in a way an audience can understand when a million things are happening, seemingly every second, during a race?*"

What Kruger was looking for during his time in Bahrain was the drama within teams and the rivalry between drivers, and he spoke to F1 personnel from up and down the paddock, not just Mercedes. "I said, 'I don't want to know about drivers who get along great. I don't want to know about the years where your car works perfectly. Tell me about all the problems.' And being the first race weekend on the calendar, it was easier to get engineers, drivers, even team principals to speak with a reasonable degree of candor about challenges that had come in past seasons."

Hamilton, too, proved an invaluable resource when it came to providing insights into a driver's rivalry with one's teammate, having experienced the situation several times during his long and illustrious career. "He had all kinds of stories about his experience with former Mercedes teammate Nico Rosberg and coming into a team as, say, the second driver, and wanting to prove you are the best, and maybe the mechanics on your teammate's car don't want you to be the best driver, they want their guy to be," says Kruger. "He had wonderful stories about competition within a team."

As the filmmakers continued to develop the script, their initial pitch transformed from being a *Color of Money*–style tale in which Pitt's character was a team principal who became a driver into the story of Sonny Hayes, a veteran racer parachuted into an ailing Formula One team, APXGP, by its owner, longtime friend, and former F1 teammate Ruben Cervantes (Javier Bardem), who pairs him with a raw but talented rookie, Joshua Pearce (Damson Idris).

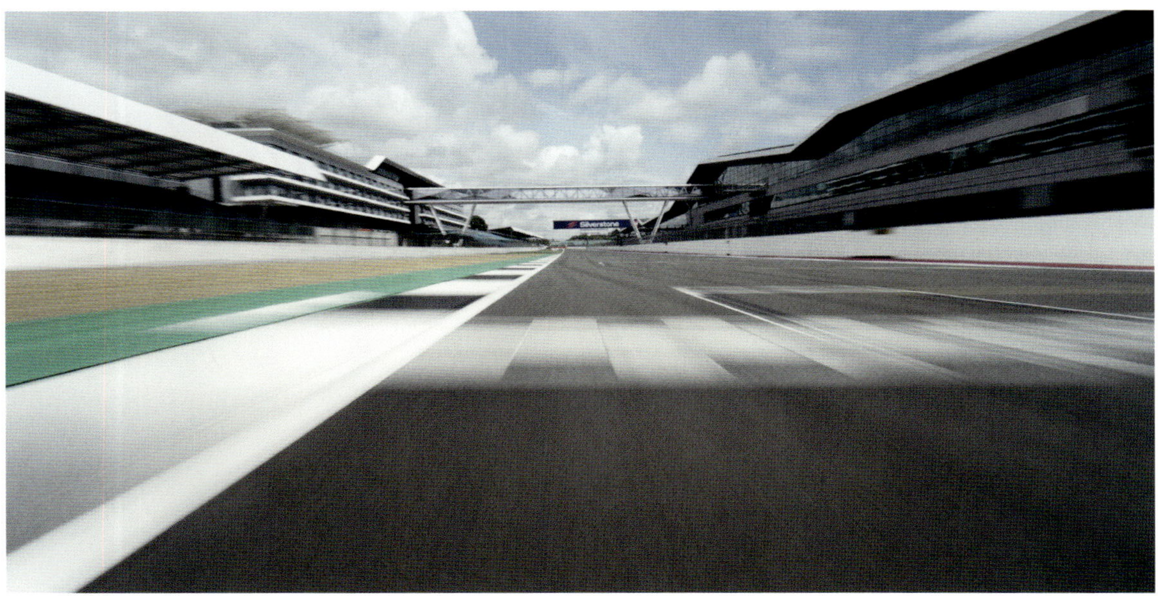

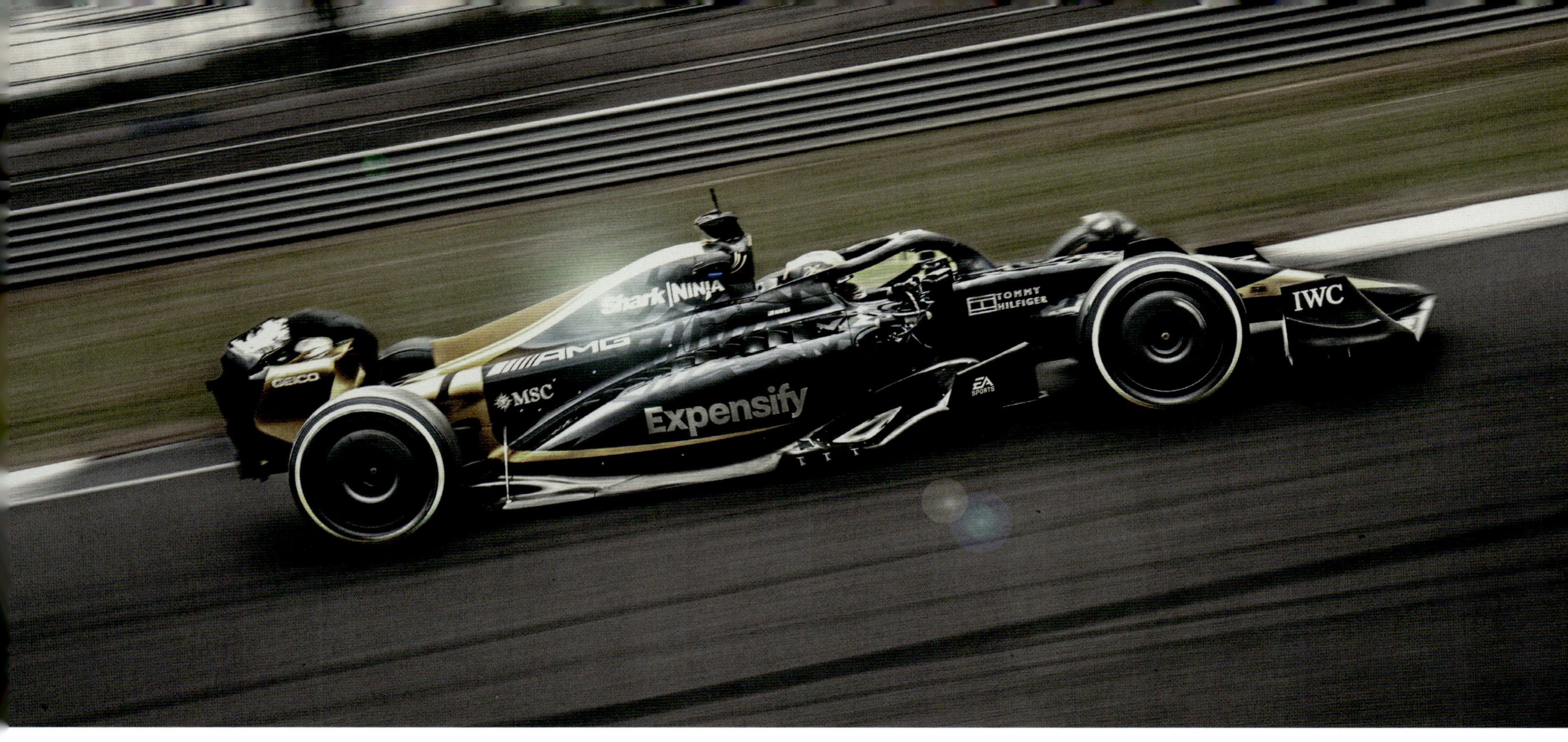

In addition to fleshing out the characters and dramatizing the rivalry between the two APXGP drivers, Kruger needed to figure out how many Grand Prix to cover over the course of the film, given that a Formula One season runs between twenty-three and twenty-four races, as well as what action could realistically occur at each race, to tell a compelling and propulsive story. He decided on ten in total: nine F1 races and one in another motorsport category at which Sonny would be introduced. Six of the nine Grand Prix would involve major action sequences, taking place in Silverstone, the Hungaroring, Monza, Spa-Francorchamps, Las Vegas, and Abu Dhabi, with a three-race montage encompassing Zandvoort, Suzuka, and Mexico City.

From a narrative point of view, the same action couldn't happen twice. More important, each race needed to tell the audience something new about Sonny and Joshua's ongoing relationship, which starts out combative and antagonistic, develops into grudging respect, before, finally, the two drivers put team first and learn to work together. "I would ask myself, *How do I want this race to end for these two characters?* And that would determine whether one performs better than the other, whether they knock each other out in a crash, whether that's accidental or intentional," says Kruger, who, during his research, looked for real-world situations where he felt Sonny could exploit the

Each race needed to tell the audience something new about Sonny and Joshua's ongoing relationship.

Top Left: The APXGP car speeds down a track at Silverstone.

Top Right: Team Principal Kaspar (Kim Bodnia) confronts Sonny (Brad Pitt), with Joshua (Damson Idris) looking on.

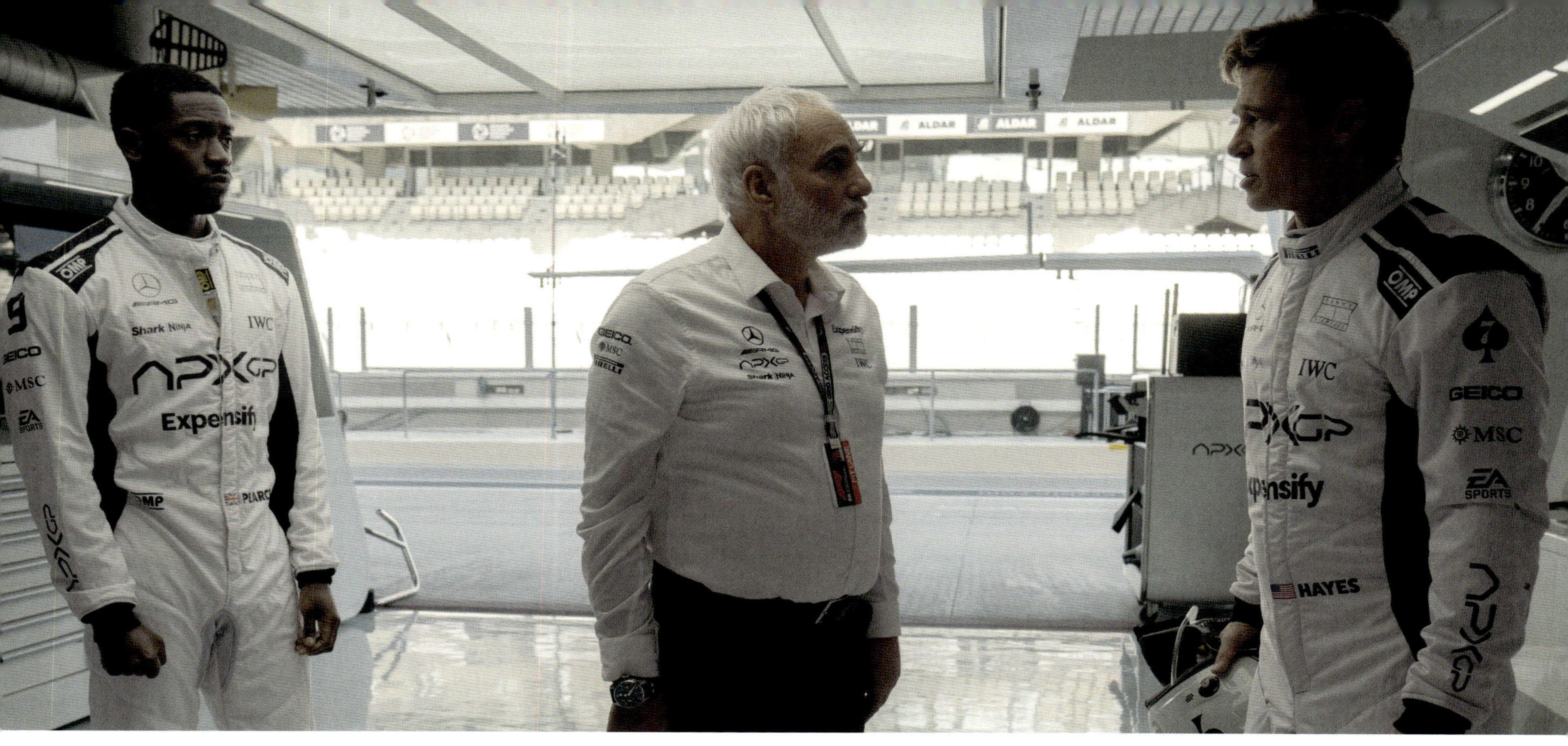

rules and regulations to the benefit of his APXGP team—be it driving excessively slowly during the formation lap to cause the tires on the other cars to lose heat or causing a safety car to come out during a race to save his teammate valuable seconds while making a pit stop.

But it was imperative that Sonny never cheated. "First of all, F1, as an organization, would never let us do that," Kruger continues. "We loved the idea of Sonny pushing right up to what is possible within the rules, that maybe an opponent might not have thought of or might have missed, whether it's another team or another driver. That's something that fascinated me about this sport; there are thousands of people poring over the regulations to find the one element that other teams might have missed or might be able to interpret it a different way. And once I knew where each race needed to end dramatically, I tried to see how many obstacles I could give APXGP in trying to get there."

When Kruger finished crafting each race, Kosinski would send it to Hamilton for his approval. "Lewis was invaluable," says Bruckheimer. "Lewis would read *everything*. Ehren would come up with things and Lewis would say, 'That's not real. You don't do that.' And so we would work with Lewis and come up with an alternative that *was* real."

"We would go through [the script] line by line," remembers Kosinski. "Lewis would say, turn six is a right-hander not a left-hander, and it has a small curb there, so you can cut the curb and shave a tenth of a second. And in Hungary, if it's hot, you can't do a soft tire strategy; you've got to start on mediums. We had the greatest driver of all time as a consultant, and he was interested in getting every detail right."

"The degree of specificity from Lewis was amazing," concurs Kruger. "I would look at a track map and say, 'I need this overtake to happen right before the main straight or the pit lane for the story,' and Lewis would say, 'That's the wrong corner. You wouldn't try to make that move there. Any die-hard fan would know that.' And we would change the story so there was authenticity."

While Kruger is credited as the sole screenwriter on *F1*, as with a lot of big studio productions, several other writers were drafted in to punch up certain characters during the filmmaking process. *F1* was no exception, with Jez Butterworth (*Ford v Ferrari*) and Christopher Storer (*The Bear*) brought in to help out. "Ehren delivered a script. He got it greenlit. It's 94 percent Kruger," says Oman. "But the main female character, played by Kerry Condon, we couldn't quite get right. Jez only worked for three weeks, but he has a knack for writing female characters that are charming, likable, and strong all at the same time. So, he helped with her and with Javier's character."

THE FORMULA ONE WORLD CHAMPIONSHIP

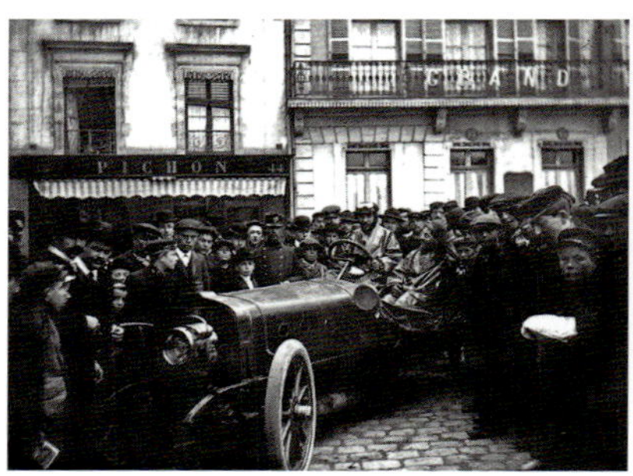

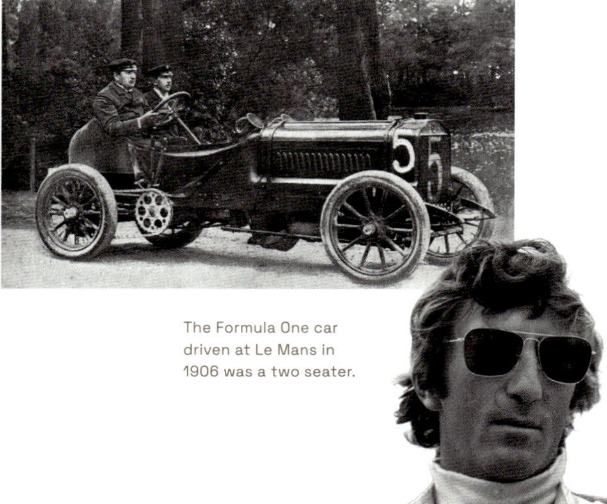

The Formula One car driven at Le Mans in 1906 was a two seater.

1906

The inaugural "Grand Prix" of international standing was held in Le Mans in 1906, and there were multiple races using the term in the years that followed, but there wasn't a consistent organization into a championship. It was only after World War II that the sport's governing body—the Fédération Internationale de l'Automobile (FIA)—defined the regulations for the top-level international single-seater racing series. Formula One is so-called due to the set of rules (Formula) and the fact it was deemed the highest category (1) by the FIA.

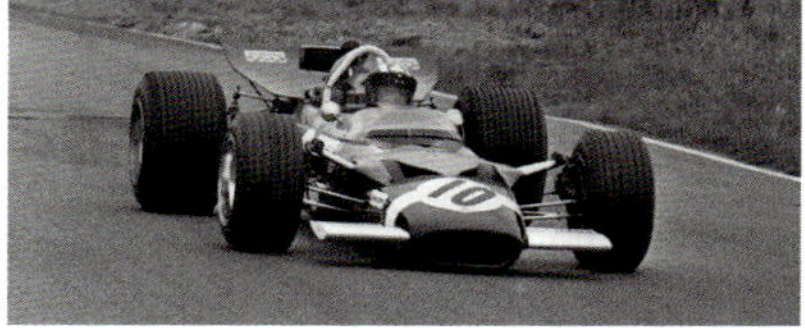

1960s

In the late '60s, the performance of the cars started to ramp up with increased power outputs and the addition of aerodynamic devices such as front and rear wings. Sponsorship became a big aspect, too, with many teams adopting paint schemes—known as liveries—in the colors of their principal backers.

The sport has always been dangerous given the speed and prototype nature of the cars, and multiple drivers were killed each season, including world champions Jim Clark—in a Formula Two race—and Jochen Rindt, in his title-winning year. But the focus on safety ramped up from the 1970s onward, with three-time world champion Jackie Stewart as one of the early campaigners.

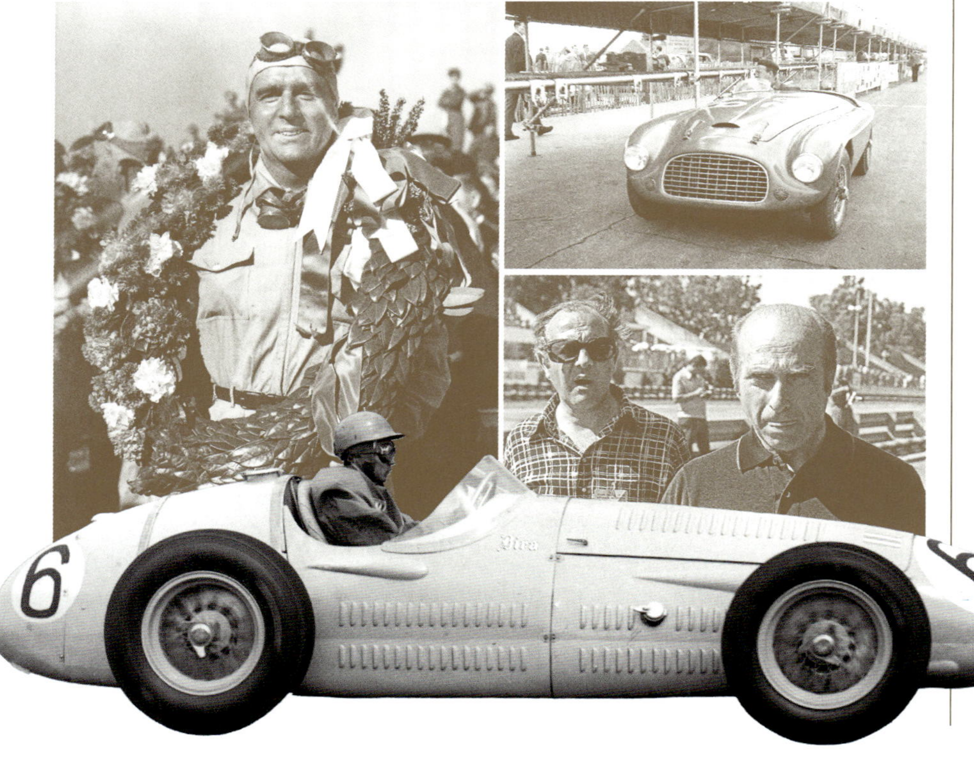

1950s

Although there have been Formula One races since the late 1940s, these were only organized into a world championship in 1950. The first world championship Formula One race took place at Silverstone in May of that year, and early seasons included major grand prix in Europe as well as the Indianapolis 500 in the United States, to create a driver's championship. The first winner was Giuseppe Farina for Alfa Romeo, before the great Juan Manuel Fangio took the first of his five titles in 1951.

Two years later, fans saw the first Formula One World Championship race (other than the Indianapolis 500) held outside of Europe, in Argentina, and the number of international races grew to double figures by the end of the decade. Mercedes dominated in the mid-'50s but then left the sport, with Ferrari the only ever-present team in the championship's history. In these early days, teams could field more than two cars at a time.

The Formula One World Championship has taken place every year since 1950, but the sport itself pre-dates that by many years.

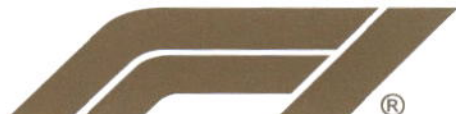

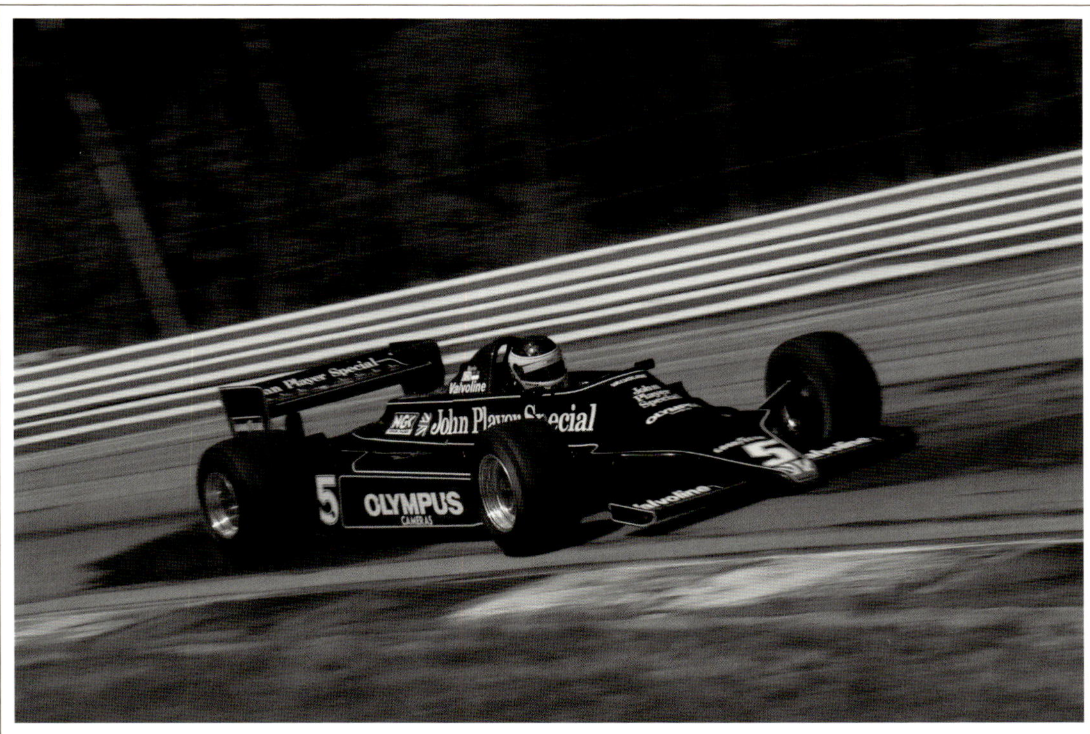

1980s

Technological development continued apace, with ground-effect car designs—which extracted performance from the aerodynamic interaction between the bottom of the car and the track surface—seeing extremely high cornering speeds before they were banned at the end of 1982. Thanks to safety improvements and advanced understanding, ground-effect cars returned to the regulations in 2022.

The sport has been through multiple eras, including turbocharged and naturally aspirated engines, and varying levels of driver aids and aerodynamic restrictions. Often these restrictions are revised on safety grounds to prevent cars from getting infinitely quicker, but they also evolve in response to the global automotive market.

1970s

By that point, the sport was becoming more commercial, with teams starting to work together as they recognized their value. In 1978, Bernie Ecclestone—who owned the historic Brabham outfit and ran an association including several teams—secured the ability to negotiate television contracts for races, eventually separating the commercial rights for the sport from the FIA.

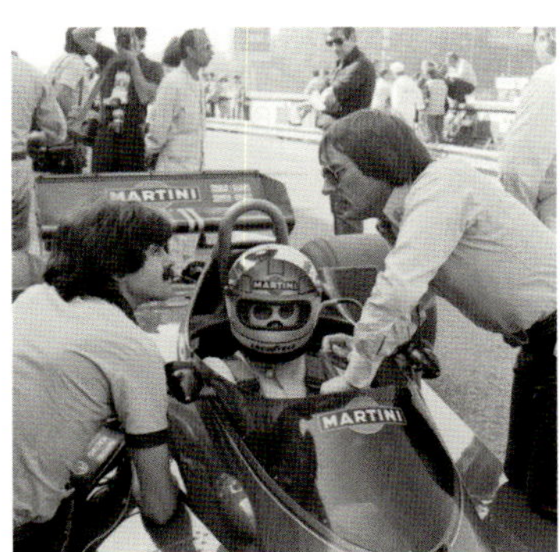

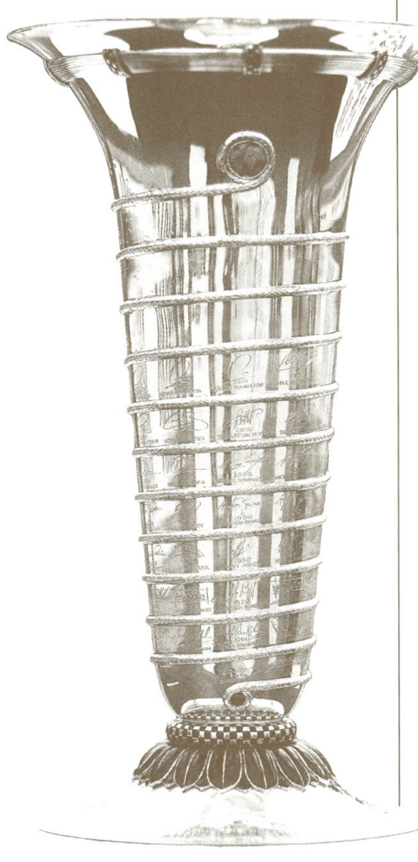

TODAY

Today, twenty drivers across ten teams* race across five continents in a truly global world championship. The points system has changed on multiple occasions, with the current format seeing the top ten finishers in each race scoring and the winner picking up twenty-five points. The driver with the most points at the end of the season is crowned the driver's champion, while the team that accumulates the highest total from both of its cars is awarded the constructors' championship.

*General Motors will join the championship with a team under the Cadillac brand in 2026, increasing the number of teams to eleven and drivers to twenty-two.

Despite having Hamilton and Wolff on board as consultants and producers, the authenticity that Kosinski and Bruckheimer required to film at real racetracks during actual race weekends could only be bestowed by the sports' owners, F1 Racing.

In February 2022, Kosinski, Bruckheimer, and Pitt flew to England to see Stefano Domenicali, CEO of F1 Racing and a former team principal of the Scuderia Ferrari Formula One team. During the meeting at F1 Racing's London headquarters, the three men outlined their concept for the film, which would require APXGP to be the eleventh team on the grid for almost half a season. It wasn't the first time that Hollywood had approached Formula One about making an F1 movie, but it was the first time an approach had been welcomed.

"We found out later, there were a couple of other producers with different pitches [in Austin], pitching to people and pitching to Lewis," says Oman. "So, we didn't know we had competition. But we ended up winning the day. I think they described it as, 'We're only going to do this if we are doing it with the best in class.'"

"The proposal from Joe, Jerry, and Brad came at the right moment with the right ingredients," says Domenicali, who joined the film as executive producer. "Coming after Covid and *Drive to Survive* and knowing who they were and the credibility they have in their world, I didn't have any doubt that this could be a successful project. So I said to them, 'Leave it with me, let me work with my ecosystem to make sure everyone understands that the movie has to be authentic.' Because, for me, that was the one thing that was essential, that the movie be authentic. So, it was a great meeting. Straightaway it was a thumbs up. Then it became a question of understanding what their need was during the race weekend. Because it was important to keep the live event and the movie separate. And from that moment on, we began a journey of daily contact. I start to speak with the teams and the drivers, because I said, 'We need to make sure that we all understand the benefit of the movie for our business.'"

"Stefano was a fan from the beginning," notes Bruckheimer. "He realized what *Top Gun* did for the Navy and what *Days of Thunder* did for NASCAR. And I think he realized that we're people of our word, and when we tell you something we're going to follow through on it. He could check with the Navy, or he could check with the Army, or anybody I've worked with, or anybody Joe's worked with, and see we're going to stand behind what we tell them."

"Jerry's reputation goes a long way," says Oman. "I think they did some checking with other studios we had worked with and with the Navy, because you must be collaborative and cooperative with the Navy. There were a lot of rules, and a lot of classified things and we had navigated those. Joe, specifically, had navigated that very well and turned a year's worth of, 'No, you can't have a camera on a jet. No, you can't have a camera inside a jet, that would be super dangerous,' into yeses. And they were absolute nos. But if you listen and understand and collaborate, you can find a way to do it. I think that went a long way with the Formula One people."

Kosinski and Bruckheimer also arranged for Domenicali and Pitt to watch *Top Gun: Maverick* in IMAX immediately after their initial meeting. "This was three months before the movie came out, so they got to be among the first people to see it," Kosinski recalls. "The reason I showed it to them was because the way we shot *Top Gun* was very applicable to how I was going to shoot *F1*. Also, Stefano was a huge *Top Gun* fan."

"I've seen that movie twenty-five to thirty times," says Domenicali. "I know every single frame. I know all the music around it. That's why we discussed having a soundtrack to be remembered for our movie. So, it was a privilege to see *Top Gun: Maverick* with them on a big screen, and really an incredible experience. After that, it was impossible to say no to their project."

"I think it showed him the power of cinema and how Formula One could be a different experience at the cinema than on TV, on *Drive to Survive*, or even in person," says Kosinski. "A large, theatrical experience can put you in that car in a way no other medium can."

Before then, there was "a year of meetings and discussions about what the film was, bringing Apple and F1 together," continues Kosinski. "I can't tell you how many meetings and lawyers and contracts and negotiations there were to pull something like this off. The sponsorship aspect of it was huge. But there's no way I could have made this movie without Formula One's participation. They've been an amazing partner, and we couldn't have done it without Stefano's support and help."

Joseph Kosinski shakes hands with Stefano Domenicali, CEO of F1 Racing and former team principal of the Scuderia Ferrari Formula One team.

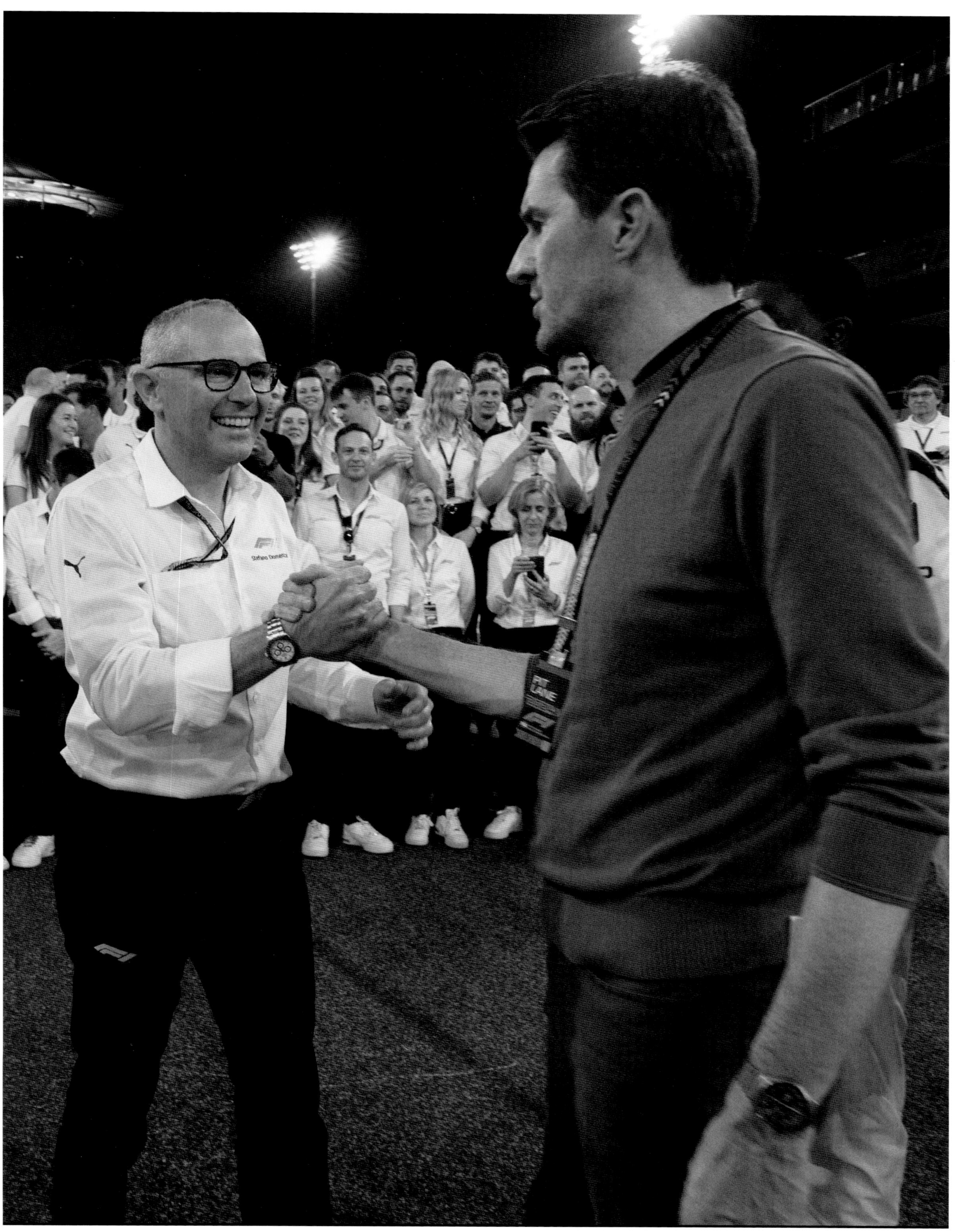
PIT
LANE

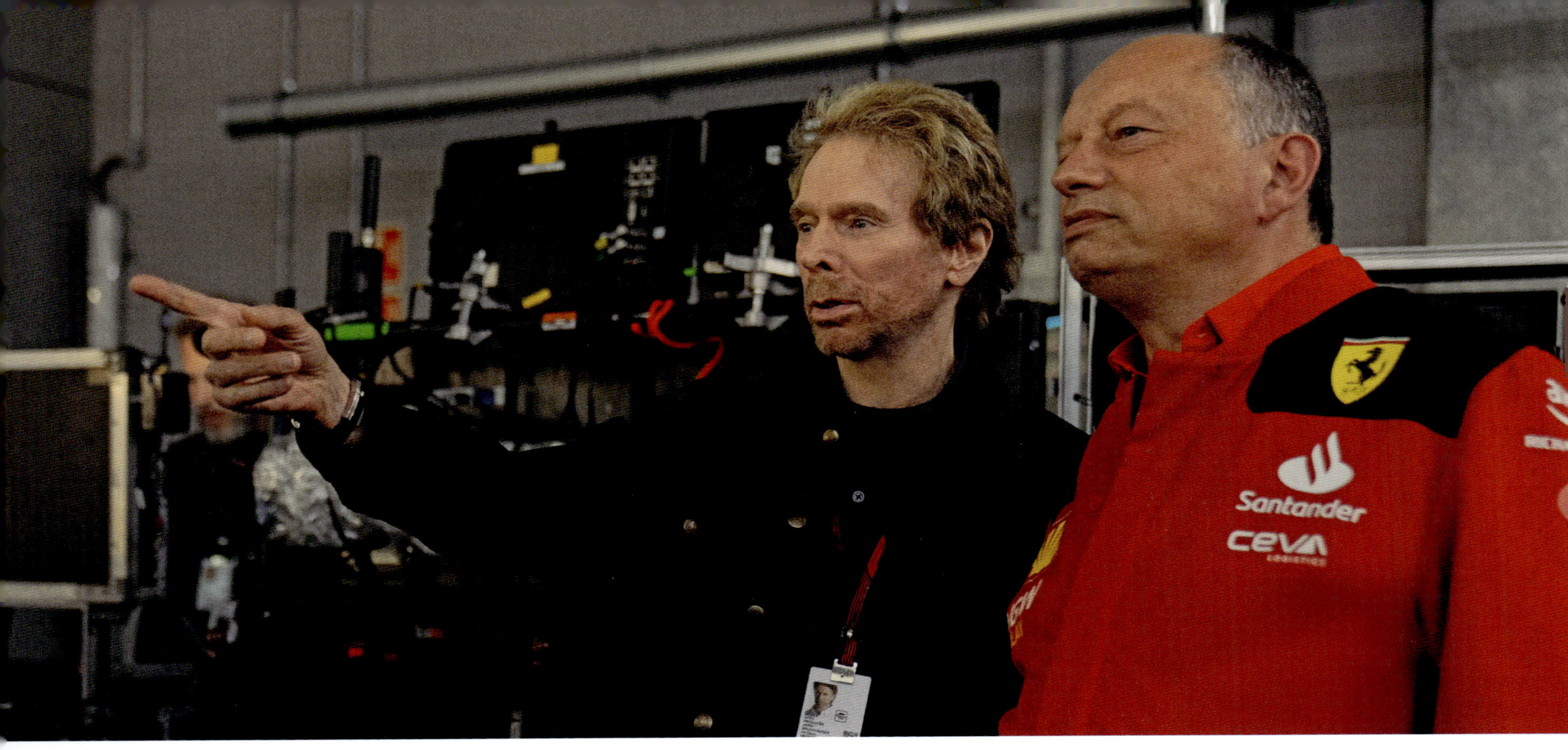

Even with F1's assistance, Kosinski and Bruckheimer still needed to get the approval of all ten teams on the grid, so they began a lengthy courtship that continued well into filming. "I had to go to every team principal, every team owner. I had to present to all of them at principal meetings. I had to present to all the drivers at driver meetings. I had to go to each driver individually," says Kosinski. "I would go to Grand Prix after Grand Prix with my laptop and show them pictures of the car that we were building and talk about how we were going to make the film."

"We were coming in as outsiders, and we were coming into very hallowed ground. Elite drivers, elite crew, elite team principals, and it's a very closed loop," says Pitt. "So, we came in with humility and wanted to hear any concerns and make sure that we wouldn't be in their way."

"It didn't take two seconds for me to go, 'This is a great idea,' given their background with *Top Gun* and Brad Pitt being a pretty famous dude," laughs Zak Brown, CEO of McLaren Racing. "Who didn't watch *Top Gun* and go, 'I want to be a fighter pilot. I want to be Tom Cruise'? Knowing Brad and Damson were going to be driving race cars, and the type of production Joe and Jerry can put together, I thought this was going to do wonders for our sport."

Still, there was some skepticism. "Firstly, it's not an American sport. So, a bunch of

"We were coming in as outsiders, and we were coming into very hallowed ground."

BRAD PITT

Top Left: The production crew, including Jerry Bruckheimer, worked hard to reassure F1 experts like Frédéric Vasseur, team principal of Scuderia Ferrari, that the movie would create something "real" for F1 fans.

Top Right: Jerry Bruckheimer speaks with the former team principal of Red Bull Racing, Christian Horner.

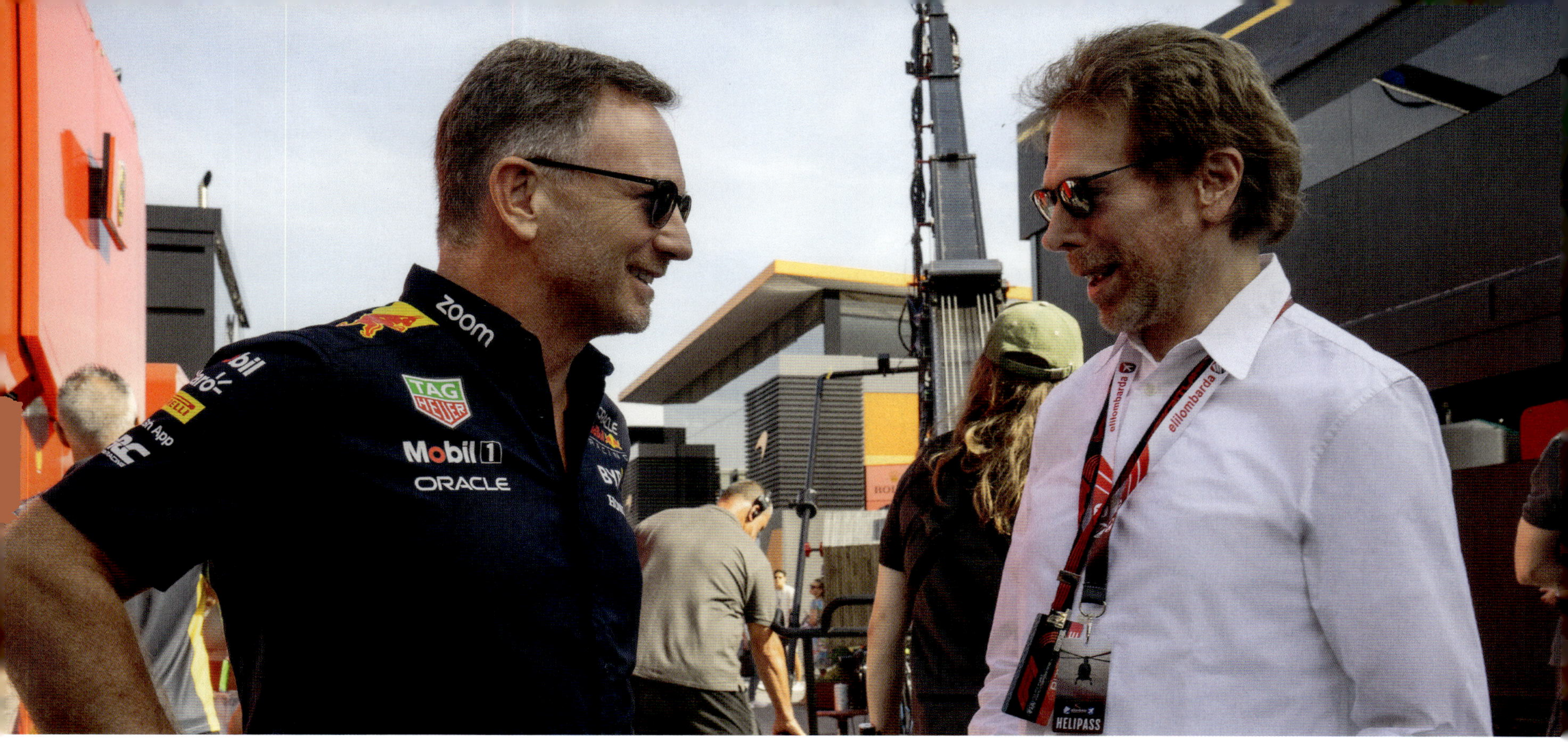

Americans walk in and say, 'We want to make a movie about Formula One,' they naturally assume it's going to be the Hollywood version," says Kosinski. "I talked about great racing movies like *Grand Prix* and *Le Mans*, but there's been a lot that are not great, certainly from a driver's point of view. I had the same experience with the Navy on *Top Gun: Maverick*. Pilots would complain about scenes in movies they felt were fake—even the original *Top Gun*. So, I was used to that [reaction]. I understood it. They don't believe you're ever going to be able to capture what it's really like. And I wasn't saying we were going to capture what it feels like to be an F1 driver, but we were going to get as close as possible."

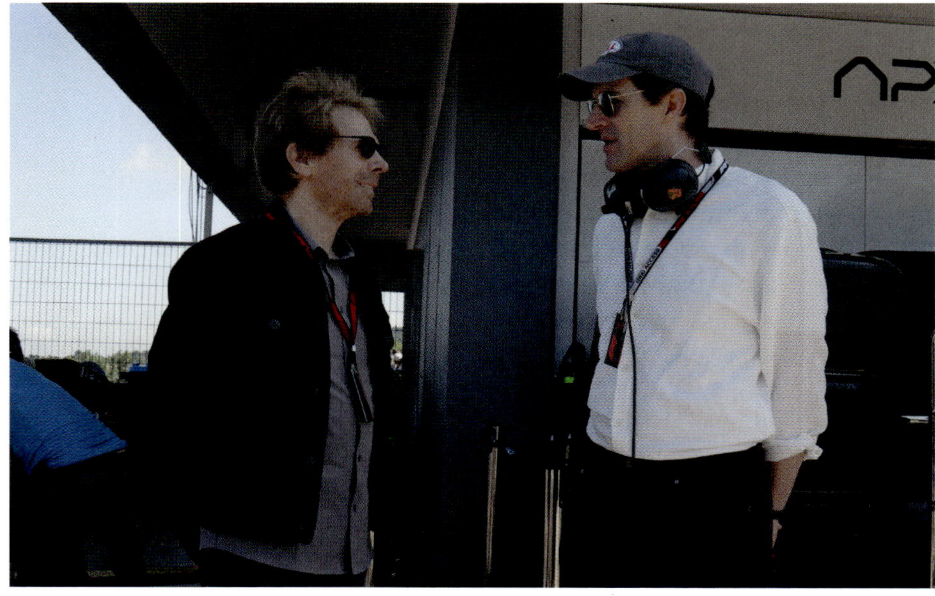

"I was a bit worried, to be honest, because it's very, very difficult to do something like this," admits Frédéric Vasseur, team principal of Scuderia Ferrari HP. "If you want to do a movie for people that are not fans of F1, I think it's quite easy. If you want to do something for the fans of F1, who know about F1, it's much more difficult, because it must be real. I was a bit concerned they would do something fake."

But that initial skepticism wasn't the sole province of the teams. "Every time you hear they're going to make a racing movie, your first thought is, *How are they going to fuck it up this time?* Because it is such a complex sport and so hard to get right," says Will Buxton, motorsport journalist and F1 commentator who joined the film as a consultant and played himself in several scenes. "Even *Ford v Ferrari*, which is one of the best motor racing movies ever made, still had the downshift on the Mulsanne straight [at Le Mans], which is going to blow your gearbox and engine out the back of the car. But very early on, it was clear they were going to do it right. Joe was talking about Frankenheimer and *Grand Prix*. He said, 'He's my North Star. How he did it in the '60s, that's what I want to do here. I want to embed us in the sport. We're not pretending our drivers are current drivers. We're creating an extra team. We're going to be a part of it.'"

The moment that helped win over any remaining doubters came during the Austin Grand Prix race weekend when Kosinski, Bruckheimer, Pitt, and Kruger met with every team principal at one time. "It was fascinating to start with all ten sitting with their arms folded and frowns on their faces," recalls Kruger. "We said, 'This is your world. This is your sport. We want to depict it as authentically as possible and show it off. But we will need your buy-in; we will need your participation. It will be your cars, your team names, and your drivers. But if you say, 'I don't want to be on-screen,' we'll honor that.'"

They began with some behind-the-scenes footage from *Top Gun: Maverick*, revealing how visual effects had put a digital skin on top of an F-18 fighter to transform it into the Russian MiGs seen in the film. "We showed them how we reskinned the various airplanes. The flying was always authentic, but the skins changed," says Bruckheimer. "And we said, 'That's what we're going to do with the F1 cars.'"

Then they played a ten-second clip of broadcast footage from that year's British Grand Prix in which Hamilton's Mercedes was racing Lando Norris's McLaren, but the Mercedes had been "reskinned" as an APXGP car. "We put together this five-shot sequence to prove that this was a very visceral, realistic, and instantly authentic way to show our car on the track with other cars," says visual effects supervisor Ryan Tudhope. "Joe graded it and had the team at Skywalker Sound do some sound design. The result was really convincing, and showed how the techniques we used on *Top Gun: Maverick* could also be used to tell this story."

The reaction in the room was utter astonishment. "You saw all ten team principals relax their guard," says Kruger.

Ferrari's Vasseur was among those present. "I think they convinced everybody with the quality of the footage and what they could do changing the livery and the cars," he says.

"When you're not making movies, you don't quite understand how the magic is," says Bruckheimer. "And what Joe did was show them behind the curtain. They couldn't believe how seamless it was and how beautiful it looked. That was a big step in them knowing that the movie was going to be, as far as the technology, on the cutting edge."

"It was a huge moment," reflects Kosinski, "because for the year leading up to that, it had been all talk. Me talking about what we'd done on *Top Gun* and how I was going to do it with Formula One. I showed [the clip] to Toto and Lewis first. As soon as they saw it, they were, 'Wow, this is going to work.' What they loved was that we were using the real sport as the baseline. The speed was there, the environment was there. There was nothing fake about it. I think the authenticity of the result was what got them excited."

While the question of authenticity had been answered, there were still some concerns from certain teams that they or their drivers would be portrayed as the villains of the piece.

"They felt if we were partnering with Mercedes, they were going to be the bad guy," reveals Kosinski. "I had to say, 'No one's a villain in this film.' It was about a bottom-dwelling team trying to score their first point or, maybe, their first victory. And the villain, if there is one, is someone internal to APXGP."

"It took a year of sitting down with all the team principals and drivers to say, 'The movie is about a competition between two drivers, it's not about you,'" says Bruckheimer, who'd been down this road three times before, having had to convince the U.S. Navy to lend its support for both *Top Gun* movies and NASCAR to help with *Days of Thunder*. "The France family [who run NASCAR] were just as skeptical when we first approached them. Fortunately, I had Tom Cruise with me, which helped enormously, and it turned out great. Once the Formula One teams knew we were being authentic, they were all in."

And so, by the time Kosinski finally began filming at the British Grand Prix on July 5, 2023, all ten teams were onboard. "At that point, they trusted that we were going to represent Formula One as the pinnacle of motor racing, which it is," says Kosinski.

To create a realistic racing film, Kosinski and Bruckheimer obtained permission from all ten Formula One racing teams to film on the grid.

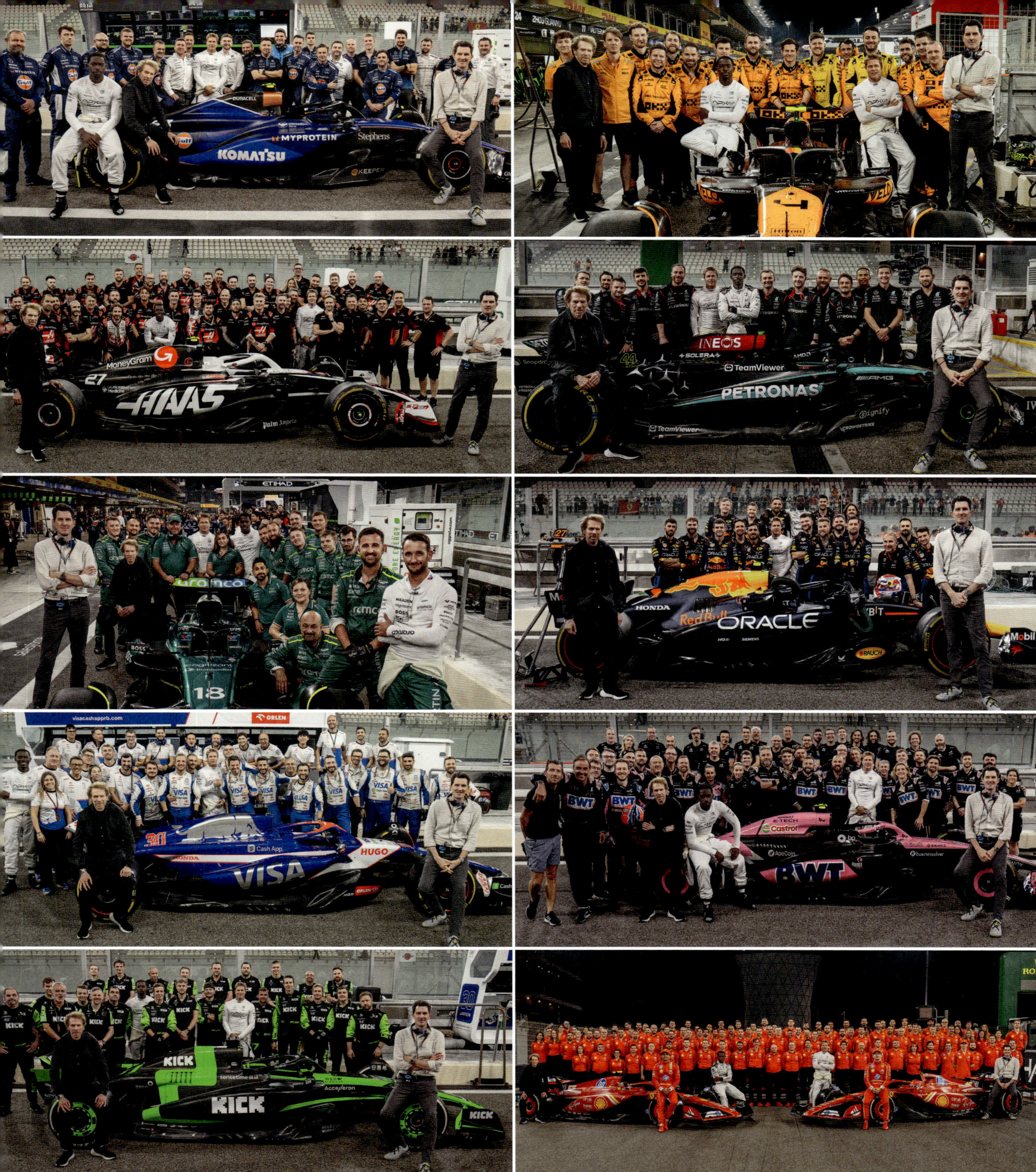
KOMATSU
MYPROTEIN
Stephens
Gulf
DURACELL
MoneyGram
HAAS
27
Palm Angels
INEOS
SOLERA
TeamViewer
PETRONAS
44
aramco
ETIHAD
18
HONDA
Red Bull
ORACLE
RAUCH
Mobil
visacashapprb.com
ORLEN
VISA
HUGO
Cash App
BWT
Castrol
KICK
sensetime
Acceleron

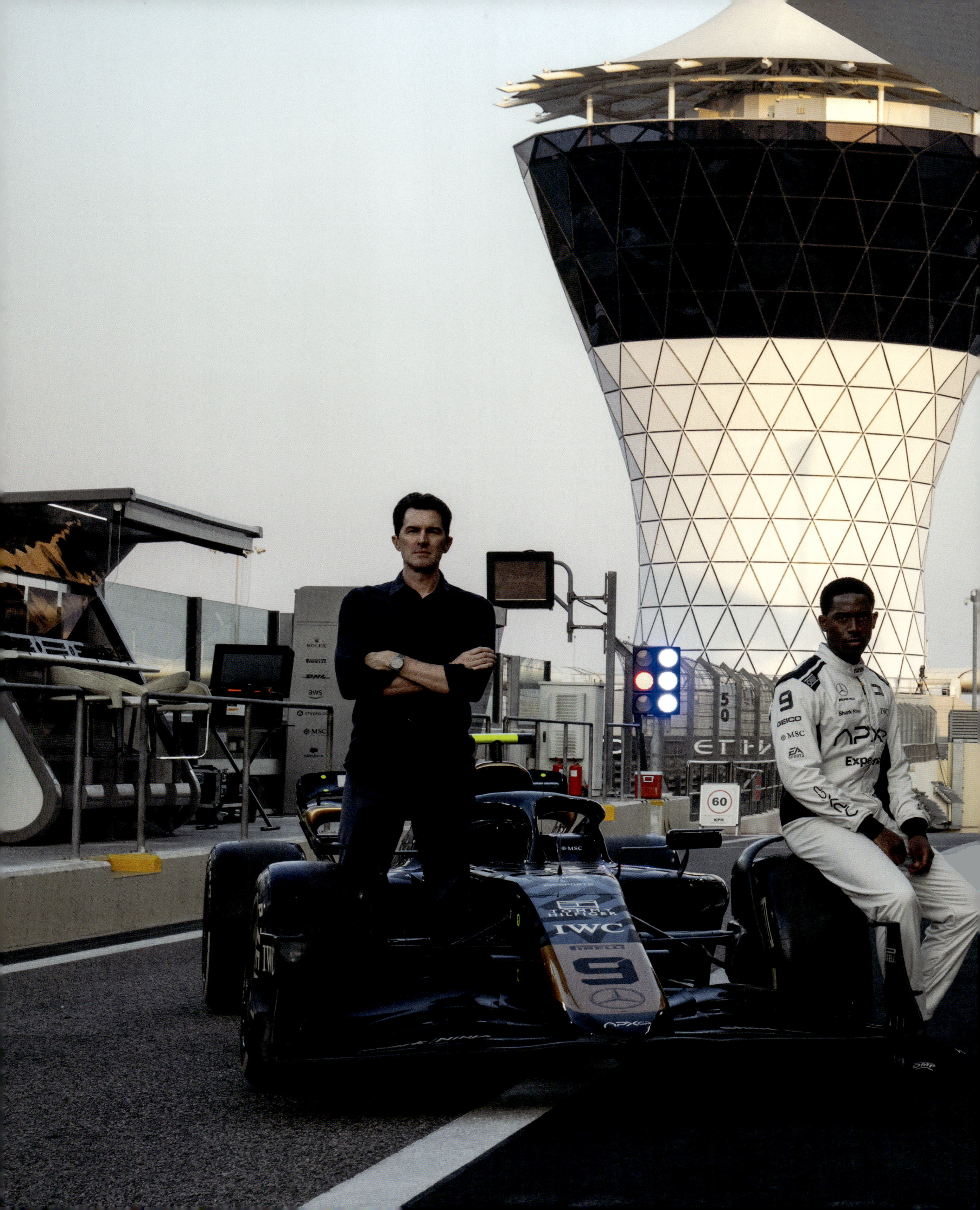
ROLEX
PIRELLI
DHL
aws
MSC
TOMMY HILFIGER
IWC
9
GEICO
MSC
EA SPORTS
Shark Ninja
60
KPH
50

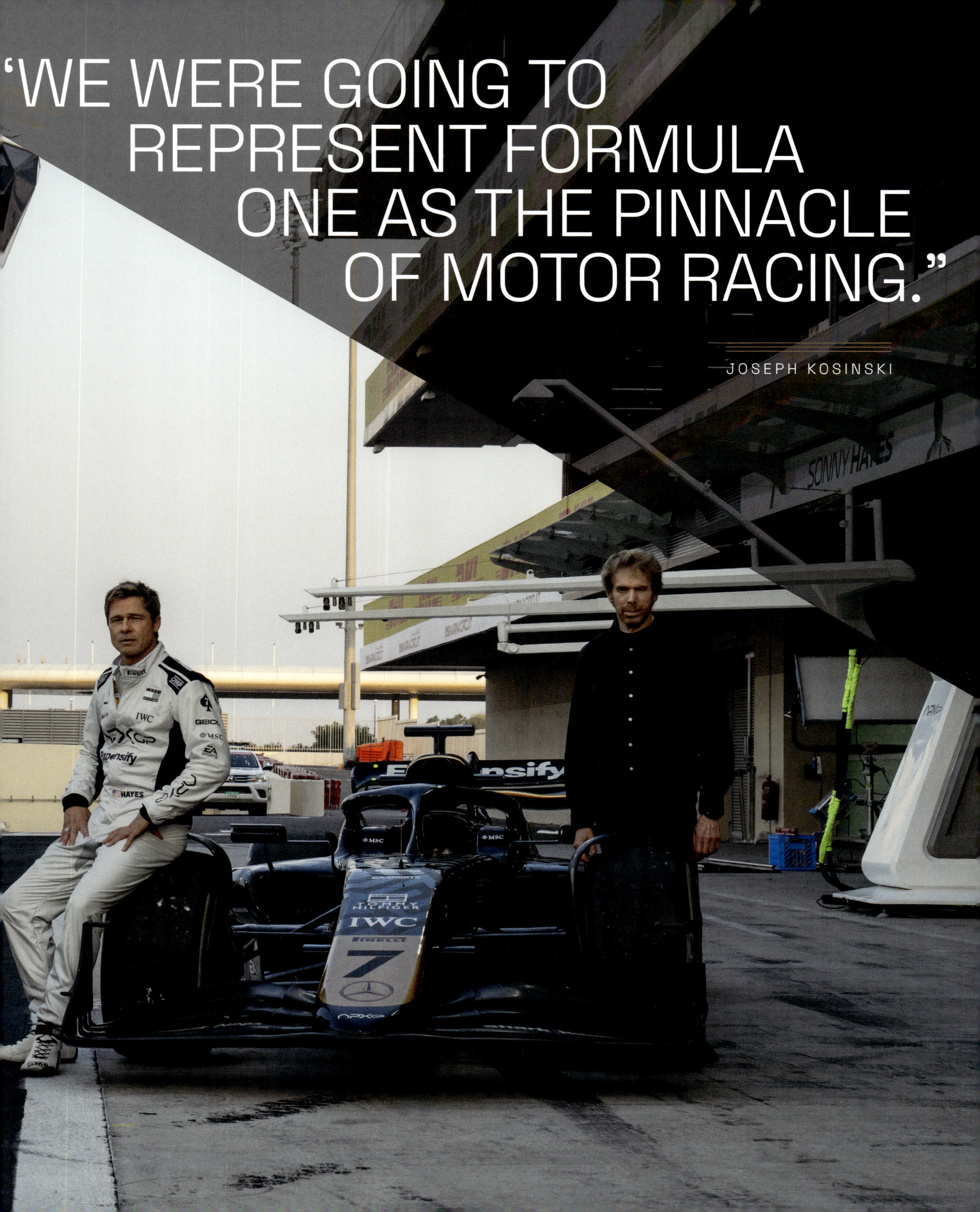

‘WE WERE GOING TO REPRESENT FORMULA ONE AS THE PINNACLE OF MOTOR RACING.”

JOSEPH KOSINSKI

CARS AND CAMERAS

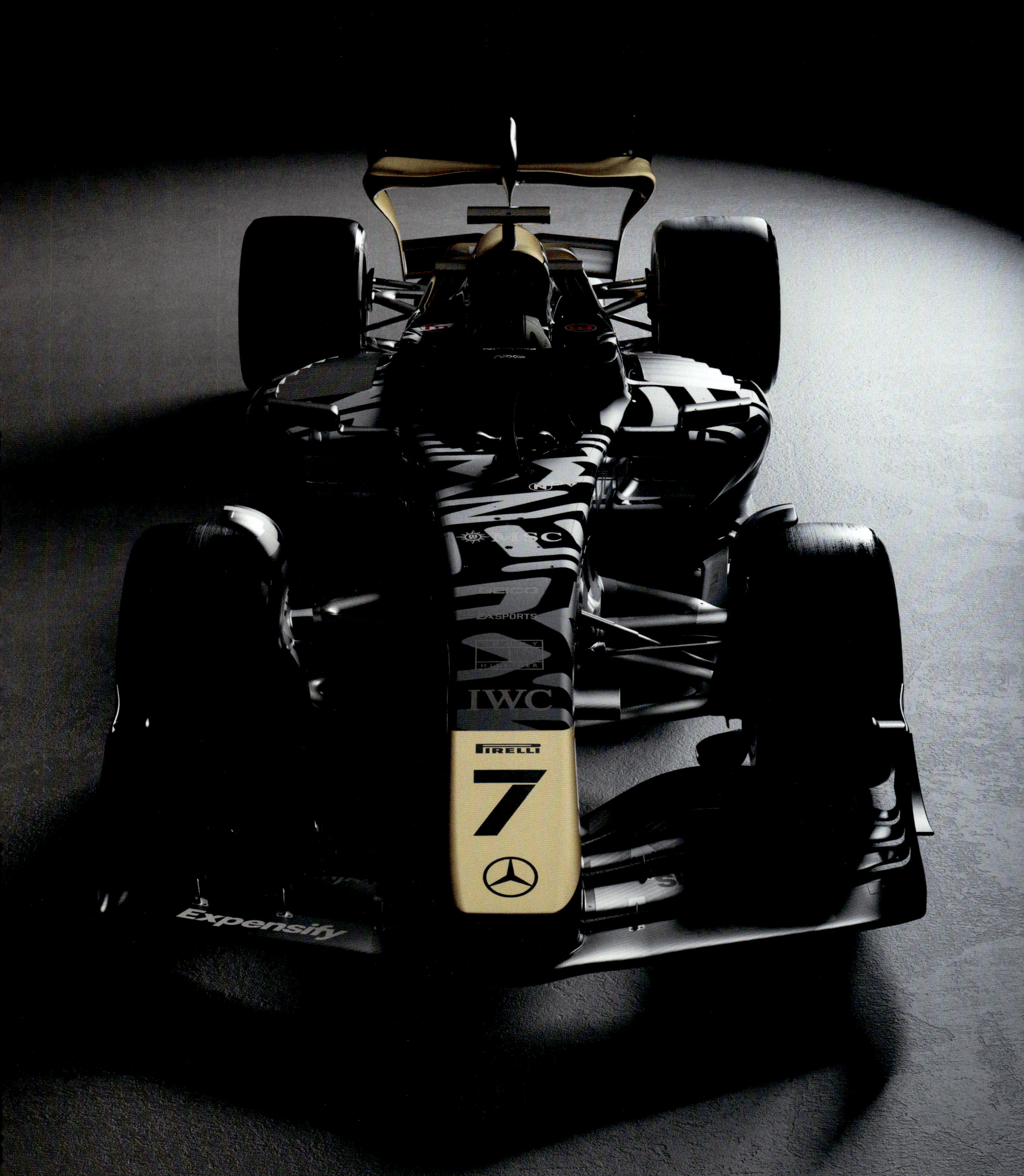
MSC
EA SPORTS
IWC
PIRELLI
7
Expensify

If APXGP was to be the eleventh team on the Formula One grid, they would need a minimum of two cars for Brad Pitt, Damson Idris, and the stunt drivers to race in. But Formula One cars are bespoke machines built to a strict set of regulations every year at a cost of tens of millions of dollars and require a vast team of mechanics to maintain, both at the track and in the factory.

Knowing his movie budget wouldn't stretch that far, director Joseph Kosinski sought the advice of team principal of the Mercedes-AMG Petronas F1 Team Toto Wolff, who suggested he take a Formula Two car—which is lighter, shorter, narrower, and slower than its F1 counterpart, but still a full-on race car with a 650-horsepower engine, capable of 90 percent of the performance—and use that as the basis for the APXGP cars.

Unlike Formula One cars, all Formula Two cars are essentially the same. Their chassis are fabricated by Italian manufacturer Dallara and cost around €450,000 each; engines are €250,000 from French engineering company Mecachrome SAS; and gearboxes are provided by U.K.-based Hewland Engineering. Wolff's idea was that Applied Science, a division of his Mercedes-AMG Petronas F1 Team, would design an F1 aero body to fit on top of this F2 chassis, so on the outside, it would look like an F1 car, but underneath, it would be an F2 car.

The design team at Applied Science was led by head of aerodynamics operations and projects Richard Bruce, composite design engineer Juan Villalba, and technology engineering group leader Evangelia Angelaki. "It was up to us to do a feasibility study and see if this was realistic," recalls Villalba. "Could we make them proportionally so they look similar, even though they are not the same size, and realistically see if we could change the dimensions to make it look like an F1 car. Wheel sizes, for example, was a big win—they both use the same wheel diameters—so we thought it was feasible and said, 'Yes, we think we can do this.'"

Below: Joseph Kosinski chats with Toto Wolff, CEO of the Mercedes-AMG Petronas F1 team.

Right: The production team, in collaboration with Applied Science, a division of the Mercedes-AMG Petronas team, worked to create an F1 chassis that would fit on a more affordable F2 car.

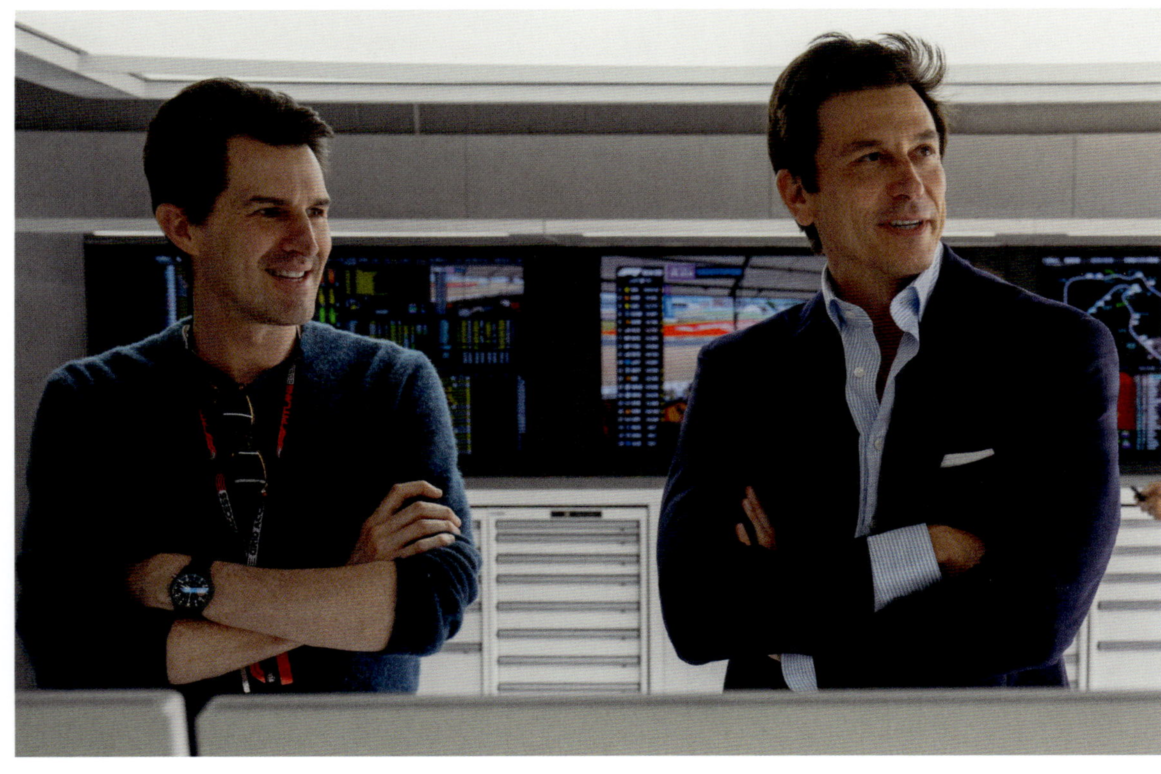

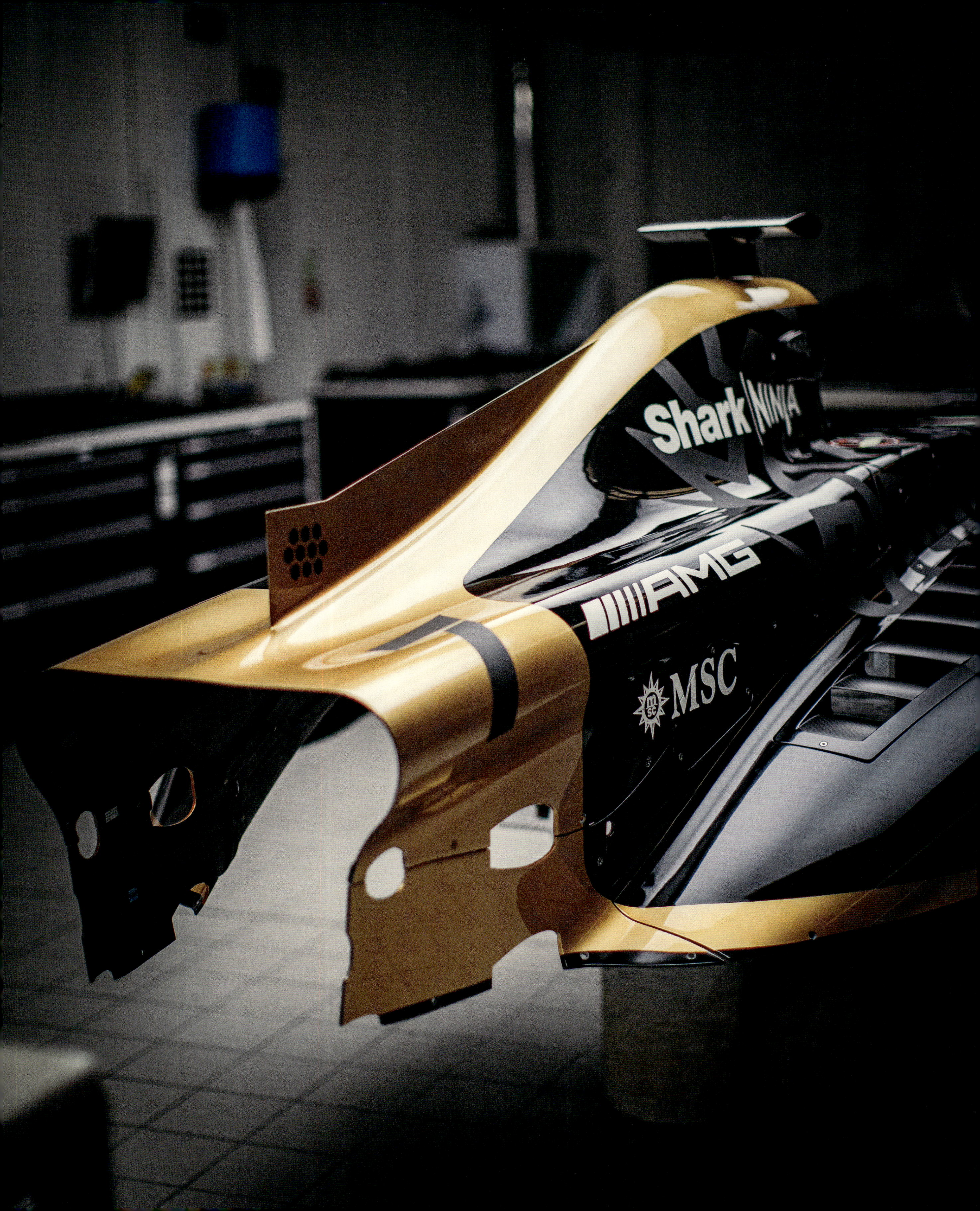

Shark NINJA
AMG
MSC

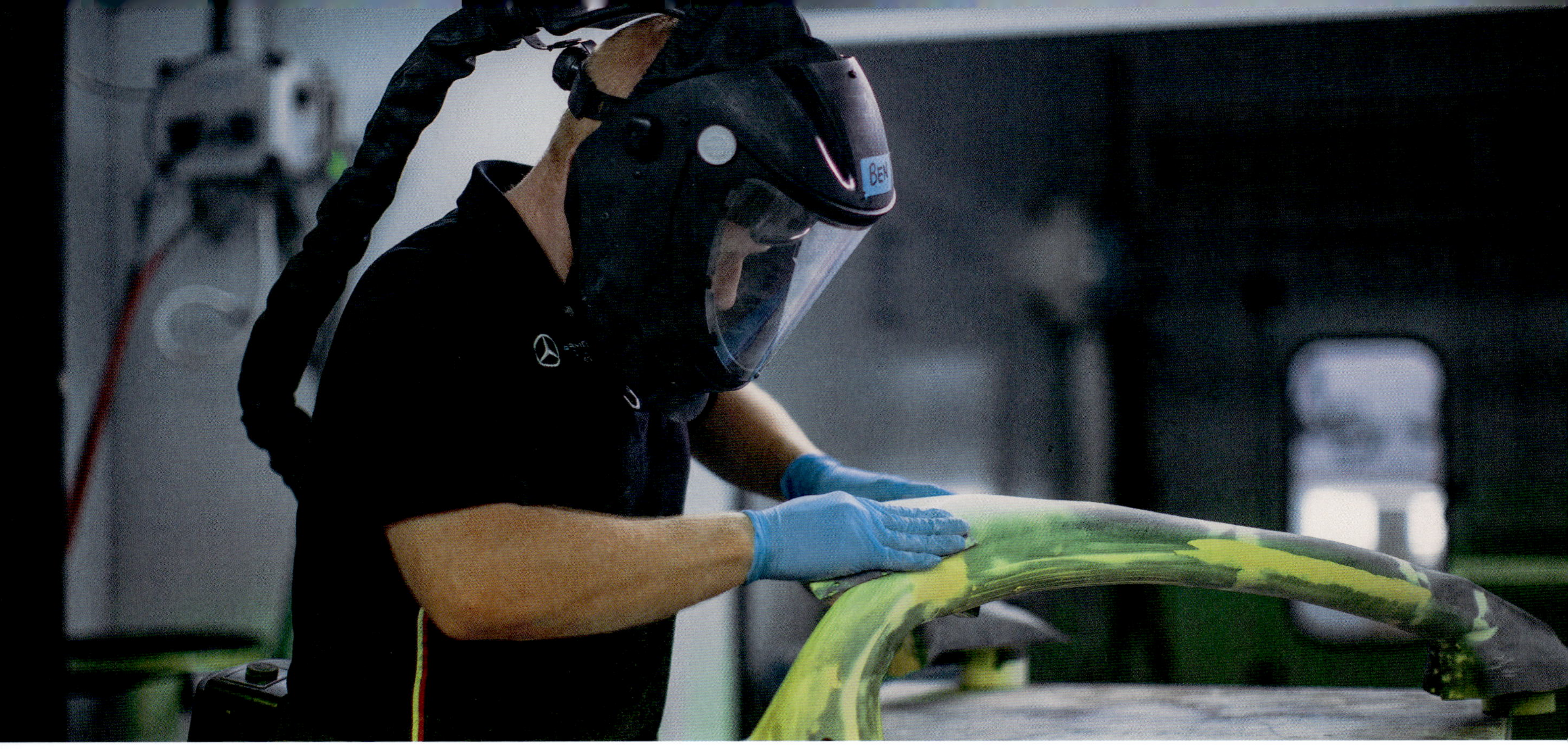

The aero design process was split into three stages, beginning with the concept phase. "Creating the shapes, to see how we can dress a car of those proportions into F1 clothes," continues Villalba. "We didn't have CAD [computer-aided design] data for the F2 car yet at that point, so we were just trying to see how the car could look with those proportions, and then if we can tweak the proportions to make it look like an F1 car. So, we created several concepts for that, and that's when we started to share this information with the filmmakers and agreed to roughly what direction we wanted to take it. Then, when we got the F2 CAD data from Dallara, we started the merging of those concepts into the car."

The biggest challenge was the timeline, with Applied Science beginning work in January 2023 and the cars needing to be ready to start filming in June at the British Grand Prix weekend in July. "So, we needed to respect some of the major structures [of the F2 car]," explains Villalba. "So, chassis, nose, rear impact structures, side impact structures, all of these are homologated, and we didn't have time to create and homologate again, so we needed to respect that. It was an exercise of blending all these clothes into existing structures, with Eva making an F1 front wing based on an F2 nose. The concept phase was mainly creating the shapes.

"Once we got a shape we wanted, then we started to find out a bit more about packaging,"

The biggest challenge was the timeline, with Applied Science beginning work in January 2023 and the cars needing to be ready to start filming in June at the British Grand Prix weekend in July.

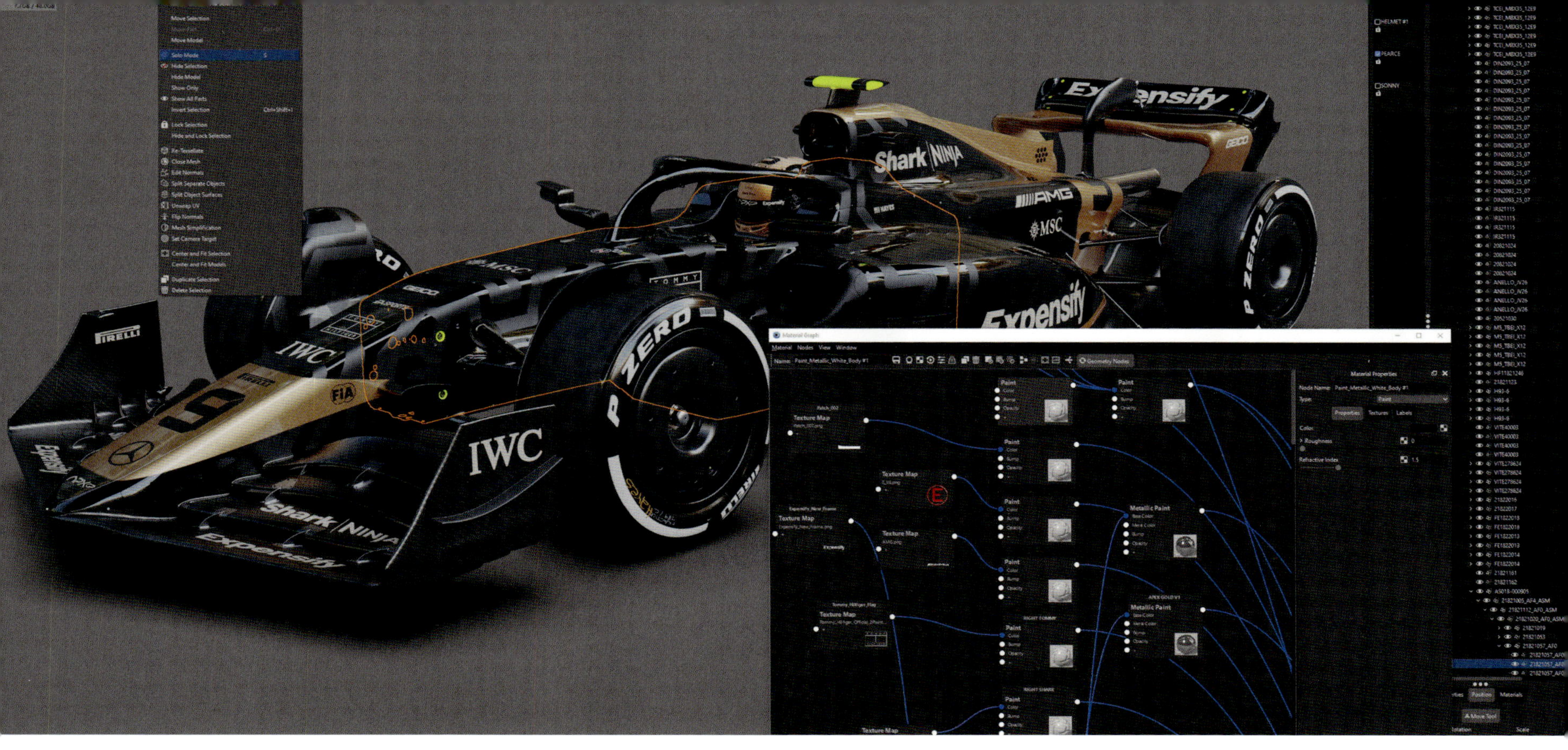

Villalba continues. "That took a fair amount of time, because this was from scratch, so we needed to match everything into an existing platform, then follow with the aero development. We changed the whole car in terms of floor and wings, so needed to make sure the car was stable aerodynamically, that it could be driven. So, we did a lot of work on aero, then cooling, because we didn't want a scenario where you do one lap, the car is too hot, and you need to stop. All that concept ate pretty much half of the time we had to design the car, although we had existing parts of the F2 we could reuse, like the Halo. But Halos in F2 don't have any fairings, carbon shrouds, so we needed to create them."

Concurrently with the aero development work happening at Applied Science, Graham Kelly, a thirty-five-year film veteran whose credits include *World War Z* and *Mission: Impossible—Dead Reckoning*, was engaged as action vehicle supervisor. It would be his and his team's job to build the cars, with Applied Science providing the bodywork. The first thing Kelly did was a side-by-side comparison of an F1 car and an F2 car, and he soon realized that F2 cars are 470 millimeters shorter than F1 cars.

"Even though the body work was going to be designed to make it look like an F1 car, if we were ever going to see this car in a paddock or near other cars, it was obviously going to be too short," says Kelly. "We sent Joe the plan of an F2 car and an F1 car and how different they would be, and he agreed that they would look ridiculous. So then we started figuring out engineering to make it longer."

To increase the car's length, Kelly decided to add a spacer—a thick piece of metal, essentially—between the back of the F2 engine and gearbox, adding 200 mm in length to the wheelbase, which was the maximum he felt was possible from an engineering point of view. "That was confirmed by Applied Science, who did a stress analysis, because any more would have put too much load on the engine," he says. "We had to design a longer [drive] shaft, which produced other issues."

"A lot of simulation took place with that spacer," says Bruce, "because when you bolt those two items together [the chassis and engine] on an F1 car, they're the structure of the whole race car. A lot of work was done before it even got onto the car, as the drive shaft had to be extended as well."

"It was a big gamble to stretch a race car by that much, then have the bodywork designed on the basis it was much longer," admits Kelly. "Ultimately, the front part was an F2 chassis slightly enhanced; the rest was all designed. The nose of an F2 car is called the crash structure; that's where the front wing bolts to. We decided to keep all the F2 crash structures intact, so we didn't have to go through hoops of R&D. All that had been done, and we were happy to go with that and design a new front wing to fit on an F2 front crash structure."

Top Left: A Mercedes-AMG Petronas team member builds the Halo, the protective structure that wraps around the driver's head, on the APXGP car.

Top Right: F2 computer-aided design (CAD) data helped to provide the blueprint for the APXGP car.

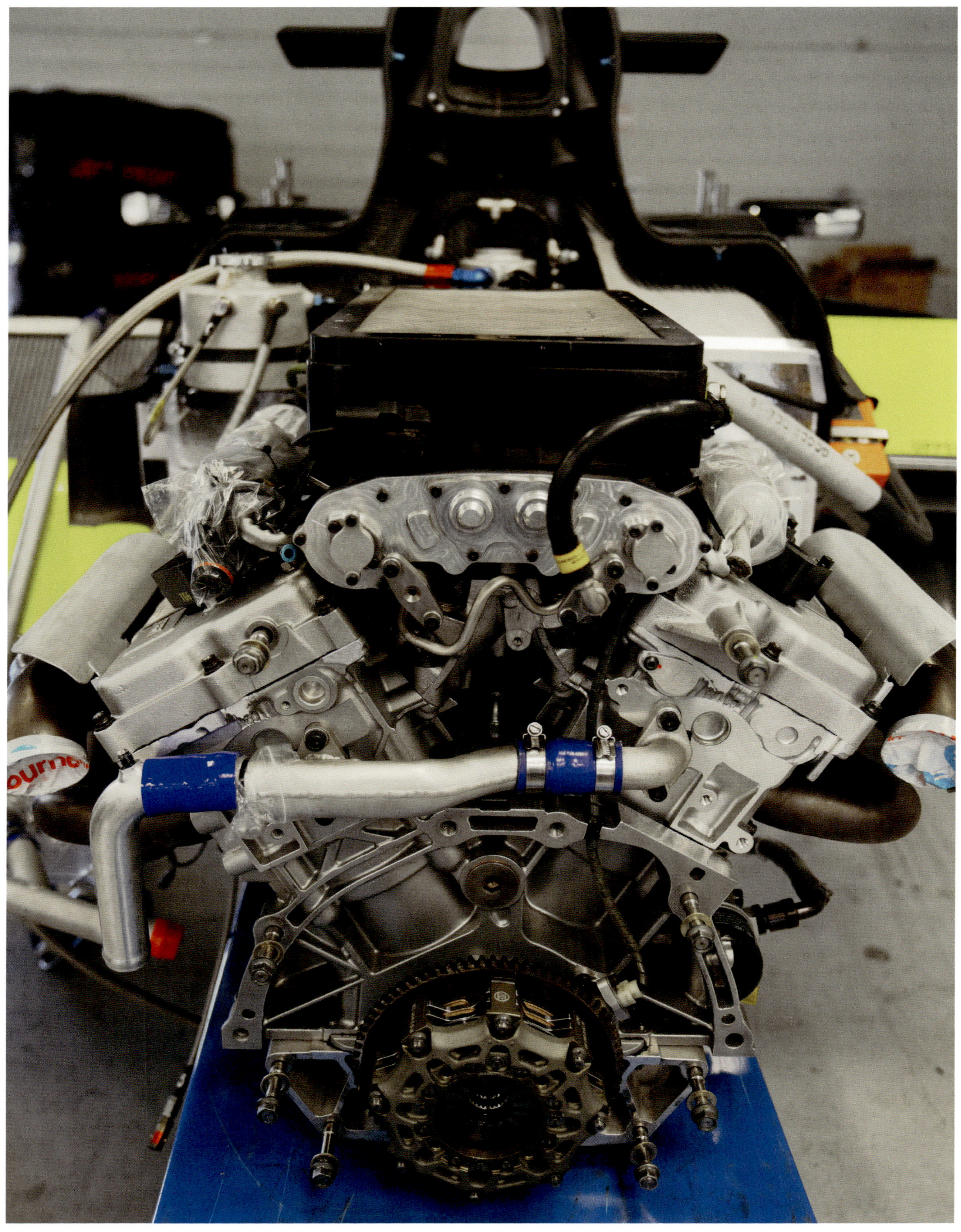

Left: A close-up of the APXGP car's engine.

Bottom Right: Gearboxes help drivers transfer power to the APXGP engine to manage speed.

To get the cars ready for Mercedes to fit the bodywork in time for testing in May, Kelly needed to start building ASAP and began ordering the required chassis, engines, and gearboxes. "Up to that point, we hadn't had a car we owned to pull apart, so all my design work was being done in CAD," says Kelly. "I did have access to a Formula Two car owned by Rodin Motorsport, so I was taking dimensions off that." But when Kelly contacted Dallara, he was told it was the last season for the chassis he was intending to use, and the company was busy making the next season's ones. "So, I'm asking for cars that are, to all intents and purposes, obsolete."

Moreover, Dallara couldn't provide Kelly with all four chassis at once. "They said, 'We can give you one now and a second at another point.' I said, 'Fine, as long as we've got two cars to start getting on with,'" he recalls. Eventually, the first one arrived, only not in the condition Kelly was expecting. "When you buy a car, you imagine a truck turns up and a car rolls out. And then you start taking it apart so you can stretch it and do all that stuff. But the whole car was supplied in pieces. It turned up in little plastic bags. So, immediate panic set in. Now we're dealing with a parts catalogue that's several inches thick. In Italian. So, we had a massive job."

On top of all that, neither engines nor gearboxes had arrived. "I was promised an engine and a gearbox by the end of April, and we needed to give one car with the engine and gearbox on to Mercedes so they could put their bodywork on," says Kelly. "Then I would take it away to test, to make sure it handled, and we could work out the characteristics of the car, which was going to happen at the Ascari circuit in Spain, because we needed good weather."

Thanks to the efforts of Kelly's team and Mercedes's Applied Science division, the production had one car to test on track at Silverstone by the second week of May. Kelly sent it out to do an install lap. "We took some data off it. It went to go out again, and the engine dropped a valve," he sighs. "We had to take the engine out and send it back to the manufacturer. Meanwhile, another car turned up in bags, and we were putting that together and getting it to Mercedes to put their bodywork on. Always looking at this deadline of filming in June and then being at the British Grand Prix in July."

So, Kelly loaded up his one car to drive to Spain, stopping at the Mecachrome factory in France to drop off the blown engine and pick up a new one, which his mechanics would fit at Ascari, so they could test the car. "And it poured for two weeks," he recalls. "Which wasn't a bad thing, because we got some good tests in the rain." Driving the car at Ascari was former professional racer Warren Hughes. "I needed somebody au fait with current Formula Two cars to give me engineering feedback on the feel of it, so we could start adjusting things and see where our parameters were in setups," says Kelly, who returned to Silverstone to put the car through its paces with stunt drivers Luciano Bacheta and Craig Dolby taking turns behind the wheel, followed by Brad Pitt and Damson Idris. "Meanwhile, the second car was just wheeling in, but we couldn't get an engine for it because Mecachrome couldn't supply two. We were begging and borrowing parts off teams to put the car together so the bodywork could go on, with the idea that eventually the good parts would turn up."

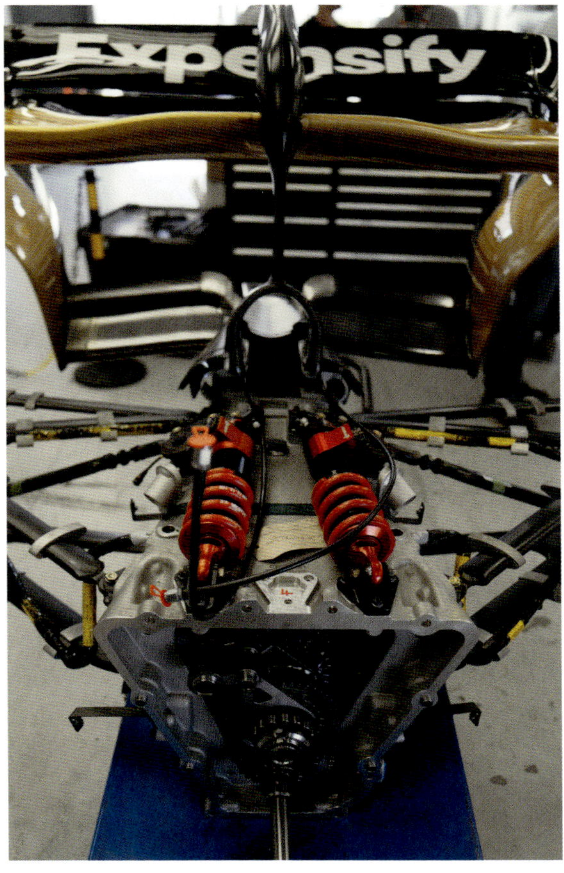

In the meantime, Kelly's second car was having the first engine that he'd collected on the way back from Ascari fitted. "That went off to Mercedes to have its bodywork done, and we now had two cars." When the actors went on strike in July 2023 and production shut down, Kelly used the time to build two more race cars, although he had to use a different engine in both, because he couldn't get ahold of anymore from Mecachrome. "I retrofitted a GP3 engine, which is from an earlier series race car and was slower than the F2 engine, which meant we had to manufacture different spacers, adapter plates, exhaust systems, and wiring to fit into the cars. We then developed another engine while we were doing this, because the GP3 engine was quite a bit underpowered compared to the F2. So, I was trying to give them more power. The GP3 engine was 420 horsepower. The F2 engine was 620 hp. And the K20 engine I built was 550 hp."

Ultimately, Kelly built six different APXGP race cars—four that were used on track by the actors and stunt drivers, two of which had GP3 engines, and the other two Mecachrome ones. A fifth had an electric motor and was used for pit stops.

"Right at the very outset, I knew that none of these traditional race engines would cope with our filming process of pulling up at a pit stop, stopping, starting, going, then doing it again, over and over again," says Kelly. "They would explode in the pit box. So, we started designing an electric version that had so many design issues to get over because of the battery size, the power of the motor, connecting it to the gearbox, and running all the power through the gearbox. But it was ready for our first day of filming at the British Grand Prix. It meant we could move straight to a pit lane car whenever we had issues with weather or the other cars."

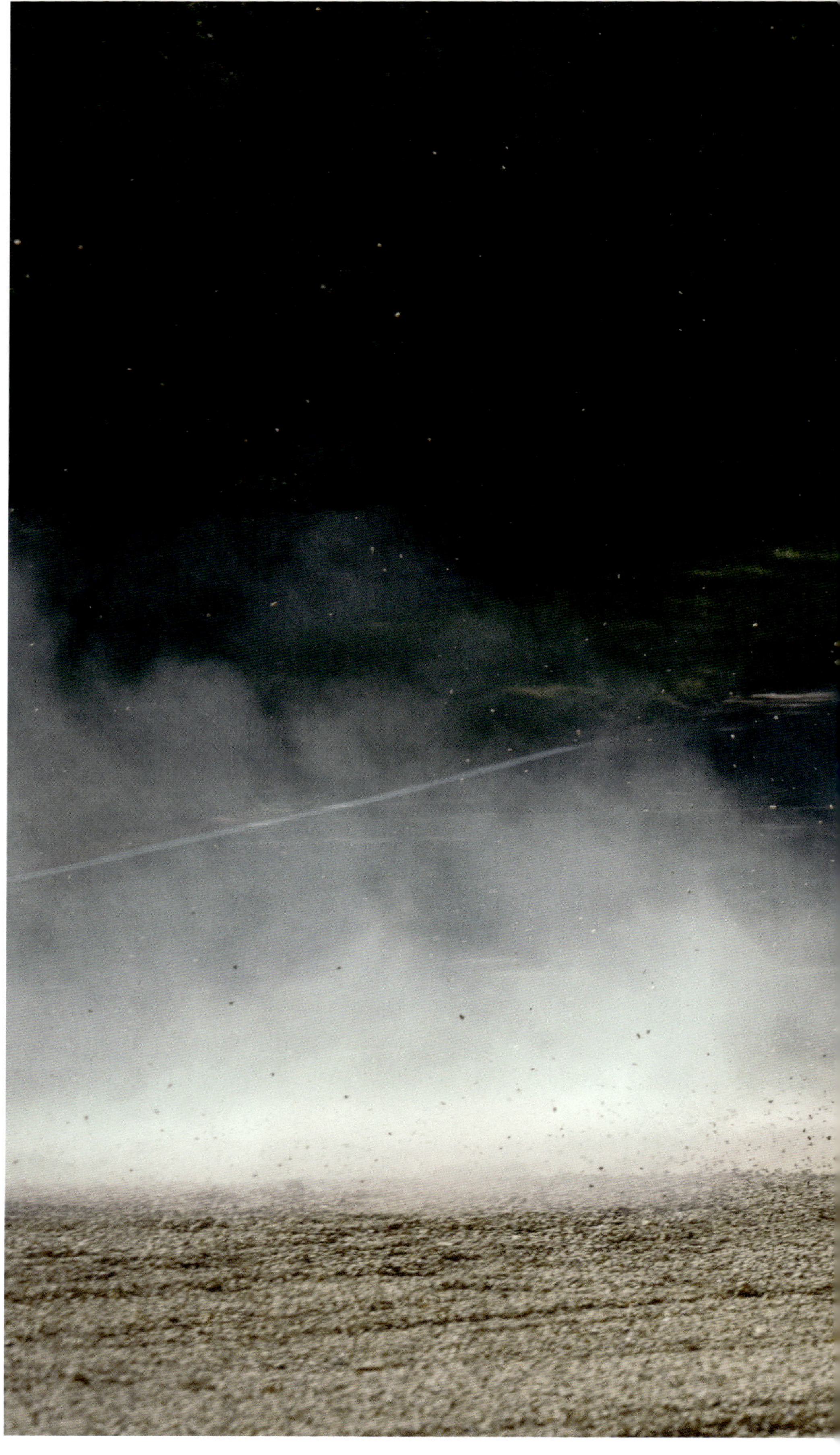

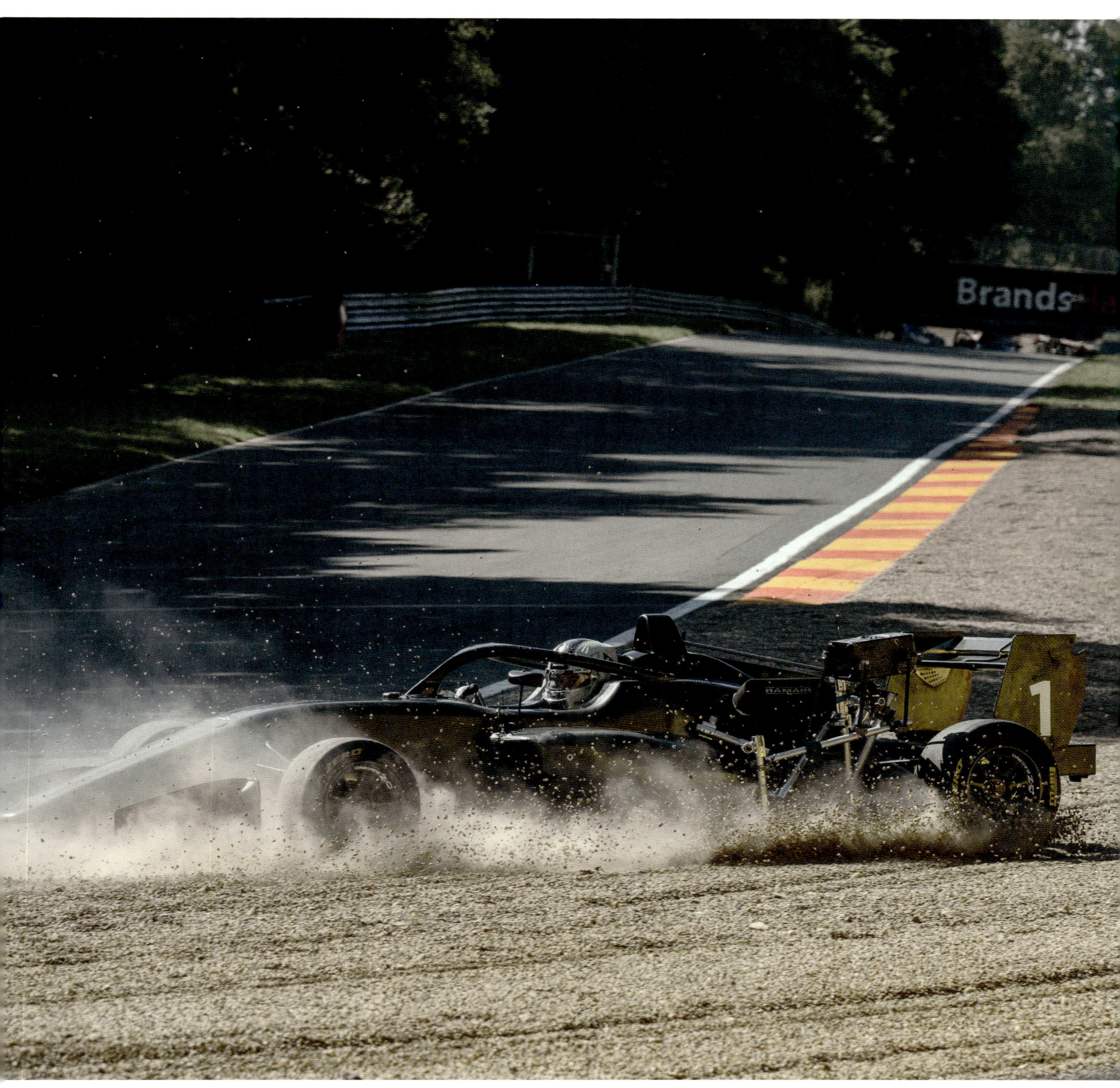

A driver tests one of the six APXGP cars constructed for the film.

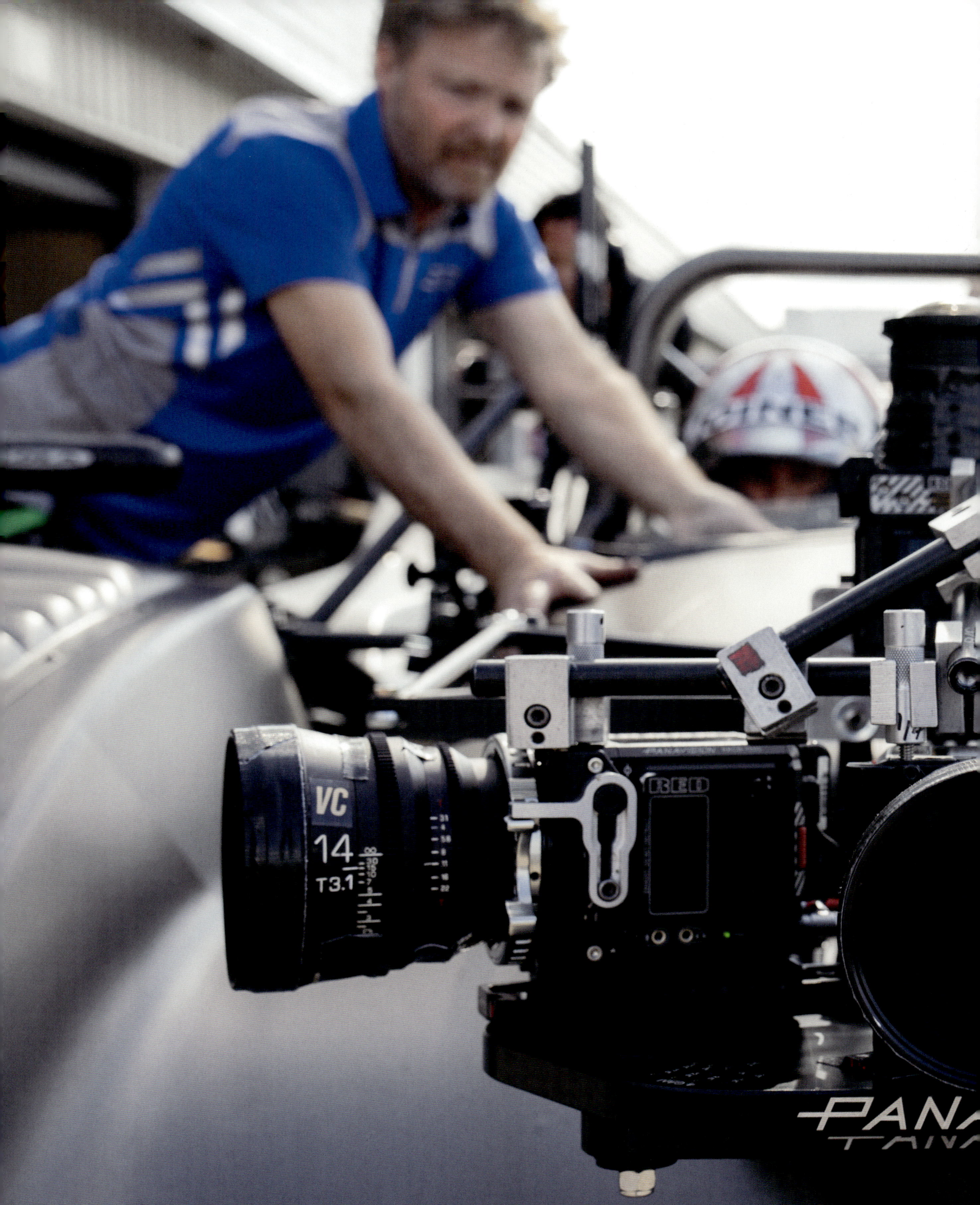
VC
14
T3.1
RED

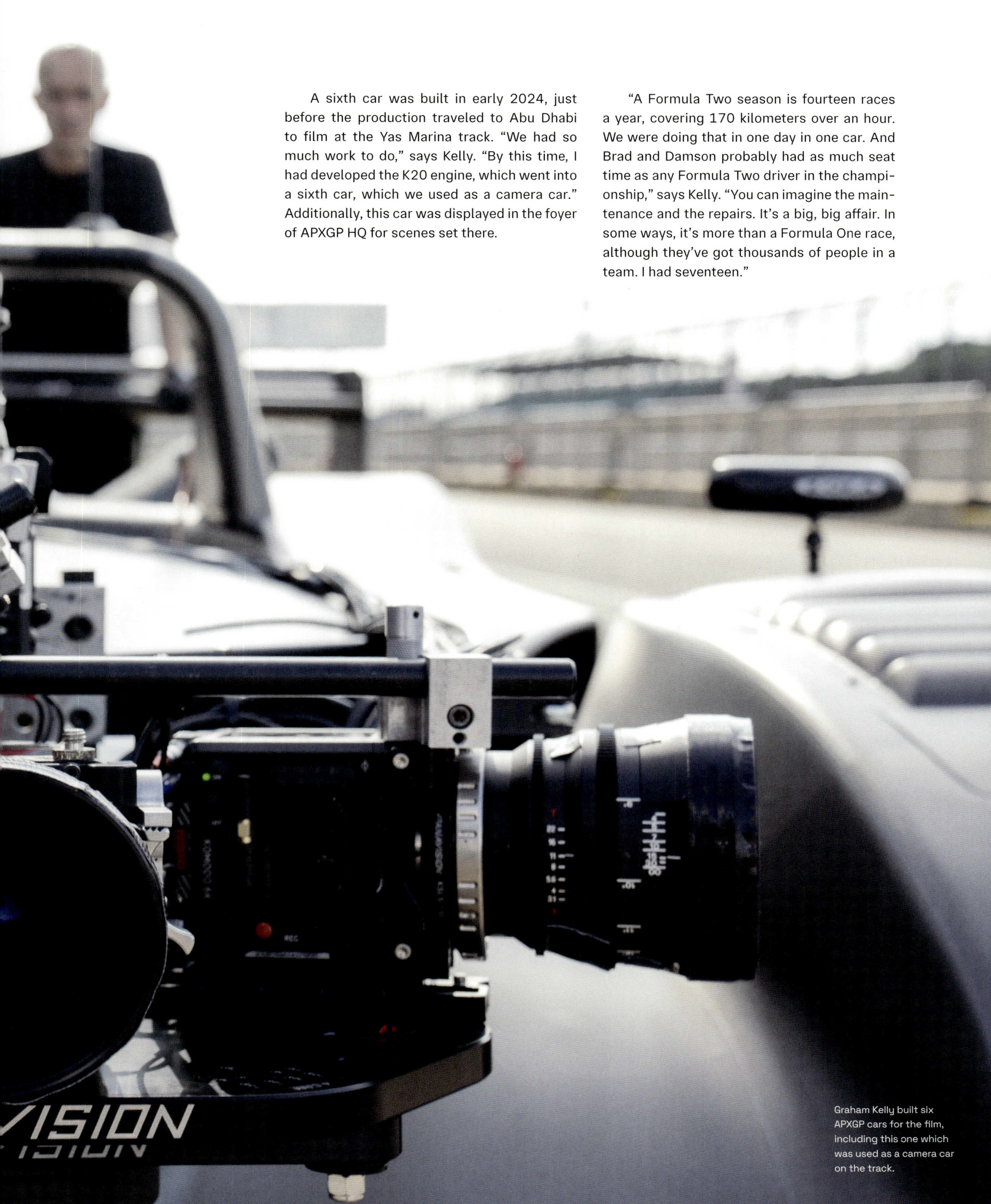

A sixth car was built in early 2024, just before the production traveled to Abu Dhabi to film at the Yas Marina track. "We had so much work to do," says Kelly. "By this time, I had developed the K20 engine, which went into a sixth car, which we used as a camera car." Additionally, this car was displayed in the foyer of APXGP HQ for scenes set there.

"A Formula Two season is fourteen races a year, covering 170 kilometers over an hour. We were doing that in one day in one car. And Brad and Damson probably had as much seat time as any Formula Two driver in the championship," says Kelly. "You can imagine the maintenance and the repairs. It's a big, big affair. In some ways, it's more than a Formula One race, although they've got thousands of people in a team. I had seventeen."

Graham Kelly built six APXGP cars for the film, including this one which was used as a camera car on the track.

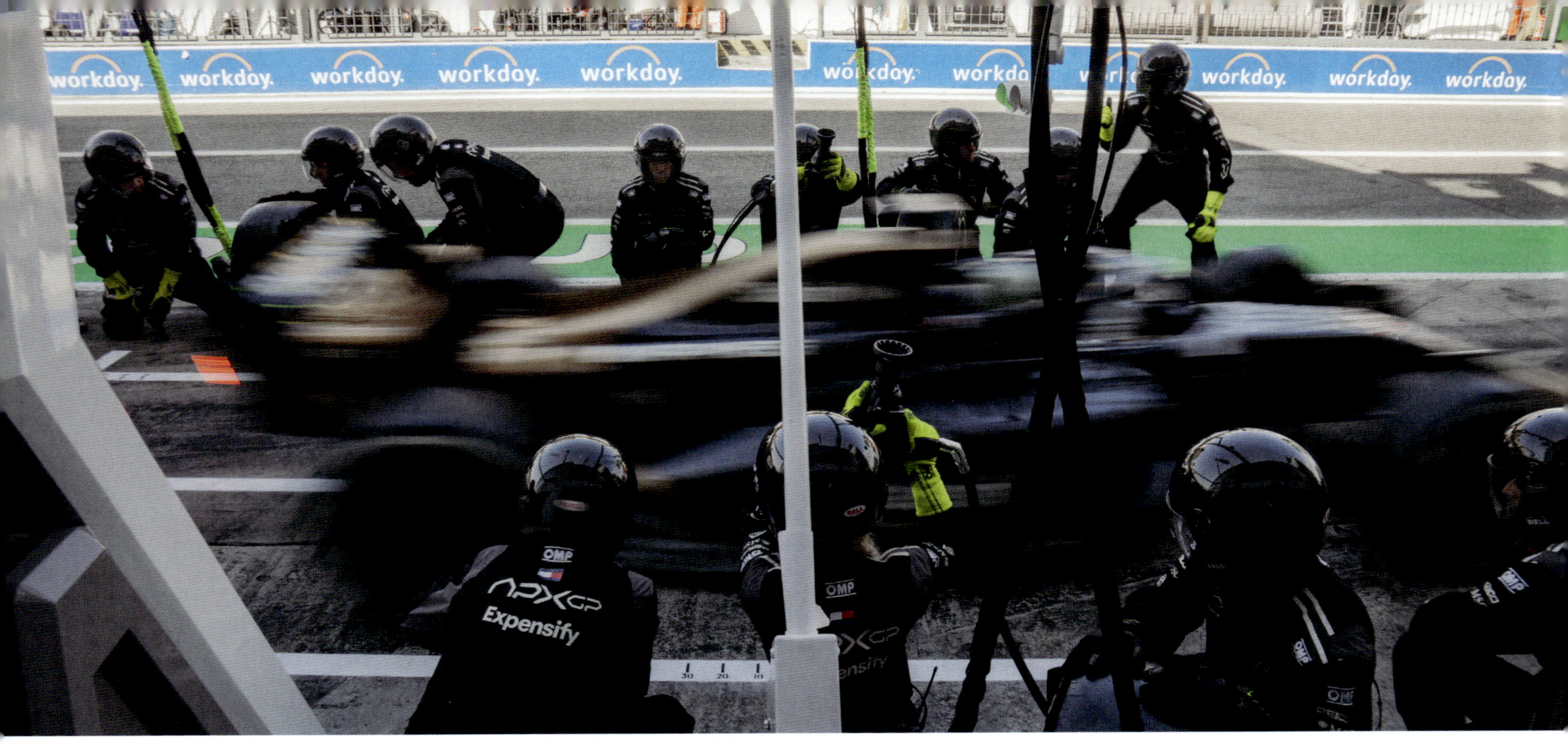

"One of the most dangerous things in a Formula One race is being in the pits and being part of a pit crew."

GRAHAM KELLY

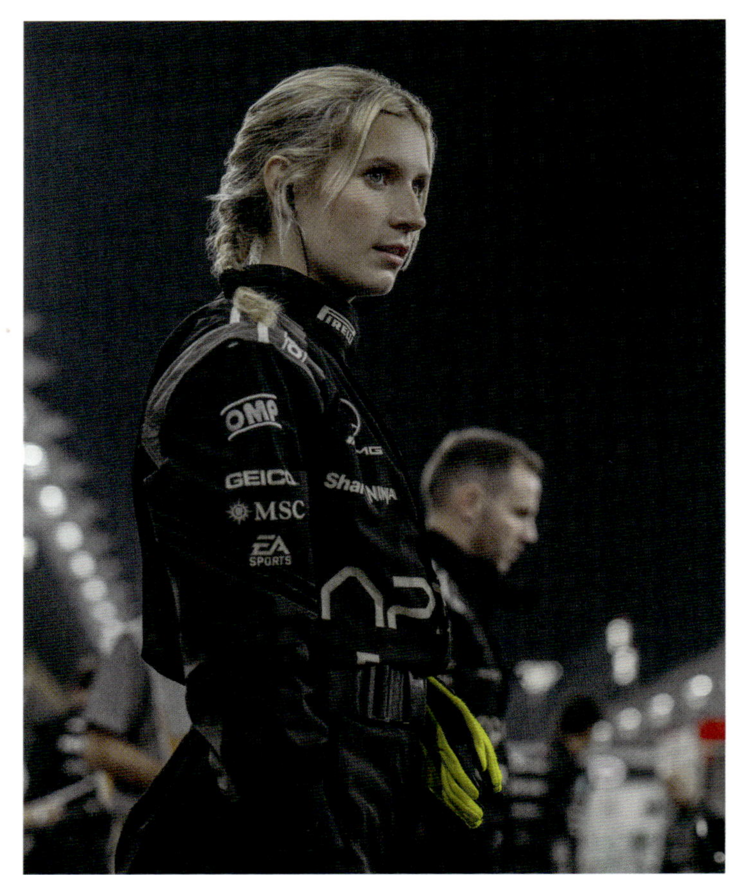

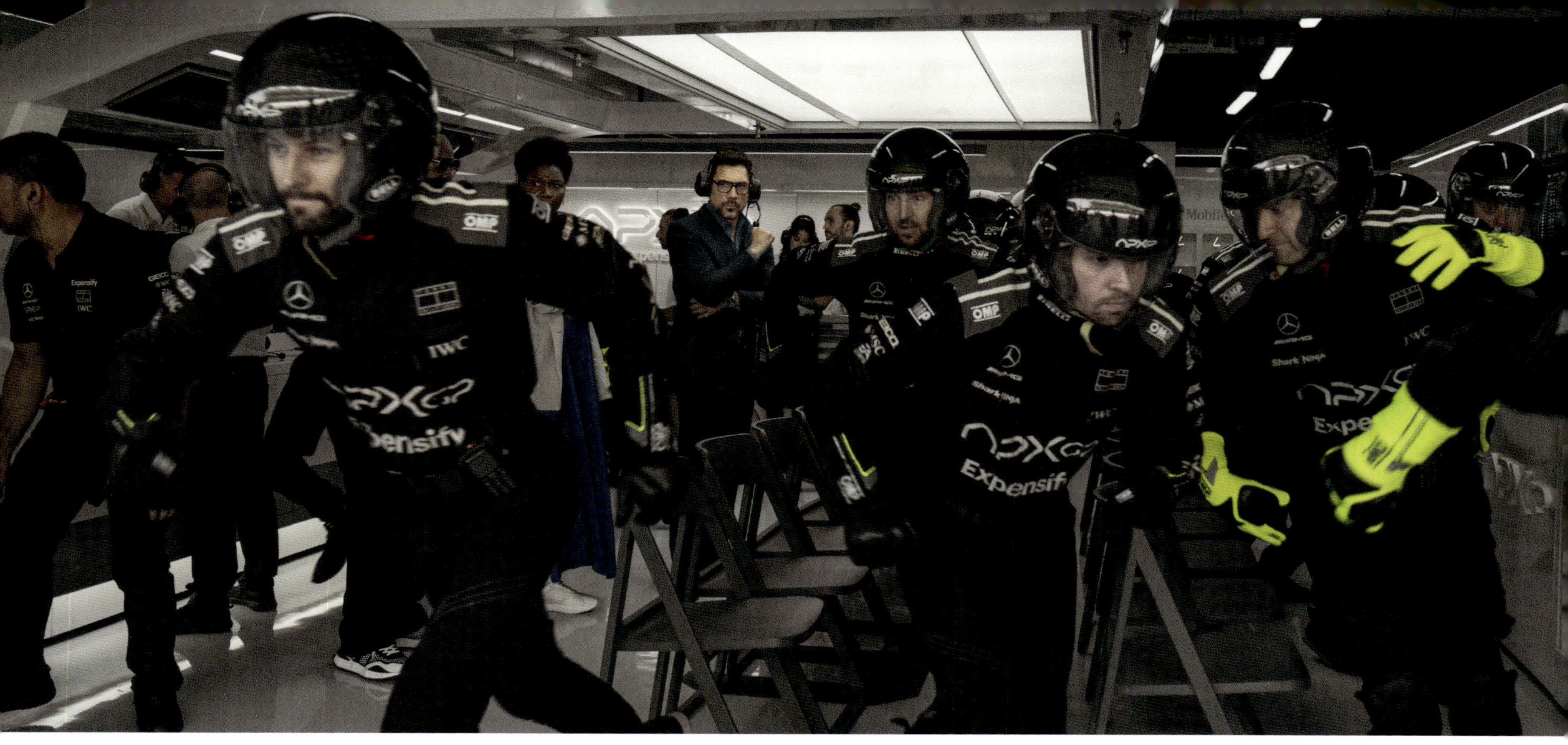

Kelly's team also played the APXGP pit crew. "One of the most dangerous things in a Formula One race is being in the pits and being part of a pit crew," he notes. "You've got a car approaching at 60-70 miles per hour, stopping in a box. You've got twenty-odd people around the car, all needing to be doing something they've been trained to do. Taking wheels off, undoing wheel nuts, putting the wheels back on, dropping the car off its jacks. It couldn't be stunt people; it had to be trained mechanics. And the only way we could do it was with our guys because there weren't any other trained mechanics available."

But Formula One pit crews are incredibly well trained and practice every day. "They get it down to a fine art but only do three pit stops, maximum, in a race," continues Kelly. "There was a day where we did twenty-five pit stops. My guys are brilliant mechanics, brilliant fabricators, but they're not the fittest people in the world. And when we were in Hungary, it was thirty degrees Celsius. They were all dressed in fire suits. In the end, I said, 'They can't do that many pit stops in a day.' The other issue was, I was losing my entire crew every time they filmed a pit stop."

The APXGP crew took about a minute and a half to change all four tires, whereas most Formula One teams can do it in around two seconds. "I was good with that, but Toby Hefferman [first assistant director] was demanding more, and I kept saying, 'They're mechanics; they're not Formula One wheelmen.'" Fortunately, that's where editing comes in. "The reality is, we all come from motorsport. But most of us haven't done it for a long time. So, you've got a crew of film mechanics trying to be Formula One mechanics and look like Formula One mechanics. And my guys weren't. They were just good at building cars."

Kelly's "guys" also included actress Callie Cooke, who was playing Jodie, one of the APXGP pit crew who wields a wheel gun. "She was great. We trained her with a static car in the workshop, putting the wheel on, taking the wheel off. And we trained her every time we rehearsed a pit stop. All she had to do was take the wheel nuts off. Then someone takes the wheel off. Someone puts the wheel on. And then you put the nuts back on. I say 'all she had to do,' but the car is approaching at sixty miles per hour. It stops in front of you, and you have to be sure the wheel nuts are on, because when the car drops and they're not on, that's a big accident."

Top Row: Graham Kelly's team not only helped build the APXGP cars, they also acted as the pit crew during filming.

Left: Jodie (Callie Cooke), a member of the APXGP team, readies herself for an upcoming pit stop.

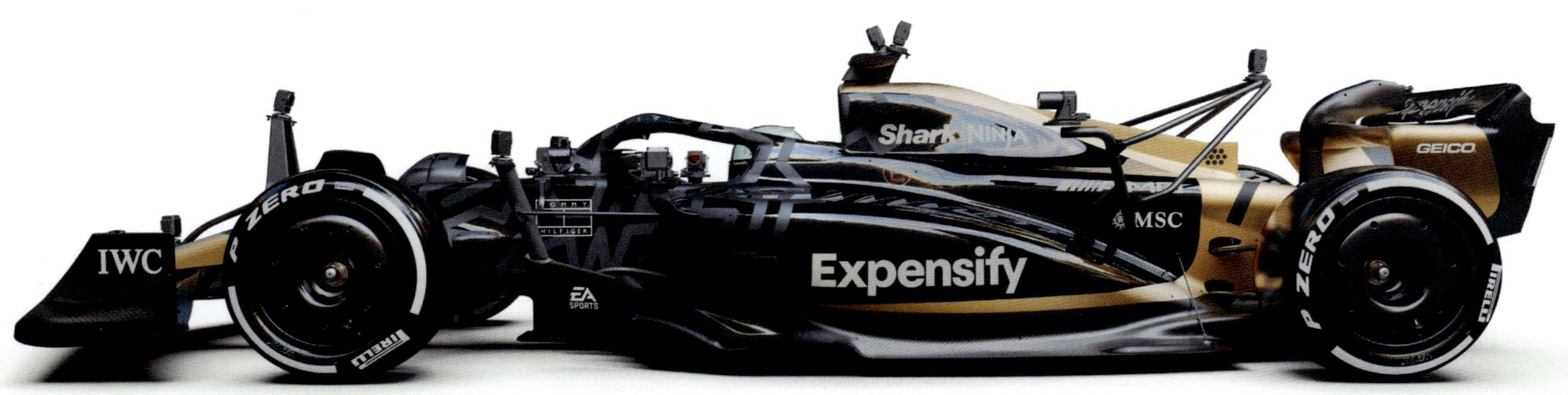

IWC
P ZERO
Expensify
MSC
Shark NINJA
GEICO

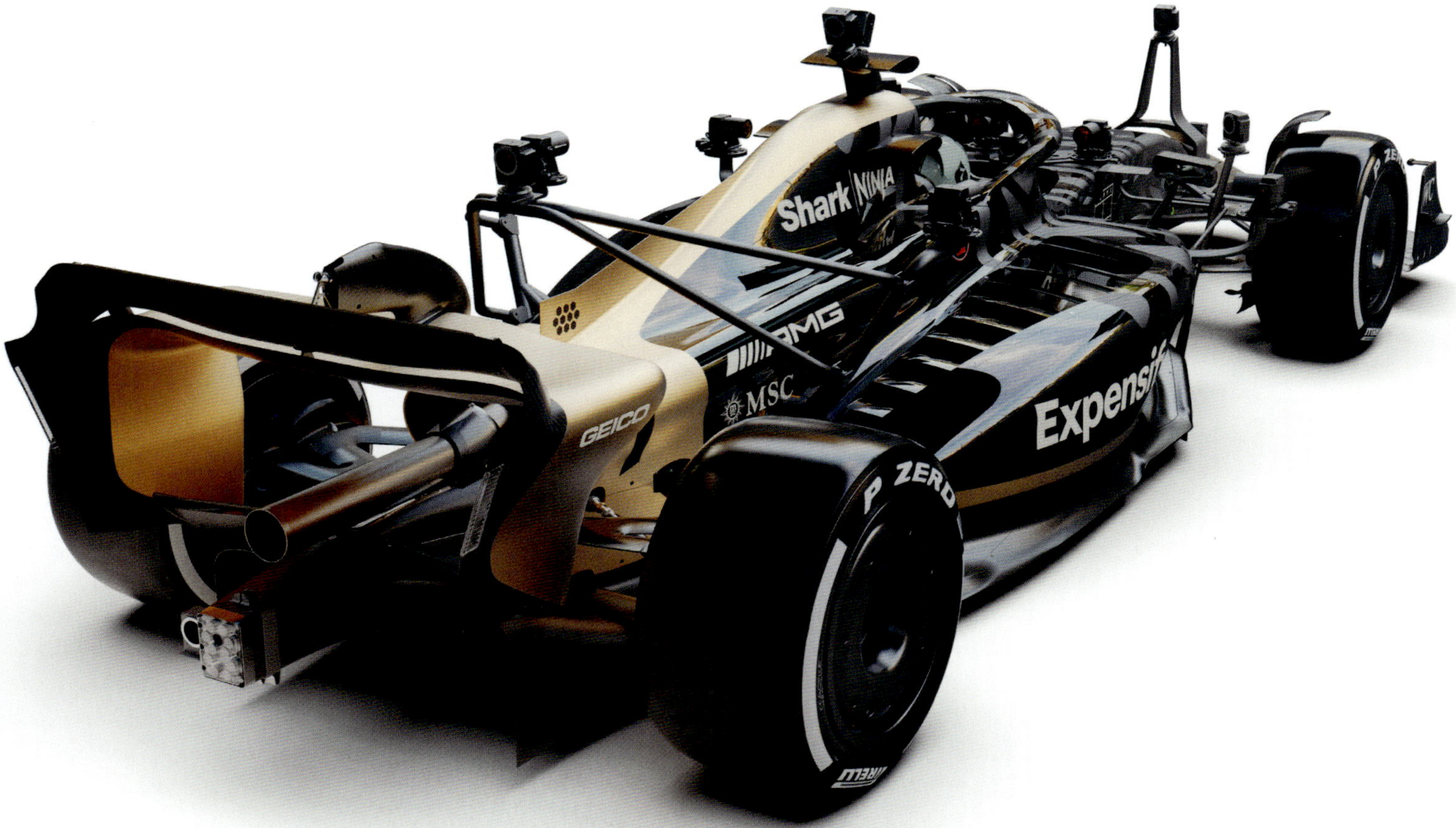

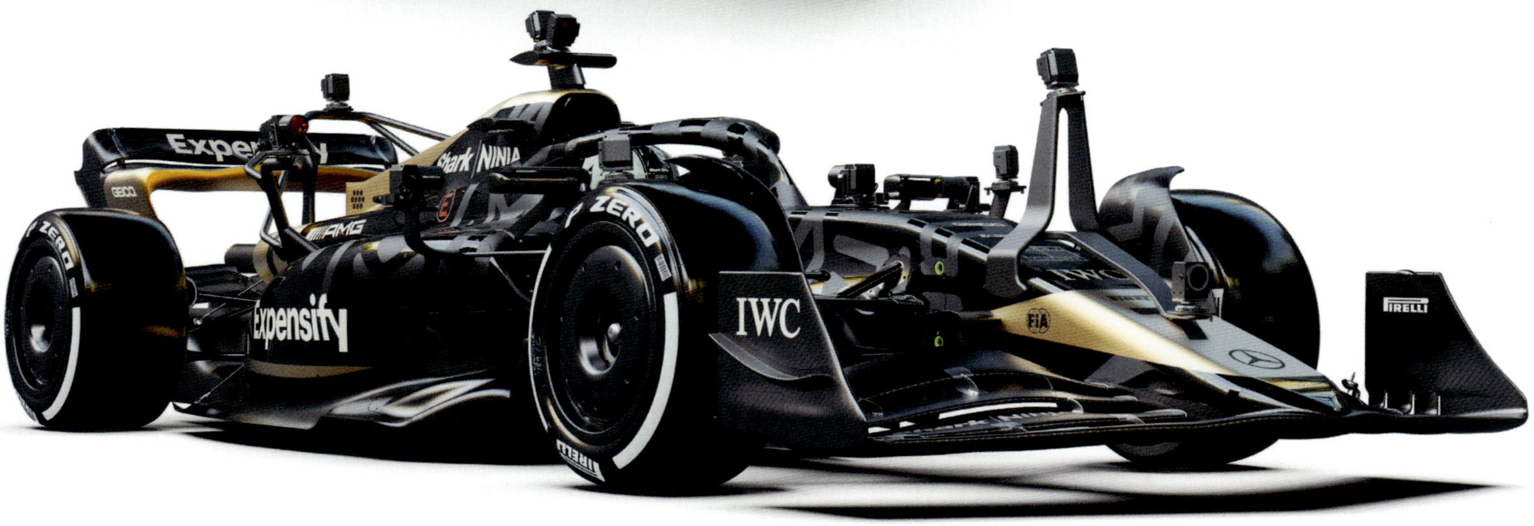

Left: Concept artist Daniel Simon's renders of the APXGP car with the various camera positions used to film *F1*.

Below: Sonny (Brad Pitt) in the camera-mounted APXGP car.

At the same time that Kelly was working through the mechanical aspects of the APXGP car's elongated engineering, and the Applied Science team was finessing the aerodynamic bodywork, Kosinski and his two-time Oscar-winning cinematographer Claudio Miranda (*Life of Pi*) started to develop the cameras that would need to be fitted onto the APXGP cars to capture the realistic race footage they were after.

"Being able to make them small and light enough so they would not slow the car down significantly was the biggest challenge," says Kosinski. "Something Lewis said from the very beginning was he hadn't really seen a racing film capture the experience of what it feels like to be an F1 driver: the speed, the violence, the physical exertion. That was something Toto echoed; they never feel fast. And the reason is because movie cameras are very heavy. If you go back and look at the making of *Le Mans* or *Grand Prix*, you'll see these giant 35-mm camera systems. Even on *Ford v Ferrari*, they had these large, sophisticated, heavy rigs to capture the image. By the nature of filming it, you're slowing it down. And if you're putting an actor in it, you're slowing it down even more, so it's not a race car anymore—it's a movie car."

But Kosinski wasn't planning to shoot his race sequences in typical movie fashion. He was intending to shoot them much the same way he and Miranda had filmed the flying sequences in *Top Gun: Maverick*. "Claudio is an artist," says Kosinski. "He's got an incredible eye. He understands how to light. He understands story. He understands tone. And he's a great collaborator. Beyond that, he's got a very technical side, so [he] can help develop these camera systems that are going to capture something that hasn't been done before. He's got that left brain/right brain thing going where he understands creatively what I'm going for, but technically, he's got the skills to figure it out. And, like me, he loves a challenge. That's what it's all about. How can we push ourselves to do something we haven't done before?"

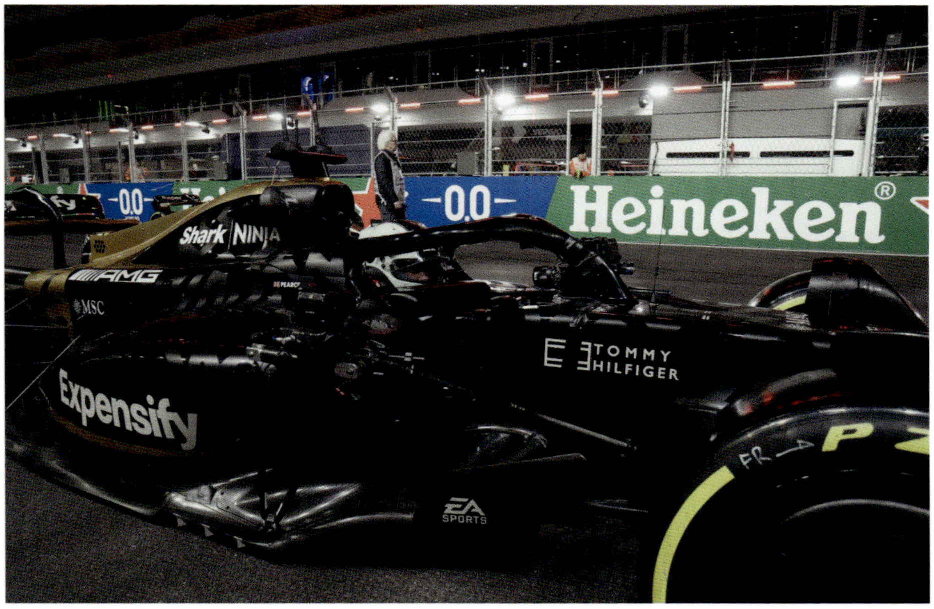

On *Top Gun: Maverick*, that meant filming the cast inside cockpits of F-18 fighter jets as they flew at speed and altitude for real, taking part in aerial maneuvers and dogfights. The results were spectacular, and audiences lapped it up. "There was a rush, a visceral excitement, when you saw Tom Cruise fly off the aircraft carrier," notes Miranda, who studied every racing film he could and felt that energy and speed were key to believability. "We looked at a lot of reference. We looked at *Senna*. We looked at some old films and shots we felt were grand and epic."

To film inside an F-18 cockpit, Miranda had developed a new camera system in conjunction with Sony, which separated the image sensor block of a Sony Venice camera from its actual body. Nicknamed the Rialto, this new camera system was able to occupy very tight spaces, allowing Kosinski to place six units inside each cockpit to capture the action both inside and out.

For *F1*, they planned to do something similar, mounting cameras on cars as they were driven at high speeds. But, in comparison to a fighter jet, a Formula One car is precision balanced, meaning every gram counts, and the Rialto system used in *Top Gun* was still too heavy and bulky for the APXGP car. "We had to make a smaller camera that didn't exist," says Miranda, who suggested taking the sensor from a Sony FX6, a full-frame, compact 4K cinema camera, and separating it from the body and putting it on a stick, dubbing it "the Carmen," a prototype made for the film that could be controlled remotely via a wireless network.

"They sent me designs of what was possible in the time frame we had. We blocked it out in 3D and thought this is something we could put on the cars and the drivers could still drive," says Miranda. "In the end, they made us twenty cameras." For Miranda, it was simply about size. "We still wanted filmic images and [to] have shallower depth of field. The idea was not to sacrifice quality for what we were doing."

ANATOMY OF A PIT STOP

One of the most crucial times during a Formula One race is the pit stop. Teams must make at least one stop per car by regulation, because the rules dictate that they use two different tire compounds during a race. There are five different Pirelli tire compounds in total, and three compounds are selected for each race event based on the demands of the track.

For circuits with an abrasive track surface and higher-speed corners that stress the tire, what are known as "harder"—more robust—compounds are used. On street circuits with a less-aggressive tarmac and slower turns, the "softer"—higher-grip but more fragile—compounds are selected.

From the three compounds chosen for any given track, these tires are labeled as the soft, medium, and hard for the weekend. The reason so many different compounds are used is to ensure there is strategic variation, which can induce differences in tire performance during a race and lead to more overtaking. Teams get to choose how they use their tires during a race and can make more than one pit stop if they wish, but they must use at least two of the three compounds at some stage.

In a sport where the aim is to complete the number of laps in the shortest amount of time, coming into the pit lane—where there is a speed limit—and sitting stationary while tires are changed is something teams generally want to avoid if possible. And they certainly want to make sure it costs them the least amount of time.

To carry out a pit stop as quickly as possible, eighteen people are involved in physically handling the car.

Once the four tires have been successfully changed, the car is lowered back onto the ground, and a green light will tell the driver to accelerate away. And based on the current world record, all that can take just 1.8 seconds.

Pit stops used to take longer when refueling was permitted during races, but this was banned in 2010. The reasons were many: It increased safety, saved on transport costs of heavy and expensive pit lane refueling equipment, and promoted greater power unit efficiency to complete a race on one tank of fuel.

Three per corner of the car. One removes the old tire, a second fits the new one, and the third person operates the wheel gun that loosens and tightens the wheel nuts using compressed air.

One each at the front and rear operate jacks that lift the car off the ground to allow the tires to be changed.

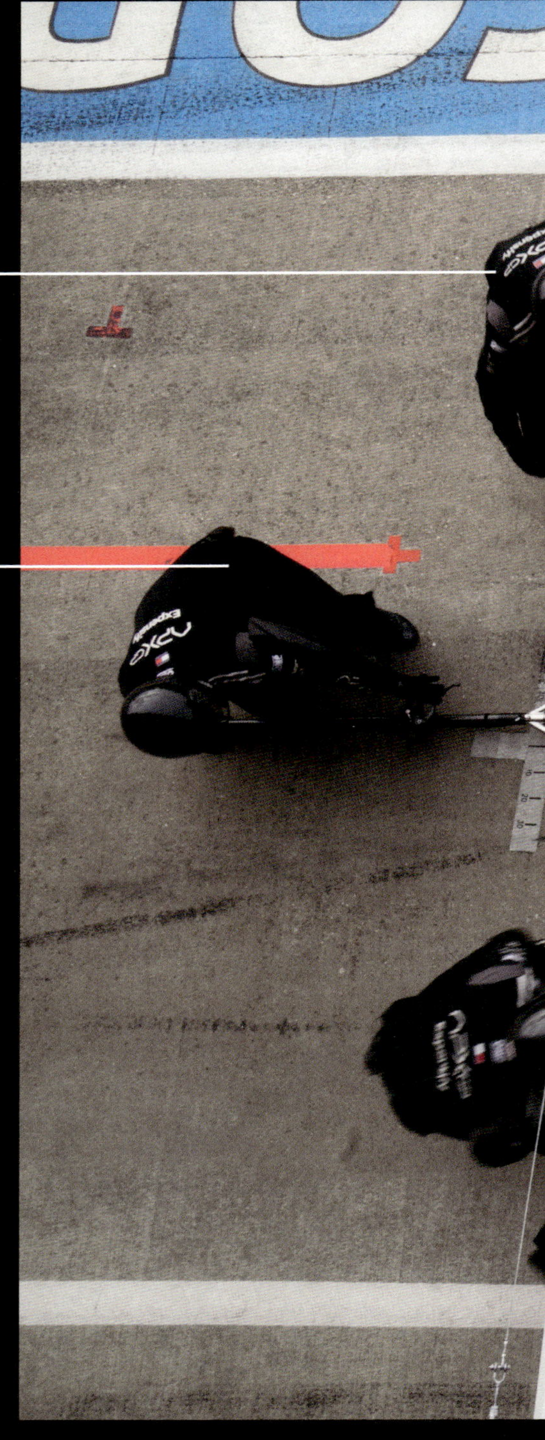

Two team members—one on each side of the car—act as stabilizers to stop the car from rocking side to side. They can also clean out debris from the side pods on either side of the cockpit, or wipe the driver's visor if necessary.

On top of that, there is always a spare front and rear jack operator in case of a failure, and a team member in charge of monitoring the pit stop and pit lane to ensure it is safe to release the car back into the race.

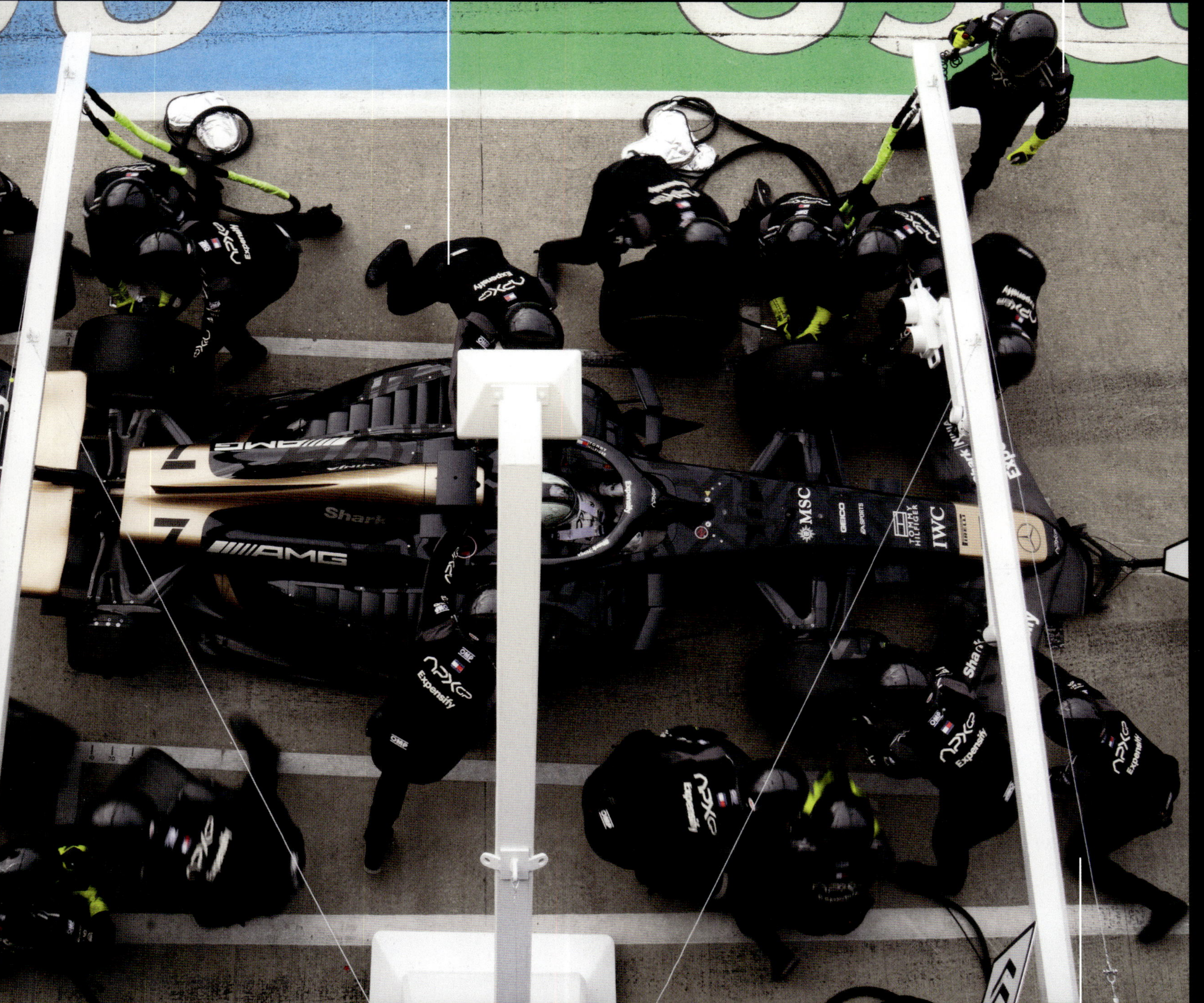

Finally, two other personnel—one on each side of the

The crew was able to capture various angles of racing footage thanks to the cameras mounted to the APXGP car. Here's a look at some shots captured by the mounted cameras.

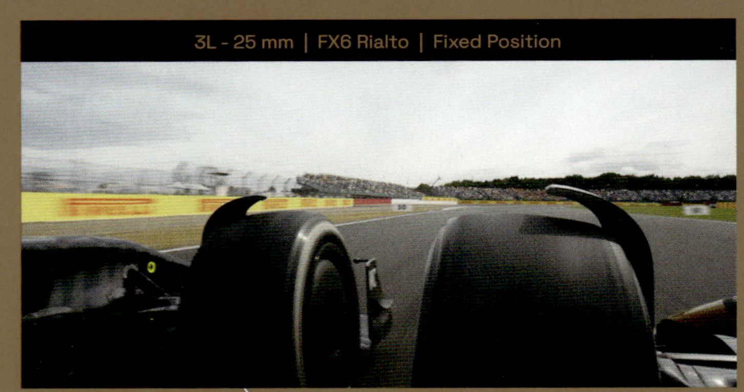

3L - 25 mm | FX6 Rialto | Fixed Position

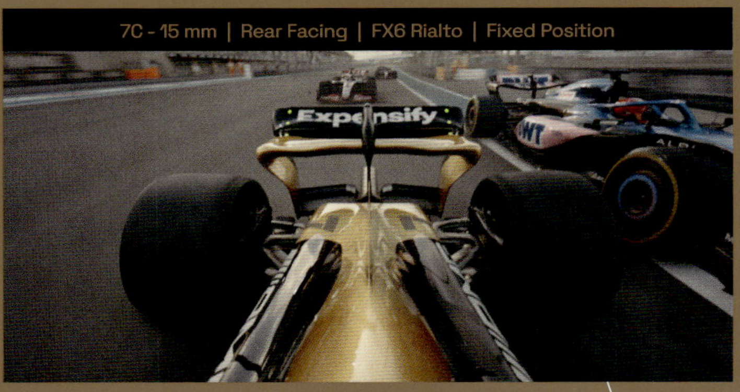

7C - 15 mm | Rear Facing | FX6 Rialto | Fixed Position

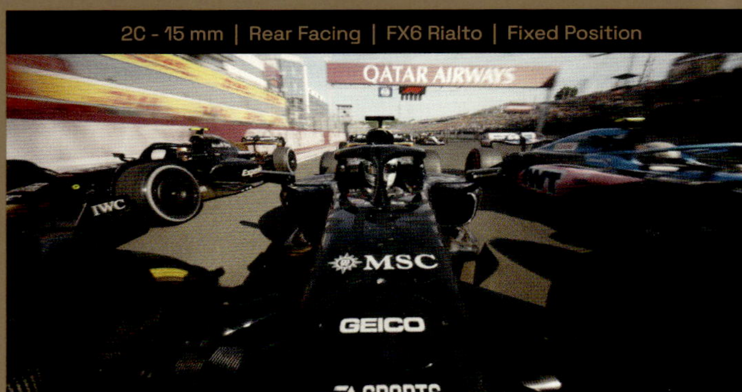

2C - 15 mm | Rear Facing | FX6 Rialto | Fixed Position

5L - 21 mm
FX6 Rialto
Pan Head
Inside 180 Pan

8L - 15 mm
FX6 Rialto
Pan Head
Outside 180 Pan

10 - 21 mm
Front Facing
Fixed Position
Possible FX3

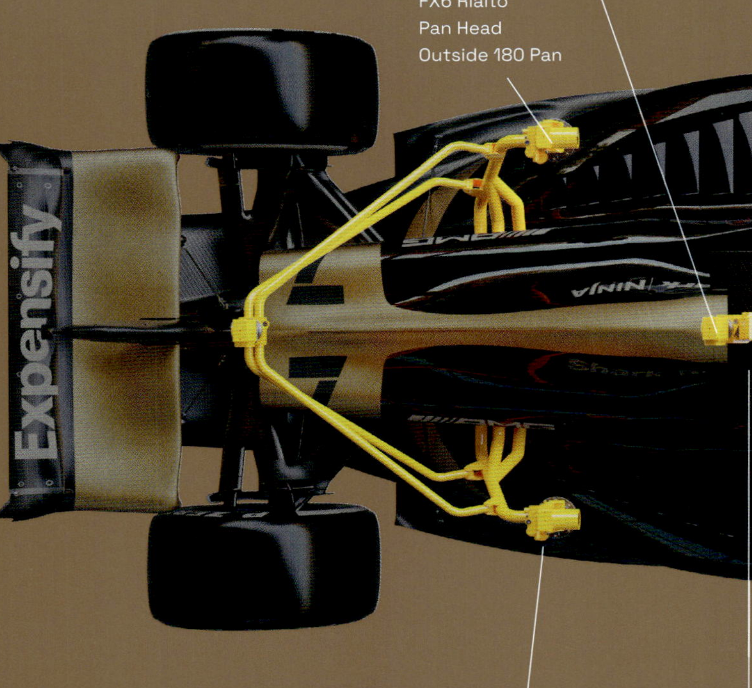

4L - 21 mm
FX6 Rialto
Pan Head
Outside 180 Pan

3R - 25 mm
FX6 Rialto
Fixed Position

6C - 15 mm
Front Facing
FX6 Rialto
Fixed Position

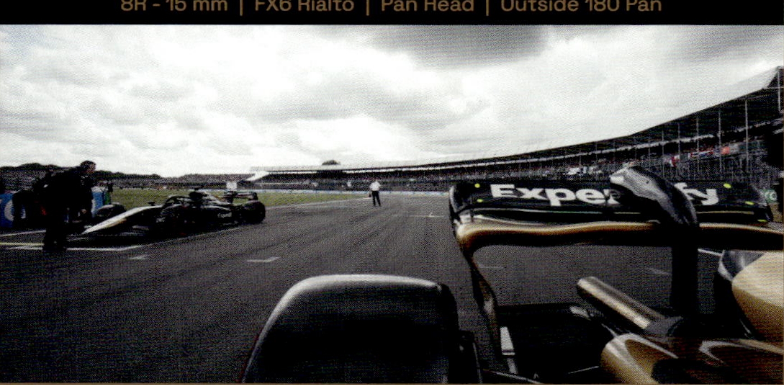

8R - 15 mm | FX6 Rialto | Pan Head | Outside 180 Pan

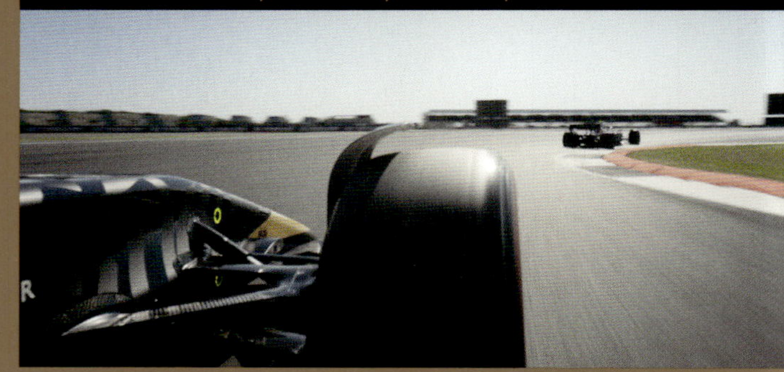

4R - 21 mm | FX6 Rialto | Pan Head | Outside 180 Pan

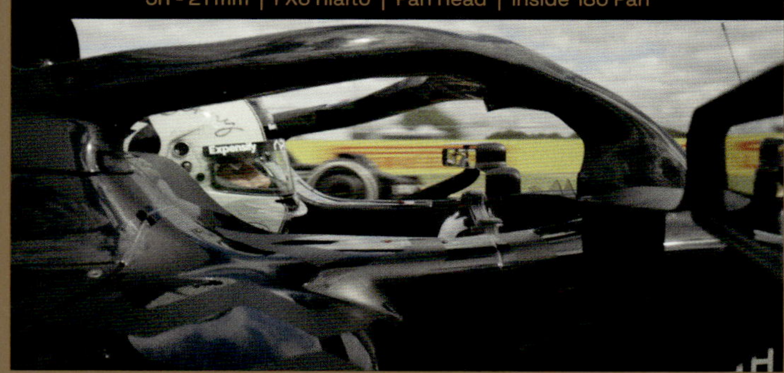

5R - 21 mm | FX6 Rialto | Pan Head | Inside 180 Pan

Right: The film crew built their own camera, the "Carmen" based on the Sony FR7 and Sony FX6. Only twenty were created for use in the film.

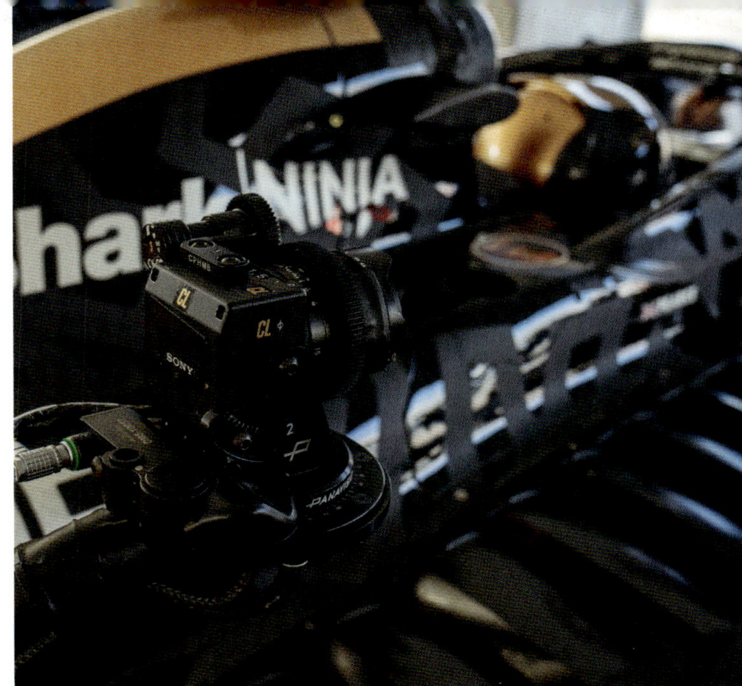

Next, Miranda and Kosinski had to work out the best camera positions, without blocking the drivers' vision. "Claudio and I went to Mercedes and spent an afternoon moving around an F1 car with our viewfinder and the camera and the sensor and lenses, looking for angles that would connect us with the driver but also give us perspectives we hadn't seen before," says Kosinski. "Applied Science built ultra-thin mounts to attach each mini-Rialto to the cars, camera mounts capable of withstanding speeds of up to 200 miles per hour. We did that with the engineers, looking for attachment points that would work both structurally and not affect the performance of the car. By building all those attachment points into the chassis, it meant we didn't have to put in a steel support structure that you normally would put on top of a car or race car. It means the cars could be as light as possible."

Visual effects supervisor Ryan Tudhope, who worked on *Top Gun: Maverick* and *Spiderhead*, also weighed in on the camera positions, using a "digital version of the car before the real cars existed" to help Miranda and Kosinski perfect camera angles, lens choices, and placement. "Claudio had determined roughly where on the car these cameras would be positioned, so we visualized that in a real-time environment, like a game engine," says Tudhope. "We placed those cameras on the car, and Joe and Claudio were able to adjust the lenses, move the cameras around, find the framing they liked of the vehicle relative to the track." Then, using footage of one of Lewis Hamilton's hot laps at Silverstone, Tudhope's team produced an "early visualization of what all these camera mounts might look like on the car. And with all that information, we were able to finalize what the cameras were and what mounts had to be designed. That went to Mercedes to engineer the proper rigs to hold the cameras in place."

The consultation between Miranda, Kosinski, and Applied Science continued throughout the design process, as any change the aero division might make to the car would impact the camera positions. "I knew what the field of view was and where all the angles had to be, so was ping-ponging back with them about the exact placement," says Miranda. "Sometimes there would be a design change, and the mirror would be an inch bigger and would completely block one camera angle, so we would have to move it."

Each car would ultimately have fifteen potential camera mounts, although four cameras on each car were the maximum used while filming. "We'd usually have two to four on Brad or Damson's car, depending on the scene," says Kosinski, "then another two on another car—a nose mount and a tail mount—shooting a clean POV, or looking out the back, or getting coverage of the cars on the track while you've got the crowd and signage in place during a Grand Prix."

Two additional camera mounts were added to the cars for the final Grand Prix at Abu Dhabi in 2024, bringing the total to seventeen. "I came up with a new one, an over-the-tire mount, which looked fantastic," says Miranda. "The film's going to be really immersive; you're going to feel like you're in a car going 200 miles per hour."

To capture close-ups of Pitt and Idris, Miranda mounted a central camera inside the car and on the Halo, looking back at them, while another was positioned on the side for profile shots. But despite the exacting camera placement process, there were times when either the central or profile camera would be in shot and would need to be "cleaned up" and digitally removed by visual effects in post-production. "As long as it doesn't cover the actors, we're okay," says Miranda. "It's so important to get the actors' performance. We had such little time with the actors on track, especially when we're running during a Grand Prix weekend. We had to be expedient."

"All of our cars ran with RF antennas and wires running down them and camera mounts and carbon fiber plates that held the cameras in place," says Tudhope. "Some of the work that nobody will notice is the cleaning up of things."

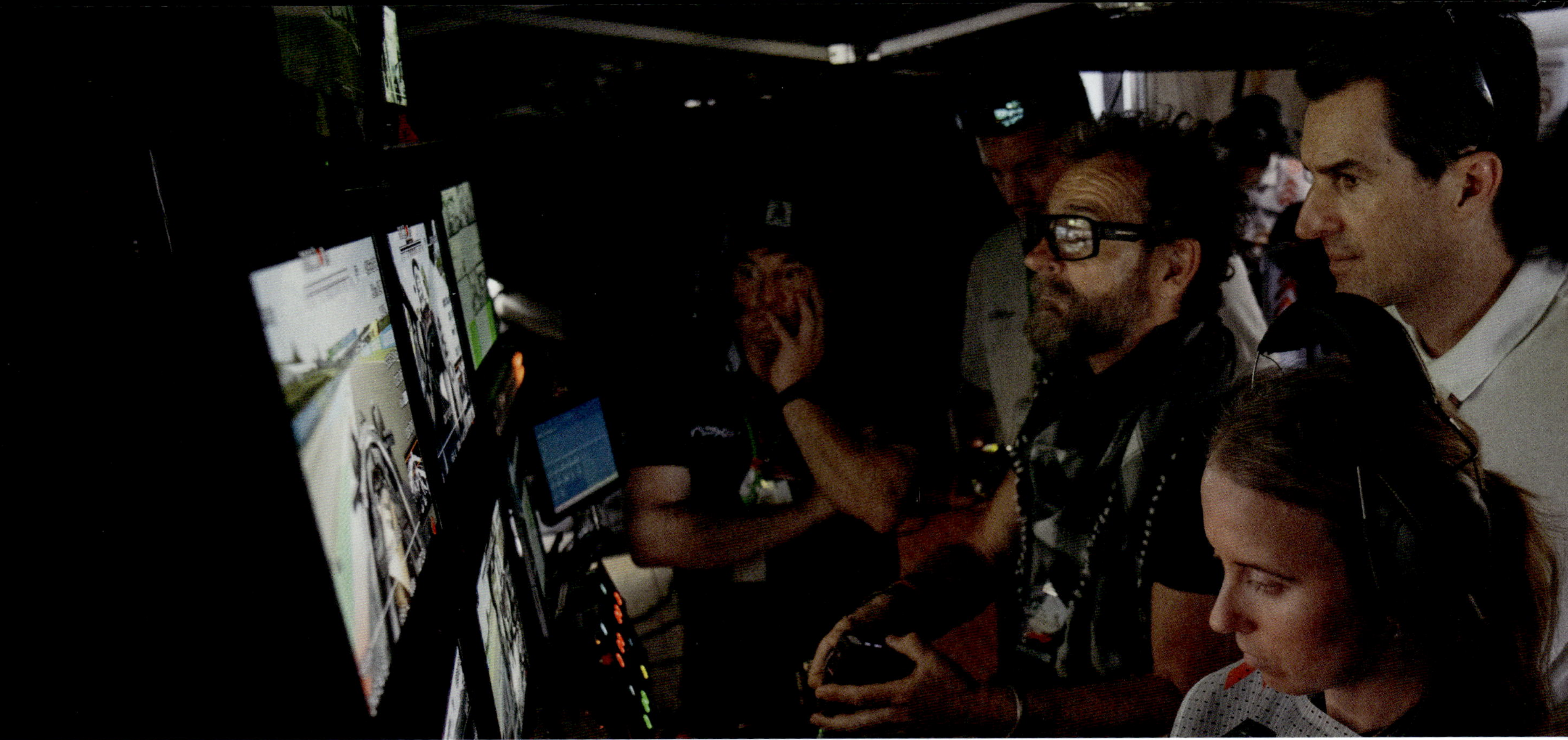

Occasionally, Miranda would stick a small DJI Osmo action camera onto Pitt's helmet. "We had a little lens made to focus on his eye. We did a chin mount too."

"We had to get used to the camera mounts," says Pitt. "Your field of vision [in the car] means you can only see, like, the top portion of your front tires as it is, and then suddenly we have this block of the camera that sits in the middle, on the Halo in front of us. So, you learn to see past that, but we also had a three-quarter/45 degree camera on either side blocking our turning points either left or right. And that was always moving. Then we had a third camera on the side. That wasn't as bad."

The camera bodies, batteries, and recording equipment were housed in a small area in front of the radiator intakes. "The first challenge was where to put highly sensitive camera bodies, which don't like vibration and heat. And we could just about get three camera bodies in there, and the batteries and all the RF [radio frequency] equipment to support it, with not an inch to spare," says Kelly. "The second challenge was seeing how the cars were going to perform with all this camera 'chutney' over it, which will break down the aero and cause a car to handle slightly differently. We tested that to make sure the cameras stayed on the car at 180 miles per hour, 190 miles per hour at times. And nothing fell off. They don't like the rain. But we didn't really shoot in the rain, because that adds a whole other level of danger."

> "The cameras stayed on the car at 180 miles per hour, 190 miles at times. And nothing fell off."
>
> GRAHAM KELLY

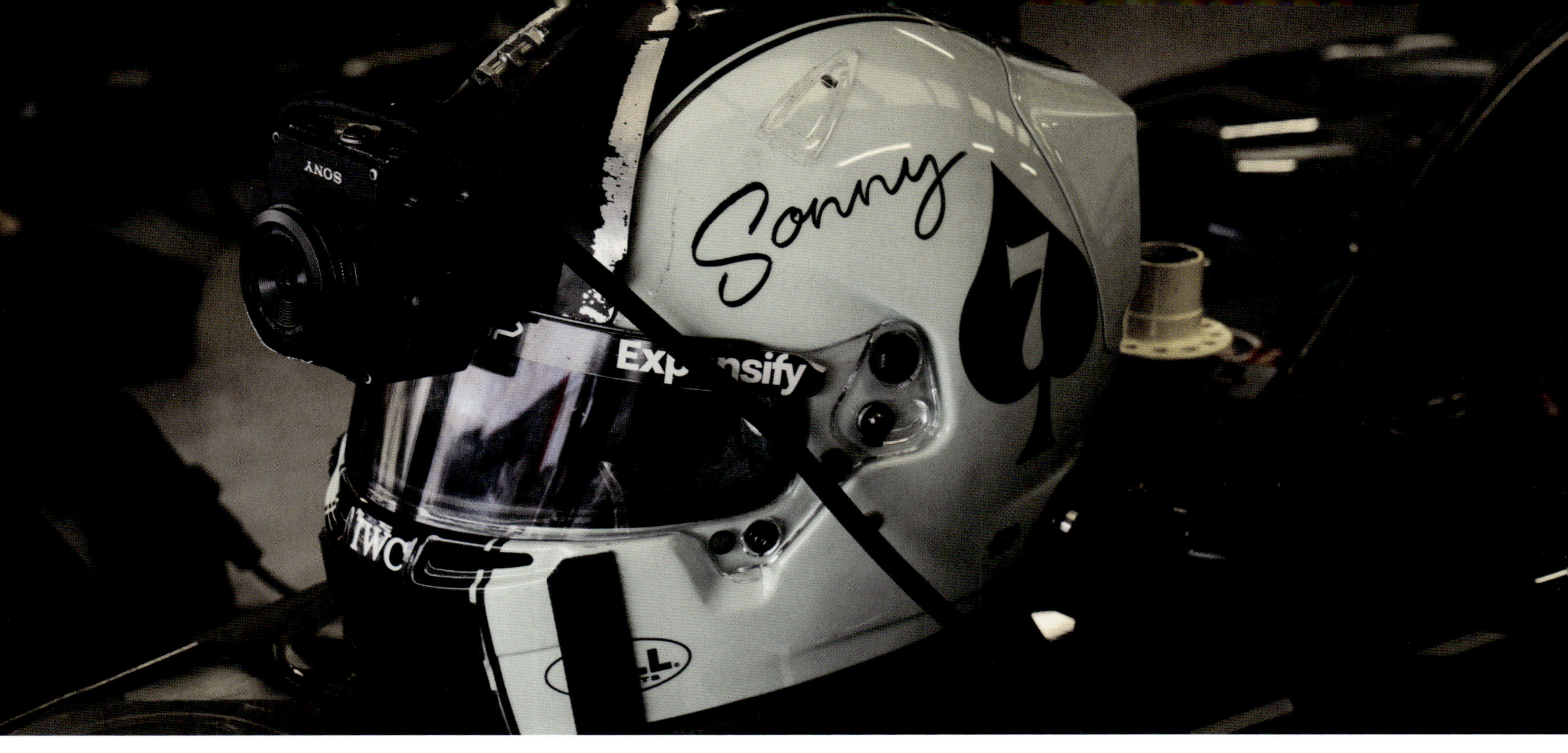

Each car was able to send "live" images back to "mission control" inside the APXGP garage, where Kosinski, Miranda, and the camera operators could watch the action on large monitors and talk with the drivers, thanks to a wireless system and kilometers of cable laid around the track. This ability to watch "live" marked a significant improvement over *Top Gun: Maverick*, where Kosinski and Miranda had to wait for the planes to land before they could review the footage shot.

Moreover, on *Top Gun: Maverick*, the six cockpit cameras had been fixed. For *F1*, Kosinski and Miranda wanted their cameras to move, giving them the ability to pan back and forth, as well as change focus, while the cars were racing. "It only needed to pan. We didn't need it to tilt," says Miranda, who had Panavision build a device to allow his cameras to move and be operated remotely. "This helped to keep it small. So, if it's in front of you, you could still drive. We wanted it to feel like we're really connected with the drivers. We could see Damson driving, then pan over and see Brad driving."

"That remote, swinging head is phenomenal," says Bruckheimer. "How we go from Brad's face to the car trying to pass him is amazing."

Another issue that needed to be resolved was how to keep the cameras steady given the cars would be racing on bumpy tracks. "They were hitting 4G to 5G around corners, so the camera needed to take a swack," says Miranda. "Any sort of traditional gimbal heads would not survive. We tried a gimbal head in our first test session, and it came back in a sack of bolts."

The solution was Sorbothane, a viscoelastic substance designed to absorb shocks and vibrations, on which the camera would be mounted. "We had to fine-tune vibration and play with different materials, different types of rubber, to stabilize the cameras, because we weren't using an active stabilization," says Miranda. "We were using more of a passive, rubber type. And every mount required a different level of rubber and stiffness. We would have to find the perfect vibration dampening for each location, and each location had a different level of absorption."

Miranda also took cameras from iPhone 12s, the last model without IBIS stabilization, and swapped them for some of the nine onboard cameras used by the F1 broadcast team to capture footage during races. That way the production could record higher resolution images than normal for use in the film.

Top Left: The production crew relied on a "mission control" center inside the APXGP garage to review all racetrack footage.

Top Right: Cameras attached to the race helmets provided the driver's point of view during filming.

Kosinski intended to insert the APXGP cars digitally into the broadcast footage to show Sonny or Joshua battling real cars on real tracks during real races. “Joe had this idea to use broadcast footage because there was no way we could ever get thirty cameras around a racetrack which we were operating,” says Tudhope. “It wasn’t financially viable. Not only that, the men and women operating those cameras are professionals at capturing action.”

“I met Joe in Barcelona,” says Jonathan Nicholas, executive producer of the F1 broadcast team. “I took him around our broadcast center—the Event Technical Center (ETC)—and showed him how we produce the coverage, got him to understand our world. Then I took him trackside, to our camera positions, showing him the lenses we use. I took him to the chicane, because he wanted to see the ride height on the curbs. Then he came to Monte Carlo, and I took him to the Swimming Pool [chicane]. I was taking him around the hearts of our tracks where you really feel cars are going to hit you and where camera positions are on the limit. Joe loved Monaco because it’s like you are touching the cars.”

To be able to use the broadcast footage in the movie and add in digital cars or reskin existing ones, the production needed the ETC to record the races in a higher resolution than normal. “They got mobile recorders that we housed in the ETC and recorded up to twenty-six cameras raw, essentially straight from the track,” says Nicholas. “So, we didn’t have to do anything different trackside.”

The broadcast team would also reassign their cameras if the production needed to capture something specific, either on track or in the grandstands. “Sometimes we’d ask them for a helicopter to follow our car for a bit,” says Miranda. “And sometimes there was an accident or an interesting moment on track that they captured that we could use in our film or as reference for a stunt.”

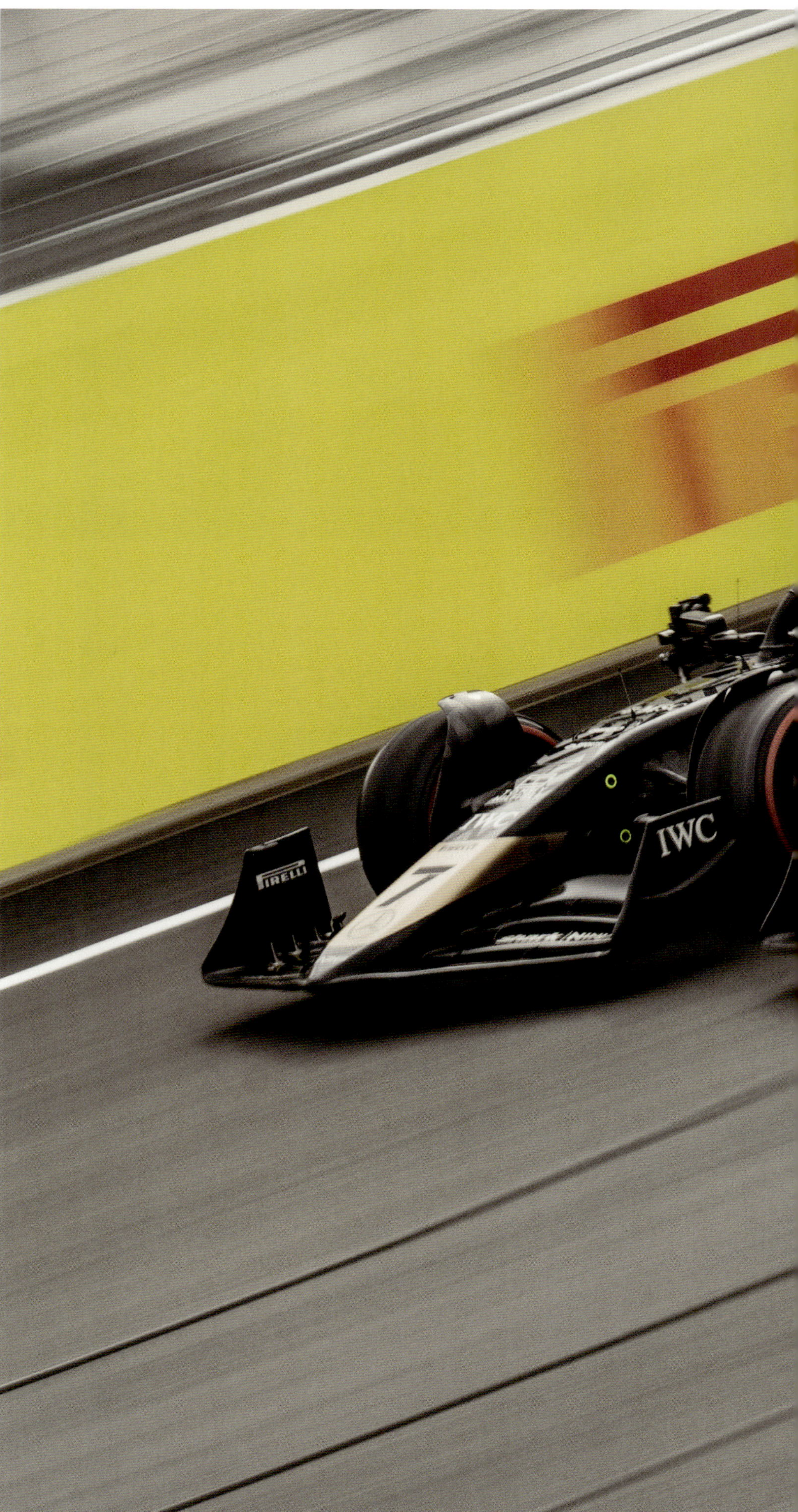

A shot of Sonny and Joshua battling on the track.

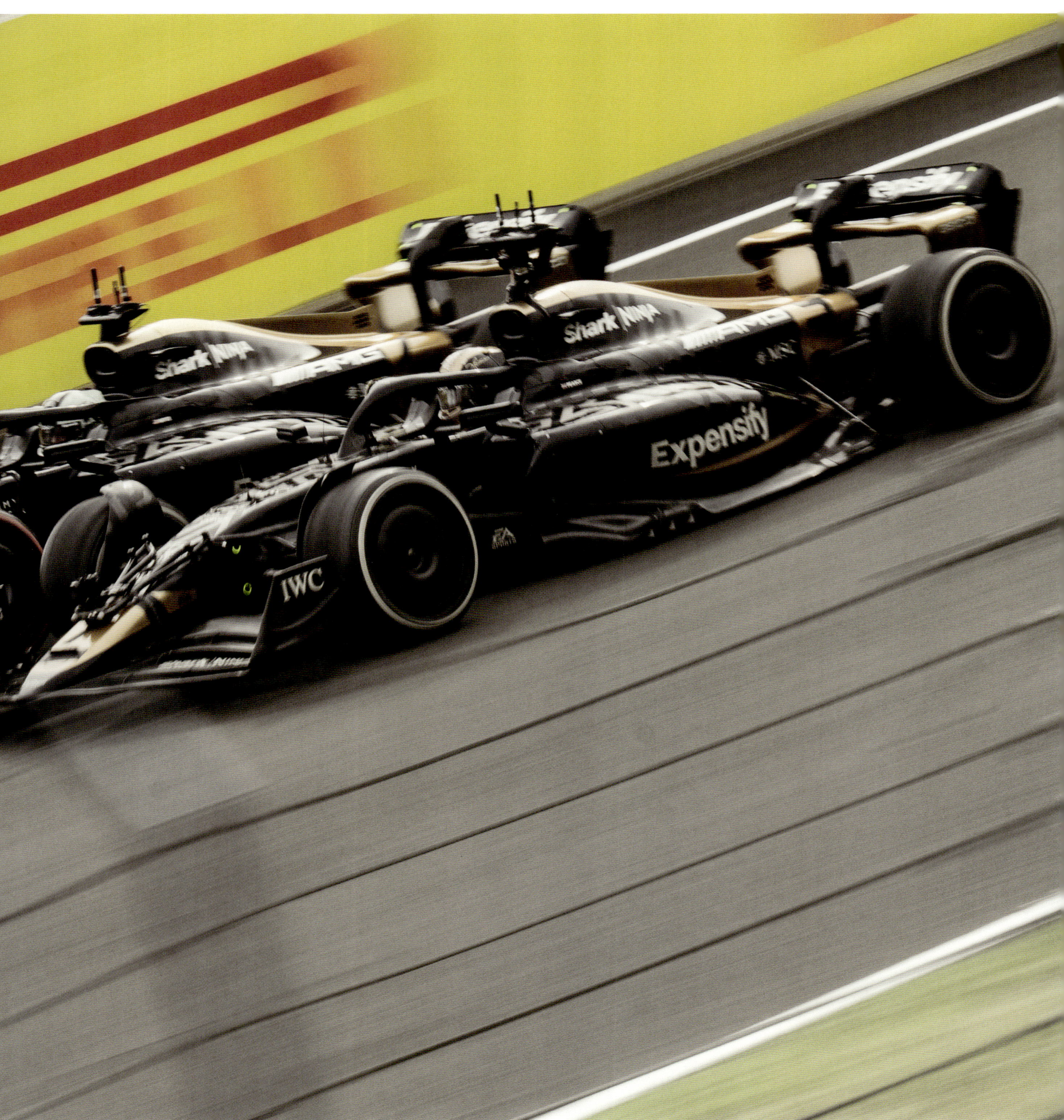
Expensify
IWC
Shark Ninja

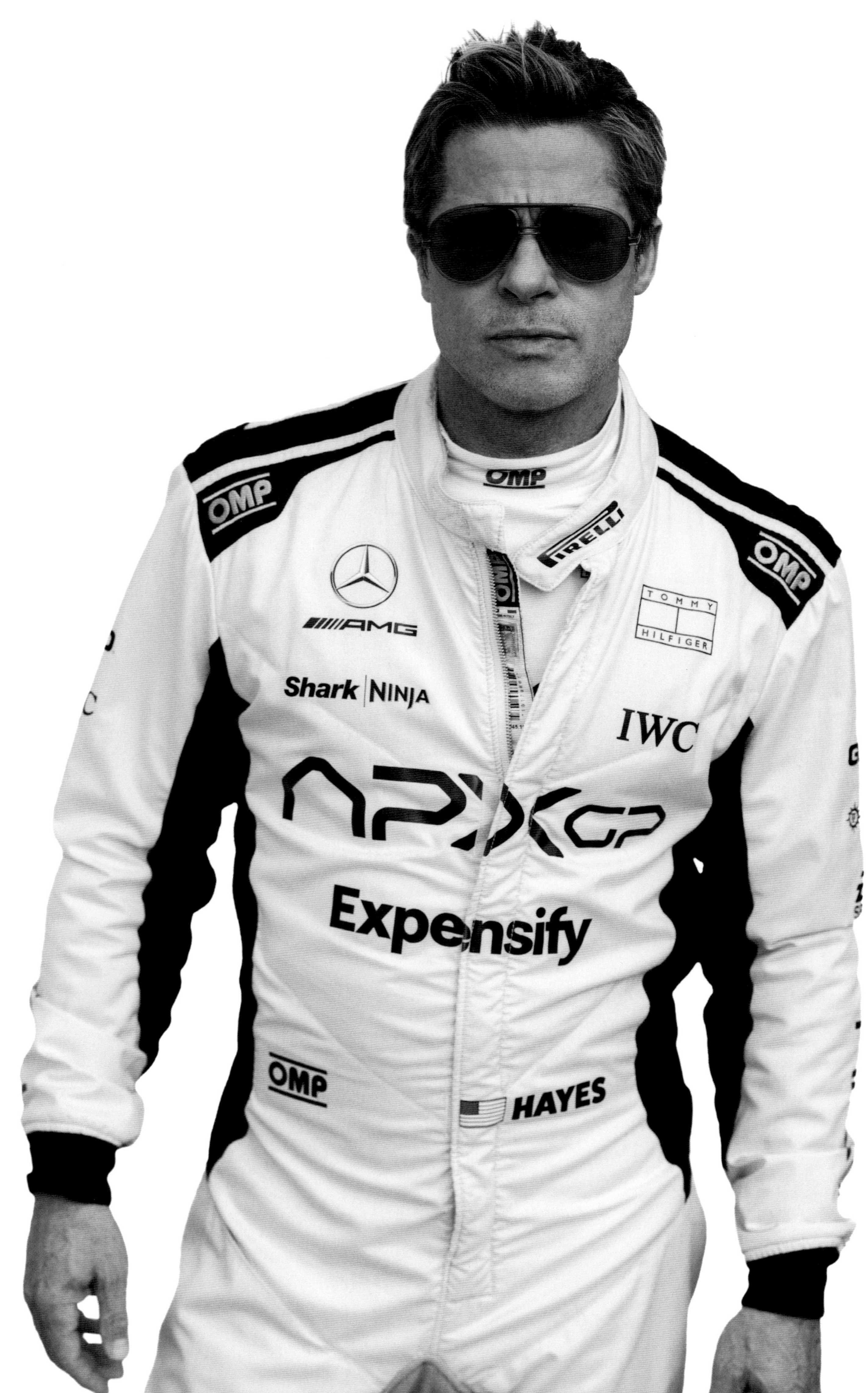
OMP
OMP
OMP
AMG
TOMMY HILFIGER
Shark | NINJA
IWC
Expensify
OMP
HAYES

THE VETERAN

SONNY HAYES

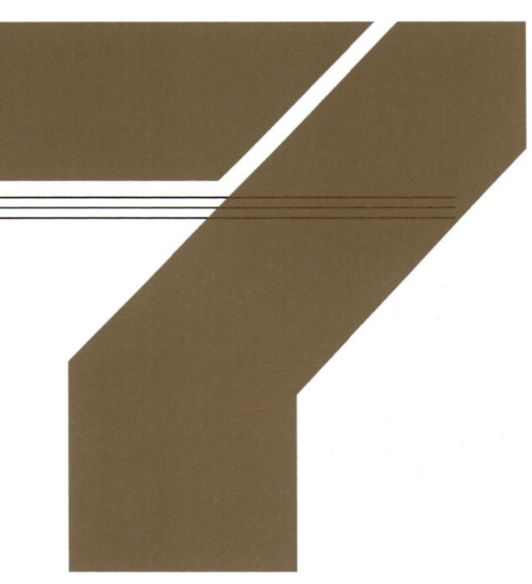

"He's a guy who had a shot in the early nineties and crapped out through a horrible accident," says Brad Pitt of Sonny Hayes, whom he plays in the film. In F1 terms, Hayes was a contemporary of Ayrton Senna, Martin Brundle, Gerhard Berger, Michael Schumacher, and Ruben Cervantes (played by Javier Bardem) before a horrendous crash at the Spanish Grand Prix in Jerez in 1993 cost him his Formula One career and nearly his life. "He disappeared for some time, then showed up again in all these other disciplines," Pitt continues. "He won Pikes Peak; he won an endurance race. He'll drive anything. And enjoy it. For the pure love of it. And this call from Ruben brings Sonny back in for this last shot, to see if they can turn this team around. He gives Sonny a chance to wake up this dragon that he still needed to slay. It's an underdog story, a redemption story."

"Sonny Hayes is a wanderer. He's been divorced. He's a gambler. But the thing he loves most is getting in a car and winning," says Bruckheimer.

"We thought of Sonny as someone who will never find contentment or satisfaction in life," says *F1* screenwriter Ehren Kruger. "We loved the idea that he's kind of a nomad and might not even be able to articulate what he's looking for, because whenever he takes on a challenge in a race and is able to meet it, he leaves that world to find another one. Losing the ability to compete as a young driver in F1 really damaged him emotionally. And none of these various racing challenges he undertakes will satisfy this existential search—and never will. He never expects to get an opportunity to race again at the highest level of the sport. So, to have that opportunity presented to him out of nowhere by an old friend is as much a potential curse as it is a blessing. Because it's a chance to confront what he feels is his greatest failure and perhaps fail even more spectacularly this time."

"His motto is 'new day, new challenge,' which in some ways is my own motto," reveals director Joseph Kosinski. "For him, it's not about being the best and staying in a certain division; it's about climbing one mountain, then looking for the next. And Formula One is that one mountain he was never able to climb. I think deep down that gnaws at him. So, when this opportunity comes up, it simultaneously draws him, but it also scares him a bit. Because if he couldn't beat Formula One before, and he gets another shot, and he can't beat it this time, does that mean he's not good enough? That's the fear. That maybe he isn't all that people thought he was."

"Sonny Hayes is a wanderer. He's been divorced. He's a gambler. But the thing he loves most is getting in a car and winning."

JERRY BRUCKHEIMER

Hayes is, in many ways, a throwback, not only to 1990s Formula One racing, with its V12 engines, lack of power steering, and manual gear shifts, but to a 1970s-style movie hero. "Sonny is a guy who's never going to change," says Kosinski, "which makes him more of a seventies-style protagonist, rather than a guy who's going to go through this giant arc and be completely changed by events. It's more the opposite. He is a guy set in his ways. He's very comfortable in his own skin and comfortable with the mistakes he's made and is going to end up changing the people around him as he moves through this story. He's more of a Western-type character, the lone gunman who rolls into town and rides off at the end, to his next adventure. That was the type of character Brad was interested in playing. So that shaped Sonny Hayes in developing his story."

"That's what I most love about seventies characters," says Pitt. "They don't necessarily learn a lesson. They're the same beast at the end of the adventures that they were in the beginning. It's just the world around him changes, or their perception of it."

In early drafts, the character went by a different name. "Teddy Gibson was one of the early ones," says Kosinski. "There was a point where he was called Guy Peppers. It was a process of Brad and I texting ideas back and forth, playing with different names, going from the boring to the insane. And Sonny Hayes was where we landed. Guy Peppers is a great name, but I was trying to imagine [F1 commentator] David Croft yelling it over the PA, and Sonny Hayes kind of rolls off the tongue."

When Kosinski and Kruger started work on the script, they were concerned that Pitt, then in his late fifties, might not be believable as a Formula One driver. "Early on, we talked about a version where he's brought in by Ruben to replace the team principal halfway through the season," Kruger reveals. "The principal has quit. The team has lost all sense of morale. Then they lose a driver. And Sonny must step in and drive again. It felt quite movie-ish, which we're trying to avoid."

But there was one driver on the grid who Kruger kept thinking about in relation to Pitt: "I kept saying, if you put Brad right next to Fernando Alonso, they look similar. They both look good. And they're both older than the average F1 driver. I said, 'I think it's going to work to just bring him in as a driver.' Then we started looking for older drivers in racing history to help buttress our case."

Right: Sonny (Brad Pitt) straps on his helmet as he gears up for a race.

Below: Ruben (Javier Bardem) finds Sonny (Brad Pitt) in a laundromat and attempts to recruit him to the APXGP team.

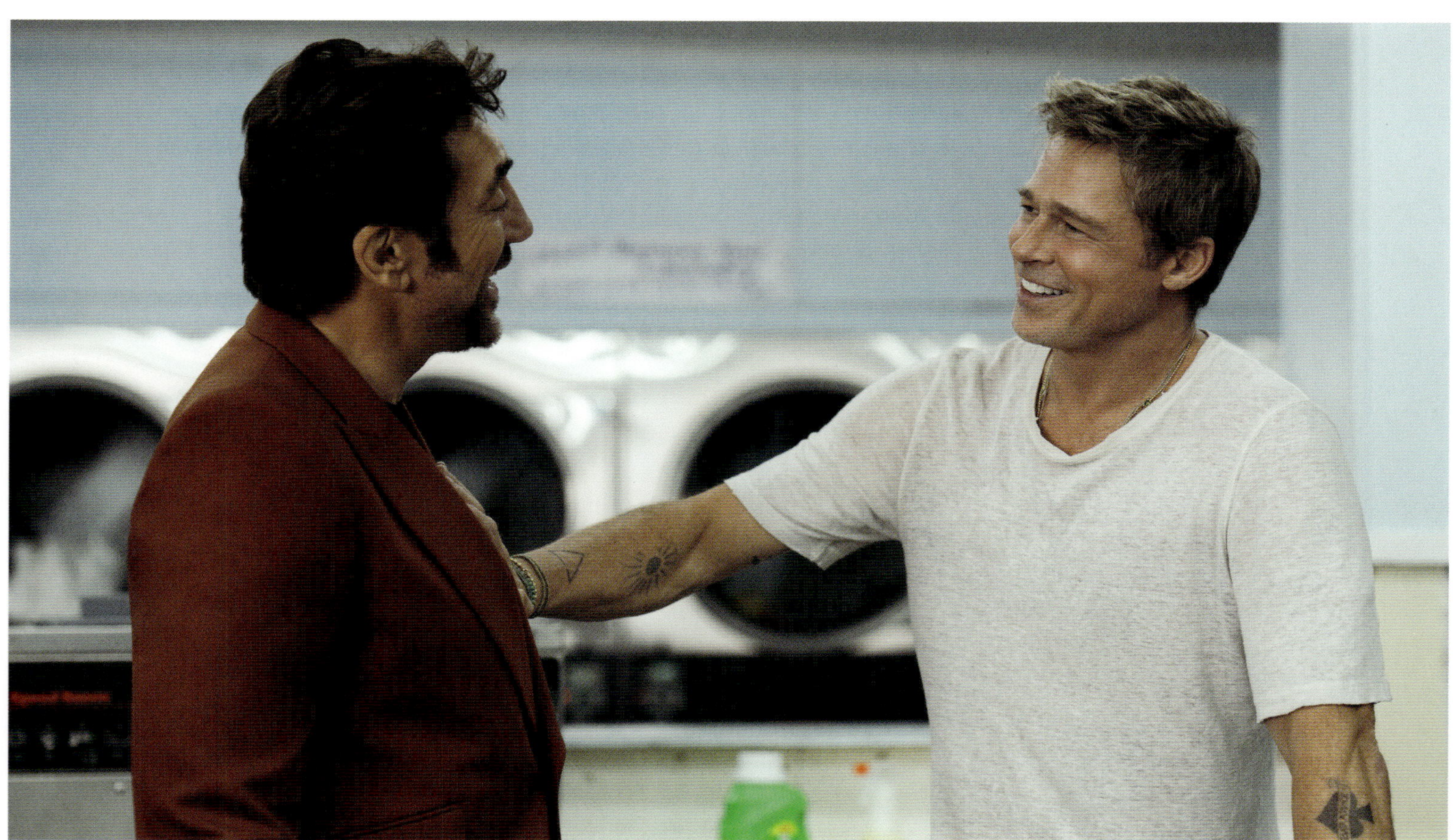

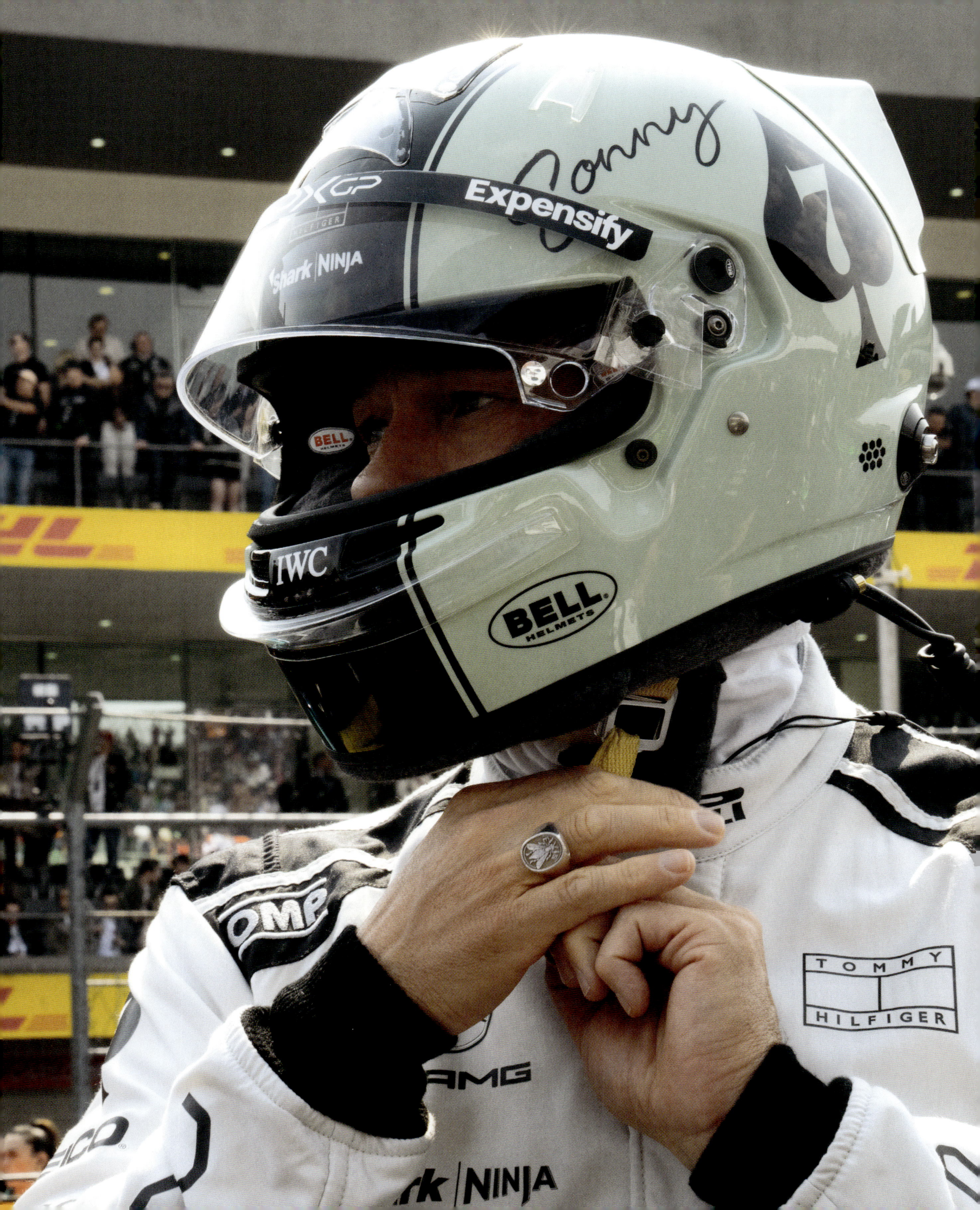

Expensify
Shark NINJA
BELL
IWC
BELL HELMETS
OMP
TOMMY HILFIGER
AMG
NINJA

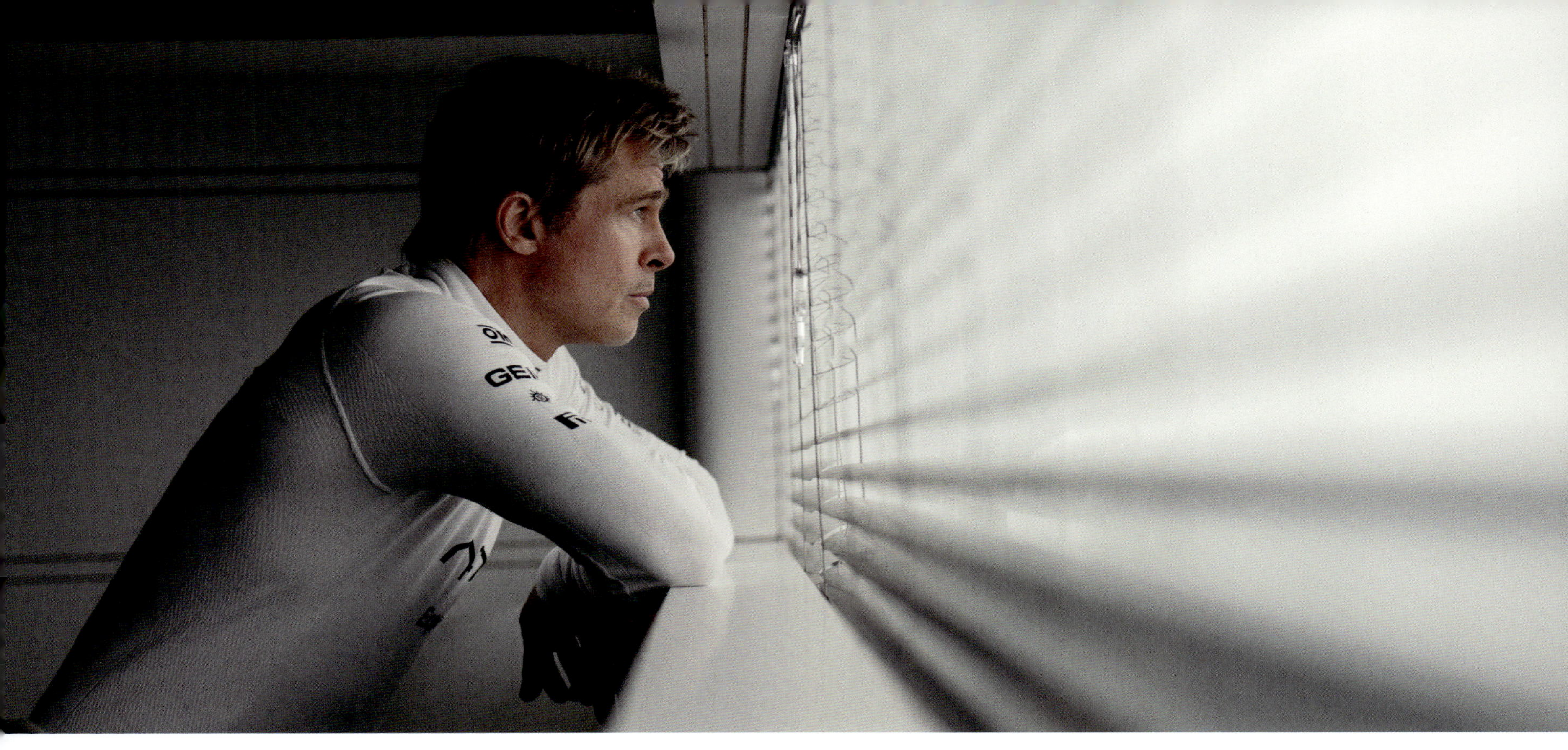

"There hasn't been a driver in their fifties since the 1960s or 1970s, so it is very unlikely that someone would be able to come in at that age and perform," admits Kosinski. "But Alonso is in his forties and performing at the top of his game. And we're seeing this across multiple sports. Athletes are now able to perform later than what was thought possible. So, Alonso was definitely an inspiration. And Lewis [Hamilton] was then in his late thirties and still performing at the top of his game. It also made us realize we should embrace that aspect and lean into it. It makes Sonny even more of an underdog when you have the racing world going, 'This is crazy. There's no way this guy can compete.' It starts them on the back foot, which is what the story is. Having an older driver helped stack the deck against APXGP even more."

Alonso was a touchstone for Sonny, not just in looks but in terms of temperament, personality, race craft, and his ability to think two or three moves ahead, as well as how wily a competitor he is. "We talked about Alonso a lot," says Kosinski. "And when we would talk to Formula One principals about the character, someone who has enough experience to know how to work within the rules but push them to their absolute limit, a number said, 'You should talk to Fernando. He's been around, he knows every trick, he knows how to play the game better than anyone. He's got the mental capacity to not only worry about his own race but

Alonso was a touchstone for Sonny not just in looks but in terms of temperament, personality, race craft, and his ability to think two or three moves ahead, as well as how wily a competitor he is.

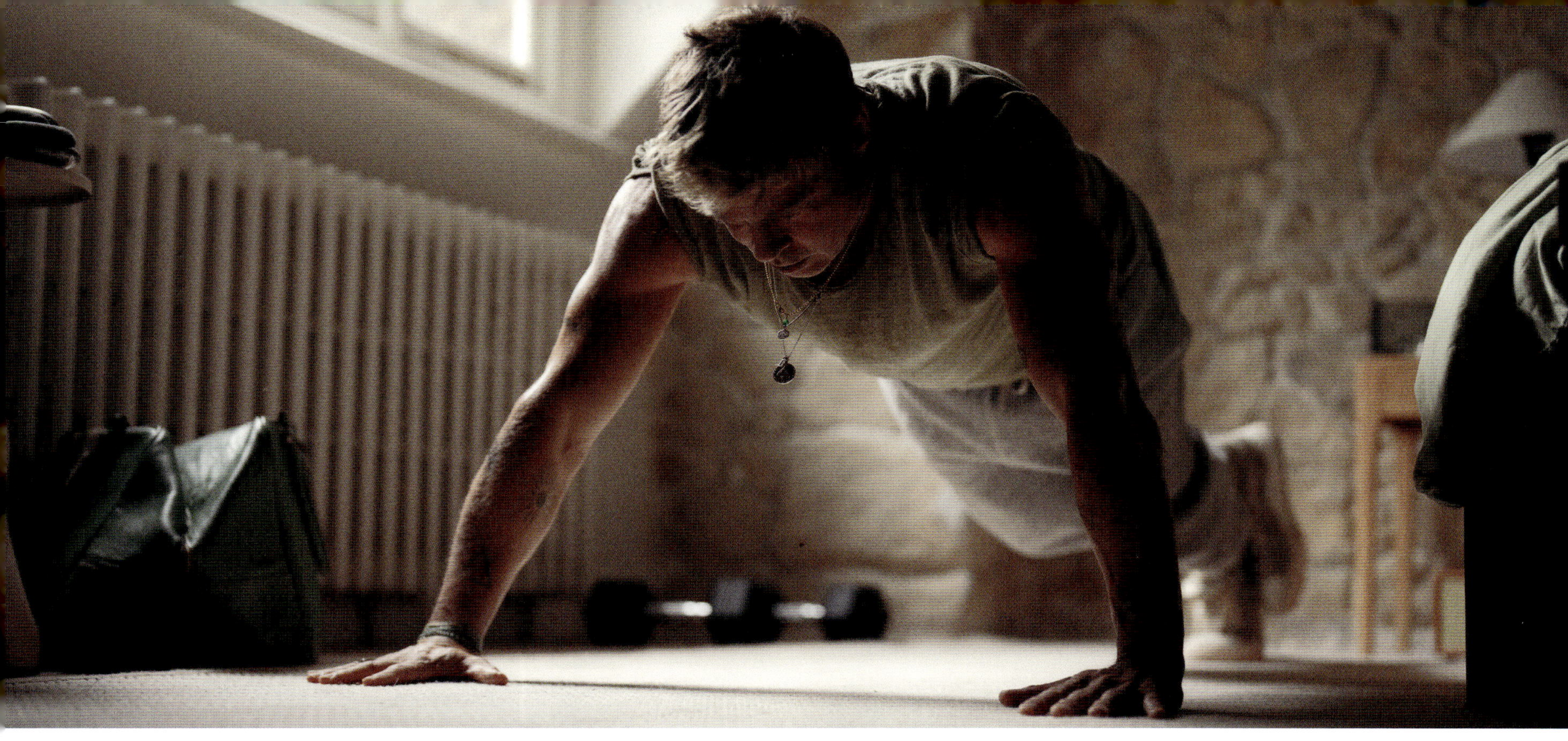

look at the big picture and understand strategy on a much bigger level, both within his team and all the other teams.' They said, 'You should look at him because he's got some aspects of the guy you're looking for.'"

"He seems to have his eye on the chessboard like few drivers ever have, always fighting for that advantage and playing with those limits and playing with the rules," says Pitt, who met with Alonso, as he did all the drivers. "He's really smart. He thinks seven, eight turns ahead. We figured being the last-place team, this is something we'd be forced to do to be competitive in any way."

But as much as Alonso was an inspiration for Sonny, according to Kosinski, the character is "an amalgam of several icons," drivers, past and present. "Martin Donnelly [whose career-ending crash at the Spanish Grand Prix in 1990 was appropriated for Sonny in the film] was one. There's a little bit of Kimi Räikkönen in there, the way he spoke his mind and didn't censor himself. Kevin Magnussen was someone people knew to stay clear of because he's very aggressive in the corners. So, there's a little bit of all these boundary-pushing drivers combined into Sonny Hayes. Brad and I had lunch with Gerhard Berger, Senna's teammate in the 1990s, and he told us a bunch of crazy stories about those days—the practical jokes, the racing and attitude of that time—which was really useful because that would have been the era Sonny Hayes started in. We also went to Toto Wolff's house for dinner with Lewis and [Toto's wife] Susie Wolff to pick their brains on who this guy was."

Left: Two-time World Drivers' Champion Fernando Alonso was one of the inspirations for the character of Sonny Hayes.

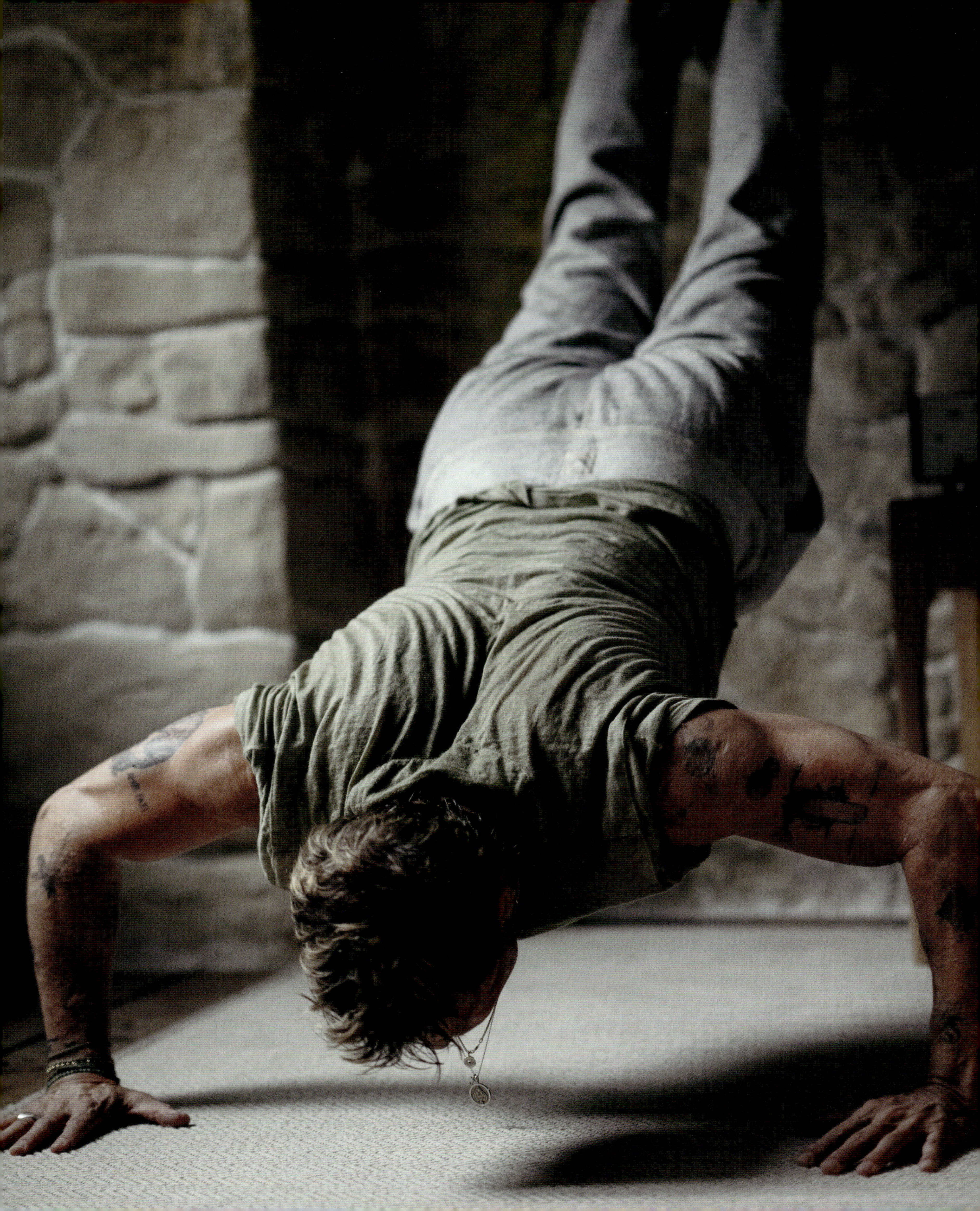

Left: Sonny's tattoos are a mix of Pitt's own body art, as well as new ones designed to represent the character's own story.

When we first meet Sonny Hayes in Daytona at the start of the film, we're introduced to him asleep in a camper van, parked next to the track, and we get a glimpse of his nomadic lifestyle, his quirks, and his superstitions—mismatched socks, a playing card cut from a pack then tucked into his race suit, a moment of quiet reflection before he gets into the car. "We wanted to hint at his period of life where he had gambling struggles and addictions, which was an essential part of his character," says Kruger. "The knowledge that there is a degree of luck that determines how things in life do or do not pan out. And it's best to be on the good side of lady luck whenever possible."

The idea of Sonny wearing mismatched socks came from a conversation with Lewis Hamilton. "When we would ask the drivers, 'Are there rituals, things you do just for luck before you get in the car,' Lewis said that odd socks or something about the wardrobe that's off is fairly common," Kruger continues. "Drivers may not tell you about it and advertise, 'This is my lucky charm,' but there are things they will wear again and again after having success wearing it one time."

Sonny's tattoos also tell their own story. "He's got a tattoo of the track he crashed at on his arm, a tattoo pointing at the scar on his back, always reminding him of that day back in 1990," says Kosinski. "I liked the idea he is a slightly superstitious character; it gives you something to learn about and hints at things you're going to discover as the story unfolds. Brad has tattoos, obviously, but Sonny's are a bit more irreverent. There are some dumb ones in there, maybe from a drunken night somewhere. Brad and I looked at hundreds of options and picked out things that felt like bits of backstory. It's a way for Brad to connect to the character and figure out who this guy is. So, we did it together, but I let him lead the choices on what Sonny would have."

"Sonny has them because the actor didn't want to spend an hour in the morning covering them up," admits Pitt. "But I added some more to make it feel like Sonny and not me."

In addition to his own tattoos, Pitt, says Kruger, also brought his own experiences to bear on his character. "Sonny having an antagonistic relationship with the press, Sonny having his past relationships picked over and criticized. The experience of living in a fishbowl, which is what Formula One drivers live in for as long as they're in the car, and their every move is scrutinized. As well as the casual confidence that Brad has instinctively, which is very important to the character, making him immune to what anyone else thinks about him."

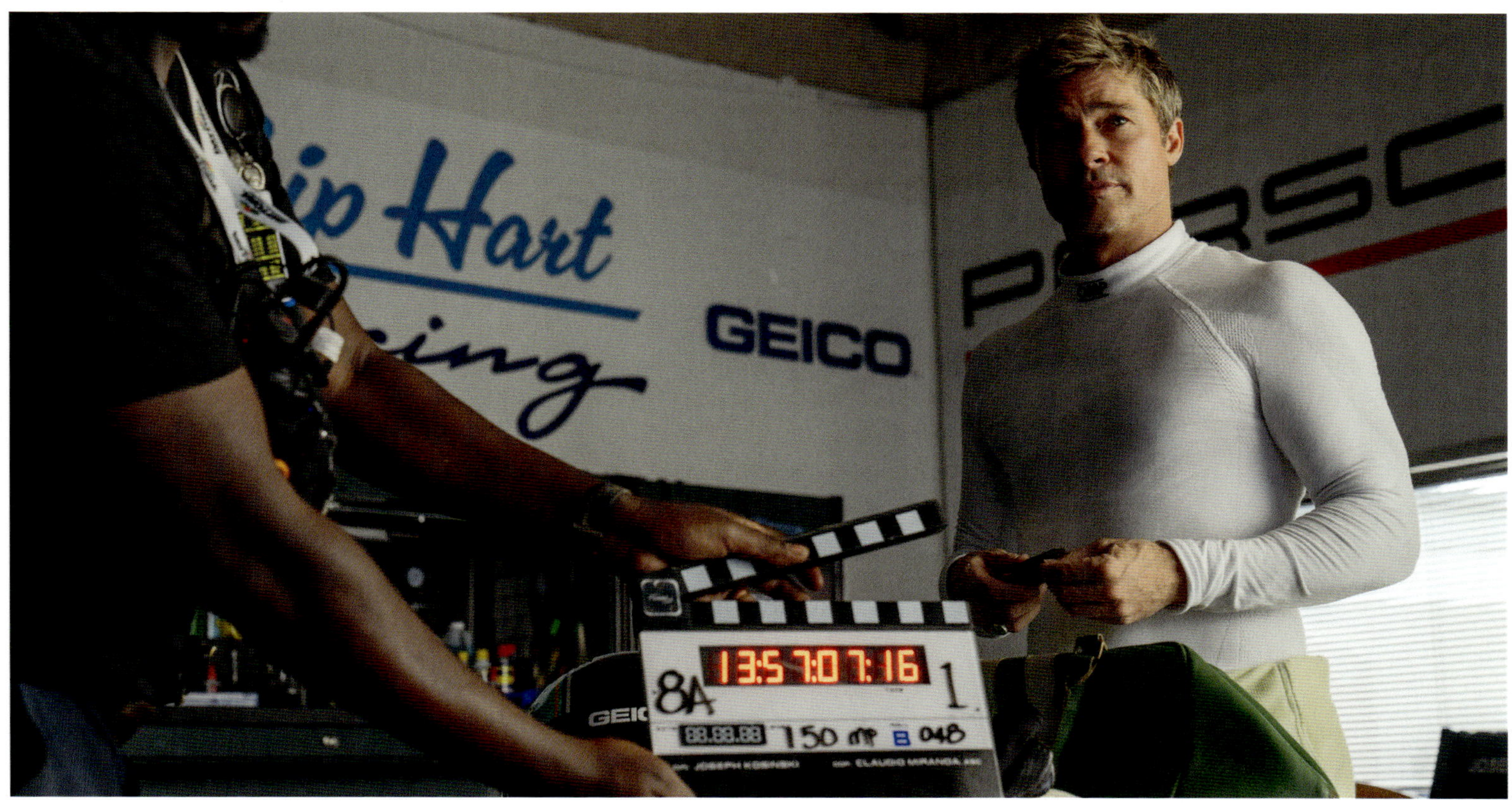

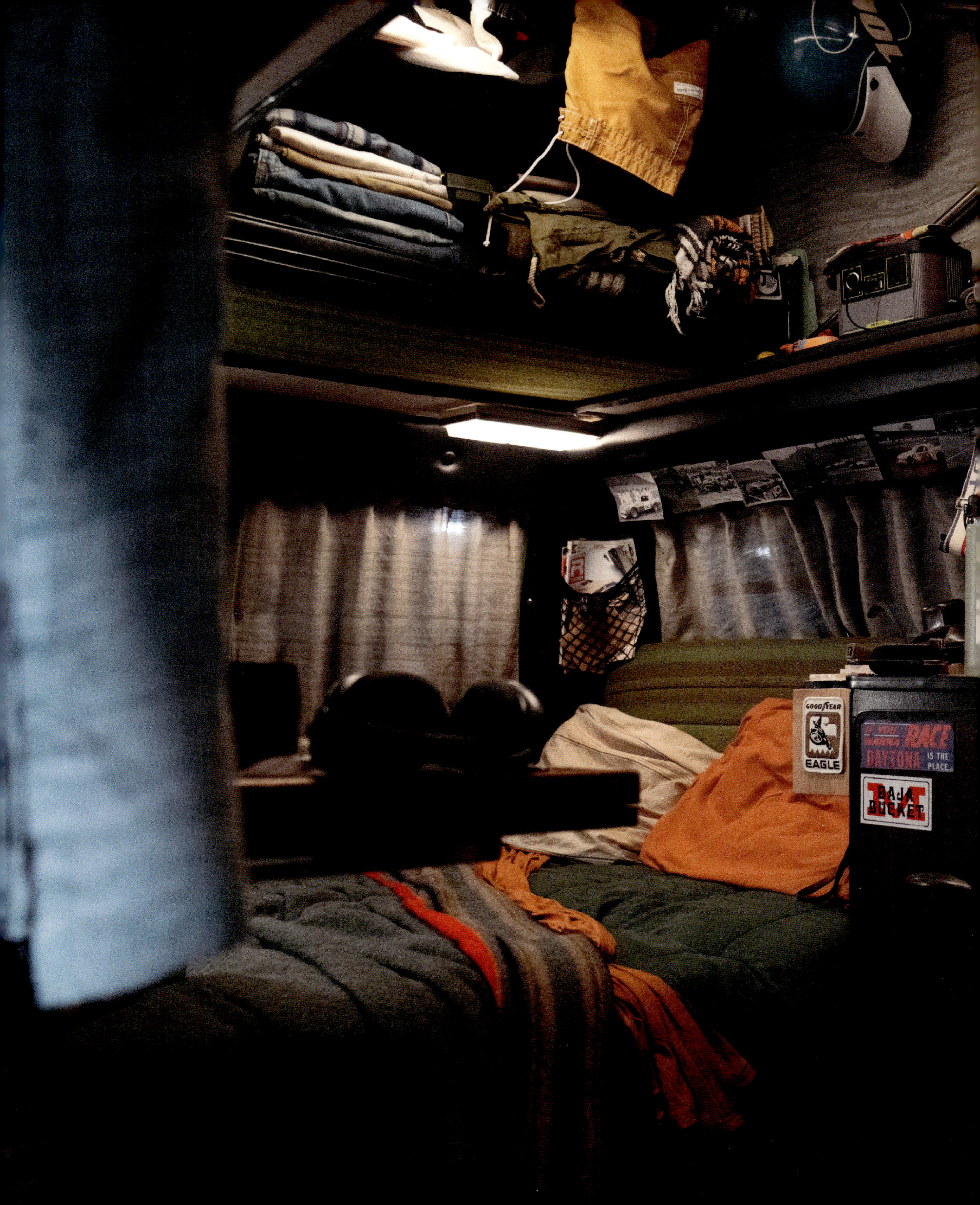
GOODYEAR
EAGLE
IF YOU WANNA RACE
DAYTONA IS THE PLACE
BAJA BUCKET

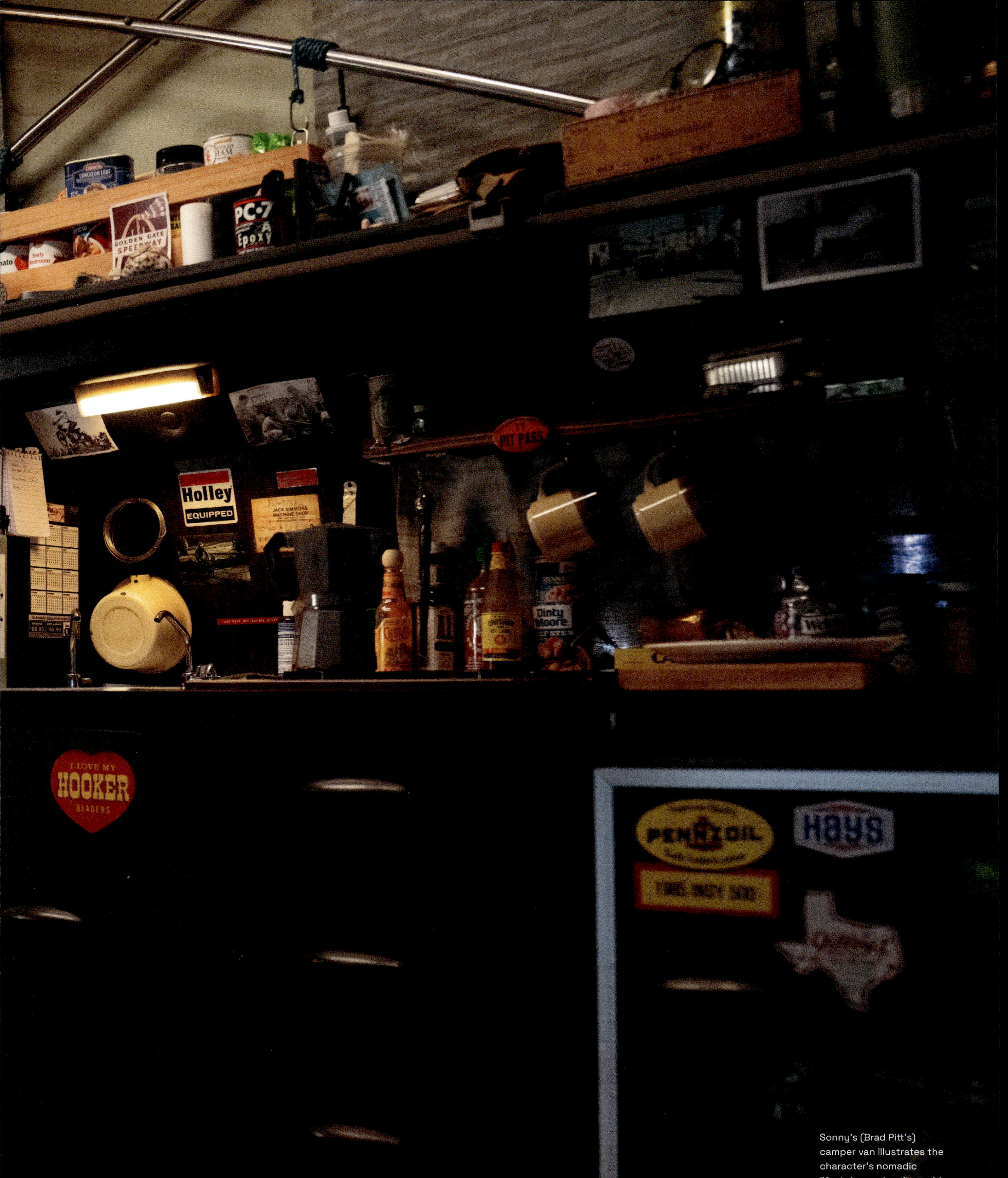

Sonny's (Brad Pitt's) camper van illustrates the character's nomadic lifestyle—and racing quirks.

> “I see him as a sensei, helping me find myself in this world of acting.”
>
> DAMSON IDRIS

That natural confidence, coupled with Pitt’s decades of experience in front of the camera, was something that rubbed off on his costar, Damson Idris. “When we were training at Silverstone, we would talk about the dynamic of the characters. Who are these two? How are these two connected?” Idris recalls. “Then I’d ask him questions about his career, where his mind was at when he first started, and he would tell stories of the time he met Sidney Poitier.

“I see him as a sensei, helping me find myself in this world of acting, outside of the film,” continues Idris. “I’m studying him in real time. I’m watching greatness. It’s constant inspiration. He’s so dedicated. He’s such a good driver. He’s an amazing collaborator. Always asking questions, like, ‘What do you think? What do you want to do?’ There’s no ego. He’s so humble. If Brad Pitt’s humble, everyone needs to be humble. There is no diva attitude. Show up and do the best work you can. That’s what I learned from him.”

Right: Sonny (Brad Pitt) and Joshua (Damson Idris) share an embrace during the Abu Dhabi Grand Prix.

Below: The relationship between Joshua (Damson Idris) and Sonny (Brad Pitt) develops into a mutual respect by the end of the film.

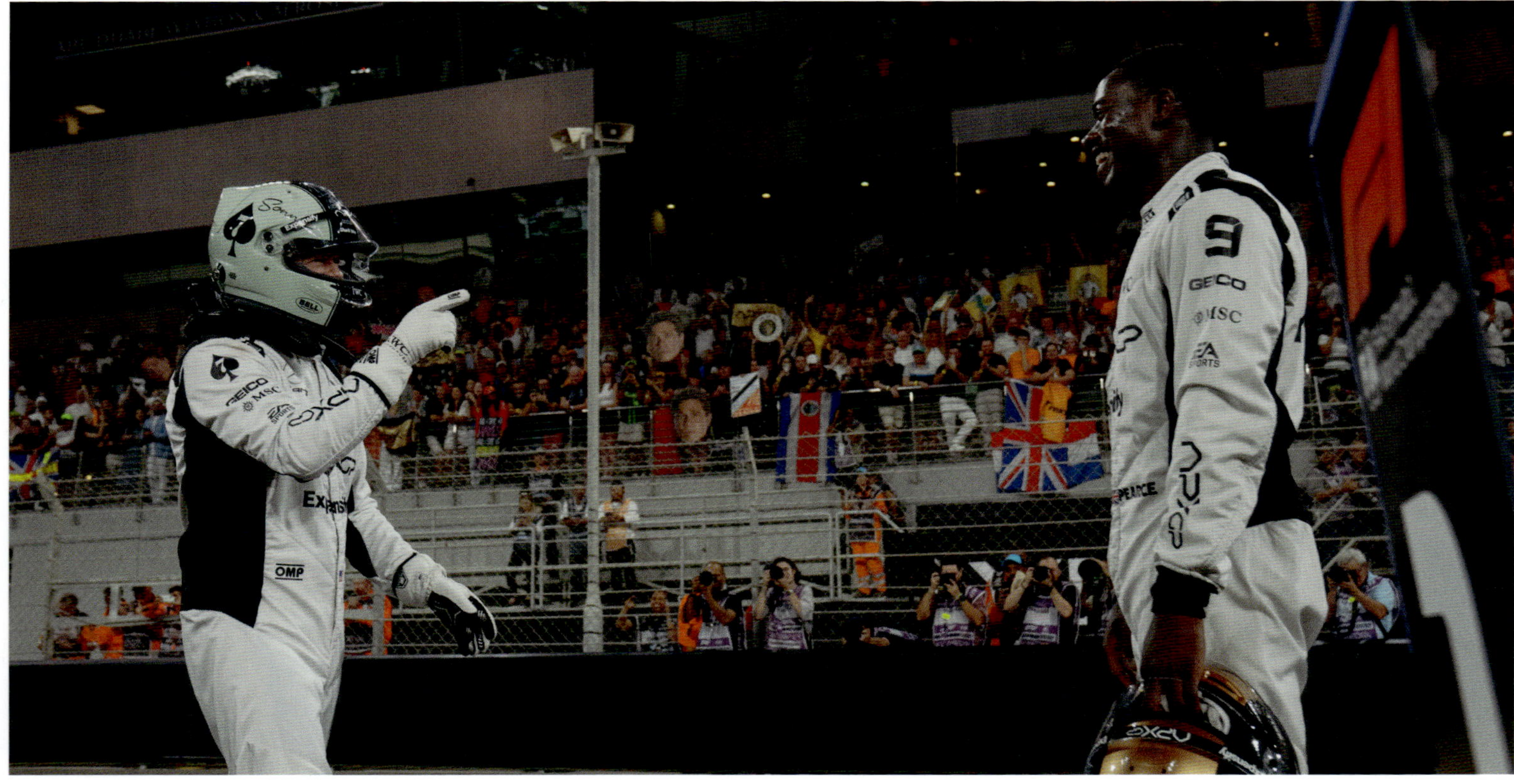

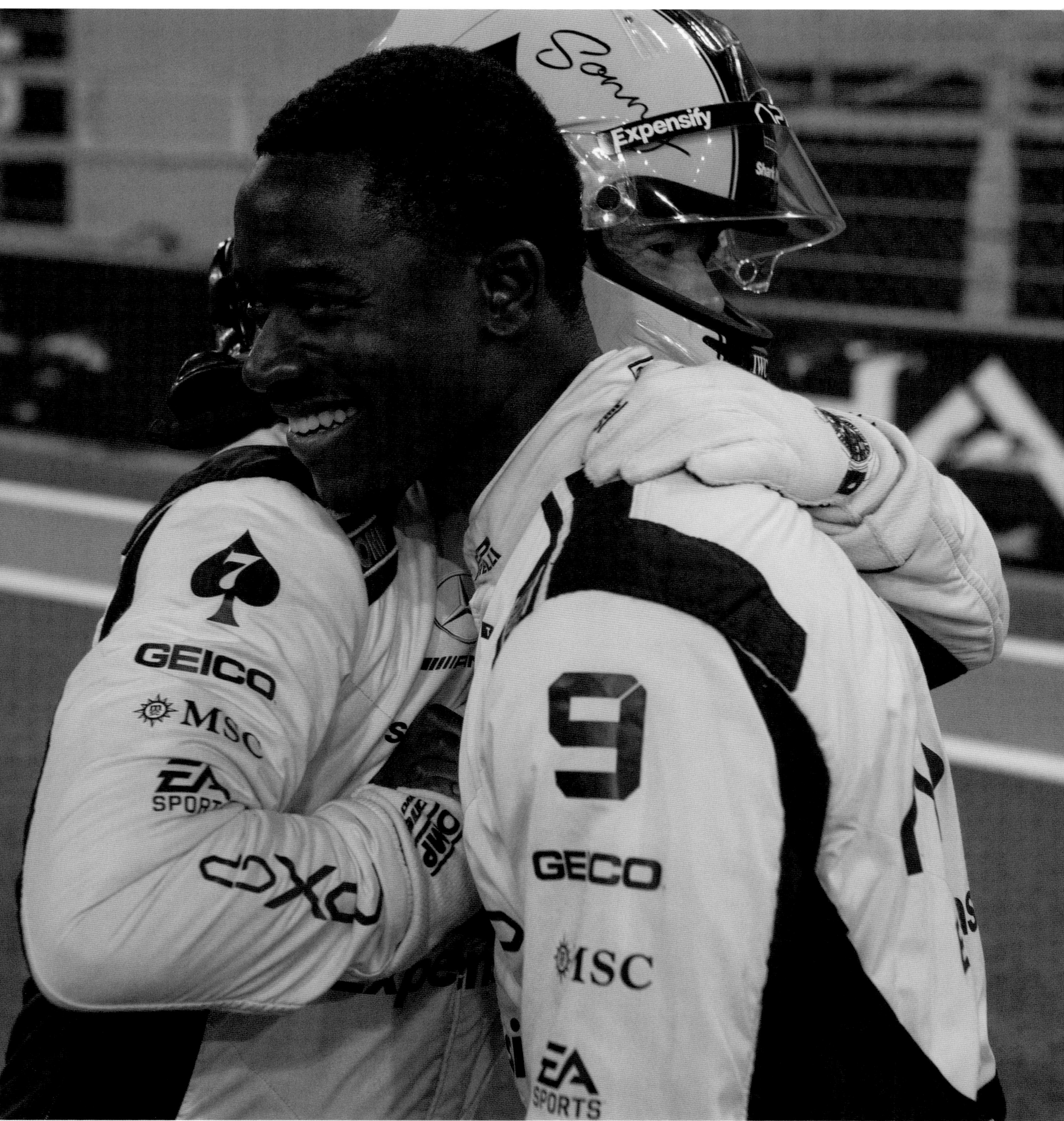
Expensify
GEICO
MSC
EA SPORTS
9
MSC
EA SPORTS

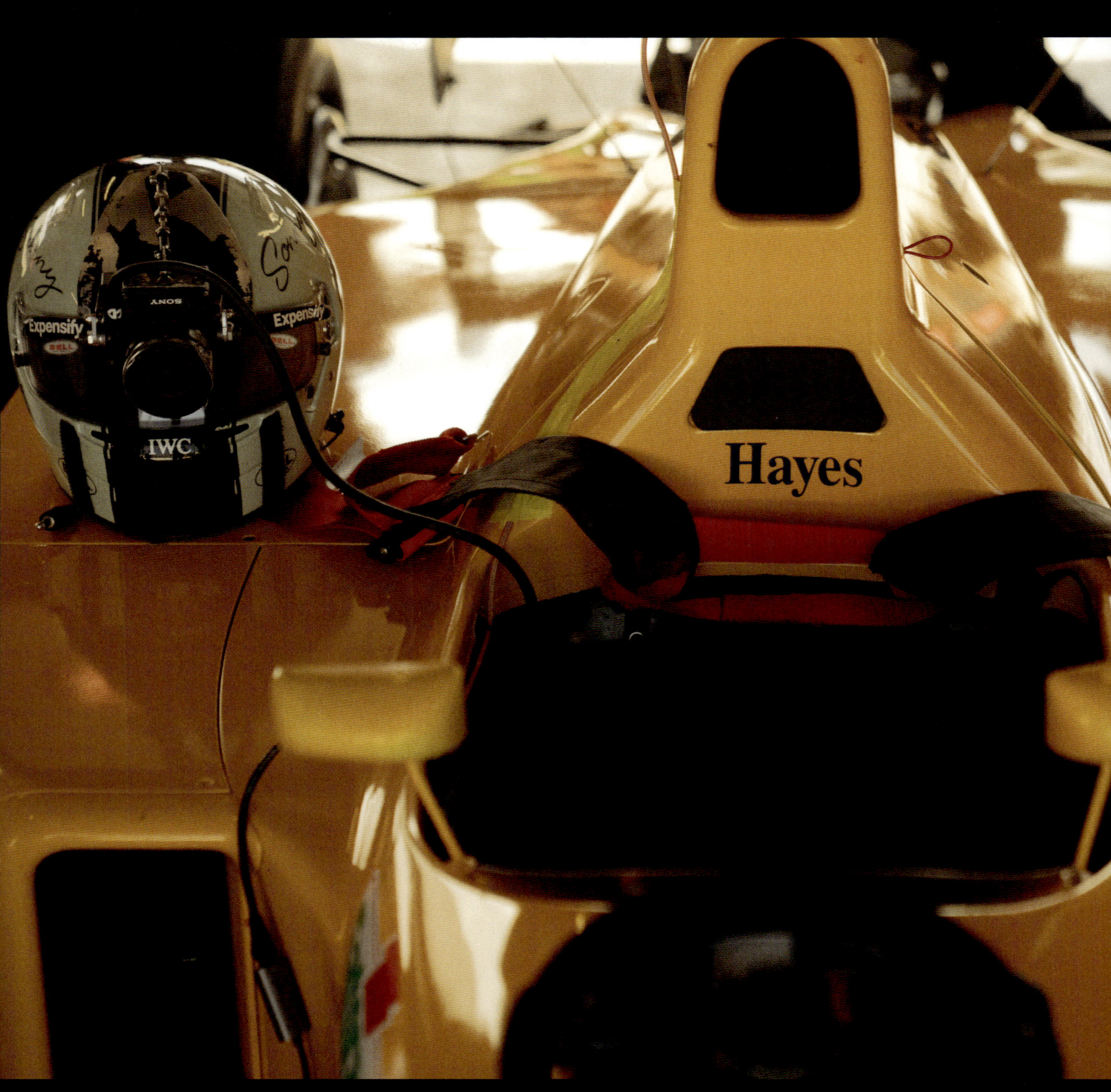

Above: Sonny Hayes's APXGP helmet sits on top of a vintage yellow Lotus like the one British F1 driver Martin Donnelly

Right: Donnelly's real-life crash at the 1990 Spanish Grand Prix was the inspiration for Sonny's (Brad Pitt's) pivotal acci-

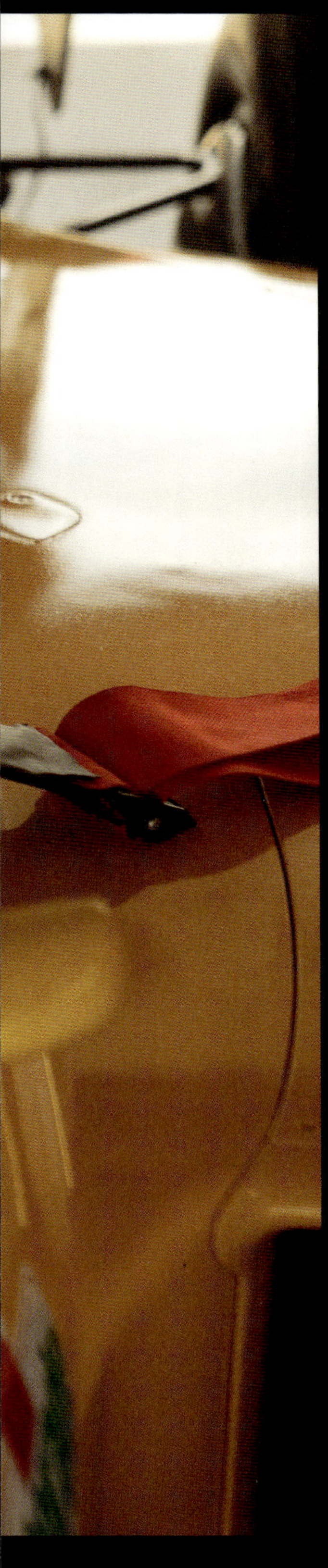

During practice for the 1990 Spanish Grand Prix in Jerez, the suspension of the Lotus driven by Belfast-born Martin Donnelly failed, causing his car to smash into the wall at 160 miles per hour. The impact split Donnelly's car's safety cell, and he was ejected across the track, sustaining multiple injuries. His heart stopped twice. He was put into a medically induced coma and was close to having his right leg amputated. At one point, Donnelly's condition was considered so grave that he was given last rites. Miraculously, he was able to walk again. But his career as a Formula One driver was over.

Director Joseph Kosinski wanted to use Donnelly's crash as the basis of Sonny Hayes's career-ending accident in *F1*, as well as footage of the aftermath of the accident, with Donnelly lying on the track. In the film, Sonny was Ruben Cervantes's teammate at Lotus and Formula One's rising star, until he suffered a horrific crash at the 1990 Spanish Grand Prix. Racing the late, great Ayrton Senna's iconic red-and-white McLaren in his yellow Lotus, Sonny overtakes Senna for the lead around the outside of turn six, but his car kicks out and snaps, careening into the wall at high speed, breaking it in two and sending him onto the track, body like a mangled puppet.

Thirty years later, Sonny carries the effects of that near-fatal accident with him every day, both physically—we see his scars when he takes an ice bath following the British Grand Prix—and mentally—he is plagued by nightmares of the crash—waking up in a cold sweat in his camper van in Daytona and in a Vegas hotel room.

Lewis Hamilton first reached out to Donnelly and sought his permission to use his image and the crash footage. "We spoke with Martin, and he was so kind, giving us permission to use what is a life-changing event for him," says Pitt. "In many ways, his story is as interesting as any champion. He was a kid from Northern Ireland who worked his way up on sheer skill, signed an option on a revised £5.6 million contract the morning before his crash, and through no fault of his own, put it in a wall, and his career was over. How does one make peace with that?"

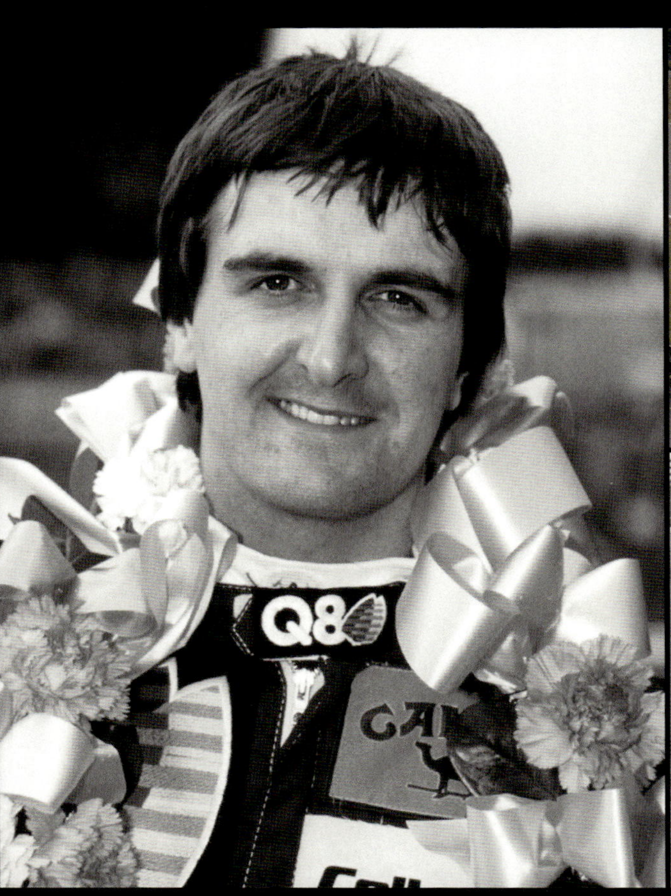

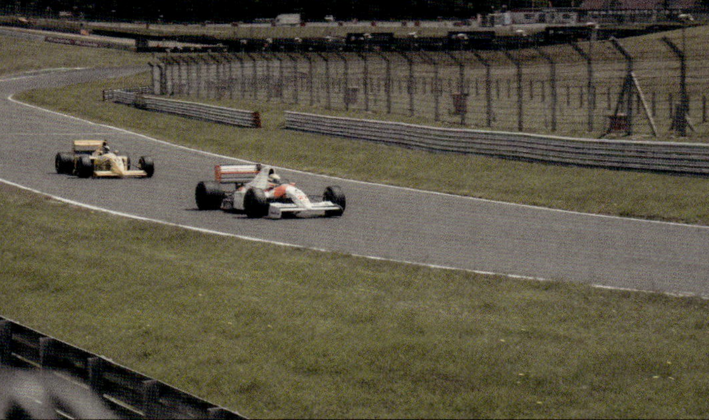

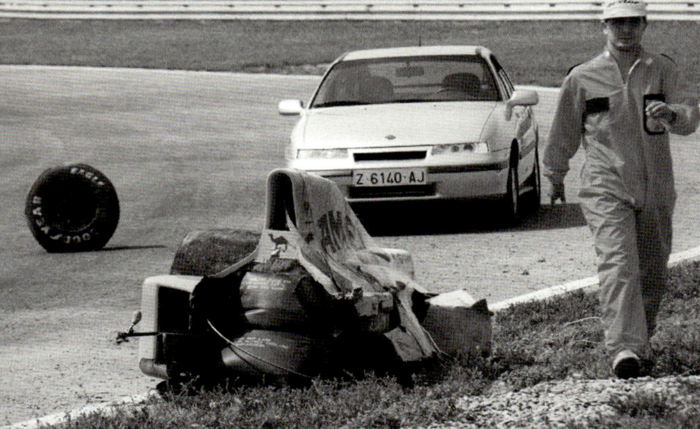

In *F1*, we see flashbacks to 1990 Sonny in his yellow race suit, alongside his bright yellow Lotus in the team's garage at Jerez. Production designer Ben Munro built the period garage at Brands Hatch, and the production borrowed a real Lotus, although it was missing its engine.

When Kosinski shot the scene in the garage and the track action leading up to the crash in June 2024, Donnelly was there to watch. "Which was very surreal for him, I think, to be in that garage and see those cars all done up in the livery of the period, and see Brad in a period suit, and then to see us work on reconstructing a version of his accident. To have him consulting and working with us was incredible."

The track action was filmed from Sonny's point of view, which is part of a dream sequence as he chases down the Brazilian driver. Alas, the production couldn't use Senna's actual McLaren. "The insurance on driving the McLaren was ridiculous," recalls Kosinski. "I mean, the real car is in the movie. It's in the display case in Ruben's office. But it's worth so much money you can't insure it to drive."

Instead, the production used a Dallara from the same era, wrapped in white vehicle vinyl, to stand in for Senna's McLaren, being chased down by a Benetton F1 car from 1990, which was wrapped in yellow vinyl to double for Sonny's Lotus. The cars were filmed at Brands Hatch and reskinned by Ryan Tudhope's visual effects team, which scanned Senna's real McLaren to create a digital version, which they used to replace the Dallara.

"The challenge there was that, in real life, Donnelly's suspension broke and turned the car into a bobsled. He had no steering control, so he just went straight off the track into a barrier," says Tudhope. "I had to find a part of Brands Hatch where the track went straight, and I could make it look like it curved. It was an exercise in location scouting, looking at the real footage from Spain, trying to understand the best possible match at Brands Hatch, and what was safe for the stunt drivers so our cars could be going full speed down the track."

Kosinski filmed the two cars going straight down the track before visual effects took over, digitally curving the track and crashing the Lotus into the barrier. "That work was being done by ILM," says Tudhope. The footage appears to be recorded on videotape, an effect achieved by using real VHS tapes and layering the footage onto them.

Before the crash, we see a twentysomething Sonny in the garage, getting ready to race. To de-age Pitt, Metaphysic analyzed videos of Pitt from the early 1990s—around the time Sonny would have been racing against Senna.

Metaphysic analyzed the archive material, and once the contemporary footage of Pitt that Kosinski shot in the garage at Brands Hatch was fed into its system, its software put out a "new, younger version onto his face," says Tudhope. "We only had to de-age Brad for about a dozen shots, and the technology is really effective at doing that."

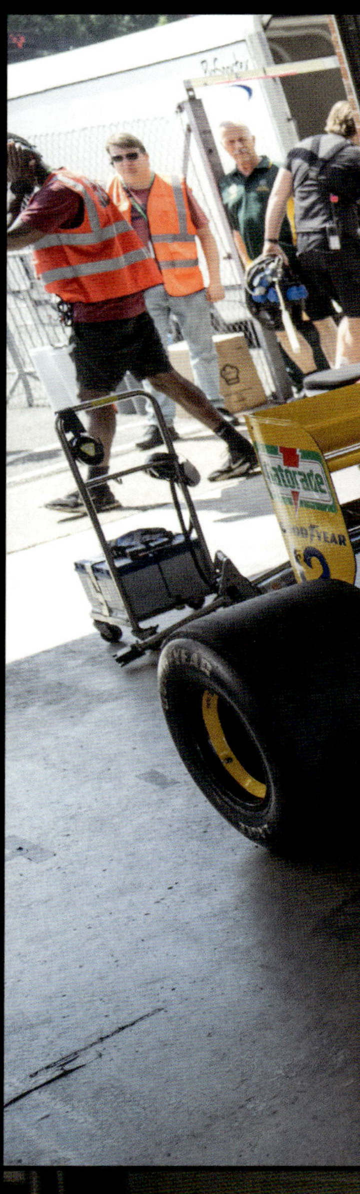

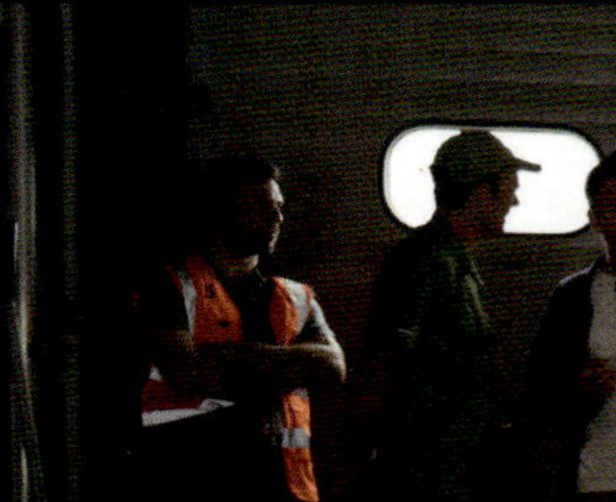

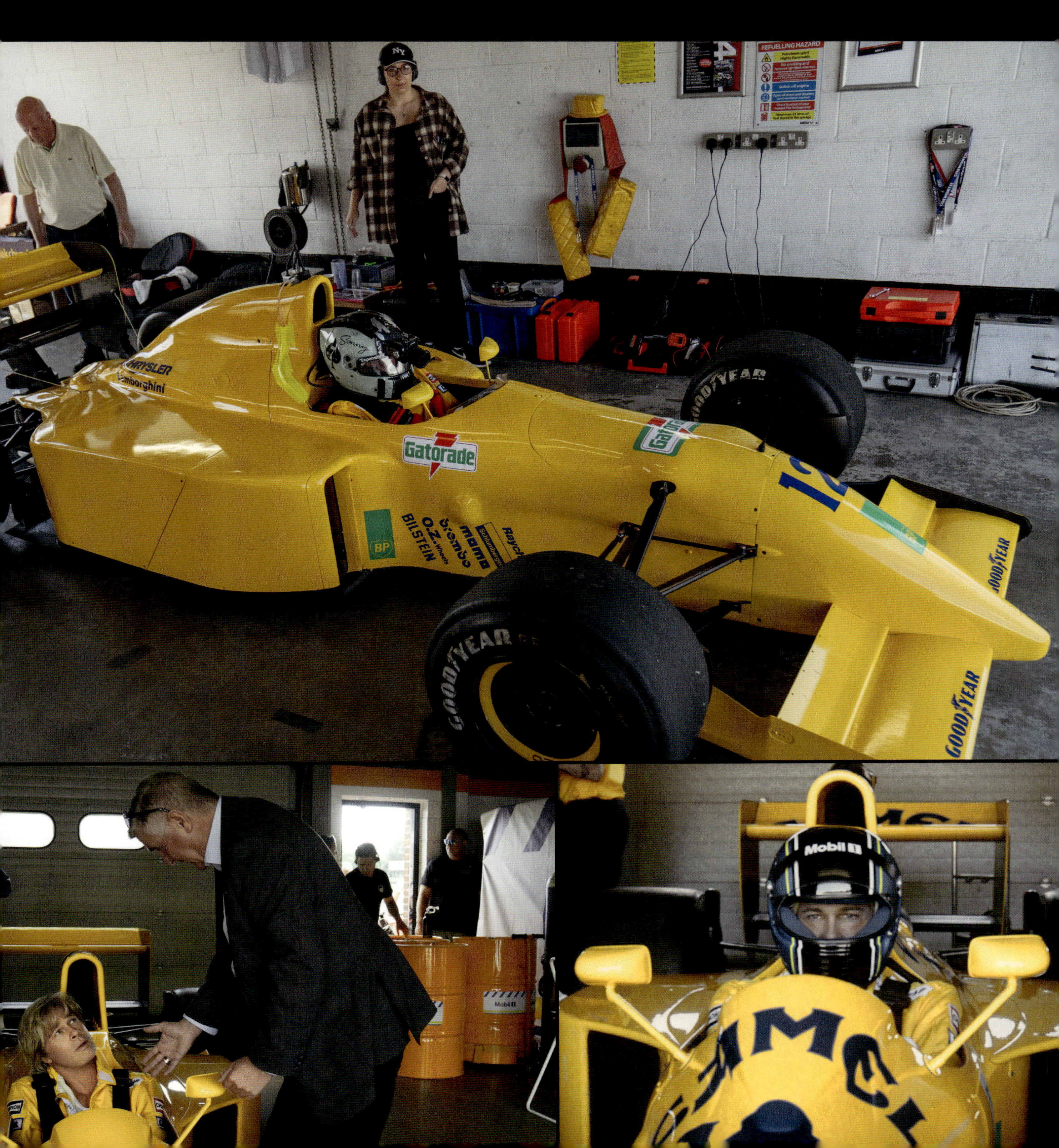

REFUELLING HAZARD
Gatorade
GOODYEAR
CHRYSLER
Lamborghini
BP
BILSTEIN
O.Z. Wheels
brembo
mama
Schlumberger
Mobil 1

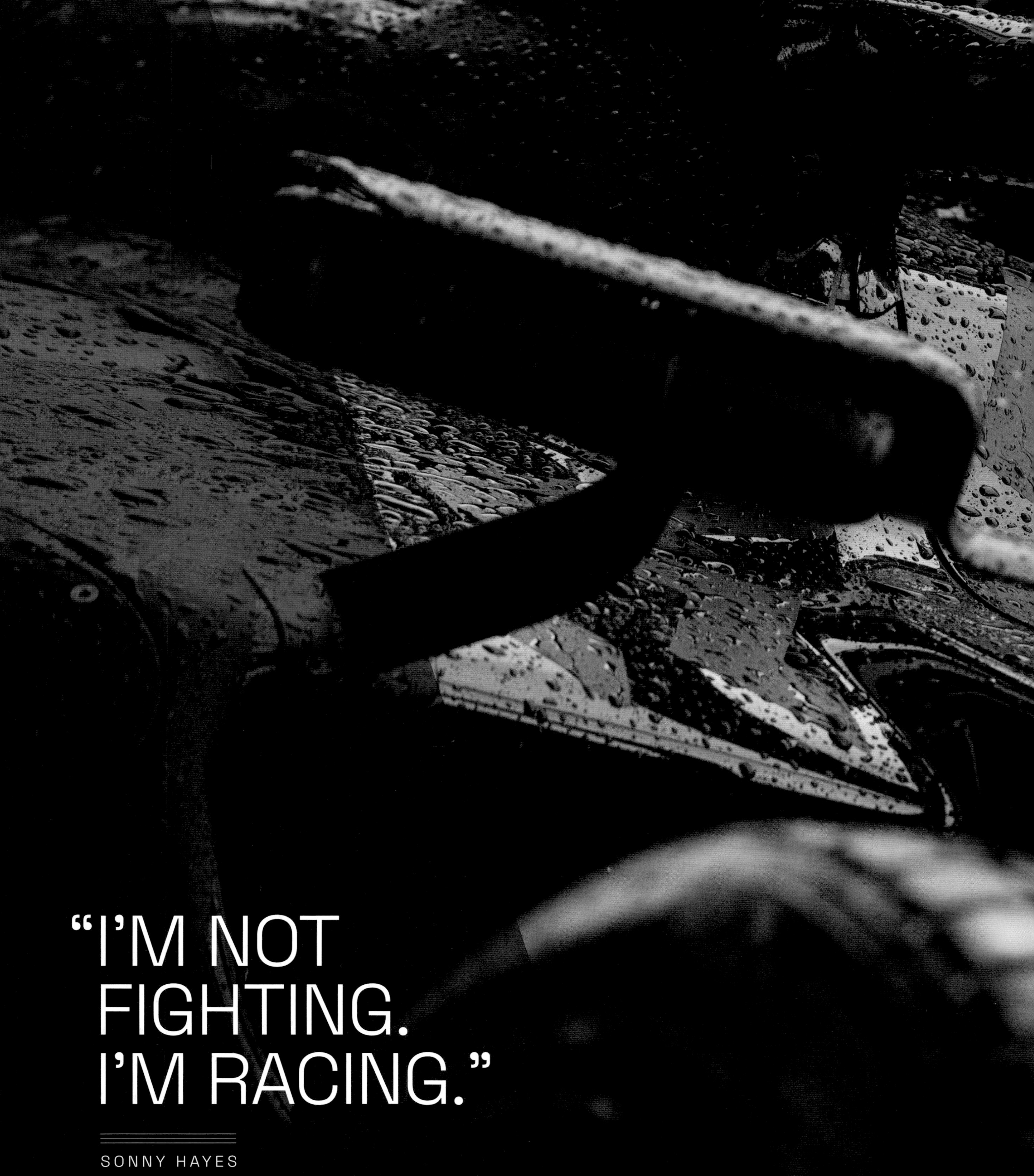

"I'M NOT FIGHTING. I'M RACING."

SONNY HAYES

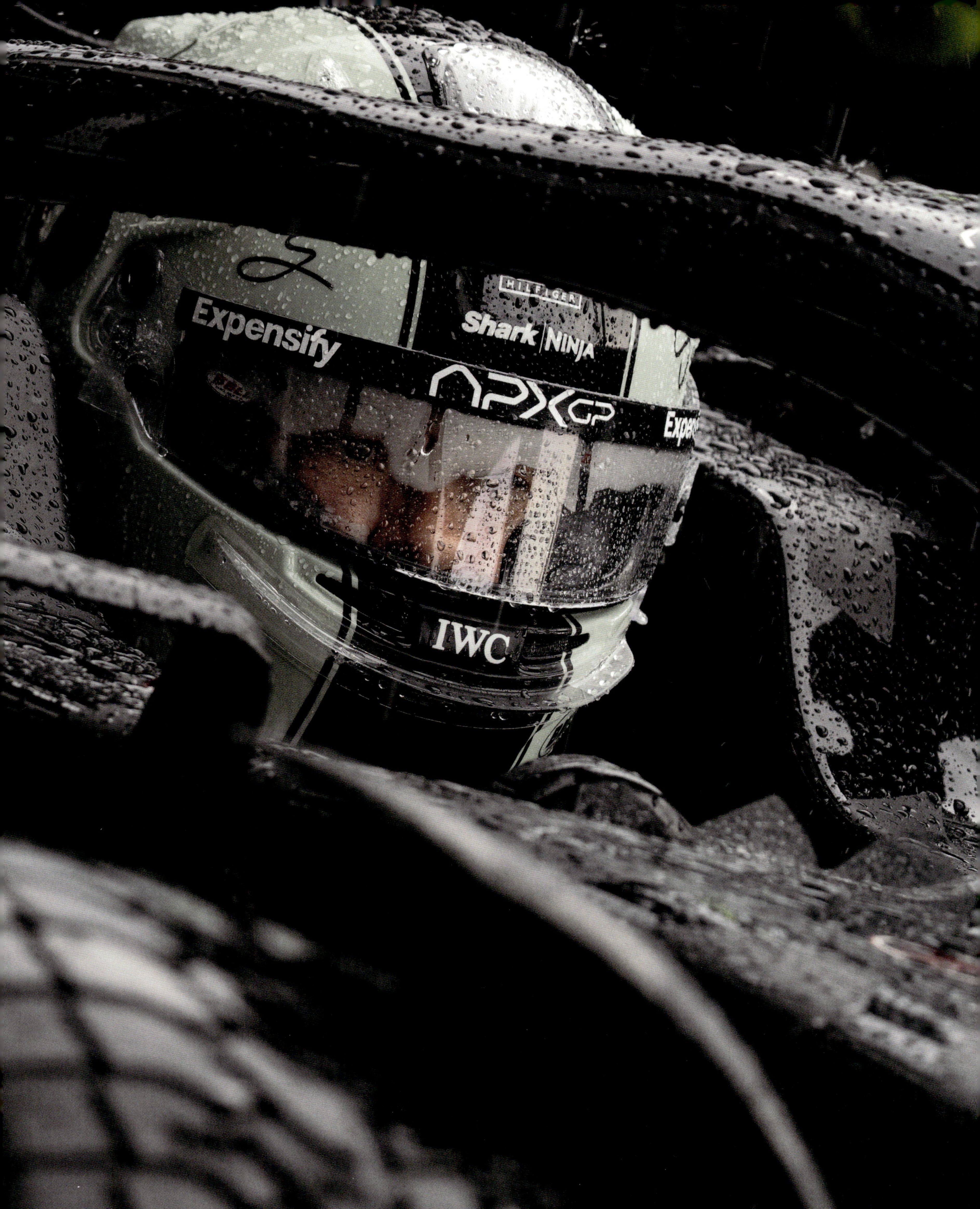
HILFIGER
Expensify
Shark NINJA
APXGP
IWC

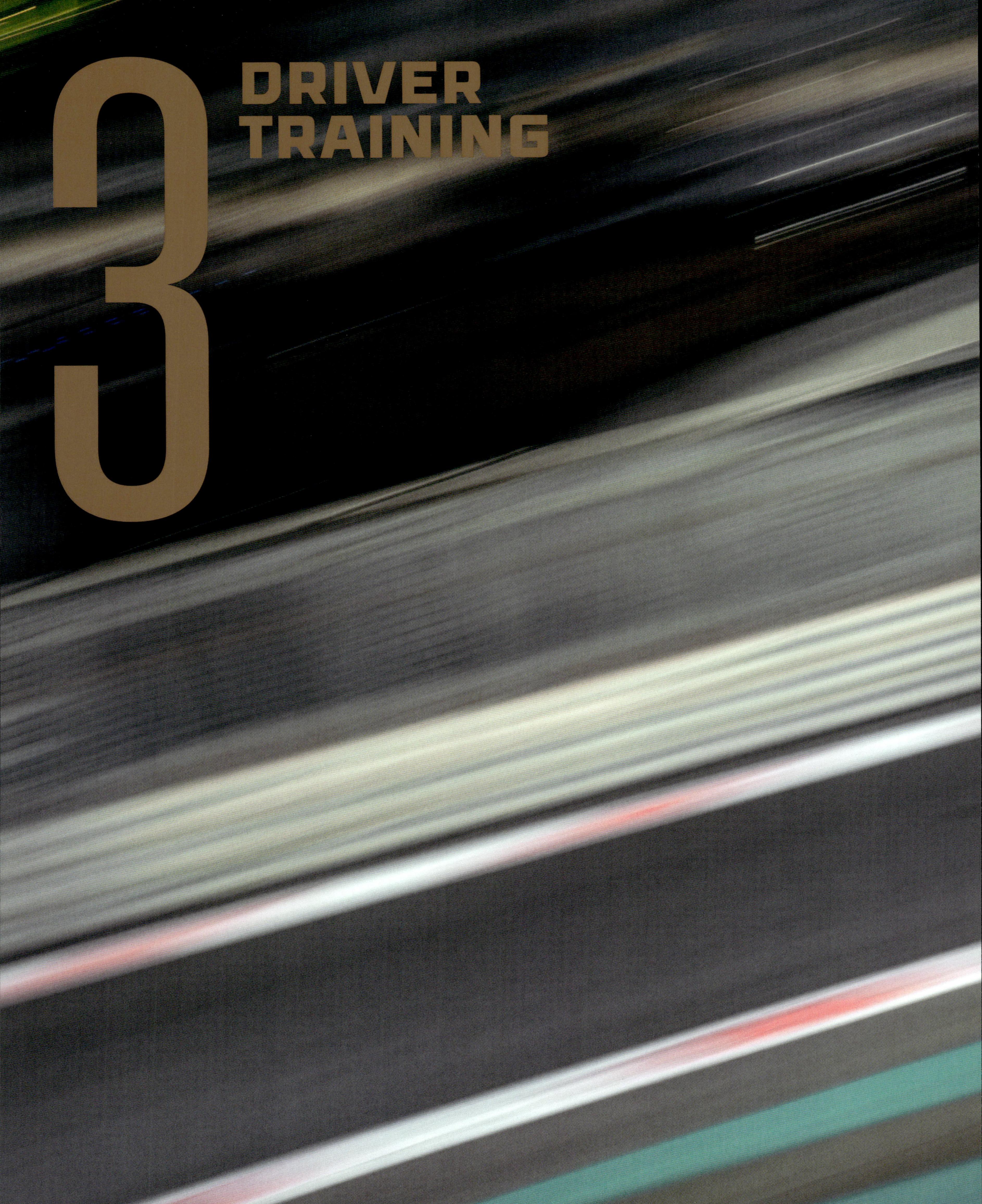

3 DRIVER TRAINING

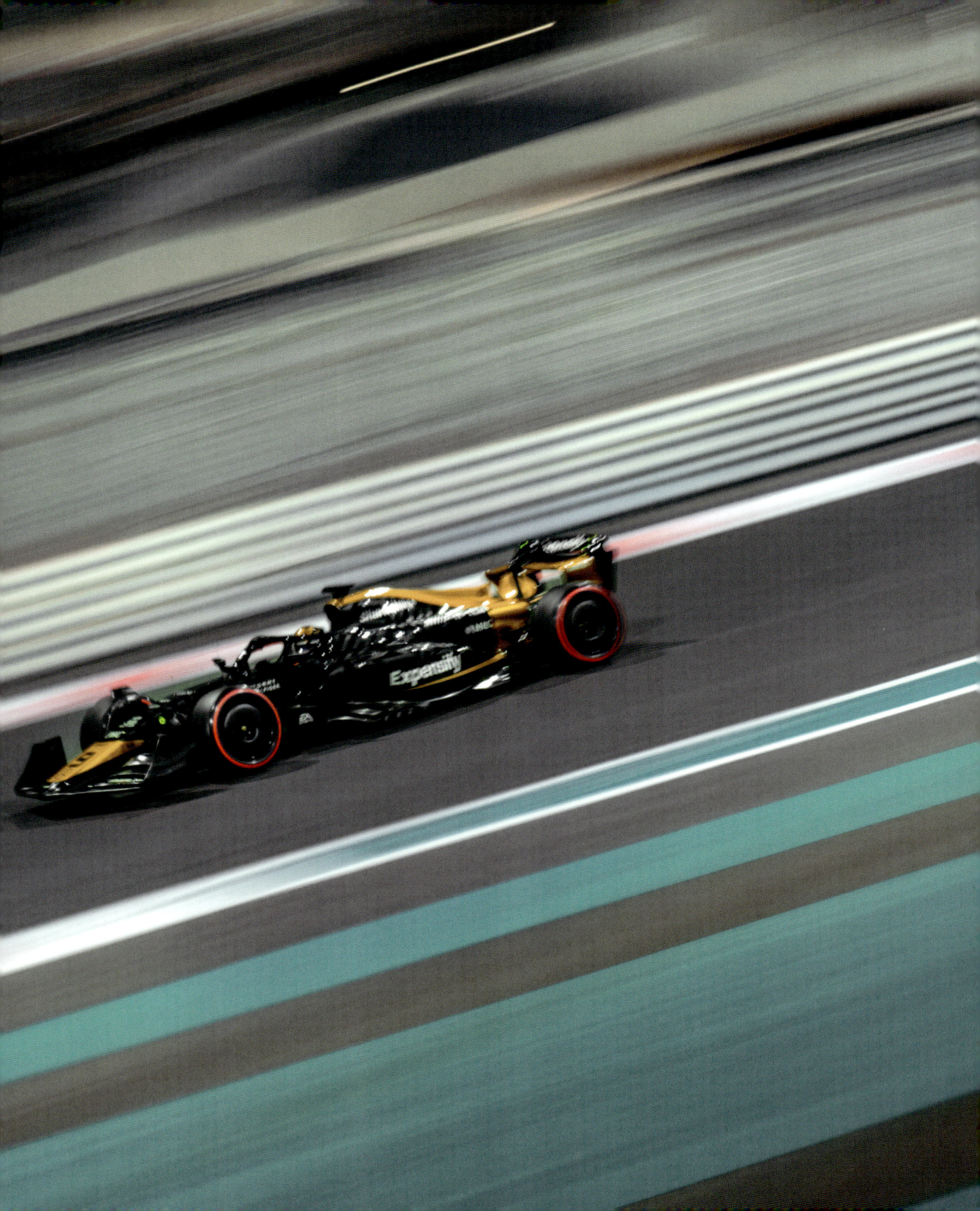
Expensify

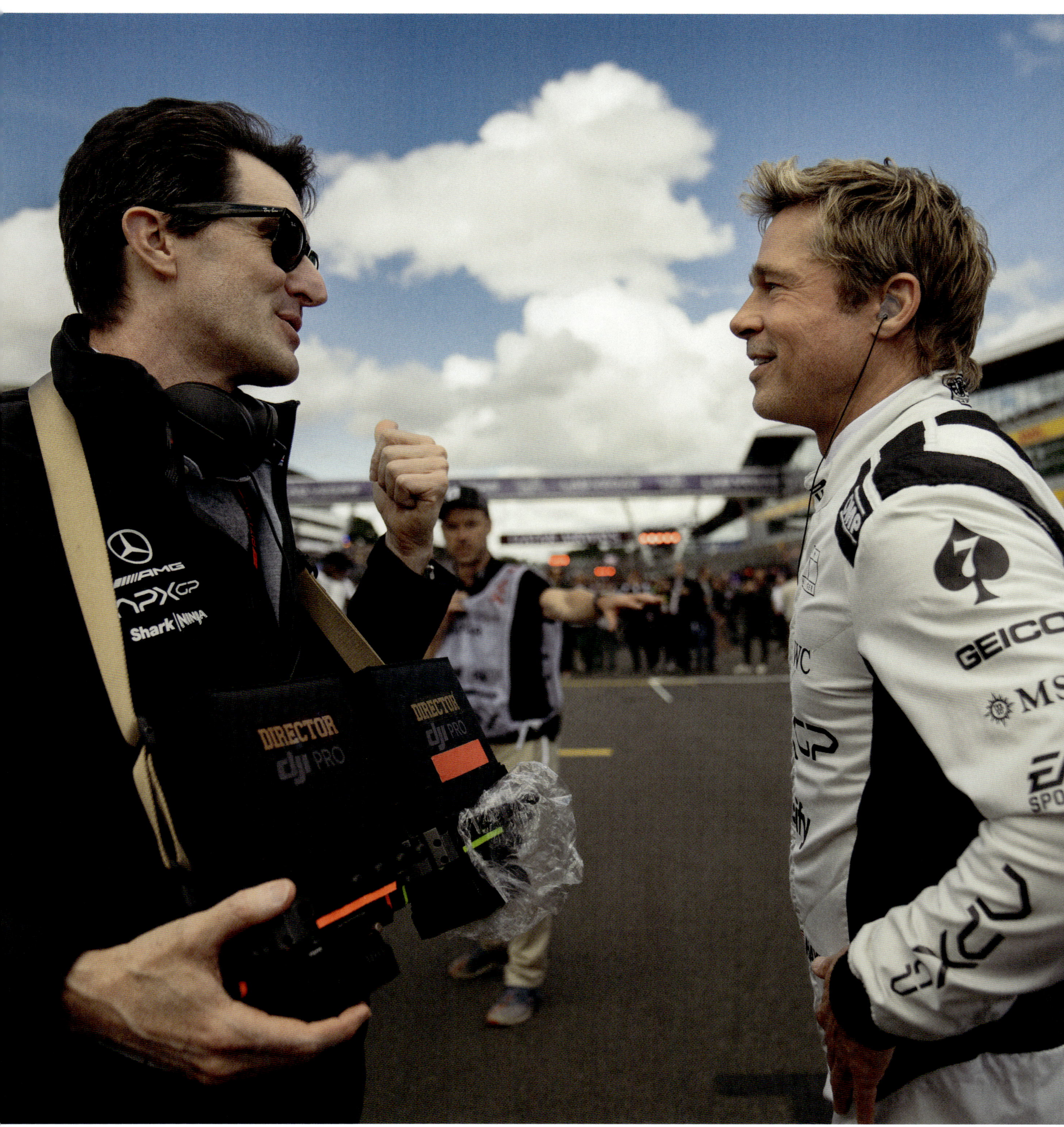
AMG
APXGP
Shark NINJA
DIRECTOR
dji PRO
DIRECTOR
dji PRO
GEICO

Left: Joseph Kosinski and Brad Pitt during the filming of the British Grand Prix race.

Below: Footage of Pitt captured by one of the mounted cameras on the race car.

In keeping with the authenticity he was striving for throughout *F1*, director Joseph Kosinski wanted Brad Pitt (Sonny Hayes) and Damson Idris (Joshua Pearce) to drive their APXGP cars for real, on actual racetracks, at speeds approaching 170 miles per hour.

"Joe's big selling point for this was, we are doing it all for real," says supervising stunt coordinator Gary Powell, whose long list of credits includes *Casino Royale* and *The Bourne Ultimatum*. "A lot of people would have filmed them on a blue screen stage, then added in CG [computer generated] backgrounds, because it's easier. Joe didn't make it easy for himself. He took the hard route, but it's the best route."

"We thought it would be nice to show the cars hauling ass," notes cinematographer Claudio Miranda. "That way we could hold onto shots longer, because you wouldn't have to disguise the car's slowness. Joe and I wanted to make sure you could see Brad is driving, going 160, 170 miles per hour, hitting those corners for real, pulling those Gs for real. The car is sliding, his body is shaking, and he's sweating. It's all real speed."

Actors are typically filmed either "driving" a stationary vehicle against a blue or green screen with the background added in by visual effects during post-production, or they're filmed in front of an LED screen on which a prerecorded background is projected. Another method is to put actors inside of a real car on a real road, but have it driven by a stunt driver in a "biscuit rig," an external pod positioned on top of, behind, or in front of the car, while the actor pretends to drive.

"The first thing I said was, 'Obviously we're going to build a biscuit rig that can go 100-plus miles per hour and is driven by a stunt guy for the actors. But Joe was, 'No, no. It's going to be like *Top Gun*. The actors are going to be doing this,'" recalls first assistant director Toby Hefferman. "The whole thing made me nervous. I mean, professional drivers crash all the fucking time. But these guys are trained to react, to crash safely. It comes with experience. But Joe was really determined. And Joe is stubborn—in a really good way. He is smart and sensible and not going to do anything that's too risky. And if it is too risky, he will listen to his people. He'll be disappointed, but he'll understand."

"Biscuit rigs were brought up," says Miranda. "People were, 'Let's be safe and use them.' But as fancy as those rigs are, they're not going to go 100-plus miles per hour, because they slow down the car. Biscuit rigs are going to get you maybe 70 mph; then you have to translate 70 to 200 mph using edits or tricks to make the car appear to go faster."

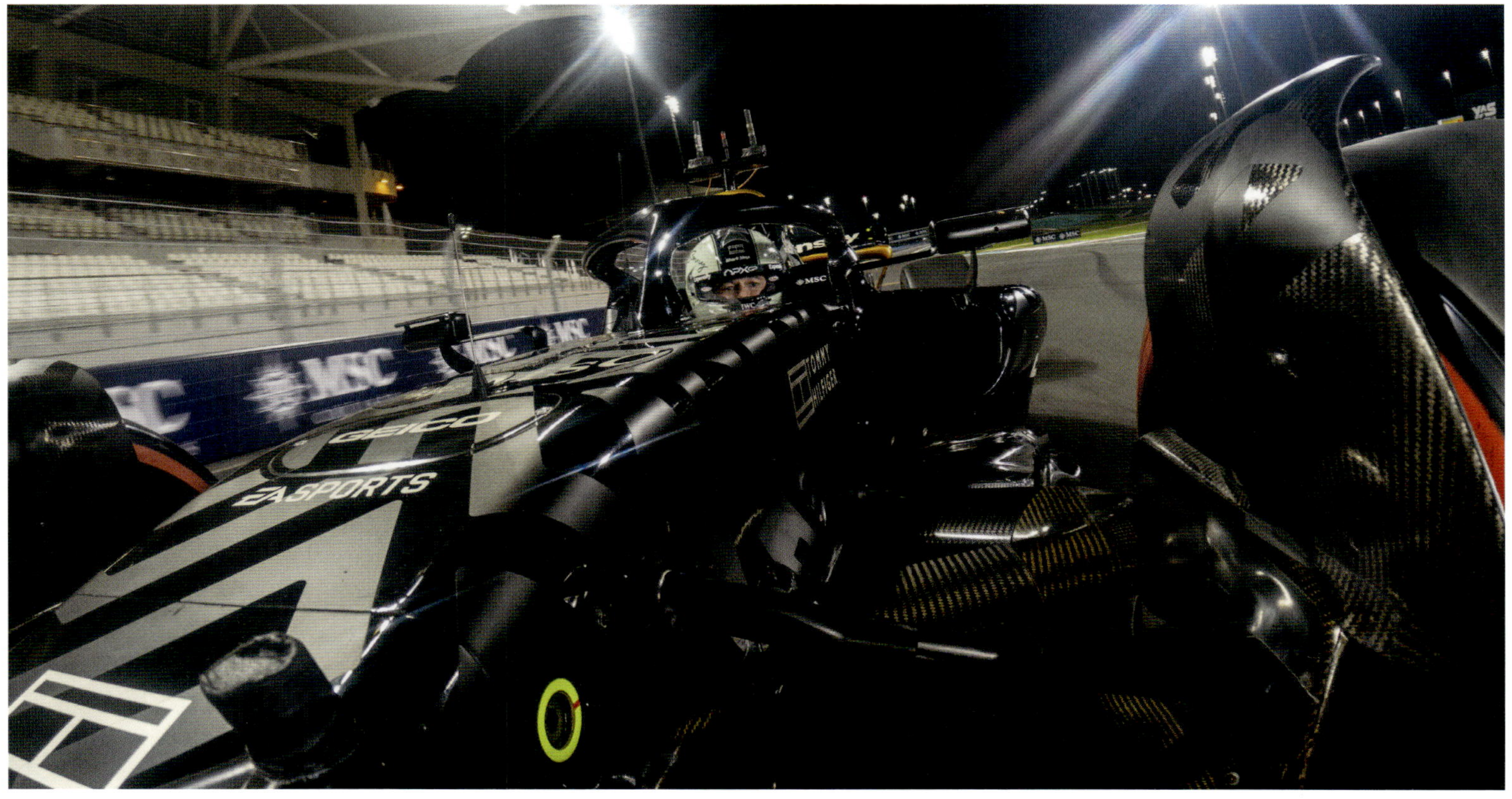

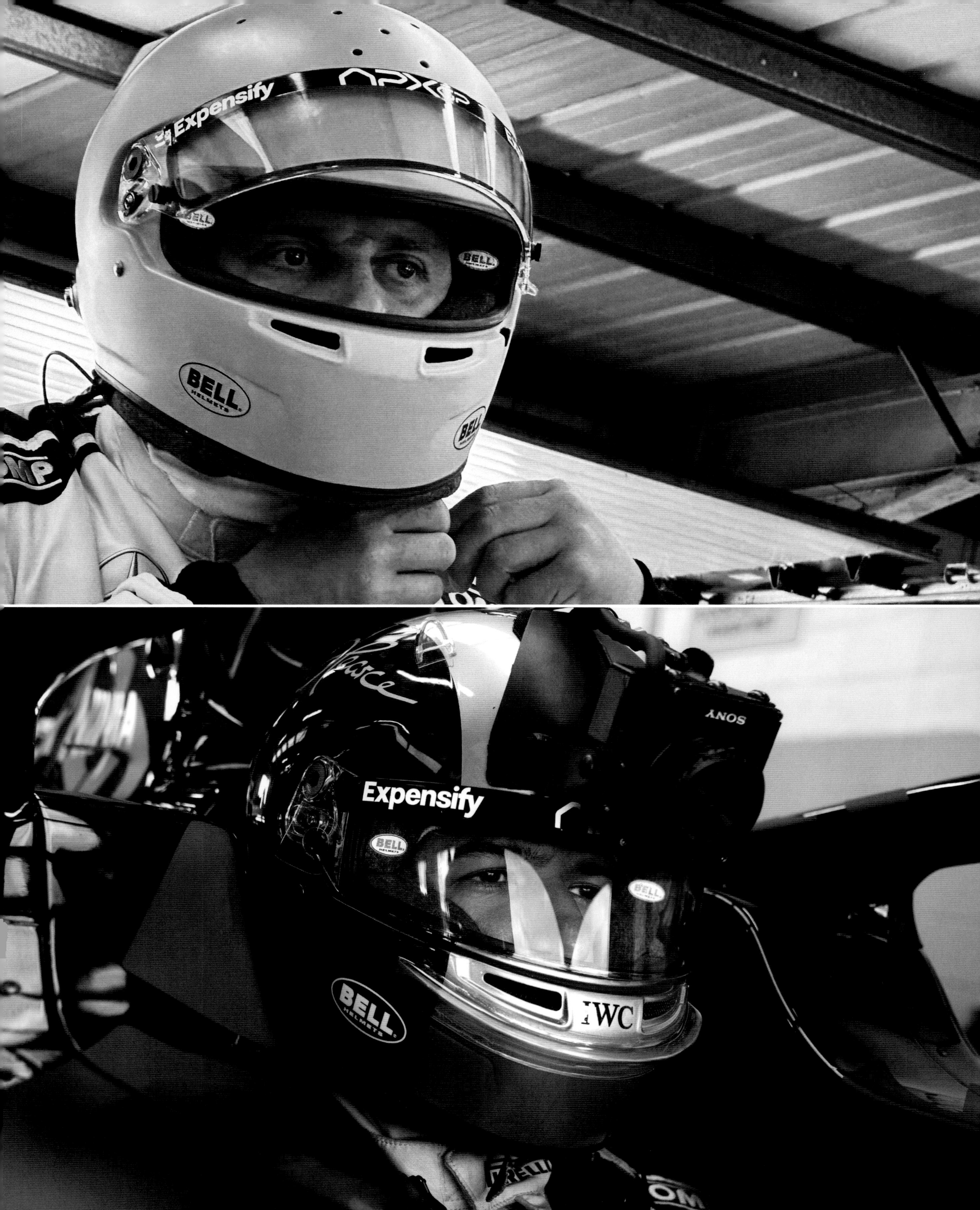
Expensify
BELL
Expensify
BELL
SONY
IWC

> “It doesn’t matter how much you train; until you drive the car, you’re not going to feel what it does to you.”
>
> LUCIANO BACHETA

Top Left: Craig Dolby, Brad Pitt’s stunt driver, straps on a helmet for an upcoming racing scene.

Bottom Left: Luciano Bacheta, who plays Luca Cortez and the stunt driver for Damson Idris, ready and waiting for the director to call action in Joshua’s car.

Below: Dolby and Idris pose with Sonny’s APXGP car.

Still, for all of Kosinski’s desire to have Pitt and Idris really drive, they couldn’t just get behind the wheel. Formula One drivers regularly experience up to 5G—the equivalent of five times their body weight pressing down on them—while cornering, braking or accelerating. The two actors would require months of training, both on the track and in the gym, to get them ready to handle not just their cars but the speed.

“I don’t think you can fully understand how physical it is until you put yourself through it,” says Luciano Bacheta, a former Formula Two champion turned stunt driver whose film credits include *Mission: Impossible—Dead Reckoning* and *Indiana Jones and the Dial of Destiny*. “Brad and Damson were both at a good fitness level when they arrived. But it doesn’t matter how much you train; until you drive the car, you’re not going to feel what it does to you. And it’s a combination of training and driving that increases that fitness.”

Together with Craig Dolby, who raced in Formula Renault before becoming a stunt driver for movies such as *Fast & Furious Presents: Hobbs & Shaw* and *Infinite*, Bacheta devised a training regimen for Pitt and Idris that began in February 2023 and lasted more than a year.

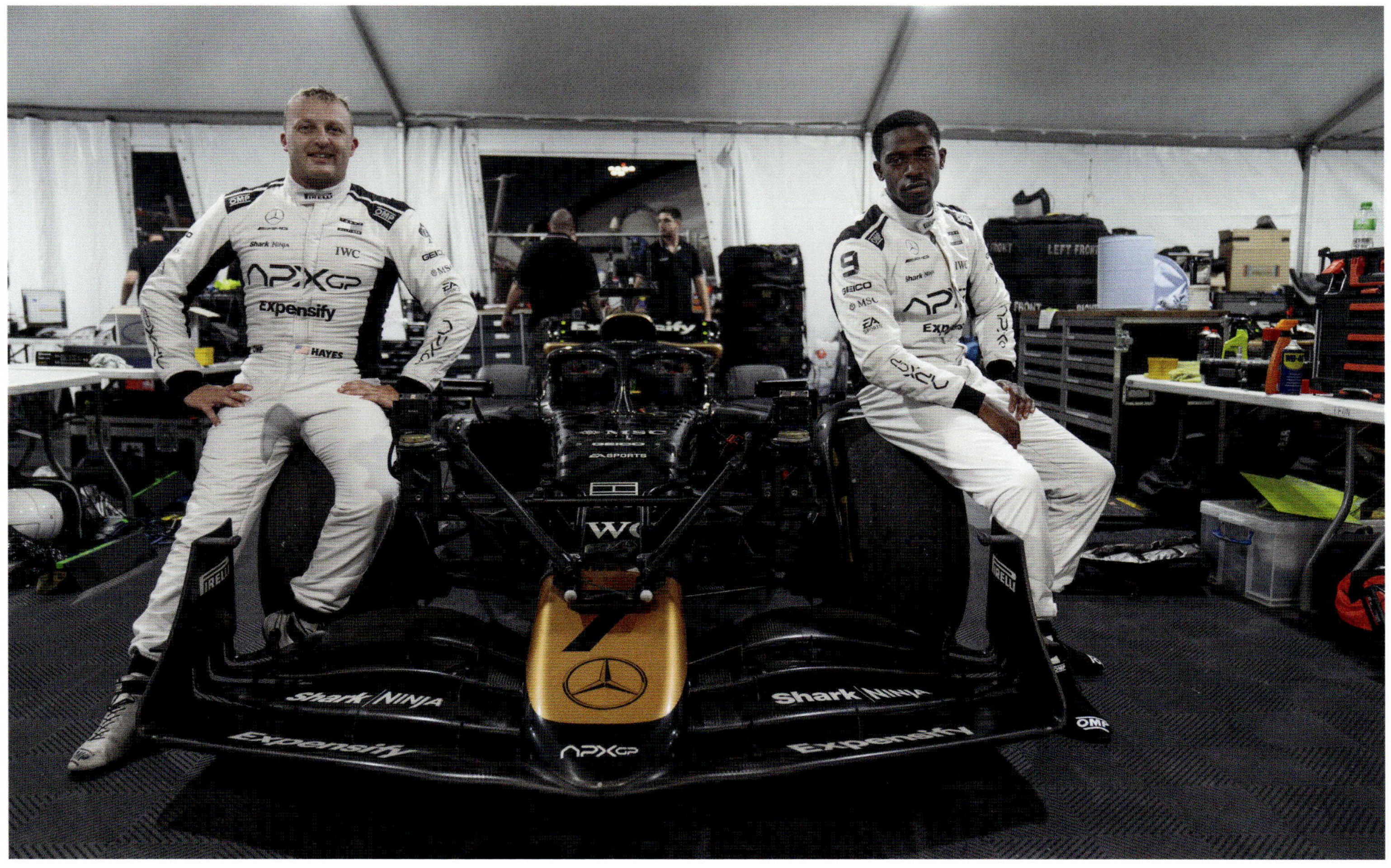

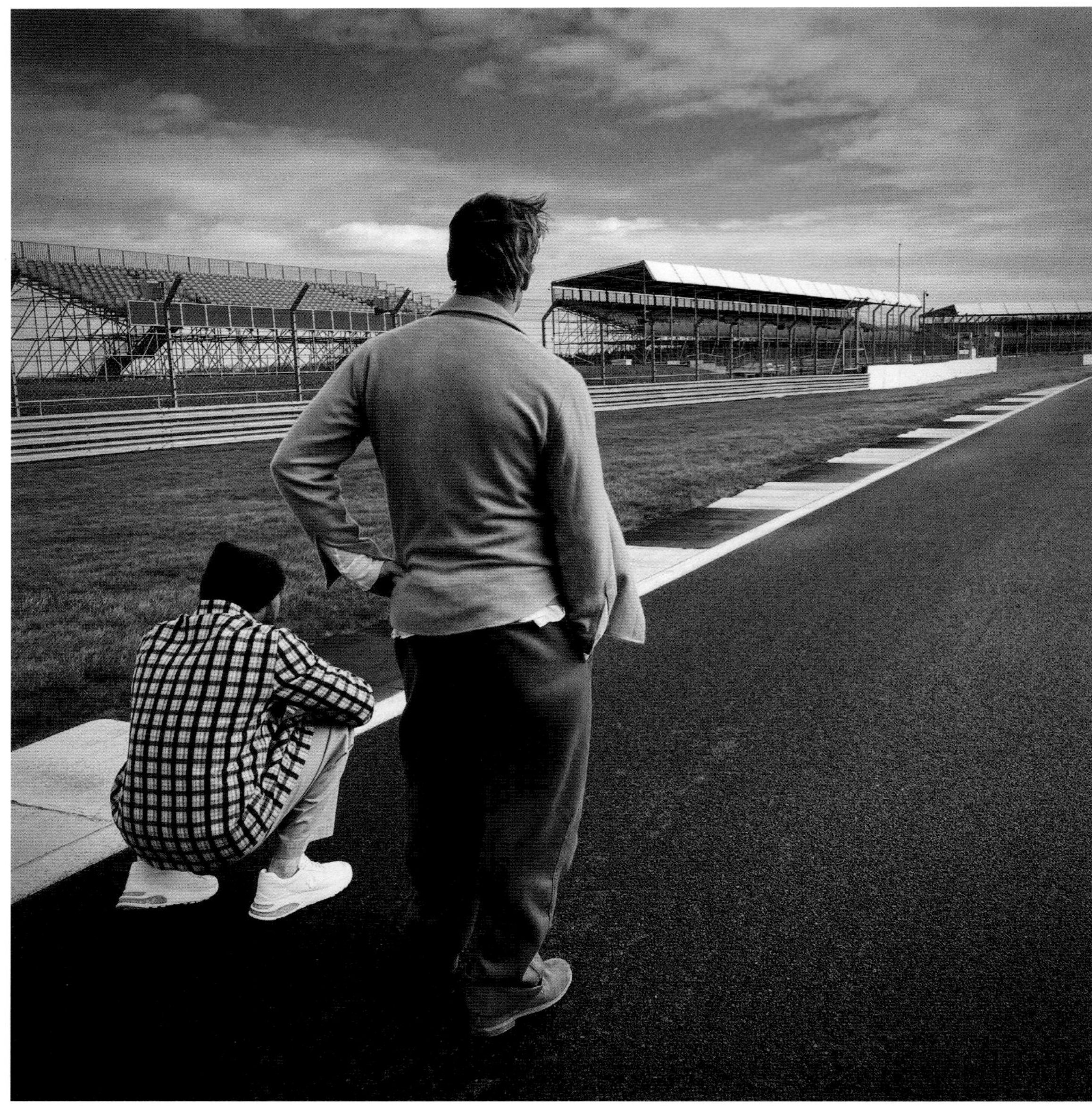

Left: Brad Pitt and Lewis Hamilton arrive at Silverstone to begin training.

Right: Brad Pitt, Lewis Hamilton, and Joseph Kosinski share a conversation with Peter Bonnington, Hamilton's engineer during his time at Mercedes.

Before Pitt flew to England to work with Bacheta and Dolby, he, Kosinski, and F1 driver Lewis Hamilton got together at the Porsche Experience Center in Los Angeles, on the afternoon of Sunday, January 30, 2022. "Brad rides motorcycles and I had an instinct he was a good driver," says Kosinski. "But the first time I saw him on the track was when I arranged for him and Lewis to meet up. They shut down the whole facility for the three of us to go out in 911 GT3s. I drove with Lewis, Brad drove with Lewis, and Lewis scared the hell out of him, which was fun. Lewis was really impressed with how well Brad drove with no formal training, and how much natural talent he had."

"First of all, Lewis was pretty brave to get in the car with me behind the wheel," says Pitt with a grin. "That was amazing. I think it was the first time he had been on a track since that controversial ending [to the 2021 Formula One world championship, which he lost to Red Bull's Max Verstappen in contentious circumstances]. I remember sitting on the curb and chatting with him, then driving with Lewis in the passenger seat, only knowing what I'm doing from being on the track on bikes. But very little training. It had to be frustrating for Lewis, but if it was, he didn't show it. They have a thing called the carousel—it's a straight, then you drop down into this little whirlpool that's banked and spits you out on the other side. I'm in the passenger seat and the [instructor] says, 'Just start out easy because there's a big bump about 200 yards down,' and Lewis was like, 'Yeah, right.' Hits the gas. We hit the bump. Get a little air. He slingshots us into this carousel and spits us out. I'm inches from the wall and he's howling. It was clear those inches that are scary to civilians are just another day at the office [for him]."

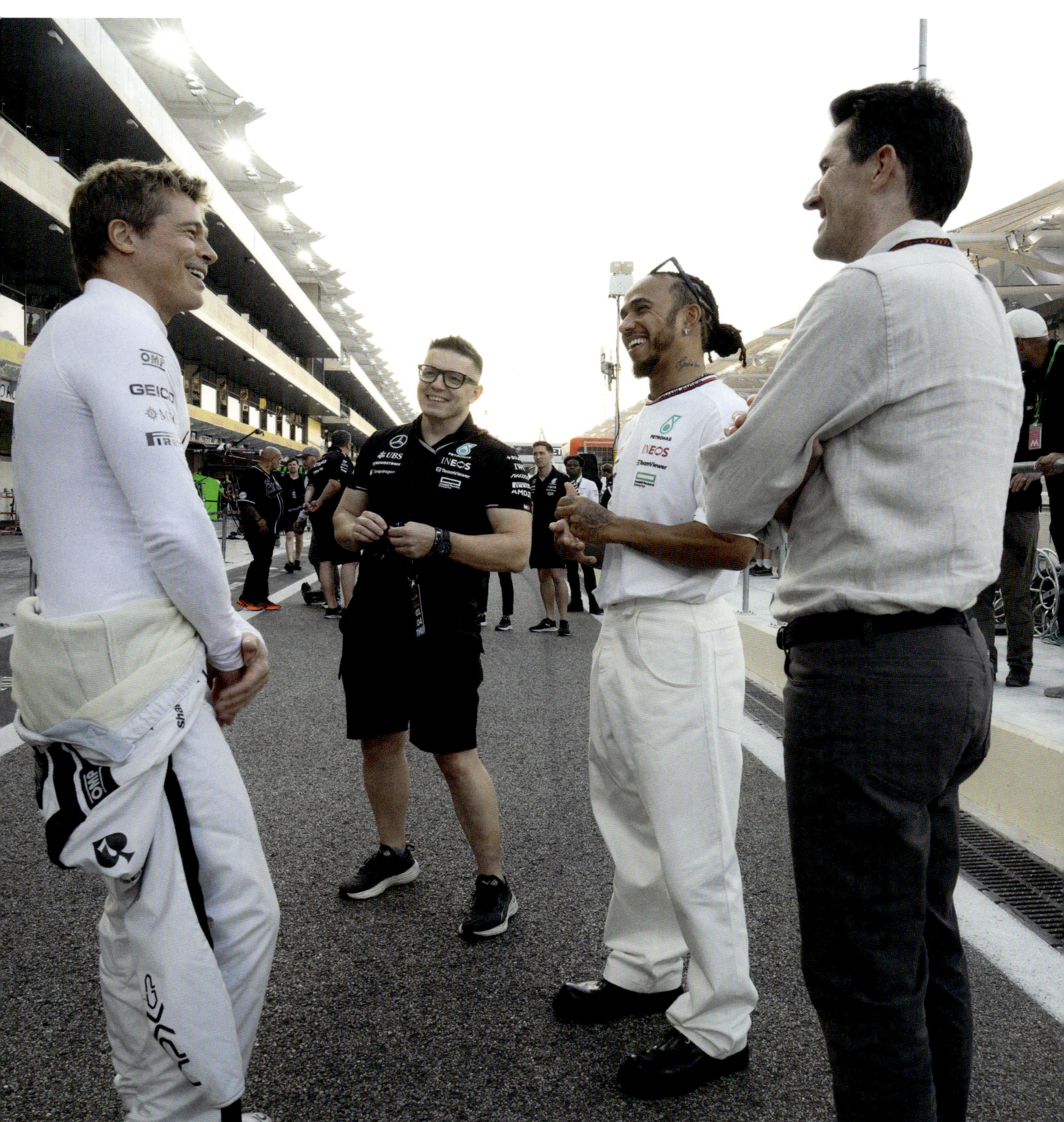
OMP
INEOS
UBS
TeamViewer
INEOS
TeamViewer

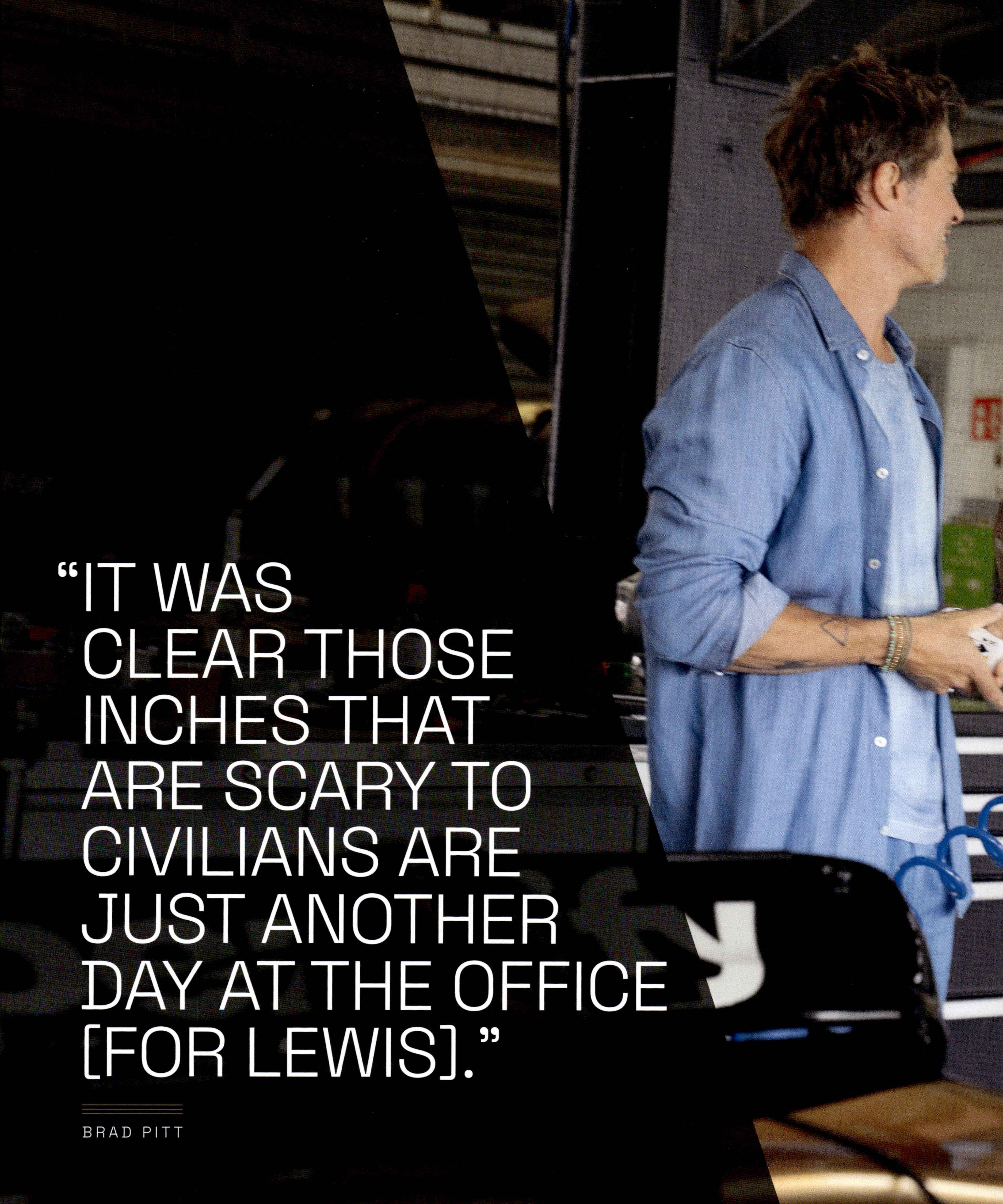

"IT WAS CLEAR THOSE INCHES THAT ARE SCARY TO CIVILIANS ARE JUST ANOTHER DAY AT THE OFFICE [FOR LEWIS]."

BRAD PITT

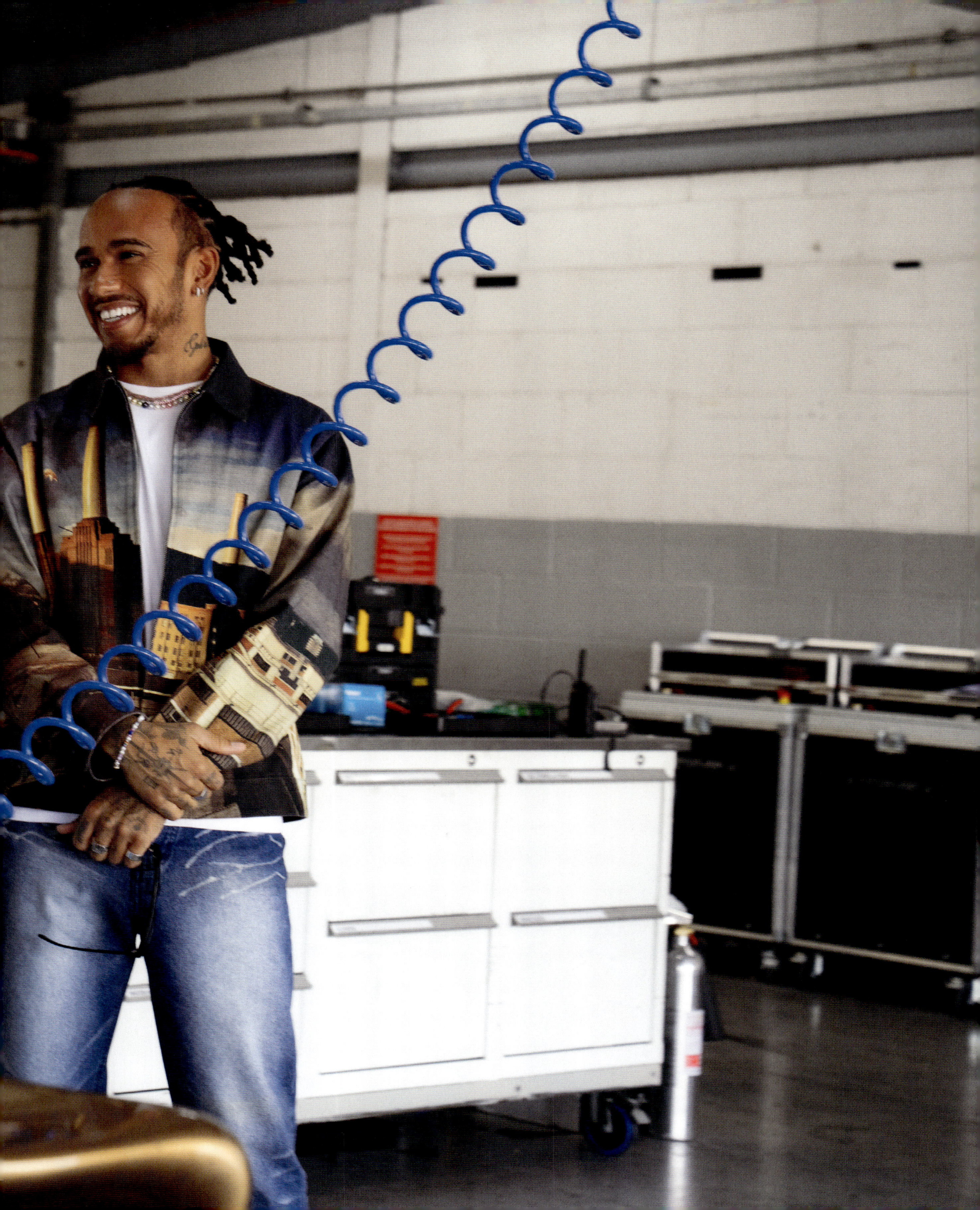

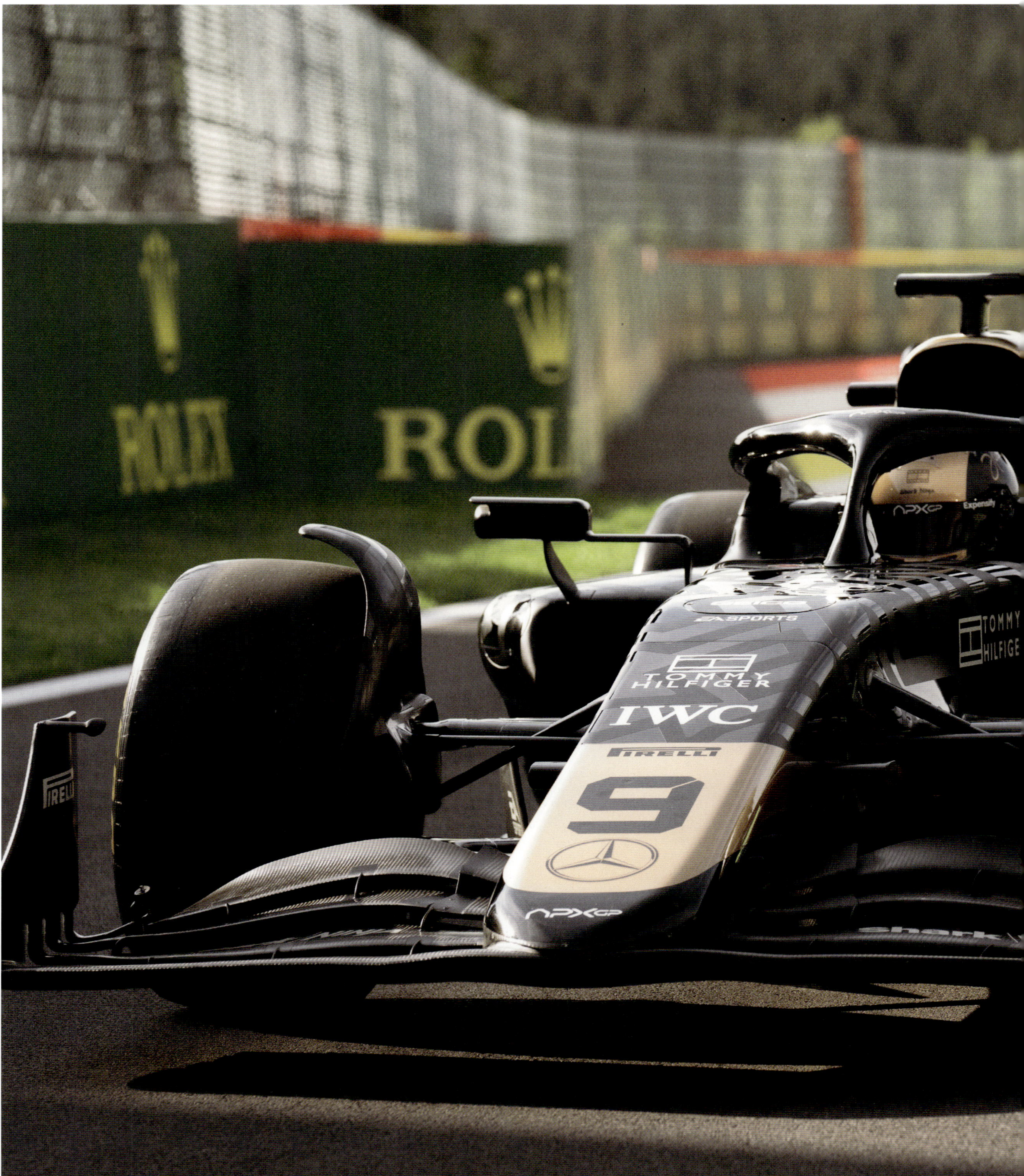
ROLEX
TOMMY HILFIGER
IWC
PIRELLI
9
TOMMY HILFIGER

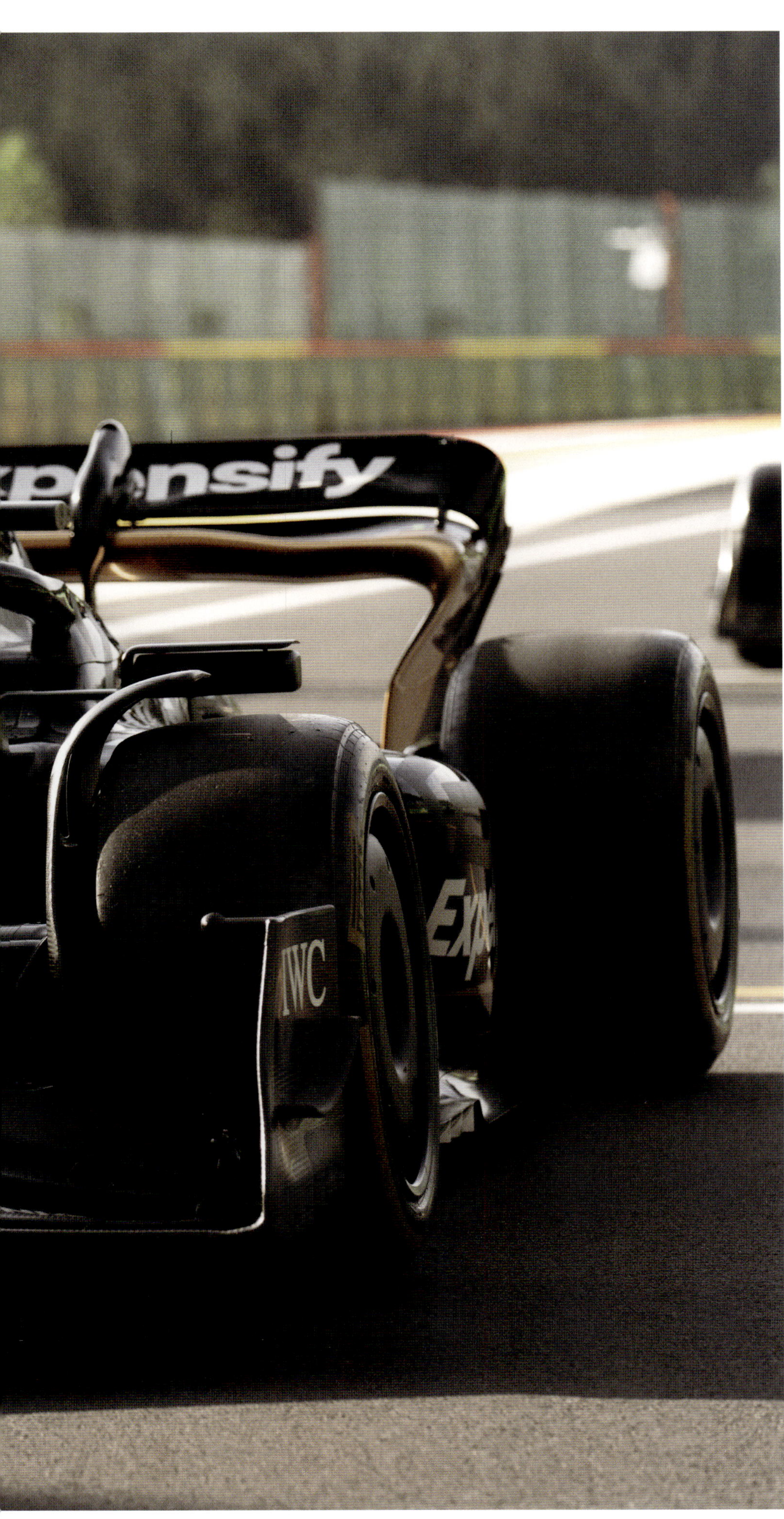

Prior to getting the role in *F1*, Idris's racing experience was limited to his audition day at Palmer Sports—where he had driven one- and two-seater sports cars—along with hours playing video games. "I bought an F1 game, created a character, named him Joshua Pearce, and won a championship with him," Idris recalls.

"When we got him, he was very raw," says Dolby of Idris. "We had to teach him the basics of driving, like downforce, getting the brakes up to temperature, turning points, racing lines. It was quite daunting—for us as well as him. But he got it fairly quickly."

"They were so patient, so understanding, so funny, and so educated on the sport of Formula One," says Idris. "They would say to me, 'Don't tell the car what to do. *Ask* it what to do.' 'Is it okay if I brake right now?' 'Is it okay if I push on the throttle right now?' 'Is it okay if I turn right now?' It really is an art."

The actor spent about a month at Rockingham Motor Speedway in Northamptonshire with Bacheta and Dolby, driving open-wheeled Dallara Formula Three cars. "In their heyday they were almost the closest thing to Formula One," says Bacheta. "They have very high downforce, very nice to drive."

"I loved them," continues Idris. "They were amazing. The track was peculiar because it's old and bumpy. You'd go down the straights and a stone might flick up or a pebble will smash off your knuckles. It's real, gritty driving. But I got to grips with high speeds and slow corners."

On Idris's first day at Rockingham, however, his car's top speed was capped at 80 miles per hour for safety reasons. But that immediately proved unworkable to the stunt team. "It was barely out of second gear," remembers Bacheta. "The tires weren't warming up, the brakes weren't warming up, and we said, 'We need to have a rethink here,' because Damson wasn't driving a car dressed up to look like a race car—it *was* a race car, and it had to be driven like one, or it wouldn't work."

Damson Idris ready to race in the Number 9 APXGP car.

"We had to explain downforce to the insurance people," says Powell. "We said, 'If a road car goes around a corner at 60 miles per hour, that's fine. But if a Formula One car goes around that corner at that speed, it's got no downforce. It needs to be going at 100 miles per hour. It was safer going faster."

"Insurance came in after they got wind of what we were doing and tried to put a speed limit on us," recalls Pitt. "It took maybe six weeks and Luch [Bacheta] and Craig and everyone putting a case together to explain how these cars work. Going 140 miles per hour sounds crazy, certainly down the freeway, but you can't look at it that way." The speed limit was initially increased from 80 miles per hour to 140, but it was still too slow. "You have to be at speed to keep heat in the brakes for them to work. These are carbon brakes. They don't start working till they're at 300 degrees and go up to a thousand degrees. And they want us to slow down. You lose all the heat in the brakes and the tires, and the car doesn't handle as well, and it becomes more dangerous. We had to keep making this point, to make the logic of how these cars work understood. And then we were free."

The 140 miles per hour speed limiters on Idris's and Pitt's cars were removed, and they could go racing. "Funnily enough, the times both actors spun out were on the slowest corners, when they were doing 30 miles per hour," remembers Powell.

Three weeks later, Pitt arrived in the U.K. to begin his training in a Formula Three car at Silverstone. "Brad is into his bikes, so he understands a lot of the dynamics about motor vehicles," says Bacheta. "But Brad's not a young driver you want to be sending into walls to learn the hard way. So, we wanted to make it fun for him but also keep it incredibly safe."

But Pitt had already started training on his own in the Circuit Paul Ricard near Marseille, France. "I kind of jumped the gun. I did a couple of days in the F4, then jumped into an F2, and then I even drove an F1, Kimi Räikkönen's 2012 Lotus. That's before the insurance team got a hold of us," says Pitt who found the whole experience of getting into a Formula car fascinating. "First, you're almost lying down, like in a bathtub, in this little bitty tube, and they put this horse collar on and screw it in place. Then it becomes a coffin. You're in fire retardant gear. You're mummified with a helmet, earplugs, and this racing suit. It's very hot and just your head is out. The first time, it can almost feel claustrophobic. But in the end, it became a place of great comfort for me.

Right: Brad Pitt slides into the APXGP car before filming Sonny's APXGP audition at the Silverstone racetrack.

Below: Sonny spins out at Silverstone.

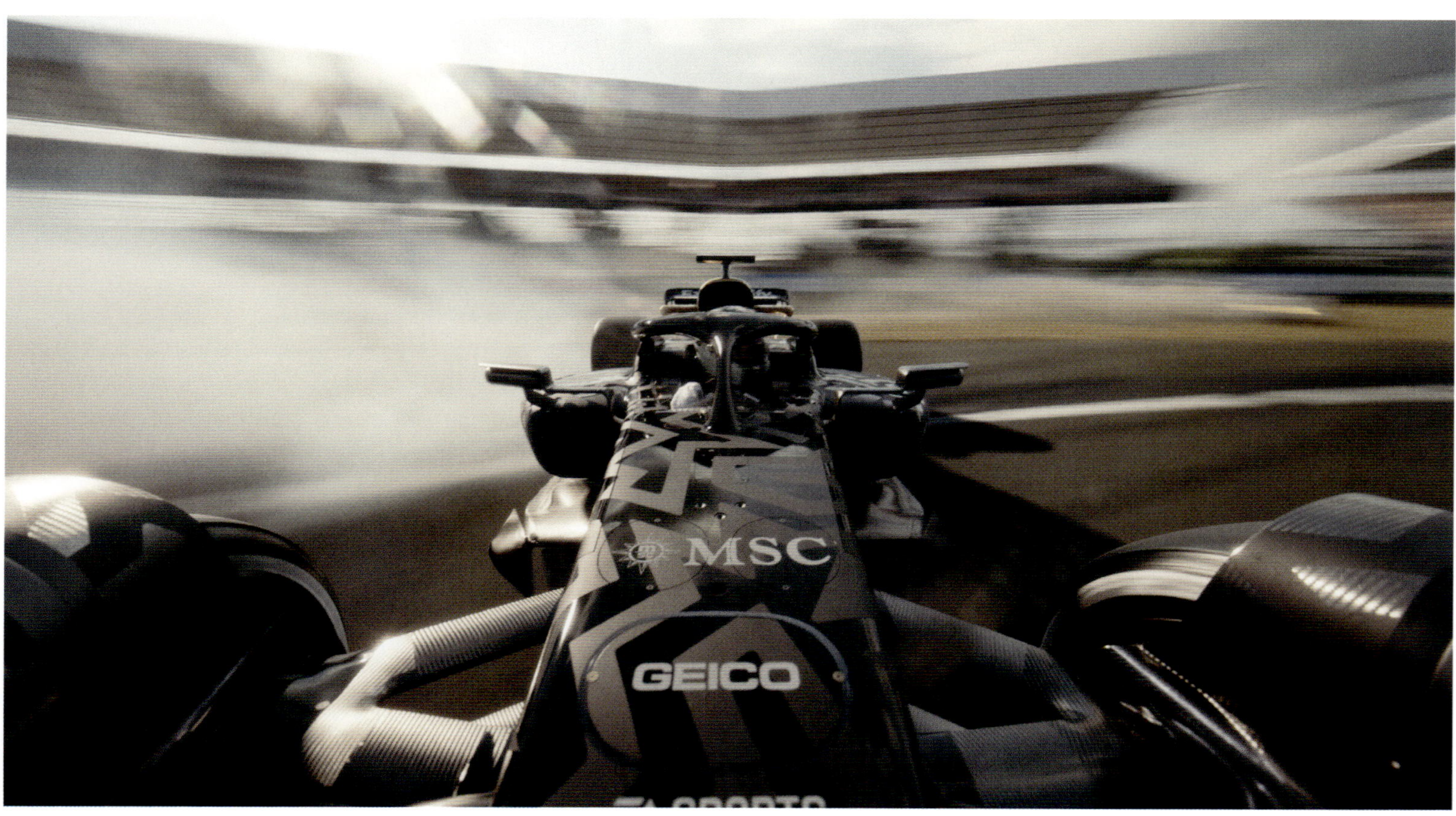

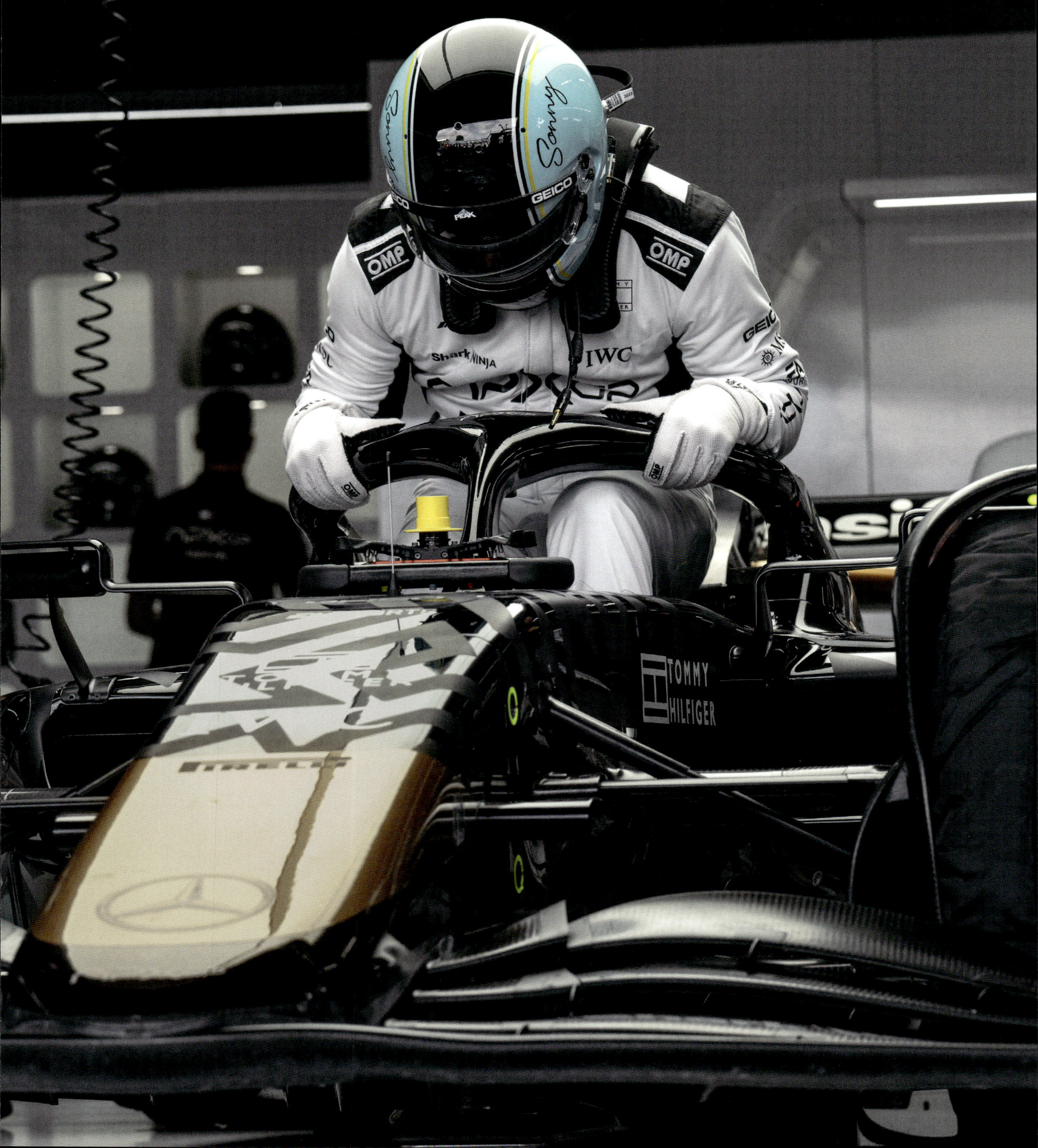
Sonny
GEICO
PEAK
OMP
OMP
Shark NINJA
IWC
GEICO
OMP
OMP
TOMMY
HILFIGER

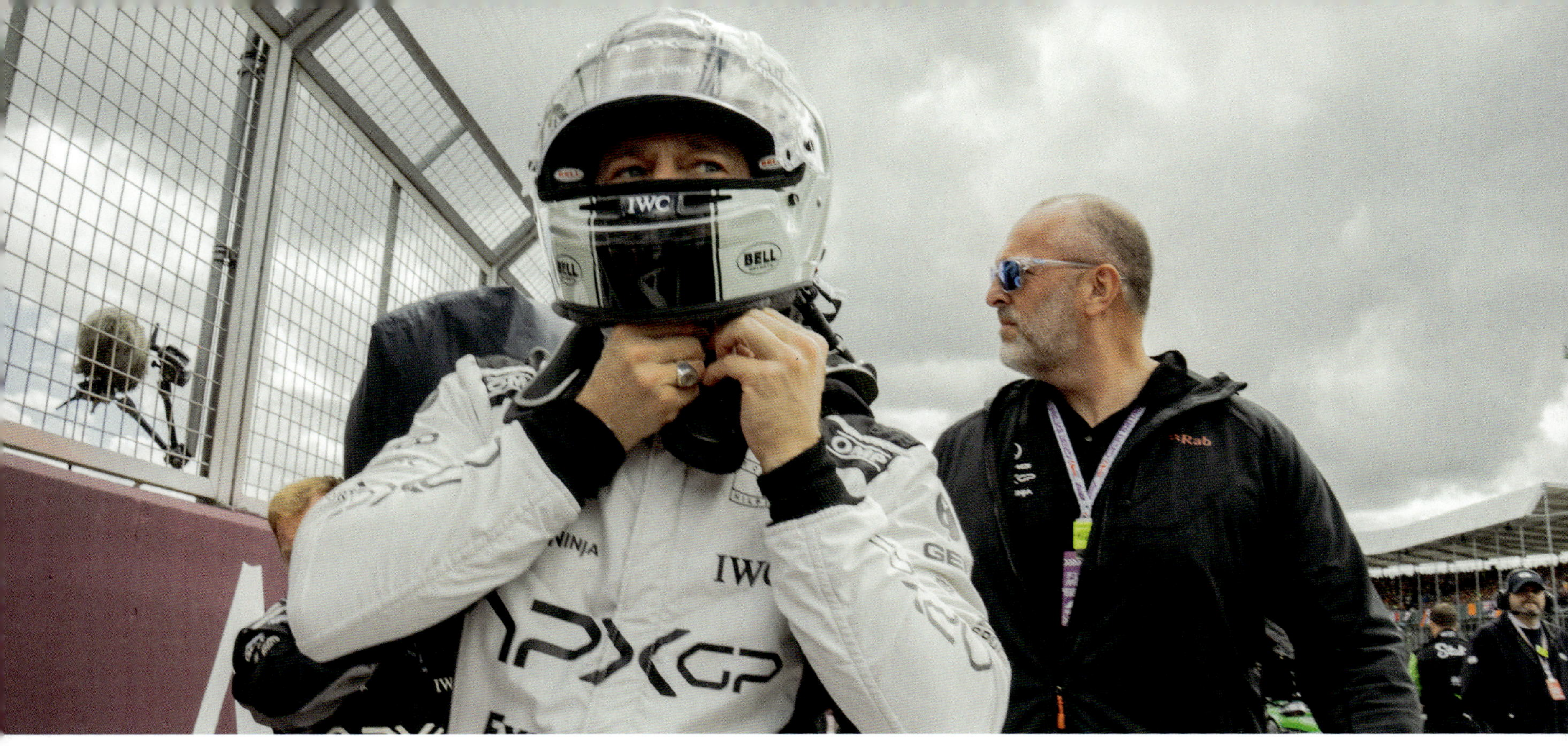

"I was already hitting 180 on a straight," Pitt continues, "but it wasn't the top speed that was so shocking—it was this concept of downforce; how the car sticks to the road. The first thing they told me was, 'If you're not on the gas or on the brake, you're not driving the car and you're upsetting the physics.' The most harrowing thing is high-speed corners. You don't think it's possible. You think you're going to flip off the track. And they kept saying, 'You've got further to go. Trust the car. Trust the car.' So, this became my mantra: 'Trust the car, trust the car.' And you dig in at a big, sweeping, double right-hander at 140 miles per hour and the thing sticks. It's a strange phenomenon to get used to, because, man, you've got to keep your nuts and dig in."

Then there was the braking. "It's shocking," insists Pitt. "It's shocking how quickly these cars can come to a stop. You're coming down the straight at 180, you jam on the brake with all your force, and you're slowing to 40 miles per hour to take that first right all within 75 yards. It is a thrill like I'd never experienced before. It is such a high. After years of that, you can start dialing it in and finding that edge. But it's hard to hold your head up [at first]. You can feel the forces of physics wanting to rip your head off your shoulders and it's why these guys have to build up their necks."

"The most harrowing thing is high-speed corners. You don't think it's possible. You think you're going to flip off the track. And they kept saying, 'You've got further to go. Trust the car. Trust the car.'"

BRAD PITT

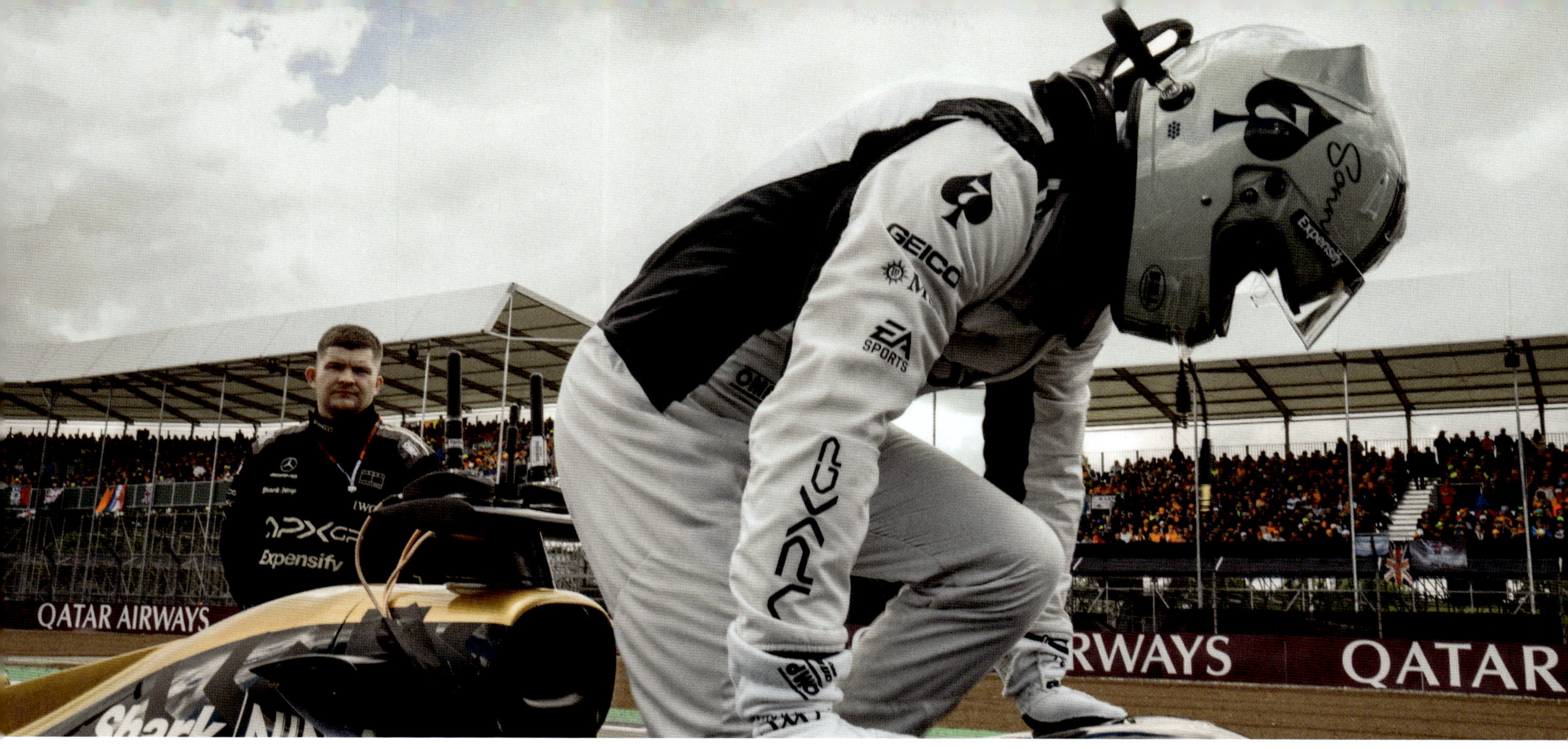

When Pitt showed up at Silverstone to start training, and the two took to the track for the first time, Bacheta was impressed by how safe, disciplined, and confident a driver Pitt was—and decided to engage him in a spot of wheel-to-wheel racing.

"I was sending it down the inside of him, and we were overtaking each other every other corner," says Bacheta. "I feel that captured not just his attention, but respect for what drivers do. Not only are you trying to get this super-heavy-to-drive car around the track, you're trying to keep an eye on your mirrors, which are vibrating, trying to see where everyone is, and trying to second-guess what they're going to do."

"I remember dicing it up and hearing him cackling over the radio because I tried to dive in on him," recalls Pitt. "I mean, I would call it a dogfight. I'm sure he wouldn't. But I remember hearing cackling because I tried to come in on him. Then I see him in the rear view, trying to come in on me. He got a kick out of that, I think."

Pitt had caught the racing bug. "Every day he turns up, he's so excited to be there. He wants to learn more," says Bacheta. "It's not just driving for him. We talk about car setups, strategy, tire pressure, ride heights, about how you can optimize a car balance. We're talking intricate technique you wouldn't do when you're coaching someone to just drive around a track. We were trying to optimize his performance and get more out of the car, be more aggressive, boss the car around."

"It's shocking what they can do to these cars," says Pitt. "Changing the camber [how the wheels are angled] or the pitch. More downforce, less downforce, pointier front end. It is so exhilarating when you start to feel these minute differences. Or when your tires are twenty-two laps in and you're sliding around, or a tailwind at a high speed corner wants to push you off the track. I think it helped that I grew up in the Ozarks, with a lot of dirt roads. Used to driving on ice, in snowy conditions and rain."

Brad Pitt readies himself for the next racing scene.

EVOLUTION OF AN F1 CAR

1906

In the early years, regulations were much more variable. A 13-liter engine, far from the biggest, was in the winning Renault of the inaugural French Grand Prix. Cars were not single seaters but had a driver and a riding mechanic, able to carry out repairs and tire changes on much longer racetracks than used today.

1960s

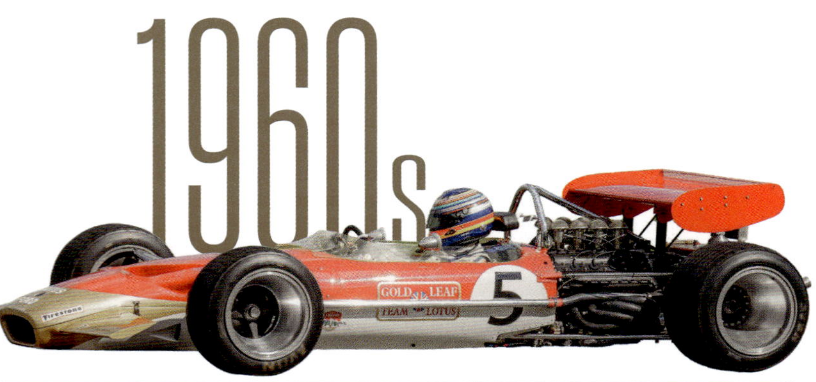

The first fully stressed monocoque reached F1 in 1962, and soon aerodynamics really started to evolve as a crucial part of the sport. Front and rear wings, of varying designs and sizes, came to the fore in the latter part of the decade, while minimum car weights were also introduced.

1950s

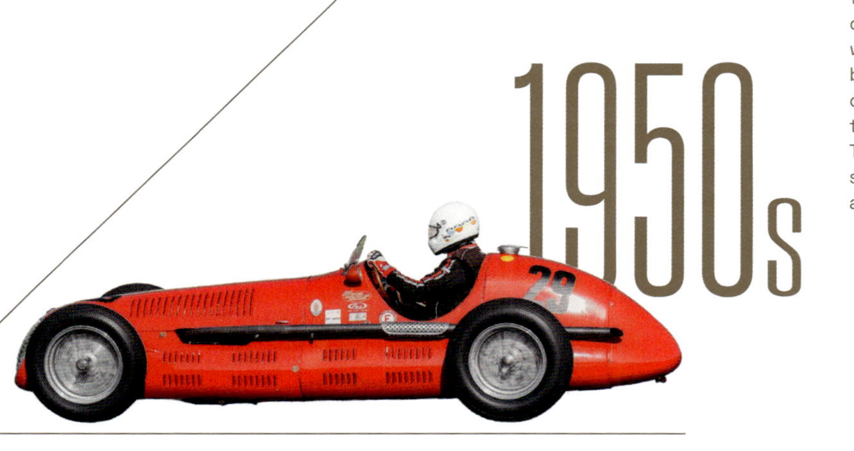

For the first half of the decade, front-engined cars were the preferred designs. Cars also transitioned to single seaters with a pit crew. Drivers were still exposed but often shunned seatbelts—preferring to be thrown in a crash rather than trapped in a burning car.

1970s

Aerodynamic development continued apace. Ground effect cars were introduced with skirts that would help seal the gap between the car's floor and the track surface. These were soon banned as cornering speeds became too high, having already climbed earlier in the decade with the introduction of slick tires. Turbocharged engines also saw an increase in power and acceleration.

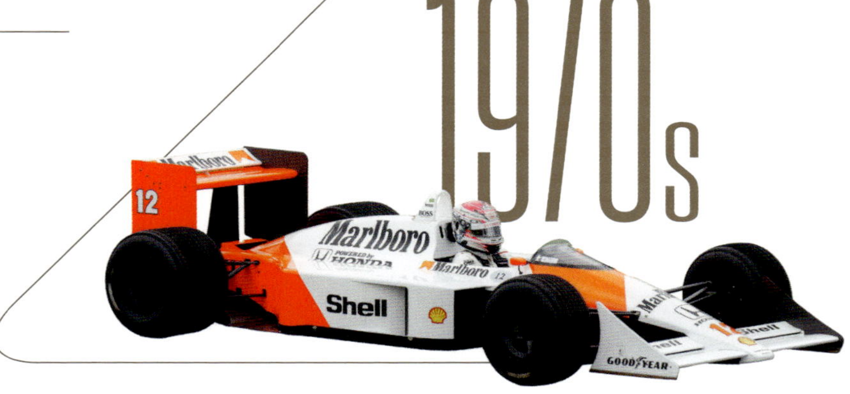

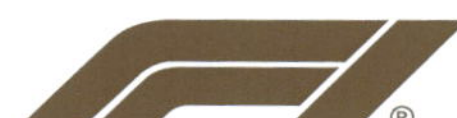

1980s

The first carbon fiber monocoque was introduced. Active suspension (later banned in the nineties) enhanced a car's stability under acceleration and braking. The semi-automatic gearbox that featured paddle shift changers on the steering wheel also debuted courtesy of Ferrari in 1989.

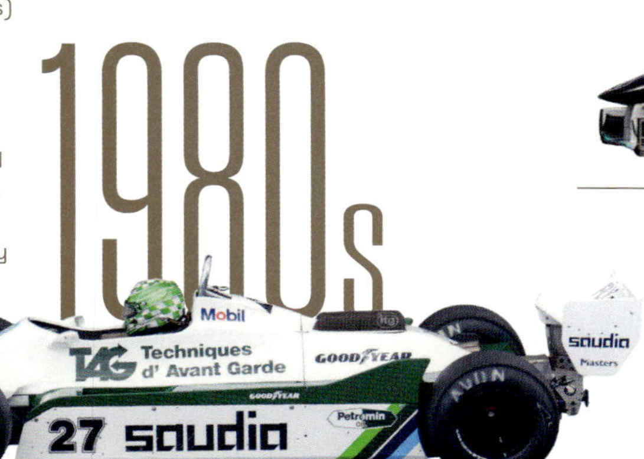

2000s

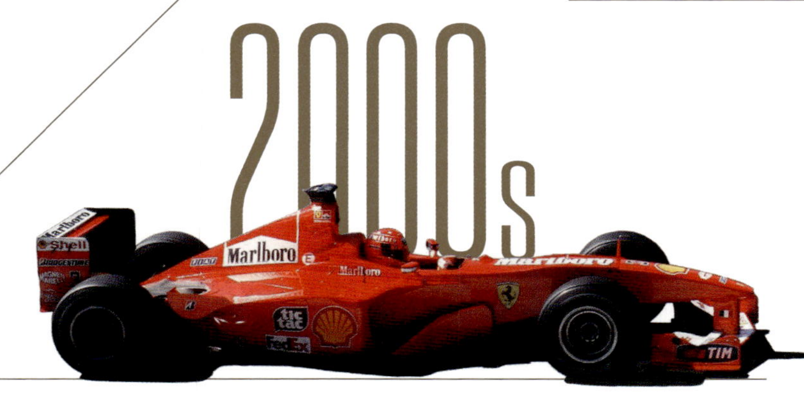

V10 engines were replaced by 2.4-liter V8s. Driver aids such as launch and traction control, along with fully automatic gearboxes were forbidden. Kinetic energy recovery systems (KERS) were introduced in 2009, at the same time as regulation overhaul resulted in wider front wings and taller rear wings.

2010s

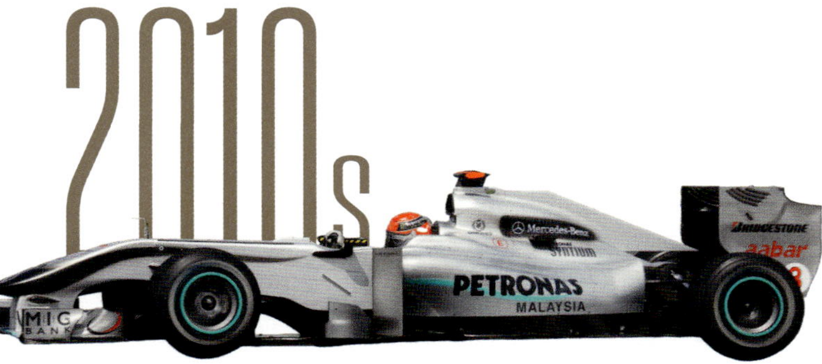

Mid-race refueling was banned. Turbocharged engines made a return as part of new regulations in 2014. A drag reduction system (DRS) helped facilitate overtaking early in the decade. Another aerodynamic change in 2017 allowed wider cars, bigger tires for increased grip, and higher-downforce designs. In 2018, the Halo cockpit protection device was made a mandatory feature.

2025

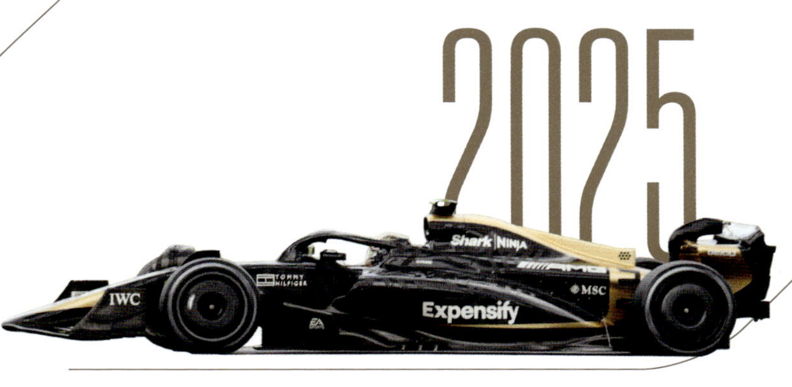

Modern F1 cars are in the final year of the current 1.6-liter V6 turbo hybrid era, while ground effect regulations have been permitted since 2022. Cars run much lower and stiffer than in previous eras, allowing increased cornering speeds and multiple track records this year. Low-profile tires are used on 18-inch wheels, and the minimum weight increased to 800kg.

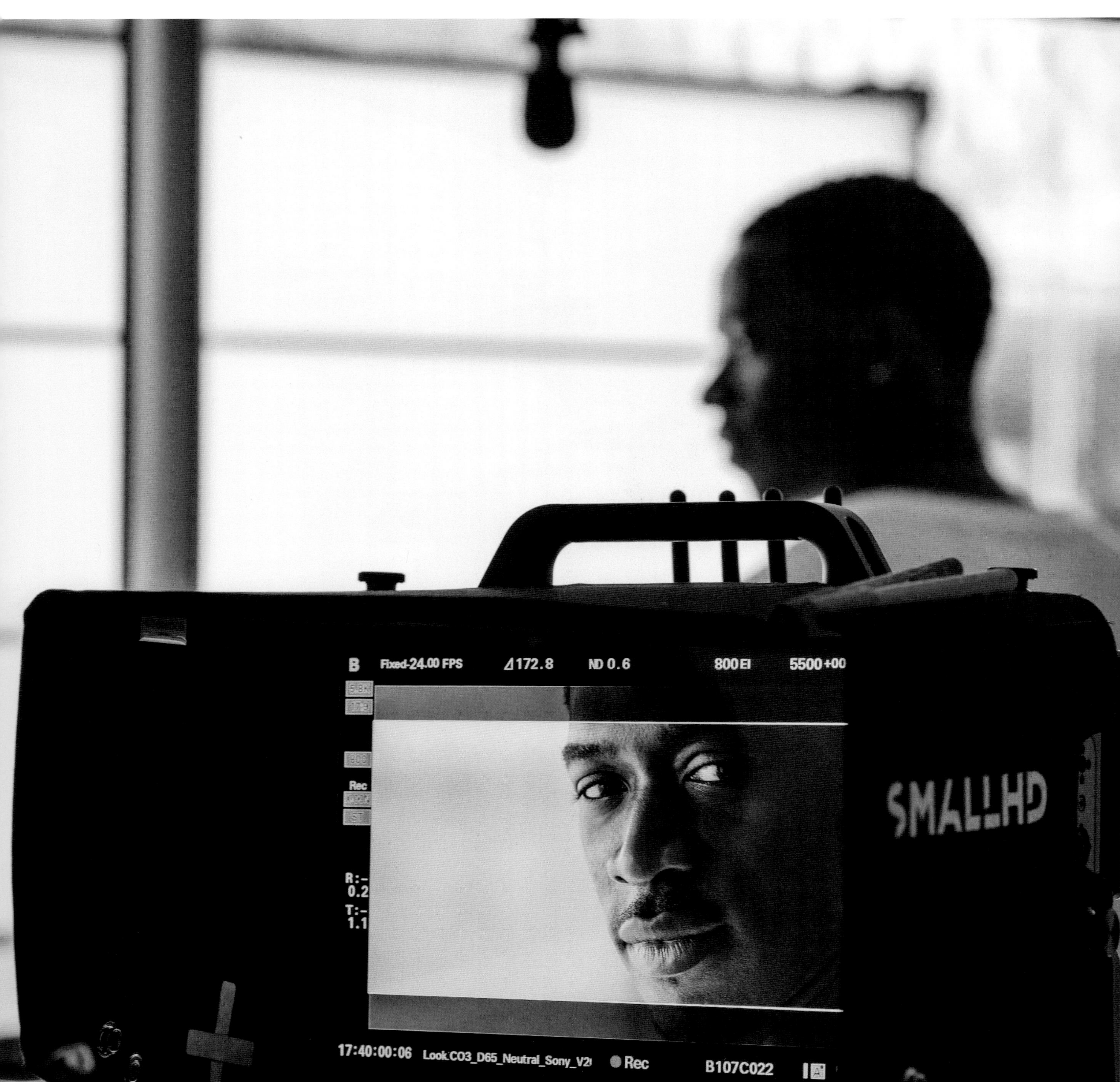

Damson Idris gets
ready for his close-up.

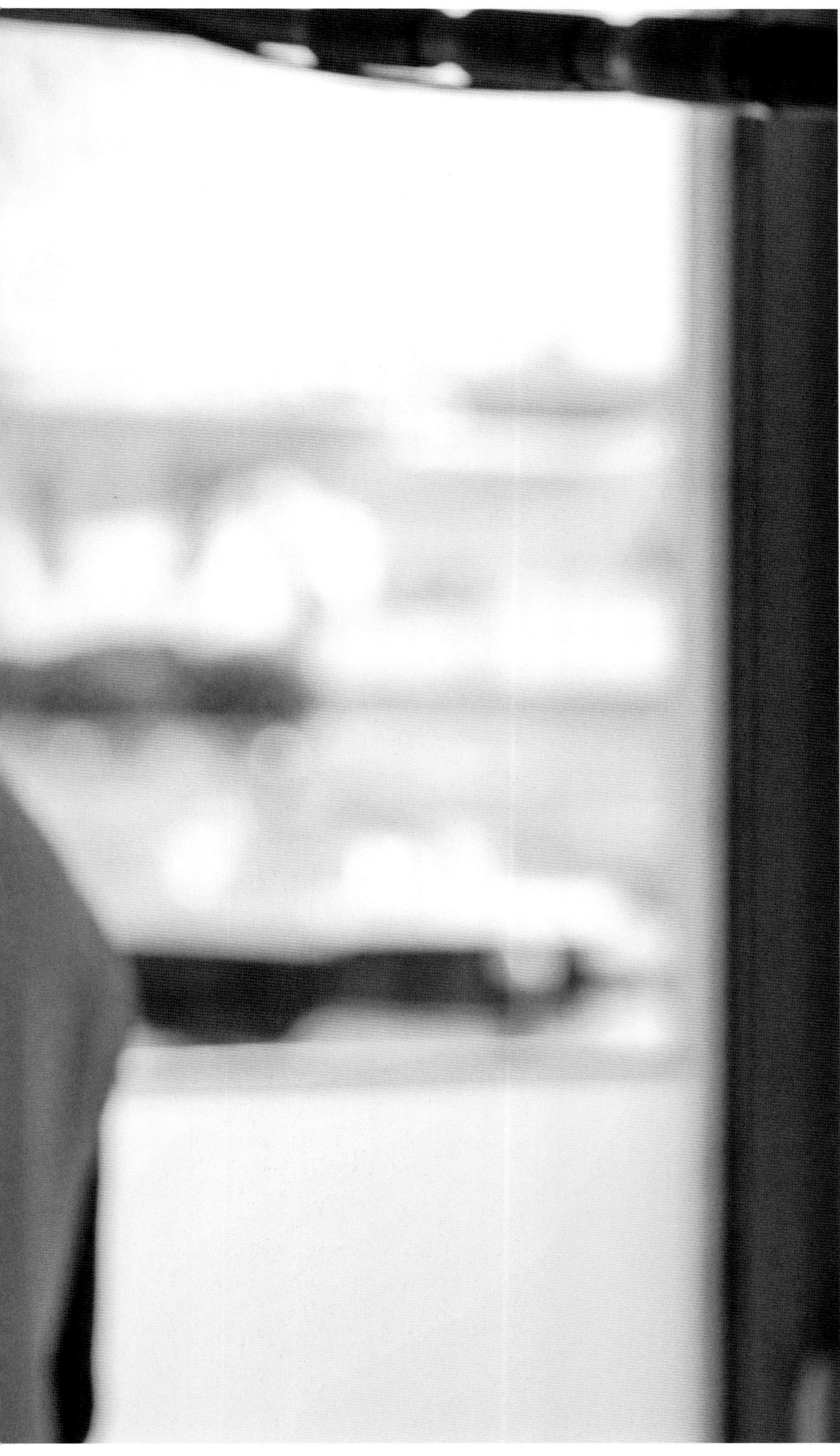

Idris also took a trip to Paul Ricard, where he got to drive an old Alpine Formula One car. “It was like I was in a spaceship,” he says. “I mean, before you know it, you’re at the end of the track and you have to smash the brakes.”

Paul Ricard was also where Idris suffered his first crash—while driving a Formula Four car. “I hated that track. I could not get the fast corners. I couldn’t get the slow corners. It was wet and I pressed the brakes, and they didn’t work. I could see the wall coming, and I’m like, ‘Here it comes . . . ’ pow.” But when the stunt crew turned up at the scene of the accident, they were all smiling. “The car’s messed up, but everyone was shaking my hand. They said, ‘*Now* you’re a driver.’”

After that, Silverstone became the main training facility going forward and Pitt and Idris continued to drive F3 cars while their APXGPs were being finished—in a garage just along the pit lane from where they were based. Eventually, in May 2023, both men got their first taste of driving the Formula Two spec APXGP car, and not even the weeks of training in F3 cars could prepare them for it. “The car was super aggressive. It’s got an incredible amount of power—600 and something horsepower,” says Bacheta, who would take to the track with Pitt, while Dolby would accompany Idris. “We were on big fat tires and used tire warmers, although F2 cars don’t normally. There’s no power steering, which made it a little more physical than a Formula One car. It’s good, but not easy to drive.”

“It was very stiff,” says Pitt. “Compared to the F1 car, which I hadn’t been driving to its limits, I didn’t have the skill at that point to even get close. This thing was like wrestling a bull. But I grew to love it. I really grew to love it.”

“The speed of it. Everything slows down when you’re doing it right,” says Idris. “And the faster I went, the less I made mistakes. It’s such a weird feeling. You can’t replicate it on a normal road, in a normal car. The first time I felt I was going extremely fast was when I went flat through Copse [Corner at Silverstone] and everyone was, ‘Whoa!’ I had watched a video of Lewis’s pole lap there. He was in a Formula One car, but I was like, ‘I want to try that.’”

“Creatively, practically, logistically, Luch and Craig were some of the most key people on this job,” says Hefferman. “They were the safety belt to the actors. They helped construct the sequences.”

"I owe those guys everything," says Pitt of Bacheta and Dolby. "They're gems of human beings. They were so patient with us. I felt absolutely safe. And when I say we got wheel-to-wheel on a straight, I mean wheel-to-wheel, like inches; even coming in between each other's wheels. And I trusted that if I cocked it up, Luch was going to get out of the way. The wealth of knowledge these guys have is staggering. It would take me ten years to catch up."

Alongside the track work, Pitt and Idris undertook a fitness regime patterned after the one Formula One drivers use. "Reflex training, tennis ball exercises, neck training, where they put a harness on your head, and someone pulls it, and you have to resist. It's excruciating," recounts Idris, who also wanted to replicate the body of a Formula One driver. "They're so skinny. I dropped from 86 kilograms to 77, which is a lot, and I was able to maintain it through fasting. We drank a lot of coffee, but fasting and driving those cars put me in this amazing mindset, where my brain felt so fresh and focused."

"The best training is spending hours and hours in the car, because that strengthens all the muscles you use while driving, the most notable being your neck," says Kosinski.

"The hand and eye coordination required is remarkable, and the stress they go through in the car, the g-forces," says Bruckheimer. "The physicality they have to go through, because it's all in your neck, your upper body and your leg. Your leg strength has to be enormous. But Brad was really rocking that car. Lewis said it, our stunt drivers said it, it's amazing how good an athlete he is, that he could adapt himself and do this at his age, to get in that car and drive at the speeds he was driving at, with the accuracy he was driving at."

Pitt and Idris also spent hours in a simulator, familiarizing themselves with the eight other Grand Prix tracks where they would be required to drive. "Pushing it to the limit," says Idris. "You can crash, and you can make a mistake, so that when you finally get out on track, you learn from it."

"I didn't like the sim unless it was Mercedes's, because then it's a real experience," says Pitt. "There you're in a cockpit and it spins 360. They have it dialed in for changes in asphalt, curb heights. It's incredible. I was sweating in that thing, which was amazing to me because I wasn't pulling any g's."

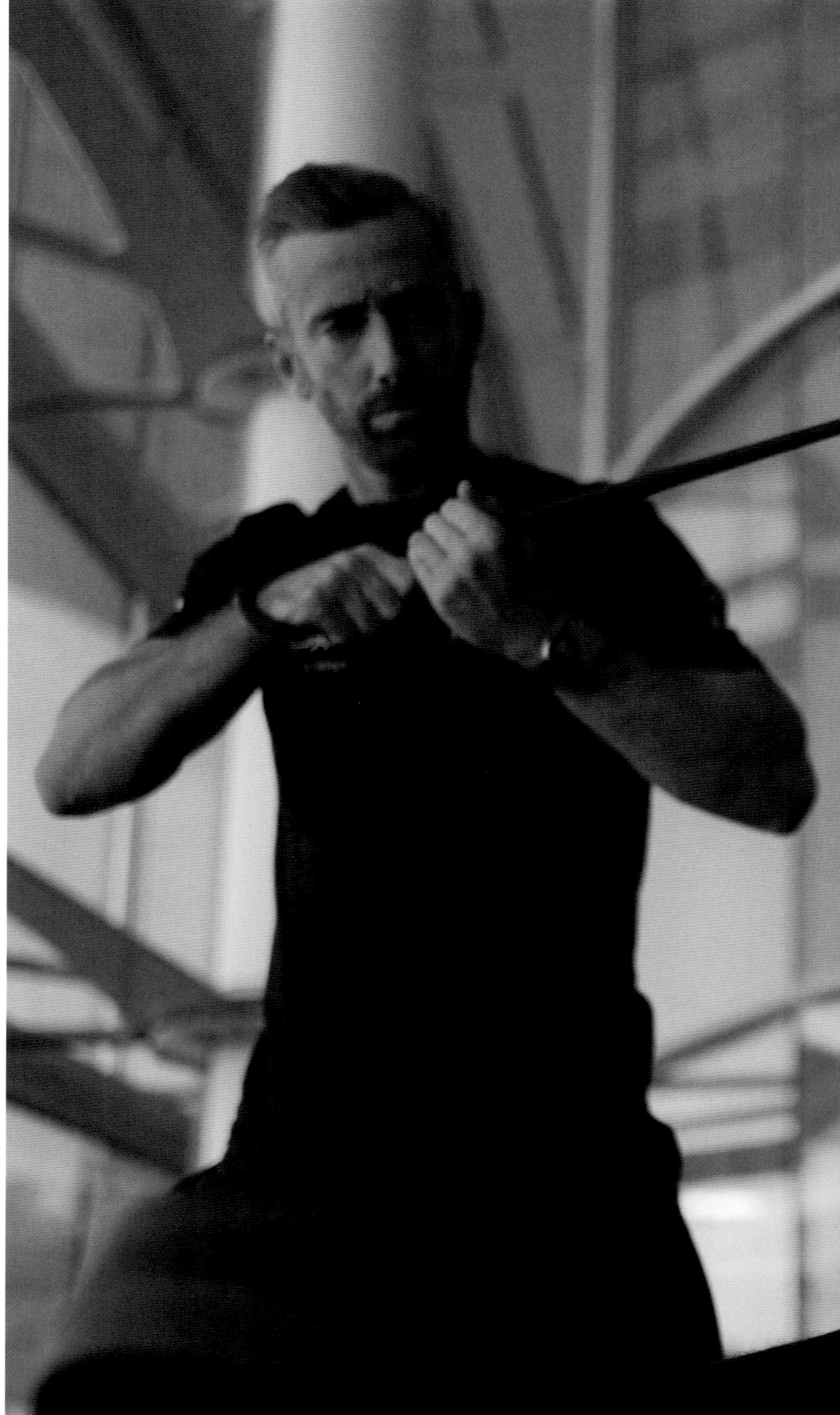

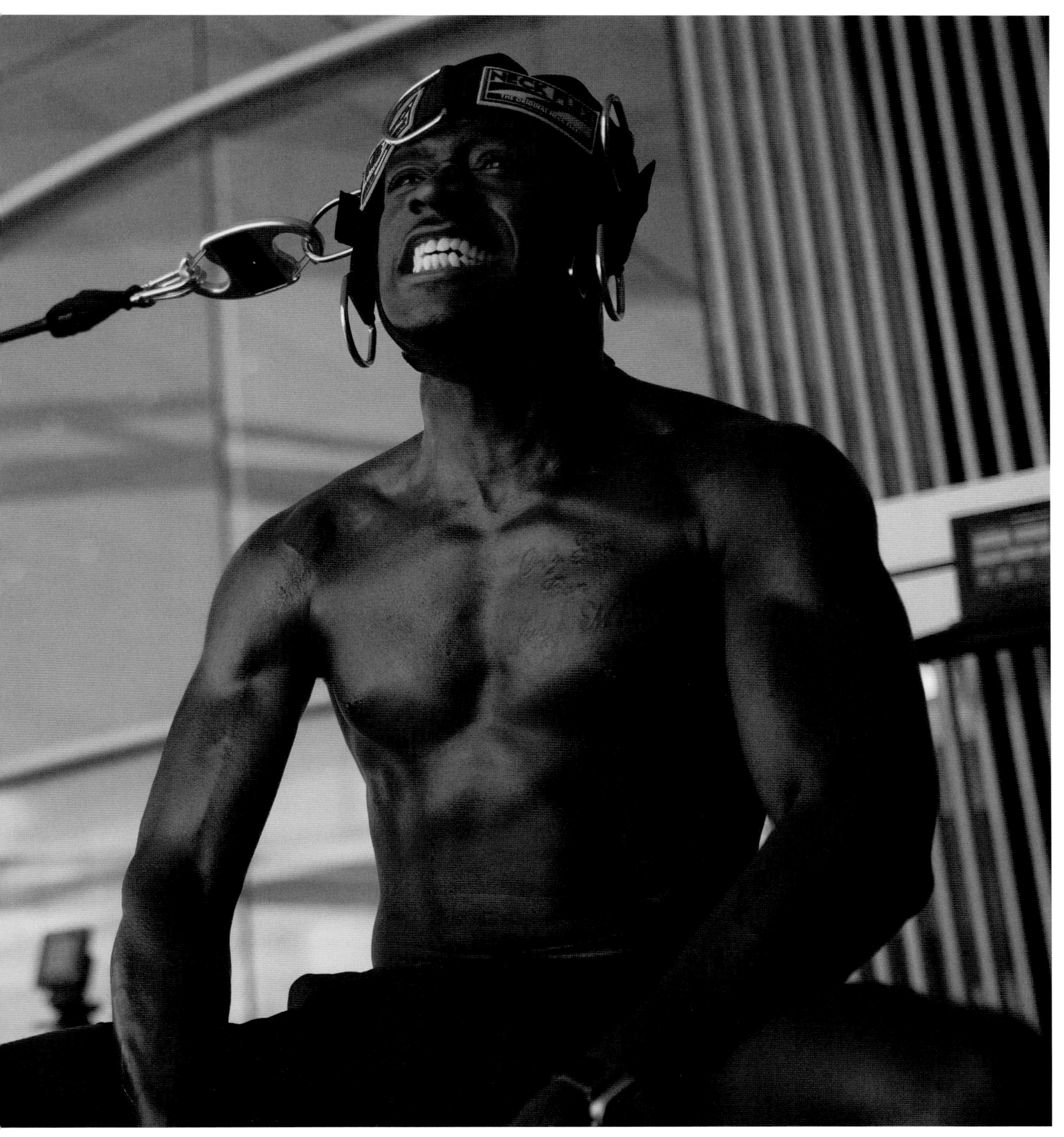

Joshua Pearce (Damson Idris) works to strengthen his neck.

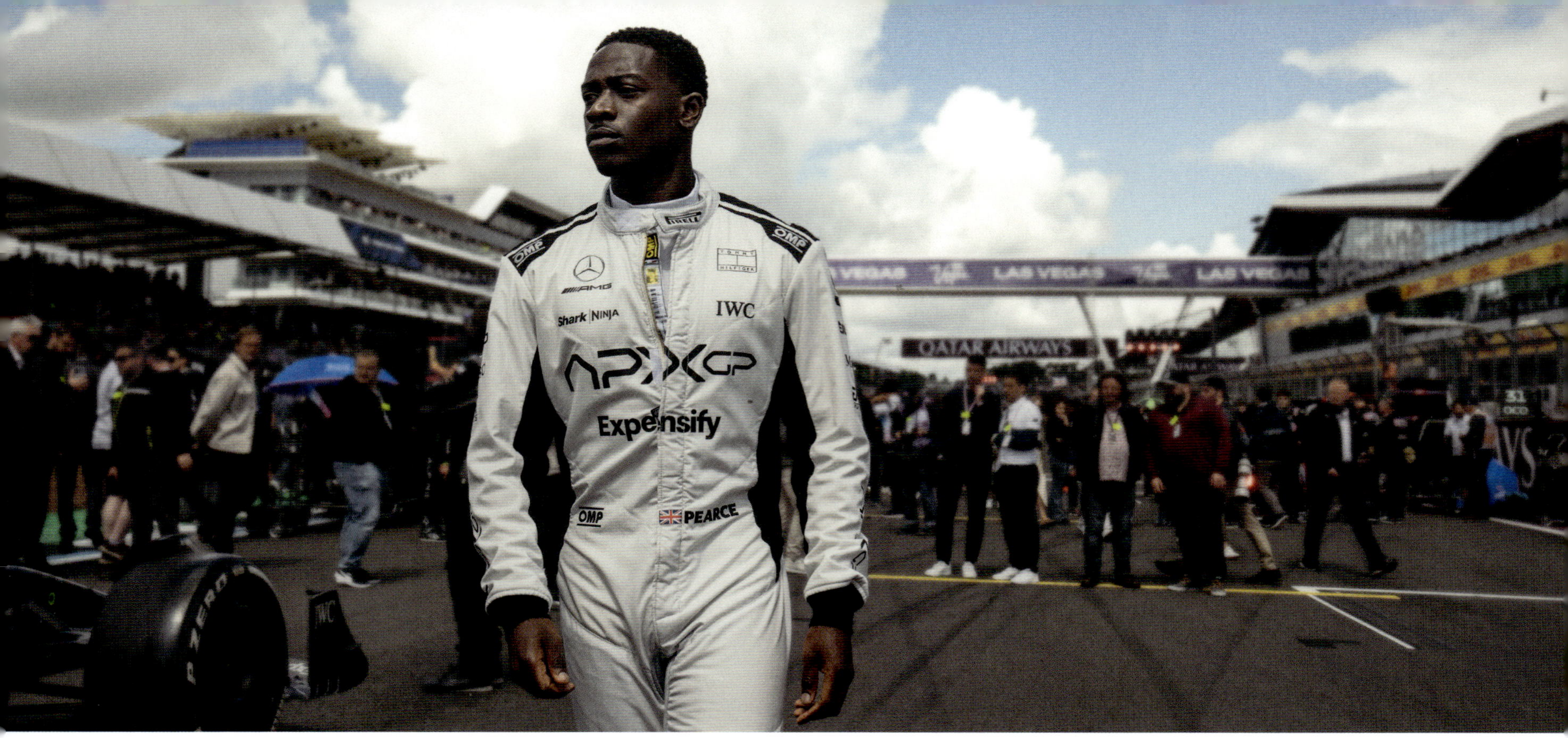

“Everything we had done the year before, we had to do again. But now it was muscle memory. I was more comfortable, even on camera.”

DAMSON IDRIS

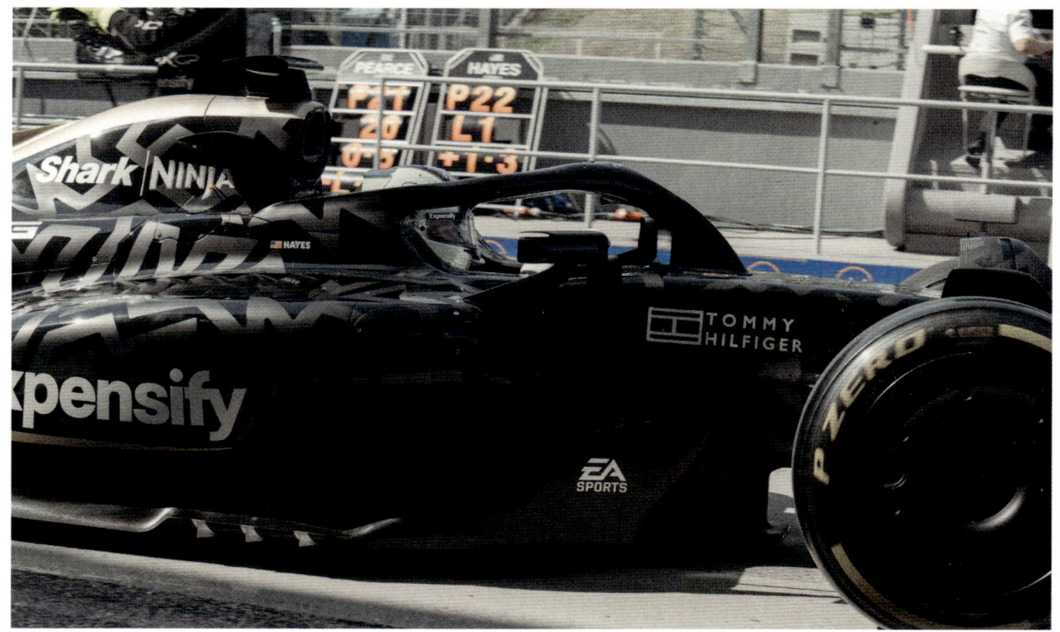

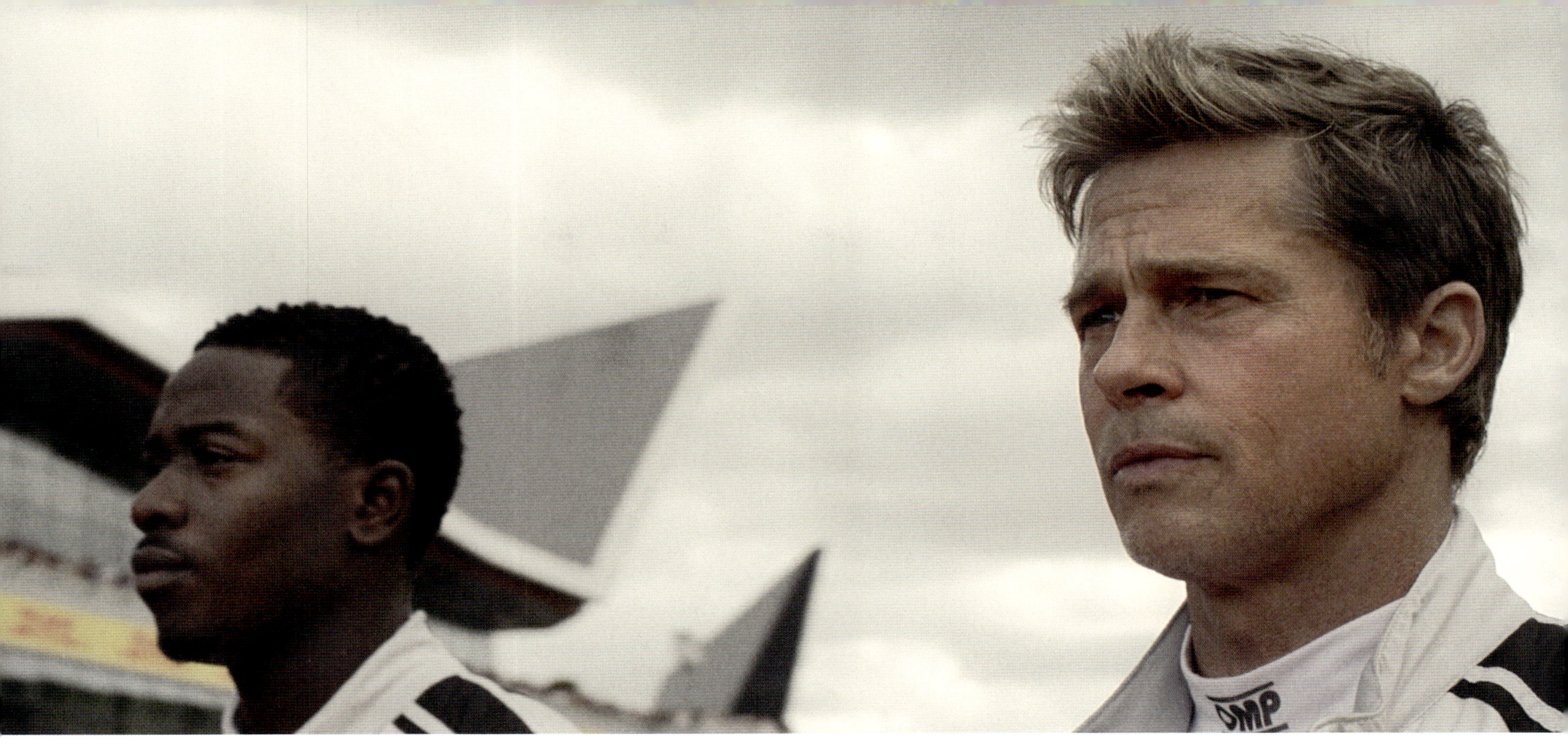

The first time Pitt and Idris got to drive their APXGP cars during a real race weekend was at the 2023 British Grand Prix which took place on July 6 through 9. But in the week that followed, the American actors' union, the Screen Actors Guild–American Federation of Television and Radio Artists (SAG-AFTRA), voted to go on strike on July 14, meaning its members, which included Pitt and Idris, couldn't work on a union project.

"When the strike hit and we were shut down, I remember bumping into the walls," says Pitt. "We just experienced this high. We had pulled off this huge race weekend at Silverstone. We were on our way. We were supposed to be shooting till the following January. And then they pulled the plug. None of us knew what to really do with ourselves for a few weeks."

"I stayed in London for a bit, because we thought, maybe, it'll be over in two weeks, and then it wasn't," remembers Idris. "I went back to L.A., ate a bunch of southern food, got fat, and waited for it to be over."

The second unit, headed up by Kosinski, continued to work without actors, filming at several Grand Prix with Bacheta and Dolby, as well as shooting several stunt sequences. But, in late November, production eventually ground to a halt.

It took until early November for the strike to be resolved, and its members were free to return to work. By then, the 2023 Formula One season was almost over, and given that filming was meant to follow the Grand Prix schedule, it was decided to pause the shoot and pick it up again the following year.

"In the end, the strike turned out to be a huge benefit, because we spent another year on the movie," says Pitt, who, in March 2024, joined Bacheta, Dolby, and Idris at the Yas Marina Circuit, home of the Abu Dhabi Grand Prix, for a fortnight's driver training. "Everything we had done the year before, we had to do again," says Idris. "But now it was muscle memory. I was more comfortable, even on camera. Joe would say, 'Oh man, you're such a better driver now,' because I'd had all these months to think about it."

Top Left: Damson Idris arrives at Silverstone to film the British Grand Prix race.

Top Right: Damson Idris and Brad Pitt stand alongside the rest of the drivers for the national anthem at the British Grand Prix at Silverstone.

The production returned to Abu Dhabi in April to shoot various driving sequences, and Pitt and Idris continued to train on and off for the rest of the year, taking to the track with Bacheta and Dolby before each race weekend—either at the Circuit of the Americas in Austin, Texas, or in Palm Springs, California.

"Training wise, it never stopped," says Idris, "even down to the exercises, the diet. There were days I didn't eat for 24 hours. And the neck exercises, man. We were in Palm Springs, in the F3s, doing 30-minute sessions, and it was hot, and after the first day my neck was killing me. This is why you must stay on it. It's the most training I've ever done for a part. But it's set a precedent going forward. The more you train, the more effortless it is to play these characters, especially a Formula One driver. Because you can tell in an instant if a driver's trained or if they haven't, down to how they look at the car."

"Selfishly, I got to drive for another year," reflects Pitt. "And the driver I became in the last month of filming, in comparison to if we had finished a year earlier is just night and day. I do think there's an alternate universe where I could have gone down this path. It was sublime. And such a joy for me at this age. Having done as many films as I have, to find something that reinvigorates all the passion and find another joy in life at my age is just incredible. Incredible. It was such a high. [Paul] Newman started in his fifties, and he won a few titles. I think I'd be competitive. I *know* I'd be competitive. I just don't know how competitive."

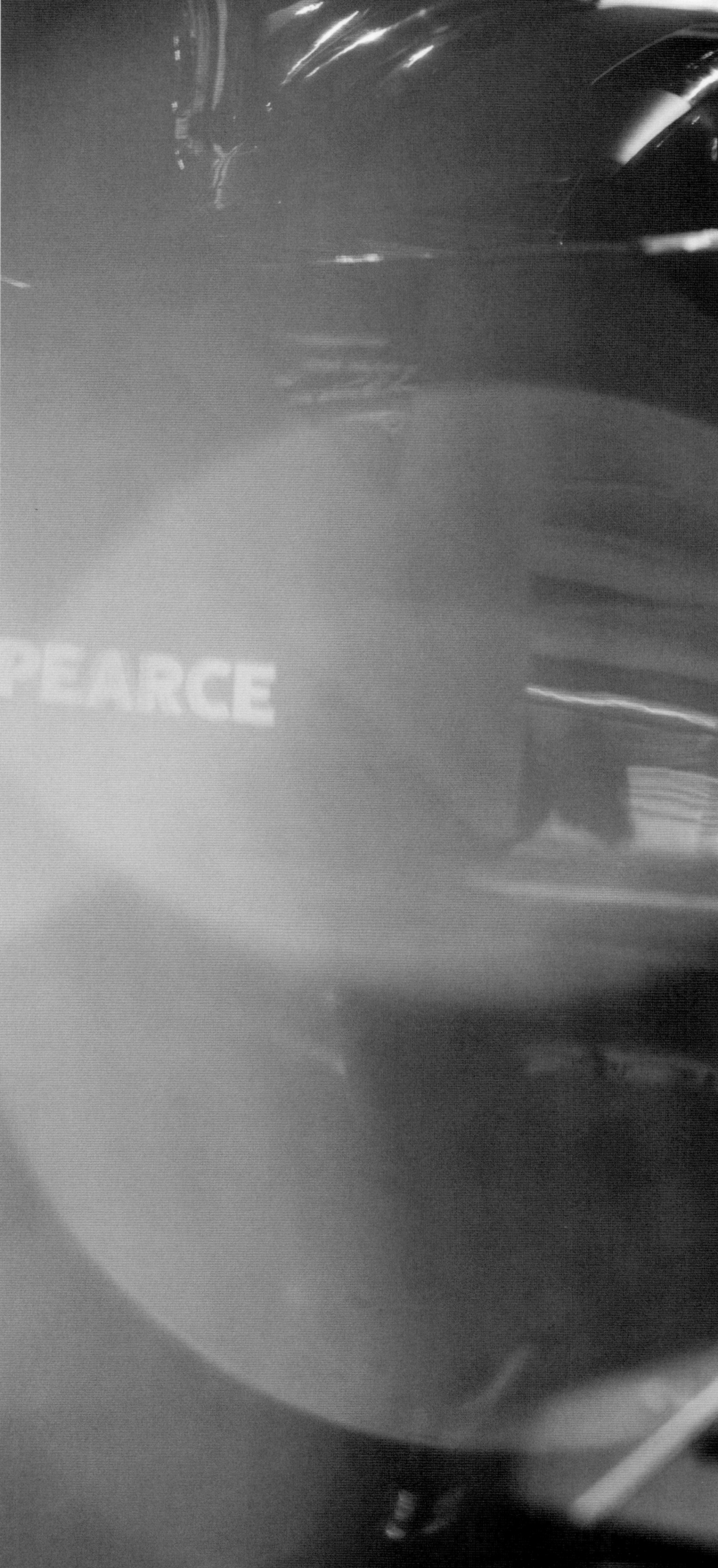

After the strike was over, both Pitt and Idris continued their driver training in F3 cars.

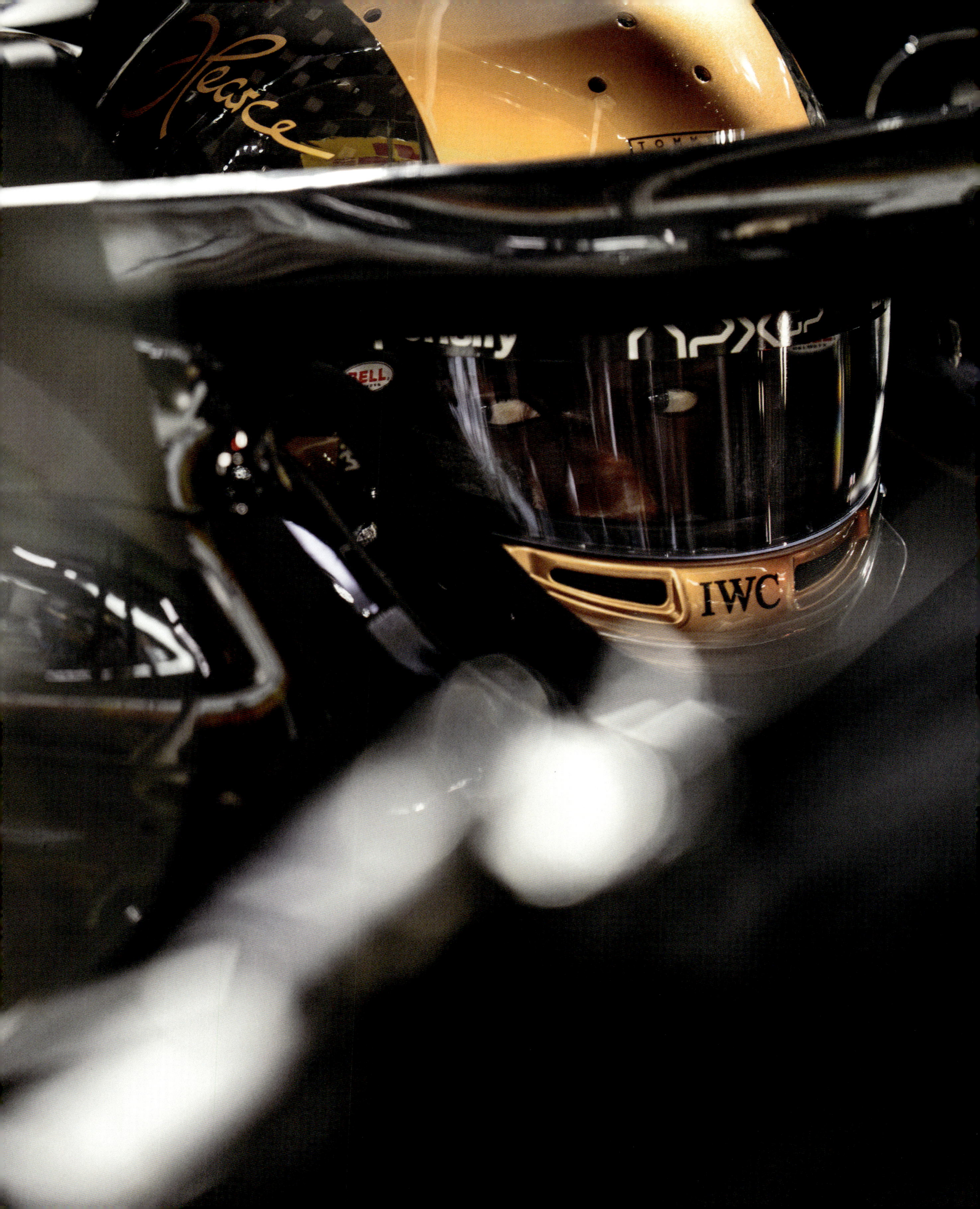
BELL
IWC

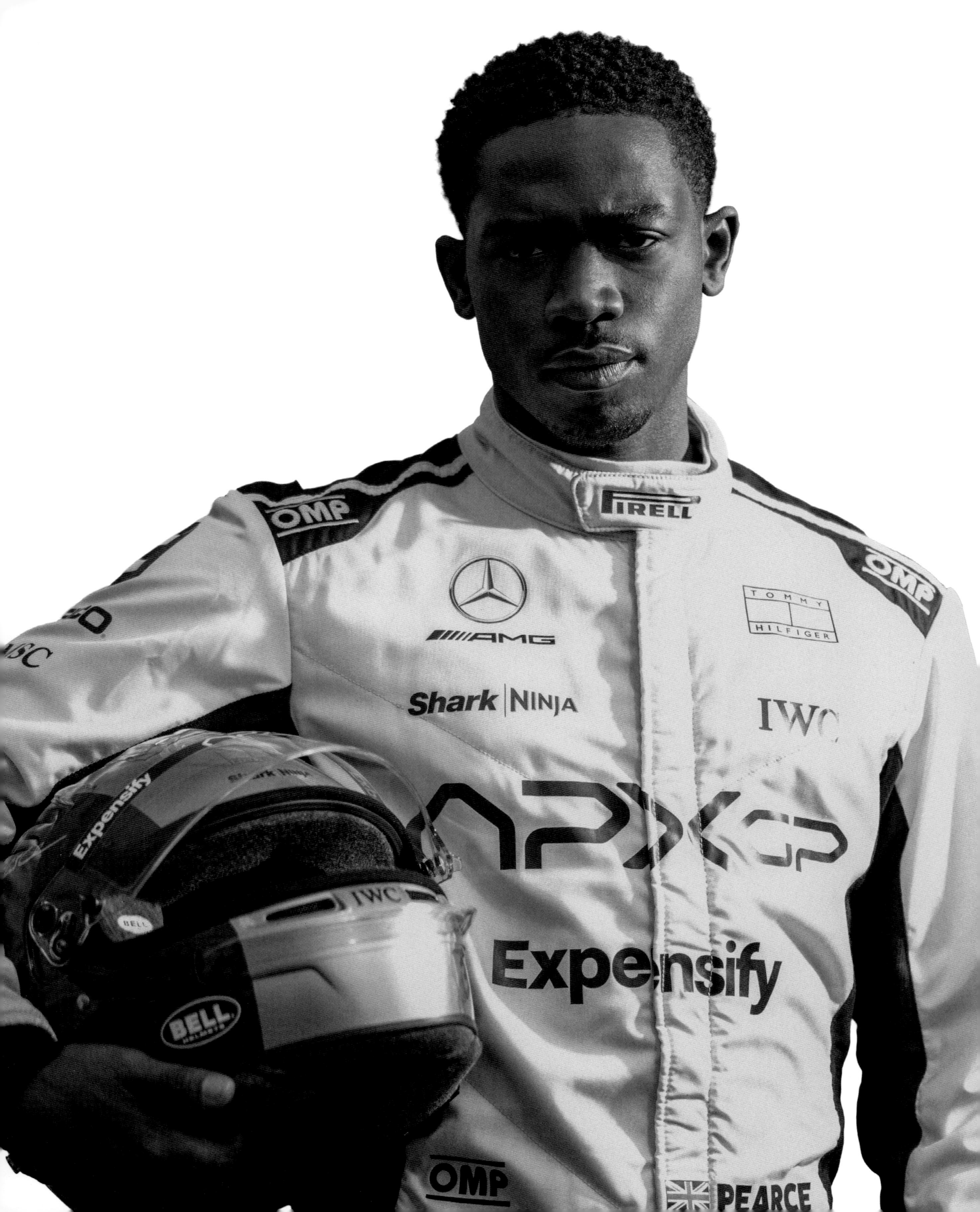

OMP
PIRELLI
AMG
TOMMY HILFIGER
Shark | NINJA
IWC
Expensify
BELL
OMP
PEARCE

THE ROOKIE

JOSHUA PEARCE

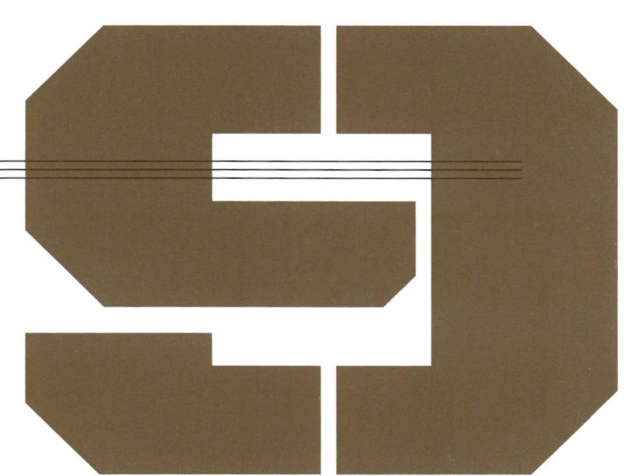

When Kosinski came up with the character of Joshua Pearce, he imagined the rookie Formula One driver to be in his early twenties. "Because my understanding was these rookies were in their early twenties, sometimes teenagers," says Kosinski, who, together with casting directors Lucy Bevan and Emily Brockman, began to look at younger actors to play him.

During their initial search, Kosinski and producer Jerry Bruckheimer met with Damson Idris, a Brit living in Los Angeles, in early 2022. "It was just a general meeting, with Joe and Jerry at their office in Santa Monica," recalls Idris. "I was thirty, thirty-one at the time. I have a babyface and look twenty, but they had in their heads that maybe I wasn't going to pull it off, so it went away."

Then, in September 2022, Nyck de Vries, a test and reserve driver for Williams, Mercedes, McLaren, and Aston Martin, stood in for Williams's Alexander Albon at the Italian Grand Prix—de Vries was twenty-six at the time. As a result, Kosinski decided to age Joshua up. "What I liked about an older rookie is that this season would really be their last chance. If it didn't work out, and they didn't perform, it wasn't like they could try again in a year or two. If you're a twenty-six, or twenty-seven-year-old rookie, this is your one shot. It makes the stakes even higher. There's a certain amount of desperation there."

Suddenly, Idris, who had made a name for himself playing a drug dealer in the FX crime drama *Snowfall*, fell back into the group of actors who could play Joshua, and Kosinski called him in for a screen test. "I knew he was a great actor; his range is phenomenal. He played a gangster in South Central LA on a TV show for five or six seasons, and you had no idea he was a Brit. I could see instantly he was our Joshua. Like Joshua, he's a huge natural talent. Exudes so much warmth, personality, charisma. He's blessed with that innate thing only certain people are born with—which is when they're on-screen, you can't help but look at them. Brad's one. Damson has it too. He is completely captivating. He's very skilled. He makes it look effortless. And that's a hard thing to find. It was not an easy role. The training side was physically grueling and mentally exhausting. But he was 100 percent committed. Came in with a smile and enthusiasm every day, which is what you want."

"He has charisma, he's a terrific actor, and he jumps off the screen. He's going to be a major movie star," says Bruckheimer.

"[Damson] has charisma, he's a terrific actor, and he jumps off the screen. He's going to be a major movie star."

JERRY BRUCKHEIMER

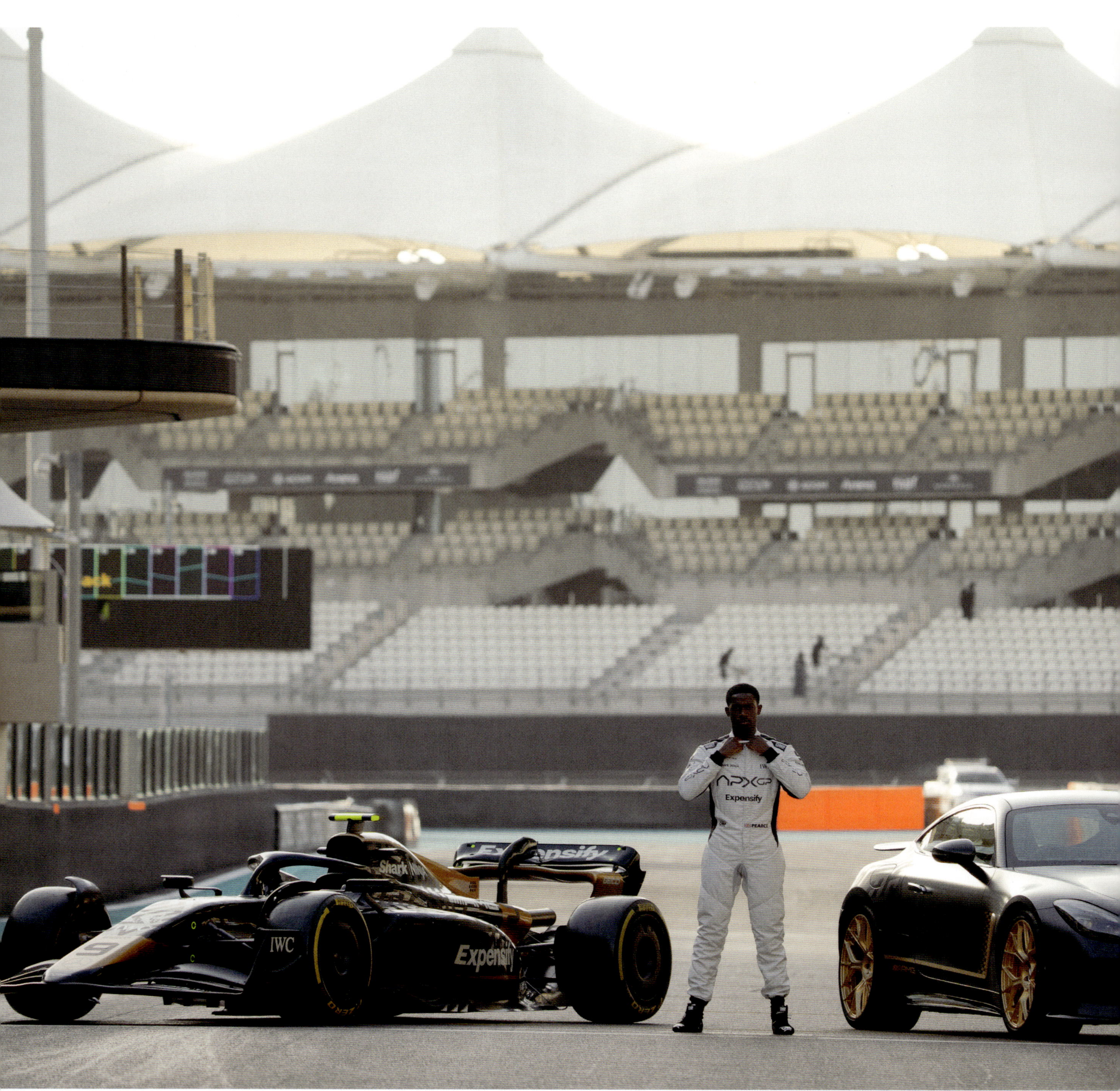

Above: Joshua Pearce poses between his number 9 APXGP car and a customized Mercedes Benz.

Bottom Right: Joseph Kosinski and Damson Idris confer before the Abu Dhabi Grand Prix scene.

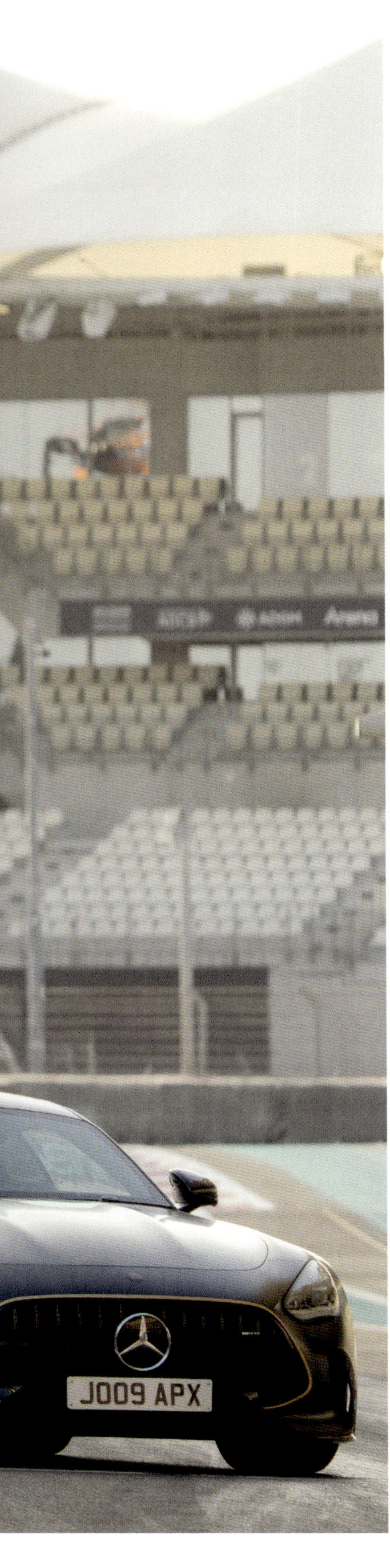

"What's wonderful about Damson is he's a very confident actor, and we needed that for Joshua," concurs screenwriter Ehren Kruger. "He's got to hold his own in this garage where he's doubted by everyone. And he made Joshua stronger than he was on the page. That was evident in the audition. In scenes with Brad Pitt, he could hold his own, and you would be rooting for him."

"I really grew to love that charming bastard," says Pitt. "He just goes for it. I also respect how he deals with everything off the court. There's even more media focus on young actors than when I started, and I really appreciate how much he's able to enjoy it. But he was great in the scenes. He's got such great reactions—and looks the business driving."

Before Idris could be officially cast, however, he had to prove a) he could drive and b) he had the mindset to undergo the months of training that were in store. "They already knew my work. That wasn't the test," he recalls. "The test was to get in the car." Idris spent the day at Palmer Sports in Bedford, England, driving high-performance cars, including a BMW M4 and a Palmer JP-LM two-seater sports car. "I was green," he admits. "I'd driven fast cars before, but never any Formula cars." Moreover, the weather was tricky. "It was wet, and I'm spinning out, thinking, *Oh, shit, I'm not going to get this.* When we got into the final car, the instructor told me the guy I was up against had spun out like crazy. He said, 'You don't want that to happen to you, so just have fun. You don't need to speed. Just get around the track safely.' So, I did. And I guess they saw maturity."

"What he showed was he picked things up very quickly and was a very good listener," says Kosinski. "The report came back that he was trainable, and it was going to work. I knew he was the actor I wanted, but we wanted to make sure he could handle himself in a car before making the full commitment. He didn't have to be an amazing driver on day one. It was more, was he going to be able to learn? And he picked it up very, very quickly. He had a natural feel for it."

(The guy Idris was up against happened to be a friend of his. "We'd meet in a bar in L.A. and laugh about how we did. That's how this game works. You become friends with people, then go out for the same stuff. But you're happy that one of you got it.")

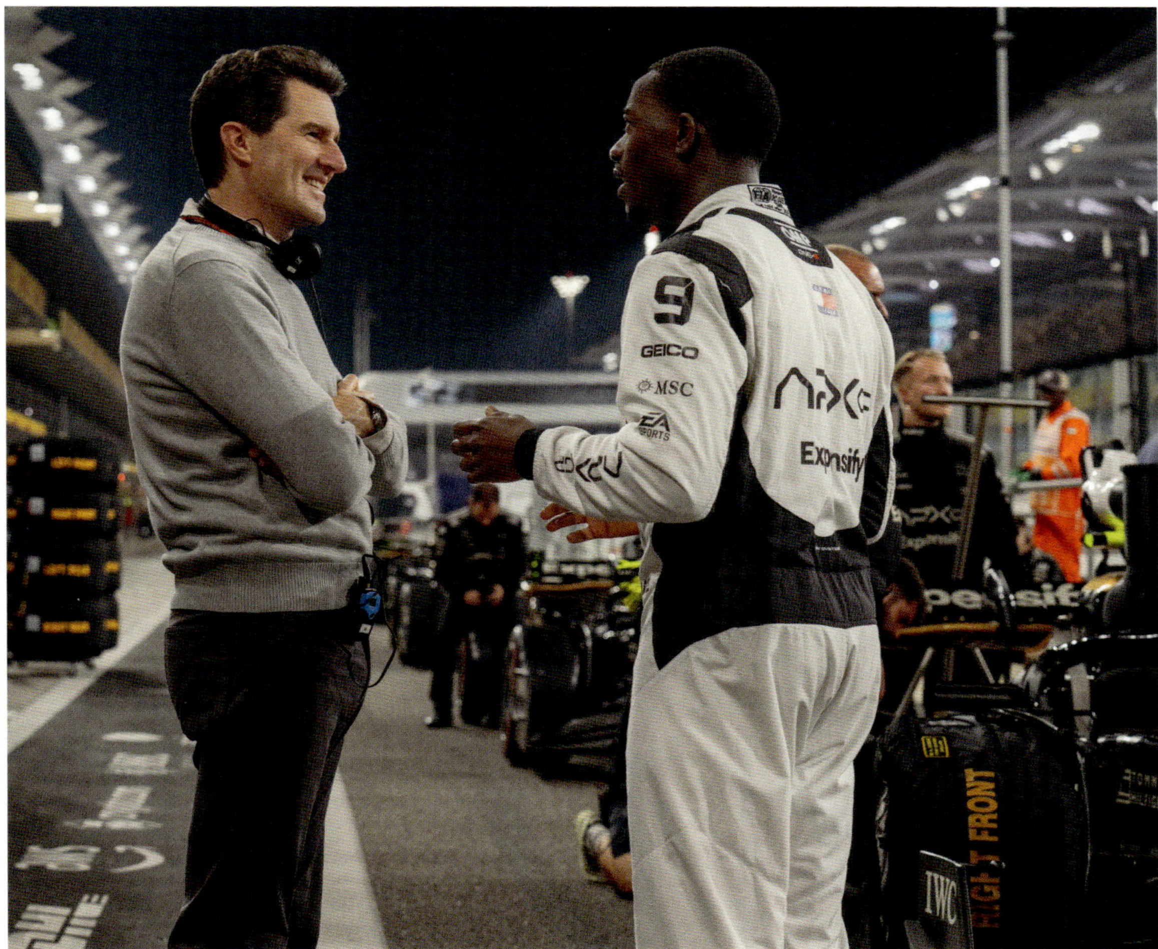

Idris was already a Formula One fan. In 2019, while filming the sci-fi thriller *Outside the Wire* in Budapest, he and his fellow cast members were invited to the Hungaroring to watch the Hungarian Grand Prix. "Lewis won that day, and it was my first time at a race. They gave us the full tour, in the garages, looking at all the cars, meeting the drivers. I stuck at it. I went to the Miami Grand Prix. I'd try and get to Silverstone. This was before the film was even a prospect. And when I knew the film was coming, I *really* got into it, watching the races all the time." He even bought himself a Porsche. "I wanted to be involved in speed as much as possible so I could be ready for when the opportunity came. And when it did, I grabbed it with both hands."

From Kosinski's very first pitch to Hamilton, Joshua was a person of color. "Lewis is a very strong proponent of diversity and is an important and inspirational symbol himself, being who he is and what he's accomplished," says Kosinski. "I think that's one of the reasons he was drawn to the project—we had a Black character as one of our leads. He's told me that when he was a kid and would go to the movies, there was never a lead character that looked like him, and that stuck with me."

But while Joshua is a young Black driver in Formula One, he was never meant to be a stand-in for Hamilton. "It was very important to Lewis that the character wasn't him," says Kruger. "But what we did want for him from Lewis's past was the fact he did not come from Formula One royalty, either family or lineage. That is one of the things Joshua and Sonny have in common and can respect about each other. They got to this level of racing the hard way. At every turn, they were doubted and told they were unlikely to reach the pinnacle or succeed. Nothing ever came easy for them."

"The beautiful thing about Joshua Pearce is he exists in a world that Lewis exists in," says Idris. "Lewis has broken down so many barriers that Joshua could just walk through. It's not, 'This is a Black driver.' It's, 'Here is a young driver every rookie can relate to. Not just in Formula One. Anyone who's trying to build something out of nothing, anyone who's trying to make a name for themselves, can relate to Joshua Pearce. He's from East London and fought his way to Formula One. Single mom. Dad passed away. So, there's that pressure of wanting to please his mom, who's sacrificed so much to get him where he is. That's something a lot of people can relate to. I can relate to [it]."

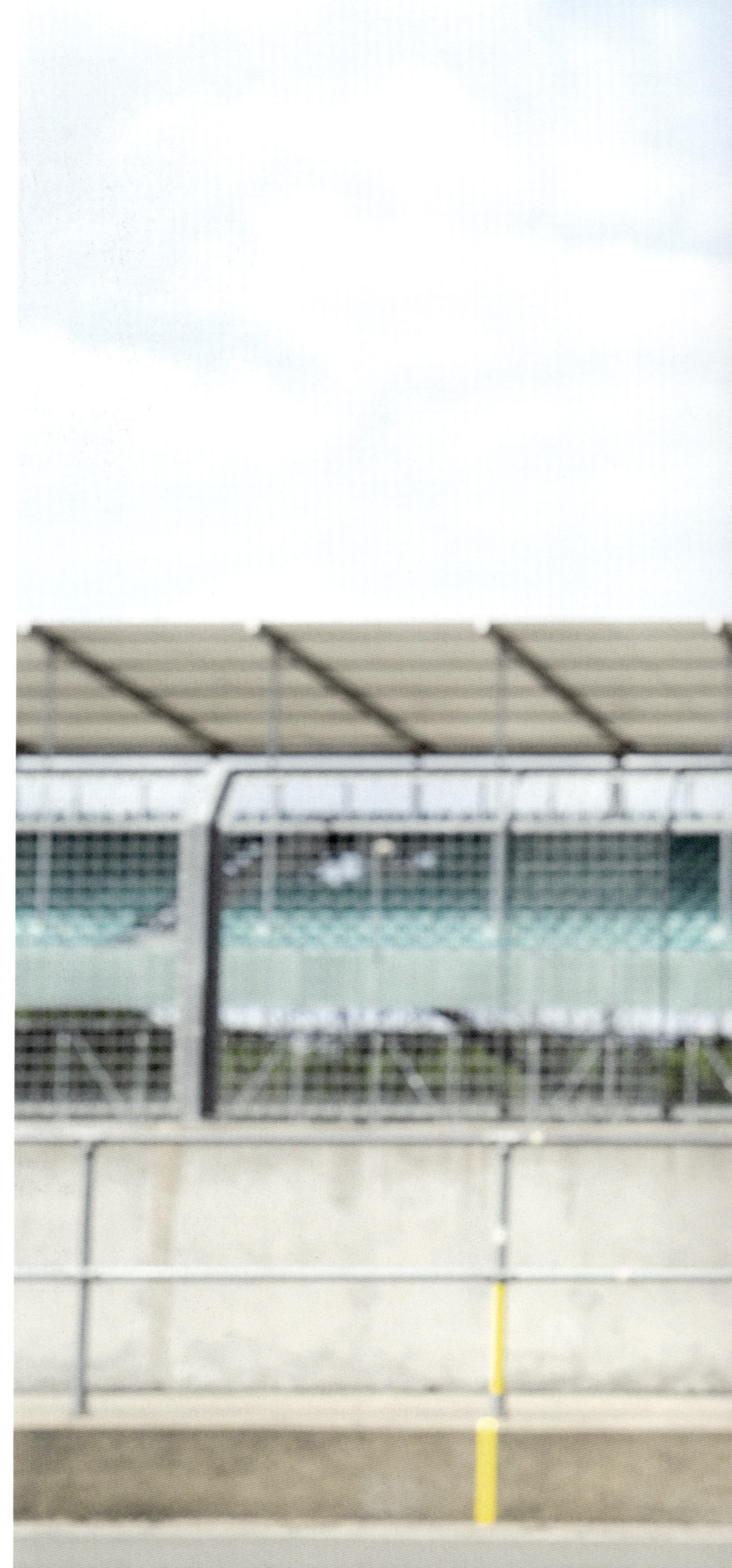

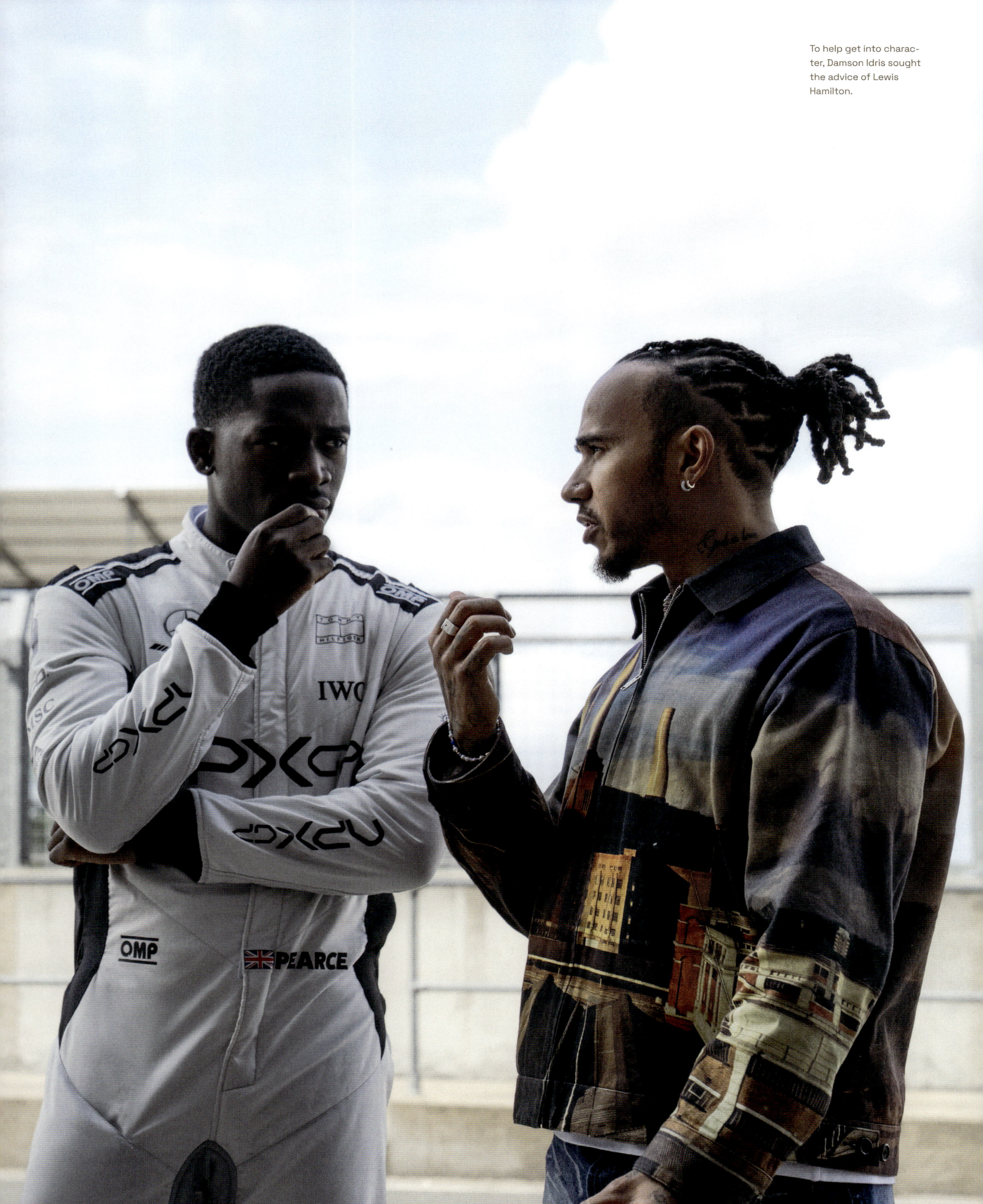

To help get into character, Damson Idris sought the advice of Lewis Hamilton.

While it took months of training to transform Idris into racing driver material, he also tackled Joshua from the inside out. "When we first meet him, he's cocky but deeply insecure, engulfed in anxiety, fearful of losing his seat, fearful his career is going to be over before it's even begun. The way I was able to figure out Joshua was to figure out real Formula One drivers and how they think. *Drive to Survive* was amazing for that; I was able to get into their minds. I saw their insecurities. I saw their dreams, their hopes. I saw how badly they loved the sport and how they couldn't do anything else. I took all of that and I put it into Joshua."

Idris would attend drivers' meetings during race weekends and would ask questions whenever he could. "We were singing the national anthem at Silverstone during the British Grand Prix, and I remember saying to Verstappen, who was standing near me, 'Do you guys zip your race suits down or do you zip it up?' And he was, 'You could do either.' He's always so serious. But the drivers are so cool, so accommodating. They've been super helpful. Anytime we see them across the paddock, they say hello. They're all excited to see the film."

He also had Hamilton to talk to. "I knew him in passing, and was a fan anyway," says Idris. "But I remember going to Joe's house and Lewis was there. We spoke extensively about the script. About the characters. About Formula One. Throughout filming, Lewis would come to set, and we'd chill in the trailer. We'd go through the script again, look at the race sequences, and he'd call bullshit on stuff. To have him as a producer on this reassured everyone in Formula One that we were not here to play. And he's incredibly proud and happy when he sees me on-screen."

Hamilton did, however, feel that Joshua was a little too cool for a rookie, and mentioned it to Kosinski. Idris found the comment funny. "I said to Joe, 'Tell him Joshua is Lewis's biggest fan. That's why he's cool. Because he wants to be like Lewis,'" he recalls. "Joe told Lewis that, and Lewis said, 'Yeah, that makes sense.' He's always teasing me."

At an event just before the British Grand Prix in 2024, Idris informed Hamilton proudly that he hadn't spun yet, to which Hamilton replied, "You're not driving fast enough."

"He said, 'Anytime I'm driving slowly, I think, *Could be worse. I could be driving as slow as Damson*,'" laughs Idris. "And then he goes on to win at Silverstone. It was raining that day, and it stopped right when we needed to film—and the *F1* trailer played while we were out on track. It was perfect. Later, I remember being in my trailer, praying to God, 'Please let Lewis win.' And everything came true. It was brilliant.

"Lewis is always giving me words of encouragement," Idris continues, "telling me how massive this opportunity is, and how he wants this movie to represent how he wants Formula One to look like in the future. And that support is endless."

Below: Damson Idris talks to the press in the media pen alongside Lewis Hamilton.

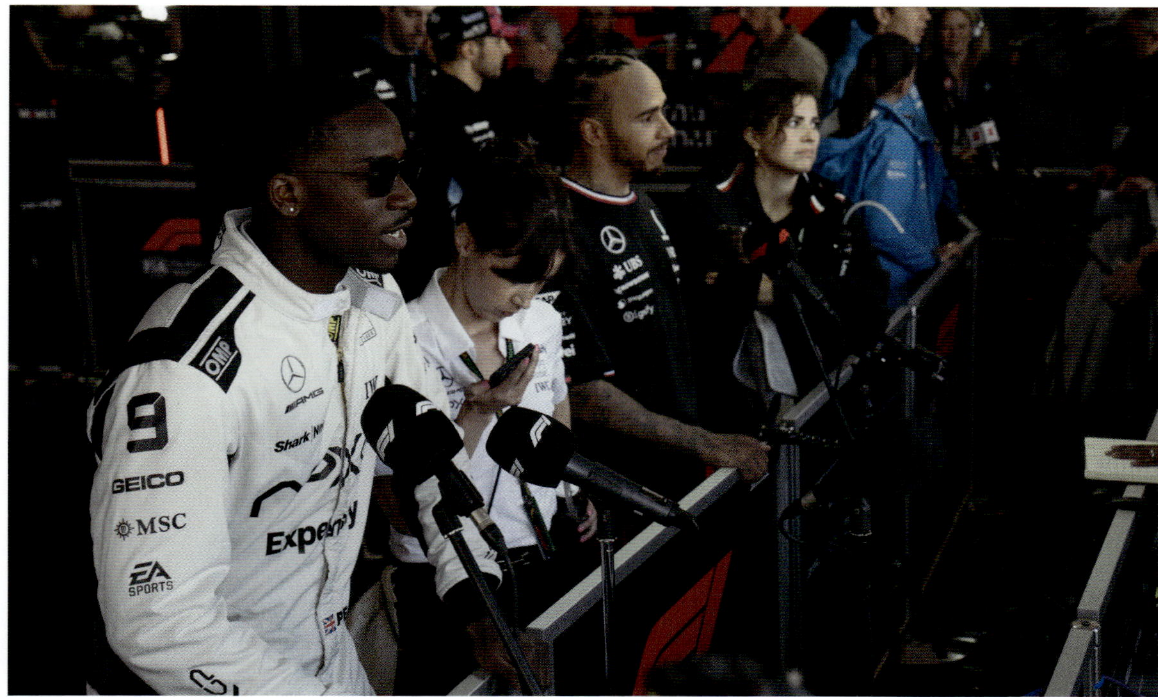

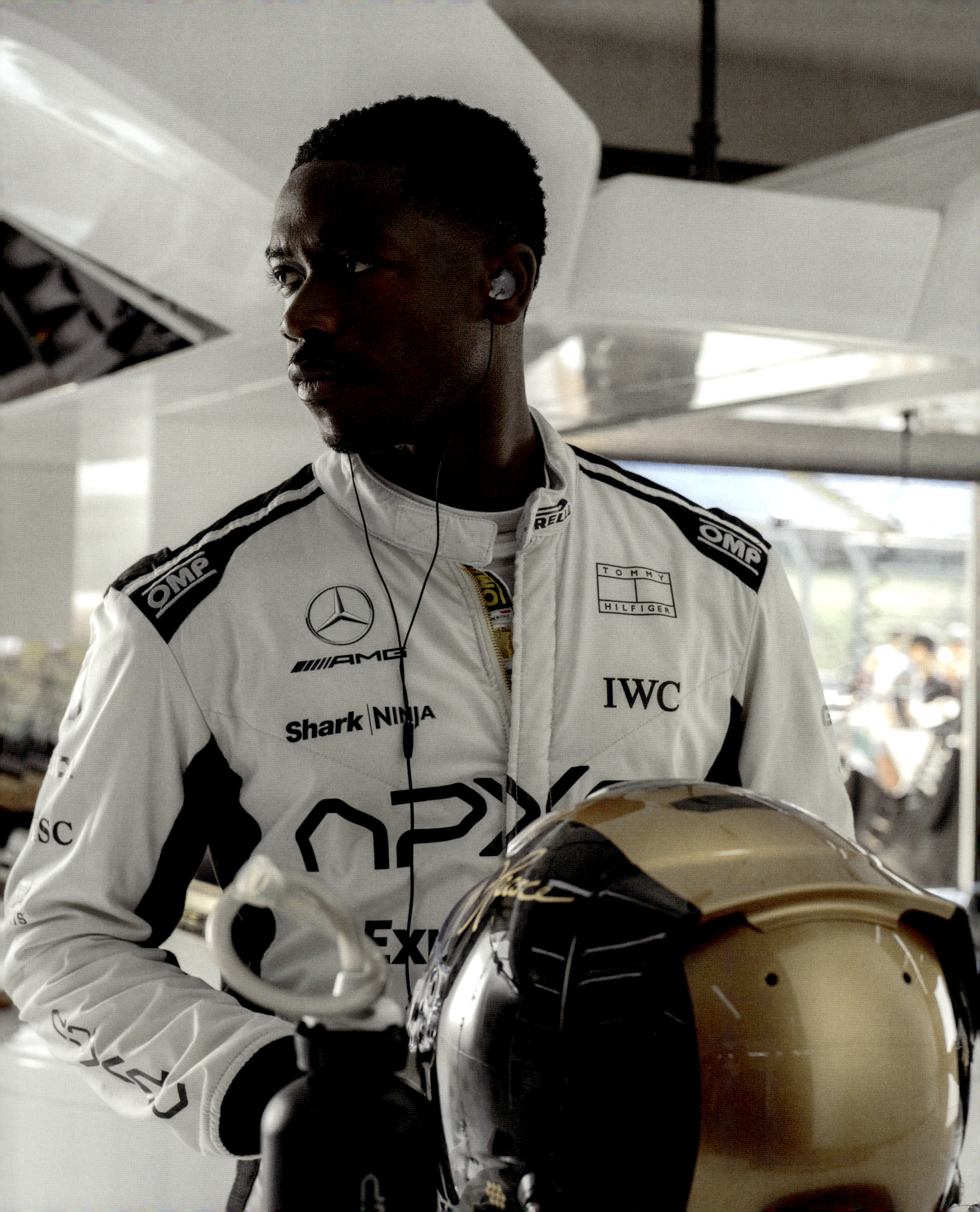

OMP
OMP
AMG
TOMMY
HILFIGER
IWC
Shark NINJA

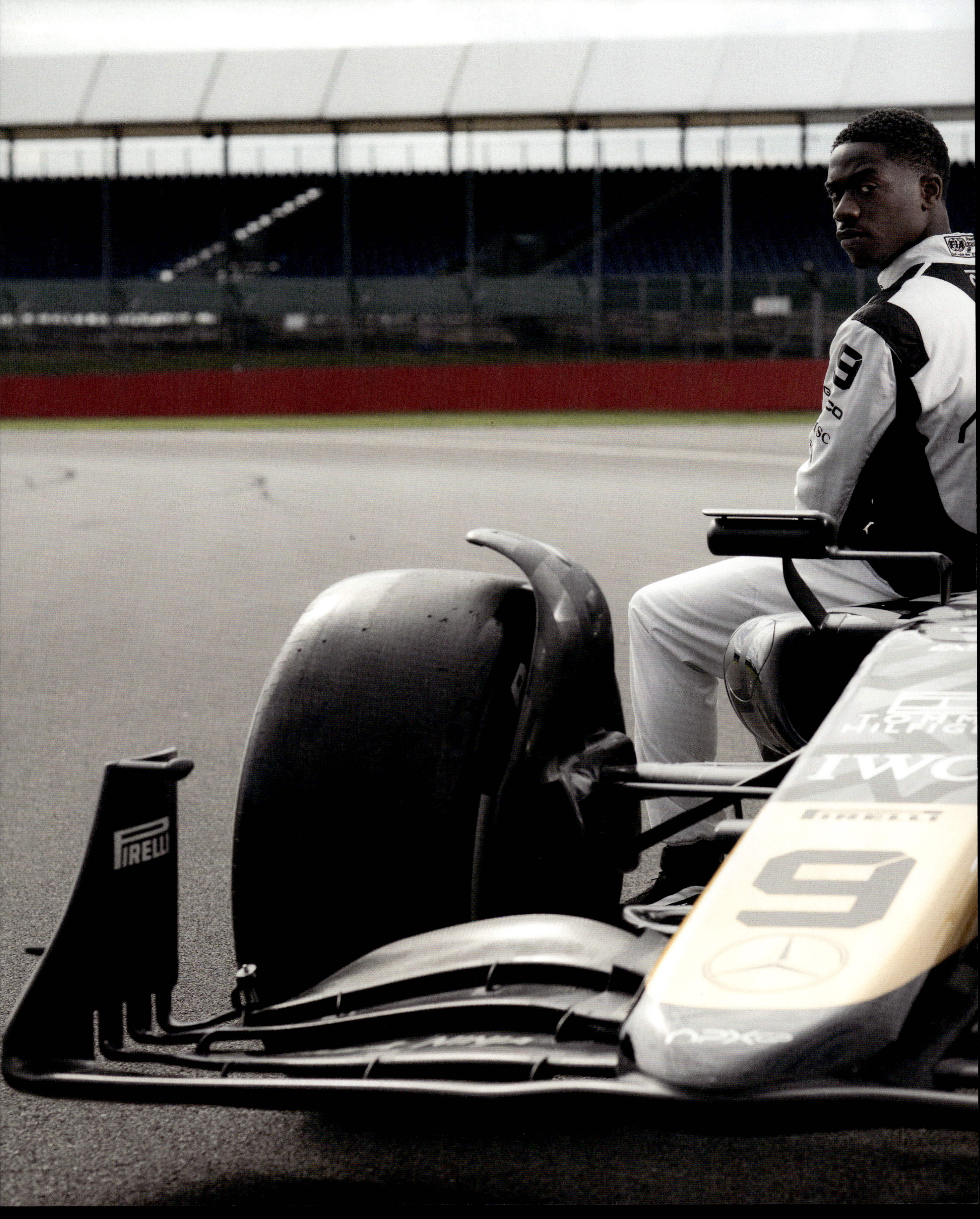

PIRELLI
9

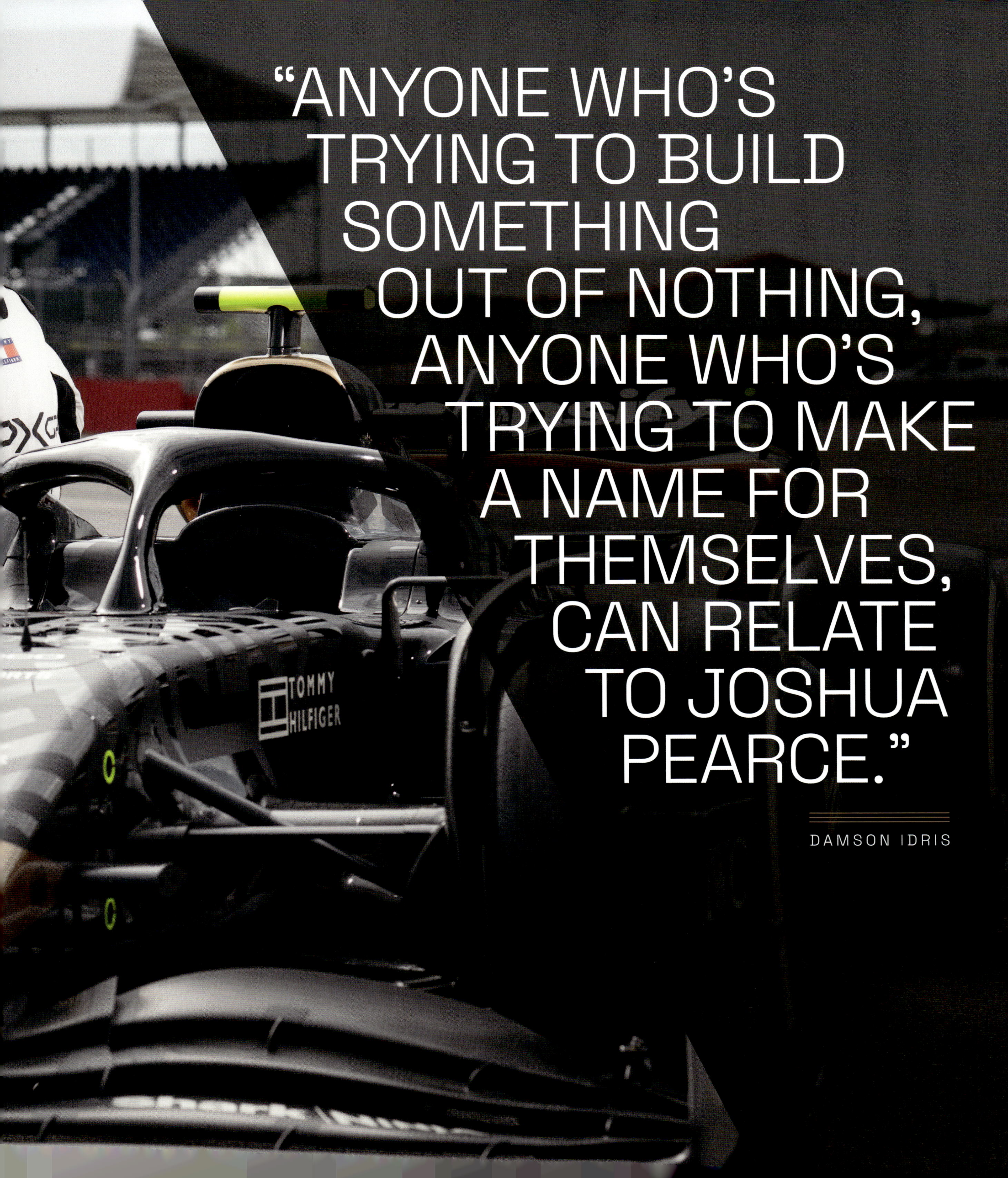
"ANYONE WHO'S TRYING TO BUILD SOMETHING OUT OF NOTHING, ANYONE WHO'S TRYING TO MAKE A NAME FOR THEMSELVES, CAN RELATE TO JOSHUA PEARCE."
DAMSON IDRIS
TOMMY HILFIGER

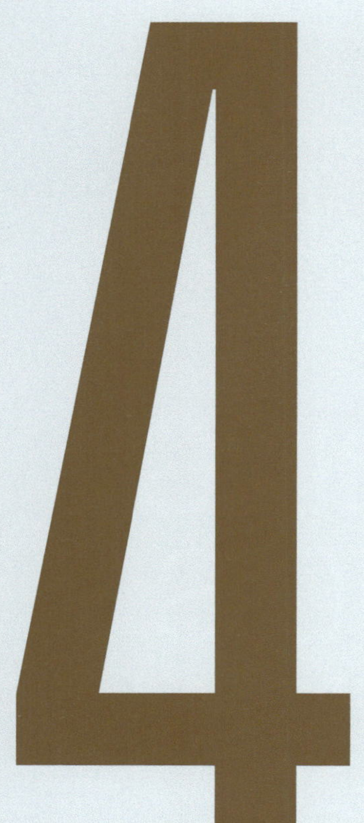

4 DESIGNING A TEAM

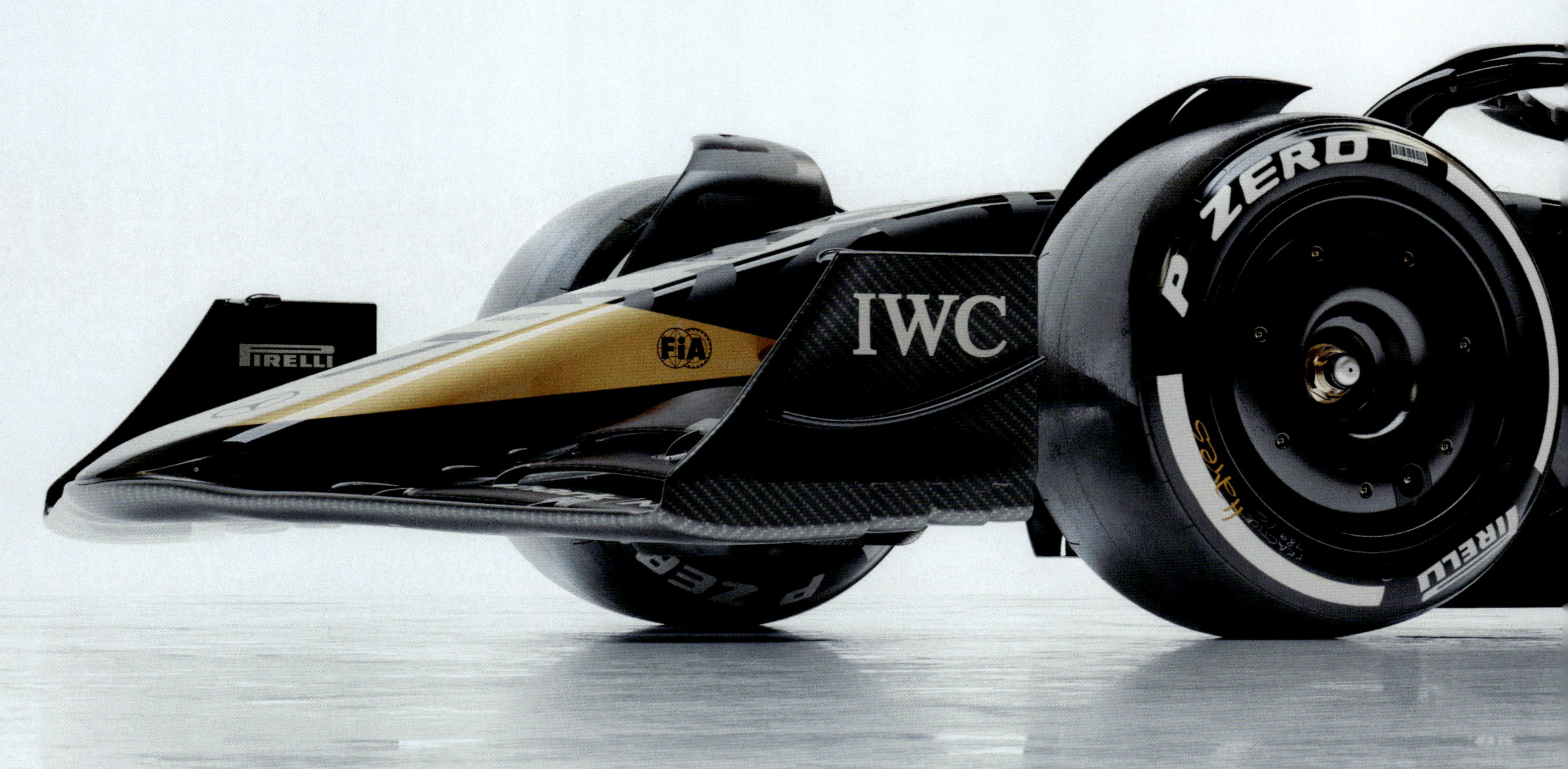

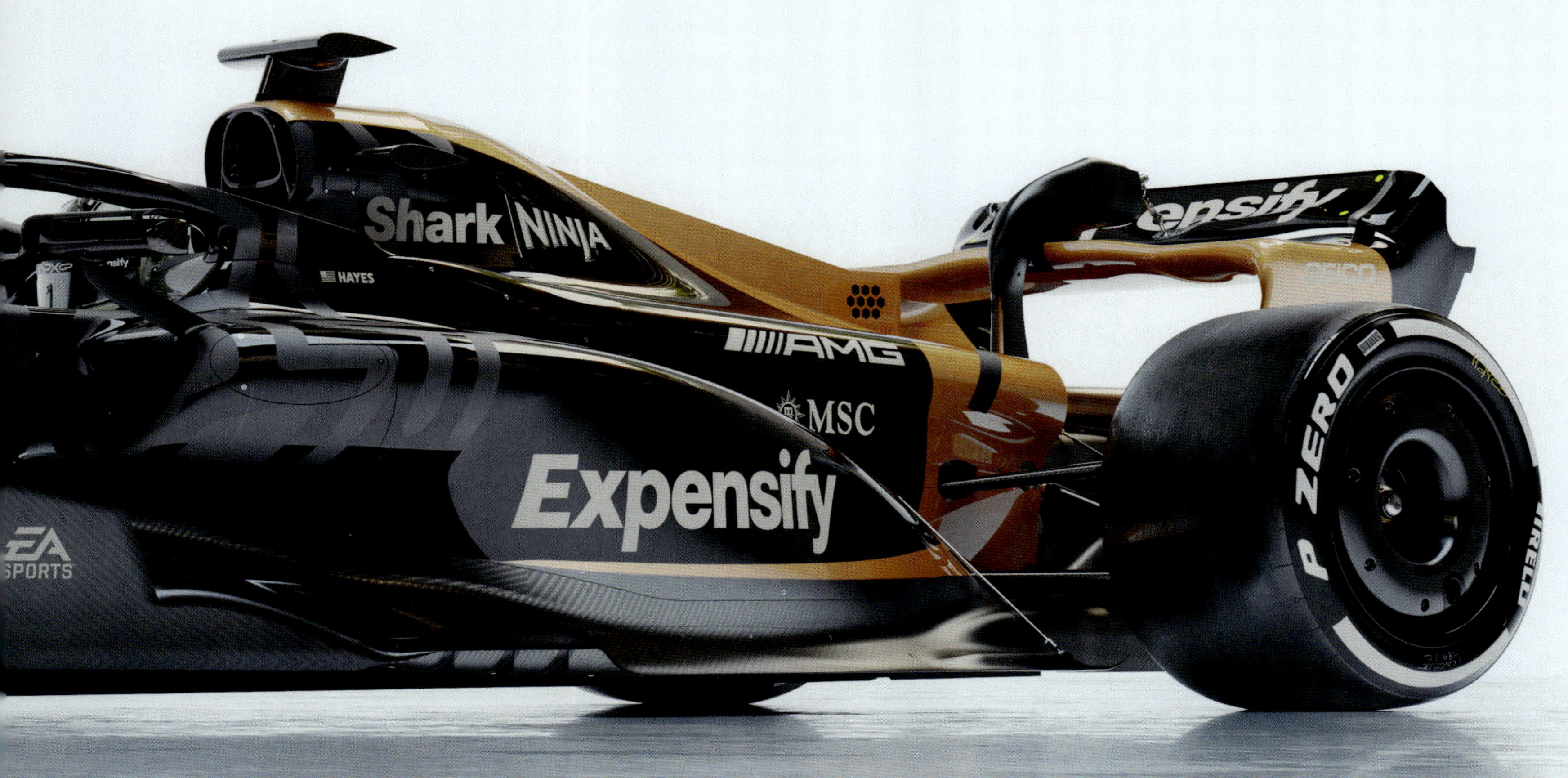
Shark NINJA
HAYES
AMG
MSC
Expensify
EA SPORTS
P ZERO

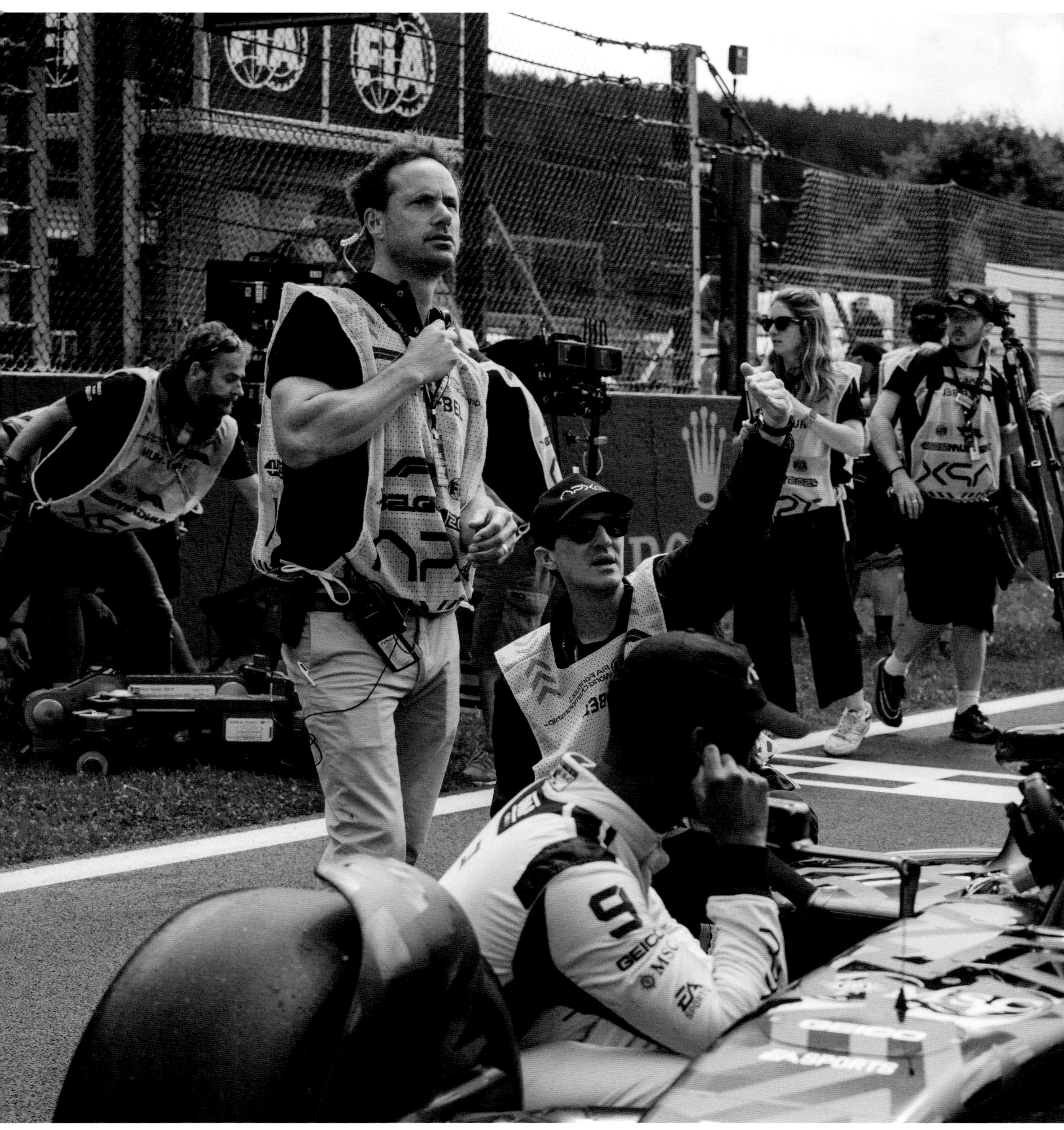

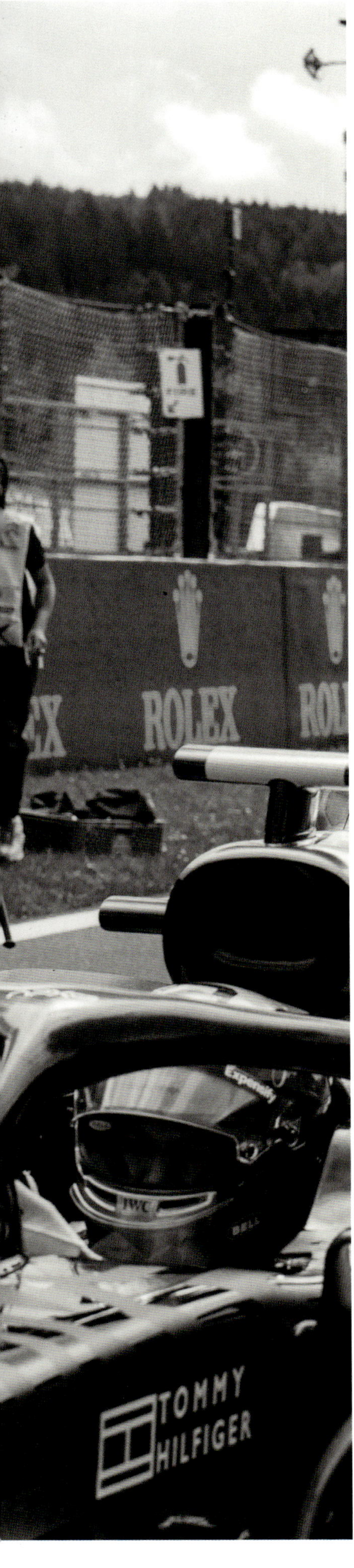

By December 2022, director Joseph Kosinski and producer Jerry Bruckheimer were beginning to piece together their core creative team, to be ready to start filming at the British Grand Prix in early July 2023. With cinematographer Claudio Miranda already attached, Daniel Lupi, a veteran line producer whose credits include *There Will Be Blood*, *Lincoln*, and *Killers of the Flower Moon*, joined as executive producer and started approaching crew in the U.K. to work on the film.

One of Lupi's first calls was to Toby Hefferman, a hugely experienced first assistant director and co-producer who had worked with Pitt on *Troy*, *World War Z*, and *Fury*, and whose credits include *Rogue One* and *The Batman*. But Hefferman had just finished Denis Villeneuve's *Dune: Part 2* and didn't want to jump straight into something new. Moreover, he wasn't a fan of Formula One. "The first thing I said was, 'This isn't for me. I've never seen an F1 race in my life. You should get the guy that did *Rush*. I'm not the car bloke. I've done car chases, but you should get somebody who's more of an expert, somebody who really likes F1.'" But Lupi wasn't to be discouraged and asked him to watch *Drive to Survive* over the Christmas break, then meet Kosinski, Bruckheimer, and himself in London in early January. "I watched *Drive to Survive* and was hooked," admits Hefferman. "It was more the politics than the driving, honestly, and how well it was put together. I took the interview, thinking it was exciting, but also super daunting."

As first assistant director, Hefferman would be the person responsible for the day-to-day operations of the production on set, acting as a liaison between the director and the rest of the crew, managing the schedule, planning each day's shooting schedule, and, in this case, liaising with Formula One and the FIA. "The real hero of all this is Toby," says Pitt. "Toby's one of the best I've ever seen. The guy is a master coordinator. I mean, he's a madman. Runs five miles every morning."

Lupi also put a call in to production designer Mark Tildesley, with whom he had worked on *Phantom Thread* and whose credits included *28 Days Later*, *The Banshees of Inisherin*, and *No Time to Die*. Tildesley wasn't a Formula One fan either, but, as with Hefferman, Lupi urged him to watch *Drive to Survive* before saying no. "I thought, *Oh my god, this is amazing. It's like* The Sopranos," laughs Tildesley of *Drive to Survive*. "These mafioso-style gangs, at each other's throats, trying to outdo each other in some super-sophisticated, high-end manner. There was clannism, secrecy, and intrigue, the business of not being able to reveal their inner secrets. And behind this is a massive sea of scientific development. So, it's not just racing, but science, money, and gamesmanship behind it. I thought, *Wow, this is a fascinating backdrop*."

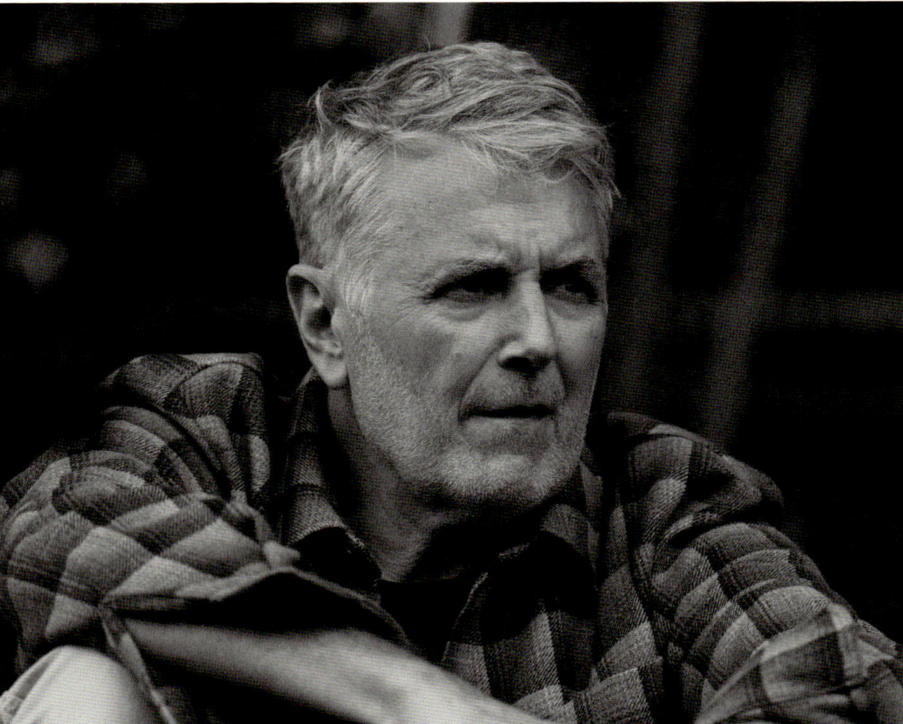

Opposite Page: Toby Hefferman, Joseph Kosinski, and Damson Idris prepare for the next scene at the Spa-Francorchamps track.

Left: Daniel Lupi, a veteran line producer, joined the *F1* production team in 2022.

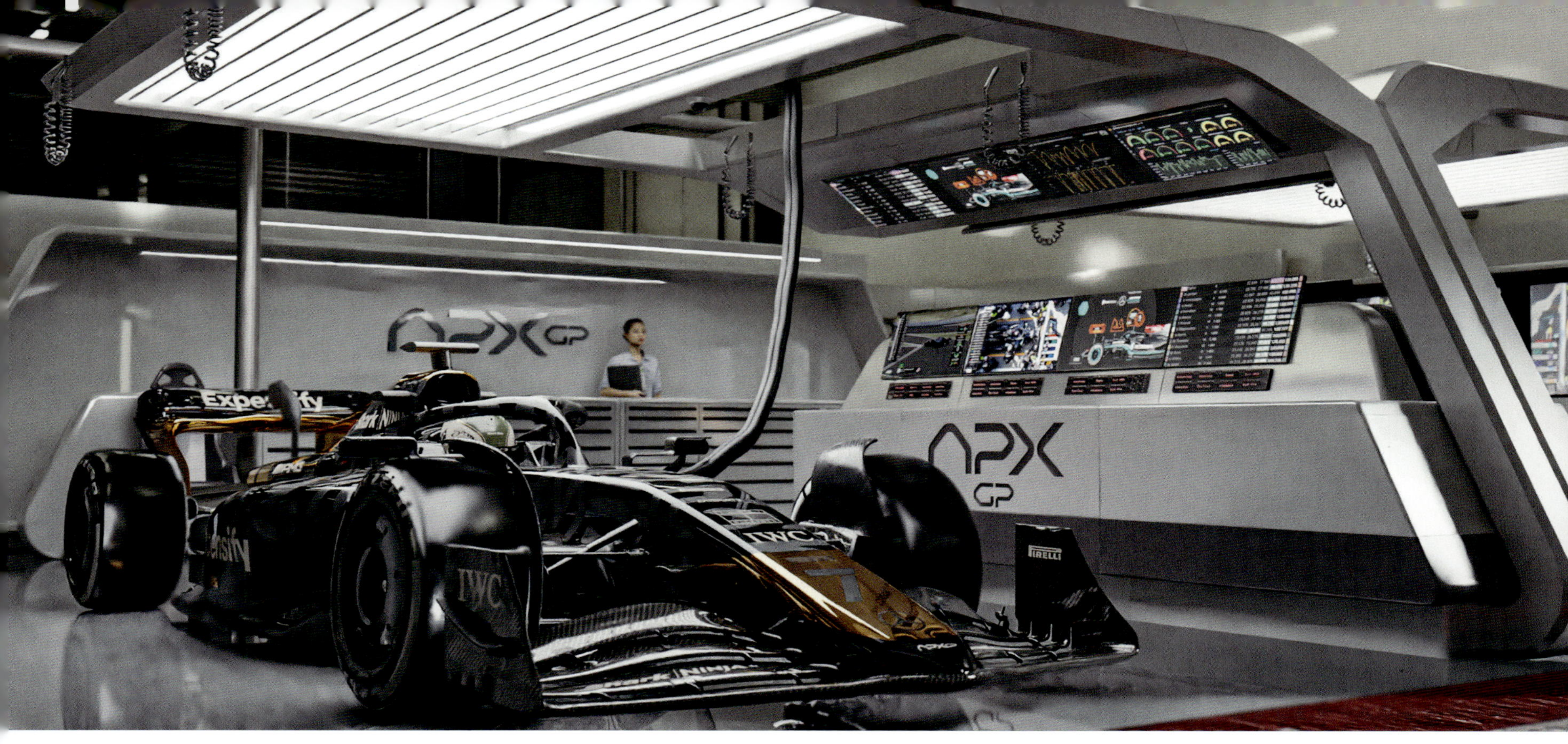

At this stage, the art department consisted of just Tildesley, supervising art director Ben Munro, concept artist Charlie Cobb, and researcher Camille Verhaeghe. Their first job was to oversee the design of APXGP. "You're building a team, building a look for the car, building a garage and a look for the drivers," says Tildesley. "We didn't go with a flamboyant new design for the costumes and car. We went for a classic black car, loosely based around the JPS [John Player Special] Lotus from the late seventies. Gold and black. Very slick. White driver suits. And a gleaming black car inside a white garage. Very monochrome in many ways."

While the APXGP car was being designed by Mercedes's Applied Science division, Kosinski drafted in German concept designer and automotive futurist Daniel Simon to work on its livery. "He was the first person I reached out to. He designed the Darkstar in *Top Gun*, along with Lockheed. He designed the bubble ship for *Oblivion*. He designed the light cycle for *Tron: Legacy*. He's an incredibly talented industrial designer."

Simon began his career at Volkswagen, before designing for clients such as Bugatti or SpaceX. Obsessed with all things racing, he also had experience in motorsport, penning liveries for the Formula One team HRT in 2011, and Lotus's Le Mans effort in 2012. "Whenever I work with Joe on a project, it doesn't feel like a movie. When we did *Top Gun*, I worked with Skunk Works, the infamous secret research shop of Lockheed Martin. When we worked on *Oblivion*, I was talking to a NASA space shuttle pilot about how it was to be in space. And here I'm swiping my security card at the gate of the Mercedes Formula One factory where Hamilton gets his car made."

Top Row: Concept art for the APXGP car and garage.

Bottom Right: Sketches of the APXGP car in a garage.

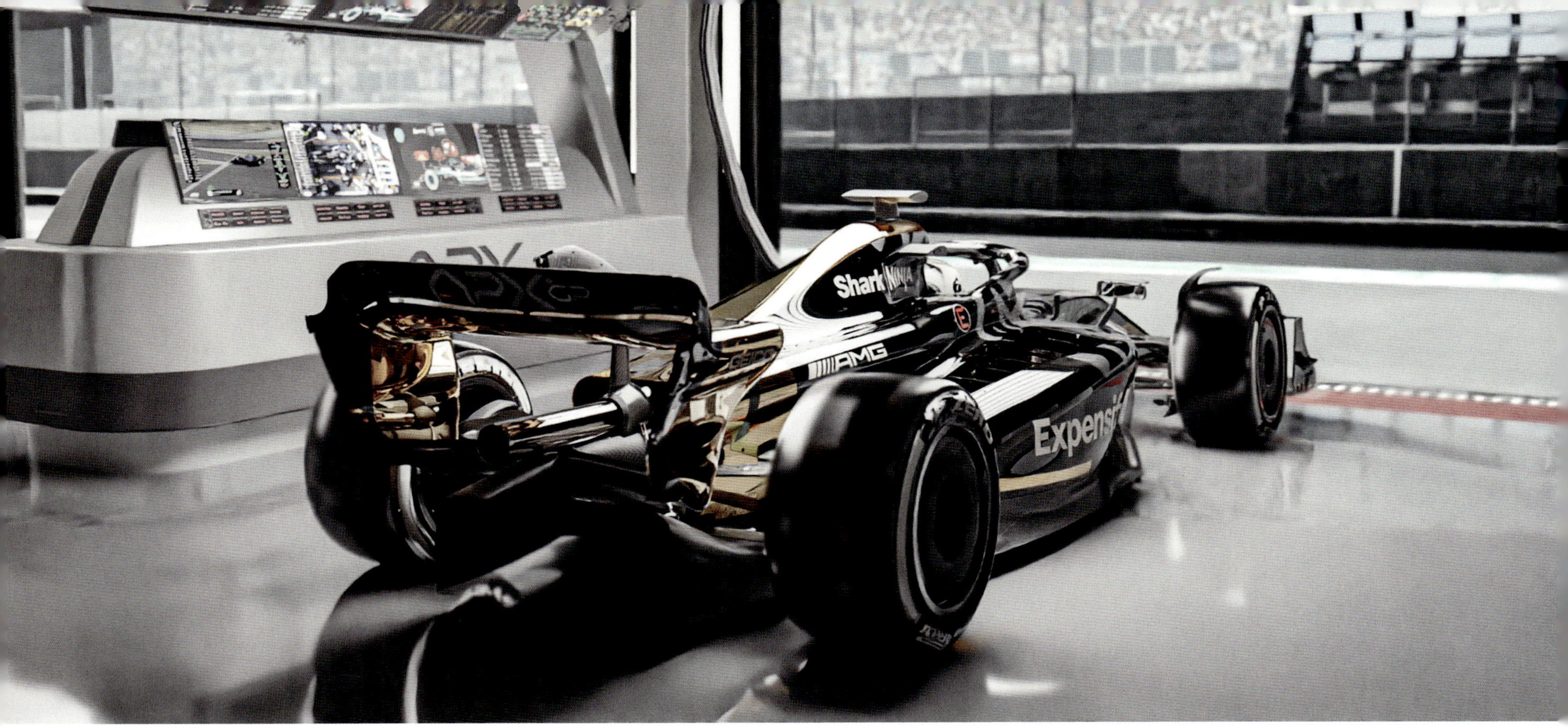

"We went for a classic black car, loosely based around the JPS [John Player Special] Lotus from the late seventies. Gold and black. Very slick."

MARK TILDESLEY

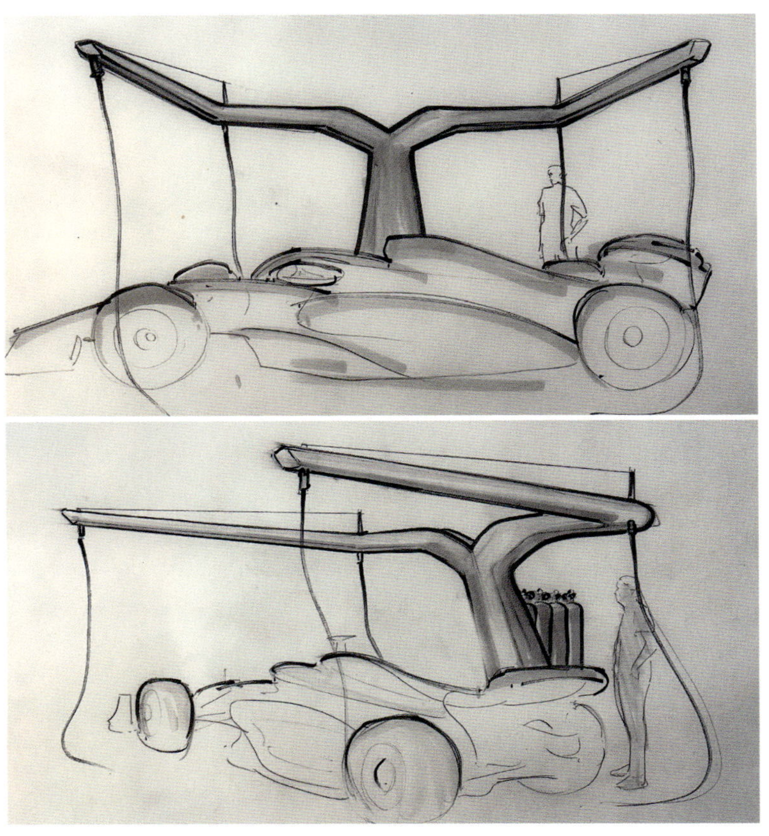

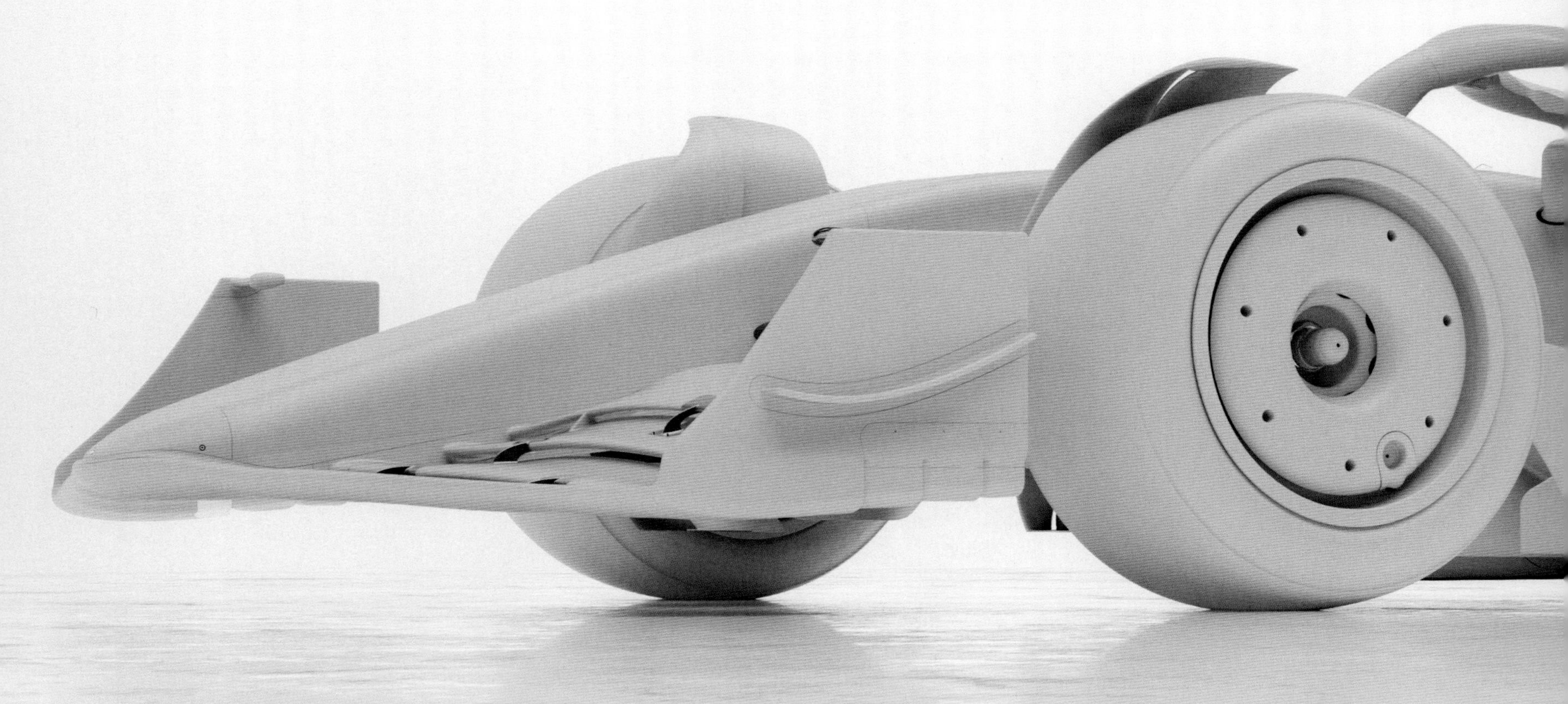

A rendering of the final APXGP model blending the livery design with the naked dataset.

Using 3D data from Mercedes's aerodynamic team, Simon started developing dozens of livery designs. "It was a blank canvas. Absolute creative freedom. But Joe is a very visual guy, so it became a question of, how does the car read in the field? Because certain colors are taken. How can we be different? My hope was we could do something that would excite viewers—but also F1 buffs—with a livery that might inspire teams to go a bit more abstract or creative. However, as sponsors came on board, it turned into a real F1 livery project. It felt no different than working for a real team."

Simon's early designs were based around Heineken or Rolex as APXGP's title sponsors. "We didn't have sponsors at the time, so it was just a matter of changing up some liveries," says Kosinski. The Heineken "sponsored car" was white, the Rolex one mostly green. But in the ten seconds of test footage that Kosinski had shown the teams at the Austin Grand Prix in 2022, the APXGP car was black, with a green Heineken logo.

"I think Joe latched onto that black. Bit of a menacing look. At that time, Mercedes was silver, so we were in stark contrast to the existing field. But then Mercedes decided to make a black car. And now we were not different anymore," says Simon, who suggested introducing a sheen to separate APXGP black from Mercedes black. "Matte and glossy are extraordinarily powerful design tools. Both blacks can shift into totally different colors depending on the light and angles, revealing invisible details. It's a great trick to give simple things a layer of complexity. So, I pitched to Joe that we could play with different sheens, which real teams can't because it's hard to multiply over many cars."

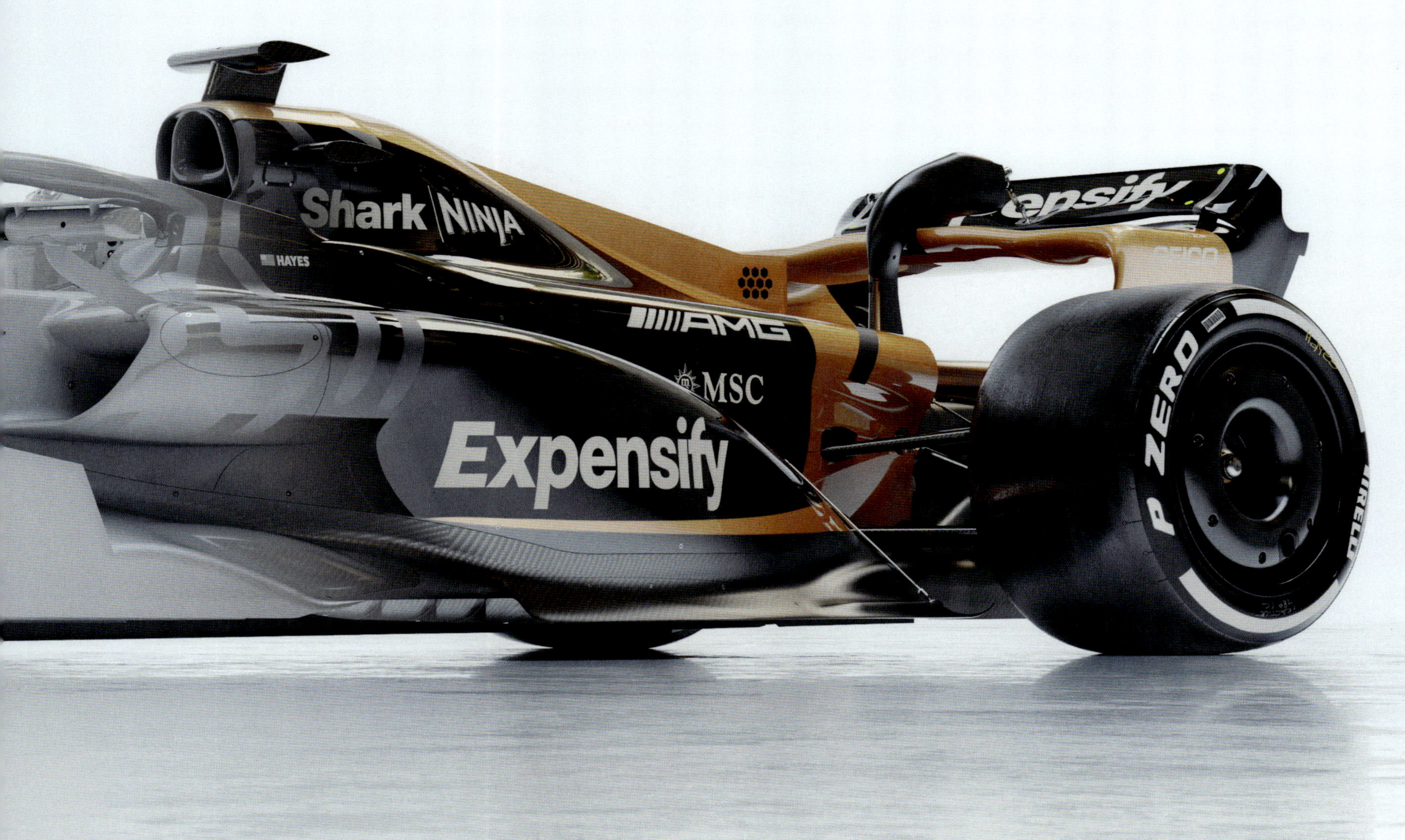

Simon was also keen on using a camouflage livery design, popular with teams during test sessions, to make it more difficult for their rivals to analyze their cars' aerodynamic design. "Most fans react positively and say they wish the teams would keep it for the season. Then the sponsors come in and say, 'We don't need to camouflage.'"

But Simon got his wish, with a black matte camo design at the front that fades out around the driver's head to become a glossy black at the back. "The pattern is custom. I drew it by hand. I was inspired by tribal face painting, with 'combat' or 'going to war' being [a] theme of the film."

But the design wasn't *all* black. The car has accents of gold. "That was Joe's idea, to add some exclusivity or high-end elegance. We didn't have any gold on the nose at first, which made us look like Mercedes from the front, so we added a gold strip in the front as well."

"Black and gold was something we felt would stand out," says Kosinski. "Particularly a gold nose in frontal shots. And because we were going to sell advertising on the car, I wanted to keep the palette to three colors, with the logos being off-white." But what gold? "We ran many tests, because Joe and I wanted a sparkly effect that looked deep and alive," says Simon, who spent a week at the Mercedes Formula One factory in Brackley, Northamptonshire, overseeing the entire paint process and application of the graphics. "We learned the gold we picked is something they would never use on a real Formula One car. It's too expensive. Too complicated to mix. And it's not easy to replicate. But Joe was for maximum effect and absolute beauty."

"They said that gold was one of the hardest things they've ever had to create," says Kosinski, "because that metallic fleck was something they had never done before."

In terms of black, Simon opted for the official Mercedes version. "We were so busy with the gold, we said, 'Nobody will know.' So, we picked standard black gloss as a base. The nose came in last; we started putting the car together without it. I only saw it completed on the last day."

For the matte camouflage on the front, Simon chose a vinyl covering. "To paint that would have taken months. With vinyl you can create a digital file, cut the shape, then peel a big sticker off. If teams don't have much budget, they use vinyl. A Formula One Mercedes is painted to perfection. We had to choose whether to paint our car or vinyl it; I chose a hybrid."

Opposite: Daniel Simon helps the Mercedes-AMG Petronas team add the camo livery to the body of the APXGP car.

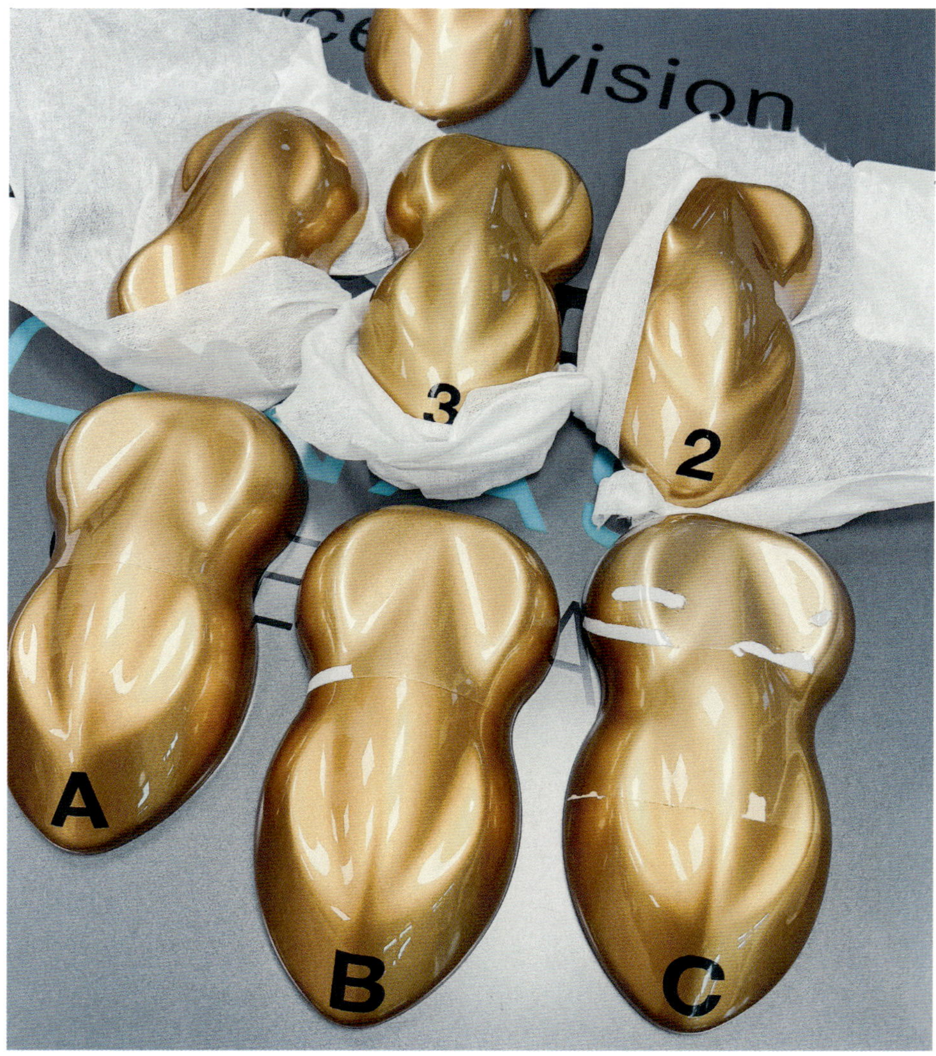

Right: Daniel Simon experimented with various automotive speed shapes to test different gold finishes to achieve maximum pearl and depth, an effect that is difficult to apply and impossible to repair if damaged.

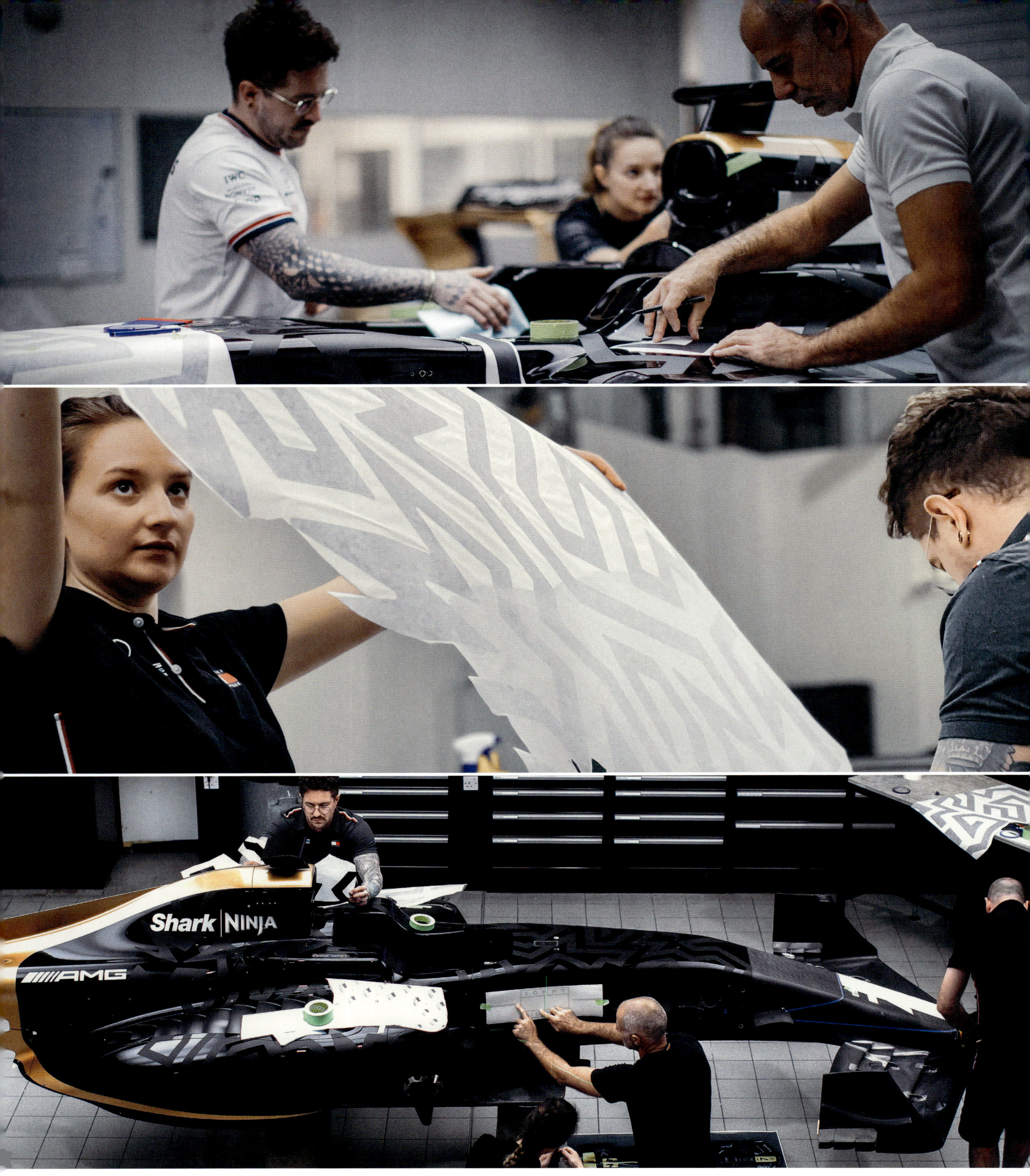
Shark NINJA
AMG

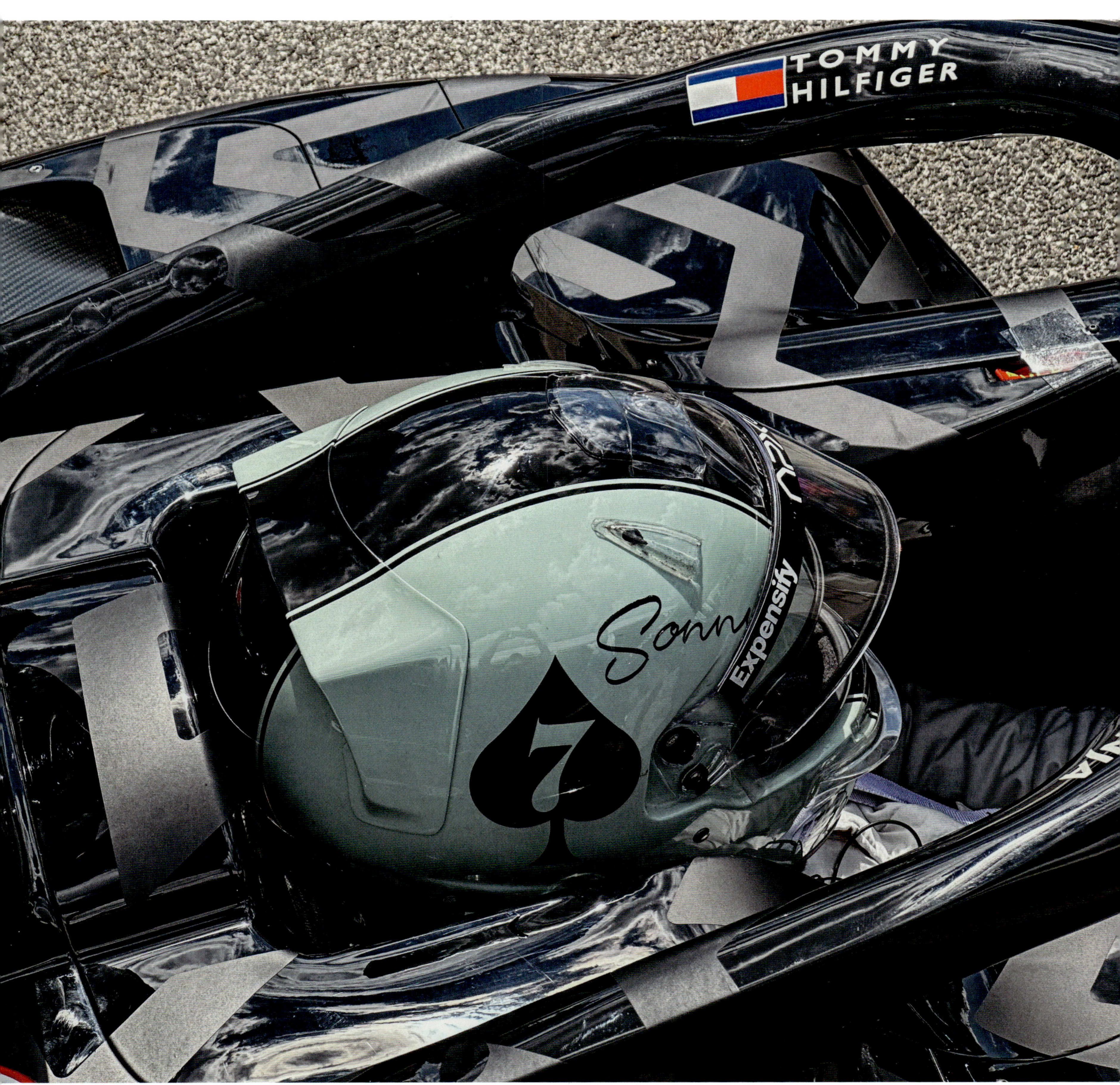

Above: Sonny's (Brad Pitt's) racing helmet features the lucky number 7 inside a black spade to represent his gambling history.

Right: Daniel Simon played with a variety of different APXGP logo designs in his sketchbook.

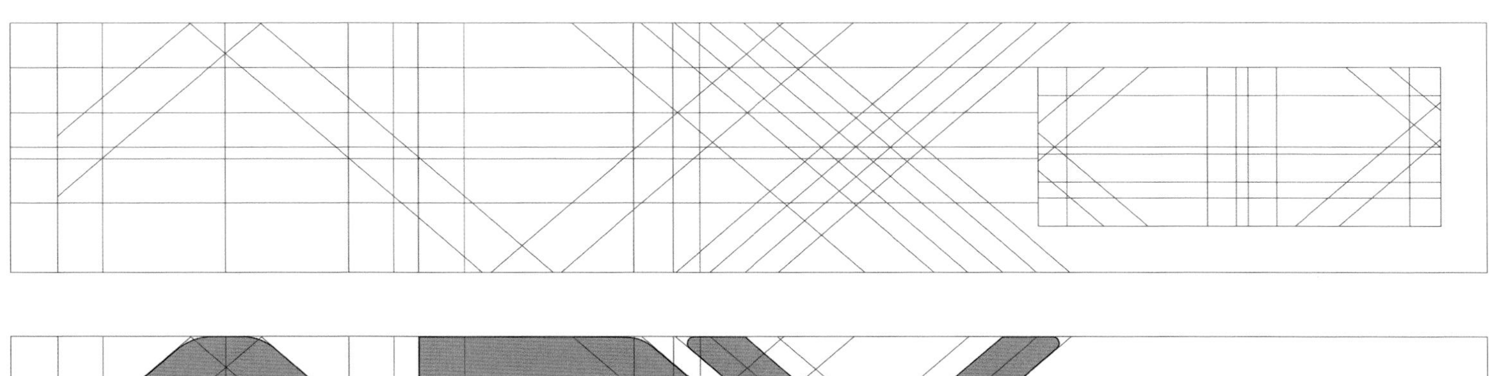

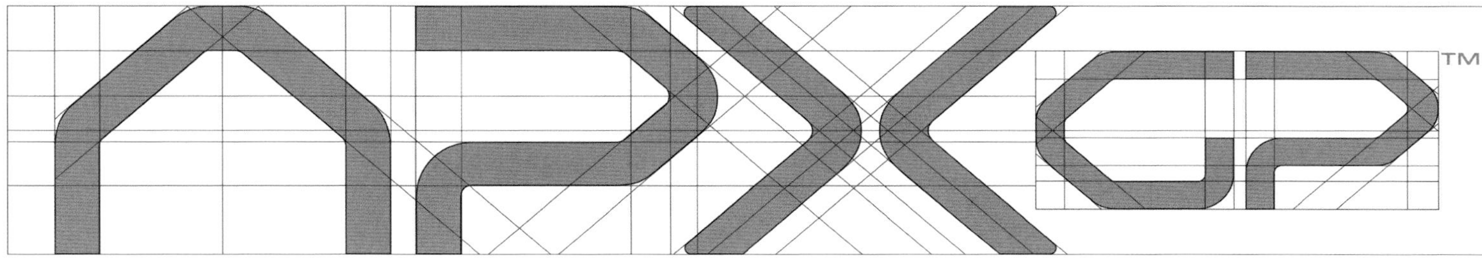

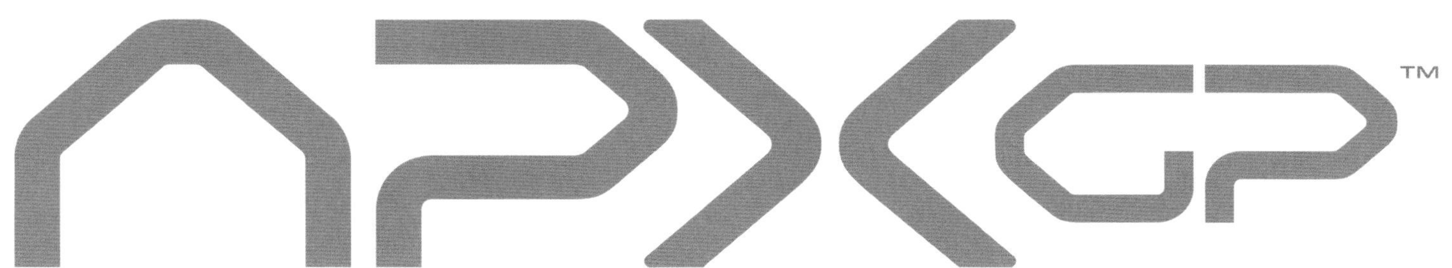

Picking numbers for the drivers was another challenge. "Formula One doesn't have standard numbers," says Simon, who custom-designed the font used on the APXGP cars. "We wanted single digits. But numbers belong to drivers. So, for example, we couldn't pick 44 because that's Lewis Hamilton's. Then it becomes, which numbers are available? You can only use a number two years after a driver 'retires' it."

Fortunately for Simon and APXGP, both 7 and 9 had been retired a few years earlier—Kimi Räikkönen had used 7 until retiring in 2021, while Marcus Ericsson used 9 from 2014 through 2018 before Nikita Mazepin took it for a spin in 2021—and were available, with Sonny taking 7 and Joshua 9.

Simon also designed the APXGP logo. "I needed a logo to put on the car and helmet, and there was none, so I proposed a few," says Simon. "As I designed the logo, I deleted the E, a creative way to make futuristic looking words, called devowelment. The result is a compact APX that works so well across the movie. I designed it painstakingly by hand, using a grid, lines, and circles. I thought of the letters as a track layout seen from above."

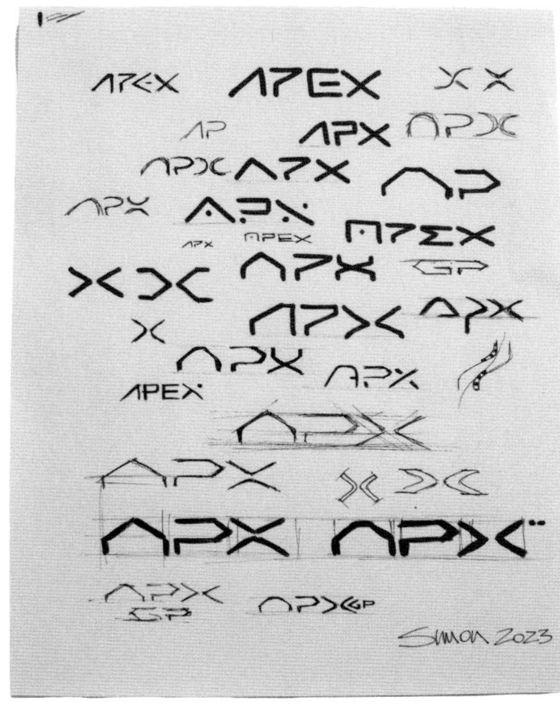

With Simon working on the livery design, Tildesley and his team turned their attention to the APXGP garage, which would house two cars, drivers, mechanics, and a pit crew. "At the beginning, the guidance or mandate we got from Joe was that we needed to provide something that sat within the real world," says Munro. "So, all the elements needed to be factually correct. We couldn't make anything up. When you look at all the other garages, there is a design element to them, but they are more about form follows function. Mark and Joe said, 'We should bring a bit of style to it as well.' Because it's not just about a car whizzing in and having its tires changed; it's going to be on the film a lot. There's going to be a lot of drama happening inside, and we're going to scrutinize it. So, it needed to be a stylish but invisible backdrop to the actors. Joe didn't want anything to stand out too much."

Given the car's black and gold livery, it made sense for the garage to be white. "Like a white cube for this black, mean machine to sit in the middle of," says Tildesley. "We went through various iterations, different colors, decorations, graphic lines, and ended up deciding white was best," adds Munro. "It had to play in daytime; it had to play at night."

"I wanted to keep it very neutral and clean, so the cars really popped in it," explains Kosinski. "The only garage I had been in at that point was Mercedes, and I remember someone said to me that if there's a scuff on the floor or a mark on a cabinet, Toto makes sure it's fixed immediately, and that he was proud the Mercedes bathrooms are the cleanest bathrooms on the grid. I liked that philosophy for *F1*, because it was very different to the Navy environment and the carrier I had just been shooting on for *Top Gun*. I also liked the idea of Sonny Hayes coming from the grit of Daytona, so when he shows up, it feels like a completely different world for him. I loved that contrast."

A major influence on the APXGP garage design was Spanish architect and structural engineer Santiago Calatrava, known for his bridges, railway stations, stadiums, and museums, whose sculptural forms often resemble living organisms. His works include New York's World Trade Center Oculus Transportation Hub, the Margaret Hunt Hill Bridge in Dallas, and the City of Arts and Sciences and Opera House in his hometown of Valencia. "I'm a huge fan," says Kosinski. "He influenced the design for *Oblivion* as well. The house in that film was influenced by the radio tower he did in Barcelona. And those flowing shapes of his you can see in the center console in the APXGP garage."

"His work is very white. It's smooth. It's clean lines. It's interesting shapes. That was our springboard, really. So, Mark and Charlie Cobb started sketching out ideas," says Munro. "Mark was very confident about it, as was Joe. I was a bit apprehensive, because bright white, historically, is quite a difficult thing to photograph. However, it wasn't *bright* white. It was off-white. And Claudio was also very much on board."

"It photographed beautifully," says Kosinski. "Claudio was involved in the design as well, especially the lighting, and he made it look beautiful, so it makes the cars look great. It was a very easy set to shoot in, and we shot all over that space. We have scenes in every nook and cranny. It was useful—and provided great cover for weather issues."

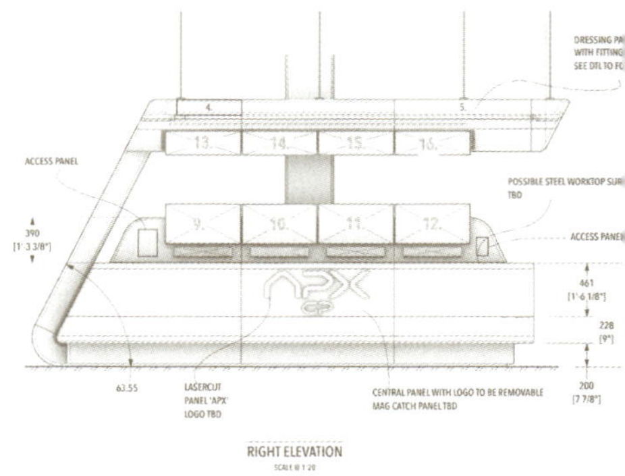

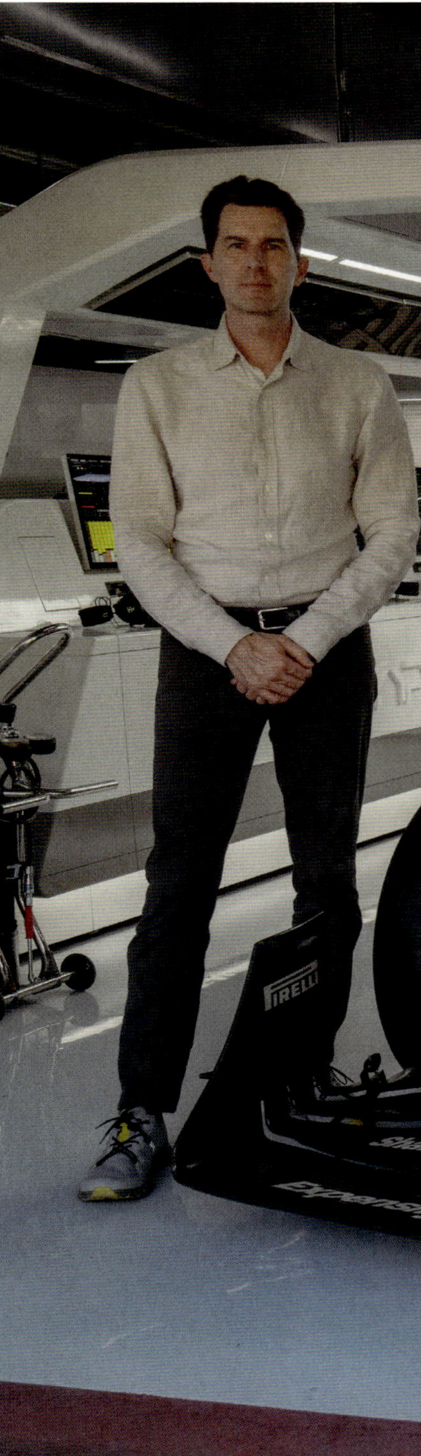

Right: Joseph Kosinski, Damson Idris, and Jerry Bruckheimer wait in the APXGP garage, which was influenced by Spanish architect and structural engineer Santiago Calatrava.

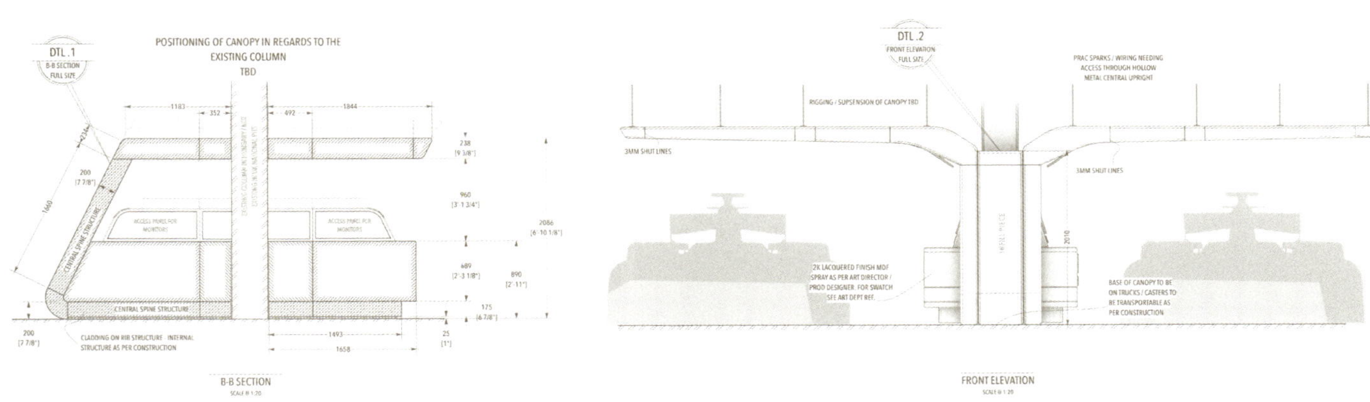

Left: The original blueprints for the construction of the APXGP garage.

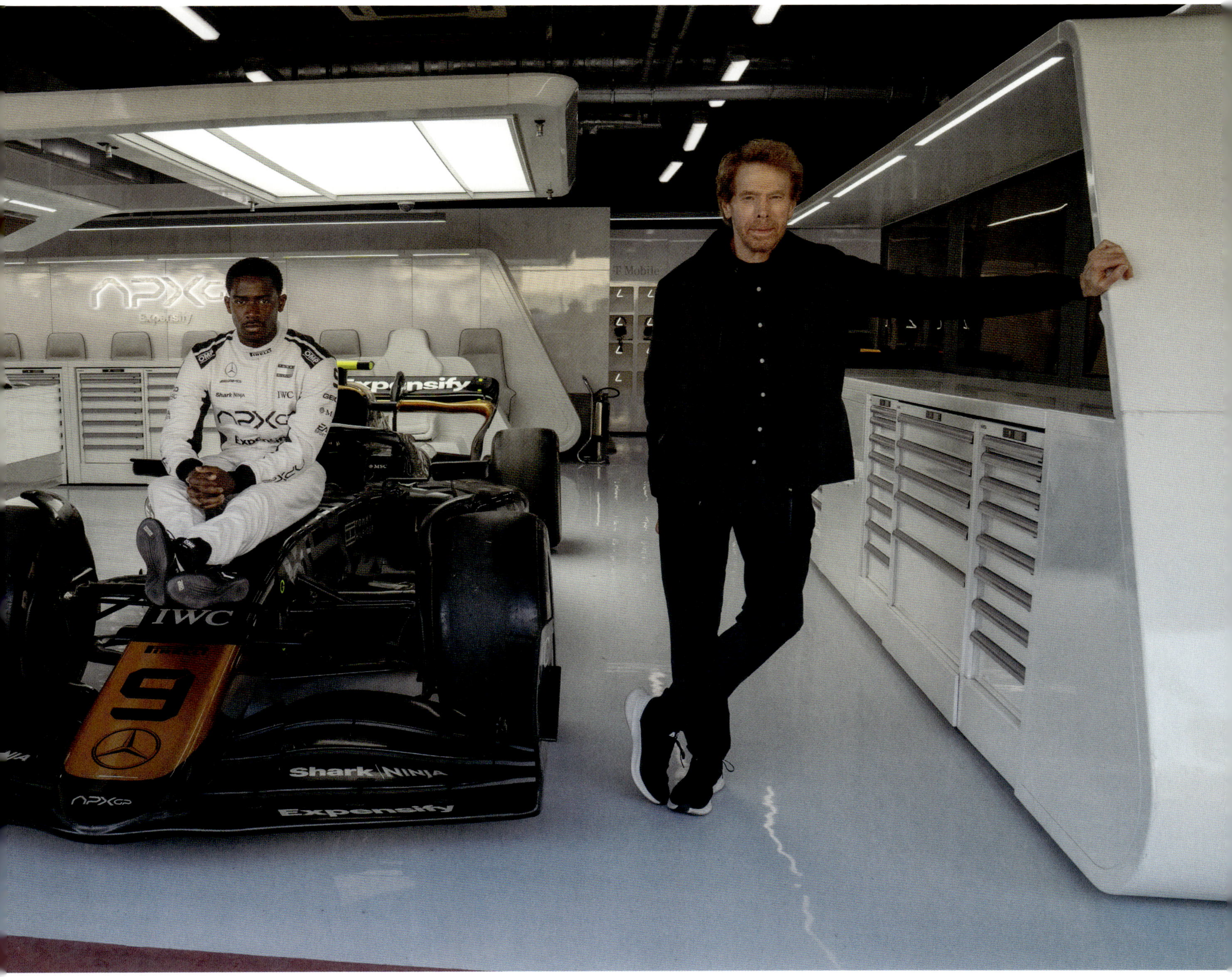

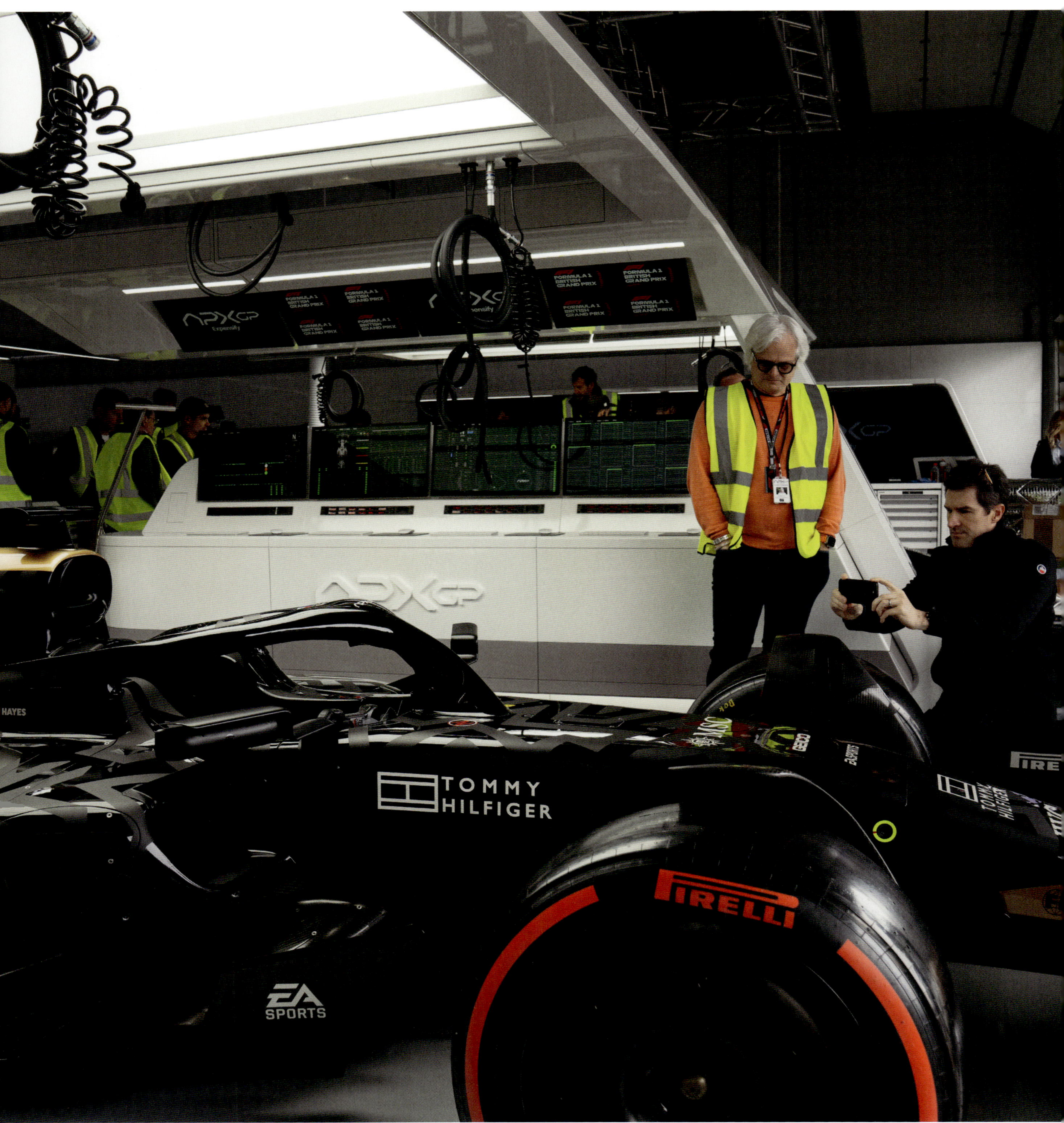
TOMMY
HILFIGER
PIRELLI
EA
SPORTS
HAYES

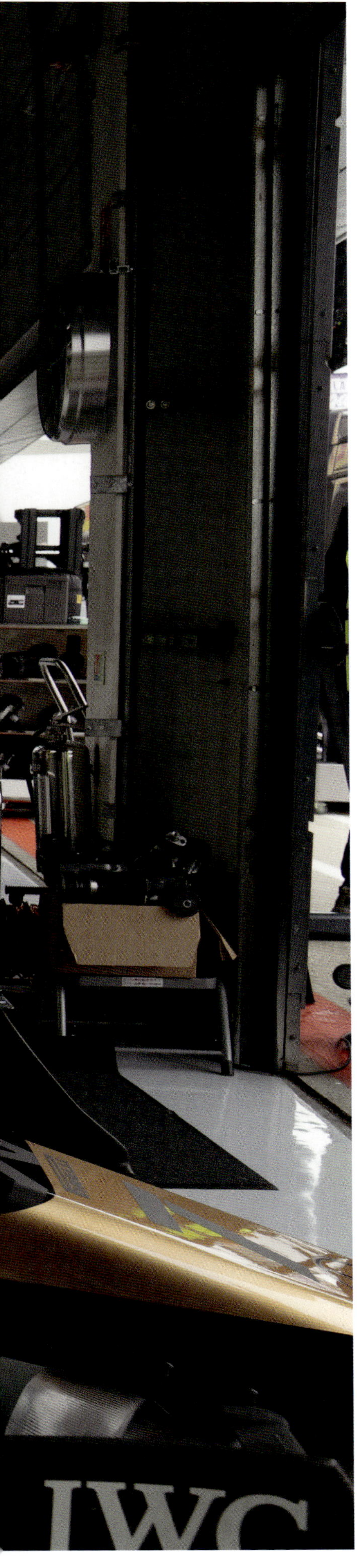

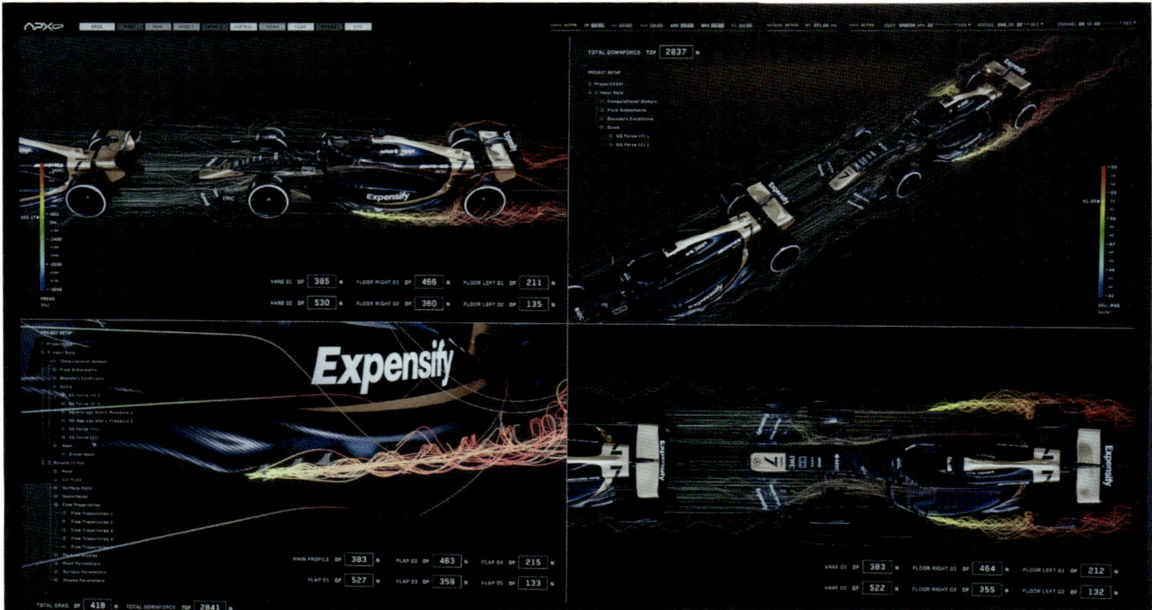

At the heart of the garage is a vast central console that contains the monitors on which telemetry—data fed to and from the cars wirelessly or via connecting cables, data pertaining to tire pressures, oil and water temperatures, the engine, brakes, etc.—is displayed and pored over by the engineers and drivers. "[On] either side of the console sit the cars, and the cars, being another character in the film, needed to be lit in a rather beautiful way," says Munro. "The design had to look good. It needed to accommodate people standing around it, it needed to have monitors, and it needed lighting. It was a process of trial and error, presenting stuff to Joe. We came up with this rather space age–looking central console, but not too out of keeping with what all the other teams did, because it had to serve all the same functions. It had all the correct elements."

"Mark did an amazing job, and unlike anything he had done before," says Kosinski. "There's a lot of research as to what's real, but then putting on his designer hat, it's about designing a completely unique identity for our team that looks different. He did an excellent job of making the APXGP garage and branding look and feel both authentic—when you walked into our garage, it felt like any other garage on the grid—but distinct from all the other teams on the grid."

From drawing board to completion took five months, with the art department, set decoration, and construction teams combining to create two garages at a cost of $400,000 each. "We didn't have the technology and space-age materials like F1, so we made them from aluminum frames clad with MDF, then sprayed with a two-part professional paint, which is baked in an oven, so it's as good as any painted surface you would buy from somewhere like Ikea," says Munro. But the APXGP garage couldn't just look good; it needed to be dismantled after every Grand Prix, then reassembled at the next, just like those of the other ten teams in the Formula One paddock. "The whole thing had to work as a beautiful set but also be functional."

Left: Joseph Kosinski and Claudio Miranda in the APXGP garage in front of the central console.

Above: Data from the APXGP cars could be seen directly on the garage's central console.

The art department also designed the various APXGP hospitality areas that would be in use at different Grand Prix, as well as the interiors of the motor homes, sometimes known as "treetops," on-site engineering trucks, or hospitality suites. These were built at Symmetry Studios in Buckinghamshire, where Apple TV+ previously shot its World War II show *Masters of the Air*, and included a strategy room, where all the pre-race meetings are held, and the driver-prep rooms. "We had advisors come in and make sure all the items we had were correct," says Munro of the latter spaces. "Massage table, somewhere they can sit and make notes. A bathroom. We had one room for Sonny and one for Joshua. Trek loaned us a bike, the only one in the world, as a bit of set dressing, which we included in Joshua's. Some drivers run the tracks. Sonny does. Joshua cycles them."

Away from the track, Tildesley was tasked with designing a headquarters and factory for APXGP, using a combination of existing real-life locations to piece it together. "We went to look at all the different factories, all the different wind tunnels and technology centers. It's like going to NASA. As someone who wasn't that keen on F1 initially, when you see the technology that goes on behind it, it's quite something."

"We wanted the APXGP HQ to be incredibly stylish, but we wanted to use real facilities, because they have all the correct ingredients in them," says Munro. "The challenge was that they all look very different, stylistically. But Mark was clever in bringing them all together, choosing certain spaces based on how the design elements of each building connected to the others."

The production shot in the Williams Racing wind tunnel at its factory in Grove, Oxfordshire, while the Mercedes-AMG Petronas F1 Team allowed filming to take place on its factory floor and race bay.

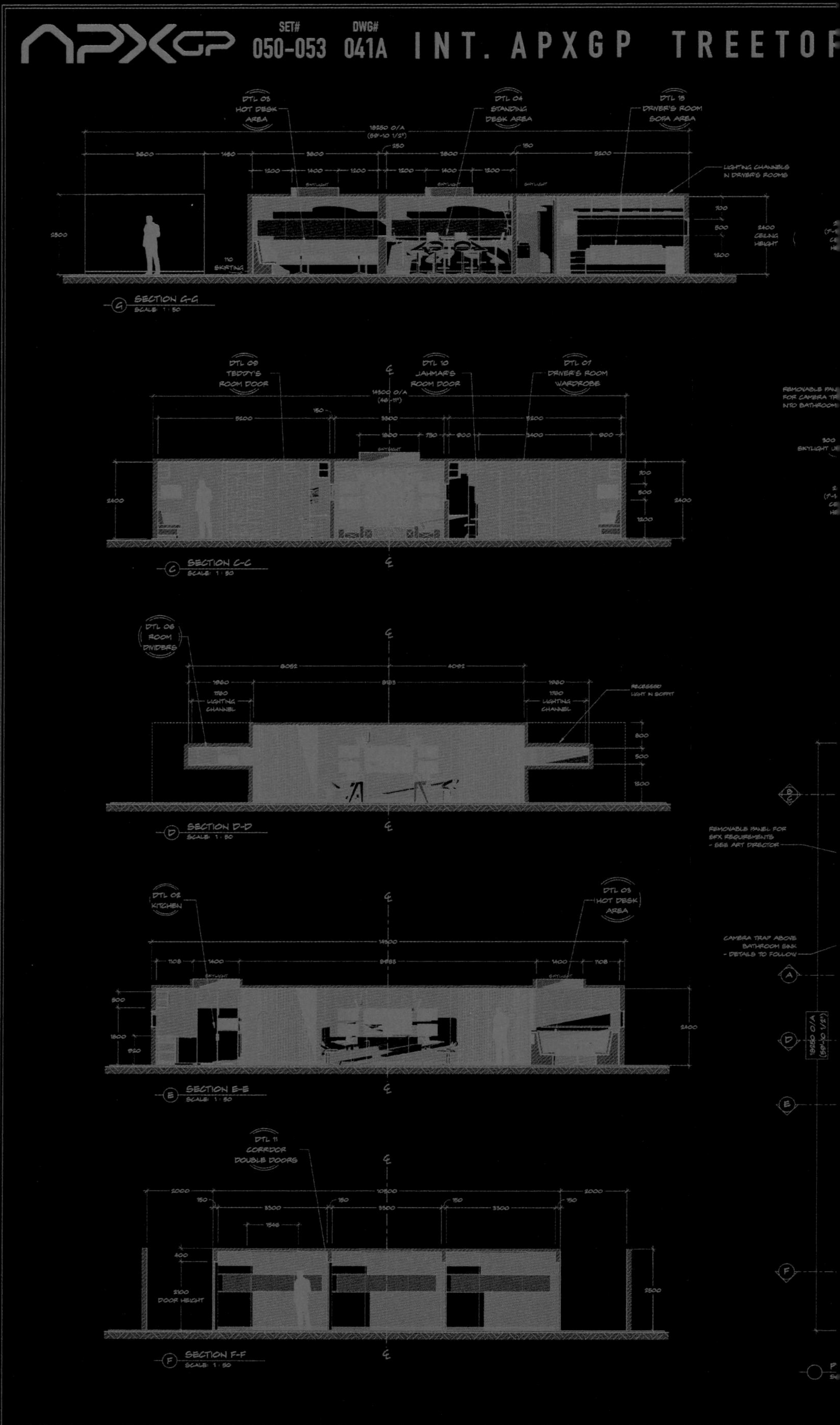

- PLAN & ELEVATIONS SYMMETRY STAGE 3 - SCALE 1:50 @ A0

DETAIL LIST

01 - CEILING PLAN
02 - KITCHEN
03 - HOT DESK AREA
04 - STANDING DESK AREA
05 - LOUNGE AREA
06 - ROOM DIVIDERS
07 - DRIVER'S ROOM WARDROBE
08 - DRIVER'S ROOM DESK
09 - TEDDY'S ROOM DOOR
10 - JAHMAR'S ROOM DOOR
11 - CORRIDOR DOUBLE DOORS
12 - WINDOWS TYPES 1-4
13 - BAMBOO PLANTER
14 - CENTRAL SEATING AREA
15 - DRIVER'S ROOM SOFA

Blueprints for the APXGP treetops, or the interiors of the motor homes.

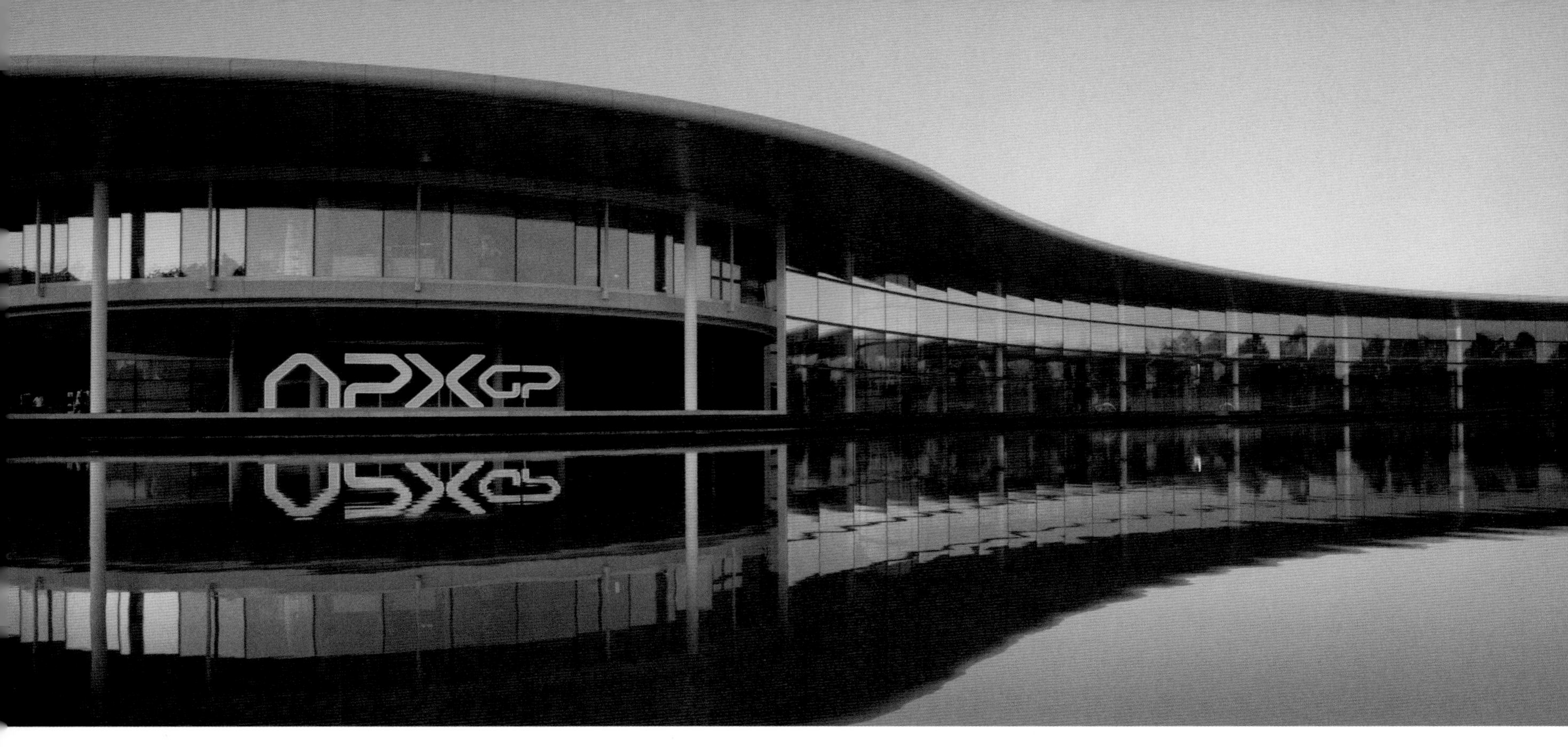

But the facility that proved the most adaptable (and best-looking) was the McLaren Technology Centre in Woking, Surrey, designed by Sir Norman Foster. "But we used it very carefully, so it wasn't so evident it was McLaren, because it's quite distinct," says Tildesley. "It has a nice modern space and values that were associated with our garage. The wonderful architecture of the building became the language for APXGP HQ."

The production used both the Technology Centre exterior and its main foyer. The latter is normally filled with McLaren Formula One cars from the company's illustrious history. "We had to clear them all out, which took a bit of convincing," reveals Munro. In their place, the art department put a lightbox featuring Sonny Hayes and Joshua Pearce together with one of the APXGP cars.

Kosinski liked the McLaren Technology Centre not just because of the steel-and-glass building's futuristic architecture, but because it had a lake on its grounds. "All of which would be very difficult to replicate on the stage. And Joe wanted to reduce as much as possible the amount of green screen by filming in real spaces and real locations," says Munro. Kosinski particularly wanted a connection between the inside and outside for two scenes set at APXGP HQ, one with team owner Ruben Cervantes in his office, another with Joshua in the gym. In the latter, Joshua would look out to see Sonny running around the lake.

"Joe wanted to reduce as much as possible the amount of green screen by filming in real spaces and real locations."

BEN MUNRO

Top Left: To transform McLaren Technology Centre into the APXGP headquarters, the production crew added a logo to the exterior.

Top Right: A lightbox image of Joshua (Damson Idris) and Sonny (Brad Pitt) on the back wall, as well as an APXGP race car display, completes the look.

Bottom Right: An interior room at the APXGP headquarters.

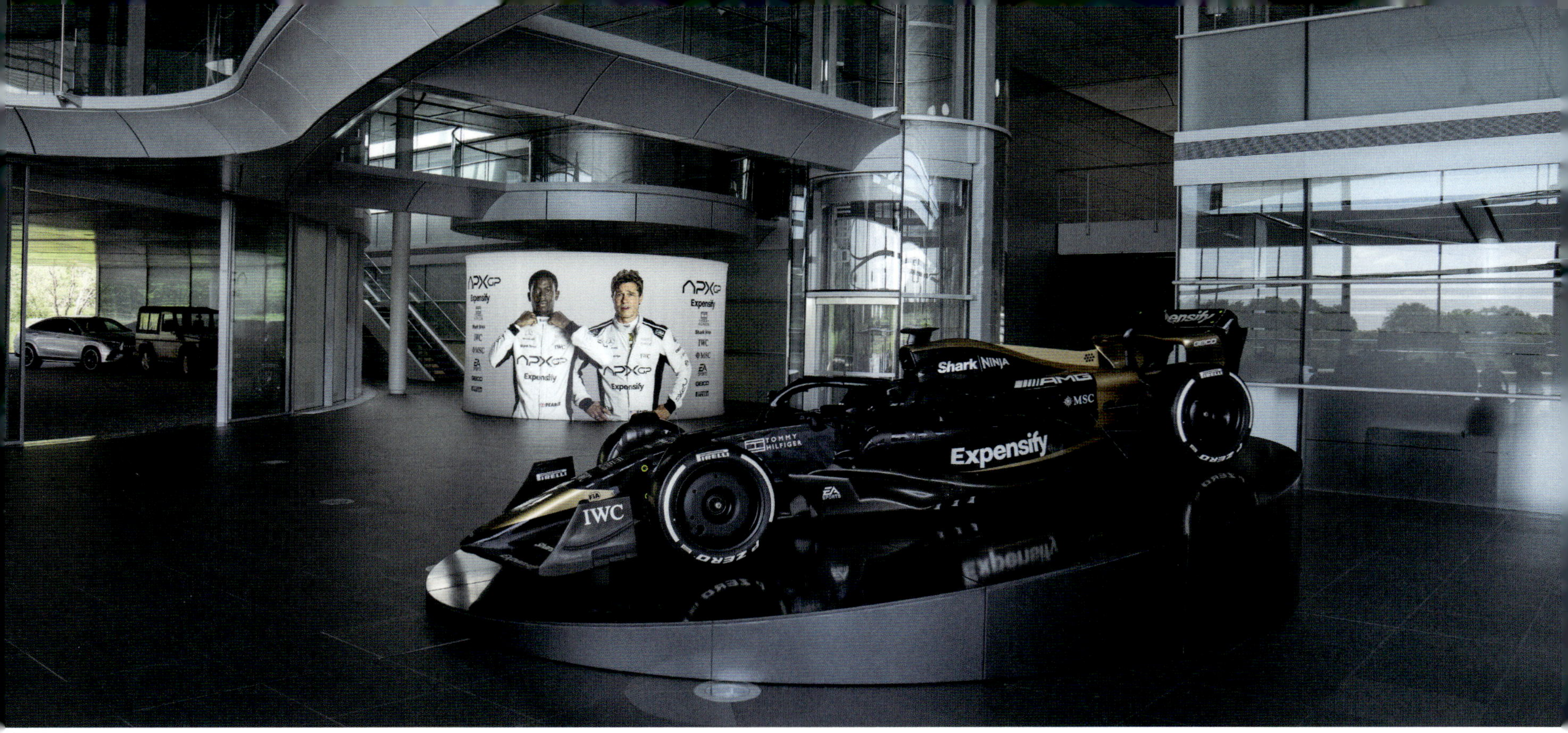

It had been decided to build both the gym and Ruben's office inside the McLaren canteen, as its large, curved windows offered the best views of the lake. Concept artist Charlie Cobb designed both sets with false ceilings as well as walls. But when McLaren realized how long the canteen would be out of commission, it said no to filming, leaving the production no choice but to build both sets onstage and create an exterior space by opening its doors.

However, neither set had been built when the actors' strike shut the main unit down. By the time the strike was resolved and the film geared up once again, Tildesley had moved on to another film, with Munro promoted to production designer. But Kosinski still wanted to shoot at McLaren, so Munro revisited the idea of using the canteen. McLaren agreed on the condition that the filmmakers be in and out in two days. "My initial response was, that's a challenge," says Munro, "and we'll have to make some huge compromises."

One of which was building both sets without ceilings to minimize construction time. The other was that they would need to build one set, then revamp it into the other set overnight. But there were some who were concerned that the view out the window would be the same in both scenes. Munro was insistent it would work. "I said, 'If you read the script, the gym scene is a series of montage beats. Ruben's office is a regular scene. I'm confident you won't tell the difference.' Joe agreed and filmed it to look like two different spaces."

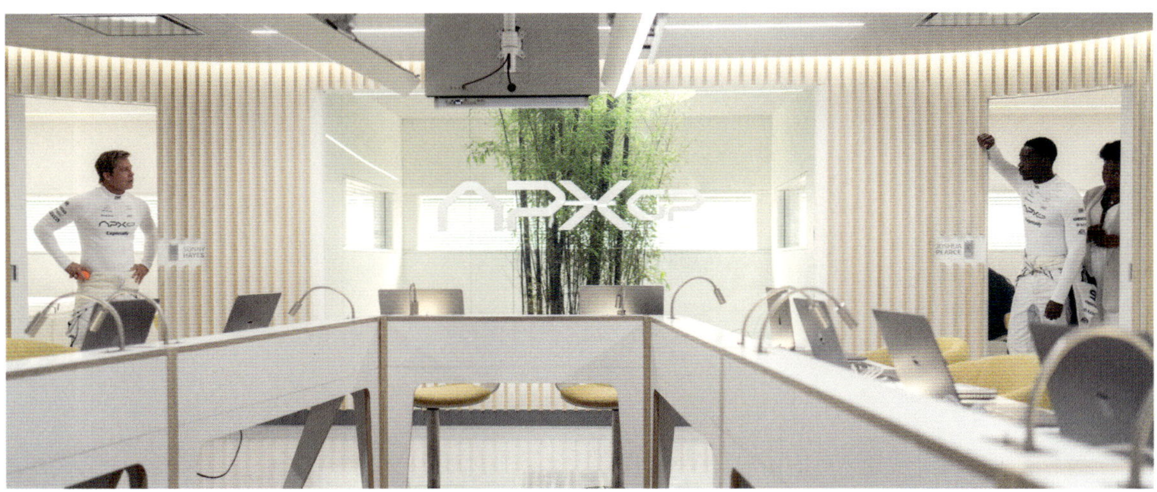

The production hit another snag when Munro discovered the land outside the canteen was being flattened and turned into a parking lot. He went back to McLaren and realized that not all of the views out the canteen windows would be affected, so suggested shifting the sets to a different part of the space. The gym set was built first. "That was the more complicated installation, because we had to put rubber flooring in, and it was easier to rip it out and dress Ruben's office than vice versa. Then, overnight, we turned it into Ruben's office."

The centerpiece of Ruben's office is Ayrton Senna's 1990 World Championship–winning MP4/5B, which is displayed in a glass box behind his desk. "Ex F1 boss Bernie Ecclestone famously had a real F1 car in glass behind his desk, and I was inspired by that," explains Kosinski. "I thought Ruben as an F1 team owner would want the ultimate office decoration. What was better than the car of the world champion when he was racing back in the day? So, we got McLaren to lend us Senna's actual car to put in glass behind Ruben's desk."

"That was another great idea Joe had," says Tildesley.

But because of the time needed to move Senna's McLaren into position, it was decided to build the car and glass box into the gym set, hidden behind paneling during the first scene. When the set was revamped overnight, the paneling was removed and the car revealed. Elsewhere in Ruben's office are trophies from his supposed racing career. "Look very closely at the trophies and you'll see they were engraved with his name for the various races he won during the nineties," says Kosinski. "Javier was eyeballing those, hoping to get one as a wrap gift."

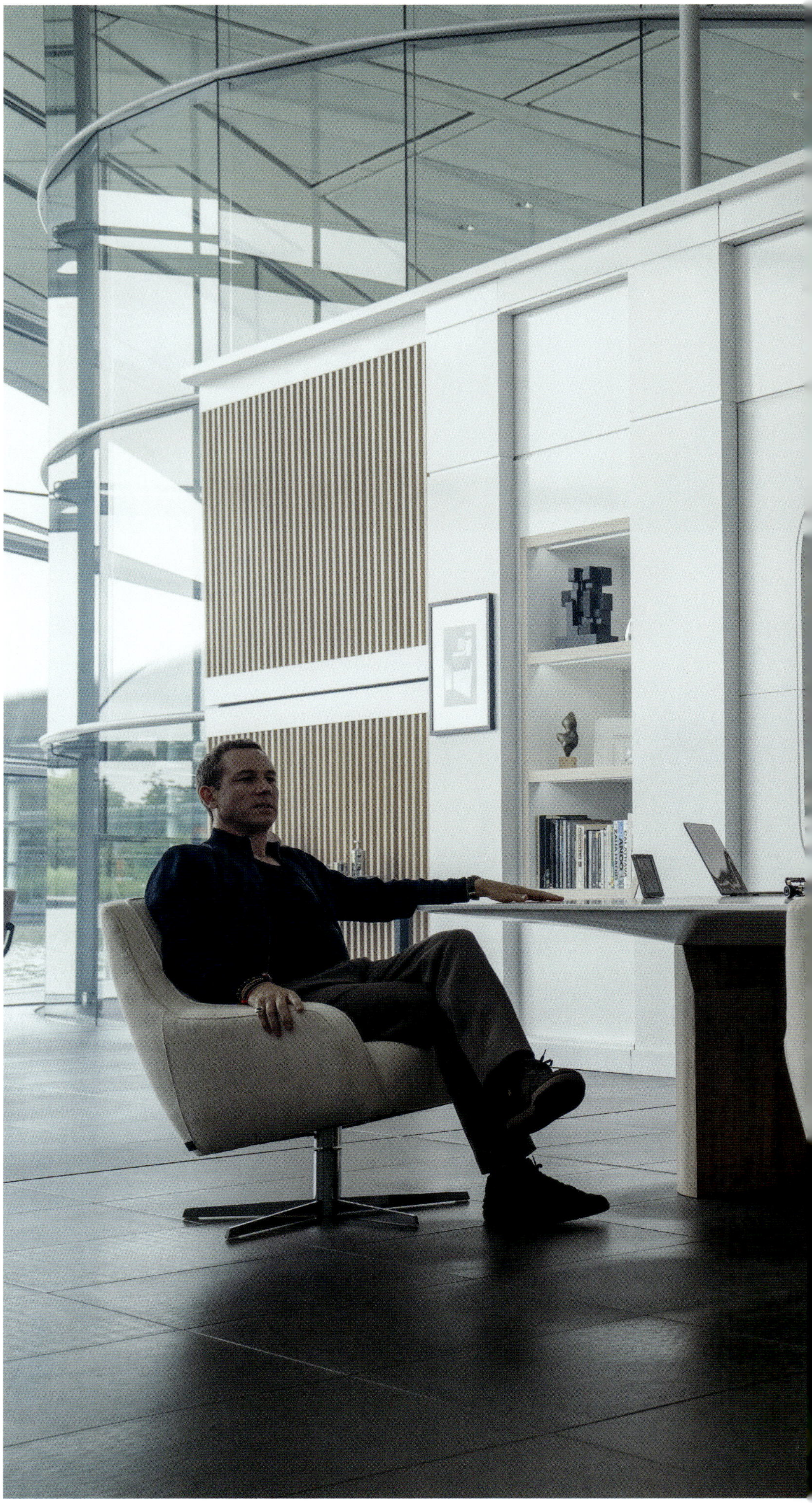

Ruben (Javier Bardem) chats with Banning (Tobias Menzies) in his office, with Ayrton Senna's McLaren MP4/5B display behind his desk.

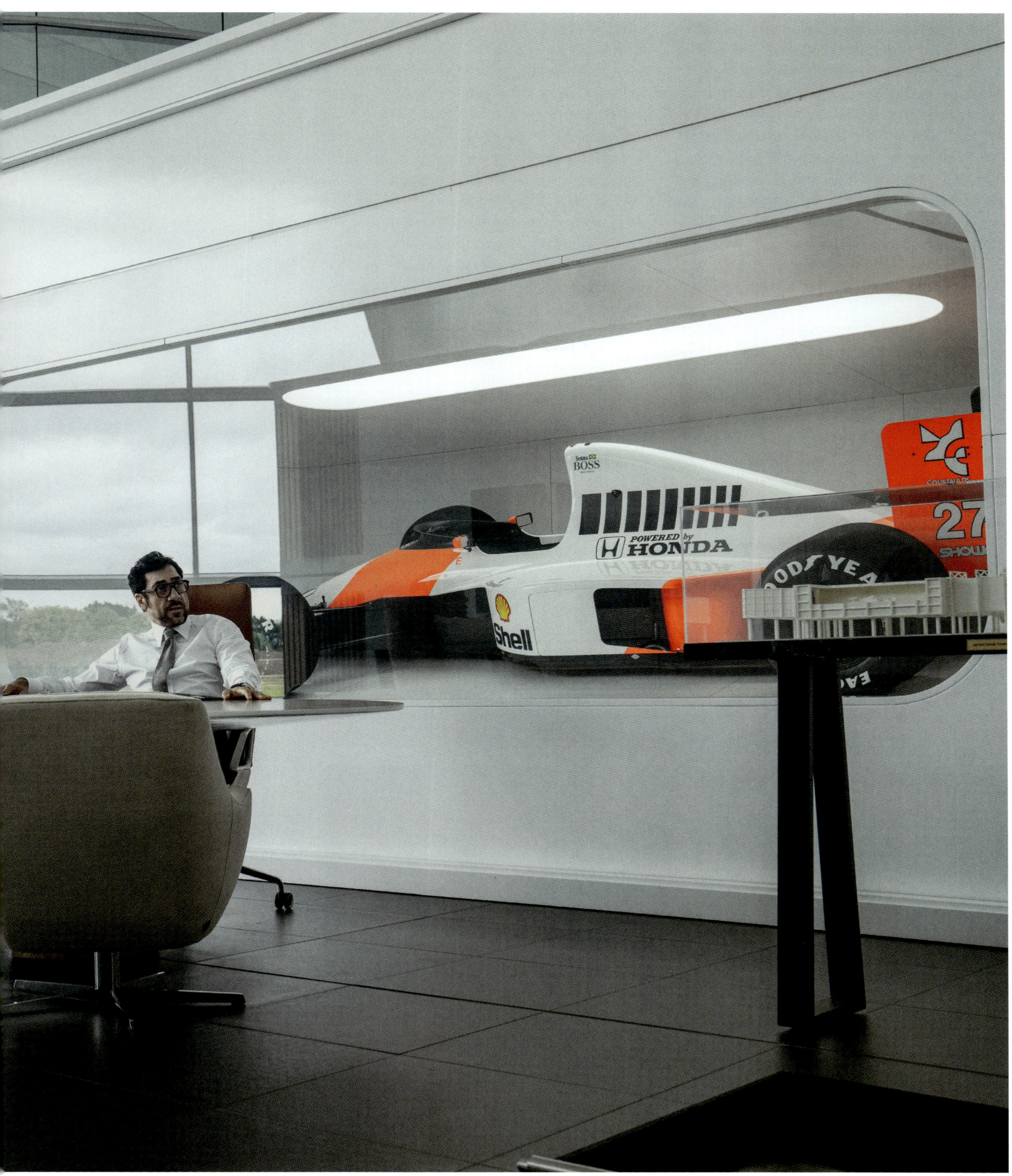
BOSS
POWERED by HONDA
Shell
27

F1 costume designer Julian Day had experience with the Formula One world having worked on Ron Howard's 2013 film, *Rush*, in which he had re-created the race suits worn by James Hunt and Niki Lauda as they battled for the 1976 World Drivers' Championship. But *Rush* was an exercise in historical accuracy. With *F1*, Day's task was designing race suits for Pitt and Idris that looked good but also served a practical purpose, namely keeping them safe in the event of an accident.

With the APXGP car black-and-gold, and the garage off-white, Day began exploring different versions of the race suits that worked with those colors. "I must have gone through sixty concepts. I did lots of gold suits, lots of black suits, and we ended up looking at three different ones—black, a classic off-white look, and the one we eventually hit upon. Joe liked the black; Brad liked the off-white. The black was a bit somber, and Sonny was a man trying to reinvent himself, so I think Brad wanted something more youthful. Maybe the off-white was a little old-fashioned. It was a bit of a throwback to Steve McQueen in *Le Mans* with the stripes, and maybe it looked *too* vintage."

Fortunately, Day had a third suit prepared. "It was the one I really liked, a silver white, that was very youthful but also very modern-looking. Brad put it on and loved it. Then we put a black stripe down the sides. It was a simple suit—clean lines, nothing fancy. Damson looked good in it, too, so everyone was happy. They were figure-hugging as well. Damson wanted it taken in to within an inch of its life. It was like a second skin to him. But Brad didn't want such a figure-hugging suit." The suits were manufactured by OMP, which provide those for the Williams Racing team and used to make those worn by Michael Schumacher and Ayrton Senna. In terms of boots, Pitt opted for white, Idris black.

The rest of the APXGP crew was decked out in white shirts and black trousers, just like the Mercedes F1 team. "You look at some of the teams, and they are quite garish, and that was never going to happen with Joe," says Day. "It was going to be monochrome. It's as simple as that. And it looks effective. Sometimes the simplest things work. Black and white."

Even the production team wore APXGP crew gear during race weekends to blend in. "F1 is all about precision," says Day. "And everyone looks, in a sense, the same. I think F1 thought that a film crew, who are not the smartest people in the world, would bring down the tone of the paddock, so they were insistent everybody wore an APXGP uniform. It was good, because you could shoot around the crew as well. You could be in shot, and no one would know. I refused to wear it, though. I always wear a hat, and I refused to wear the crew uniform."

Sonny's Daytona race suit was white with a blue stripe, while his co-drivers wore the opposite, blue with white stripes. "I think Daytona is a lot less strict than Formula One," says Day. "And his helmet was a duck-egg green."

Below: Costume designer Julian Day looks over Joshua's (Damson Idris's) racing suit.

Right: Brad Pitt opted for an APXGP race suit with a looser fit.

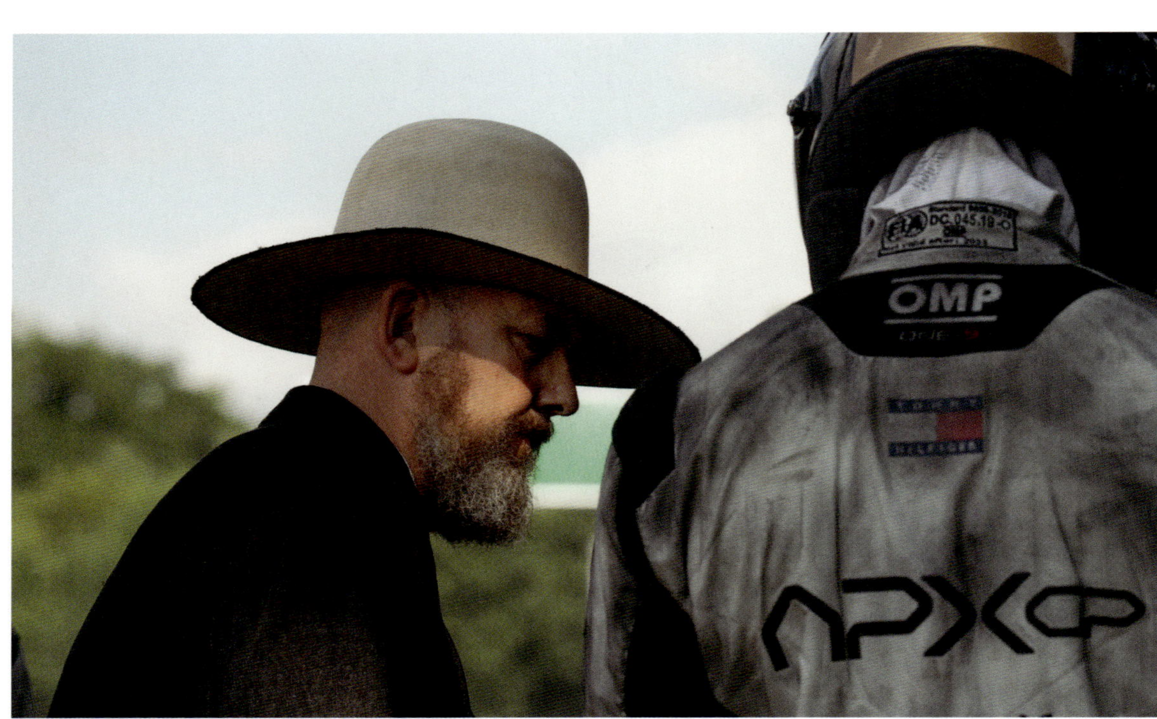

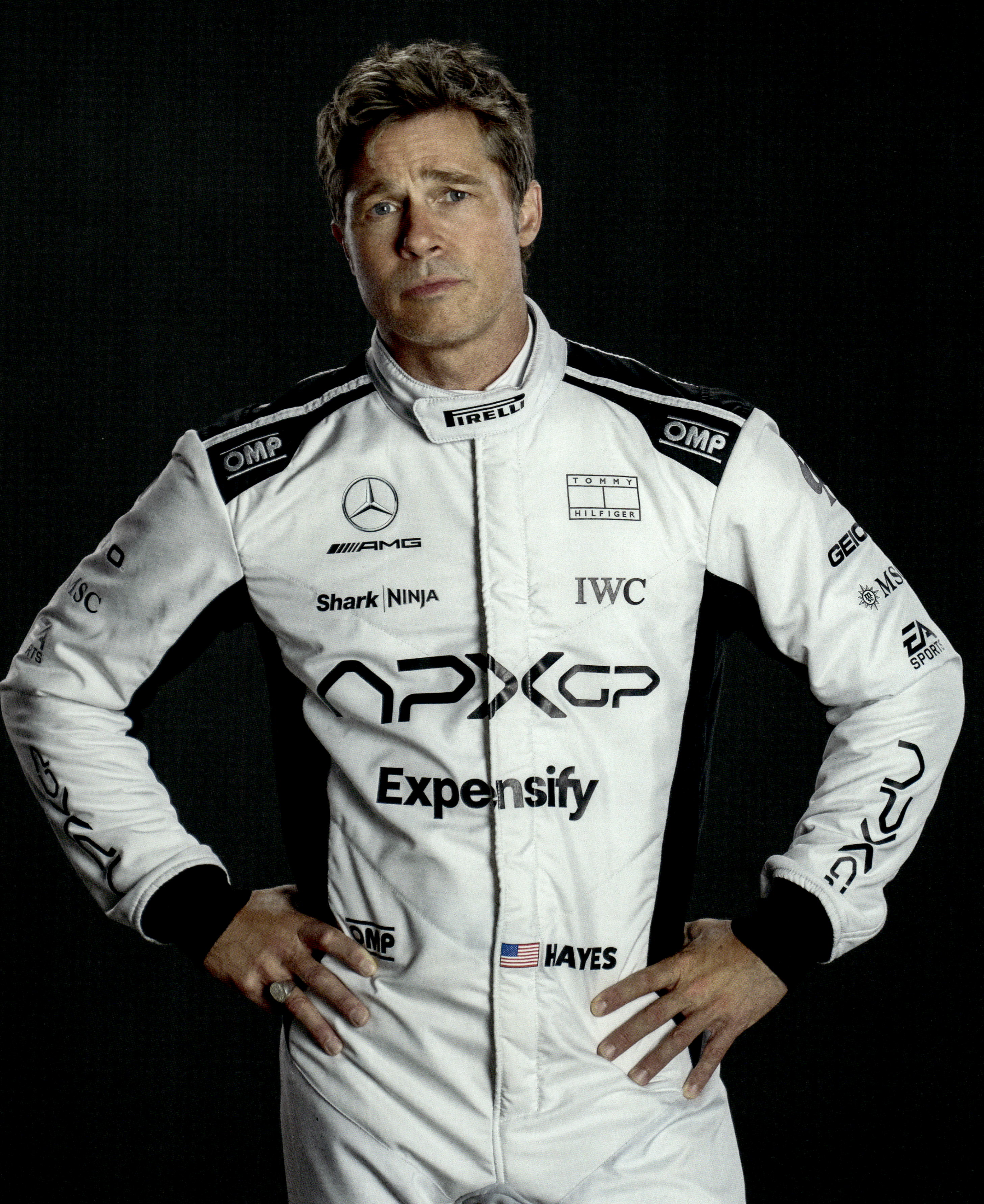
PIRELLI
OMP
OMP
AMG
TOMMY HILFIGER
Shark NINJA
IWC
APXGP
Expensify
OMP
HAYES

Formula One is a heavily sponsored sport, with all the teams relying on the financial benefits of advertisers to offset the huge costs of racing. To fit seamlessly into the world of Formula One, APXGP would also need to be sponsored.

Tasked with finding sponsorship was associate producer David Leener, whose day job is head of alliances for Jerry Bruckheimer Films. Leener began by meeting with the head of sponsorships at F1 Racing. "When companies normally sponsor a car, the sponsorship lasts for two to three years. I was offering not only sponsorship on a car, but in a movie. It's going to last forever, and it's going to be highly visible because we were going to be at actual races," says Leener.

In keeping with other Formula One teams, APXGP offered potential sponsors various options. While Kosinski had initially wanted a watch manufacturer or a multinational brewing company to be APXGP's main sponsor, he soon realized that a lesser-known company made more sense. "An up-and-coming brand was more realistic to an up-and-coming team," he says. In the end, Expensify Inc., a software company that offers an expense management system alongside a business credit card, become APXGP's presenting sponsor.

With Expensify onboard, Leener brought on Swiss watch manufacturer IWC Schaffhausen, which also sponsors Mercedes F1, clothing manufacturer Tommy Hilfiger, another Mercedes sponsor, and SharkNinja, the global product design and technology company, to be an additional sponsor, while EA Sports, a division of Electronic Arts that develops and publishes sports video games; Geico, an auto insurance company; and MSC Cruises, a Swiss-Italian Cruise line that has been a global partner of F1 since 2022, joined as sponsors as well.

Additionally, telecommunications company T-Mobile became the team's technology partner, while tire manufacturer Pirelli provided APXGP with a million dollars' worth of tires in exchange for branding.

For Leener, the next challenge was the positioning of the sponsors' logos on the APXGP cars. "Once you get the 'yes,' the next element is: 'Where does my logo go? What's it going to look like?' Again, we looked at the other teams and how they did it."

Given the APXGP cars were black and gold, all the sponsors' logos needed to be white. "I didn't want to create a rainbow of colors, which I know a lot of the manufacturers struggle with," says Kosinski. "Because everyone wants their logo full color."

"Is it a glossy white sticker? Is it matte? Is it satin?" recalls concept designer Daniel Simon. "A glossy sticker looks glamorous when you photograph it. However, there are light situations where it blurs out and you can't read the name. IWC has very bold, big letters, whereas Hilfiger is a very small font. IWC you see from a hundred meters away; Hilfiger you don't. Once we had the final car design, I spent three or four months moving logos around by the millimeter."

"Hands down the biggest challenge was Tommy Hilfiger, because Tommy Hilfiger's logo is a colored flag," says Leener. "Tommy and Jerry are friends for years and, ultimately, they agreed to doing it black and white. But Joe agreed to put it in color on the Halo, as well as on the back of the uniforms, which are all white. That's how Mercedes does it."

As title sponsors, Expensify's logo is on the cars' side pods as well as rear wing, Halo, driver uniforms, and helmets, with IWC and SharkNinja also on the helmets.

Since the film was shot in chronological order, following the racing season, the

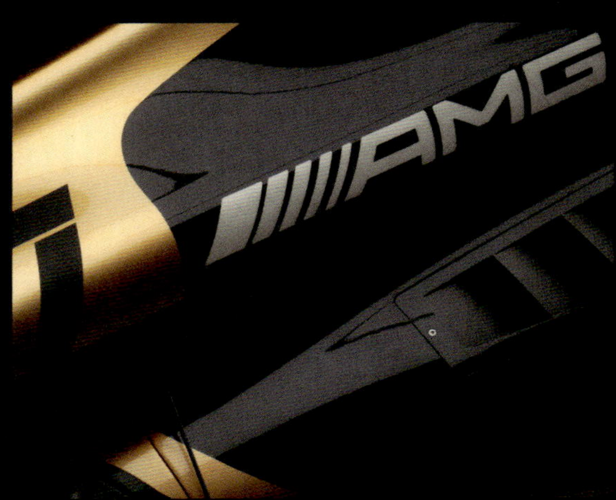

Below: The nose of the APXGP car prominently features sponsors including MSC, Geico, EA Sports, Tommy Hilfiger, IWC Schaffhausen, Pirelli, SharkNinja, and Expensify.

Left: One of APXGP's sponsors, Mercedes-AMG.

production could update and amend sponsor logos as required, without any continuity issues. "For the last two races, we put the MSC logo in the driver cockpit on either side," says Leener. "It's a very, very prominent location.

The sponsorship Leener raised for APXGP, he says, was all invested back into the film. "Dave did a phenomenal job," says producer Jerry Bruckheimer, "getting all these advertisers to believe in us that we were going to treat them properly."

"It worked out better than any of us could have ever, ever hoped," reflects Kosinski. "I'm grateful to Expensify and SharkNinja and Tommy and IWC and the rest for sponsoring the APXGP car, because it was a risk. But they trusted us, and hopefully when the movie comes out, they all get the exposure they were hoping for."

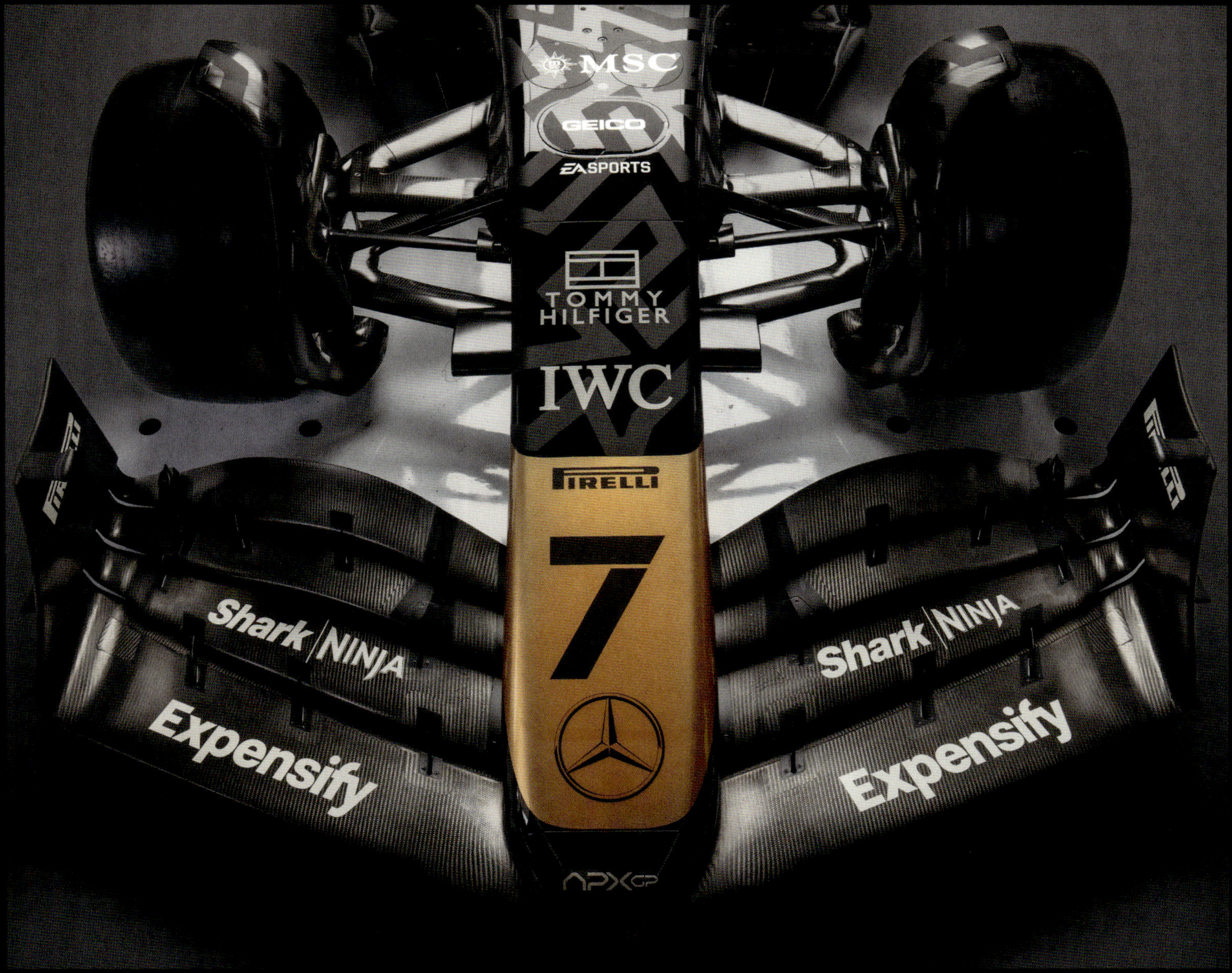

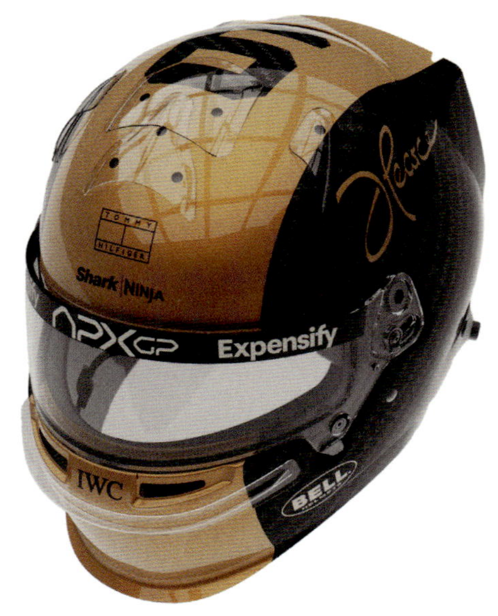
Shark NINJA
APXGP
Expensify
IWC
BELL

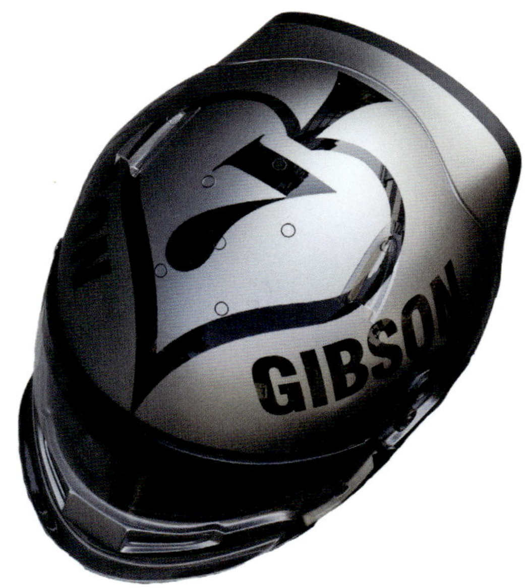
GIBSON

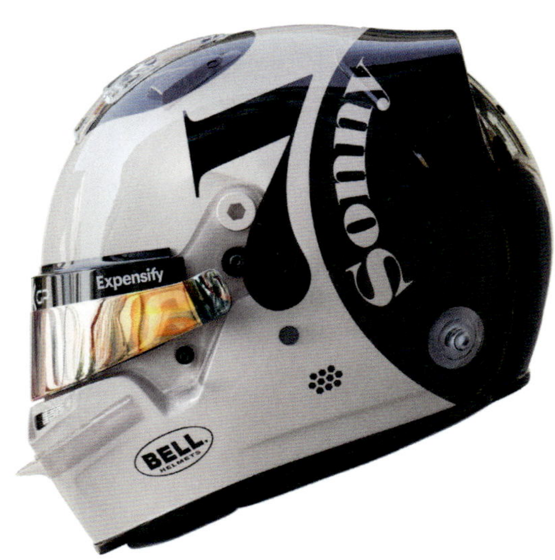
7
Sonny
Expensify
BELL

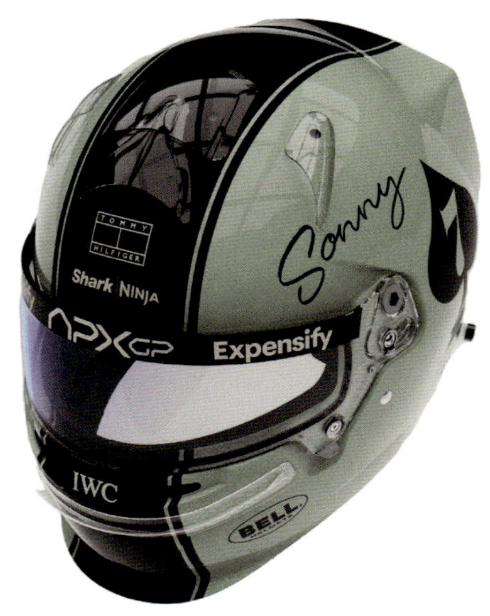
Shark NINJA
Sonny
APXGP
Expensify
IWC
BELL

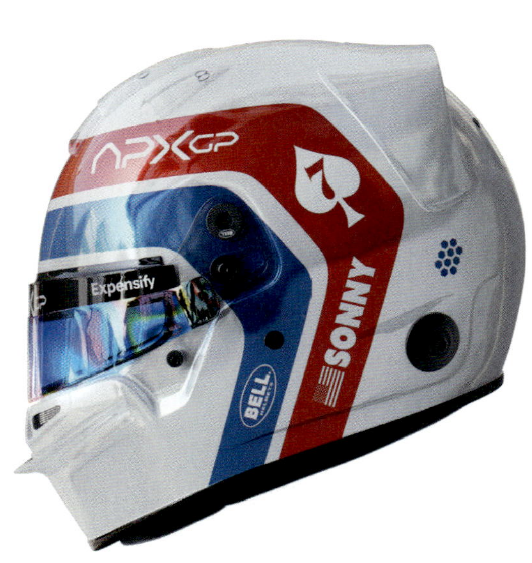
APXGP
Expensify
SONNY
BELL

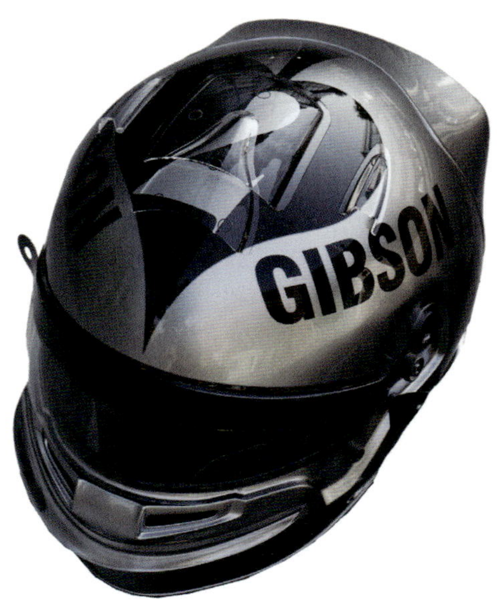
GIBSON

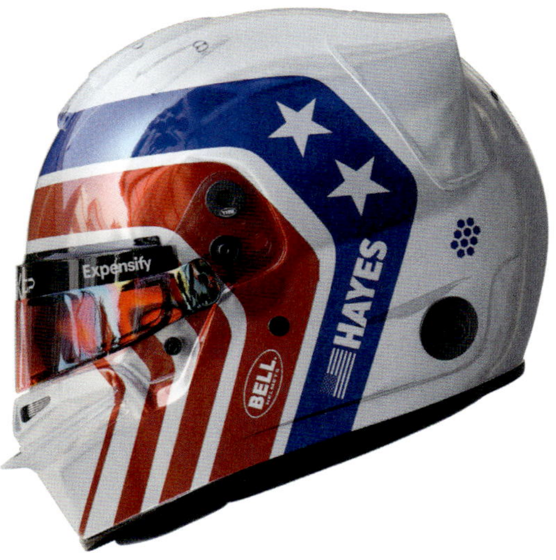

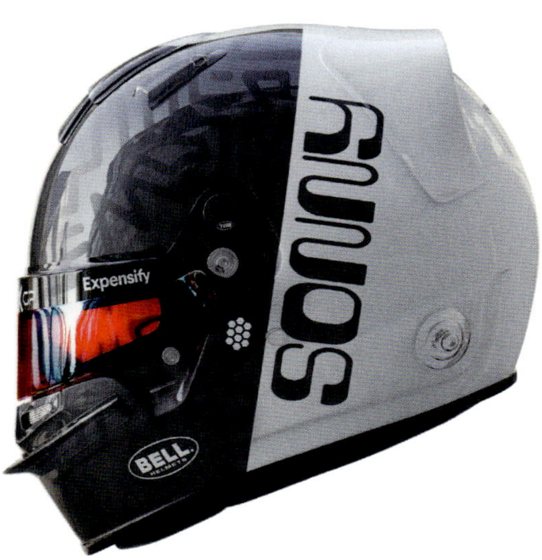

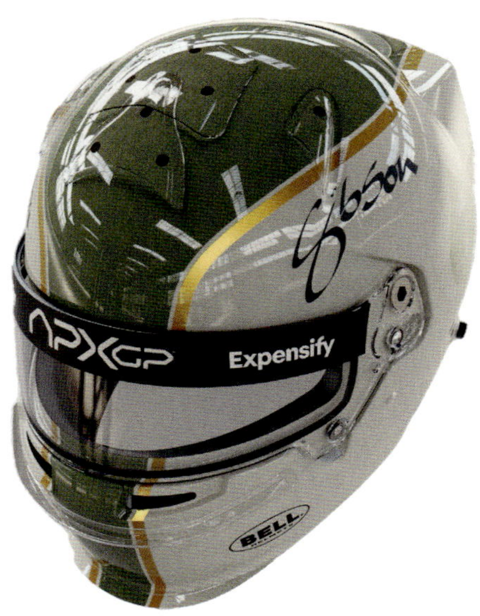

When it came to his character's Formula One helmet, Pitt collaborated with Kosinski and concept artist Daniel Simon on the color and design. "Modern helmets are extraordinarily complicated and have become like a canvas for drivers; they present a new helmet every race," says Simon. "I come from a time when drivers like Senna had one helmet their whole career. So, I wanted Sonny's to be classic and recognizable. I had dozens of other designs, but Joe likes very clean, iconic, simple things that once they're done, you think anybody could have done it. But getting there is quite a process."

A desaturated olive green with a black stripe through the middle, Sonny's helmet featured his name (hand-drawn by Simon) and a spade with his number inside, a nod to his gambling nature. "I really wanted to celebrate this. It's such a beautiful shape, and, initially, it was massive on the helmet. But we shrunk it down, step by step," says Simon. "Then the question became, which way does the spade point? Days go by for those decisions, and it ended up on the side." Joshua's helmet shared much the same design, but gold and black, echoing the APXGP livery. "It's literally a twin of the car."

All the helmets were manufactured by Bell Racing in Bahrain. "We had twenty-two versions of Brad's hero helmet, because we had three or four stunt drivers, we had helmet cams, we had helmets for fire, we had spares," says property master Steven Morris. And each needed its own set of foam cheek pads. "Brad's head size was fifty-seven, but we had the inner pads manufactured to the millimeter, so it was a perfect fit. Because if there was a slight uplift in his cheeks, it just didn't look right. And we want his face looking as perfect as it can be, because of the speed and the g-force in these cars. It was Lewis who flagged the thing with the cheeks."

The APXGP drivers' visors were also unique to the film. "Visors are usually tinted and look mean and menacing, but this is a movie, so we need to see the eyes of the actors," says Simon. "We had an antireflective covering across the visor that's specific for cameras, so when Joe or Claudio looked through the lens, there was no bounce-back," adds Morris.

F1 helmets are more than just sophisticated safety equipment—they also tell you a lot about the drivers who wear them. Early helmet design options explored different color schemes, and even featured the name Teddy Gibson, which was originally considered for Brad Pitt's character.

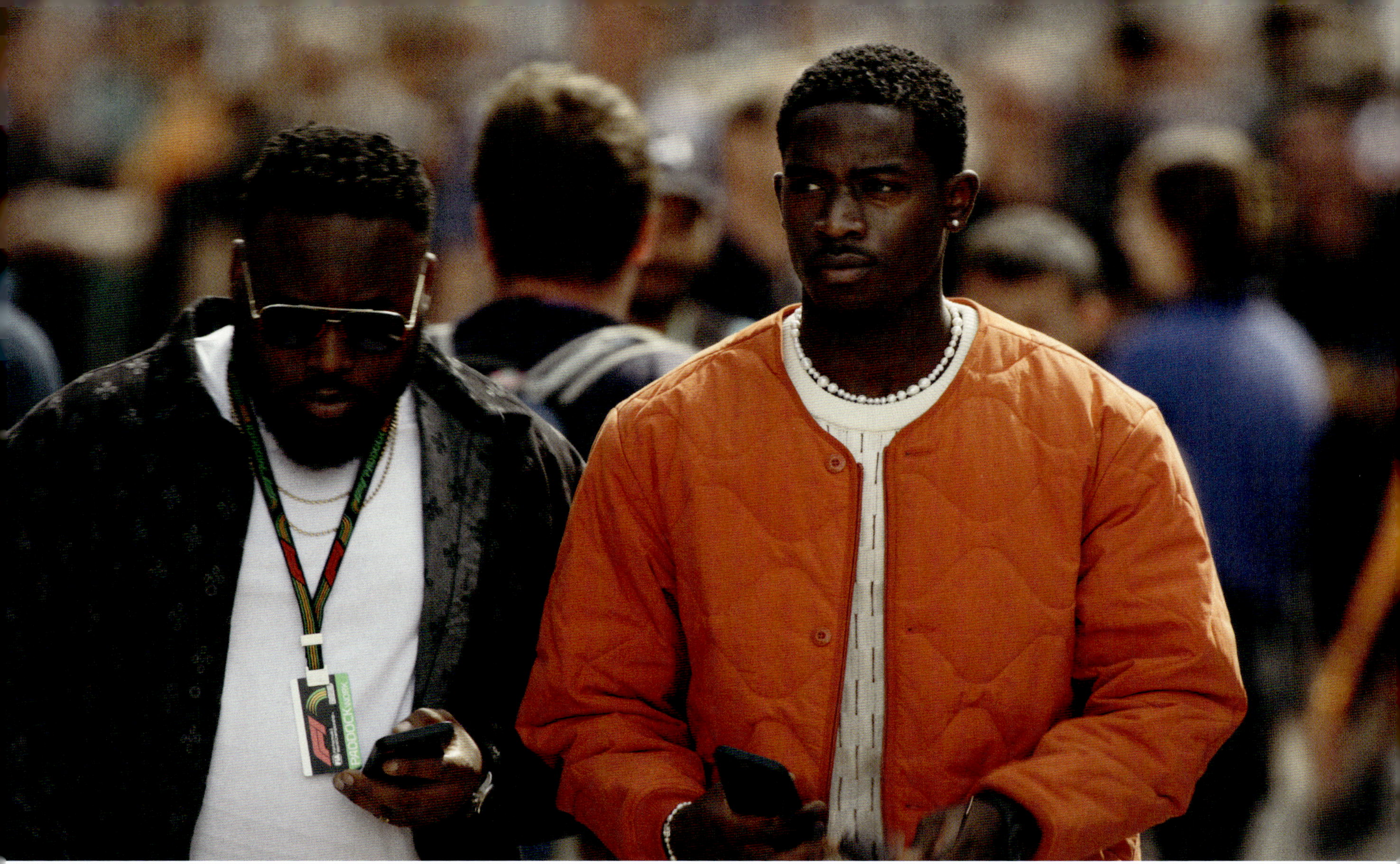

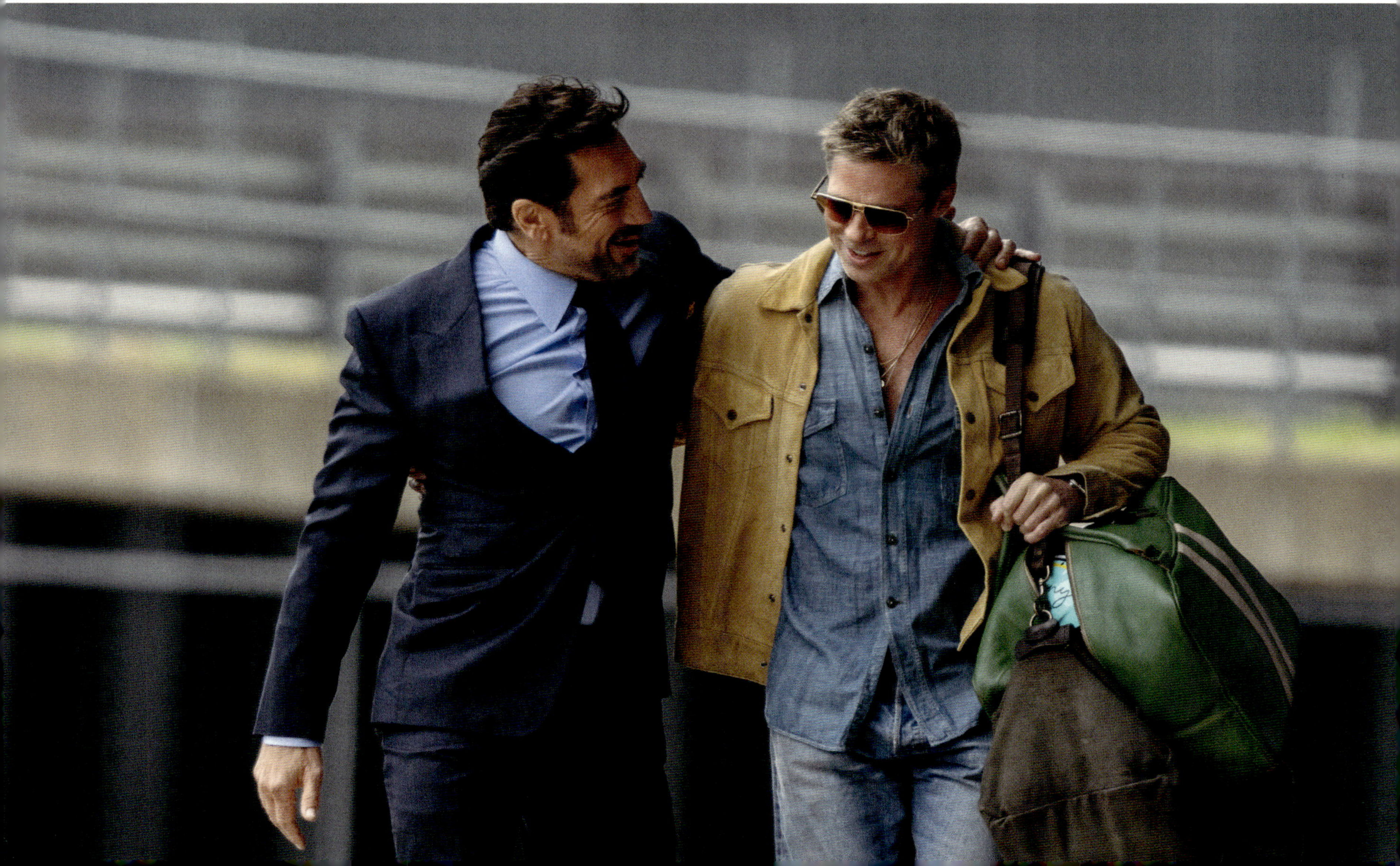

Top Left: Joshua (Damson Idris) in his orange Tommy Hilfiger jacket.

Bottom Left: Ruben (Javier Bardem) walks with Sonny (Brad Pitt), whose wardrobe consisted of several pieces from Pitt's own closet.

Bottom Right: Sonny's (Brad Pitt's) watch was designed in collaboration with IWC Schaffhausen, one of APXGP's sponsors. The face is the same color as Sonny's helmet.

Away from the track, Sonny's wardrobe was a combination of things Pitt brought with him and clothes Day sourced. "One of the references was Kris Kristofferson. The maverick cowboy, denim and cowboy boots, but a contemporary version of that, a laid-back Americana look," says Day. "I bought lots of denim from the sixties, original jeans, and Levi and Wrangler shirts. His color palette was denim, greens, blues, browns, nice earthy colors, with a pop of color. Green was very much Brad's color for the film. A lot of his suede jackets were green. Some of the stripes on his socks were green." Day estimates he bought somewhere between sixty and one hundred pairs of socks from Japanese brand Rototo for Pitt to pick from for the mismatched pairs Sonny always races in. "All types, all colors, different every scene. He rather liked them and would say, 'Can I have a few pairs?'"

Pitt also designed Sonny's watch, in conjunction with IWC—another APXGP sponsor. "The color of the face was the same color as his helmet," reveals Day. "He co-designs a jewelry brand and brought some with him. He likes things that are comfortable. And if Brad feels comfortable in what he's wearing, then you've succeeded. Filmmaking is all about collaboration and the pooling of ideas."

Sonny's props—his leather kit bag, his camper van, even his iPhone—all had a beat-up quality to them. "The reason Brad is so successful is because he has really great taste, and once he gets into a character, a really strong sense of who that person is," says Kosinski. "From designing the watch to the helmet to the playing cards to his medallions and tattoos, there were hundreds of choices to make for Sonny Hayes, and it was a fun collaboration. I love it when an actor has a point of view on that, because it shows how invested they are in getting this character right."

As for Idris, who models for Prada, Day opted for a combination of outfits from APXGP sponsor Tommy Hilfiger, along with "a lot of street clothes, including Carhartt, and a lot of Indian brands: Kartik Research, 11.11. They're really of the moment. Damson was good fun to dress.

"I have to say, all the men were so great to dress," Day continues. "Javier was brilliant. He wore Tom Ford, Armani, a throwback to eighties Armani, and Gucci. Obviously, he had to look like a billionaire, but a very precise billionaire. So, we used a lot of nice brands of suits. And he looked fantastic."

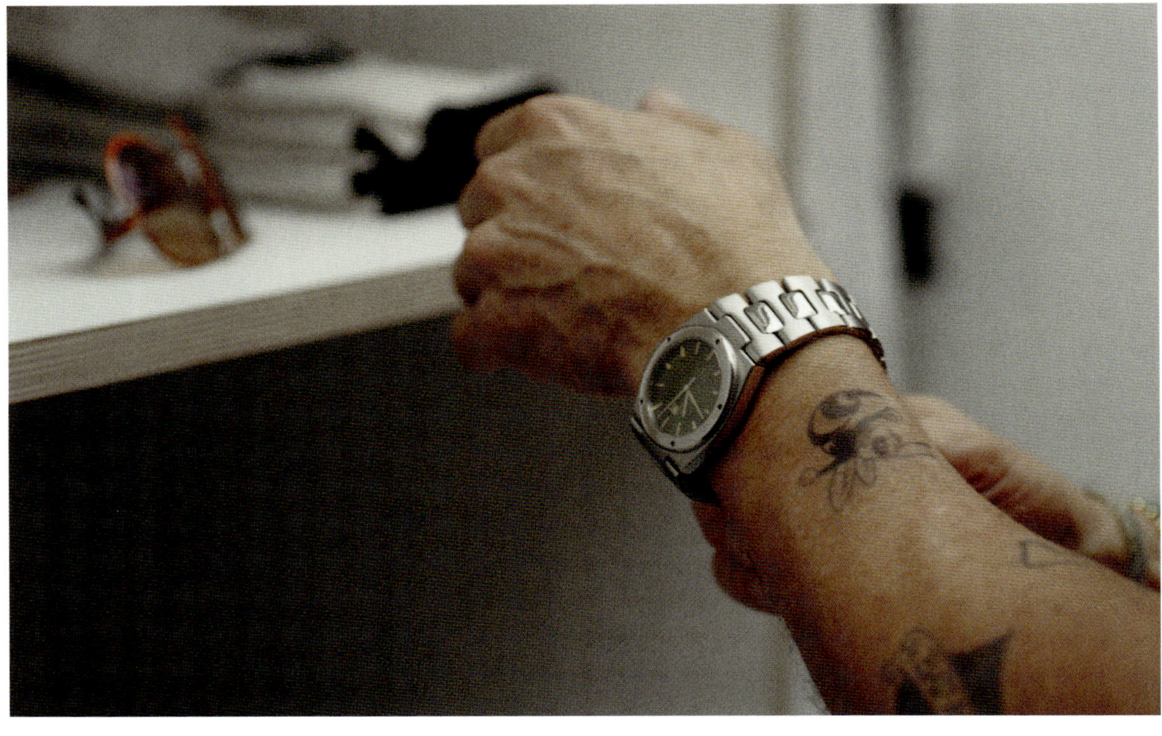

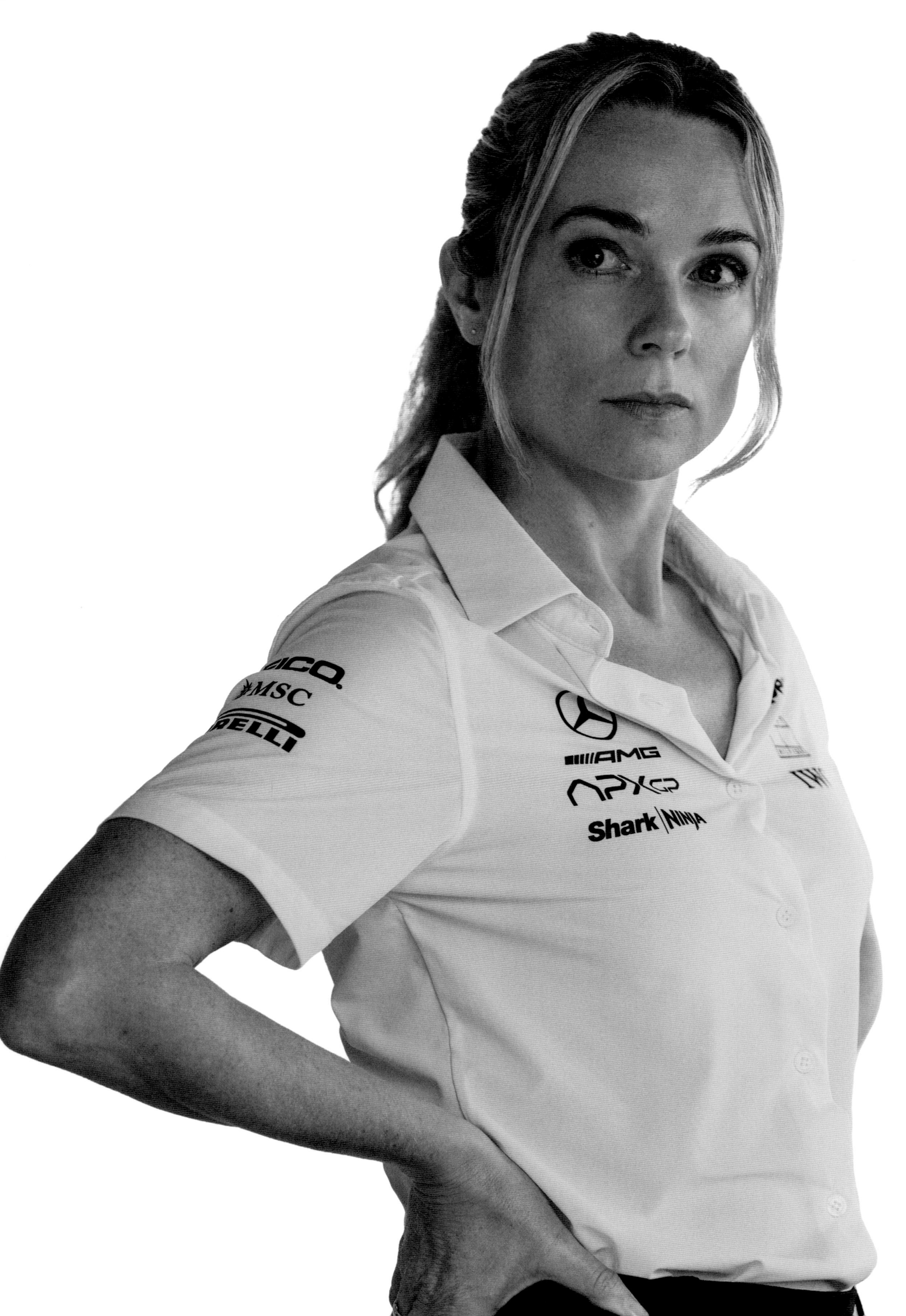
MSC
AMG
Shark NINJA

THE TECHNICAL DIRECTOR

KATE McKENNA

"With APXGP, we were trying to make every major personality an underdog in some way," says screenwriter Ehren Kruger. "Not just feel they were working for a team that hadn't scored a point, and that's demoralizing, but that these characters had something to prove, personally. Like, maybe people think it's not the car that's bad, it's not the drivers. Maybe it's the technical director. Maybe it's the team principal. Everyone needed to have some sense of being doubted. And we wanted that for Kate."

In filmic terms, Kate McKenna is the first female technical director in the Formula One paddock—responsible for the day-to-day engineering of the APXGP team cars—in what is still a male-dominated sport. But Irish actor Kerry Condon, Oscar-nominated for *The Banshees of Inisherin*, who portrays her, didn't want to play the "woman card too much." For Condon, her starting point for Kate was "coming from a work point of view," she says. "The team is not doing well, and she is overly sensitive to criticism. They're calling the car 'the shitbox,' and I imagined she'd take those things personally. When you're losing every weekend, it must be soul-destroying and hard to show your face along the paddock."

"Kerry has the perfect combination of qualities I wanted Kate to have," says director Joseph Kosinski. "She's very bright, very, very smart, but tough, a woman who's not going to back down, who will tell you what she thinks, as she does to Sonny. She's not afraid to give him a piece of her mind. I needed a very strong actress, someone willing to dive in and do the research and immerse themselves in this world. And Kerry was the perfect actor for that."

Although Kate isn't based on any one person, Bernie Collins, a former F1 strategy engineer for Aston Martin, McLaren, and Force India, now a strategy analyst for Sky Sports and F1 TV, was "a huge influence," according to Kosinski. "They spent time together, in person, on Zooms, going through the script, understanding her, where she's coming from, getting the language right. I wanted Kate to speak in the jargon of the job, so it felt real. The terminology, how they would say things and what their tone is, on the pit wall, speaking with drivers and dealing with the other engineers in the garage. Kerry spent a lot of time figuring out that dynamic, going to races and observing."

> "[Kate's] very bright, very, very smart, but tough, a woman who's not going to back down, who will tell you what she thinks, as she does to Sonny."
>
> JOSEPH KOSINSKI

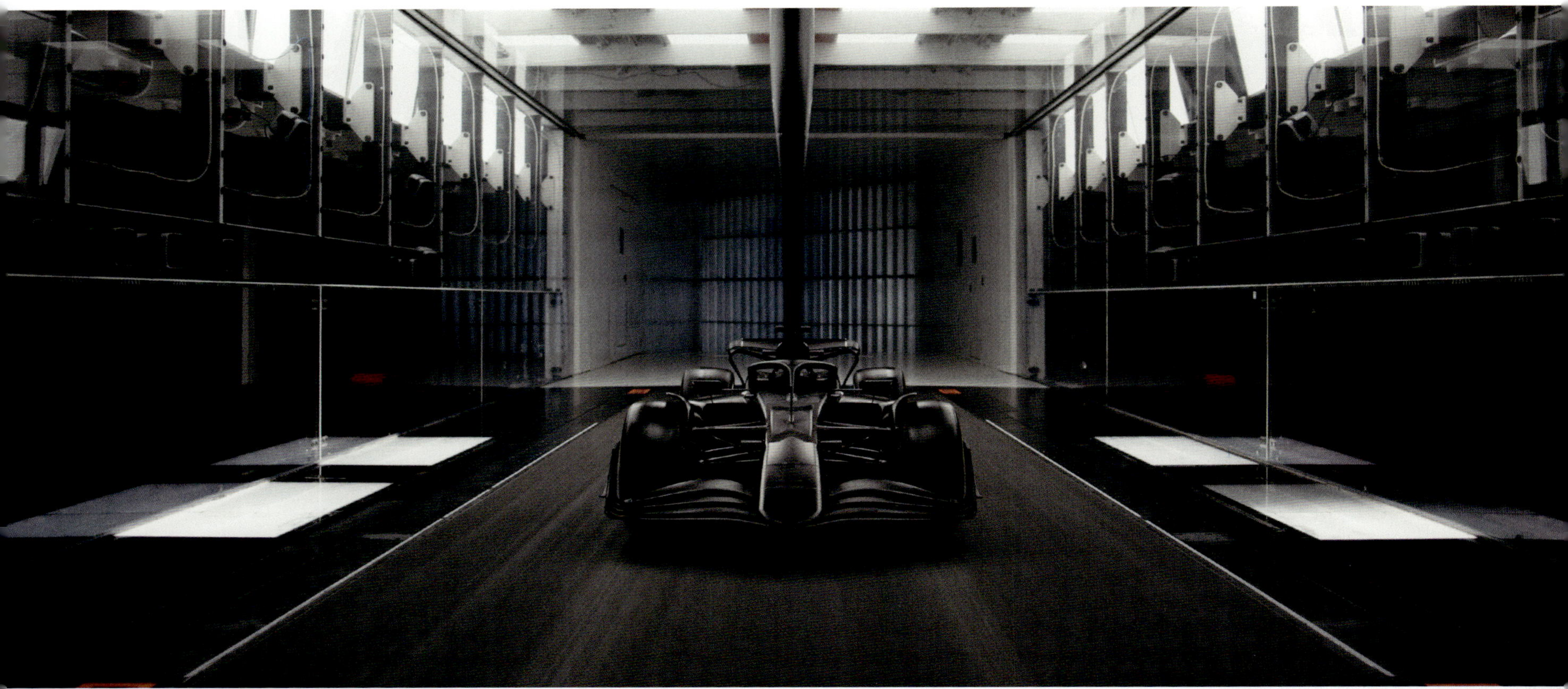

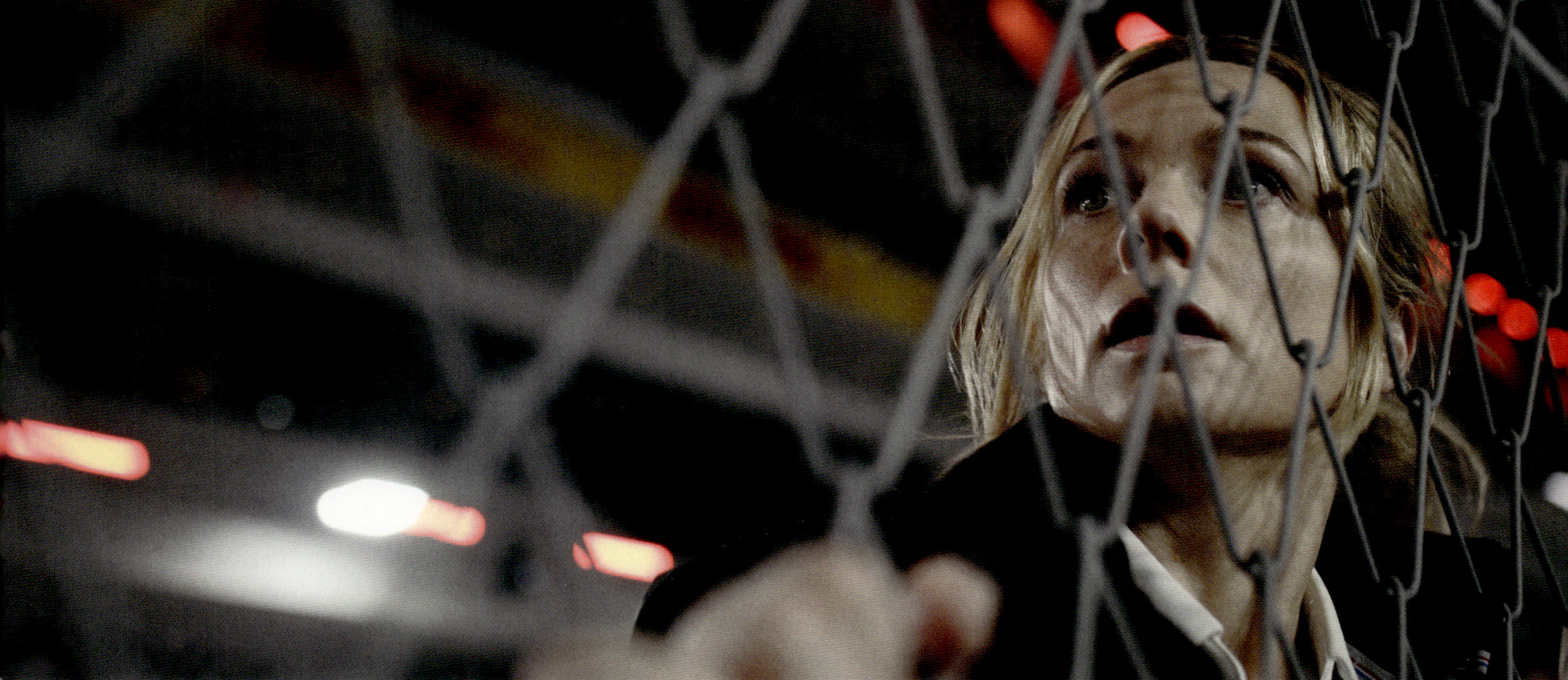

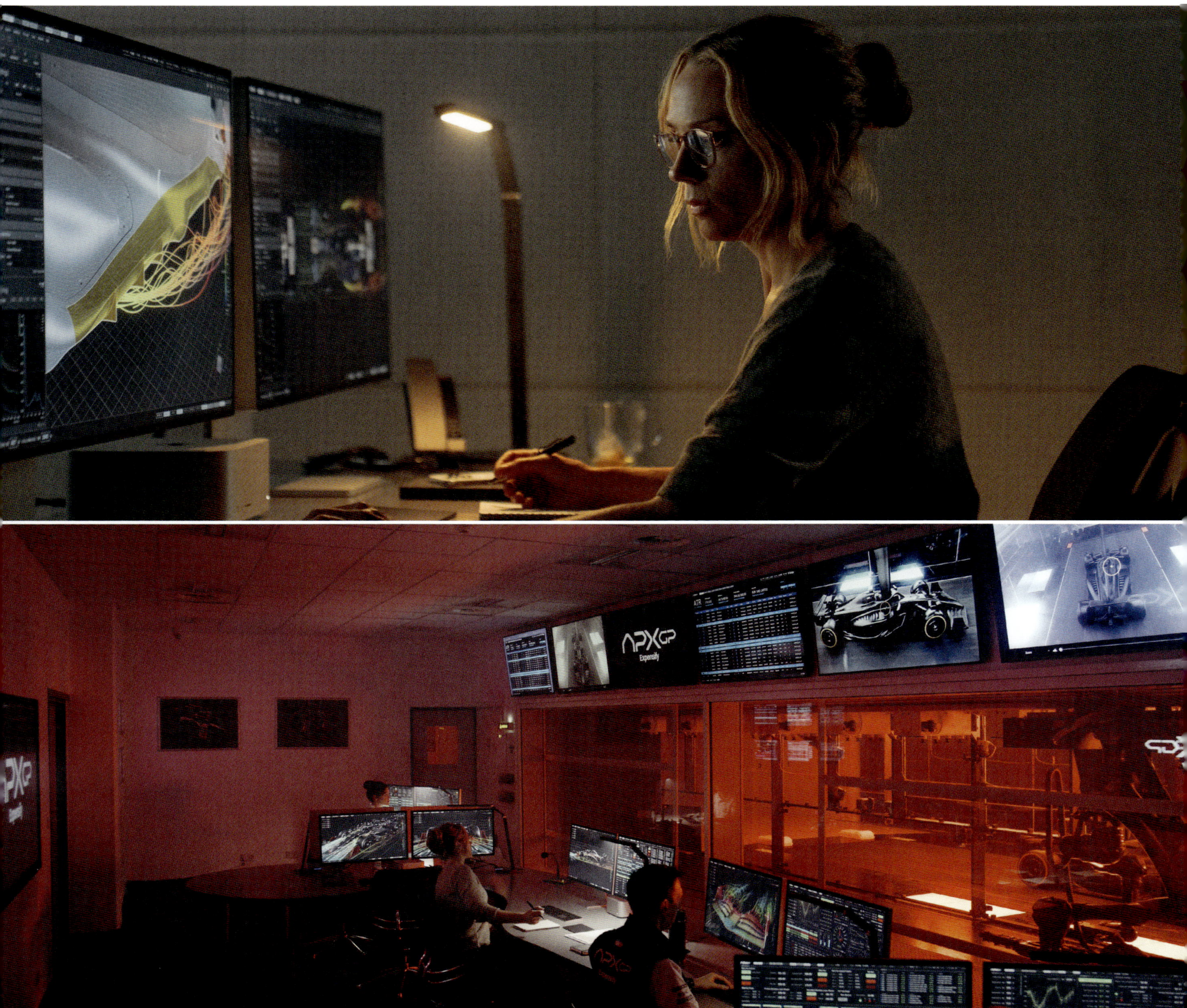

Top Left: The APXGP wind tunnel.

Top Right: Kate McKenna (Kerry Condon) works on an upgrade for the APXGP car.

Bottom Left: Kate reacts in horror to Sonny's crash in Las Vegas.

Bottom Right: Kate working in the control room for the wind tunnel.

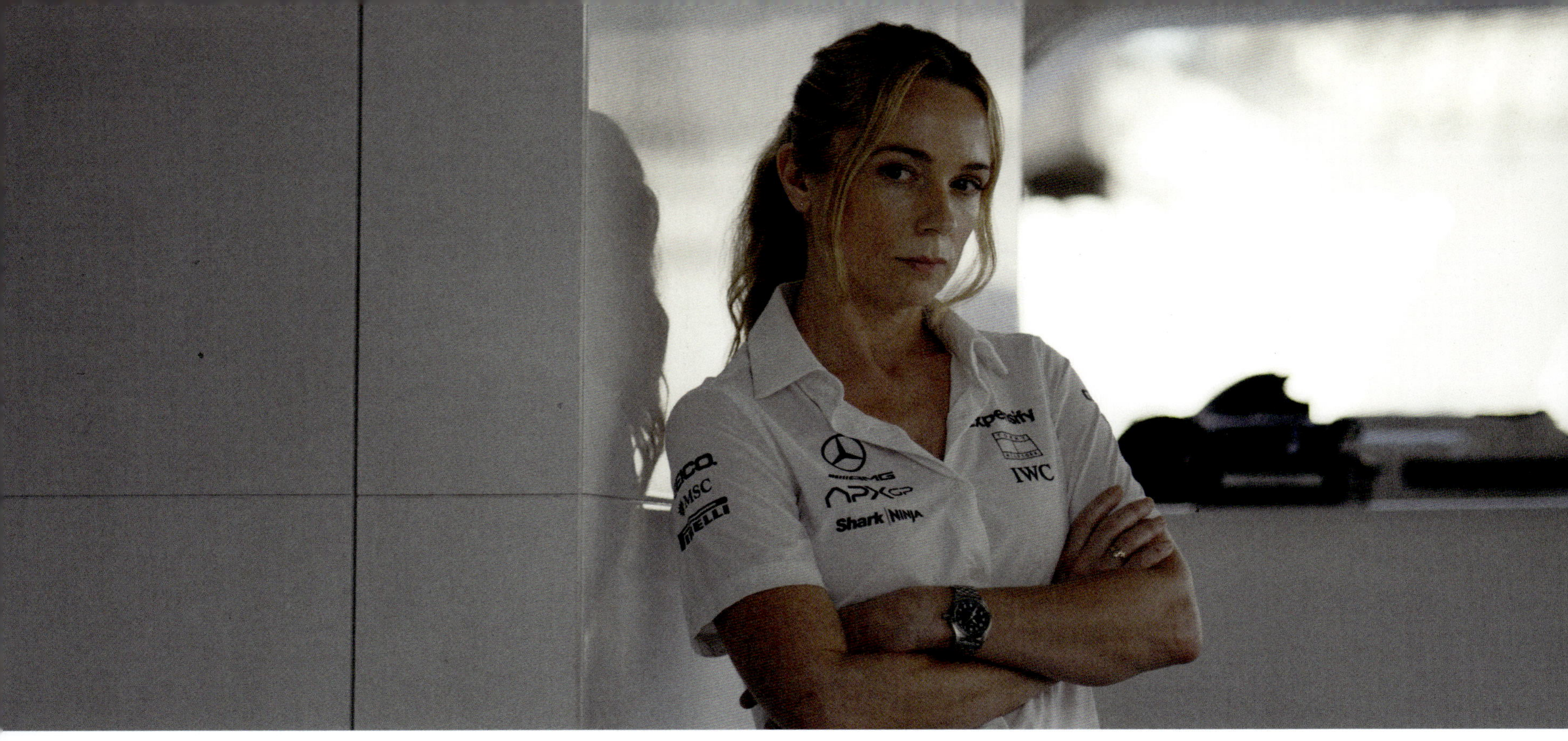

"We wanted a character who could call Sonny on some of his shenanigans and some of his attitude and throw things back."

JOSEPH KOSINSKI

"Bernie was the first person I met when I got the job, and we were sent to the Grand Prix in Barcelona," recalls Condon, who also spoke to British motorsport engineer and F1 TV presenter Ruth Buscombe and read former Red Bull Racing chief technical officer Adrian Newey's book, *How to Build a Car: The Autobiography of the World's Greatest Formula 1 Designer*. "I'd never been to an F1 race in my life, and she was going to explain everything to me. The best part was she was super relaxed. She didn't bombard me with a million things I had to learn."

More than that, Collins reminded Condon of the smart girls she went to school with. "I went to an all-girls Catholic school, same as she did, and she was one of those who were good at physics and good at maths. I was desperate at physics. To do this job, you must be very, very smart and super confident in your decisions, because it is a gamble. You get all this info and go, 'Okay, this is the plan. Let's hope it works.' So, I kept her close to the background I had. And that informed everything then going forward." She also watched *Drive to Survive*. "For the pit wall stuff. To look at some of the mannerisms and the way they stand and the way they sit, things like that. That was very helpful. Plus, the drama of it was really interesting."

If Condon had a specific question, she would text Collins. "Stuff like, 'When you walk to the pit wall with your notebook, what's written on the front page?' Just in case the camera

Top Left: Kate McKenna (Kerry Condon) looks on in the APXGP garage.

Top Right: Kate (Kerry Condon) monitors the race from the pit wall.

Bottom Right: As part of her research, Kerry Condon spoke to former Aston Martin strategist Bernie Collins.

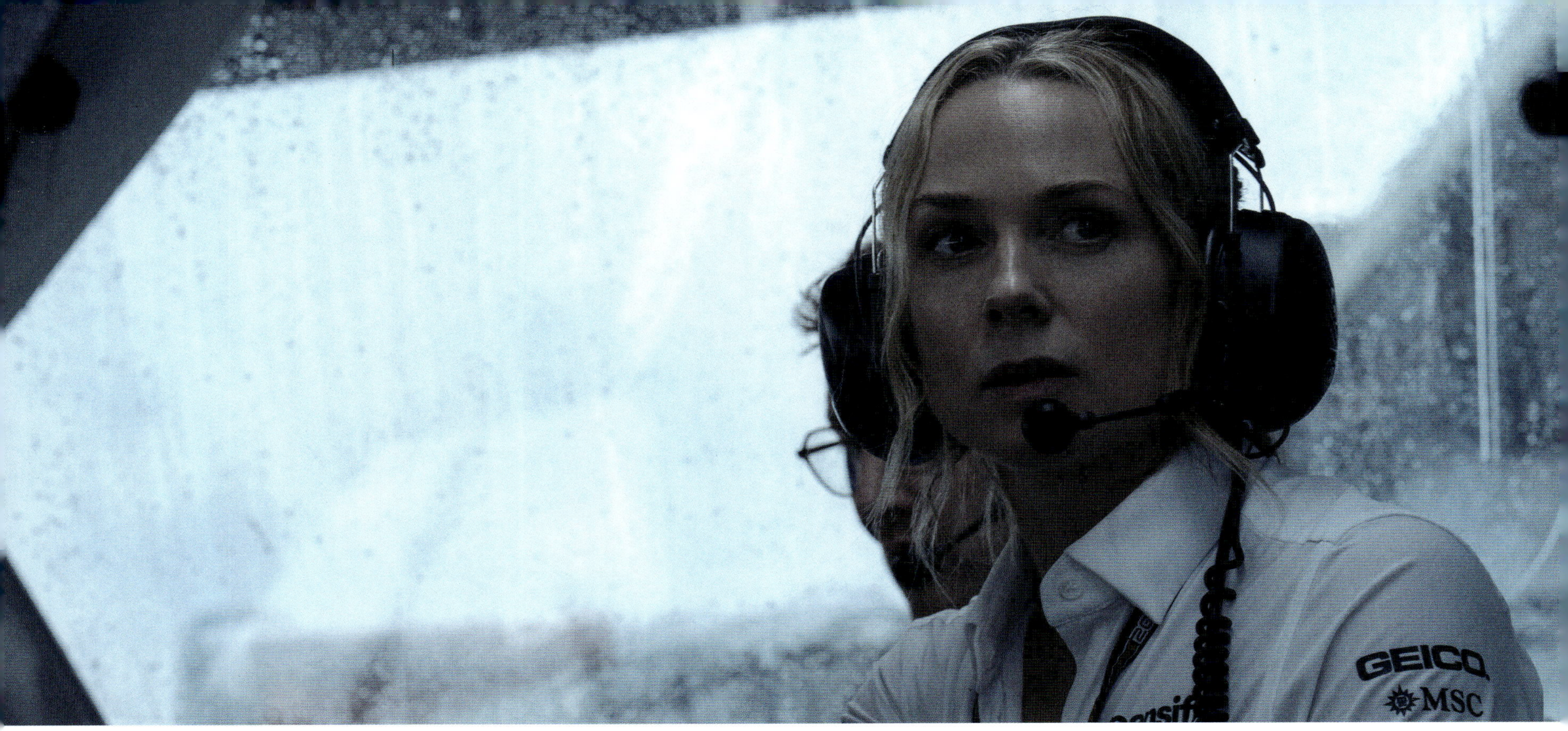

sees it. I copied what Bernie would have. I only needed one or two things. Kate was a pen and paper girl, because, in college, she would have written everything down. It was more things to sell it as opposed to technical stuff. How she carried herself. How would she wear her headphones. At the end of the day, these are human beings. I'm a human being. How far wrong can I go? Otherwise, you can overthink it and get too into the details. Ultimately, I'm acting. I'm not building a car."

Kosinski and Kruger also met an aerodynamicist during a tour of the Mercedes factory whose method of transportation impacted Kate. "She told us she rode her bicycle to work every day, and that was the inspiration for Kate doing the same thing in the movie," reveals Kosinski. "She said she needed to 'feel the wind,' which became a line in the movie."

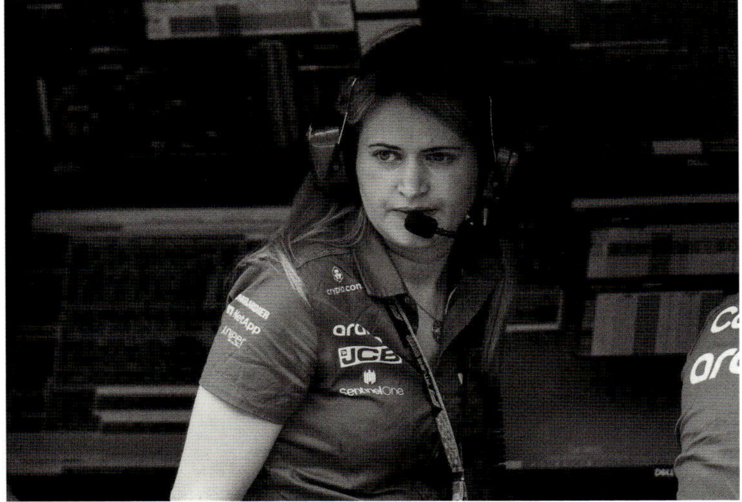

Kate spends most of her time on the pit wall or in the APXGP garage. The latter location was a familiar one for Condon. "My dad is a haulage contractor; he had lots of lorries and a garage when I was growing up. So, I was aware of cars and the garage scene. The F1 part was strange, but the garage and cars weren't a crazy leap for me." When Sonny arrives at APXGP, his relationship with Kate begins rocky—"the Yank telling them what to do"—although she is one of the few people able to get under his skin. "They complement each other, even though it starts from a place of conflict," says Kosinski. "We wanted a character who could call Sonny on some of his shenanigans and some of his attitude and throw things back."

Eventually, Kate and Sonny find a degree of mutual respect. "They help each other get better and help the team get where it needs to be," Kosinski continues. "She also embodies the classic conflict that exists between engineers and drivers, where, if a team's not performing well, the engineers will say it's the driver not driving the car, while the driver will say, 'The car's not working properly.' So, you've got two people pointing a finger at each other as to what's not working."

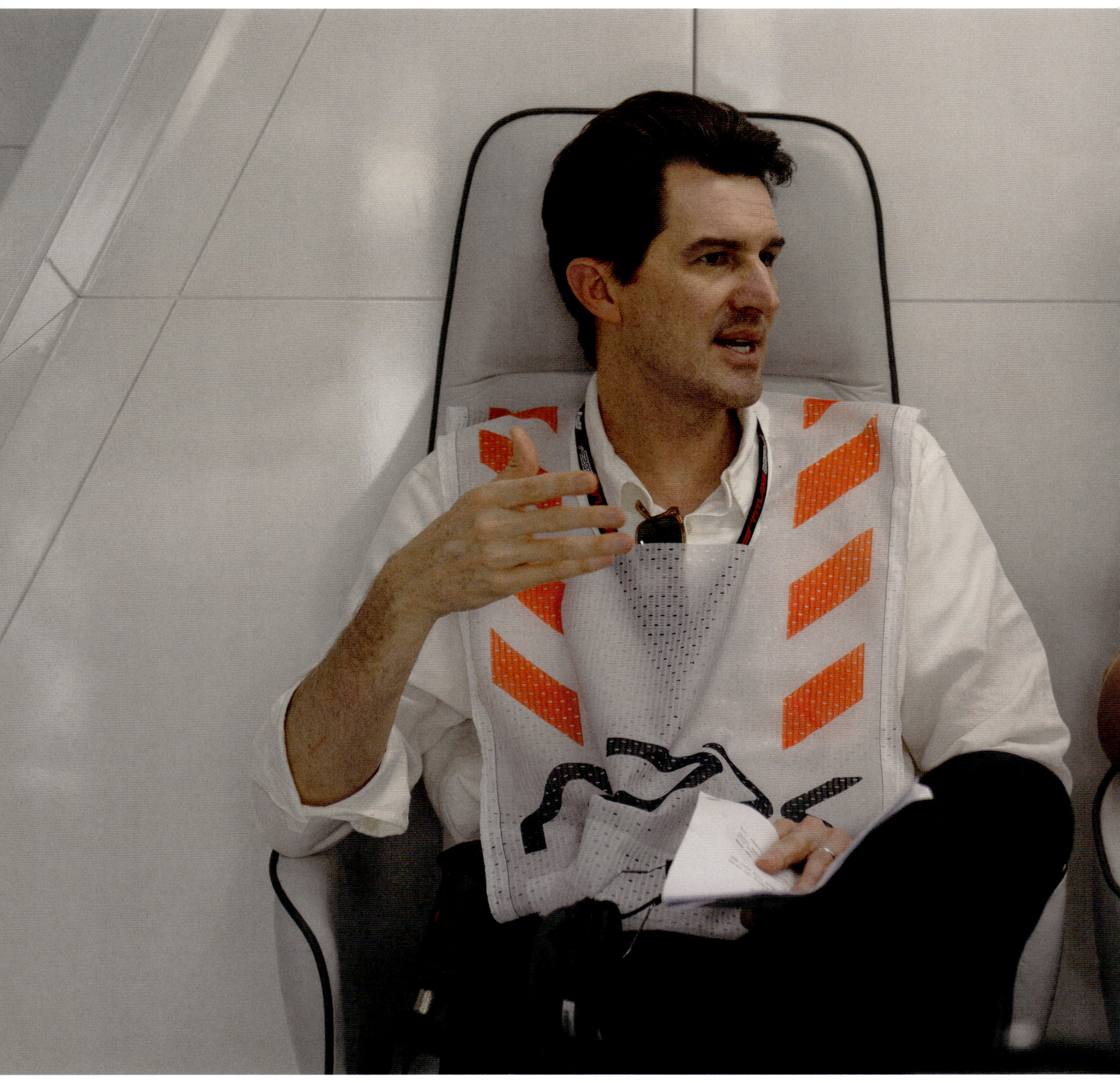

Above: Kerry Condon speaks with Joseph Kosinski behind the scenes.

Top Right: Sonny (Brad Pitt) and Kate (Kerry Condon) share a moment in Las Vegas.

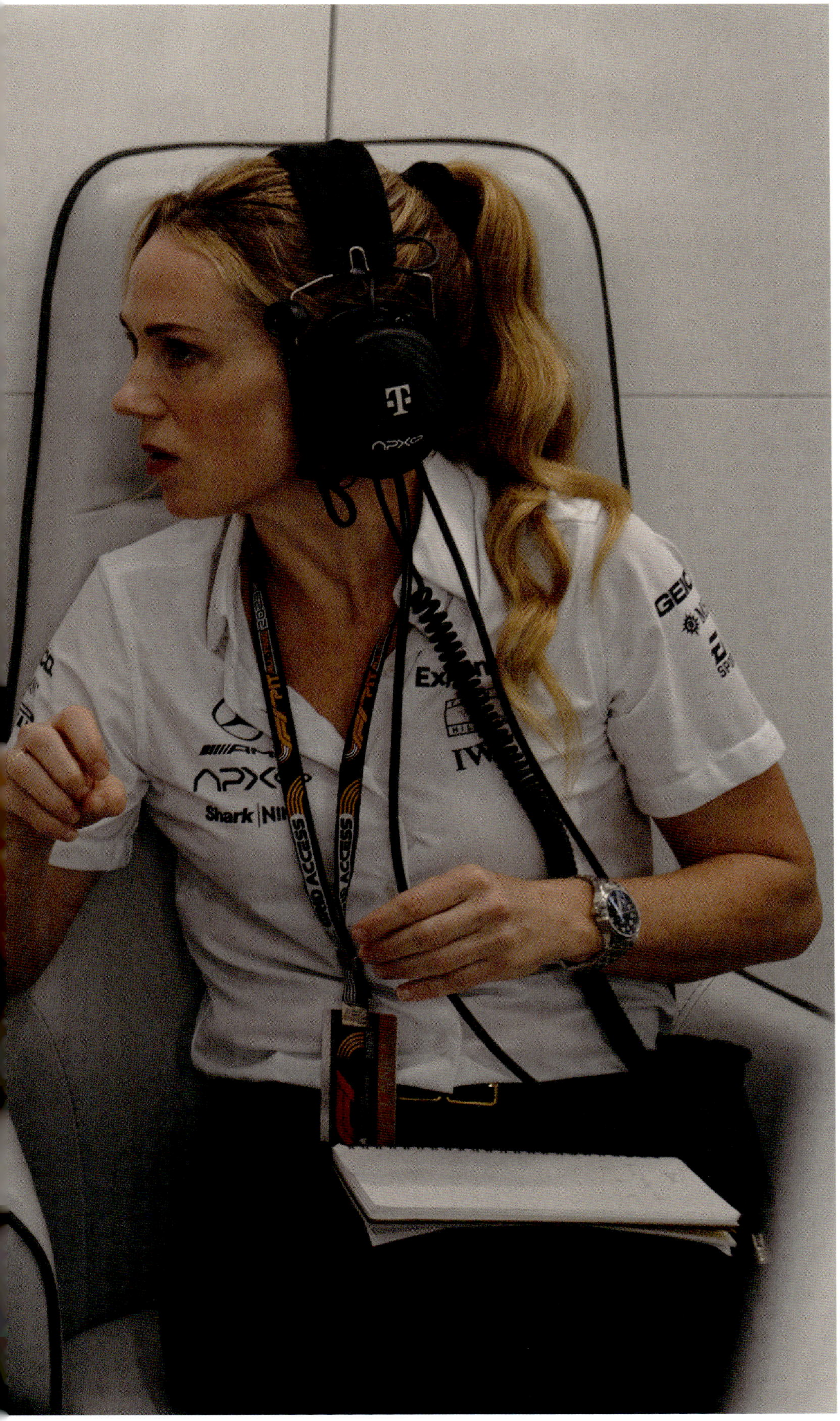

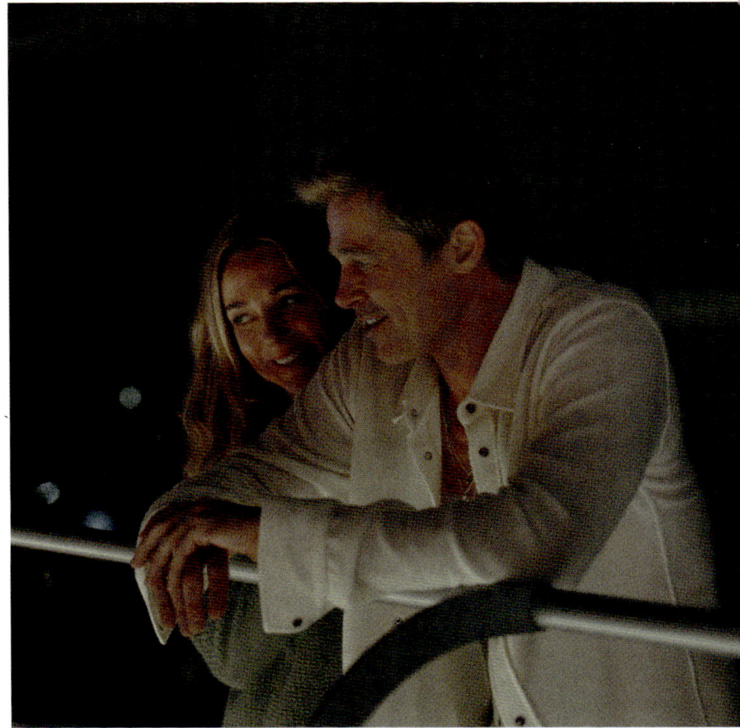

"But with Sonny, they're very similar," says Condon. "They're both loners, both love their jobs, and are both obsessed with it. So, when he gives Kate the tip about how to improve the car, she says, 'Hey! Hang on a minute. Don't tell me how to do my job.'"

In the end, Kate accepts Sonny's advice—as well as his romantic advances—and together they propel APXGP onto the top step of the podium. "From the very first time they meet, he's funny and has that thing about him, where she's like, 'Who the fuck is this?' He's just so cheeky and bold," Condon laughs. "It's also talent. Talent is very attractive, and someone who can tell her about the car, and what to do with it in a way no one else has done, is super attractive."

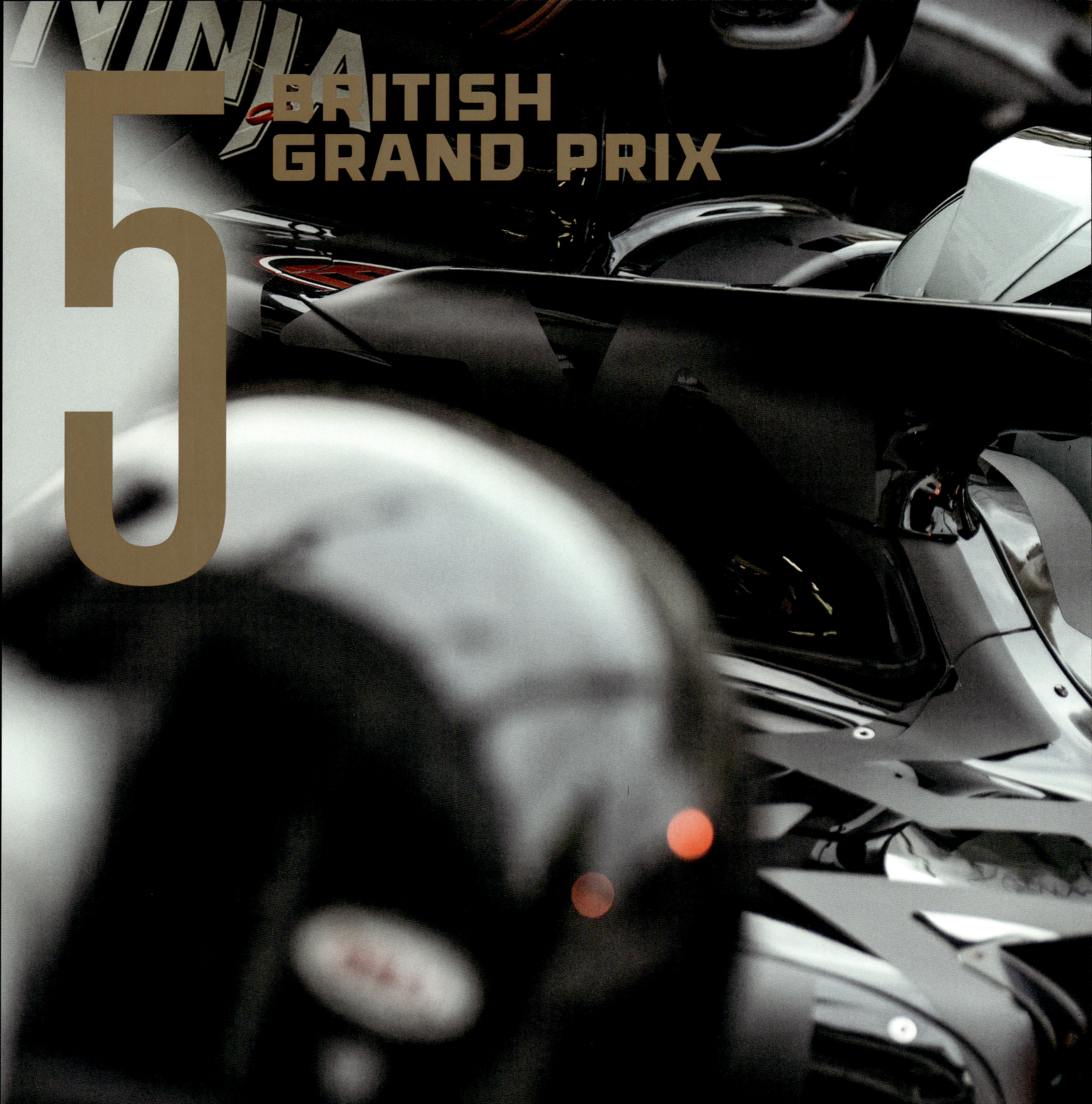

5 BRITISH GRAND PRIX

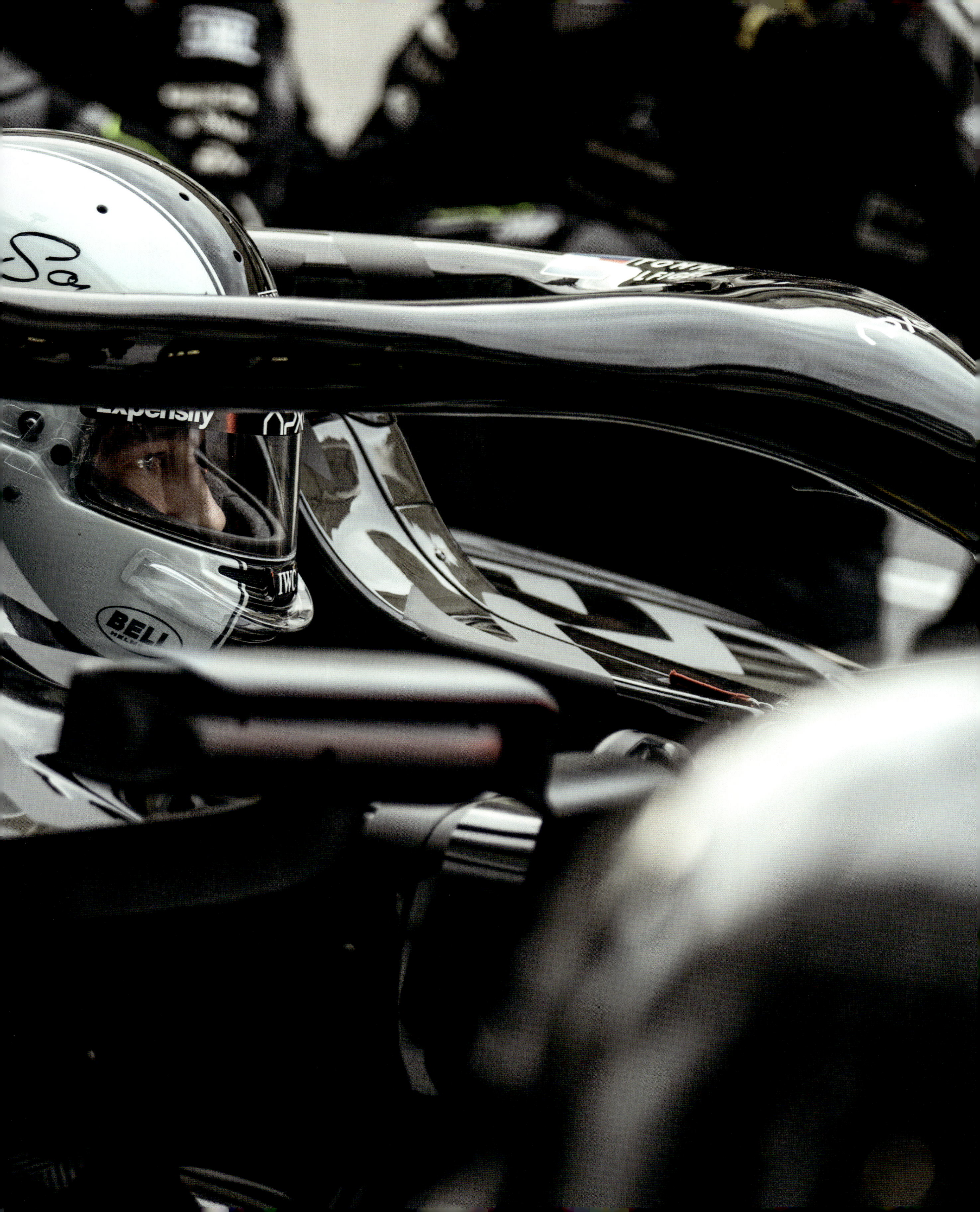
Expensify
IWC

From his earliest conversations with F1 driver Lewis Hamilton, director Joseph Kosinski had an ambitious plan to film at Grand Prix weekends, with his cast and crew embedded in the Formula One paddock in much the same way he had shot at the Navy Fighter Weapons School and aboard the USS *Abraham Lincoln* and USS *Theodore Roosevelt* for *Top Gun: Maverick.*

But integrating a massive Hollywood production into the middle of a Formula One season wasn't without its challenges, with first assistant director and executive producer Toby Hefferman responsible for breaking the script down into a shooting schedule and, in conjunction with F1 and the FIA, working out what could reasonably be achieved during race weekends and what would have to be re-created away from the tracks. "Joe was always, 'We're doing this.' But I started from a place of, '*Can* we do this?' I'd watched *Le Mans* and *Grand Prix*, but, in this day and age, I thought, *This seems crazy.*"

For starters, Kosinski's storyboards—sequential drawings breaking down the action into individual panels, much like a comic book—showed Brad Pitt's character standing at the back of the grid at the British Grand Prix, putting on his fireproof balaclava and crash helmet before strapping himself into his car, with a crowded grid and packed grandstands around him.

"I knew we were going to digitally reskin cars, and I knew we could do the grid as a set extension. That's the easiest way," says Hefferman. "But it wasn't just the cars we would have to re-create. It was the people around them, the mechanics, team principals, and the drivers themselves. That's animation on a scale we'd never be able to create."

The solution, and Kosinski's preferred method, was to do it for real. That meant during the British Grand Prix at Silverstone on July 9, 2023, shooting scenes on the grid just before the race, having Pitt and Idris stand with the drivers during the singing of the national anthem, as well as having both APXGP cars at the back of the grid then pulling away with the rest of the field on the formation lap. Any one of those elements was a huge ask; all of them together seemed like overreaching.

Enlisted to act as a conduit between Formula One and the production was Tim Bampton, former chief communications officer for McLaren Racing, who joined the film as executive producer. "They embedded him with us," says producer Jerry Bruckheimer, "and he's been a vital part of everything we do."

"It was inspiring to work with Joe and Jerry, in different ways," says Bampton. "As a director, Joe's so calm, meticulous, and technical in the way he goes about things. He's clearly got a strong vision, but he's very open-minded in how you get there. The good thing about Joe was, he was so particular about making sure the authenticity was strong but also knew where to apply discretion and creative license. And Jerry is just a force of nature. I'm in awe of his whole approach. He's made so many amazing movies, yet was so invested in this one. Anything he could do to help and support us as Formula One, he would do, whether it was meeting with teams, drivers, the media, or the FIA. I understand what being a producer like Jerry is about, and his energy levels are boundless. They're the Formula One of the movie industry; that blend of Joe's forensic eye and Jerry's experience and storytelling nous was the perfect combo."

Right: Storyboards showing part of the action to be filmed at the British Grand Prix.

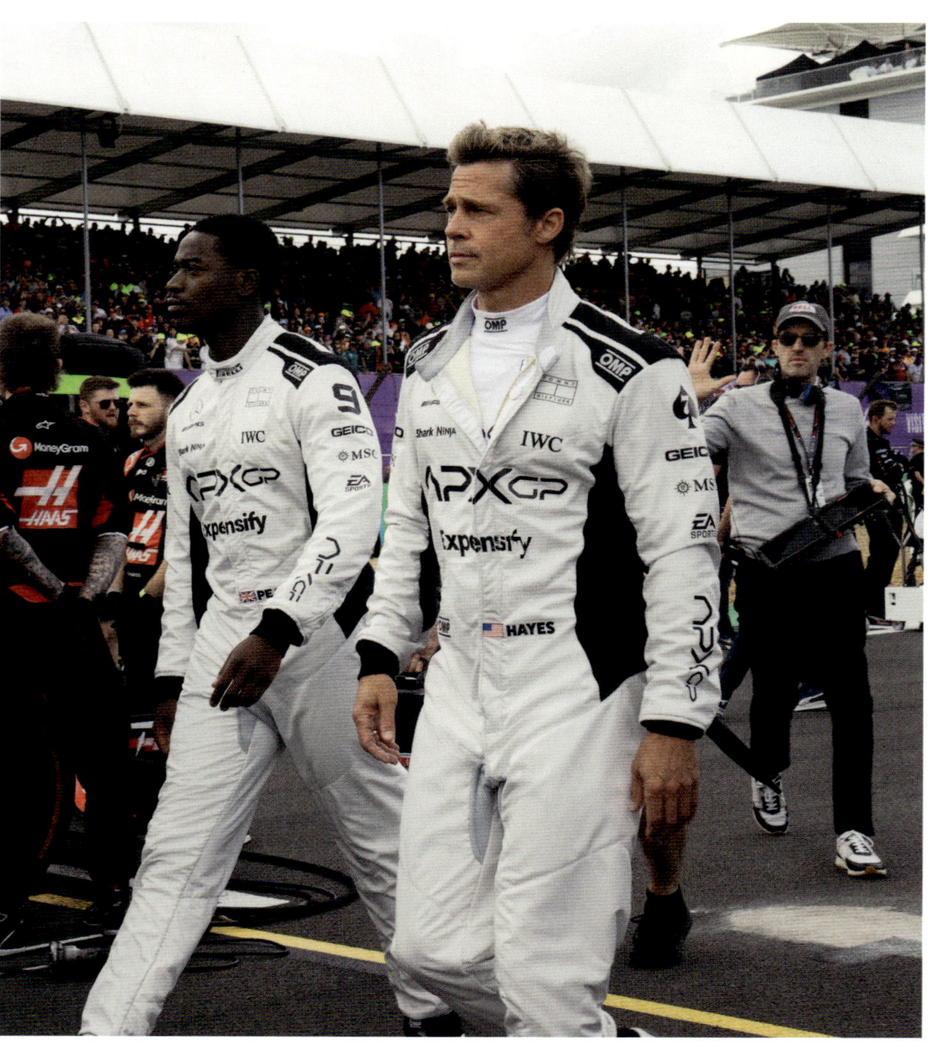

Below: Damson Idris and Brad Pitt make their way through the grid at the British Grand Prix at Silverstone.

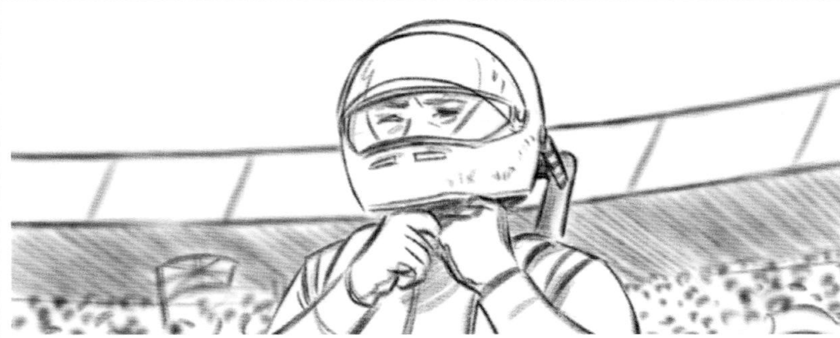

MAIN SILVERSTONE 13
Sonny puts helmet on.

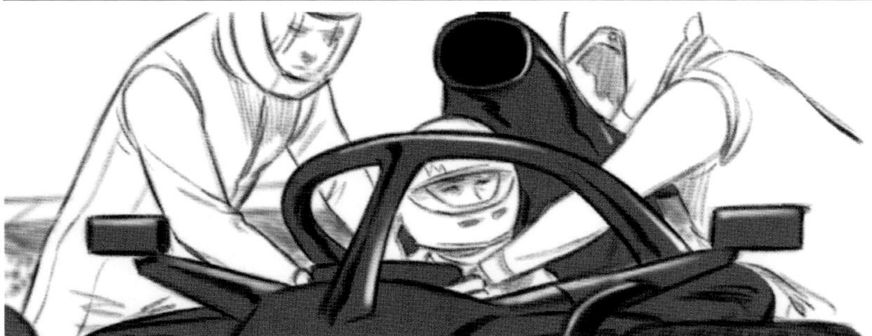

MAIN SILVERSTONE 14
He climbs in his #7, SNAPS ON wheel. Mechanics lock him in.

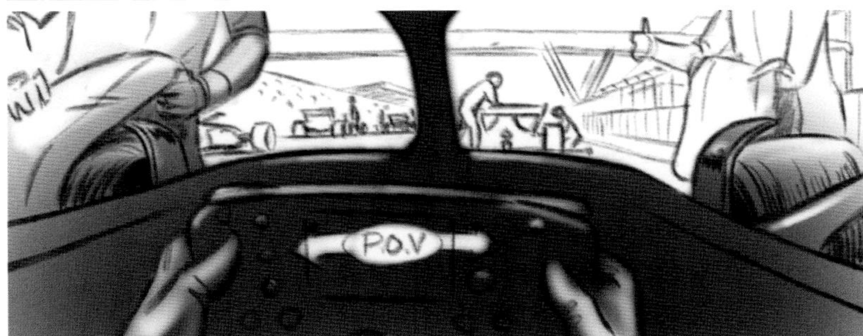

MAIN SILVERSTONE 15
Sonny's POV.

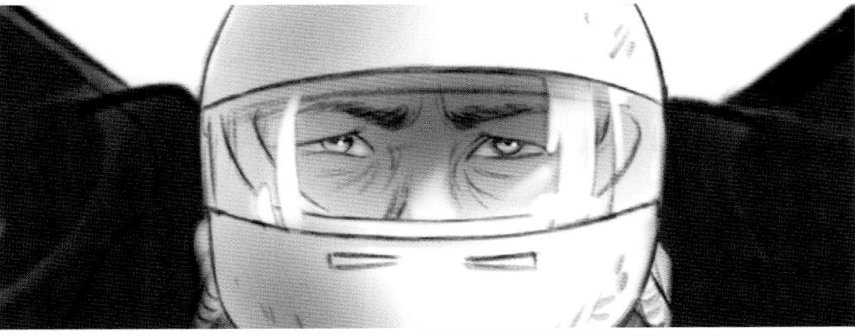

MAIN SILVERSTONE 16
Sonny focuses.

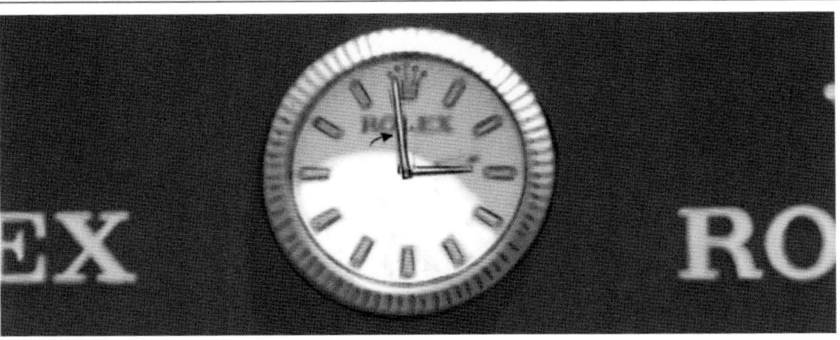

MAIN SILVERSTONE 17
A CLOCK advances to "12:00," triggering FIVE GREEN LIGHTS . . .

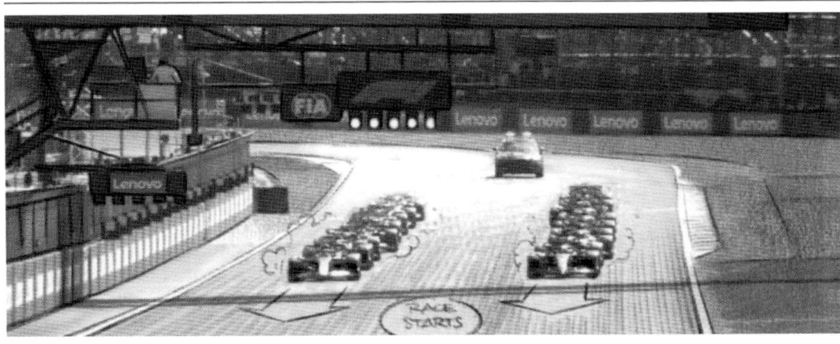

MAIN SILVERSTONE 181
TELECAST (V.O.)
And we're ready to race at Silverstone, as the field sets out on the Formation Lap—one trip around the track for them to warm up tires . . .
ON TRACK:
The twenty-two cars begin their lap, pulling away like a daisy chain . . . except for Sonny, whose car hasn't budged.

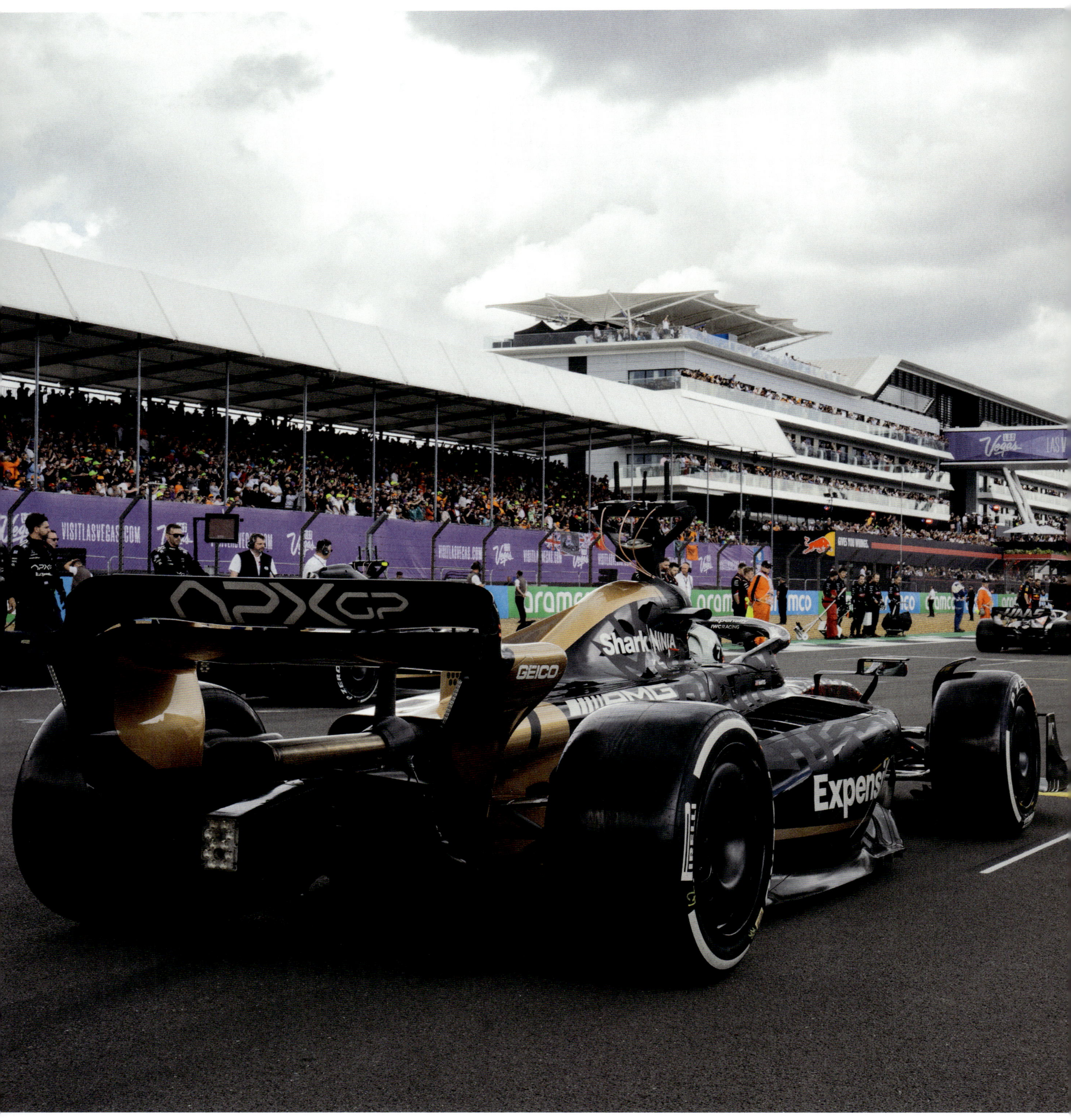
VISITLASVEGAS.COM
GEICO
AMG

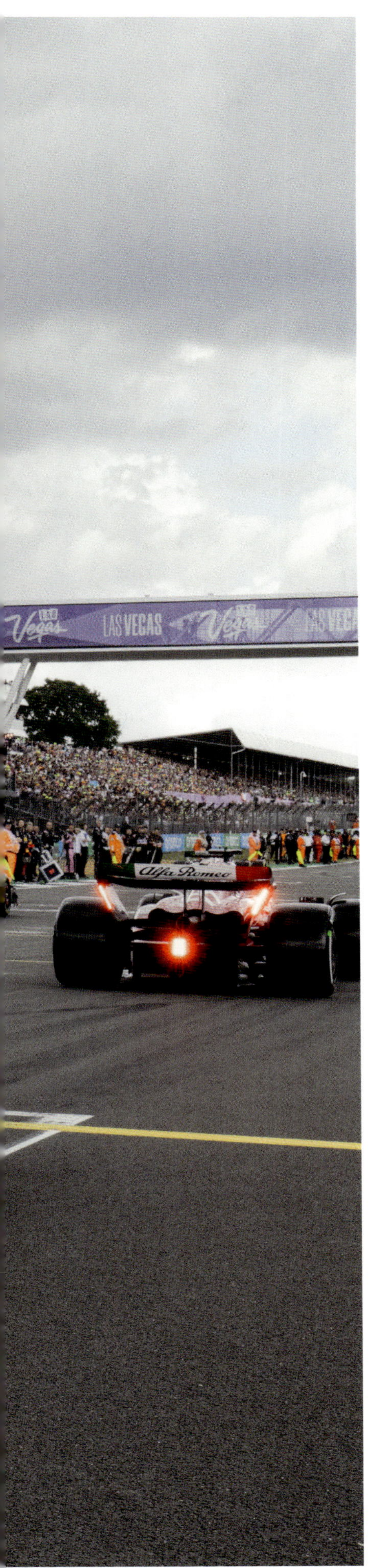

In March 2023, however, Hefferman still needed to know what, if anything, was possible before reporting back to Kosinski, Bruckheimer, and line producer Daniel Lupi at a methodology meeting the following month. Together with production designer Mark Tildesley and supervising art director Ben Munro, he sat down with Bampton to go through the storyboards. "I said, 'This is Silverstone just before the formation lap. This is Brad putting his balaclava on, getting in the car, and the cars pull away. And there's a whole scene with Javier Bardem and Tobias Menzies beforehand. Before that, we're at the national anthem, and we need our drivers to line up with them.' I said, 'If we were to do this at the Grand Prix, how would you do it?' I remember saying, 'How much crack do you think we're smoking?' Tim laughed. But he didn't say, 'No, that's impossible.' He said, 'Maybe. We need to talk to the FIA, and we need to talk to the teams.'"

"I understood the ambition from the outset, just by looking at the storyboards, talking to Toby, talking to Joe, Jerry, et cetera," says Bampton. "It was clear the ambition was that large and there would be some big asks. But to make this movie as special as it could be, we needed to do our very best to achieve them. They were being ambitious, nothing was going to be done by halves, and that's very Formula One."

Even putting the two APXGP cars at the back of the grid was a huge, logistical hurdle. "They needed assurances that our cars weren't going to leak oil or break down, and if they did, how were we going to get them off the grid. But if we could do it, it would allow us to get shots and scenes you just couldn't get any other way, the point of view of what it's like to sit at the back of the grid, looking at a half a billion dollars' worth of machinery."

The filmmakers needed to prove to both F1 and the FIA that they would not interfere with either the race itself or the TV coverage of it. And if they could do that, then the rewards for the production going forward would be immense. "We knew if we played our cards right and gained the trust of the FIA, F1, and the teams, they were going to allow us to do more," says Hefferman, who, in June 2023, traveled to the Spanish Grand Prix in Barcelona with Kosinski and cinematographer Claudio Miranda on a technical reconnaissance to see what the back of the grid looked like on race day.

And so Kosinski spent two weeks at Silverstone rehearsing the grid scenes on the track. "We parked twenty cars on the start/finish straight, regular cars belonging to the crew, and rehearsed it with the cameras," says Hefferman. "Once we got shots we liked and did it with stand-ins, then we brought the actors in. I had a mike set up and was calling the time back from three o'clock, when the formation lap would start."

"We did a lot of work researching the formation lap time," says Bampton, "working back from what point the leader got to Stowe corner, as in that's when we want to be clear of the track. We went through five years of data within Formula One and what was a quick formation lap, what was a slow formation lap, and worked through that with the FIA."

"We rehearsed it and rehearsed it and rehearsed it," says Pitt. "Because not only were we trying to get something for the film, but this was our first proving ground that we could operate within the F1 ecosystem and not fuck up the flow."

Eventually, the production did a fully timed dress rehearsal for the FIA, F1, and F1 broadcast team, knowing that nothing could compromise either safety or the integrity of the Formula One world championship. "Full credit to the FIA for their open-mindedness and can-do attitude," says Bampton. "Without the FIA many of these moments would not have been possible."

The filmmakers also had to show they had a contingency in place should the APXGP cars not start on the formation lap. "We videoed Graham Kelly's mechanics pushing the cars off the grid before the rest of the cars got round the track for the race start," says Hefferman. "It took forty-five seconds."

Finally, F1, the FIA, and the F1 broadcast team were satisfied. "And we were off to the races, quite literally," says Hefferman.

The APXGP car lines up with the other teams on the starting grid for the British Grand Prix.

Due to take place across the weekend of July 7–9, 2023, the British Grand Prix would mark the first race where the APXGP would be part of the Formula One paddock, with the team given a prime spot between Mercedes and Ferrari for their garage.

Not knowing exactly how long it would take to build the garage on site—up until then it had been put together only in the studio—the art department and construction crew arrived at Silverstone on June 19 to begin work. "Initially, we thought it would be a two-week installation, but F1 teams were doing their garages in five, six days," remembers Munro. "Some people were asking why ours was taking so long. And the answer was, we haven't done it before. We've got fifteen people to do it, and F1 teams have three hundred people. By the time all the other teams arrived to start installing their garages, we were ahead of schedule and had our garage pretty much erected."

Once their garage was up, Kosinski and Bruckheimer held an open house on Thursday, July 6, inviting the other teams to stop by. "We invited them to come over, to open our drawers and make sure we got everything right," says Kosinski. "They saw the lengths we were willing to go to make it feel real. And I think they were very impressed with what we did. It was a big hit on the grid."

"Toto Wolff was taking notes, saying, 'We must make ours look like this next year,'" says Tildesley. "We got the sign-off from all the teams. They said, 'You've done a fantastic job. It looks like the real deal,' which was always Joe's ambition."

It was also, for all intents and purposes, a working garage. The art department, alongside the set decoration team, led initially by Véronique Melery and later by Andrew McCarthy, had pulled out all the stops, down to the appropriate tools. "Everyone was blown away by the detail," says Munro. "When Lewis Hamilton came in, he said, 'This is way better than mine.' And Jackie Stewart said it's the best thing he'd seen in the sixty years he'd been in F1." Even the monitors showed the correct data. "Everyone started focusing on what was on the screens, thinking it was going to be made up and nonsense, and it was all correct," says Munro. The graphics were provided by BLIND, a company that provides motion graphics for film and TV.

And, as with all the other teams, the APXGP garage had the names and photographs of its two drivers above the doors. "It was insane," says Idris. "There's my picture. I was able to bring my sister and my niece and nephews to the garage. My niece was like, 'My gosh, Uncle Damson, it's you.'"

"You got these two jackasses who got their pictures up on the pit lane, and they got their own garage as well, sandwiched between Mercedes and Ferrari" laughs Pitt. "We're walking along like we're supposed to be important, while everything else actually important is going on."

Right: The APXGP pit crew prepares Joshua's car for the upcoming race.

Below: Joshua's mother, Bernadette (Sarah Niles), Ruben (Javier Bardem), Dodge (Abdul Salis), and Jodie (Callie Cooke) watch the race from the APXGP garage.

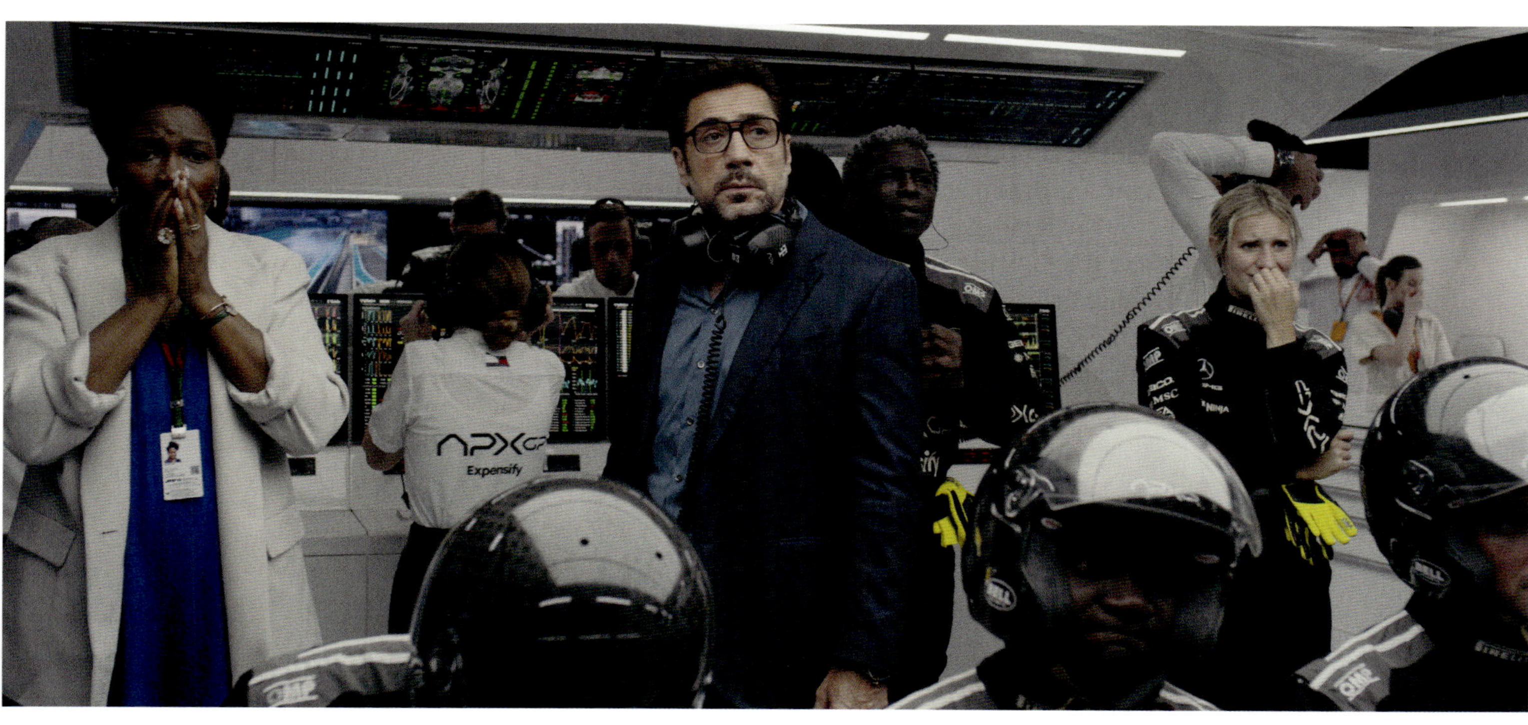

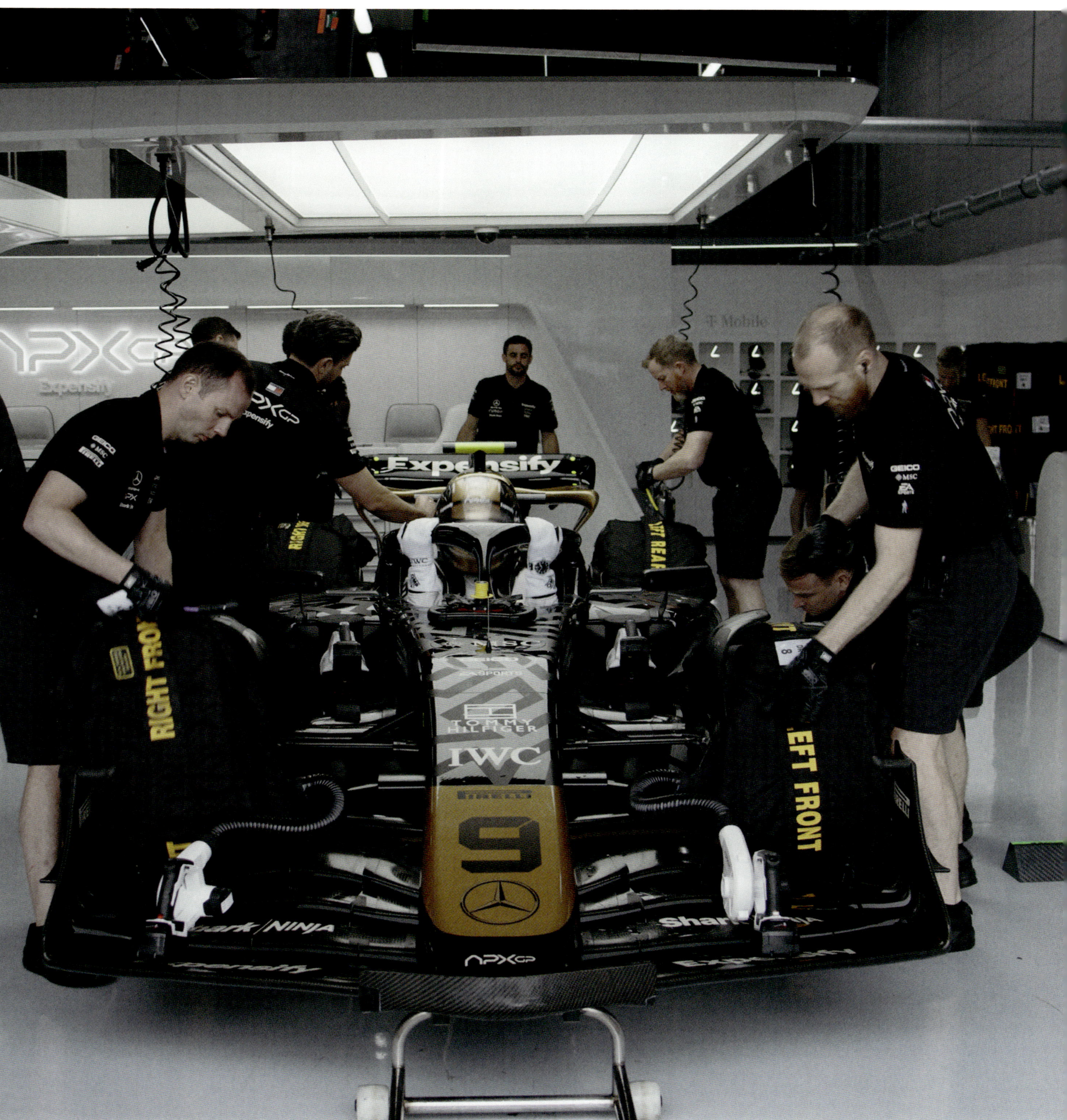
Expensify
RIGHT FRONT
TOMMY HILFIGER
IWC
PIRELLI
9
Shark NINJA
GEICO
MSC
T Mobile
Expensify

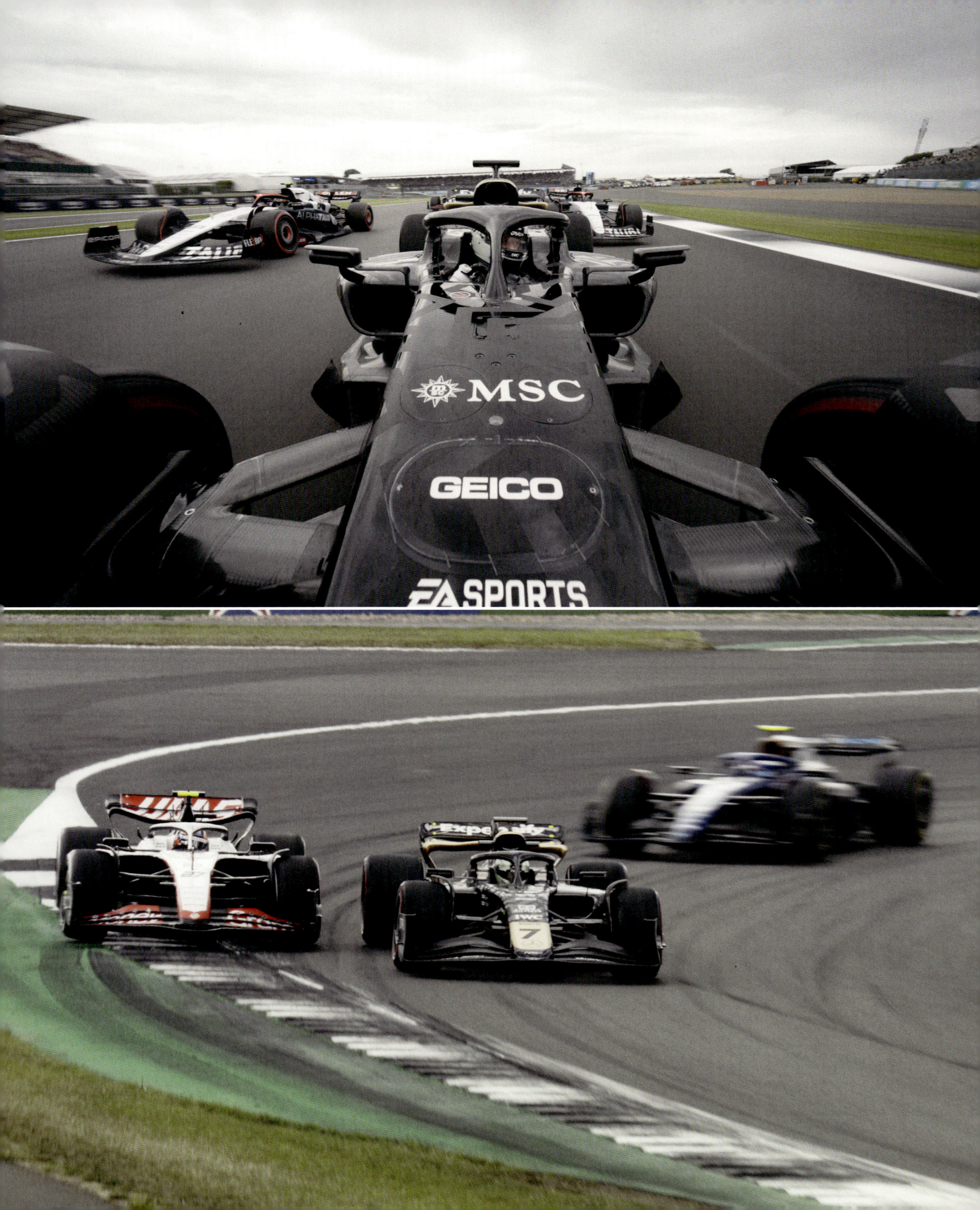
MSC
GEICO
EA SPORTS

“The British Grand Prix had to tell a story about two drivers who end that race at more odds than they started the race with.”

EHREN KRUGER

In narrative terms, the British Grand Prix *was* important, not just in establishing Sonny and Joshua’s rivalry on the track—with the drivers taking each other out during the race—but off it. For screenwriter Ehren Kruger, it was a sequence that presented many challenges. “It had to tell the story of what an F1 race looks like for anyone who has never watched one before—Why do they have to pit? Do they have to refuel the cars? Why are they changing the tires? Why are the drivers not helping each other? How can you draft someone’s slipstream to get a tow?—but we also had to be cognizant that we needed to tell a realistic, authentic race story for fans who watch F1 every week. We had to introduce a lot of ideas very quickly, and in simple terms, so an audience can grasp what’s happening, even if they’ve never seen an F1 race.

“Another aspect was, we’ve said this team has not scored a point, is the worst team on the grid, so we need to depict that somehow,” Kruger continues. “We need to show why this team doesn’t work well together. It can’t just be that the car is designed poorly. We need to show their struggle. And then we need to depict who Sonny is during a race and who is Joshua through the way he races? So, the British Grand Prix had to do a lot. And then it needed to tell a story about two drivers who end that race at more odds than they started the race with.”

Additionally, the race needed to show that Sonny will employ unconventional methods to get ahead. In this case, trying to slow down the rest of the field on the formation lap by delaying his getaway. “Using what seems like a disadvantage in your positioning on the grid and turning that [into] some small advantage,” says Kruger. “That’s the way the character thinks, so he’s going to consider the most counter-intuitive things. And if he does that the very first time you see him in a car, he’s capable of doing that at any time during the movie. Doing the opposite of what you would think would make the most sense. So, the notion became, how long could you do that without getting penalized or disqualified? And could that get you into the midfield at the start? Then we had to clear it with not just Lewis but Toto and F1, saying, ‘Is this within the rules but up against the rules that one could call it an unorthodox strategy?’ And if the answer is yes, then it can be in the movie.”

Scenes from the British Grand Prix race, which needed to highlight Sonny’s (Brad Pitt’s) unconventional racing style.

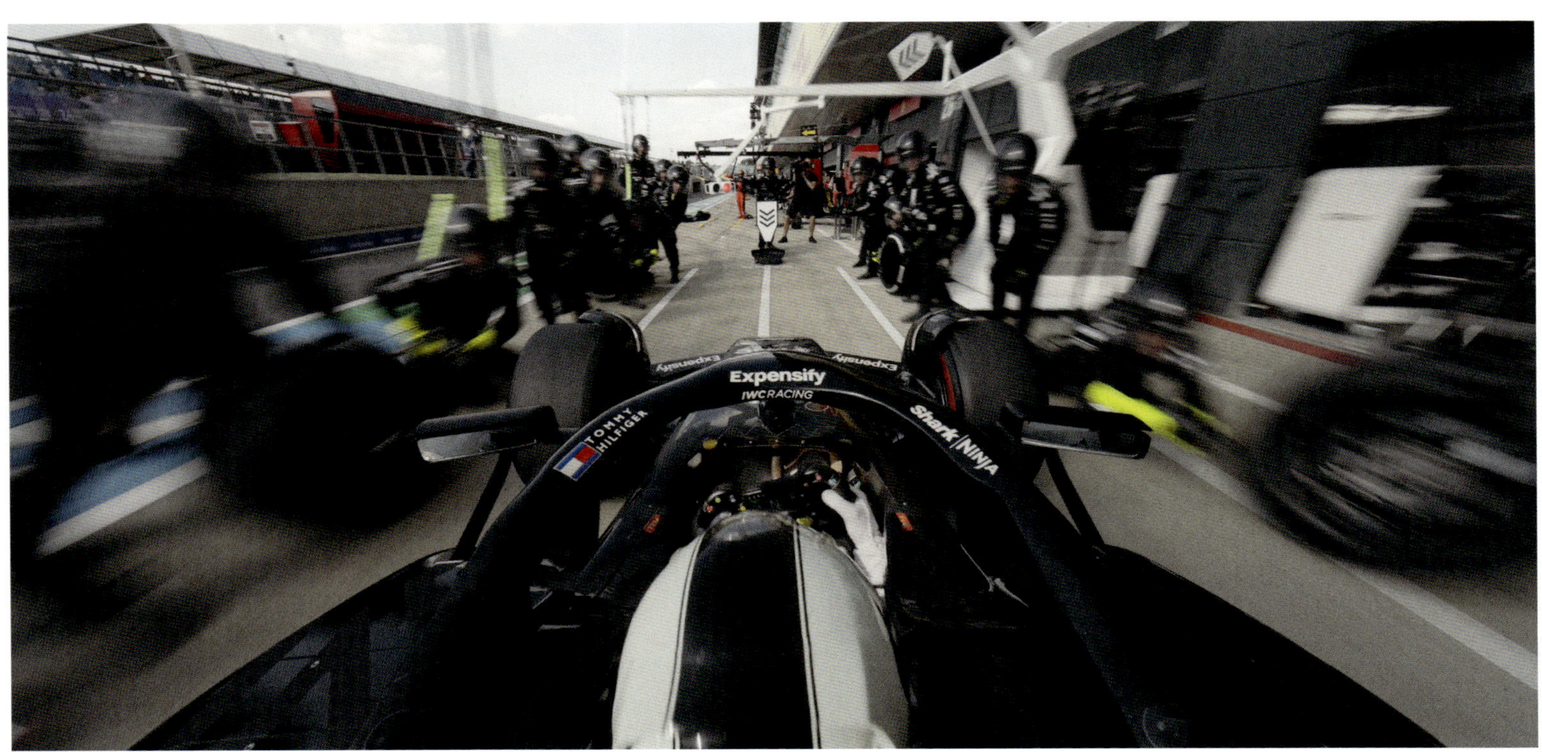

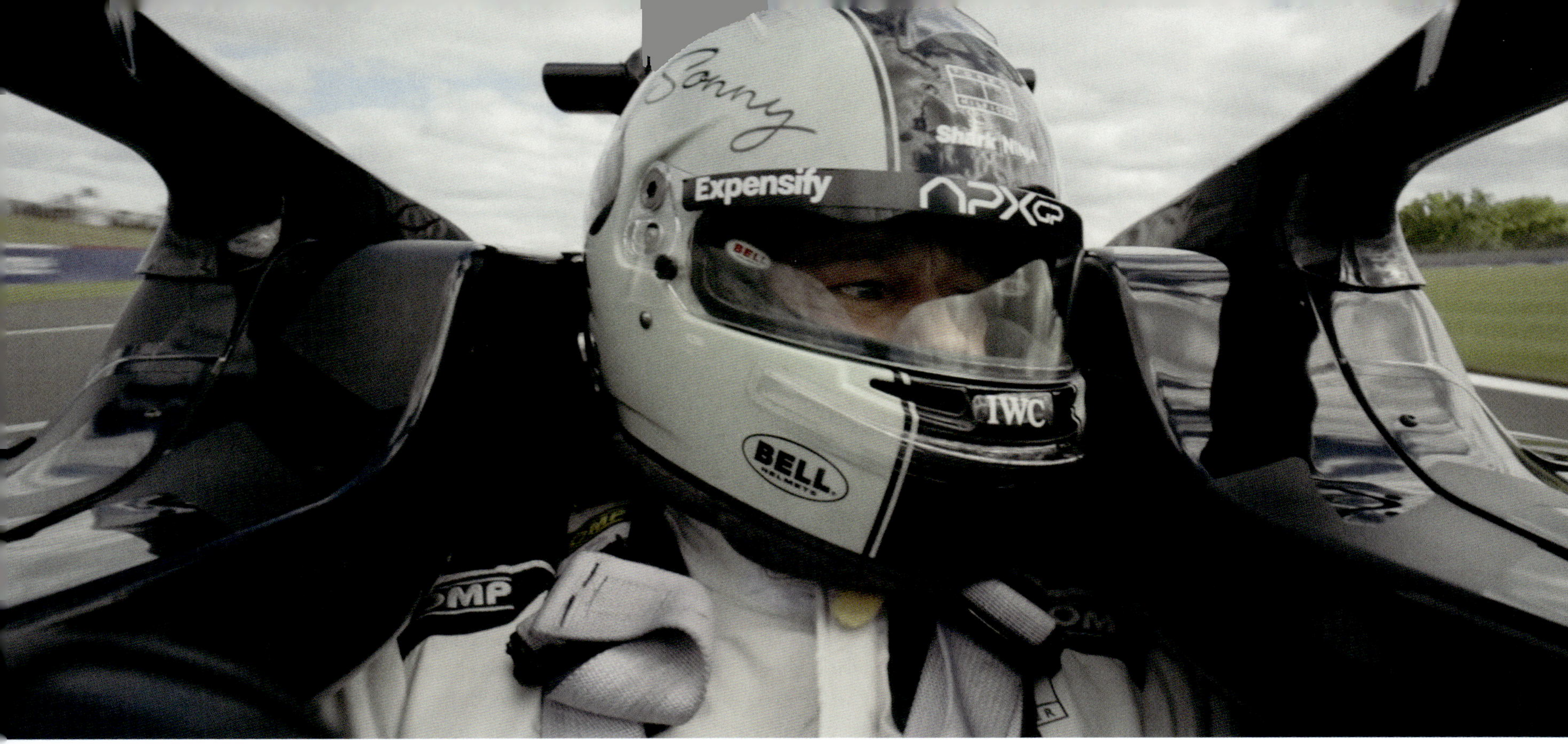

When Kosinski started filming at Silverstone on Wednesday, July 5, 2023, he had a lot to achieve in a short span of time, beginning with a scene involving Joshua arriving at the APXGP garage, only to find Sonny already there, drenched in sweat from a run around the track, immediately putting Joshua on the back foot before the race has even started.

In addition to filming on the grid on Sunday just before the start of the race, the British Grand Prix would also mark the first time that Pitt and Idris would drive their APXGP cars on a "live" track during an actual Formula One race weekend, with Bampton having negotiated with the FIA several short windows during which the production could run its cars on the track. "One of the great things Joe and Jerry did at the beginning was connect me with Christopher 'Pops' Papaioanu, [commanding officer of the U.S.'s Navy Fighter Weapons School aka Top Gun]," says Bampton. "I learned there were a lot of similarities with what we were doing. If you take the Top Gun analogy, our race track was the carrier deck. Anything outside of mission critical activity was 'white space.' It's not just thinking about cars on tracks, but inspections, transition times, driver parades, and pit lane walkabouts. So it was, 'Where is the white space? Let's work from there.' What can we shuffle? Because they would be shooting choreographed moves, not just running around the track for the sake of it. They were shooting against storyboards."

> "If you spin, you might affect the time of the actual qualifying, because they would have to wheel you off. It was the one time when the entire crew got the jitters. But when it worked, it was the greatest thing in the world."
>
> DAMSON IDRIS

"The windows could be any time from eight in the morning to four in the afternoon," says Kosinski. "Generally, we tried to get some warmup laps on Thursday to get the drivers accustomed to the choreography and the track we're shooting at. The hero shooting times—with Brad or Damson in the car—were the ones that usually corresponded to race times. So, 2 to 4 p.m. were the most valuable slots from a shooting point of view, and so we tried to get those hot laps spread around Thursday, Friday, Saturday, maybe one Sunday morning.

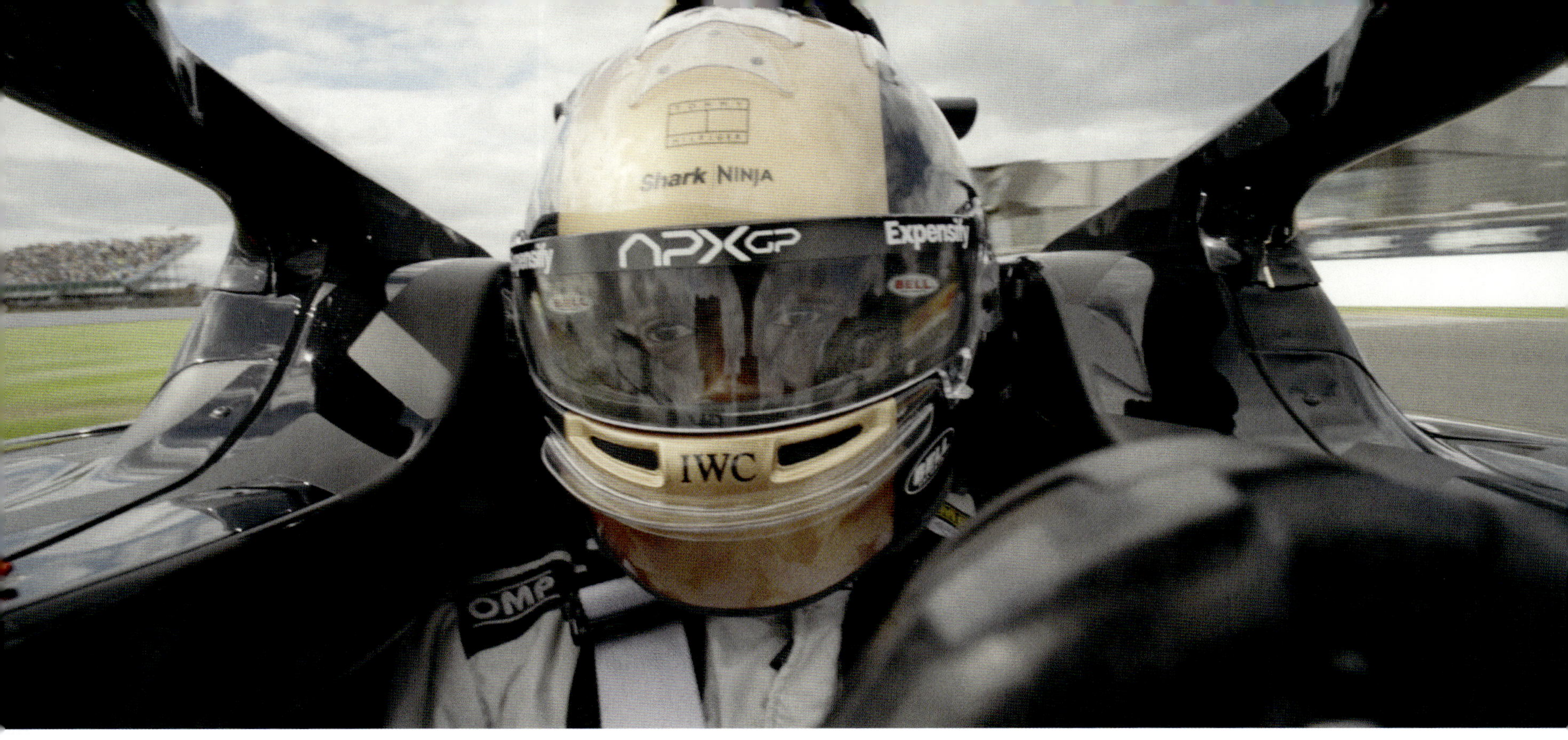

Shots of Damson Idris and Brad Pitt the very first time they drove their APXGP cars on a live track during the British Grand Prix.

But Sunday was mostly reserved for dramatic scenes or the start of the race."

These "hot laps" or "performance laps," as the filmmakers would call them, would involve Pitt driving with stunt driver Luciano Bacheta or Idris driving with Craig Dolby. The two actors never drove on track together.

"We'd have these eight- to ten-minute slots," says Idris. "Ten minutes, I'll go out; ten minutes, Brad will go out. That might be 12 to 12:30 p.m., then, at 3 p.m., we might go again. The importance of those times was because we have the crowd there. So it looks real." But, due to the unpredictable nature of racing, these slots could be curtailed at any moment, by bad weather or accidents in the sessions beforehand. "In between, the real race weekend is happening. There might be red flags. There might be safety cars. It might rain. I got rained on three times during races, so couldn't go out," Idris continues. "Those were the moments when I had the most anxiety, because we had eight minutes. If you stall the car when you start, that's a minute gone. And if you spin, you might affect the time of the actual qualifying, because they would have to wheel you off. It was the one time when the entire crew got the jitters. But when it worked, it was the greatest thing in the world."

Preparation was key. Each driving scene was tightly scripted, storyboarded, and previsualized by the visual effects team in conjunction with Kosinski, cinematographer Claudio Miranda, and the stunt team, with Hamilton signing off on every beat for authenticity and realism.

"Joe storyboarded every scene, especially every action scene," says Bruckheimer. "And they became so proficient at it. Sometimes they only had a five-minute window or a ten-minute window to shoot. Joe trained as an engineer and as an architect, so everything is very precise with him. That's why he was the perfect person to direct this movie."

Hefferman would then break down the required action into, first, a beat sheet, then a master document, complete with track map, detailing what would happen—a line of dialogue, an overtake—and where it took place. "We'd whittle it down to, this is just Damson or this [is] just Brad, so Brad could see that at turn four he had to say this line, so he could focus on driving," says Hefferman. "But there were times where Luch [Bacheta] would turn around to Joe and say, 'I know it says turn four, but turn six would be better.' So, there was always that creative thing going on. And then if there was a stunt, we'd work out how many times the drivers would have to go around the track, because they needed to get the tires up to temperature and get them focused. Same with the actors, before they started their 'performance laps.' It was the most complicated part of the shoot."

Bacheta and Dolby would choreograph and record each sequence in the simulator, then play them back in a pre-brief meeting. Then, on the Thursday of each race weekend, Bacheta and Dolby would drive Pitt and Idris around the track in a four-seater BMW to further familiarize the actors with the circuit. “We also had Hot Wheels model cars on a miniature track set up in the production office where we would drive them around, like boys playing toys, and go over the choreography, turn by turn,” says Kosinski.

“Brad and Damson would know the lines they would have to say at any given point on the track as well as what action—if they’re going to get overtaken at turn one or if they’re going to be overtaking at turn one,” says Bacheta. “Down to the tiniest details, like we might want Brad to look in his left mirror along a particular straight. Everything was written down before we went on track, which allowed the camera team and Joe to know how they were going to shoot it. Then, once we’re filming, we might get a note from Joe—get closer, get farther away, be more camera right—normal movie stuff. But generally, we knew exactly what we were going to do before we drove out.”

“It’s high pressure, high stakes,” says Kosinski. “And for the actors, it’s probably completely nerve-racking and exhilarating because, as with live theater, you’re in front of a live audience performing and acting. On top of that, you’re trying to drive a race car at 150 miles per hour and not crash in front of everyone. That was our biggest fear. Nobody wanted to spin off into the gravel or go into a barrier. So, there was a lot of nerves involved, and a lot of planning.”

Given the limited access the drivers had to the track, production would utilize every second available. If Pitt and Bacheta were out on track for a predetermined set of hot laps, Idris and Dolby would wait in the pit lane, ready to replace them on track as soon as Pitt and Bacheta came in to have their camera mounts changed.

“Part of our job was to make sure the actors were focused,” says Dolby, “to make sure they understand what they’re doing, and make sure they’ve got their specific moves down. But it changed all the time. You could be delayed, so then it’s about keeping them calm, making sure they’re in the car early enough, making sure everybody’s prepared. Because as soon as we go green, we’ve got an eight-minute slot to shoot something that, on a normal film, we’d probably have a couple of weeks to shoot. So, it was getting them in the right frame of mind beforehand.”

Sometimes, the actors would have to combine dialogue from different scenes into one hot lap. “They could be doing lines from one scene in turn four and lines from another scene in turn eleven,” says Kosinski. “That required a little bit of mental jiujitsu on the part of the actors to memorize all that.”

“It wasn’t tricky at all,” says Pitt. “We were so comfortable in these cars. These were *our* cars. And these became *our* tracks. And the camaraderie with Luch and Craig was such that it felt like, okay, this is today’s work, this is what we got to knock off, like any other kind of shot list. It was about pulling off the choreography. But there were things that *were* hairy, like if you had to run it off track onto the sausage curbs. That would get your attention. But we just went for it until we’d get the word from ‘mission control’ saying, ‘Got that bit. Move on to the next.’ And that’s what we do.”

At other times, Bacheta and Dolby would go out for stunt-only sessions—without Pitt and Idris—either battling each other or a third car, with a fourth operating as a camera car. During these stunt sessions, Bacheta and Dolby would double for Joshua and Sonny, respectively, repeating the same on-track action the actors would do, but driving a little faster and harder. To create the moment of Sonny and Joshua racing wheel-to-wheel before their cars collide required a combination of practical stunt driving and digital effects. “There are a variety of techniques mixed in,” says visual effects supervisor Ryan Tudhope. “There is a shot looking at the tire, where the tires are right next to each other, and that second car is digital for safety reasons. But you don’t question it because you just came off the real thing, and this is the type of movie where the visual effects are meant to be hidden.”

Occasionally, Bacheta and Dolby would also be required to play a driver for another team. “Halfway around a lap, I would turn into a Ferrari or a Haas or any other car on the grid,” says Dolby. “So, in one lap you might end up playing two or three different cars. It was a busy time. Those eight minutes could be a blur.”

When the cars were on track, Kosinski, Bruckheimer, Miranda, and Hefferman would sit in mission control in the APXGP garage, viewing

The production team used model cars to help them plan the filming of each race.

the action captured by the multiple cameras on large monitors. "There was a silence when the actors were on the track, a real moment of concentration," notes Hefferman, who would shout out a minute-by-minute countdown for both drivers and crew to let them know how much time was left. "Not just because we were shooting. Joe would watch all the screens and call out to the operators, who were next door, asking them to pan whichever camera at specific times. But because the actors were out on track, I don't want to say you had your fingers crossed, but these guys were driving so fast and doing lines and acting, as well as concentrating on the track. Brad was super good. He is smart and sensible. At the same time, it never got easier. You were always on tenterhooks whenever they went out. I take my hat off to them. It was incredible what they did."

At the end of each stint, the cars would come into the garage, and Kosinski, Bruckheimer, and Miranda would review the footage as best they could in the time available. "We'd often go again in forty minutes, so if we wanted a lens change, we had time," says Hefferman. "For close-ups, there were three different lenses we could play with. So, Joe might be, 'Tight lens on Brad's car, leave Damson's where it is.' Then they'd go out again. Meanwhile, the script supervisor and her assistants are there trying to log it all to make sure editorial has some idea of what was going on, because it's a huge amount of material to understand and ingest."

"Anytime you sent a car out, you had hours of prep time," recalls Kosinski, "but you could also have up to four cameras on each car. That's eight cameras reporting, which is a lot of prep for the camera department. It was like NASA getting ready for a space mission. And that's not the only thing you're doing that day. In addition to those driving sequences, you've got a couple of dramatic scenes that our actors are going to have to jump into. So, it's a lot of balls in the air. But it was also exciting. By the end of the day everyone was wiped out. But the footage we were getting was undeniable."

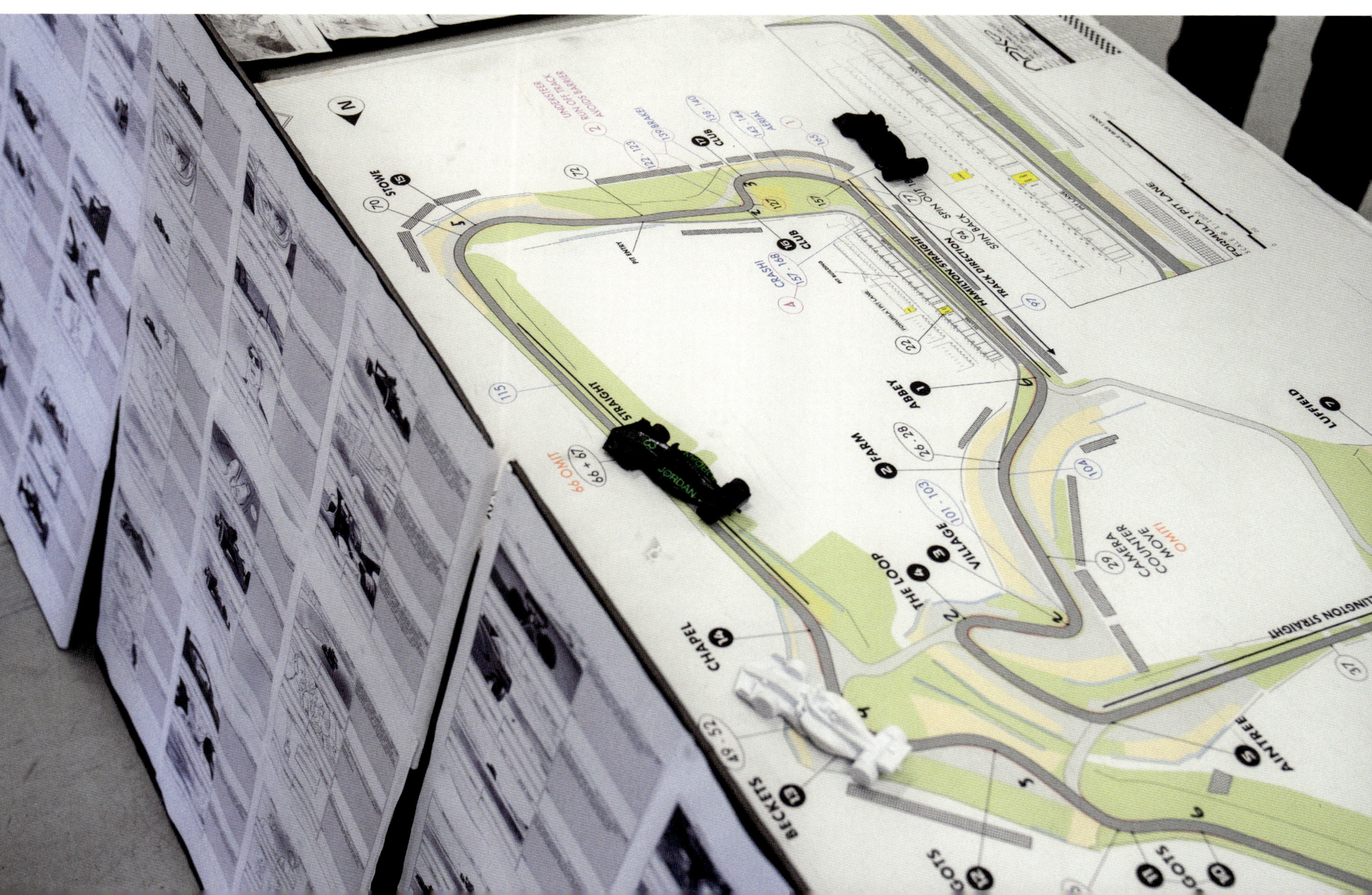

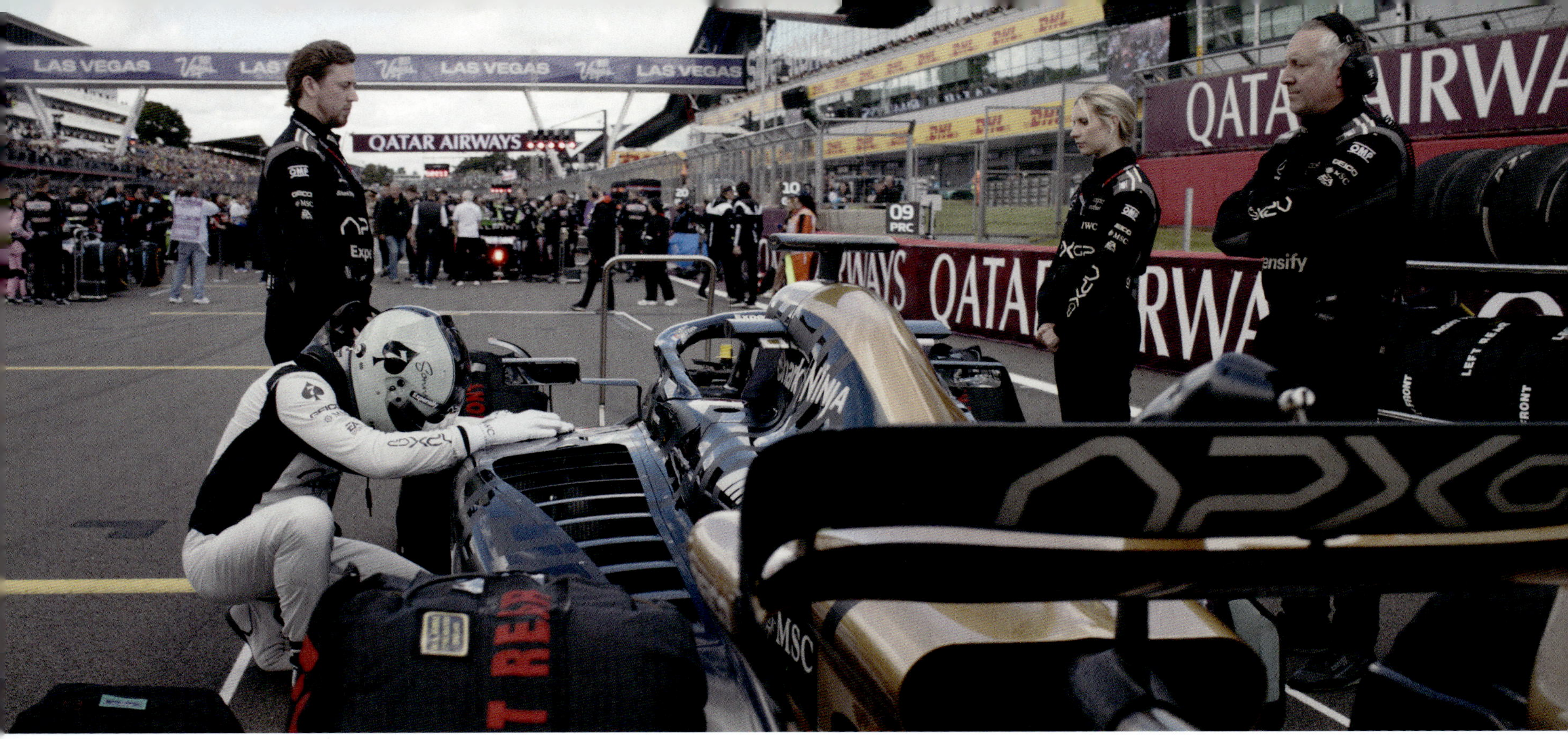

The production's first "hot lap" session at the British Grand Prix in 2023 saw Bacheta and Dolby take to the track for fifteen minutes between 2:45 p.m. and 3 p.m. on Thursday, July 6. "When we turned up at Silverstone, everyone was so nervous, because you just didn't know what to expect. But when we finished the first session, it was a huge relief. Firstly, it looked good. Secondly, we didn't get kicked out," says Bacheta. "Apparently, mission control went silent, then erupted," says Dolby. "After we finished, we got taken to mission control to be congratulated. But that pressure is what we thrive on."

Idris's first hot laps were the following morning between 9:30 a.m. and 9:50 a.m., with Pitt getting on the track for twenty-five minutes on Saturday at 8 a.m. "I was pretty intimate with the track by now, so knew the trouble spots," Pitt recalls. "So, I was just telling myself, 'Don't cock it up, man, don't cock it up.' They put me in the car a half hour early. It's hot as dog balls, and you're sitting in this coffin, waiting to go out, knowing we got this short window, knowing that if there was to be some kind of cock-up, it would delay the whole race weekend. Not wanting to do any of that. So I said to myself, 'I'm going to brake ten yards earlier [than normal]. I'm going to be easy out of the corners.' The first one was just about getting through it."

But once Pitt got onto the track with Bacheta in the other car, he realized his radio

"I had to tell myself to calm my nerves and enjoy it. I saw the stands full of spectators and tried to block them out and make sure I was focused on my turning points, my breaking points, just thinking about the next corner."

BRAD PITT

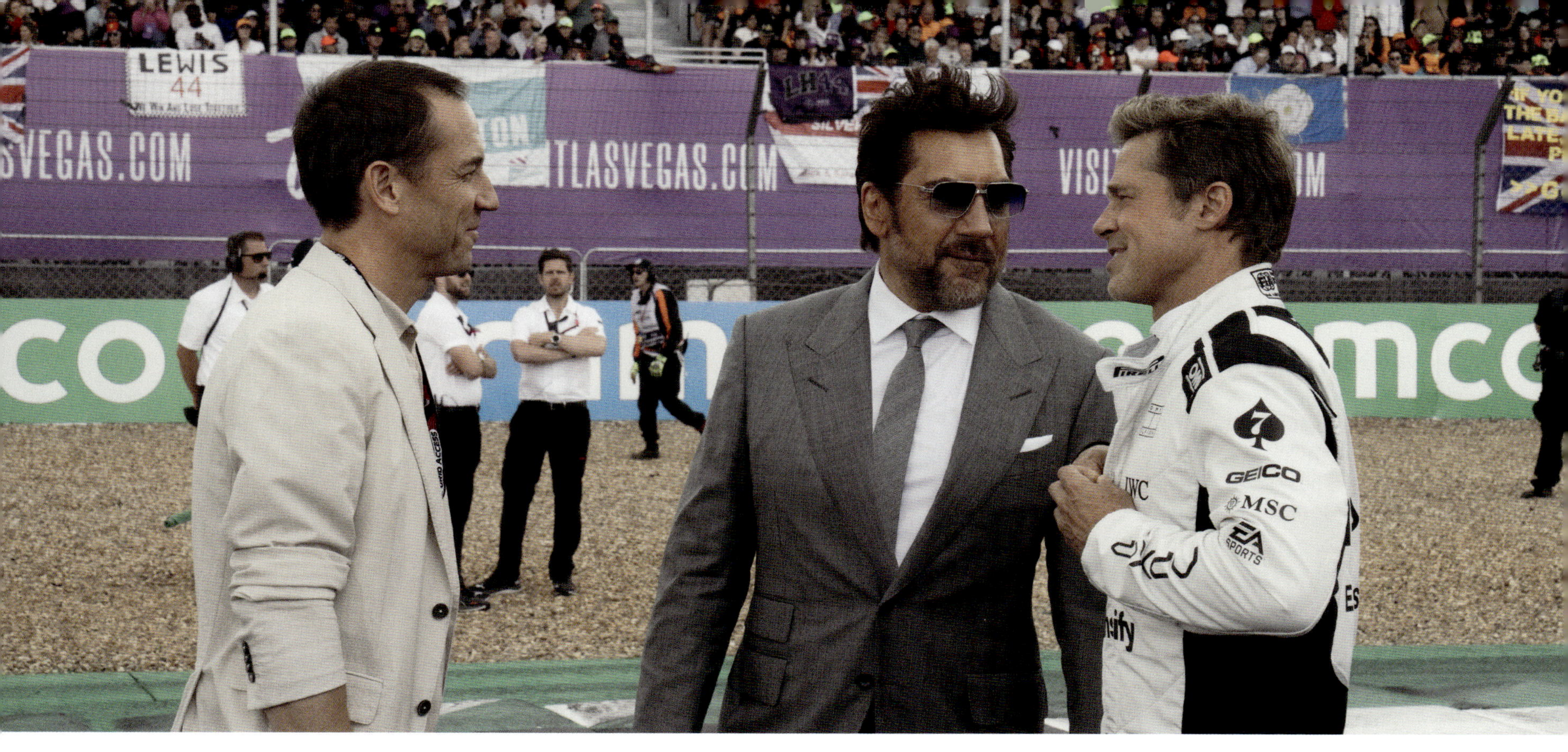

didn't work, so he couldn't speak with either Kosinski in mission control or Bacheta. "I'm driving deaf. Of all times for it to go out, it goes out for that first time out in front of all that crowd. Couldn't believe it. But you've just got to go. It was our one shot."

This was where all the training and preparation kicked in. "I just followed what I knew we had to do, and we were able to pull it off because we had gone over it ahead of time," Pitt continues. "At turn eleven, you need to say this line. On the straight, you got to hit this. This is where Luch was so good. He could drive these things and keep one eye on me in the mirror, keeping me safe. It's like he was driving two cars. I can't say enough about those guys."

Footage from that initial session was used in the film's first trailer, which aired during the British Grand Prix the following year. "I can see the difference in the driving," says Pitt. "And it's a disappointment for me, because I see it's very calm and calculated. But I had to tell myself to calm my nerves and to enjoy it. I saw the stands full of spectators and tried to block them out and make sure I was focused on my turning points, my breaking points, just thinking about the next corner. And it worked out all right."

Besides the on-track action, Kosinski also had to shoot a number of dramatic scenes before race day involving Joshua, his mom, Bernadette (Sarah Niles), and his manager/cousin, Cashman (Samson Kayo), walking through the busy paddock; scenes with Ruben (Javier Bardem), Banning (Tobias Menzies), and assorted VIP guests watching the race in the APXGP hospitality suite; as well as scenes on the APXGP pit wall with Kate (Kerry Condon), Kaspar (Kim Bodnia), Nickleby (Will Merrick), and Rico Fazio (Joseph Balderrama). "We also had cameras in the stands to get reactions from the crowd. We had scenes on the balcony with Javier next to real fans, watching the race. There was stuff happening everywhere during the whole weekend," says Kosinski.

Top Left: Sonny (Brad Pitt) kneels before his car for good luck in a pre-race ritual.

Top Right: Ruben (Javier Bardem) introduces Sonny (Brad Pitt) to Peter Banning (Tobias Menzies), a member of the APXGP Board of Directors.

Sunday, July 9, 2023, marked the seventy-fourth running of the British Grand Prix. "It's like the Super Bowl, only bigger, because of the people that hang out at the track and their enthusiasm and how they wear the colors of all the different drivers," says producer Jerry Bruckheimer. "It's amazing the level of fandom the sport has there."

But for the film crew, the British Grand Prix was the most pivotal day of the production so far—and not just in terms of what he had to film. If they screwed up, it was possible that their plans to shoot at more Formula One races would be severely curtailed.

Crew call that day was 8 a.m. "I'm not sure if I've ever done a day like it," remembers Hefferman. "The jeopardy here was, what happens if our cars don't pull away from the grid? I knew we had a [backup] plan, but those things start getting in your head."

The production was told it would only be allowed nine people on the grid but ended up with sixteen. To help keep the crew small and nimble, and to minimize their presence, Miranda had developed a small, handheld camera rig using the DJI Ronin R4D 8K fitted with Sony G series lenses, which the production dubbed "turkey heads." "We just needed a little gimbal because a Steadicam is too big and awkward. We had such limited time and had a bunch of things to get, so we needed to be quick."

Between 2 p.m. and 2:10 p.m., the *F1* cast and crew assembled on the grid. Kosinski had two "turkey head" cameras—one operated by Miranda, the other by Lukasz Bielan—and he could view what they were filming on two handheld monitors. Each camera had its own focus puller and grip. They were joined by production sound mixer Gareth John, a boom operator, and F1 liaison Tim Bampton.

At 2:20 p.m., the film crew headed to the front of the grid, where Kosinski had lined a tracking shot across the track. Five minutes later, the two APXGP cars were moved into position at the back of the grid.

At 2:41 p.m., the twenty drivers started to make their way to the front of the grid where the British national anthem was about to be sung by actor and musician Damian Lewis.

Meanwhile, Kosinski moved into position, ready to film the driver lineup, which this year would include the APXGP duo of Sonny Hayes and Joshua Pearce.

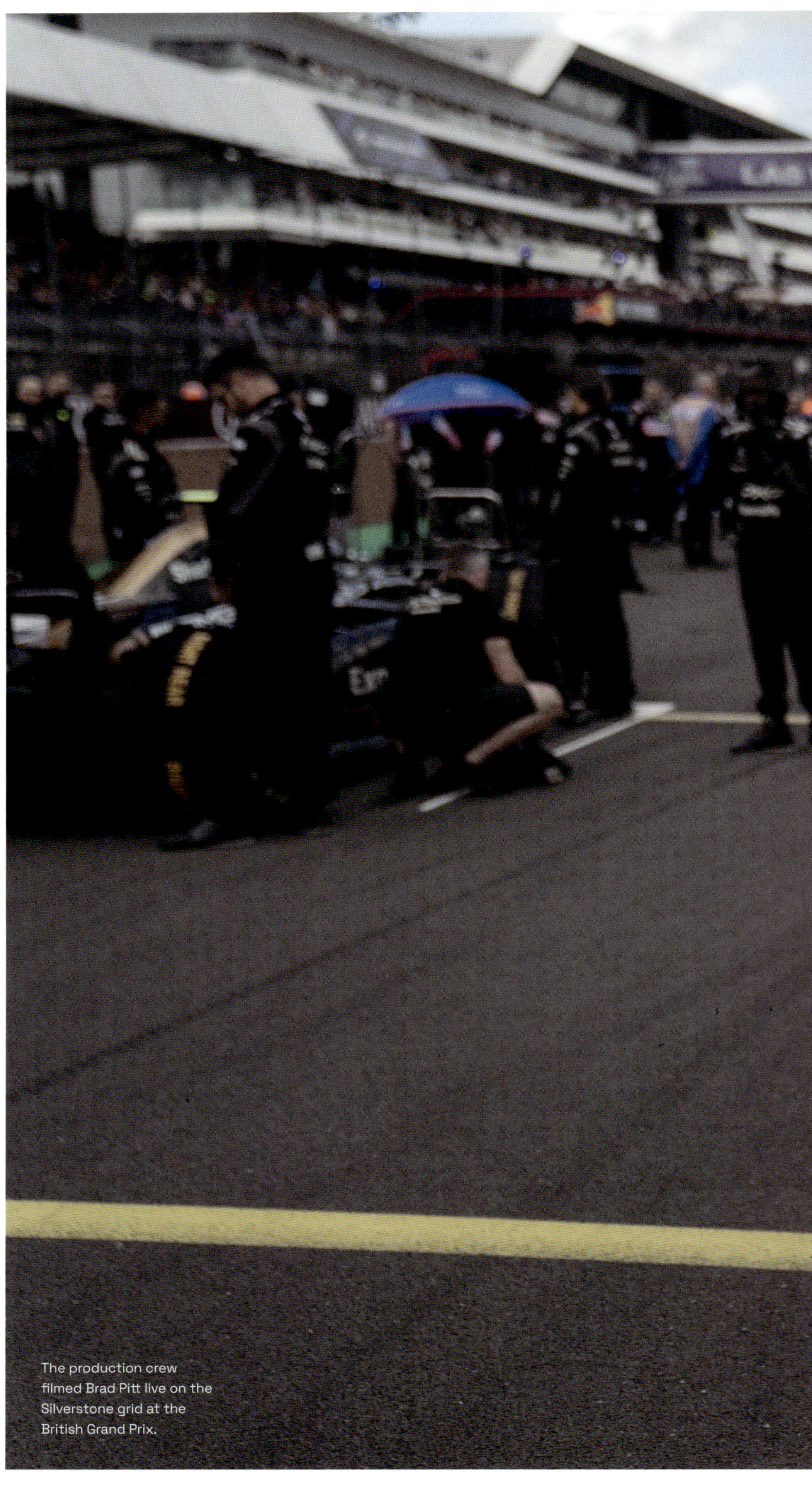

The production crew filmed Brad Pitt live on the Silverstone grid at the British Grand Prix.

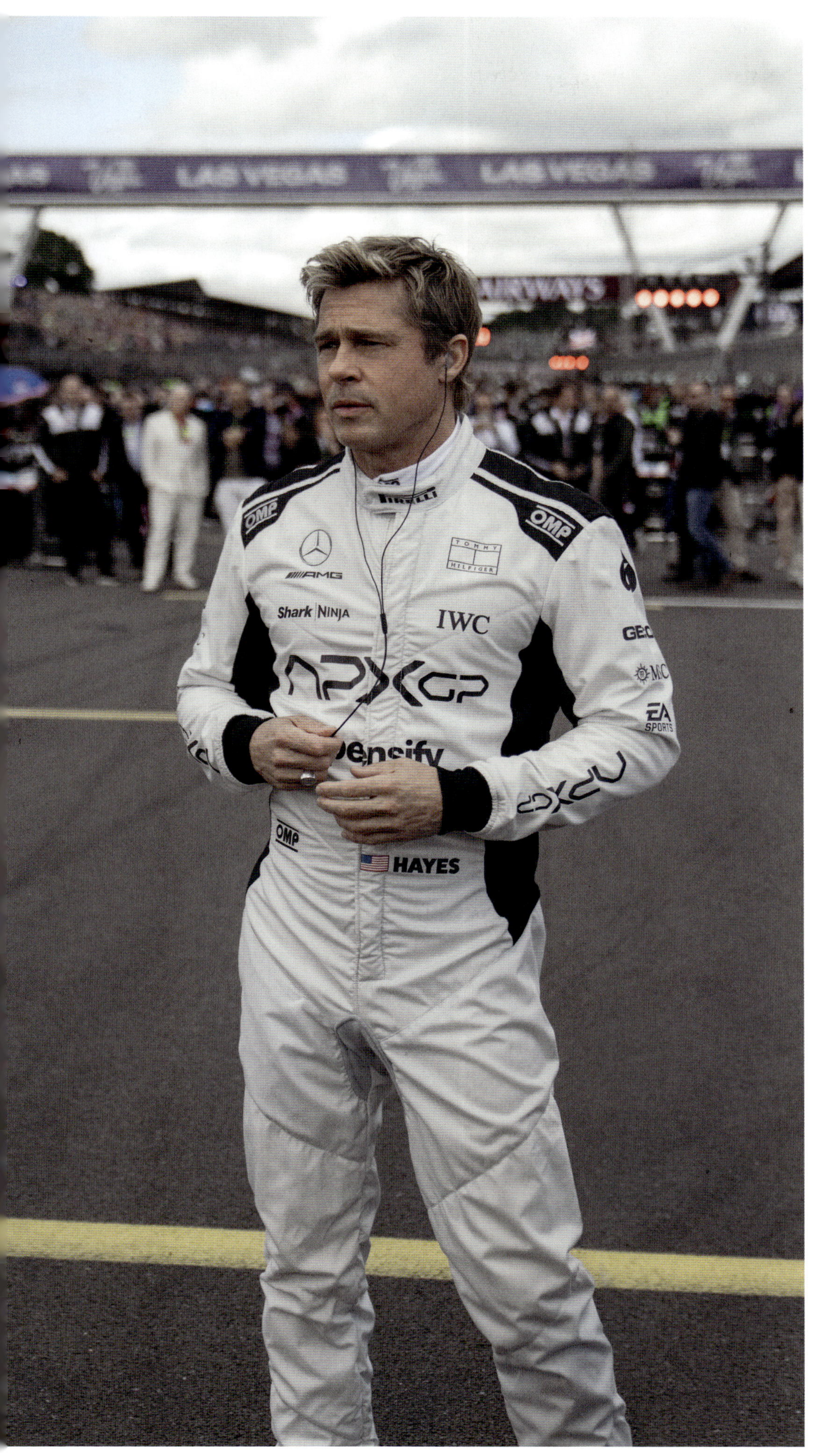

At the same time, Hefferman summoned Pitt and Idris to the grid. "I called Brad five minutes early because I was so afraid he was going to get mobbed. He came on, and I was standing on the grass with him. This is the fourth movie I've done with Brad, and I remember saying, 'We've done zombies, you've killed Nazis. This is going to be easy in comparison.'"

At 2:45 p.m., Pitt and Idris took their positions at the end of the driver lineup, standing next to Red Bull driver and current world champion Max Verstappen. "Fucking big balls to stand there next to Max Verstappen and sing the national anthem before he's about to go race," laughs Pitt. "Because I'm in such awe of the sport, and because these drivers are so revered, by me included, I was a little tentative. But you've got to shake out any embarrassment and get on with it."

If you were one of the millions of viewers watching on television, you wouldn't have seen either Pitt or Idris standing there. "Everything was choreographed with the F1 broadcast team so we could get our shots without them shooting us," says Kosinski. "Because it wouldn't make sense for people who tune in to watch a sporting event to see Brad and Damson standing next to Max. We didn't want anything transmitted that infringed on the purity of the actual sporting event."

At 2:46 p.m., actor Damian Lewis started to sing the British national anthem, "God Save the King." "I remember the note was: Joshua Pearce isn't supposed to be smiling; he's supposed to be ready and focused for the race. But I couldn't help it. I was teeth and smiling," says Idris. "I remember Brad looking at me and saying, 'This is fucking insane.' At that point you're not acting. You're just *there*. It's so real and authentic, you don't need to do anything but be."

At 2:48 p.m., as soon as the national anthem was over, Pitt, Idris, Kosinski, and co. made their way through a crowded grid toward the back of the grid, filming as they went. "When we rehearsed, it was just me and Brad," says Idris. "There was no one on the grid. There was all this space. But when we got there, there was no space. There are tires where I'm supposed to walk. There's a car here. There's a bunch of fans, so we're having to maneuver through people. And Carlos Sainz is right in front of me, where I'm supposed to be walking. That's why there's that picture of Brad, me, and Sainz, because he got in front of me."

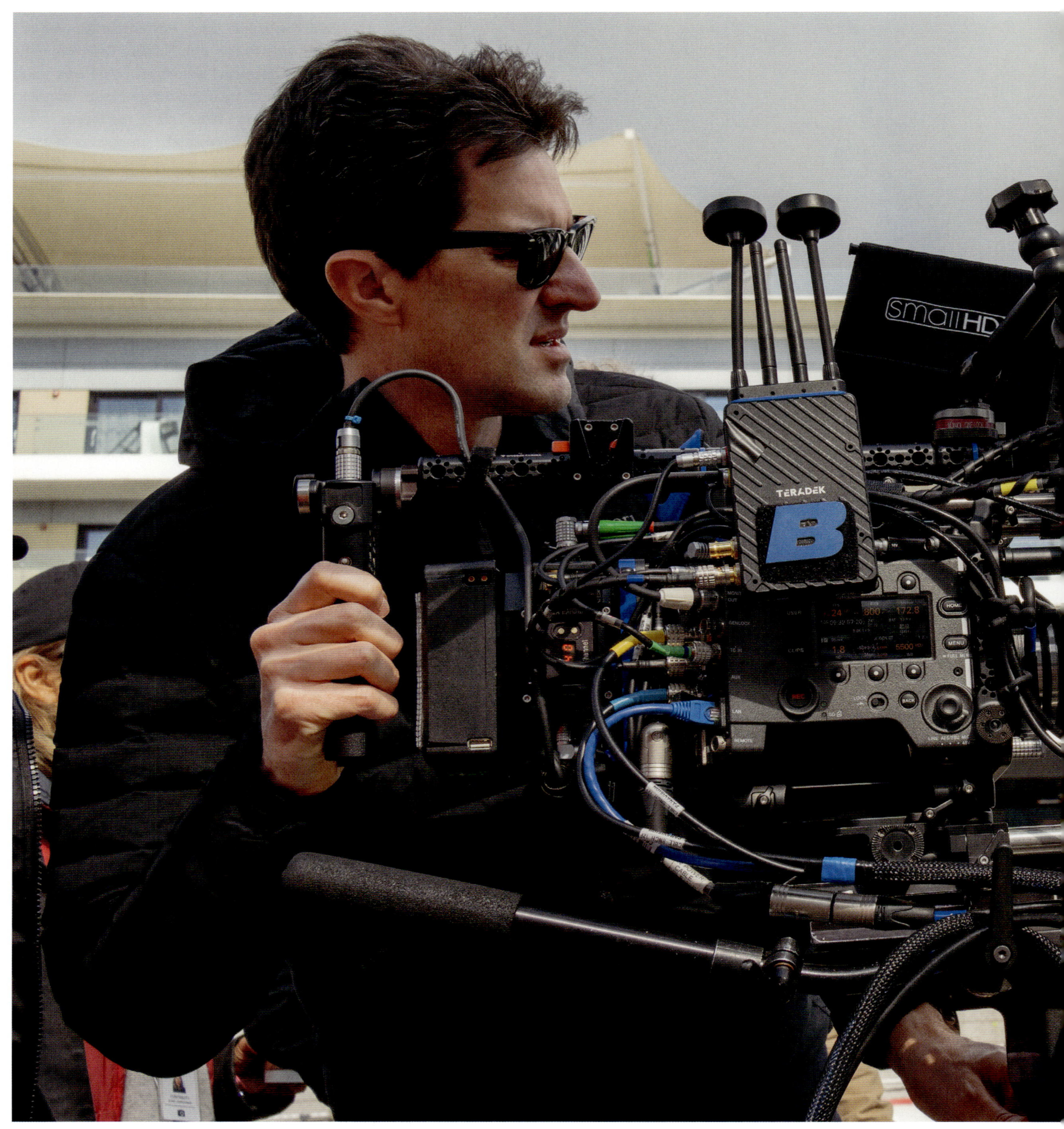

Joseph Kosinski captures the action on the track.

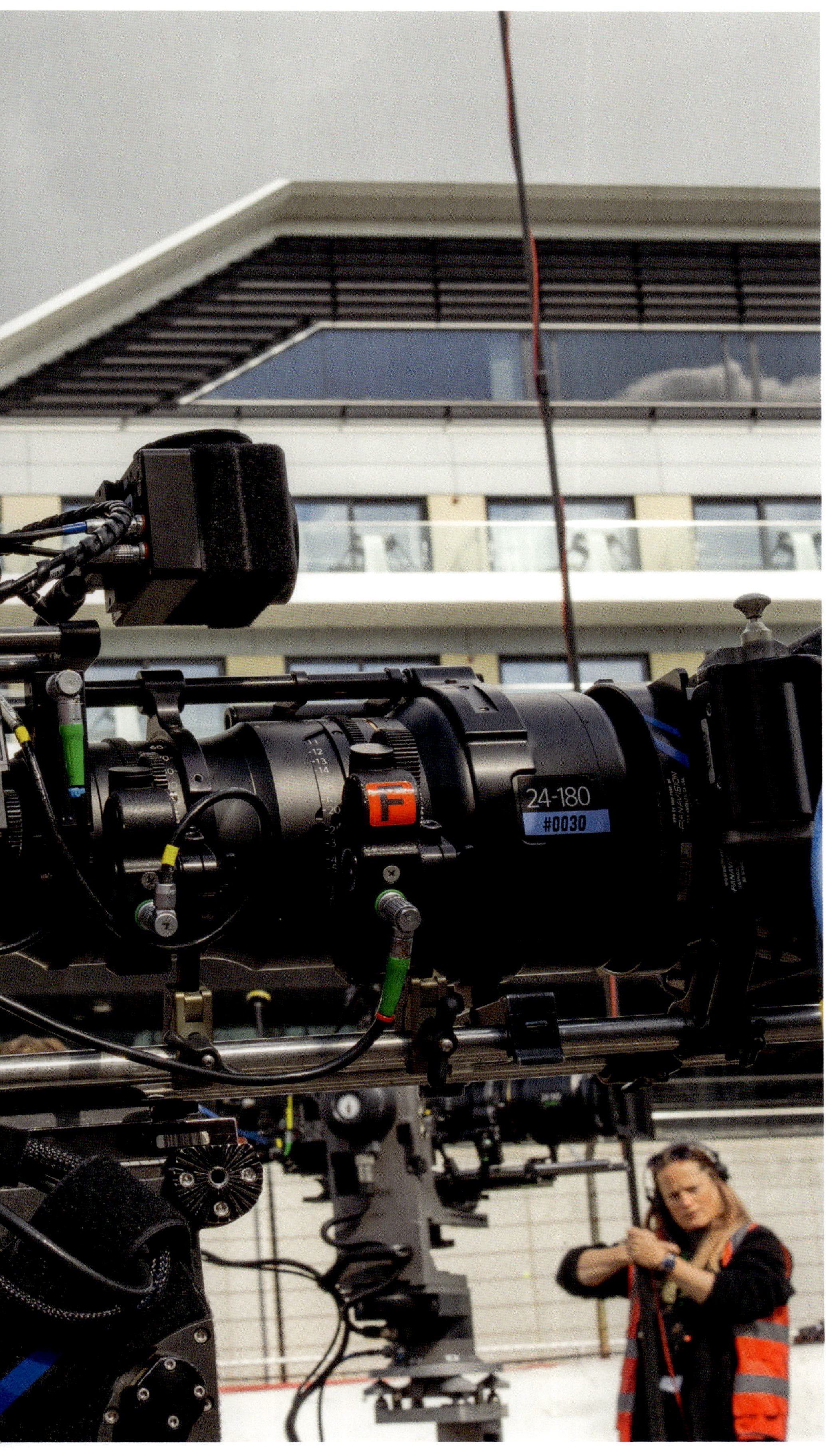

En route to the back of the grid, Kosinski picked up actor Simon Kunz, who plays the reporter Cavendish, to film a walk and talk with Pitt. "We got two takes of that," says Kosinski.

Finally, Pitt, Idris, Kosinski, and co. arrived at the back of the grid to find Javier Bardem and Tobias Menzies waiting for them. "Brad and Damson stepped into the third scene, at which point the two cameras were repositioned to shoot that," says Kosinski. "I had three scenes to shoot back-to-back-to-back over the course of ten minutes. I'm listening through headphones, running beside everything, watching on two monitors, seeing what we're getting, then resetting, giving the actors notes and having them go again, instantly. Calling out different coverage. We were able to get three takes of the final scene before I jumped to another camera position, behind the APXGP cars, ready to shoot them as they pulled away down the grid, which was the fourth scene. It was like a live show. We probably spent two weeks planning those ten minutes."

"I liked the energy of it all," says Pitt. "I've always felt a day on set is like a prize fight. The bell rings, and you're doing your thing, and then it's off, and you get to sit in your corner and catch your breath. This film felt like that more than ever. I loved the energy and the propulsion of these moments, like we got to get it here, then we're moving, moving, and we're in position, the bell rings, and we go. There's something exhilarating about that. It's do or die. Whatever we get, success or failure, is going to be it, carved in stone."

"The energy, the power, the noise, the crowd, the fact you have a long dialogue scene to do among the real drivers, the real cars, and you have only three minutes to do it, gives you such an adrenaline rush," says Bardem. "At the same time, for them, it's normal, they're used to it. So, you have to digest it, normalize it, and play with it, not making a big thing about it. Like, this is my life. This is my world."

"We had eight minutes to shoot that last scene," says Hefferman. "We'd rehearsed and worked out the angles, so we're not dicking around. Some directors might turn around and say, 'It's not enough. I need more time for performance.' And if that was the case, we'd have worked out how to do it again. Joe was always faced with, 'We can absolutely do this. *But* you've got six minutes to shoot it.' And he was, 'Okay.'"

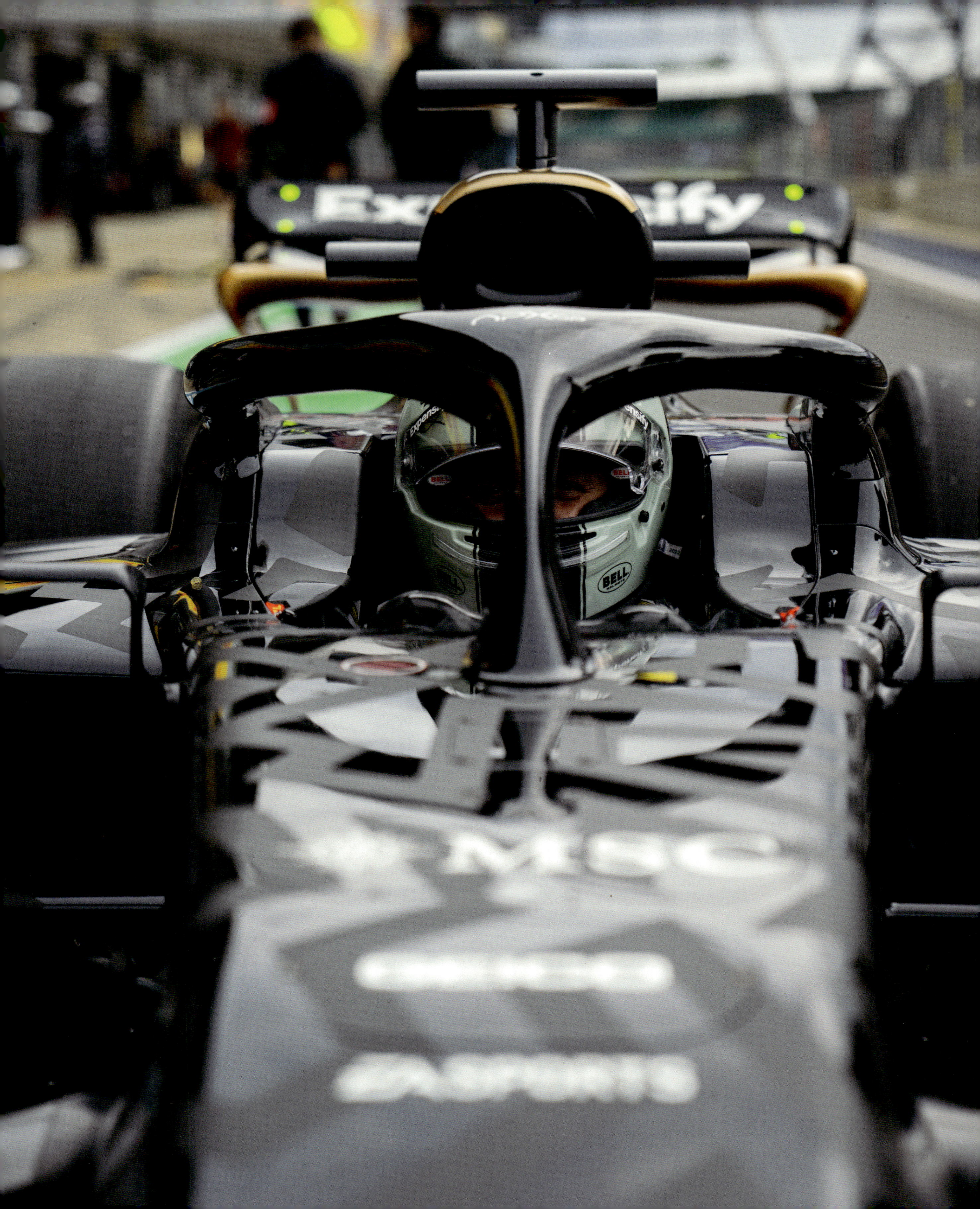
BELL

“You want to get the shot. My big thing was, don’t stall, don’t delay the start.”

CRAIG DOLBY

But Kosinski’s work was still not over. As Pitt, Idris, Bardem, and Menzies exited the grid, the APXGP mechanics readied their two cars, in twenty-first and twenty-second positions, for the start, strapping Bacheta and Dolby into their seats in preparation for the formation lap. As agreed with the FIA, Bacheta and Dolby would follow the twenty other cars along the start/finish straight before veering off the track and driving through a service gate at turn one.

For the formation lap, both APXGP cars and their drivers had been covered in cameras. But Kosinski wanted another camera to start high then boom down as the cars pulled away, a shot that would have normally been done with a camera crane.

“We couldn’t put a crane on the back of the grid. There was no time to get it off,” says Hefferman. “This is where Claudio’s brilliant. He said, ‘I’ve got an idea. We’ll do a “turkey kebab.” I’ll get a stick, a boom pole, and attach a turkey head to the end, and we can literally boom down.’ He wanted to change lenses, which would take ninety seconds, so we built that all into the schedule. It worked a treat, and we were all ready to go.”

At 3 p.m., the green lights on the grid indicated that the formation lap was about to begin. The Red Bull of polesitter Max Verstappen led the pack away, followed by Lando Norris’s McLaren in second, Lewis Hamilton’s Mercedes in third, and the rest of the field, including Joshua, who was being doubled by Bacheta.

In the script, Sonny, in last place, delays his getaway until the last possible moment, to try to eke out a tire advantage over the cars directly in front of him.

On the grid, Dolby was playing Sonny. “The cars start pulling away, and Sonny has to wait to give some tension,” says Dolby. “F1 were saying, ‘No, no, no, you can’t wait too long,’ and I had Joe going, ‘Craig, wait as long as you can.’ So, I sat there and thought, *I’m going to get in trouble here*. But you want to get the shot. My big thing was, don’t stall, don’t delay the start. Then pull off to the side, jump out the car.”

However, when Bacheta eventually tried to pull away, his car stalled because of a hydraulic issue, which delayed Dolby pulling away as he was supposed to go after Bacheta. “Time stops at that point,” admits Hefferman. “All I could see was a little bit of fluid kicking out from the back of the car, and I’m like, ‘Fuck, the car’s not moving!’” Fortunately, the production had planned for any such issue at the start and quickly sprang into action.

Once again, TV viewers around the world were none the wiser, with the F1 broadcast team cutting away from events at the back of the grid to follow Verstappen and co. around the track.

“James Boughton, our brilliant track supervisor, said, ‘We got to go.’ Because the rest of the cars were going to be back around in two and a half minutes,” continues Hefferman. “Graham Kelly’s mechanics were brilliant. They jumped on the back of Luch’s car and pushed it off the grid, through a crash gate in the pit lane. Meanwhile, the other car did its thing. It drove off as planned, then pulled out at the first turn and got pushed into the FIA garage.”

Bacheta’s car had suffered a catastrophic loss of pressure because of its DRS [drag reduction system]. “The DRS in a Formula Two car works in a different way to a Formula One car,” reveals action vehicle supervisor Graham Kelly. “It runs on less pressure as well, so in designing this car with a new Formula One rear wing, Mercedes had designed a ram that was bigger than a Formula Two ram to work the DRS. So, when Luch went to grab a gear, the car stalled, and he had no oil pressure, because the DRS was draining all the pressure out. He didn’t have any gears and couldn’t restart the car, because Formula Two cars don’t restart.

Craig Dolby, Brad Pitt’s stunt driver, in the pit lane.

Fortunately, we'd rehearsed pushing the car off in the event of something going wrong. Thankfully, we weren't pushing two cars, we only had to push one. But from that moment on, I changed the whole DRS system to work in a very different way."

Once the race was underway, Kosinski sprinted down the pit lane to where Kerry Condon, Kim Bodnia, and the rest of the APXGP pit wall crew were waiting in the team's "Wendy House," to film scenes throughout the Grand Prix, as they monitor their cars during the race, with the field roaring past them. "When I got the job, I had been briefed by Joe that 'live' filming was one of the aspects of it, and we were only going to get so many takes," says Condon. "And there was going to be an element of pressure that was unusual to regular filming. I love stress in the sense that I like a rise to the challenge. So, I was excited about it. At the same time, once you're on that pit wall, you can't really get a makeup or hair check." Denise Kum was the film's hair and makeup designer. "We couldn't have crew crossing the pit lane," continues Condon. "Once you're there, you're there, and you had to let go. It was so much adrenaline. And so much fun. My biggest fear was not I would fuck up a take, but we would do something that would disrupt F1. Like if a piece of paper went flying and landed in a car. Things like that terrified me."

The production had even gotten permission from the FIA to fix a Technocrane with a Sony Venice attached to the pit wall. "It was able to reach up over the fence and shoot the real race, then boom down and reveal our team on the pit wall," says Kosinski. "We set the crane up three days before and had to put all our technicians, including me, on the wall, squished up against it, during the race. It's crazy when you think about it, but I've learned to not take no for an answer. That's something I learned from Tom Cruise on *Top Gun*."

In addition to scenes of the pit wall, Kosinski had to film a tense moment in the APXGP garage between Pitt and Idris while the race was running in the background, as other teams brought their cars in to change tires. "It was production value you just couldn't re-create because our garage was in the middle of the pit lane," says Hefferman. "It was incredible."

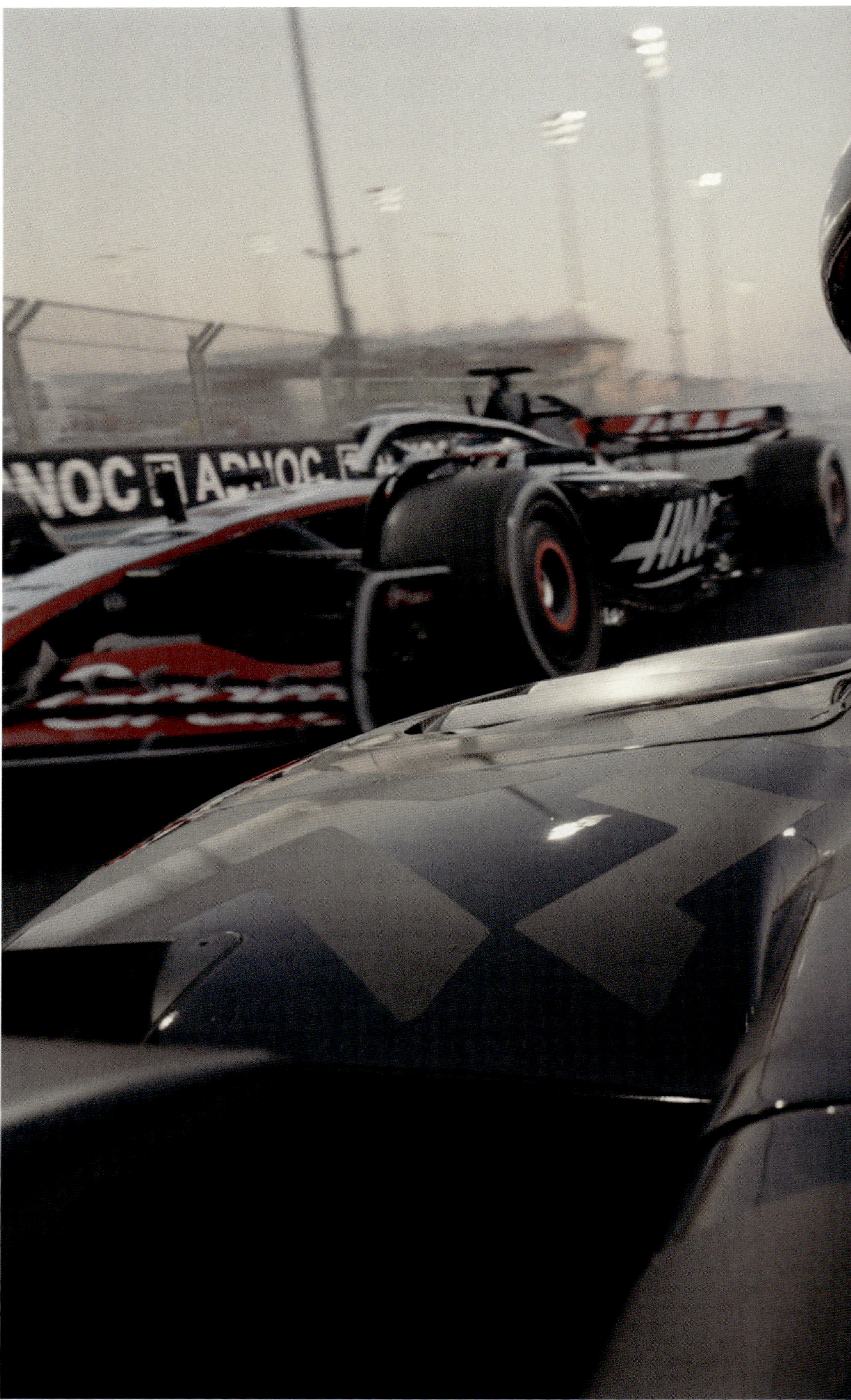

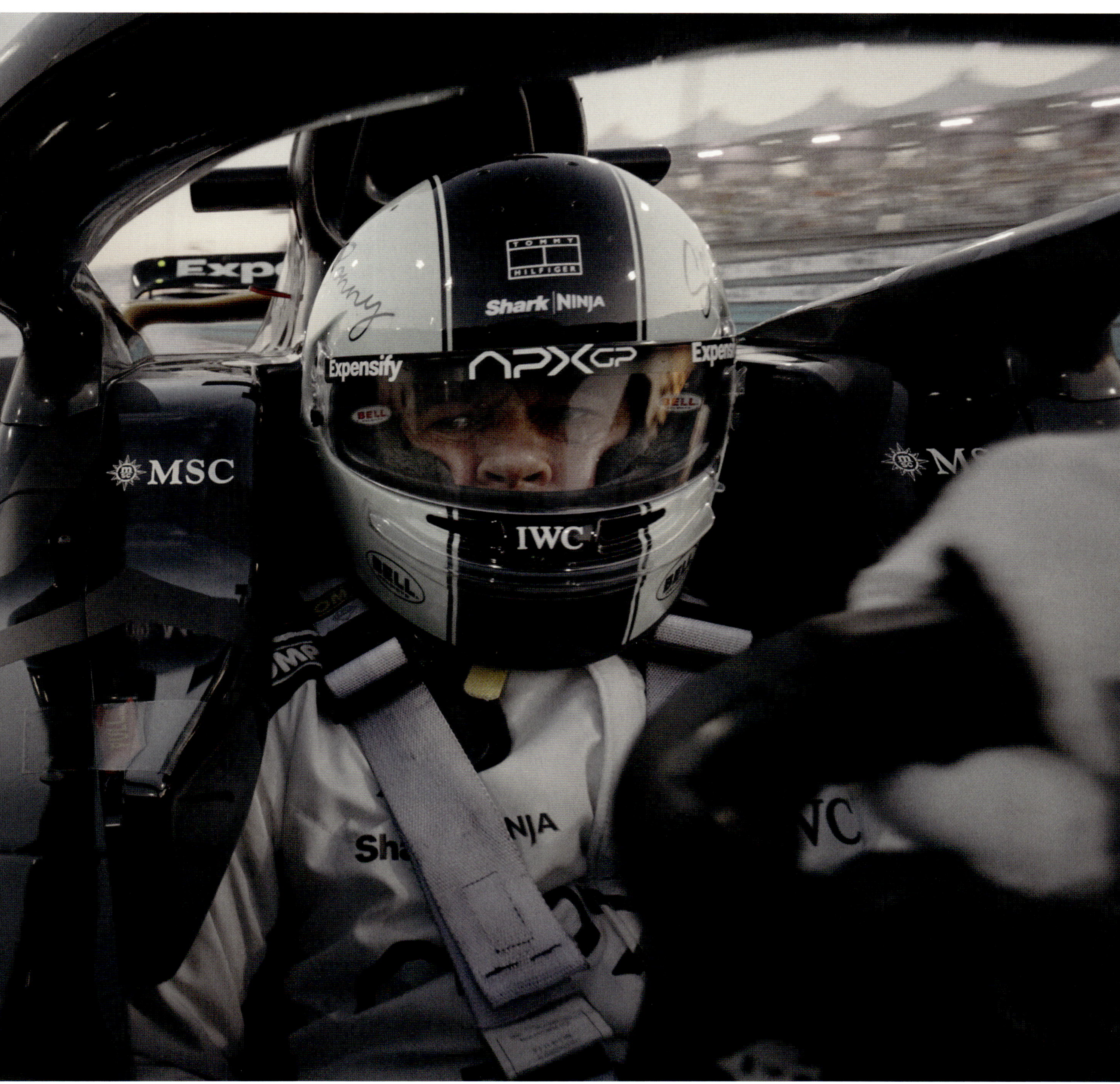

Sonny (Brad Pitt) dukes it out with the Haas car.

During the "race," Sonny and Joshua are battling each other on track before committing the cardinal sin of racing, taking each other out, with Bacheta and Dolby doubling for the APXGP drivers as they get increasingly close on track before making contact. As their cars touch wheels, Sonny spins off into the gravel, leaving his car beached.

Close-up shots of Pitt spinning in his car were shot using a 360 Plus rig that special effects supervisor Keith Dawson (*Back in Action*) manufactured. "It was, effectively, a biscuit rig," says Dawson. "We built a replica APXGP Formula One chassis with fully finished bodywork and mounted cameras on the front and side, then had a stunt driver tow the rig along and with the actor in [it]. It could do a revolution in two seconds and had smoke coming from the tires, so it was a massive help for visual effects and obviously Joe. But it was also good for the actors to be in the moment. We got up to speeds of 85 to 90 miles per hour, which, depending on the section of track, was quite hairy. We used it multiple times on the movie. I rode it myself at a slow speed, and it was disorientating. Obviously, you didn't have a big breakfast before you got in, but both actors nailed it."

The actual spin into the gravel was filmed at a later date using an F3 car, so as not to damage any of the "hero" or picture vehicles. "We didn't have an unlimited number, and they were valuable," says Tudhope. "F3 cars are still expensive, but, from a movie standpoint, damaging them is less of a risk, financially. So, we would send our F3 cars into these situations, then digitally replace them with our APXGP car, with a digital driver. What you get by doing that is, the camera operator is following a real car going into a real stunt, and you get all the dust coming up from the gravel, and even though we might enhance it, you're starting with something real."

Right: Sonny's (Brad Pitt's) APXGP car spinning out during the race.

Below: Keith Dawson built a special rig to film Sonny's (Brad Pitt's) pivotal spin-out scene.

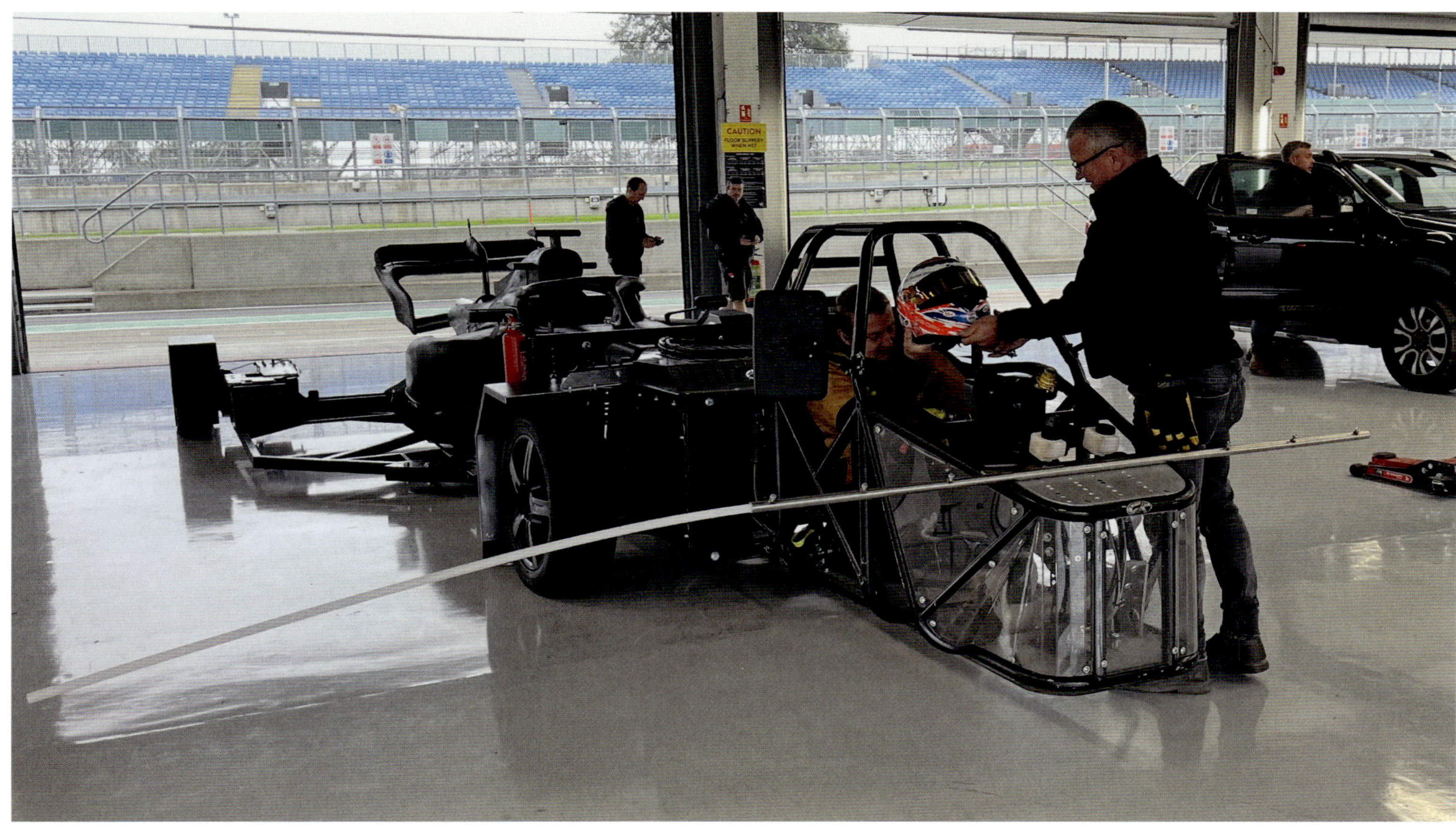

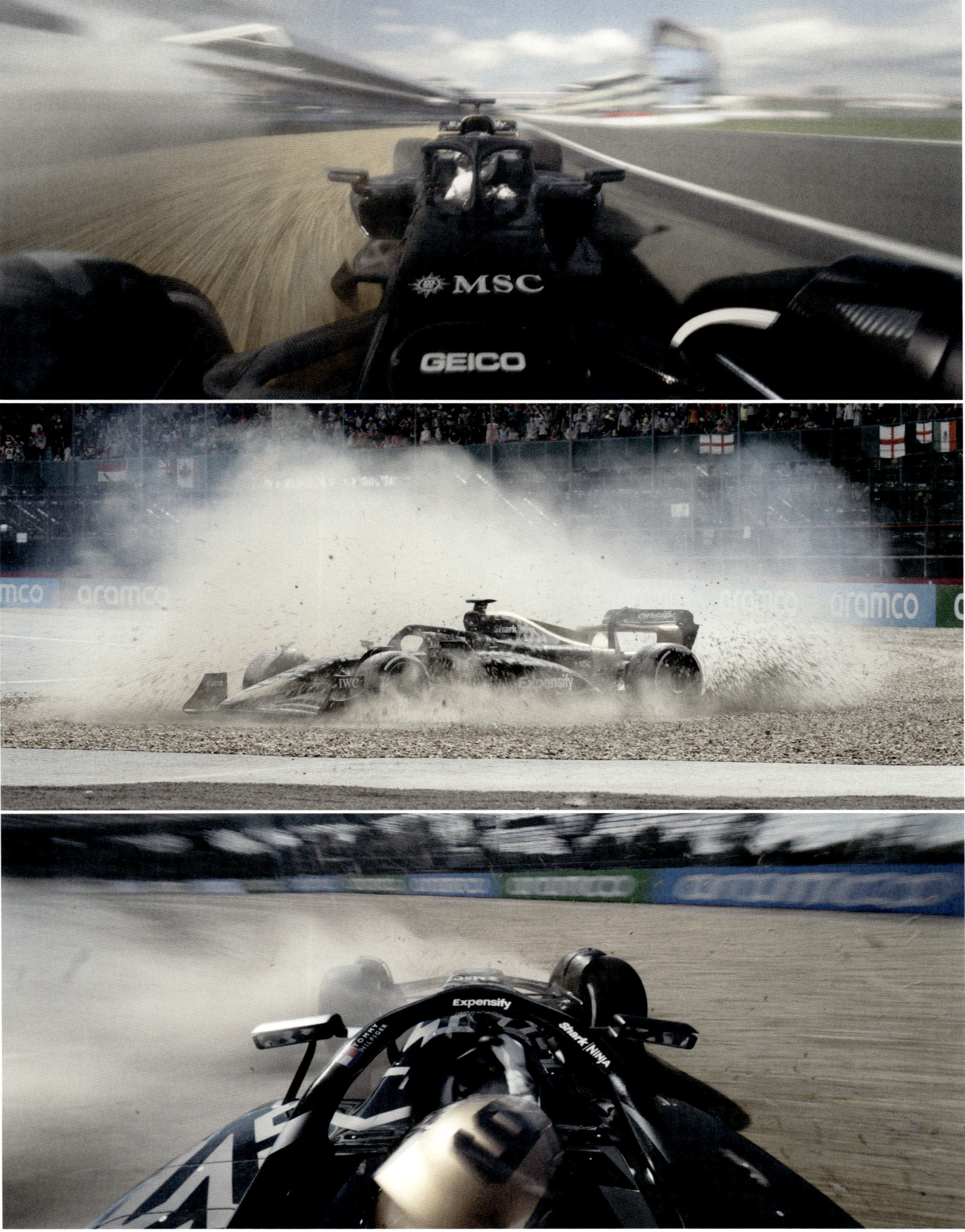
MSC
GEICO
aramco
Expensify
Shark NINJA

As technical a sport as Formula One is, it is the human aspect that makes it so compelling. From designers to team principals, engineers to mechanics, there are so many stories to connect with on a personal level. But nothing resonates like a true rivalry between two drivers. Often these revolve around fights for the World Championship, where both are duking it out on the track for the right to call themselves the best. For fans, it usually means picking a side, and there have been some legendary battles over the years, including between teammates.

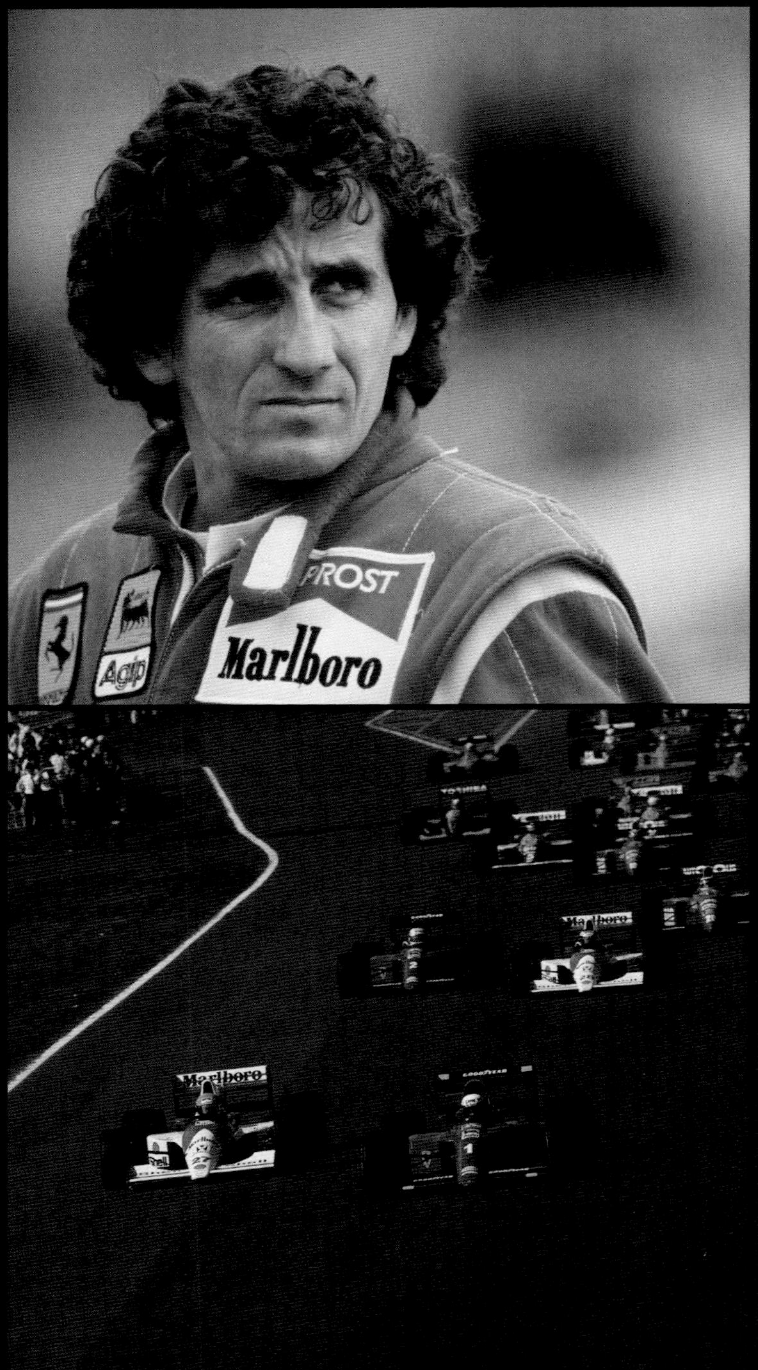

AYRTON SENNA VS. ALAIN PROST

Arguably the most famous rivalry the sport has seen, Ayrton Senna and Alain Prost were teammates at McLaren during a dominant period in the late eighties and early nineties. Senna joined Prost—who was already a double world champion—in 1988 and duly won that year's championship.

The following season, their relationship really soured, and the title was decided in Prost's favor when the pair collided at the penultimate race in Suzuka. The Frenchman left McLaren for Ferrari in 1990, but they collided once again in Japan, this time at the start of the race. But, on this occasion, Senna was champion.

In the nine seasons from 1985 to 1993, the duo won seven titles between them, with Prost's final title in 1993 coming with the Williams Racing team, a year in which he vetoed Senna from becoming his teammate again. Prost retired at the end of that season, allowing Senna to take his seat, and the pair reconciled their relationship before Senna's death at the 1994 San Marino Grand Prix.

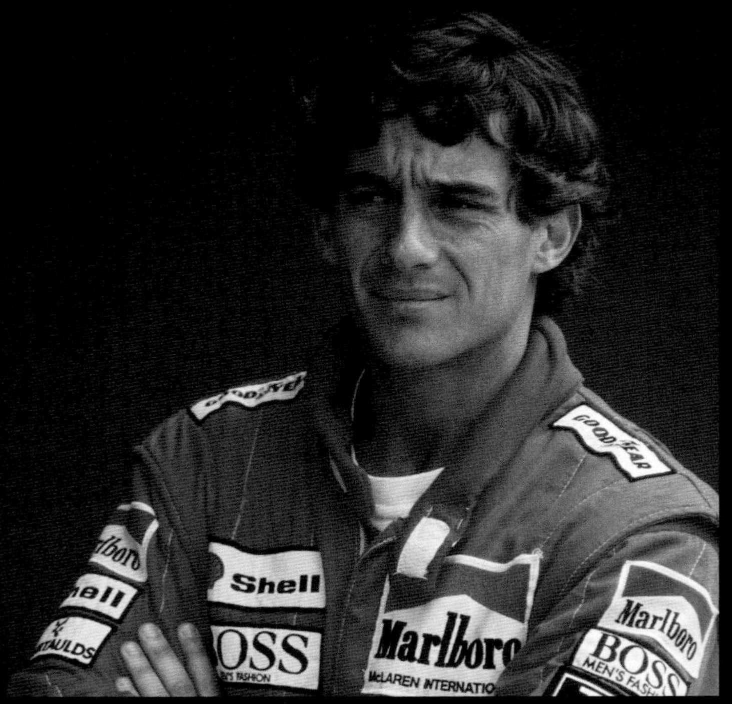

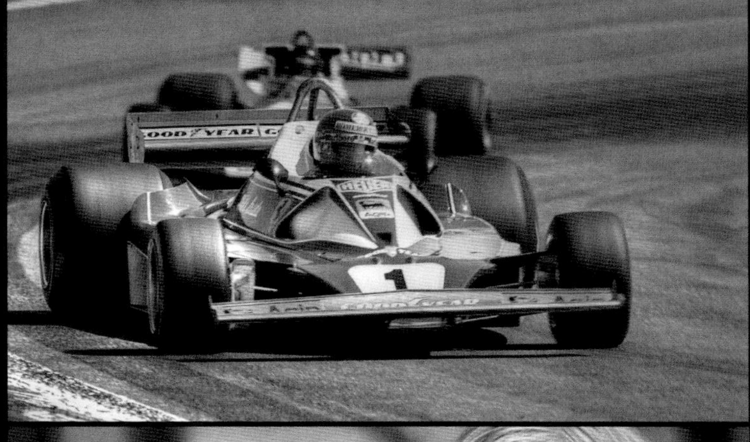

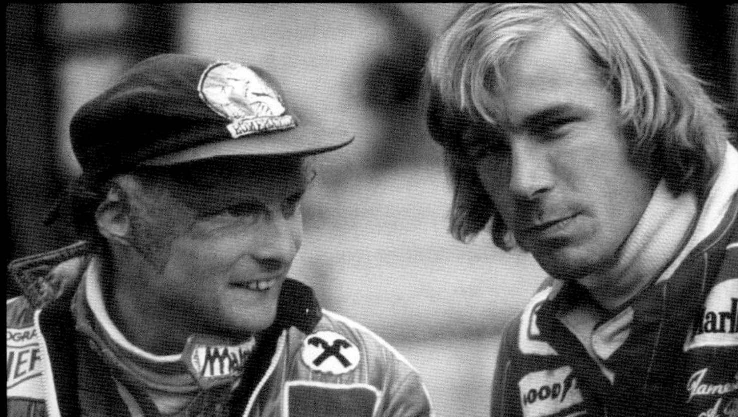

JAMES HUNT VS. NIKI LAUDA

Not all rivalries involve bitter feuds. James Hunt and Niki Lauda provided a thrilling championship fight in 1976, but it was one that was underscored by immense courage. Lauda was leading the championship by more than two race victories when he suffered a horrific crash at the Nürburgring, sustaining severe burns, among other injuries, and was even read his last rites as he lay in the hospital.

Hunt won in Germany following Lauda's crash and took another win and fourth place from the next two races, but Lauda made an astonishing return after just six weeks to finish fourth in Italy.

The championship went to a deciding round, and in treacherous conditions in Japan, Lauda withdrew after just two laps as one of many drivers saying it was too dangerous to race. With the championship leader out, Hunt dramatically secured the third place he needed to win the title by a single point. The season was dramatized in the film *Rush* in 2013.

MICHAEL SCHUMACHER VS. MIKA HÄKKINEN

Such was Michael Schumacher's dominance in the sport that he had a number of rivalries over the years, including with Damon Hill in the mid-nineties and Fernando Alonso a decade later.

But with two World Championships already to his name when racing for Benetton, the legendary German was looking for a third after joining Ferrari in 1996. It didn't take long for him to be in regular title contention, but in 1998 and 1999, Schumacher came up against a formidable adversary in the form of the "Flying Finn," Mika Häkkinen. The McLaren driver had fought back from a life-threatening crash at the Australian Grand Prix in 1995 and would go wheel-to-wheel with Schumacher in thrilling fashion on more than one occasion.

Two titles went the way of Häkkinen at the final round in 1998 and 1999, the second of which saw Schumacher trying to help teammate Eddie Irvine win the championship, having broken his leg in a crash midseason. Schumacher finally triumphed with Ferrari in 2000, and Häkkinen took a sabbatical at the end of 2001 that turned into full retirement.

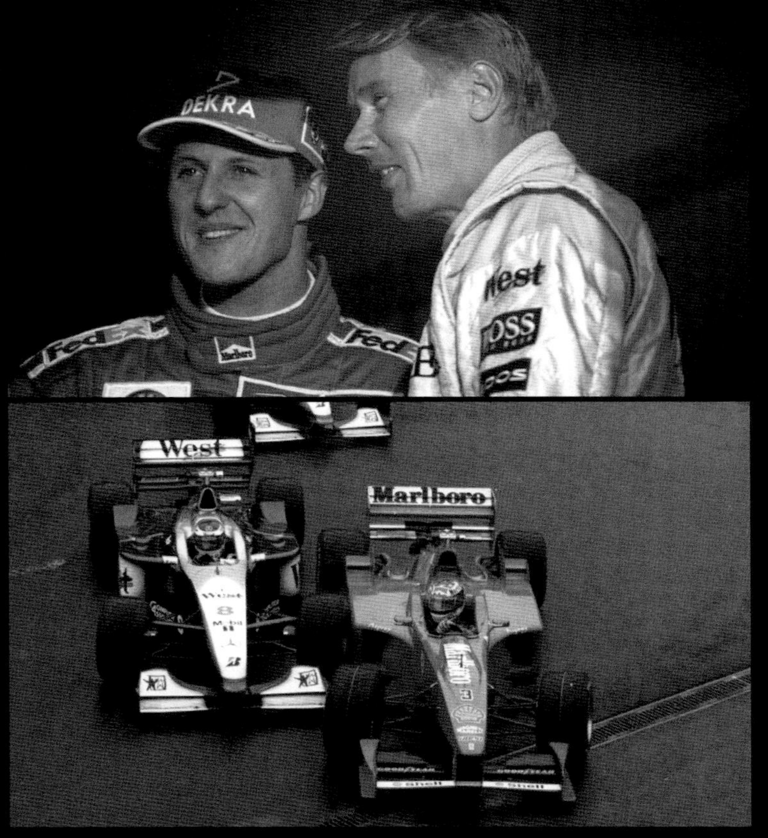

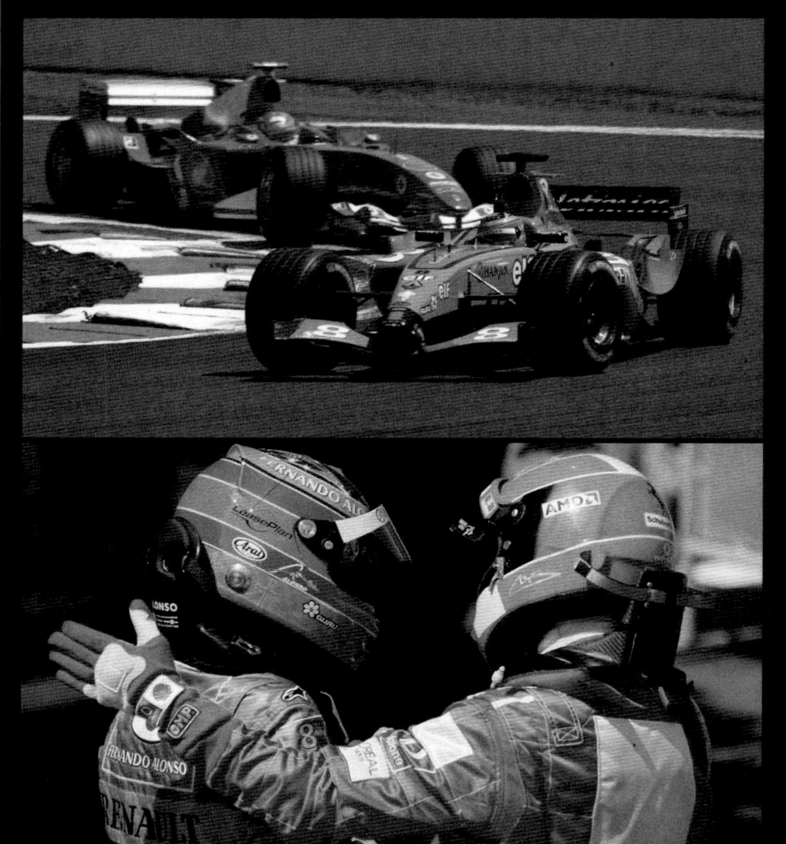

MICHAEL SCHUMACHER VS. FERNANDO ALONSO

Such was the level of Schumacher's success with Ferrari that he won five straight titles from 2000 to 2004. Then came a formidable opponent in Fernando Alonso, who had started winning races with the resurgent Renault team.

Alonso combined immense speed with an outstanding racing IQ, and it was soon in evidence when he had a car capable of fighting for the championship, as he held Schumacher off in a thrilling battle in Imola in 2005. That season, Ferrari was off the pace, and Alonso's main threat was the McLaren of Kimi Räikkönen. But with better reliability, the Renault team—with Alonso at the wheel—won out.

The following year, Schumacher was able to mount a stronger challenge. In a true Renault vs. Ferrari battle—the two teams won all but one race that season—there were on-track scraps and controversies throughout the season. Schumacher's win in China moved him level on points with Alonso and into the championship lead based on having won more races, but he failed to finish the next Grand Prix in Japan, which Alonso won, the Spaniard wrapping up a second successive title in the final round.

Finishing runner-up to Alonso was not the fairy-tale ending Schumacher had hoped for, as he retired from Formula One at the end of the season, though he would later return for a three-year stint with Mercedes from 2010 to 2012.

LEWIS HAMILTON VS. FERNANDO ALONSO

Prior to the 2006 season, Alonso announced he would be joining McLaren a year later, and, as the reigning double world champion, he was expected to lead the team.

He would be driving with rookie phenomenon Lewis Hamilton, who had been handed a rare opportunity to start his F1 career on a front-running team but was seen as Alonso's understudy. That dynamic didn't last long, as Hamilton—who had been part of the McLaren young driver development program—reeled off nine straight podiums, including two wins, to start the season in sensational style.

A clear title challenger, Hamilton unsettled Alonso, and the two drivers took steps to undermine each other. On track, their battles became increasingly heated, to the extent that each driver blocked the other to hurt their qualifying times for the Hungarian Grand Prix.

Alonso soon confirmed that he would be leaving the team one year into his three-year contract, and both he and Hamilton fell a single point short of winning the driver's title, losing to Ferrari's Kimi Räikkönen in a thrilling finale.

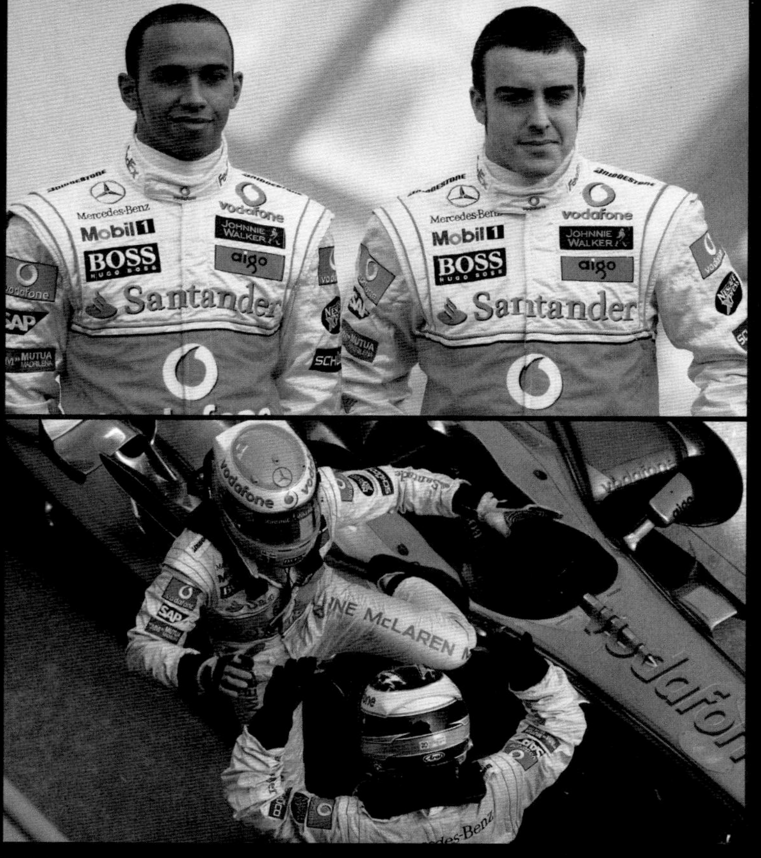

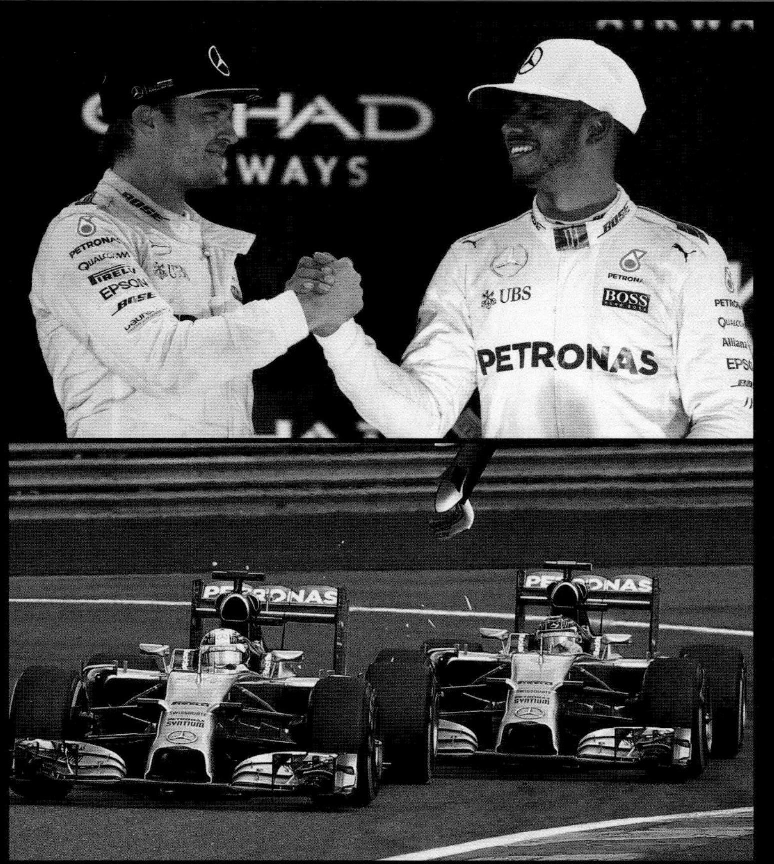

LEWIS HAMILTON VS. NICO ROSBERG

Following his remarkable rookie season, Hamilton won his first driver's championship the very next year but could not add to that tally while still a McLaren driver. A move to Mercedes in 2013 was seen as a gamble, as the German team had not yet been successful. But new regulations in 2014 marked the start of a dominant spell for the Silver Arrows.

Hamilton triumphed in the next two seasons as only teammate Nico Rosberg could provide any threat, winning at the final race in 2014, then wrapping the title up early in 2015. That second success saw Rosberg win all three races after Hamilton was crowned, and the German came out of the blocks in similar fashion in 2016 to win the first four races. Hamilton had ground to make up, but a first lap collision in Spain wiped both drivers out and added further tension to the situation.

For the third straight year, the driver's title came down to a battle between the Mercedes teammates, and Rosberg took advantage of some poor starts from Hamilton, plus reliability issues, to put himself in a strong position with four rounds to go. From there, he simply did what he needed to do and finished second to the defending champion at each race, including a tense decider where Hamilton backed his teammate into the chasing pack in the hope of overturning a significant points deficit.

The battle took so much out of 31-year-old Rosberg that he retired from F1 five days after the end of the season, becoming the first champion to do so in nearly twenty-five years.

LEWIS HAMILTON VS. MAX VERSTAPPEN

Hamilton's fights with Alonso and Rosberg were dramatic but took place within the confines of the same team, whereas the interteam battle provided by the 2021 season was as intense as it gets.

Red Bull had a car to end Mercedes's dominance and provide a true challenge, with Max Verstappen chasing his maiden championship. A rising star and the sport's most successful driver, the pair had numerous collisions, including a huge crash for Verstappen at Silverstone, and both retiring after coming together at Monza, with Verstappen's car coming to rest on top of Hamilton's. The rivalry was not only between the two drivers but also their respective teams—it even expanded to sections of their fanbases in polarizing fashion.

Verstappen and Hamilton finished one-two in each of the last six rounds as the tension grew further; in Saudi Arabia Hamilton won to ensure they entered the final round level on points. Hamilton was on course for an unparalleled eighth title when, one lap from the end, a hugely controversial decision regarding a safety car overshadowed the race, with Verstappen pitting, putting on fresh tires, and beating Hamilton in a one-lap shootout to take his first title.

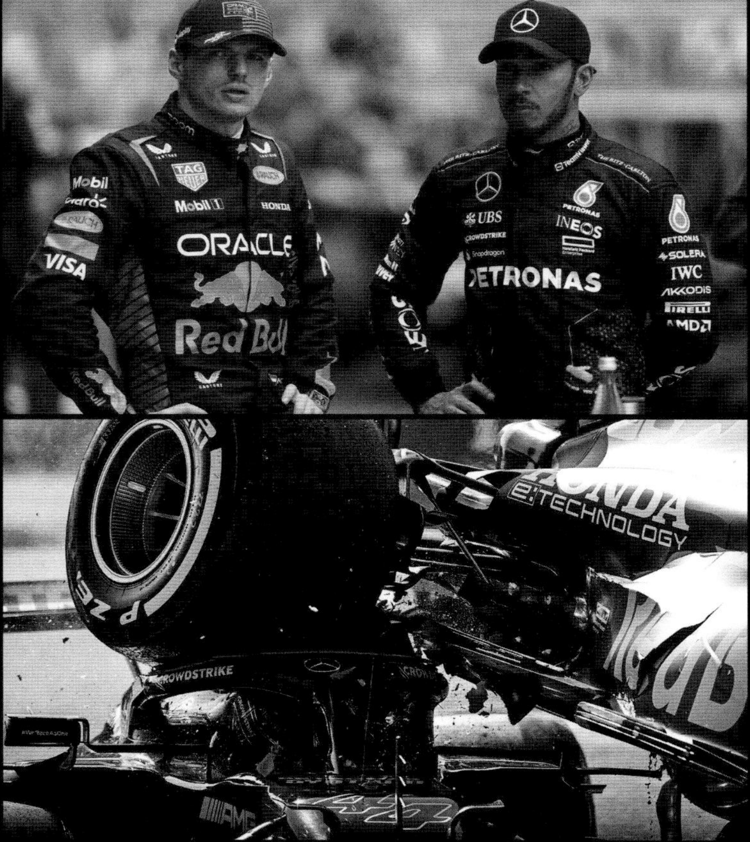

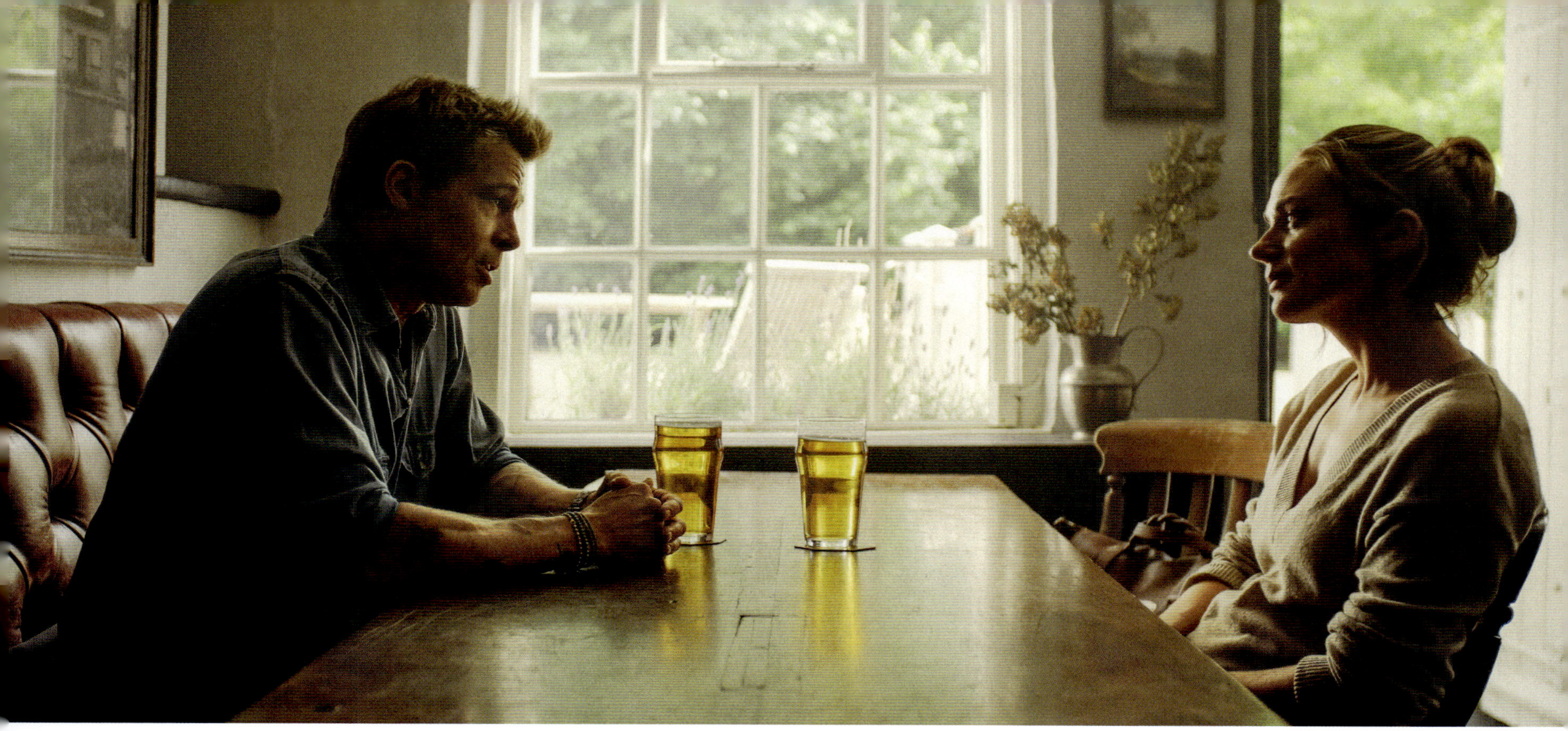

"Red Bull, Ferrari, Mercedes, Aston, McLaren all have a speed on the straights. Our shot is battling in the turns. We need to build a car for combat."

SONNY HAYES

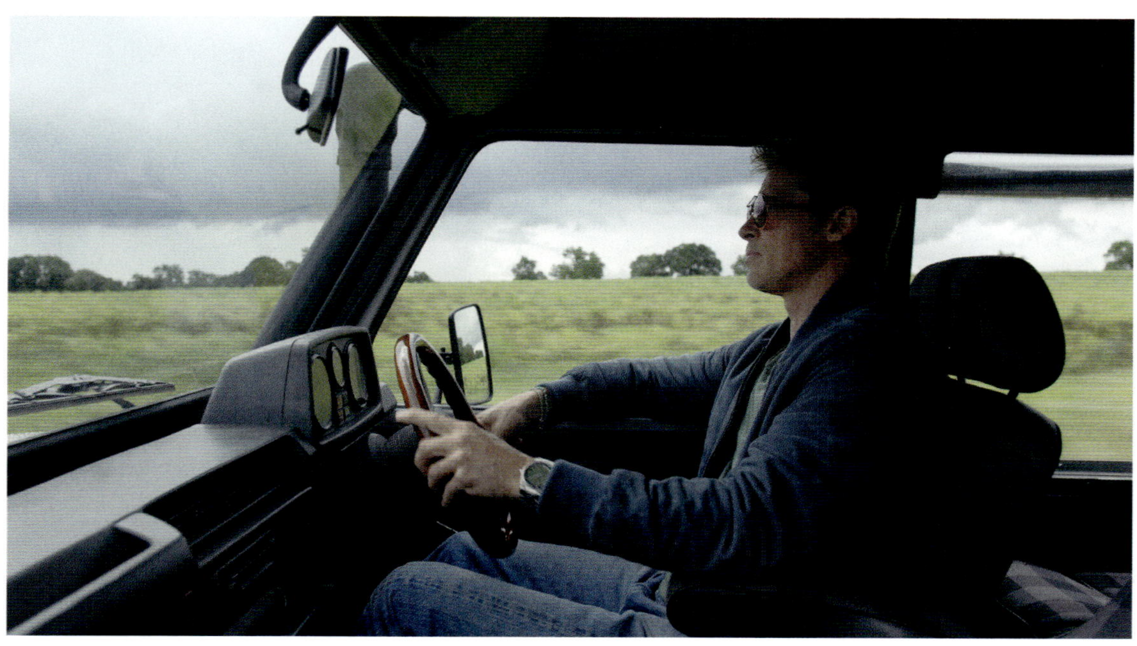

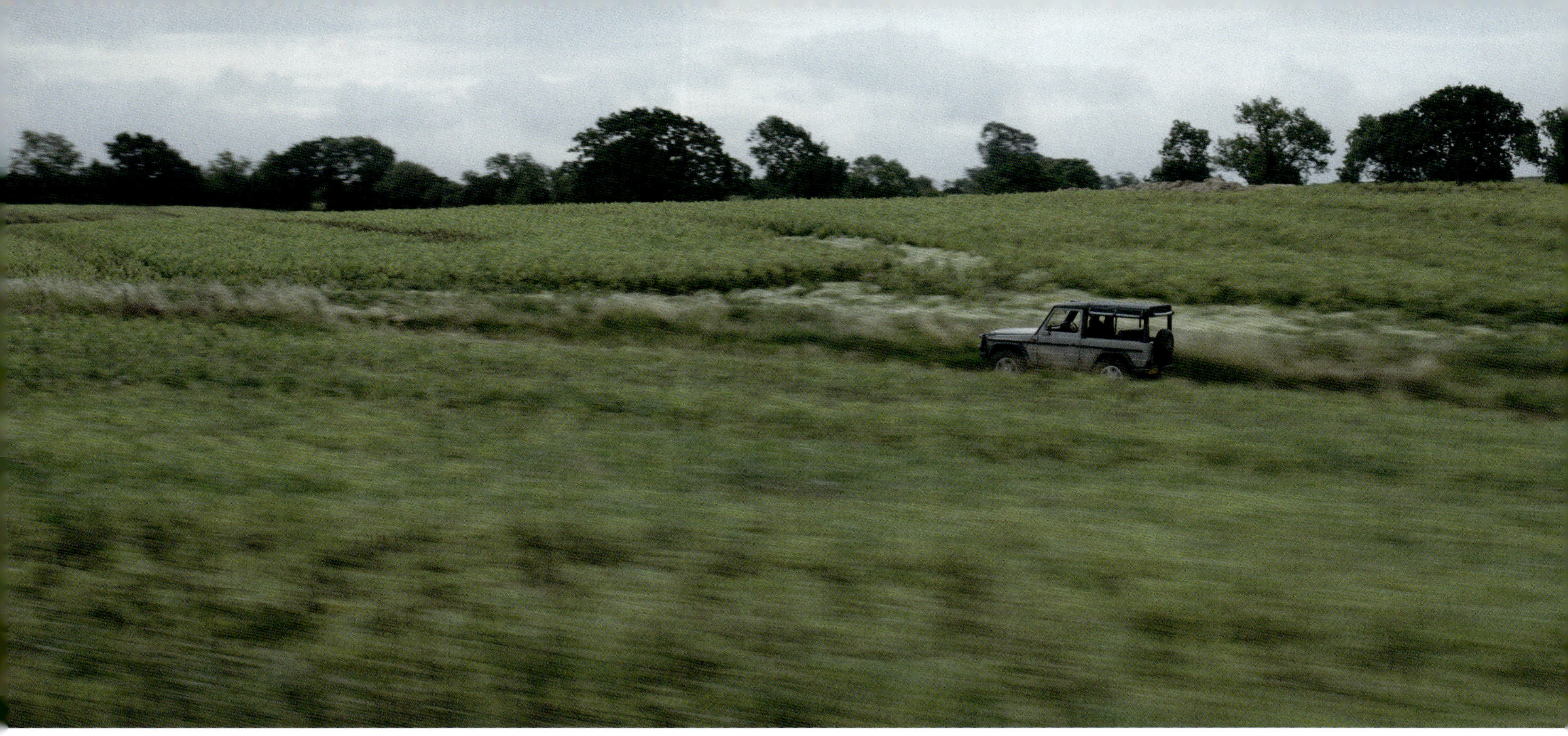

Bacheta's stalled car aside—it would be replaced by visual effects supervisor Tudhope's VFX team with a digital version that pulls away as planned in the finished film—the British Grand Prix had shown F1 and the FIA what the production could achieve without any impact on the event itself.

"It was the moment when the people behind the scenes at F1 saw how coordinated and professional we were, and that's thanks to Joe and Toby," says Bruckheimer. "We had rehearsed it ad nauseam until we had it down flawlessly."

"That was a pretty epic day," reflects Kosinski. "You can feel it in the movie. You can feel it when you see our pit stops with the other teams around and when you're looking out of the garage and seeing fans in the stands and cars whipping by. It all adds to this feeling of being *in* the sport. And when we're at those races, we really do feel like we're one of the gang in a way that's pure make-believe."

With Silverstone unavailable to shoot at on the Monday and Tuesday, the production took those two days as leave, although Kosinski spent Monday reviewing the footage they had shot during race day.

Filming recommenced on Wednesday to shoot the scene in the pub with Sonny and Kate, where he asks her to build a car for "combat" and she storms out. The following day, Thursday, July 13, Kosinski filmed Pitt driving through the English countryside, coming upon Kate, riding her bicycle. But then, after lunch, the U.S. actors' union, the Screen Actors Guild, went on strike.

"As soon as they did, all of our SAG actors had to go home," says Kosinski, who immediately pivoted to shooting second unit, action, and stunt sequences, which are typically the remit of a second unit or action director. "I continued shooting for another thirty-two days. I focused on everything in the movie that did not involve those four actors and shot it myself, which was an amazing luxury, because on a giant film like this, you might have a second unit director doing that type of work. But I got to do it all. Whether racing shots or a tight shot of a wheel gun putting on a wheel, I did everything, every single shot in this movie. I did as much work as I could without SAG actors. That was the positive way to look at a negative of losing our actors for what turned out to be months."

Kosinski also used the time to work with the film's Oscar-winning editor Stephen Mirrione, "putting the movie together with the pieces I had." The footage appeared in the first trailer, released during the British Grand Prix the following year.

Top Left: Sonny (Brad Pitt) asks Kate (Kerry Condon) to build him a car ready for "combat" to drive in future races.

Top Right: Sonny (Brad Pitt) driving his Mercedes G-Class SUV through the English countryside.

At the end of July 2023, Kosinski's second unit touched down at the Hungarian Grand Prix to shoot hot laps with Bacheta and Dolby, as well as both cars in Parc Fermé—the secure area at circuits where cars are checked over by FIA examiners for legality and safety. "Full credit to the FIA embracing this and understanding the need, because it's unprecedented," notes Bampton. "Again, the stakes were high. It's a sterile environment. You've got drivers walking past, having just finished a Grand Prix. No one's filmed in there before. But we rehearsed it with the FIA, we prep-positioned the cars and executed it well. I remember the euphoria I saw in the crew when they wrapped was a measure of what they had achieved. They were buzzing."

"It was epic," says Hefferman of Parc Fermé at the Hungaroring. "It was like *Apocalypse Now*. There were flares. A track invasion. Ticker tape flying everywhere. Jo Bauer from the FIA, he's really into filmmaking, and he called in one of our cars onto the scale. The FIA weighed it as if it was a regular car in the race, gave it the thumbs up, a ticket came out, they put on the car, which then got pushed out. We hadn't asked for it. We were so fortunate. We were there for wide shots, knowing we were going to come back with the actors the next year. Then we stayed in Hungary, did some pit stop work and more driving. Because we weren't expecting the strike to last so long."

After Hungary, Kosinski moved onto the Italian Grand Prix in Monza, where he filmed Bacheta and Dolby doing more hot laps, some hospitality area and pit wall work, as well as moments of Charles Leclerc, Lando Norris, and Carlos Sainz on the grid as they prepared for the race, along with shots of the Ferrari drivers arriving at the track.

Post-Monza, the SAG strike was no closer to being resolved, leaving the production with a dilemma, given that the events of the film were meant to follow the 2023 Formula One calendar. Best case: The strike would be over soon, and they could continue shooting. Worse case: It dragged on, and they would need to hit pause and go again the following year.

By the time the strike ended on November 9, the production had already decided to start again the following season, although they did send a reduced crew to both the Las Vegas and Abu Dhabi Grand Prix in November to shoot reference material.

In the meantime, Kosinski and Bruckheimer prepared to welcome back their actors, with principal photography set to resume in January 2024 in Daytona, Florida, with Pitt spending several days in December at the Willow Springs Raceway in Los Angeles, working with endurance racing legend Pat Long, getting ready to drive a Porsche GT3 at the world-famous Daytona speedway for the film's opening sequence.

Below: The post-race celebration at the Hungarian Grand Prix.

Right: Storyboards showing Sonny's refusal to drive off during the Hungarian Grand Prix, after a disagreement about the team's tire choice.

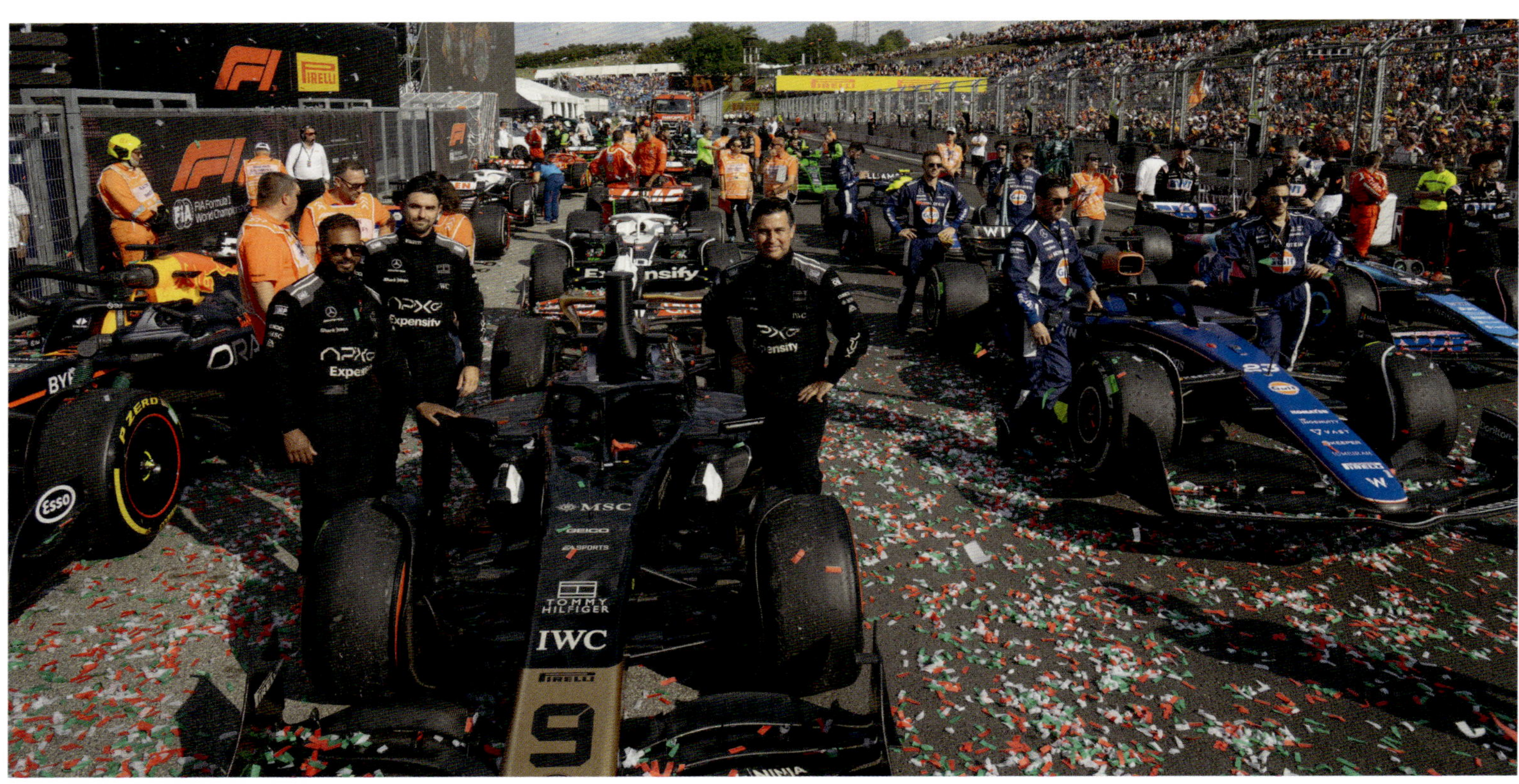

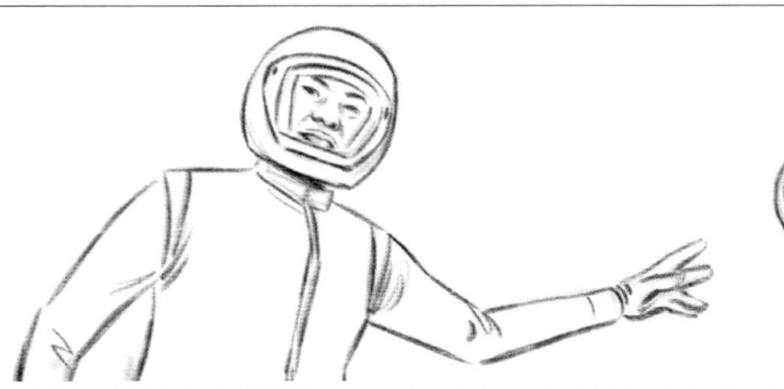

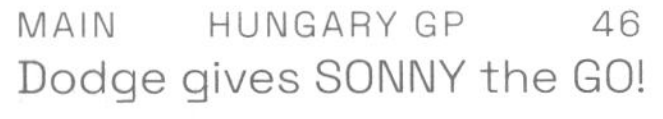

MAIN HUNGARY GP 46
Dodge gives SONNY the GO!

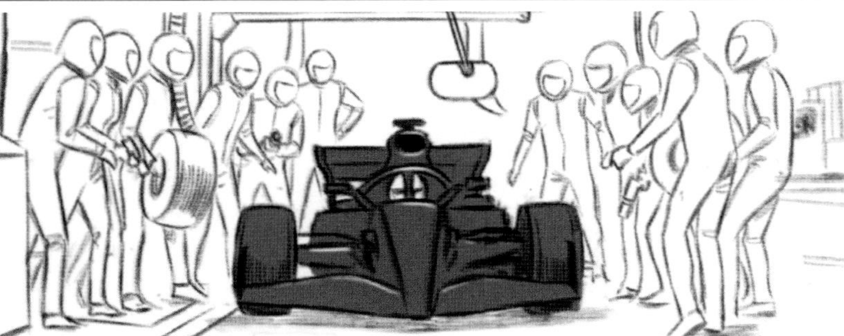

MAIN HUNGARY GP 47
Except Sonny's car doesn't move.

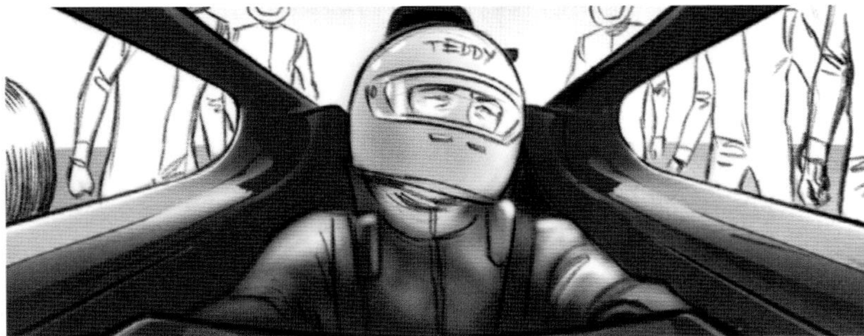

MAIN HUNGARY GP 48
Sonny just stares down his Engineers.

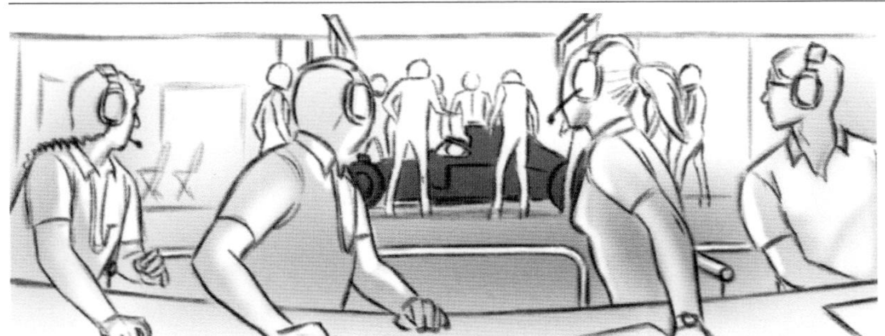

MAIN HUNGARY GP 16
Kate scans data:
KASPAR:
What is wrong with the CAR?!
KATE:
The guy sitting in it.

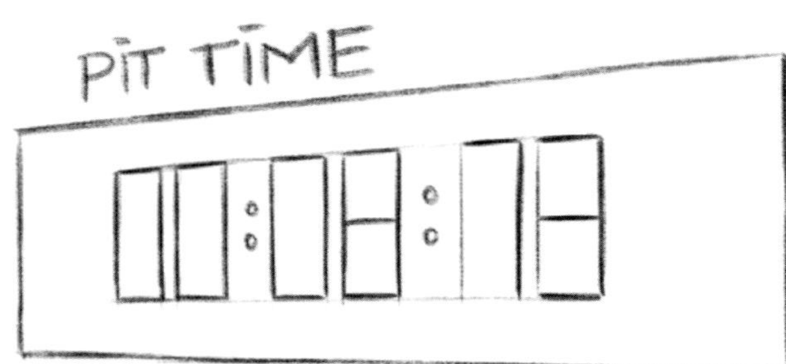

MAIN HUNGARY GP 49
The Pit timer is FLYING: 7 seconds, 8, 9.

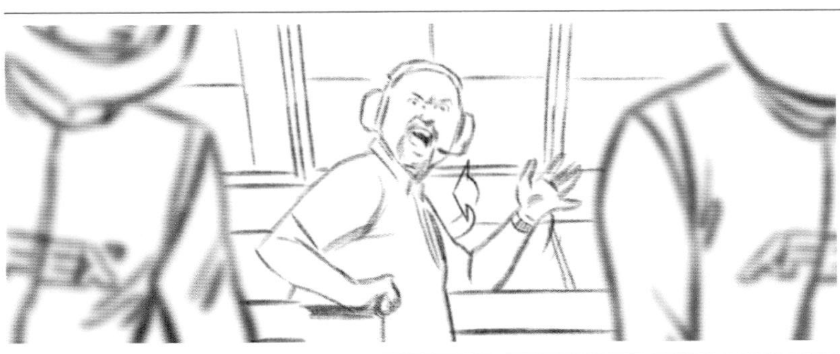

MAIN HUNGARY GP 50
Kaspar spins.
KASPAR:
ARE YOU INSANE? We need hard tires!
Everybody here is on a one-stop race!

6 DAYTONA

WRIGHT Motorsports
WRIGHT Motorsports
04
PORSCHE
120
GEICO
IMSA
PEAK
PEAK
MOTUL

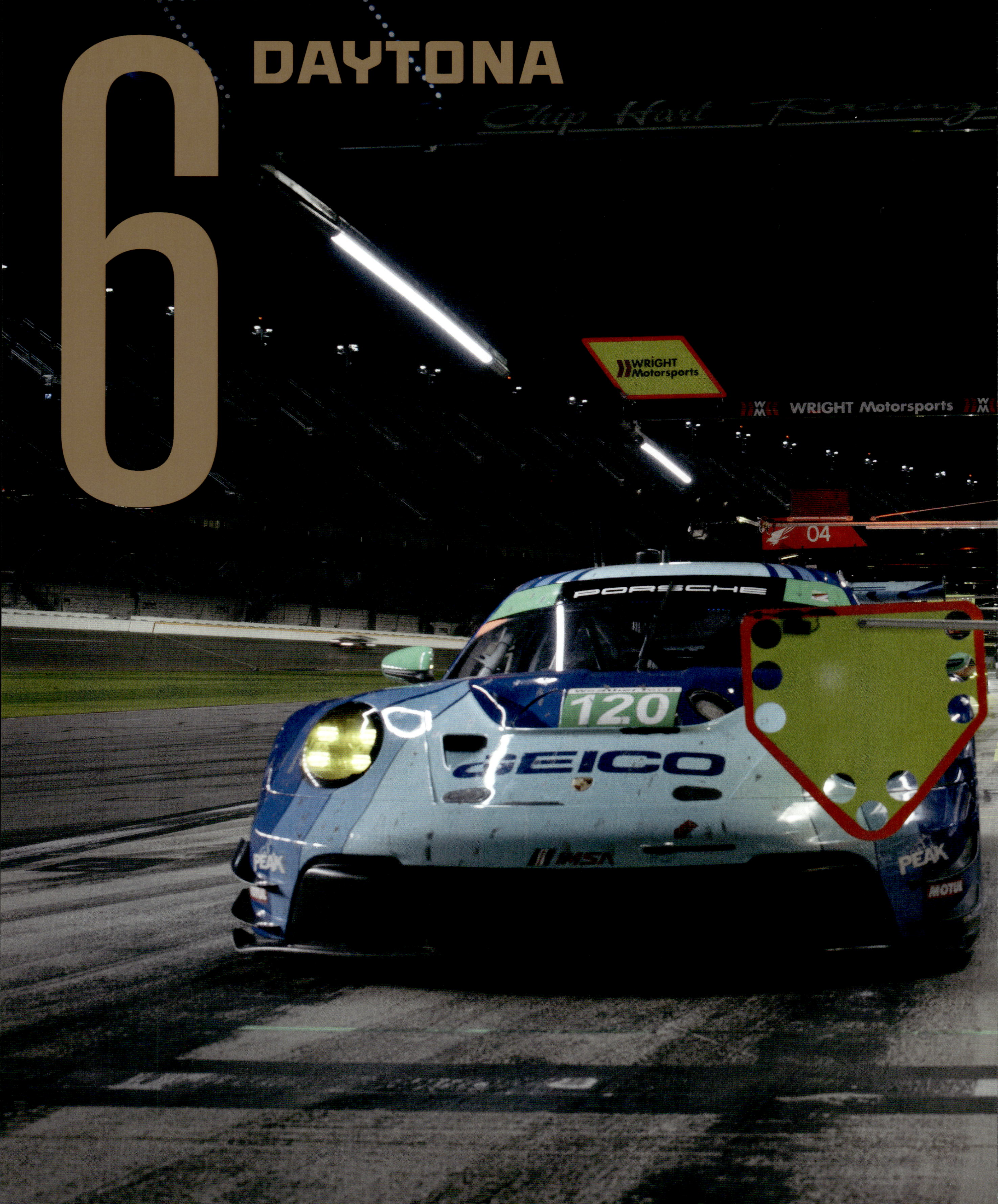

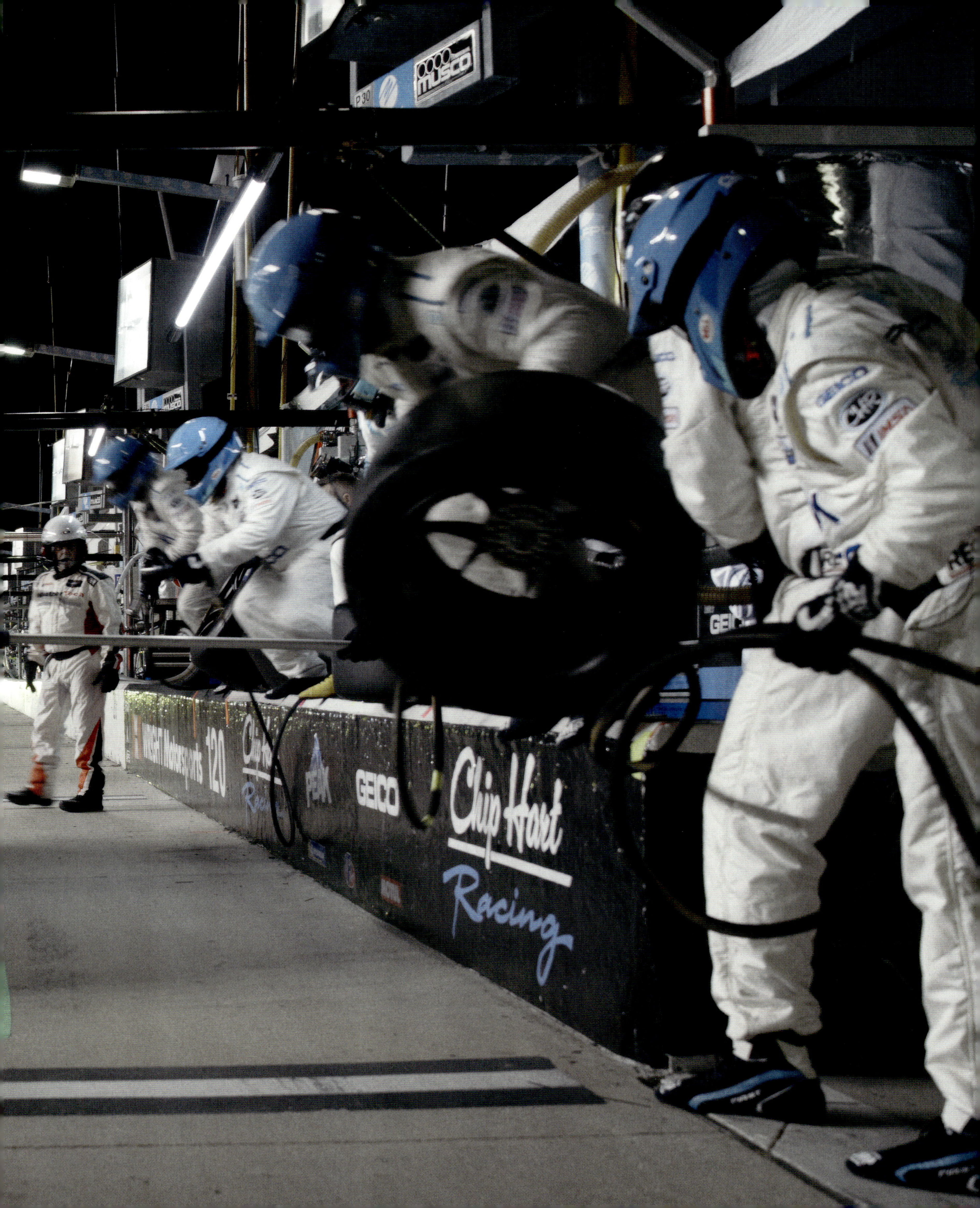
MUSCO
WRIGHT Motorsports 120
GEICO
Chip Hart
Racing

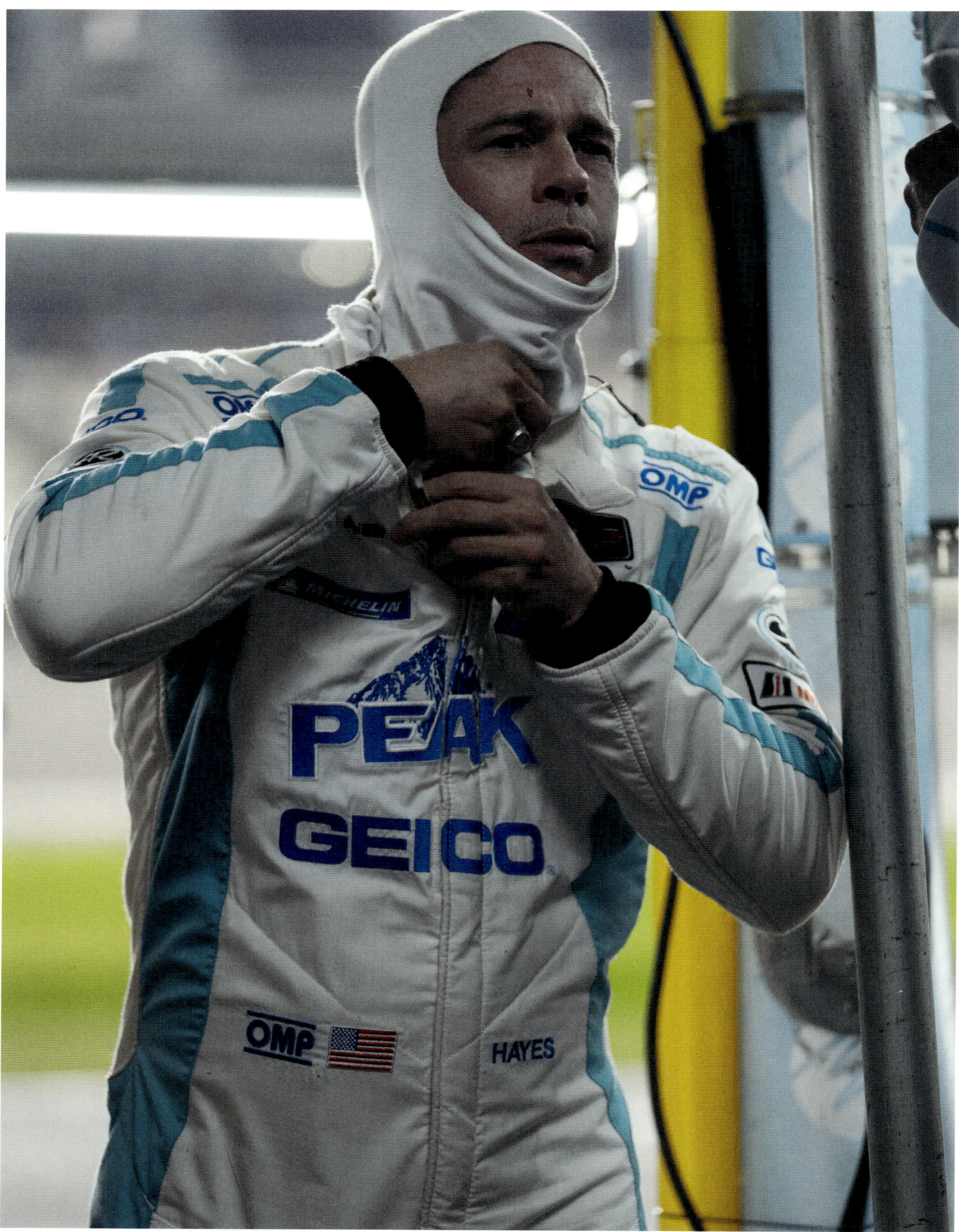
OMP
MICHELIN
PEAK
GEICO
OMP
HAYES

Left: Sonny (Brad Pitt) zips up his blue Chip Hart race suit before racing in Daytona.

Below: Sonny (Brad Pitt) wakes up in his camper.

F1 opens with Sonny Hayes (Brad Pitt) in his camper van, a 1970 green and beige Ford Econoline, parked next to the Daytona International Speedway in Florida, where the 24 Hours of Daytona, aka the Rolex 24 at Daytona, race is underway. "He's a gun for hire, sleeping at the track. It's almost midnight, and he's driving the graveyard shift," says director Joseph Kosinski.

Awoken by a pounding on his window, Sonny glances up and sees a mechanic hold up five fingers to indicate it's almost time for him to race. He swings his legs out of bed, revealing a pair of mismatched socks, plunges his face in a sink full of ice water, shuffles a deck of playing cards like a professional gambler, then extracts one for luck, tucking it into his race suit without even looking at its face.

Sonny grabs his crash helmet and weaves his way through the pit lane, heading toward the garage of the Peak-Geico Chip Hart racing team, just as Patrick Long, a former winner of both the 24 Hours of Le Mans and Rolex 24 at Daytona, slows his Porsche 911 GT3 R into its pit box and leaps out. As the mechanics slam on a new set of hot tires, Sonny straps on his helmet and goes through his pre-race routine, kneeling down, almost in prayer, before slipping behind the wheel and gunning the accelerator.

The Porsche blasts onto the track, with Sonny immediately joining the vehicular fray, veering between a cluster of cars, scrapping metal, and forcing his way through, before attacking the first corner, many hours of hard racing ahead of him.

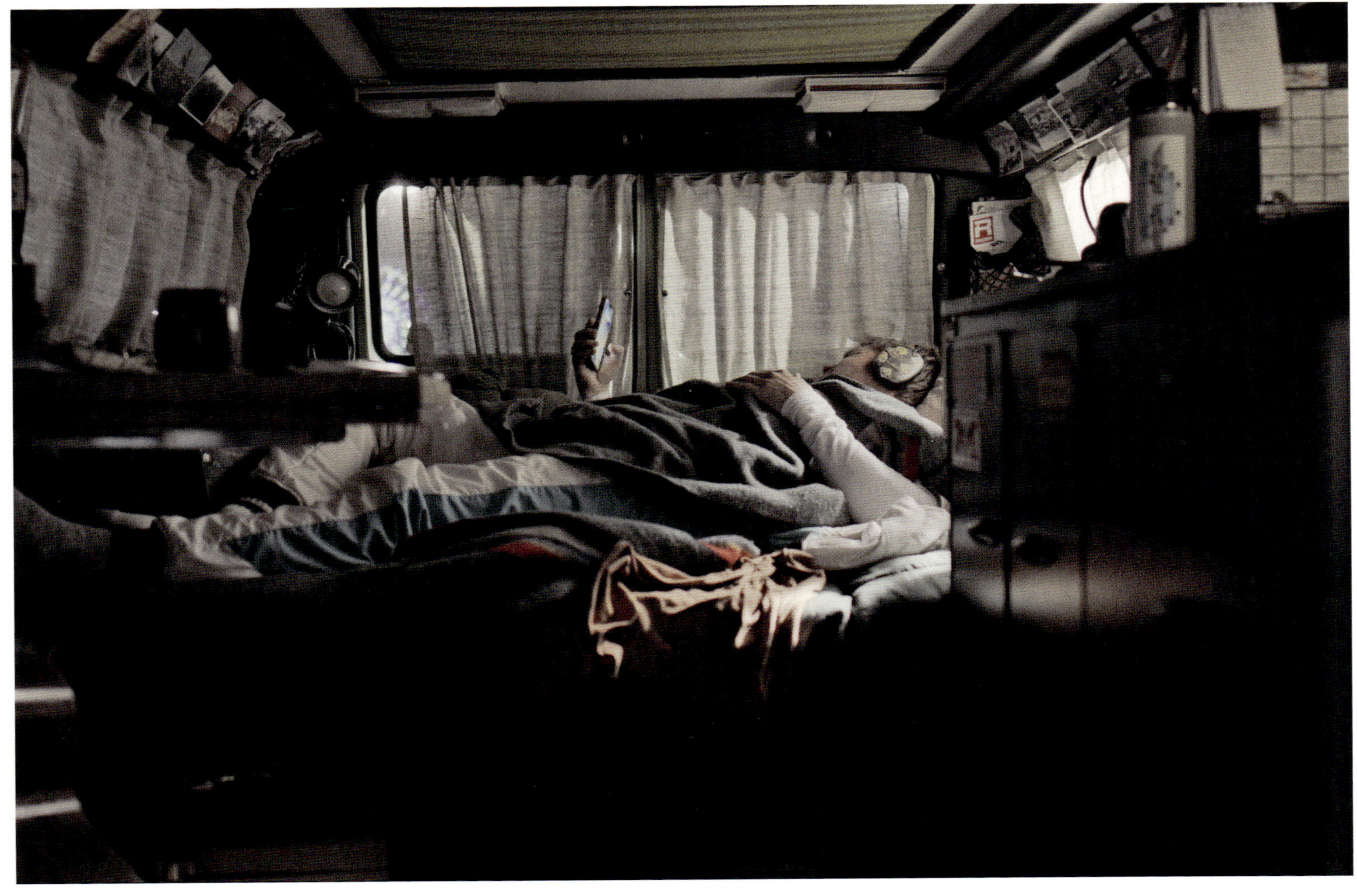

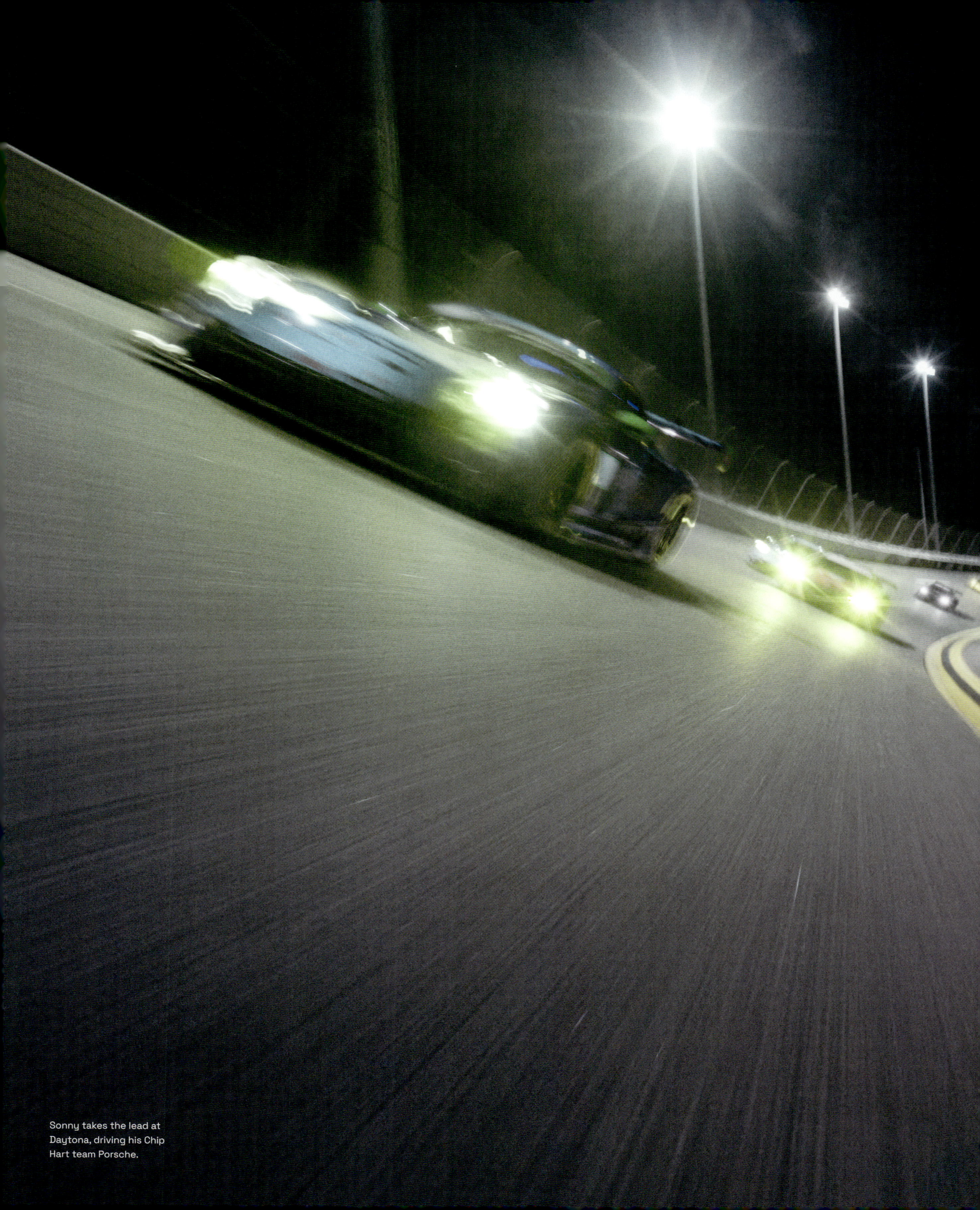

Sonny takes the lead at Daytona, driving his Chip Hart team Porsche.

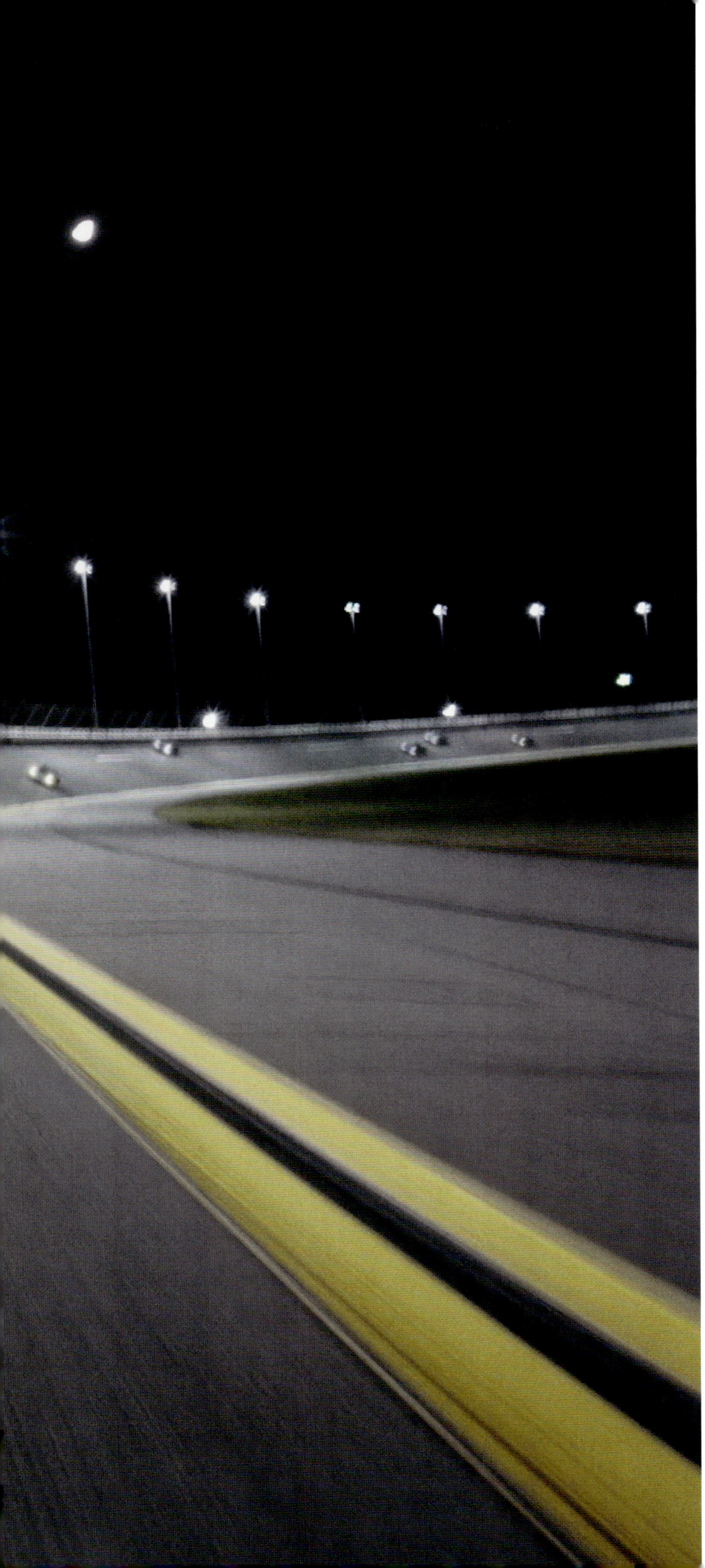

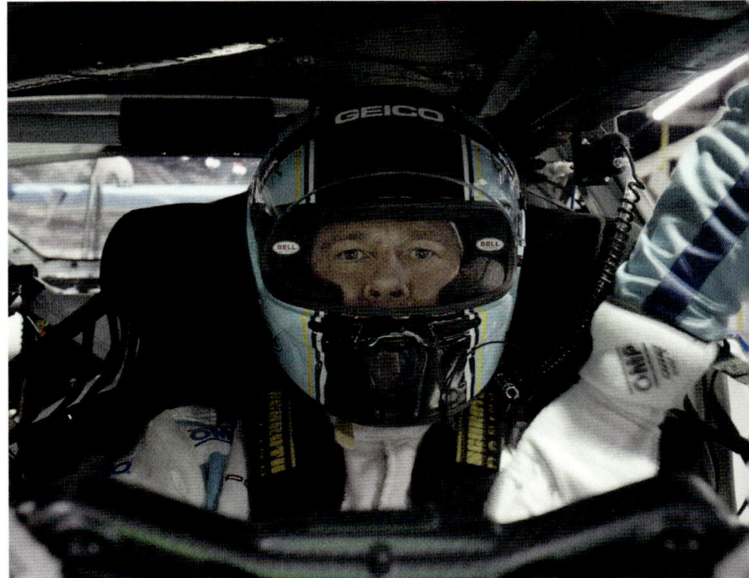

In Kosinski's initial pitch and Ehren Kruger's first draft screenplay, Sonny's story began in Baja, Mexico, where he was driving the Baja 1000, an annual off-road motorsport race. But when Kosinski ran the idea past team principal of the Mercedes F1 Team Toto Wolff and F1 driver Lewis Hamilton during dinner at Wolff's house, both men said the race setting wasn't right for the character's introduction. "Lewis felt very strongly it was the wrong place to meet him. To be able to get into a Formula One car midseason and be competitive, we needed to find Sonny racing some more appropriate and challenging race circuit," says Kruger.

"Toto said, 'You can't go from Baja 1000 into Formula One. That's impossible. It's too different,'" adds Kosinski. "So that's where we came up with the idea of starting him in endurance racing at Daytona instead."

"Daytona needed to show us who Sonny is through the way he approaches the race, the way he drives, and what the race means to him," reveals Kruger. "We had a fun sequence for Baja, but once it was Daytona, what I loved about it was the idea that it's an endurance race, and drivers may or may not recharge between stints. I loved the idea of Sonny waking up, walking straight out to work, and hopping in a car and driving off at crazy speeds to show who his character is and how he approaches life and racing. He's done all the prep and can just throw himself into profound danger and seem comfortable and casual about it, showing a fearlessness and a willingness to rub people the wrong way on the racetrack, showing he's a great driver, if a little reckless."

"We're establishing he's a phenomenal driver," says Kosinski. "Does things his own way. Not afraid to get his elbows out and get dirty. Races hard. He's got a reputation for it. Pisses some other guys off. But that's who he is."

Moreover, after helping his team win, Sonny doesn't stick around for the prize giving. "The most important thing coming out of Daytona was to show the trophy didn't mean anything to him," notes Kruger. "He doesn't even want to touch it, because it would represent achieving something and being satisfied. And he's always onto the next challenge."

"He has no interest in picking up the trophy," concurs Kosinski. "That's not why he does it. That's not why he's racing. He's happy to take the paycheck, because it means he's going to keep racing, but then he's off to his next adventure. He's a man always on the move, looking for a new challenge."

Playing Chip Hart was Shea Whigham (*Boardwalk Empire*, *Mission: Impossible—Dead Reckoning*). "Shea was born, I think, only ten or fifteen minutes away from that racetrack," says Kosinski. "He's a central Florida boy in addition to being a brilliant actor, so I was thrilled to have Shea in the part. His scene opens the movie, so it has that much more weight and pressure on it, because, as an audience member, you're sitting there with your arms crossed, wondering if this is going to be a real authentic race car movie, and I think Shea fits into that world like a glove. He really helped set up Sonny's ethos for the movie. The notion of this guy, who spends his whole life starting over and moving on from one race to the next. I love Chip Hart, and I hope Sonny gets to see him again somewhere down the road."

Sonny's latest challenge arrives in the form of his old friend and former Formula One teammate Ruben Cervantes (Javier Bardem), who reconnects with Sonny, first at a laundromat, where he's plotting his next move—a trip to Baja—following the 24-hour race, then in a shower block, and finally in a truck stop diner. There, Ruben offers Sonny a seat with his struggling F1 team, APXGP, in the hopes that he can not only turn their fortunes around but also be a mentor to their phenomenally talented, if immature, rookie driver, Joshua.

Below: Chip Hart (Shea Whigham) celebrates after his team wins at the 24 Hours of Daytona race, featuring a cameo from Porsche factory driver Pat Long.

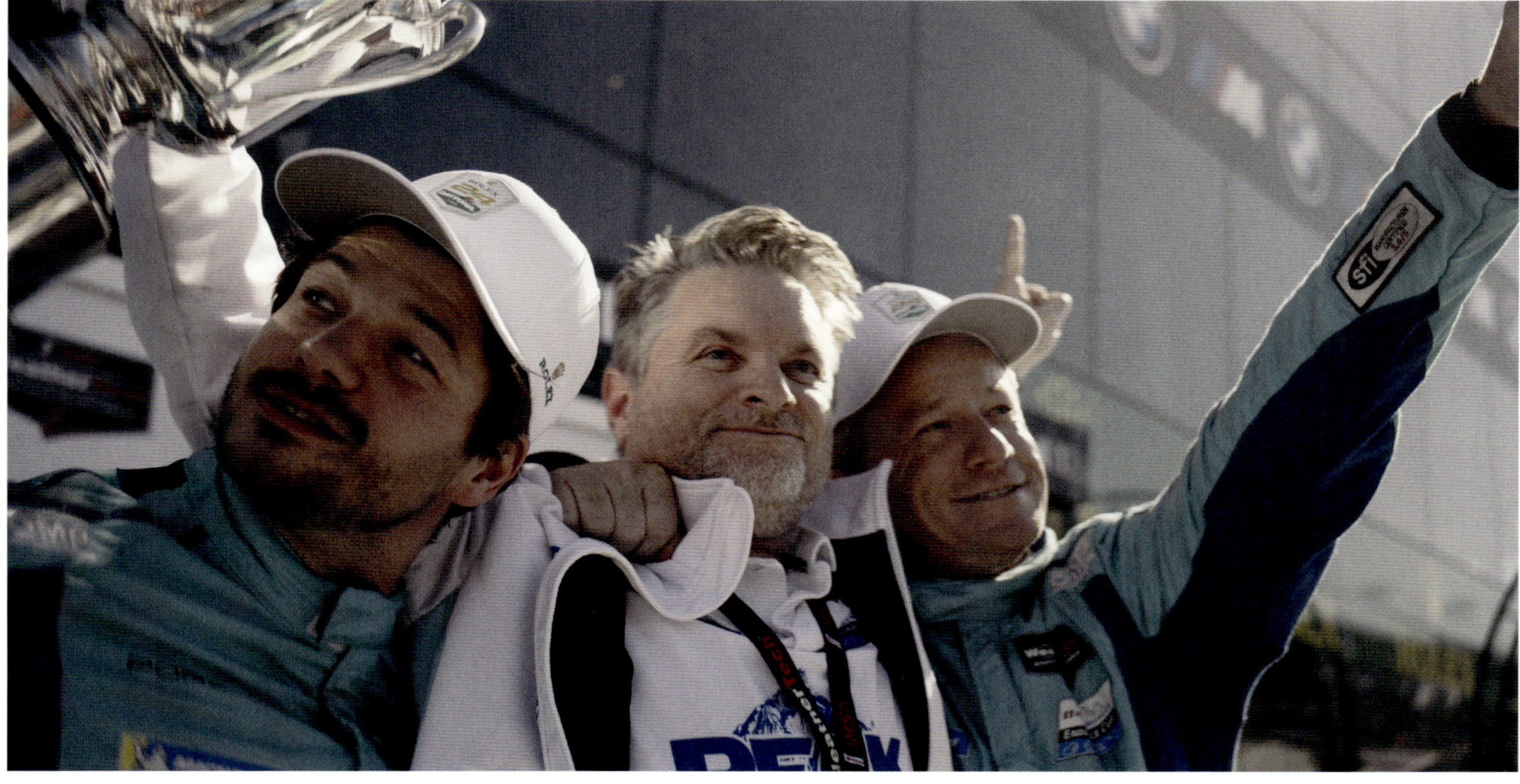

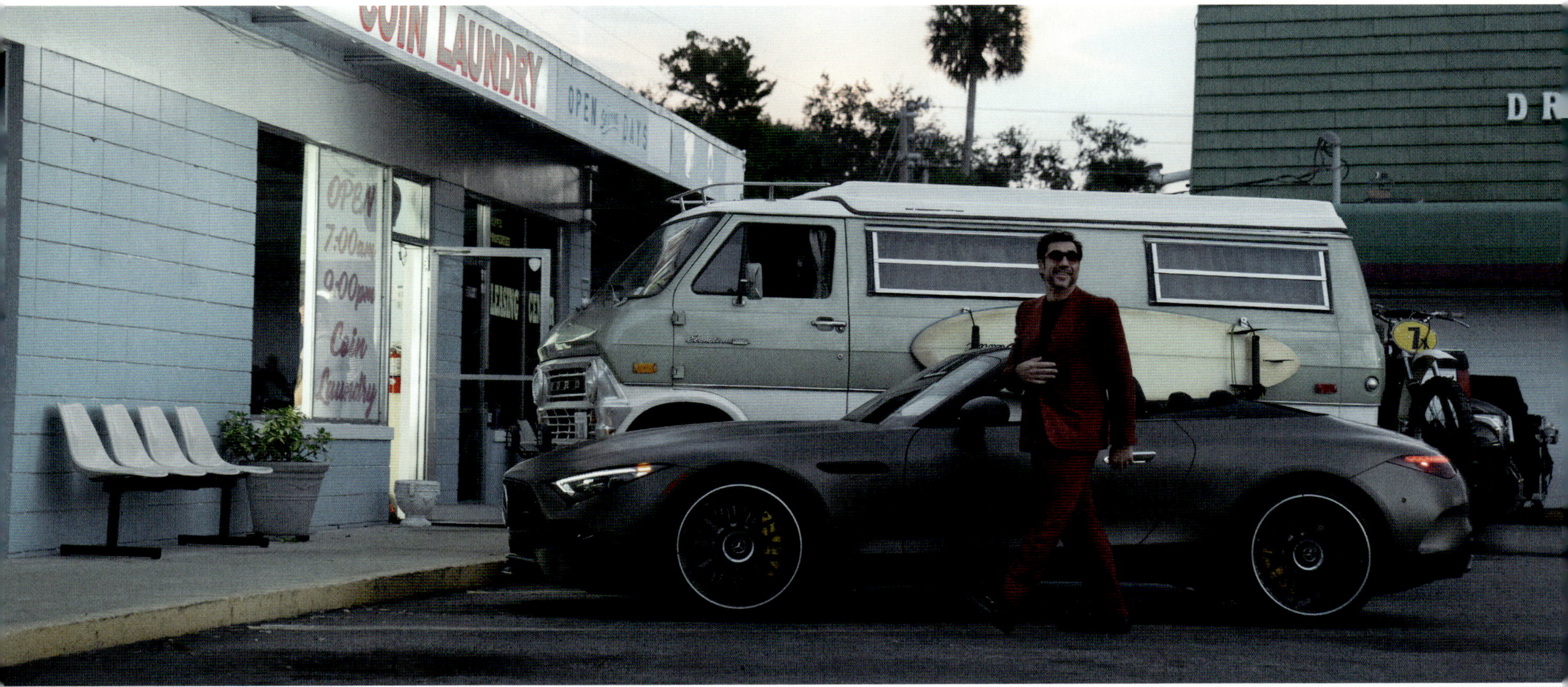

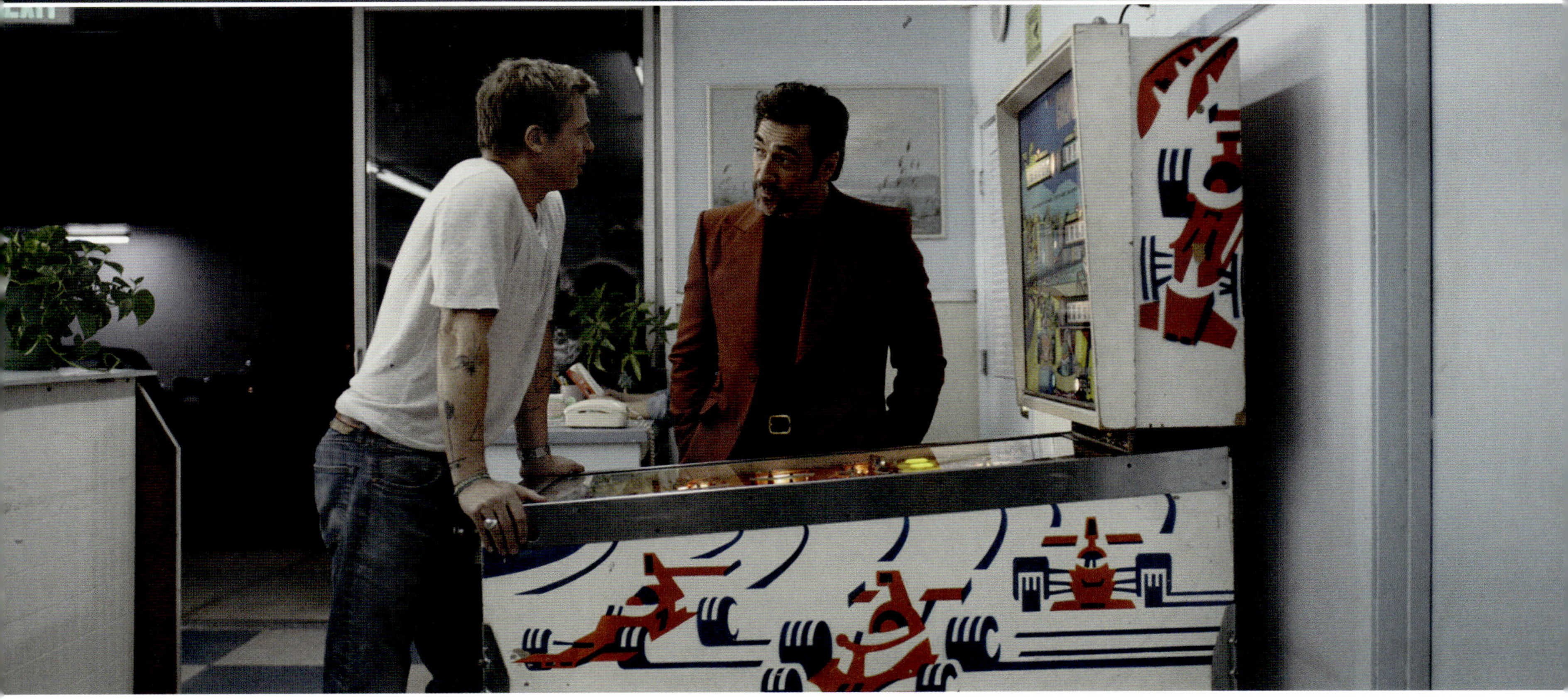

Above: Ruben (Javier Bardem) arrives in Florida with the hopes of recruiting Sonny (Brad Pitt) to the APXGP team.

VETERANS

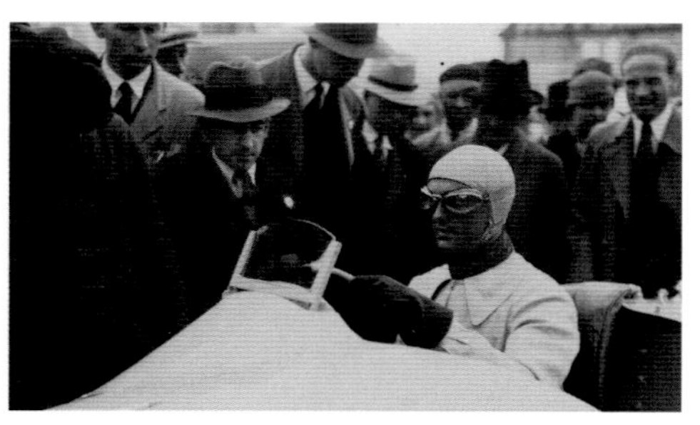

LOUIS CHIRON

The oldest driver to start a Formula One World Championship race at almost 56, when he finished sixth in the 1955 Monaco Grand Prix, Chiron also attempted to qualify for his home event three years later, when he was closing in on his 59th birthday. While he failed to qualify, Chiron remains the sport's oldest entrant, and he might have set an even higher record in terms of oldest starter had his engine not blown up in practice for the 1956 Monaco Grand Prix. And until Ferrari's Charles Leclerc won in 2024, Chiron was the only Monégasque driver to have triumphed at his home race.

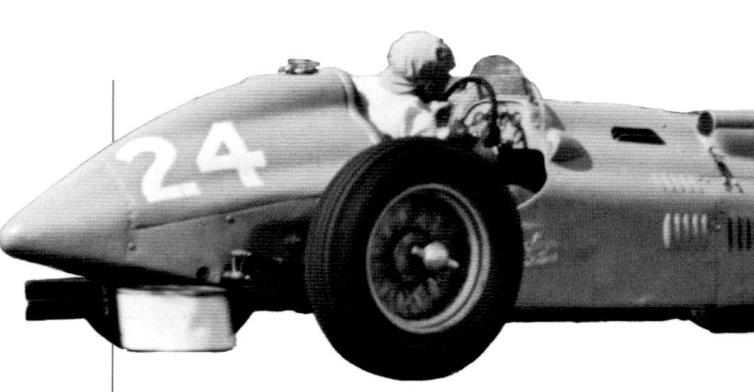

PHILIPPE ÉTANCELIN

While Luigi Platé was slated to enter the 1950 Italian Grand Prix, he never took part, so Étancelin is the second-oldest driver to both enter and start a round of the World Championship. Another to race on either side of the Second World War, the Frenchman finished eighth in his final appearance, driving a Talbot-Lago in a race in his hometown of Rouen. A Le Mans 24 Hour winner in 1934, Étancelin also holds the record as the oldest driver to score a point in Formula One, having finished fifth in back-to-back races at the end of the 1950 season, the latter result coming at Monza when he was 53 years and 249 days old.

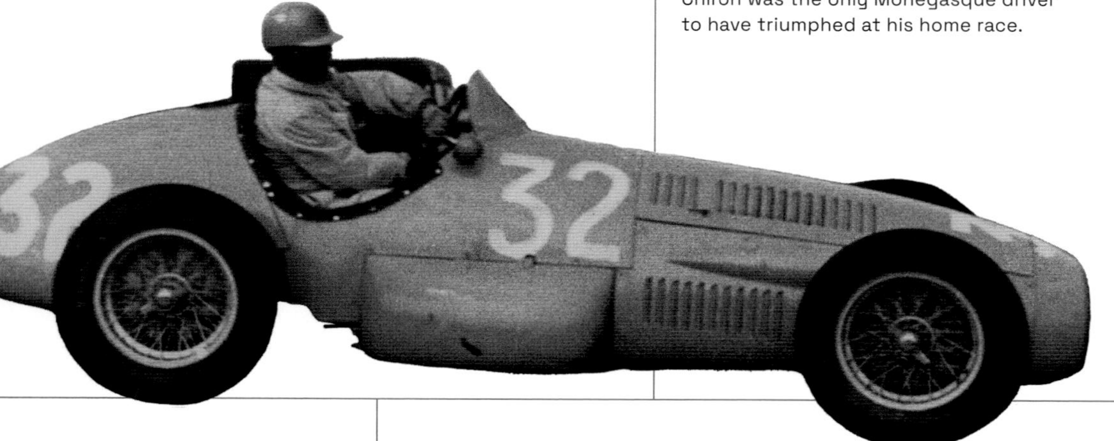

LUIGI FAGIOLI

An Alfa Romeo works driver in 1950, Fagioli finished third in the driver's championship with four second-place finishes and a third from the six rounds he competed in. He only entered one race the following year, the 1951 French Grand Prix, which saw him qualify seventh, directly ahead of Louis Chiron, as the slowest of the Alfa Romeos. Fagioli climbed into the top three when championship contender Juan Manuel Fangio's car hit trouble, and the Italian was ordered to hand over his vehicle to Fangio. The Argentine duly went on to secure the victory, with the points shared between both drivers and the pair credited as joint winners. It proved to be Fagioli's last Formula One race. But, at 53 years and 22 days old, Fagioli set a record that looks unlikely to ever be broken.

FERNANDO ALONSO

Alonso made his Formula One debut in 2001 for the Minardi team and won two championships driving for Renault in 2005 and 2006. Since then, a third title has eluded him, but as one of the finest drivers the sport has ever seen, he continues to perform at the highest level in search of it.

Spells with McLaren, Ferrari, and more recently Alpine saw victories and podiums but no championship, so he joined Aston Martin for the 2023 season and enjoyed a brilliant start, finishing fourth in the driver's championship. Although 2024 was tougher, Alonso signed a contract extension to take him through the end of 2026, when he will be 45. On top of starting more than 400 races in Formula One, Alonso has won at Le Mans and Daytona and had multiple attempts at the Indy 500 in addition to competing in the Dakar Rally, a remarkable racing resume that keeps growing.

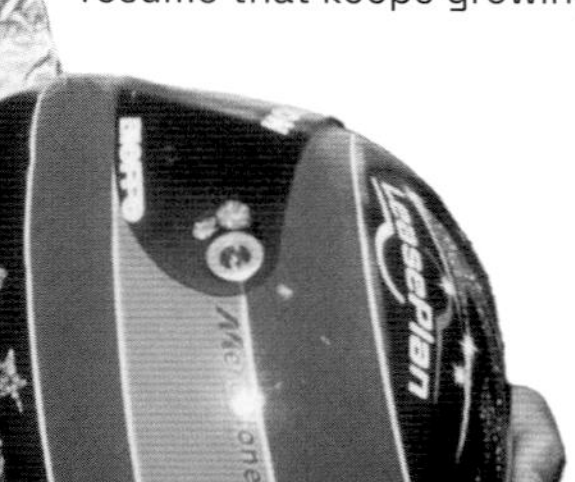

While it might seem far-fetched for Sonny Hayes to be competing in Formula One at age 54, he still lags behind a number of other drivers who entered race weekends over the years.

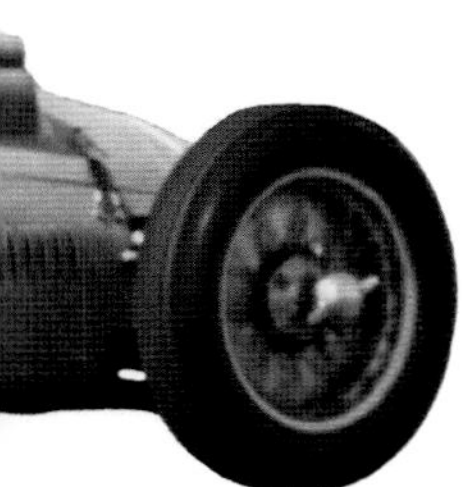

ARTHUR LEGAT

As with many drivers of the time, Legat was a local entrant into his home grand prix. Making just two appearances, the Belgian finished 13th at Spa-Francorchamps in 1952, driving a Veritas as a privateer. A year later he qualified 19th—two spots higher than his first attempt—but failed to complete a lap, retiring from his second and final race at 54 years and 232 days old.

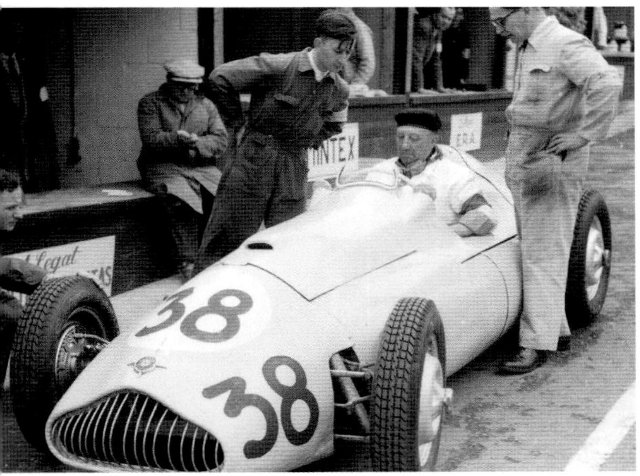

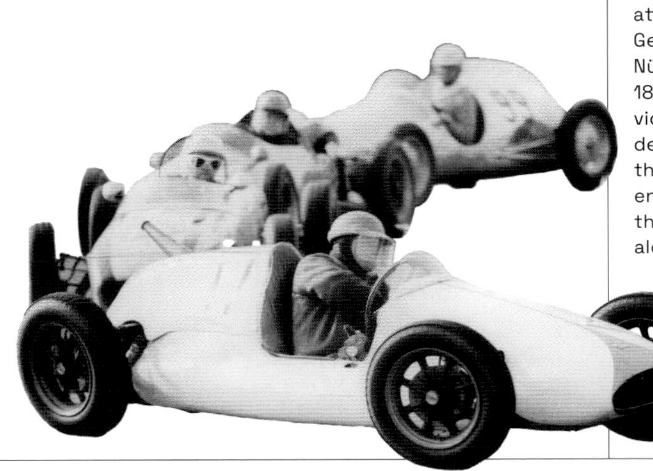

KURT KUHNKE

At 53 years and 92 days, Kurt Kuhnke attempted to qualify for the 1963 German Grand Prix on the infamous Nürburgring Nordschleife, driving a Lotus 18 that had taken Stirling Moss to four victories in the opening years of the decade. Powered by a Borgward engine, the car was no longer competitive enough, and Kuhnke failed to set a time that would make the grid. He was not alone, as two other entrants in Lotus 18's also failed to qualify, but Kuhnke did manage to start several non-championship Formula One races, the last in Sweden a week after his attempt at the Nordschleife.

LEWIS HAMILTON

Not far behind Alonso in terms of race starts is Hamilton, who has been ever-present on the grid since making his debut alongside the Spaniard in 2007. Since then, Hamilton has won a record-equaling seven driver's championships—one with McLaren and six with Mercedes—and finished the 2024 season with an astounding 105 victories. He also holds the record for most pole positions, with 104, 36 more than Michael Schumacher. Hamilton spent the first six years of his career with McLaren and won the driver's championship in his second season before moving to Mercedes ahead of the 2013 campaign. It was an inspired move, as he won further titles in 2014, 2015, 2017, 2018, 2019, and 2020 to match Schumacher's seven. After missing out in a controversial title showdown in 2021, the next two seasons were the first in which Hamilton did not win a race. But he showed that age was not a factor with two victories in his final season with Mercedes in 2024. Hamilton made the decision to move to Ferrari ahead of the 2025 season, signing a multiyear contract that will keep him racing in F1 well into his forties, as he goes in search of an eighth championship.

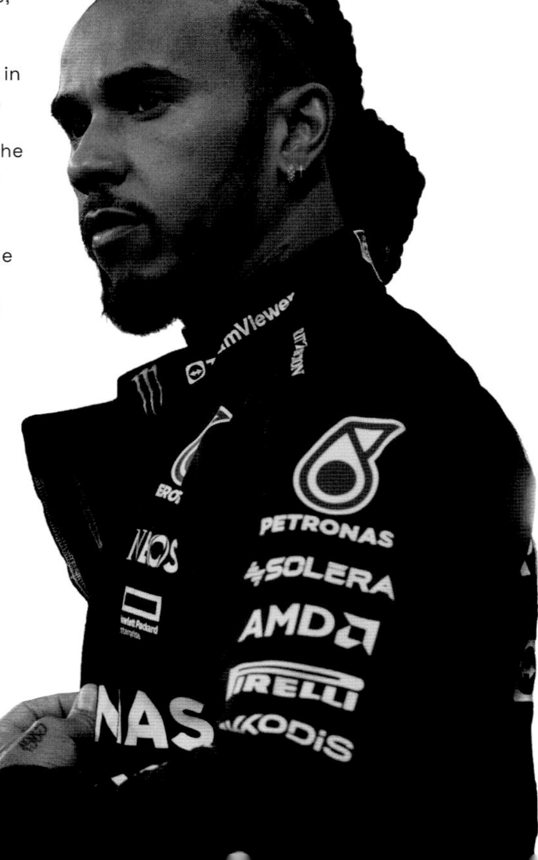

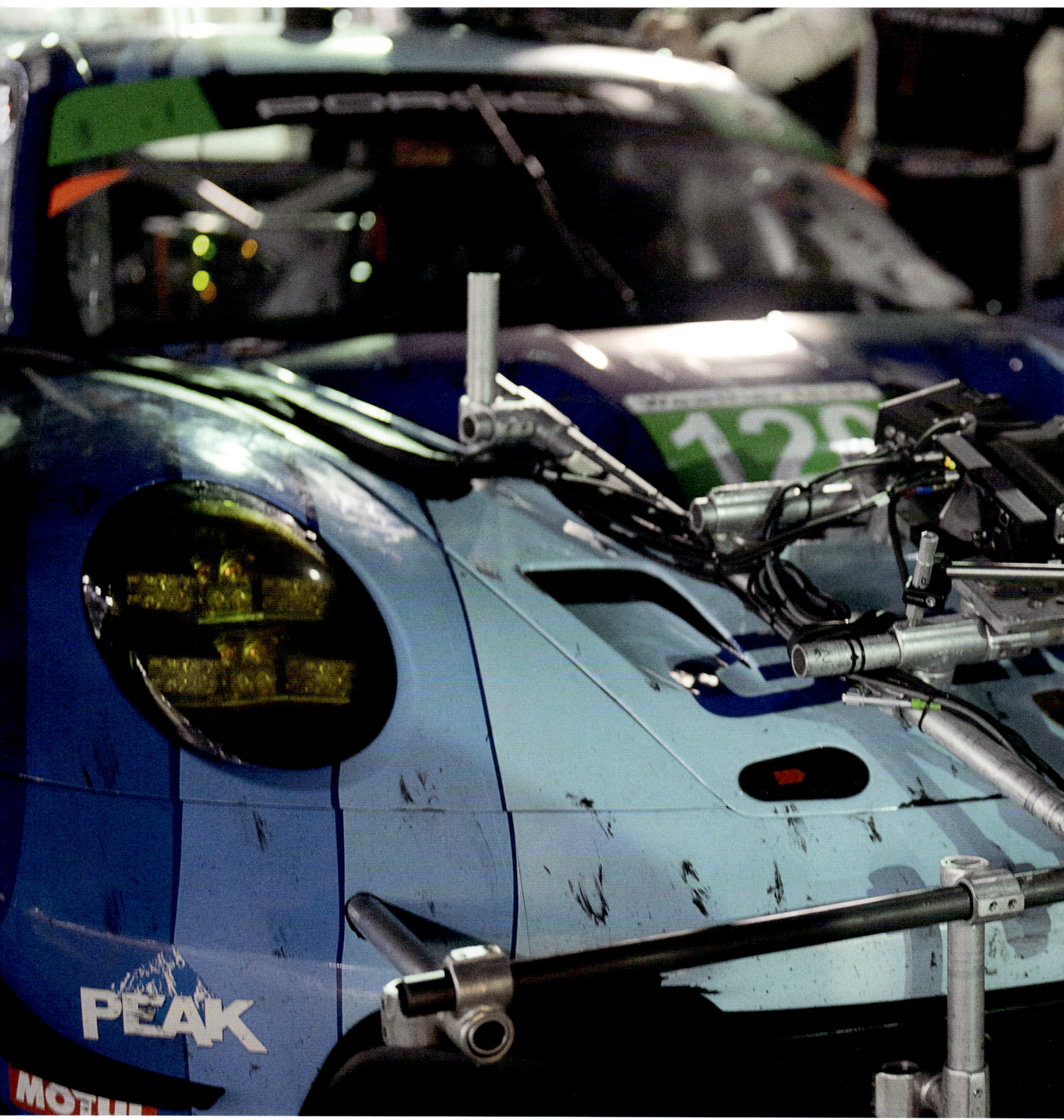
PEAK

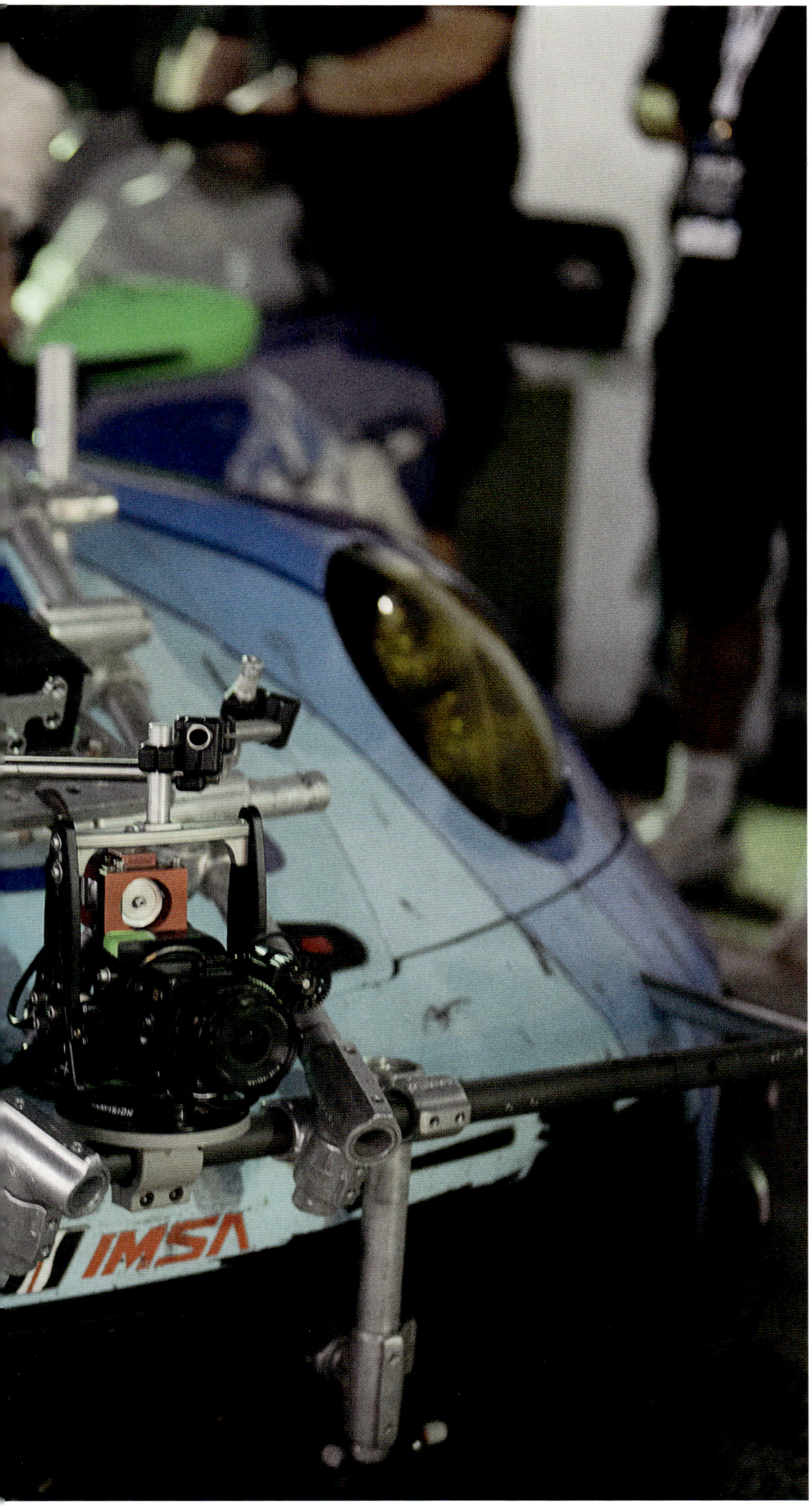

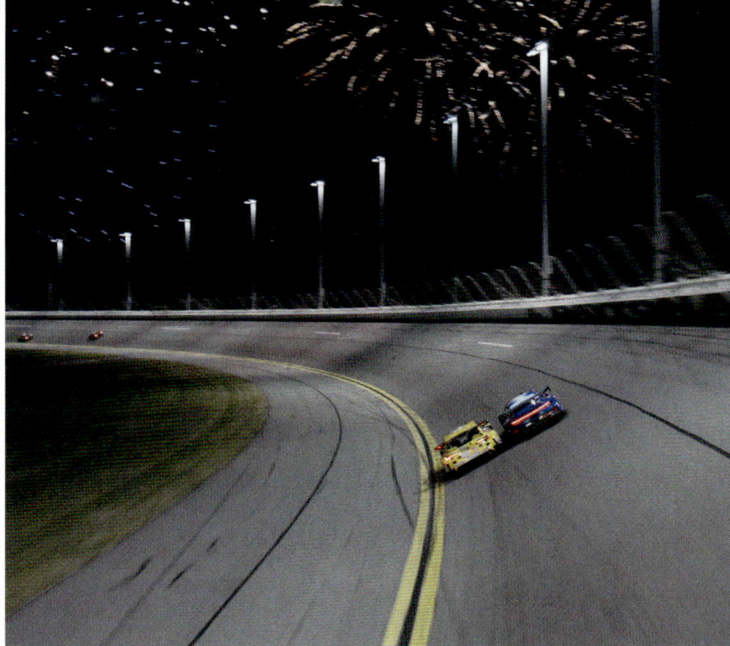

The production arrived in Daytona, where Bruckheimer had shot scenes for *Days of Thunder*, in mid-January 2024 for several days of prep and rehearsals, with filming set to begin on Saturday, January 20, during the Roar Before the Rolex 24 event, and continuing through the Rolex 24 Hours of Daytona race the following weekend and beyond.

"We shot before, after, and during the 24-hour race to get that sense of being at the real race while it's happening," recalls Kosinski, who wanted the Daytona race scenes to look and feel very different from those in Formula One. "It doesn't have the polish and sophistication of F1. It's a little more down-and-dirty, and I wanted to embrace the Americanness of it all."

"It's hallowed in its own way," says Pitt of Daytona. "And this 24 Hours race is our Le Mans. So, being able to shoot within that was crazy cool. Different discipline, fun, scrappy, just spin the wheels and spin the car around, much looser. More what I was accustomed to, having grown up driving on dirt roads."

Just as the filmmakers had partnered with Mercedes for Formula One, they joined forces with Wright Motorsports, an American racing team based in Ohio, run by John Wright, to enter their own Porsche GT3 into both the Roar and 24 Hours of Daytona races. The car would be driven by Long and three others, with a camera mounted on the roll cage, filming an over-the-shoulder shot throughout both races.

Left: The production crew mounted a camera on to the hood of the Chip Hart car in order to capture first-person POV shots during the race.

Top Right: Sonny races neck-and-neck with a yellow BMW at Daytona, striving for first place.

All four men wore Sonny's blue-green helmet, while the car was decked out in the striped blue livery of the film's fictional Chip Hart racing team, although both sponsors were real. "I love stripes," says concept artist Daniel Simon, who designed the livery, "and Porsche has a strong connection to stripe liveries with the seventies Porsche 917 Le Mans winning cars. A lot of stripes there, and color gradients, which is like a seventies vibe. And blue was set because we had Peak and Geico as title sponsors. All the red I put in was canceled by Joe. I love red. That's the only thing we disagree on. It was designed from a top view, and the team who put the livery on did a great job keeping those stripes nice and organized."

With time on the track limited between the Roar and the 24 Hours of Daytona race, the production focused on the scenes between Sonny and Ruben, which took place at the Pappas Drive-In & Family Restaurant in New Smyrna Beach and neighboring Christina's Coin Laundry. The art department also constructed a shower block within the restaurant and laundromat complex for the scene in which Sonny washes.

But Kosinski was mostly in Daytona to film at the Roar Before the Rolex 24 and 24 Hours of Daytona, shooting the scene of Sonny waking up in his van then heading down to the Chip Hart garage in one continuous take while the latter race was running, alongside several other scenes of Pitt on the pit wall, in the pit lane, and inside the team garage. "We had to soak up all the production value we could, because you can't re-create that stuff after," says Hefferman. "Mentally, it was challenging, because it's constant noise and so hard to communicate." Fortunately, the Chip Hart garage was positioned next door to the Wright Racing team. "Their cars would pull in, they would do a driver switch or a tire change, and we'd shoot it, because it was absolute gold." Kosinski also filmed in the broadcast booth with racing commentator Leigh Diffey, who narrates the on-track action.

Once the real 24 Hours of Daytona race was over on Sunday—in the movie, the Chip Hart team is victorious—the production was allowed to shoot on the actual winner's podium. "It took some negotiation," admits Hefferman. "Brad, Joe, and Jerry were instrumental in making it happen, meeting the team who organized it, saying, 'After you've done your presentation, please, let us move our car in. We're used to doing things in small time windows. We don't need an hour and a half. Give us ten minutes. Give us eight.'" The pitch worked, and Kosinski was allowed to film on the podium while the crowd was still there. "We piggybacked onto that live environment and did it within the limitations we were told. Again, you can't re-create that stuff, because there's so much going on: they got confetti cannons; you've got the cars moving in and out." Although, true to form, Sonny has already left, on his way to pastures new.

Below: Assistant Director Toby Hefferman relays instructions for the opening scene at the 24 Hours of Daytona race.

Right: Daniel Simon's concept art for the Chip Hart team Porsche features a blue striped paint scheme.

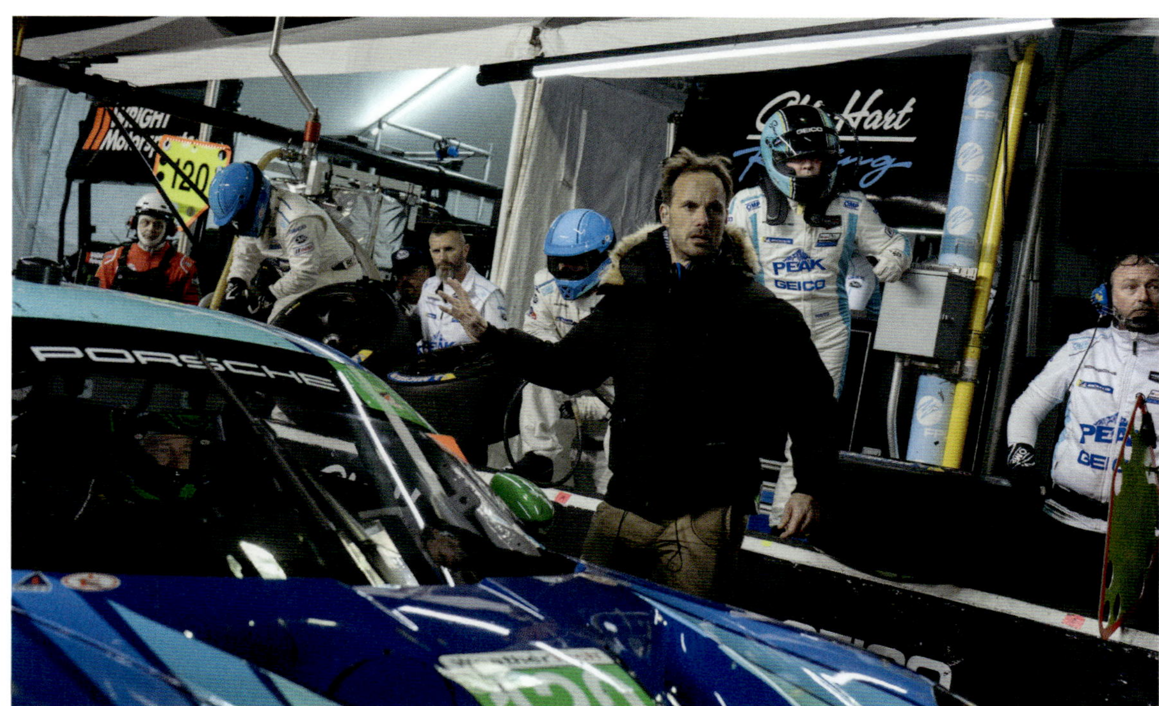

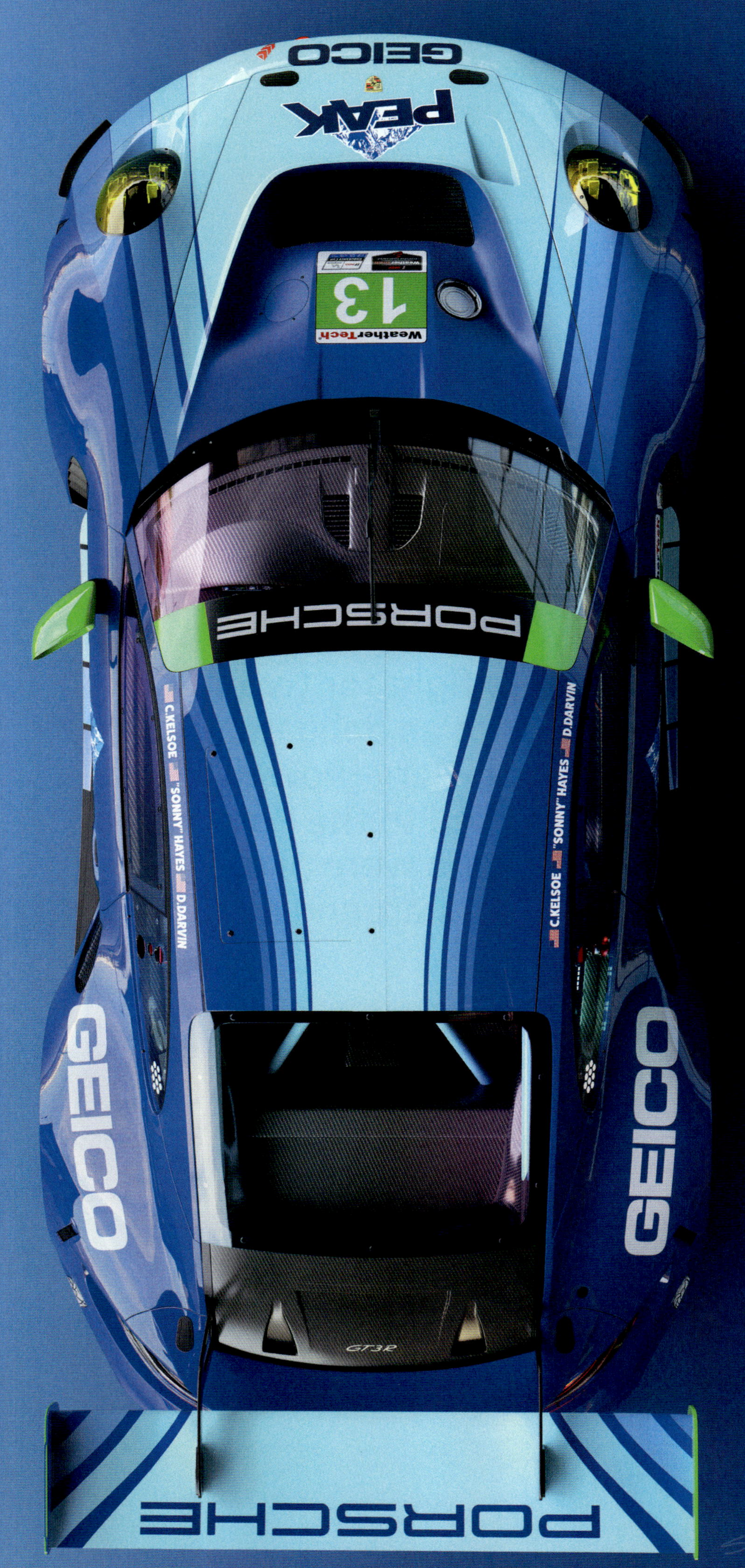
GEICO
PEAK
13
WeatherTech
PORSCHE
C.KELSOE "SONNY" HAYES D.DARVIN
C.KELSOE "SONNY" HAYES D.DARVIN
GEICO
GEICO
GT3 R
PORSCHE
SIMON

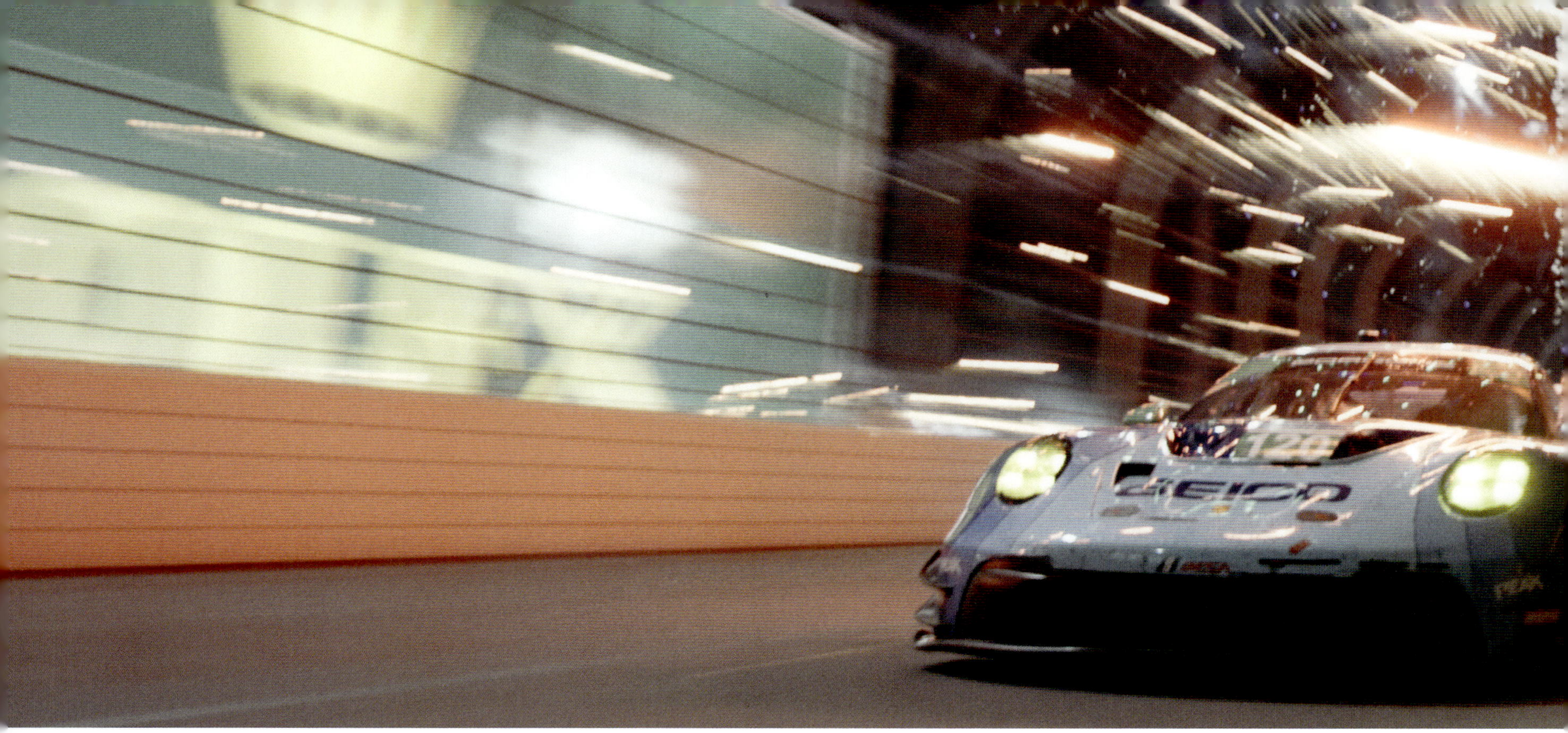

“These cars are made to fight for twenty-four hours, so they’re not as delicate as Formula One cars. Once Gary [Powell] brought that up, we talked to the Porsche guys about it, and Porsche were okay with us banging their cars around a bit.”

JOSEPH KOSINSKI

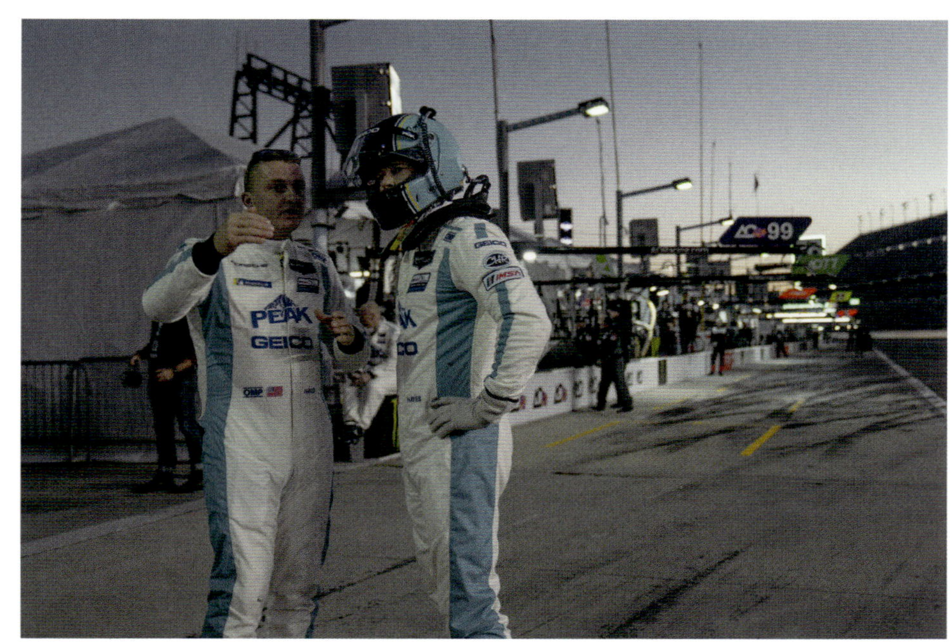

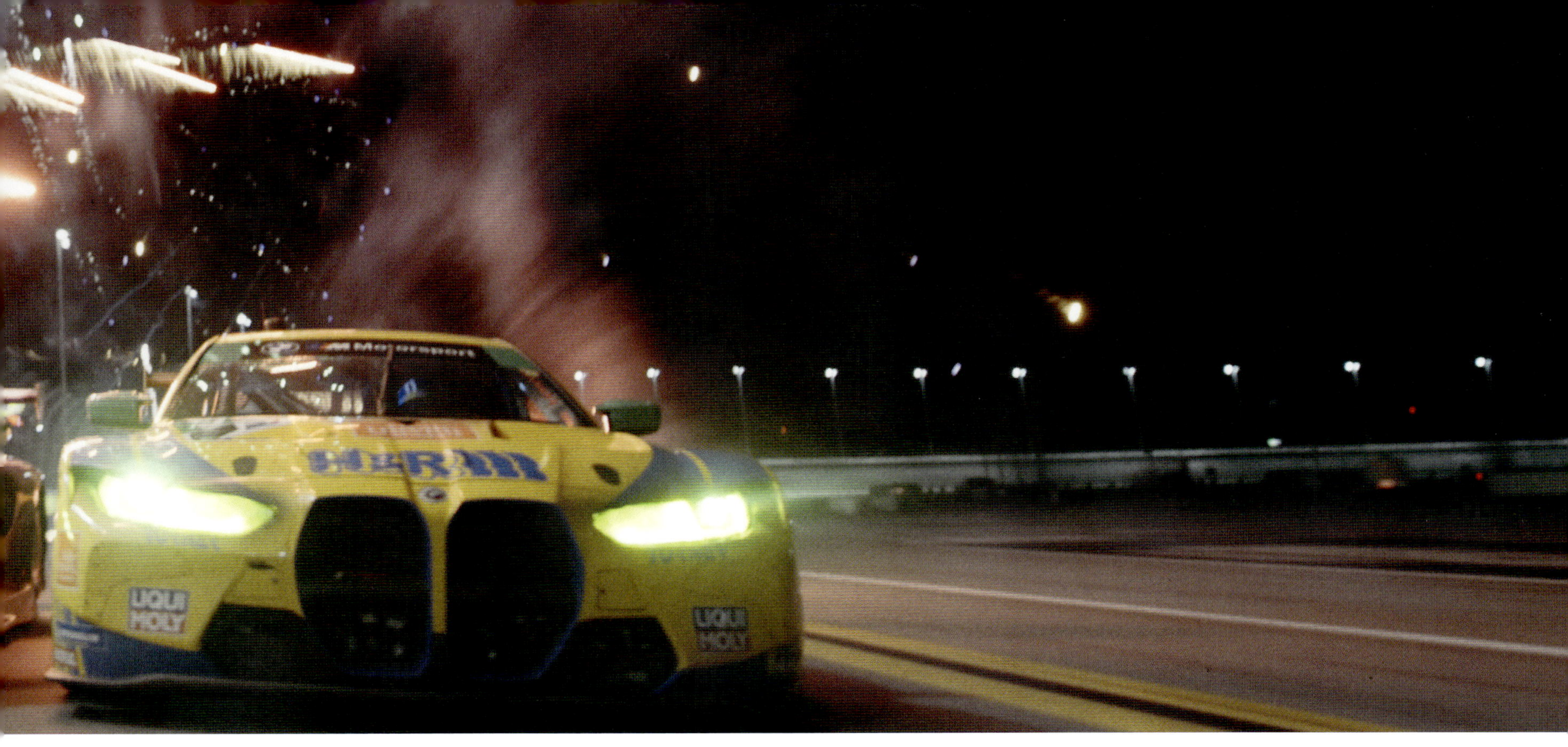

In addition to filming on track between sessions for both the Roar and the 24-Hours races, Kosinski returned to the Daytona speedway the following week with Gary Powell, who had recently joined the film as supervising stunt coordinator, replacing original stunt coordinator Adam Kirley, to shoot various action beats that, at times, required up to eight cars on track and included the returning Luciano Bacheta and Craig Dolby.

"We had our own track sessions to shoot the spins and bumping and the specific stuff from a better angle and camera car work," recalls Bacheta, who drove the yellow BMW M4 GT3 that tangles with Sonny's Porsche, which was driven by either Pitt or Dolby, depending on the level of risk involved.

"That was fun," says Pitt, "because you've got the two ends of banked ovals, which is a whole other experience to hang on. But once you've experienced the downforce from the Formula cars, these are much looser. Still fun, but not able to do what those other cars could do. I did enjoy it. It was a high. But a much scrappier style of driving for me."

To make the track action as realistic and exhilarating as possible, Powell felt the cars should bump while racing. "We started going through the choreography, getting used to the cars, and, to my mind, they were playing it safe, because they weren't allowed to rub," says Powell, who voiced his concerns to Kosinski. "I was nervous because these cars, even though they look more traditional, are still million-dollar race cars, so I was very wary of wrecking anything," admits Kosinski. "But these cars are made to fight for twenty-four hours, so they're not as delicate as Formula One cars. Once Gary brought that up, we talked to the Porsche guys about it, and Porsche were okay with us banging their cars around a bit."

"They were real GT3 race cars we borrowed from a European team because it was their off-season," explains action vehicle supervisor Graham Kelly. "I took them apart and put in some strengthening, so we could get two cars side to side and wouldn't damage the chassis. We did the same with the BMW, which needed push bars on the side and front."

Left: Stunt driver Craig Dolby discusses the 24 Hours of Daytona race scene with Brad Pitt during the shoot.

Above: The blue Chip Hart GT3 demonstrates that "rubbing is racing" while trying to pass the yellow BMW on the Daytona racetrack.

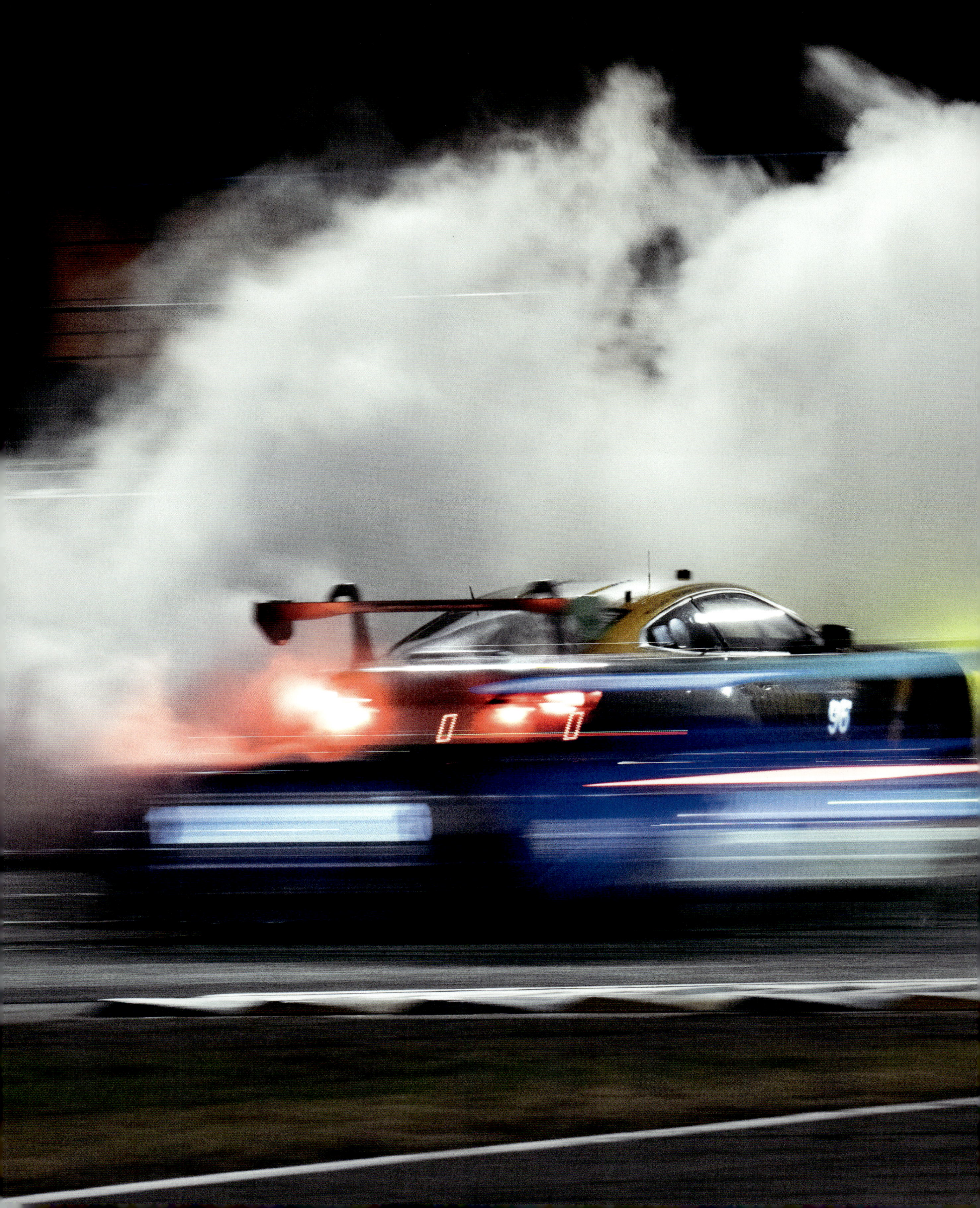

For the scene of Hayes's Porsche rocketing out of the pits before squeezing between two competing cars, it's Dolby doubling for Pitt and Bacheta driving a Mercedes he clashes with. "We were filming from a helicopter, and Craig drove out of the pits, through the middle of two cars," recalls Powell. "I said to him, 'That was good, but can you get *closer*?'"

Dolby went again, this time making contact. "Craig started nudging and scraping the other cars, and suddenly it becomes real," says Powell. "Because you can't replicate real racing unless you're racing for real and doing what real racers would, and, in that scenario, they would scrape, push, barge, and bump, and that's exactly what they did going down the back straight at 160 miles per hour. Craig and Luciano were bumping and rubbing each other, and it looked amazing."

"Because we were in GT3 cars, you can make contact without it being super dangerous and also without it killing the car," concurs Bacheta. "So, we made the most out of our opportunities there. Gary would come on the radio and say, 'Get closer,' and we'd radio back saying, 'We're touching! We can't get any closer!' And he'd say, 'Get *even* closer! Touch more!' That was on day one of working with him as well. We were banging wheels at 170, 180 miles per hour, going round the oval [track] and seeing 191, 192 miles per hour on a dash, with the cameras rolling. It was amazing to have cameras on the cars at that speed, filming what we were doing."

This included a spinout, when a BMW, driven by Bacheta, is battling Sonny's Porsche, driven by Dolby. "We were hitting wheels, and my BMW ends up having a spin," continues Bacheta. "Obviously, that's risky to do once, but we did it about twelve times, where I had to do a high-speed spin into oncoming traffic. We had about eight stunt drivers working with us, and everyone was really on it, avoiding accidents, but getting close enough to make it look good and repeatable."

Stunt driver Craig Dolby, driving Sonny's Chip Hart GT3, pursues the yellow BMW through a thick cloud of smoke.

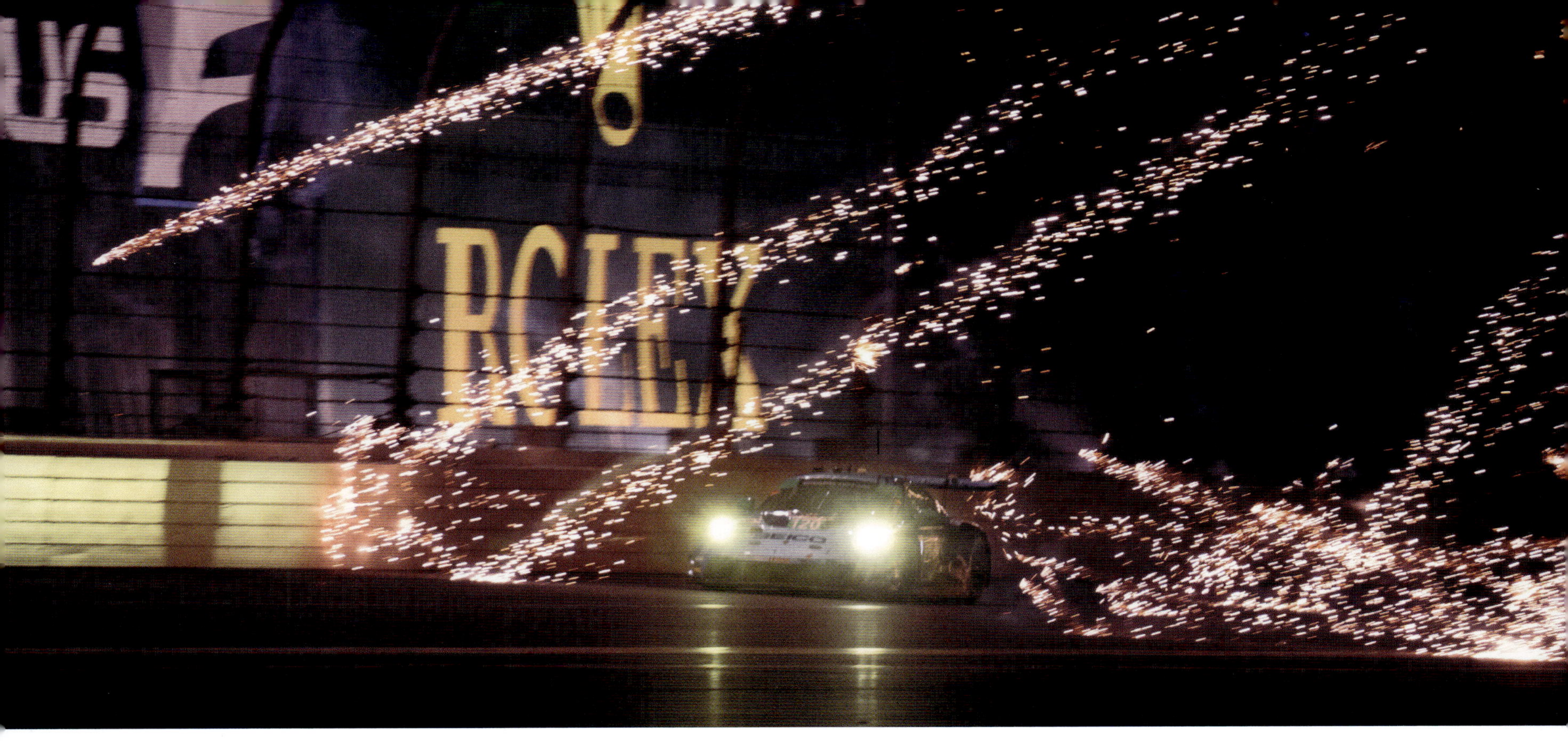

One idiosyncratic quirk of the 24 Hours of Daytona is that fireworks are let off around the track during the actual race, and not, as in Formula One, at the end to celebrate the victor. As such, Kosinski wanted to show the fireworks interacting with the cars while they were on track, beyond just being reflected in their windscreens. “Joe said it would be cool to have fireworks bouncing on the road and the cars going through them,” recalls special effects supervisor Keith Dawson, who worked with a local pyrotechnic company to create fireworks that could be launched at the track itself.

To test the effect, Dawson took to the track with Powell. “Gary doesn’t drive slowly. So, we drove around at 170 miles per hour, and I had my firework team launch a couple across the track so we could video it ourselves and see what the dangers might be. Shells were bouncing off the windshield or went off in front with the car driving through them. It was so dynamic. Then we spoke with Graham Kelly about any potential damage that might happen. We always knew we would cause a little bit of damage to the vehicles, but not hurting any of the artists or stunt crew was our main concern.”

Kosinski filmed the firework sequence in the week following the 24 Hours of Daytona, with Pitt behind the wheel of the Porsche. “It turned out way better than we anticipated,” says Dawson. “We had fireworks going aerial.

Kosinski wanted to show the fireworks interacting with the cars while they were on track, beyond just being reflected in their windscreens.

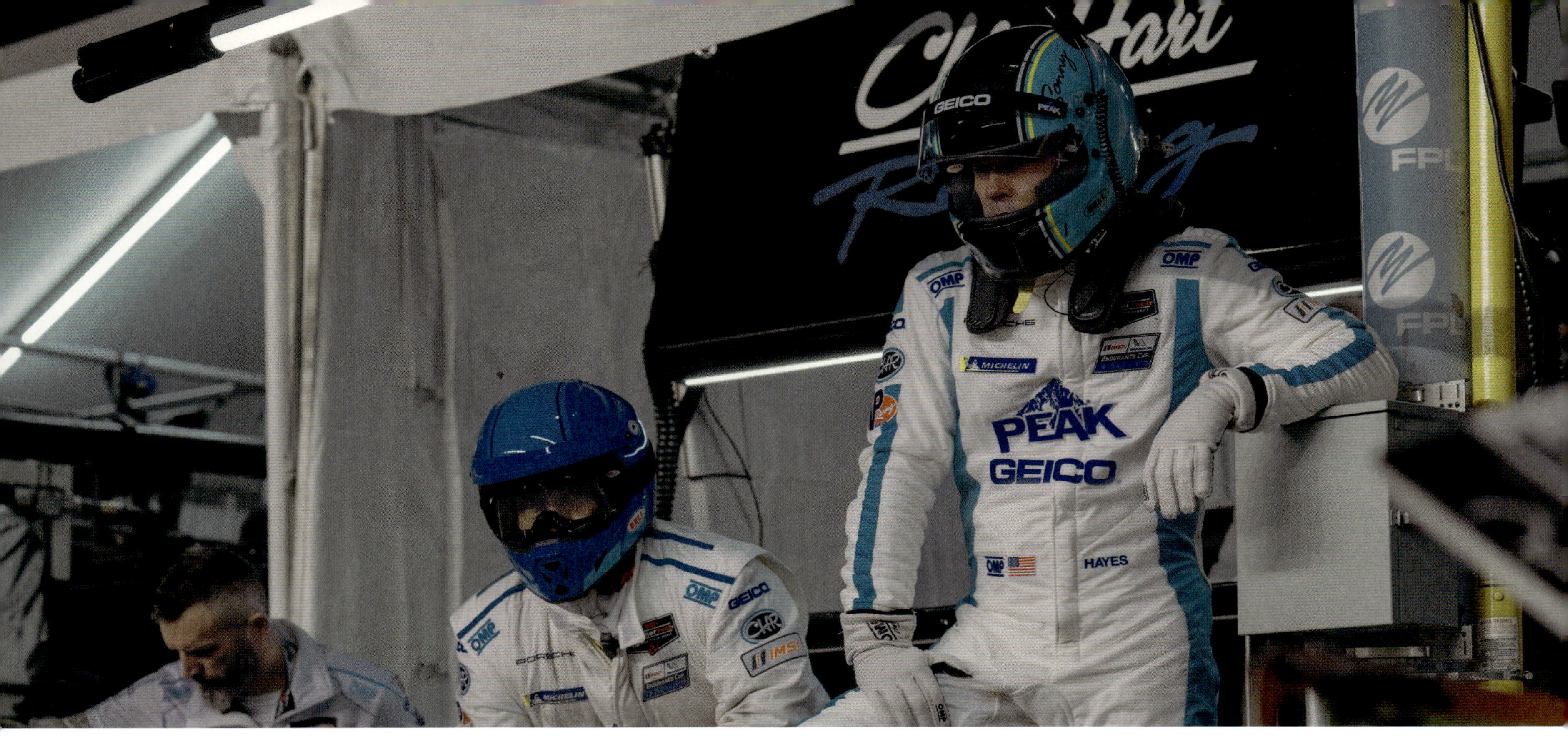

We had some side mounted. We got some great moments with Brad driving, going through showers of sparks and fireworks bouncing off the cars in front of him and the ground. Timing-wise it was very tricky. We managed it when I was in the car with Gary, but when you've got real race action going on and cars speeding, we had to get our timings right. Ninety-nine percent of the time, they bounced in front of the cars as they drove through."

Unfortunately, one tracer found its way into Bacheta's BMW. "It came through my headlight and blew up inside the car," he recalls. "It exploded in the chassis. But all the smoke was in the car. It was pretty funny."

"Luckily, it was Luch it happened to, and he could deal with it," says Dawson. "But the shots we got were amazing. Everyone was blown away. Joe was over the moon. Being able to do it for real, with real drivers in a real location, you're not going to beat that. You wouldn't have got the same effect using CG. You wouldn't have got the same interaction with Brad."

At another point during his stint, Sonny must contend with the car in front of him leaking oil onto the track, which causes him to careen toward the banked curve. "We mounted some smoke grenades on the car in front and put some spark effects on it," says Dawson. "In situ with that, we put a little washer bottle on the front of Brad's car and made a thick, oily, viscous liquid that would splat onto his windscreen and obscure his vision. He could still see where he was going, but you could tell the car in front was spitting oil at him."

While Bacheta, Dolby, and the stunt team did most of the driving during the track sessions at Daytona, Pitt did his fair share. "We were bumping and grinding," says Pitt. "I don't know how fast we were going there. I would guess 160. I'm probably inflating a little bit, but I remember going 160 and hitting the bank. That'll get your attention, man. Real fast."

"He was getting bumped along the straight. He was bumping *me* on the straight. He was doing overtakes, getting overtaken, and a car hit him," says Bacheta.

"You knew Brad was having a good time, 'cause even though he's got a crash helmet on, you could see the smile through the helmet," laughs Powell.

"Whenever you see Brad's face, it's him driving. Whenever there's a car battling wheel-to-wheel with him, it's real," says Bacheta. "It's unbelievable what he was doing, and what we were doing collectively. Everything was turned up to eleven for Daytona."

Top Left: Kosinski filmed a sequence with fireworks being launched across the track at Daytona.

Top Right: Sonny (Brad Pitt) waiting to get into his GT3 in the Chip Hart box.

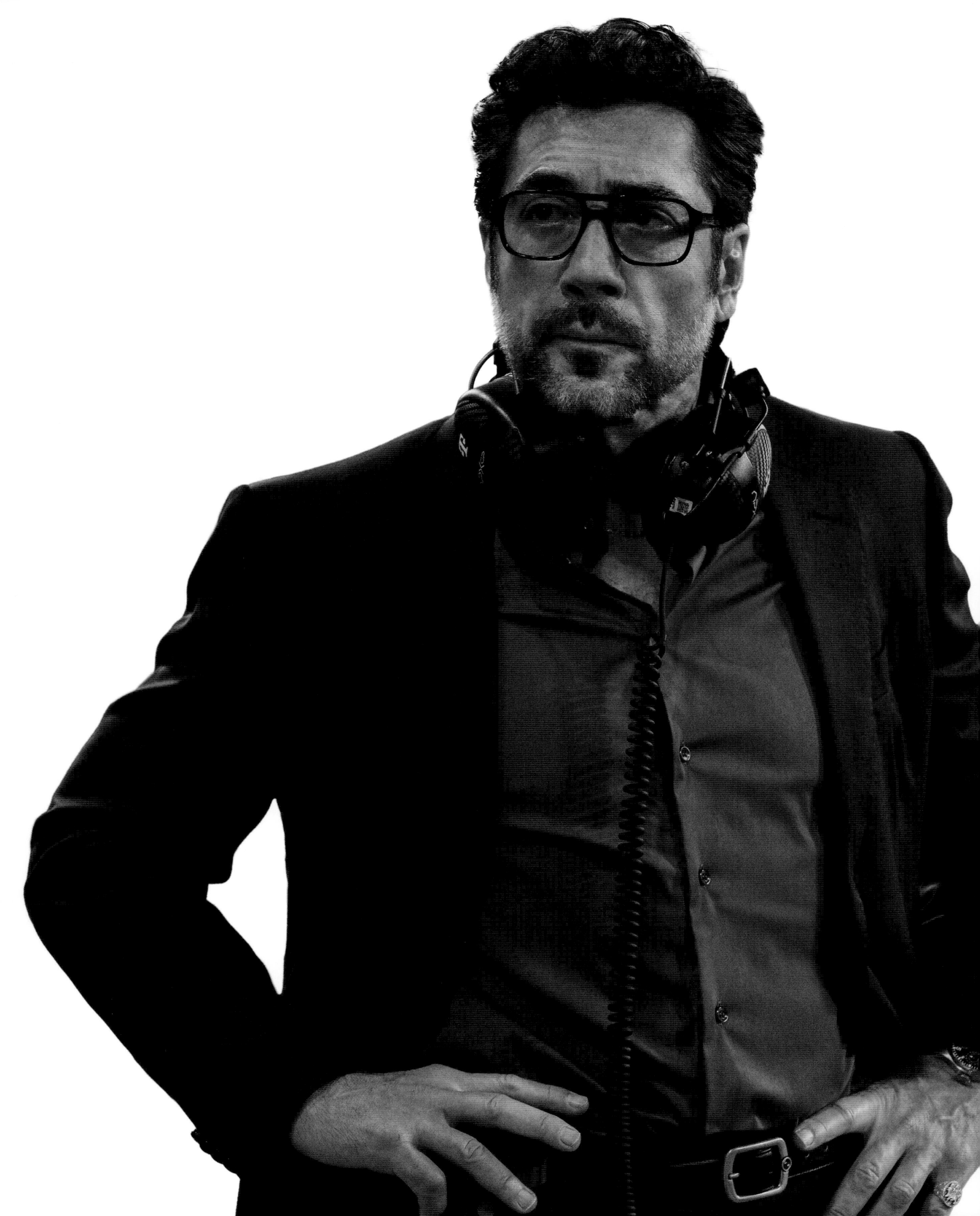

THE BOSS

RUBEN CERVANTES

APXGP owner Ruben Cervantes (Javier Bardem) was Sonny Hayes's (Brad Pitt) teammate the year he crashed out of F1 following his horrific accident at the Spanish Grand Prix. But while Sonny sought solace in gambling and women, Ruben transformed himself into an entrepreneur and businessman, building himself a very successful company, Cervantes Capital. "Then he was able to buy his own Formula One team, which is a very, very expensive endeavor, because he loves racing and he had the means to do it," says director Joseph Kosinski. "He's put together this unlikely group of people and is trying to figure out a way to do it better than everybody else, going up against the titans of the sport. But he made a deal with his shareholders/board that if APXGP didn't win a race in the first three years, he would sell the team."

To play Ruben, Kosinski and Bruckheimer cast Spanish actor Javier Bardem, who won the Best Supporting Actor Oscar for his terrifying portrayal of hitman Anton Chigurh in the Coen Brothers' *No Country for Old Men* and starred in the Bruckheimer-produced *Pirates of the Caribbean: Dead Men Tell No Tales*. Bardem had also co-starred with Pitt in Ridley Scott's *The Counselor*, although the two men didn't have any scenes together. "I needed someone who felt like an equal to Brad," explains Kosinski. "Javier is a phenomenal actor, phenomenal presence. At the same time, he has a warmth that is instant. He doesn't always play it in his characters, but it was evident the first time I talked to him. I needed someone who could walk in and feel like an old friend, and Javier brings that. You feel these two have a friendship that goes back decades."

Which is why, when Ruben is faced with the prospect of losing APXGP, he turns to his friend to help save him. Unlike Sonny or Ruben, however, Bardem is not remotely interested in speed. "I only got my driving license six years ago," laughs the 56-year-old actor. "Why? Because I lived all my life in the city, in the center. Then, ten years ago, I moved out of the city. At first, I tried to cope by using taxis, underground, or buses, but it took so much time, so I said to myself, 'I must learn to drive.' Now I drive. I like it, but I'm not good at speed. Making this film, I was asked, 'Would you like to be driven in a two-seater F1 experience car?' I said, 'No.' I rejected that. When I told my friends who are huge Formula One fans, they said, 'Are you fucking crazy?' But I'm not a huge speed fan."

> "[Ruben has] put together this unlikely group of people and is trying to figure out a way to do it better than everybody else, going up against the titans of the sport."
>
> JOSEPH KOSINSKI

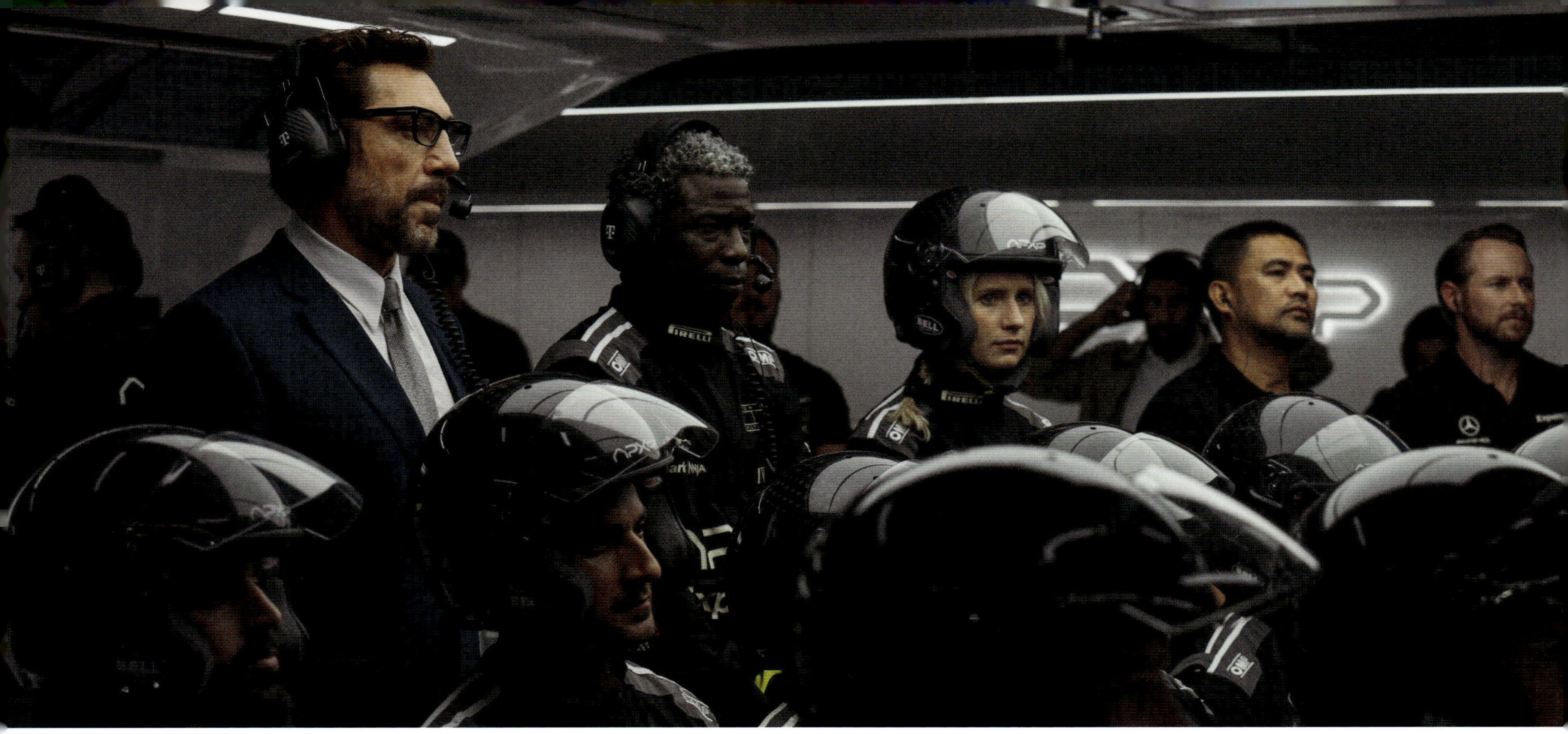

“Ruben is ruled by the need to compete . . . I like competition. I competed myself.”

JAVIER BARDEM

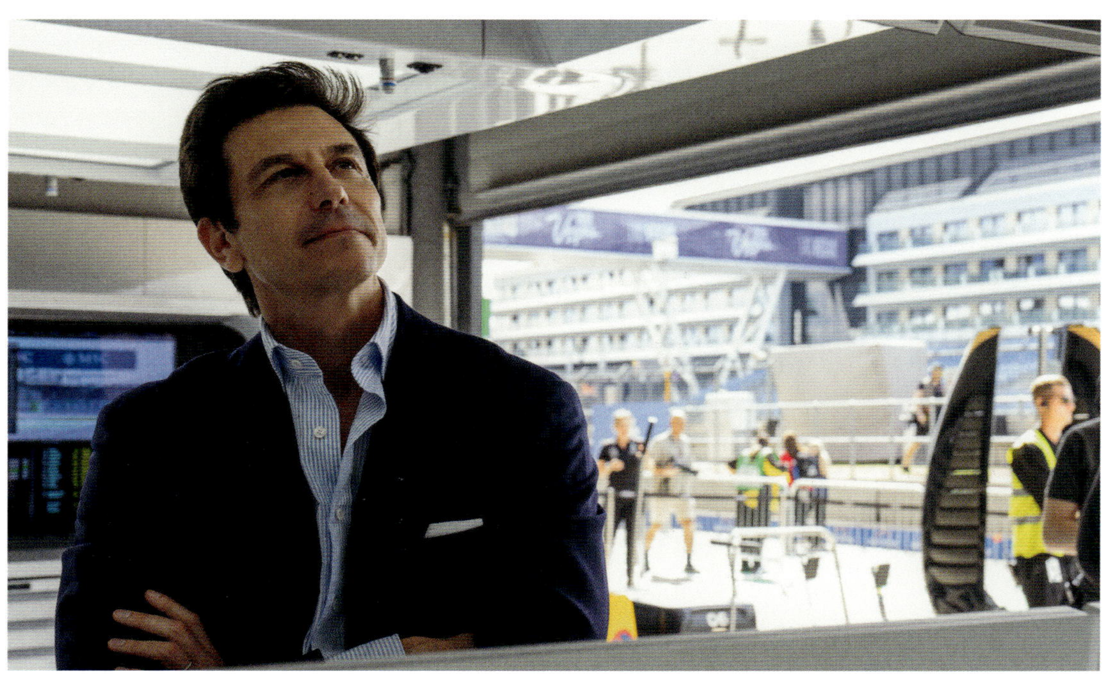

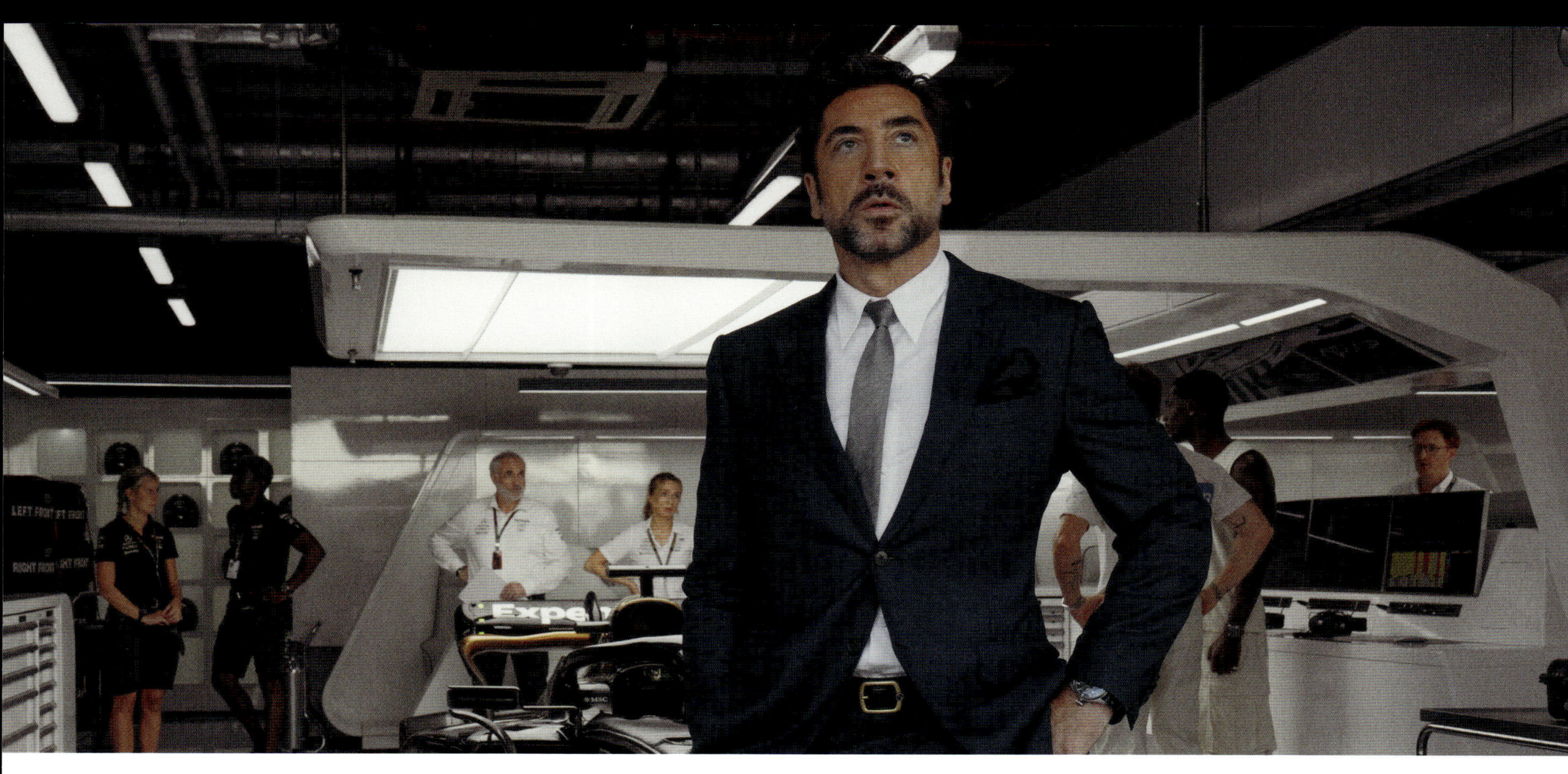

As part of his research, Bardem talked to as many of the current F1 team bosses as possible and, of course, watched *Drive to Survive*. "When I met these guys, I knew who they were because of the series, which was very helpful to understand the world behind the F1, because it was very accurate in many aspects. But speaking with Joe, I wondered if I should focus or be more aware of one [team boss] above the others. And we decided no. Ruben's a mix of all of them, and no one in particular, because he was a driver himself, and that's what makes a difference."

But one owner did make an impression on Bardem and fed into his portrayal: Mercedes's Toto Wolff. "I watched the British Grand Prix sitting next to him in his garage, with headphones on. I was looking at him and his focus, his way of owning the place, owning the garage, owning the team, at the same time being very gentle. I mean, he's very gentle, very attractive, and has a beautiful presence, but he would lose it in a snap. So, I thought, *Okay, I'm allowed to do that. If he does it, I can do it.* And they fucking lose it. They get nuts. They get crazy. Then they come back into this focused state. As an actor, I love to play that range of emotions. If I had not seen *Drive to Survive*, or been with Toto in that garage, I don't know if I would have had the courage to go crazy."

While Bardem is not a fan of speed, he did understand his character's competitive nature. "Ruben is ruled by the need to compete. I played rugby for seventeen years in Spain. I was the captain of the national rugby team when I was sixteen and seventeen. I like competition. I competed myself. But those drivers put their lives on the line. Once you are in one of those seats, you are putting your life at risk every race."

Nevertheless, Bardem says the most challenging aspect of playing Ruben was "imagining the amount of money he's dealing with daily. He may lose millions of dollars just because he still wants to race. Ruben's a gambler. What I wanted to bring to the character was this sensation of making the next bet even stronger, without the fear of losing. And calling upon Sonny is a very strong bet indeed. I don't know much about the F1 world, but the drivers I've met are calm, focused, and fearless. I wanted to bring that into Ruben's actions, Ruben's reactions, Ruben's decisions."

Top Row: Ruben (Javier Bardem) watches the race with members of the pit crew.

Left: Toto Wolff, CEO of Mercedes-AMG Petronas, plays himself in a cameo.

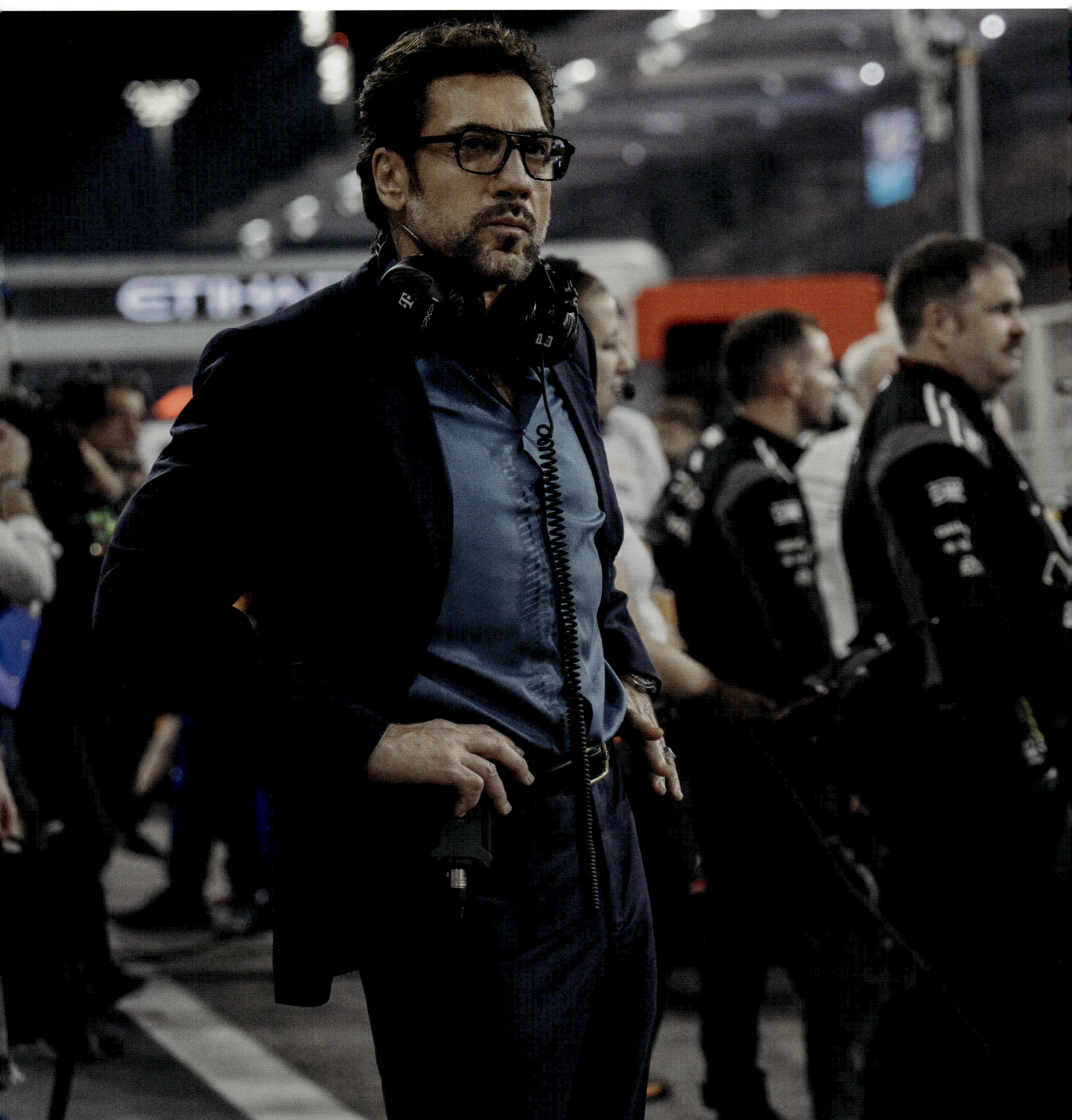

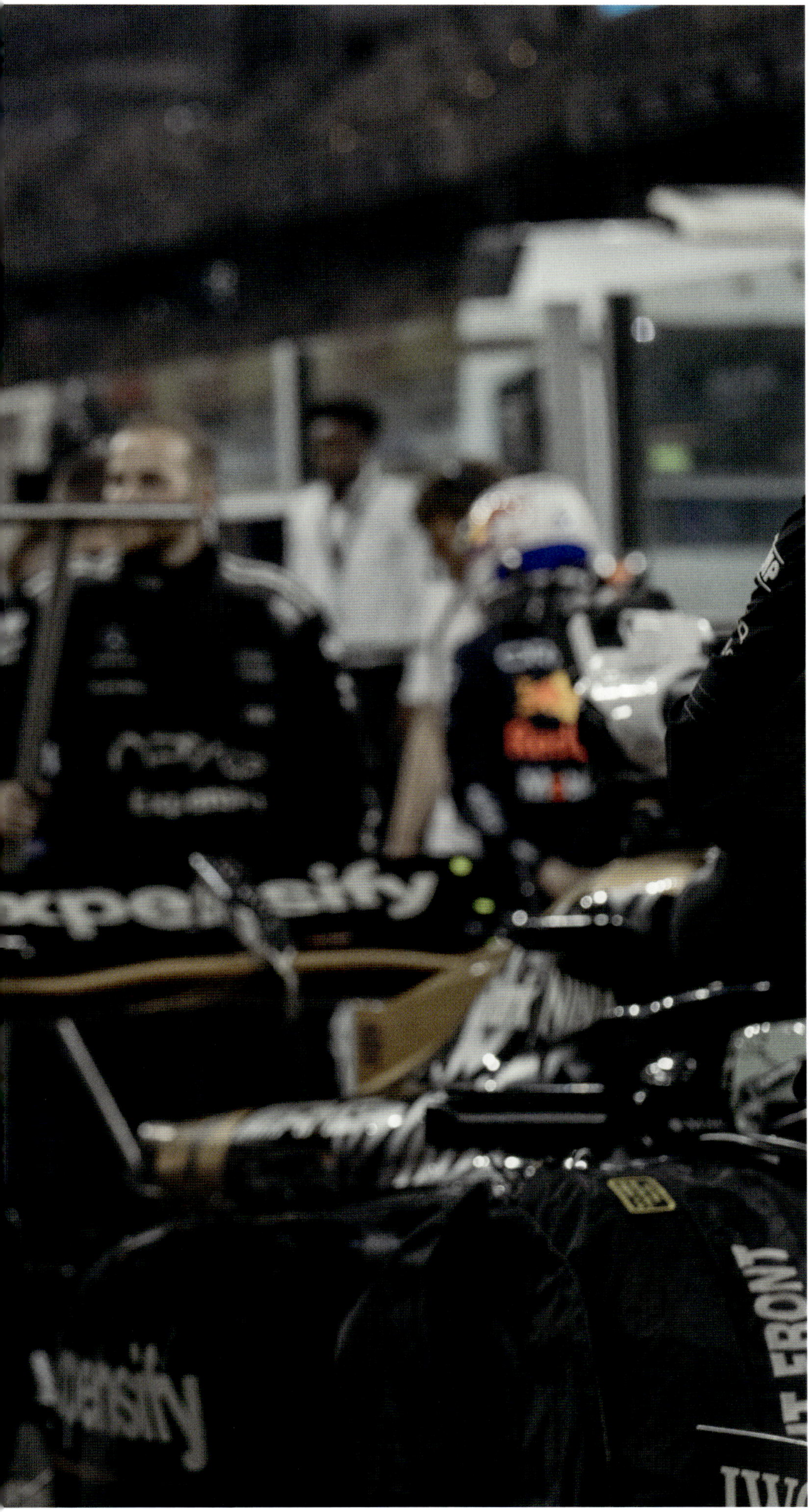

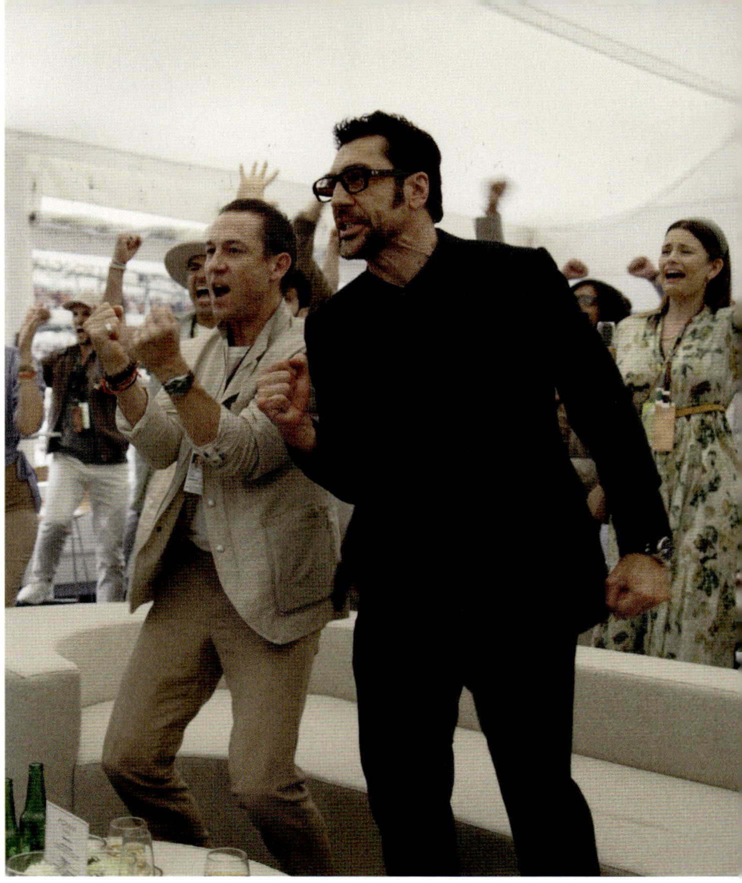

His character's suits helped, too, with Ruben always impeccably attired in either Tom Ford, Armani, or Gucci. "I only dress well when I go to premieres and red carpets. The rest of the time I am very relaxed," admits the actor. "So, I'm not used to wearing suits for a long period of time. But when you dress nicely, your body changes, your posture changes. Your way of moving, walking, relating to others changes. At the same time, you must be comfortable in it. The fact I was wearing those beautiful suits helped me understand Ruben's power, his money, but also the way he has to be relaxed within that world. He can't be stiff. Sometimes, when I'm wearing a suit, because I'm not used to it, I get stiff. But the people who are very comfortable with their own money really own it. It's like royalty. So, I had to be relaxed."

Left: Ruben (Javier Bardem) out on the pit lane after a red flag is signaled during the Abu Dhabi Grand Prix.

Top Right: Ruben (Javier Bardem) and Banning (Tobias Menzies) cheer as they watch a race.

7 SILVERSTONE AUDITION

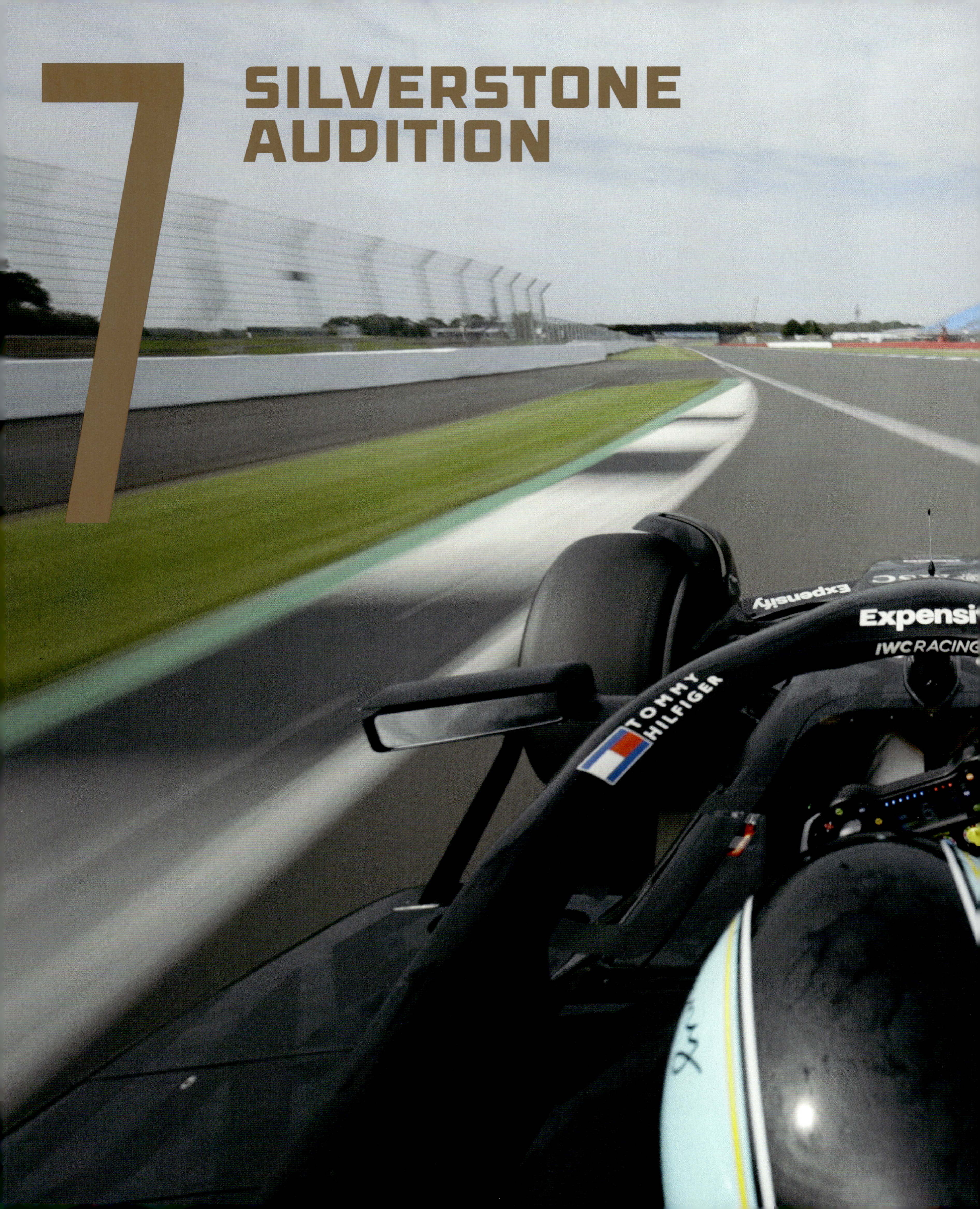

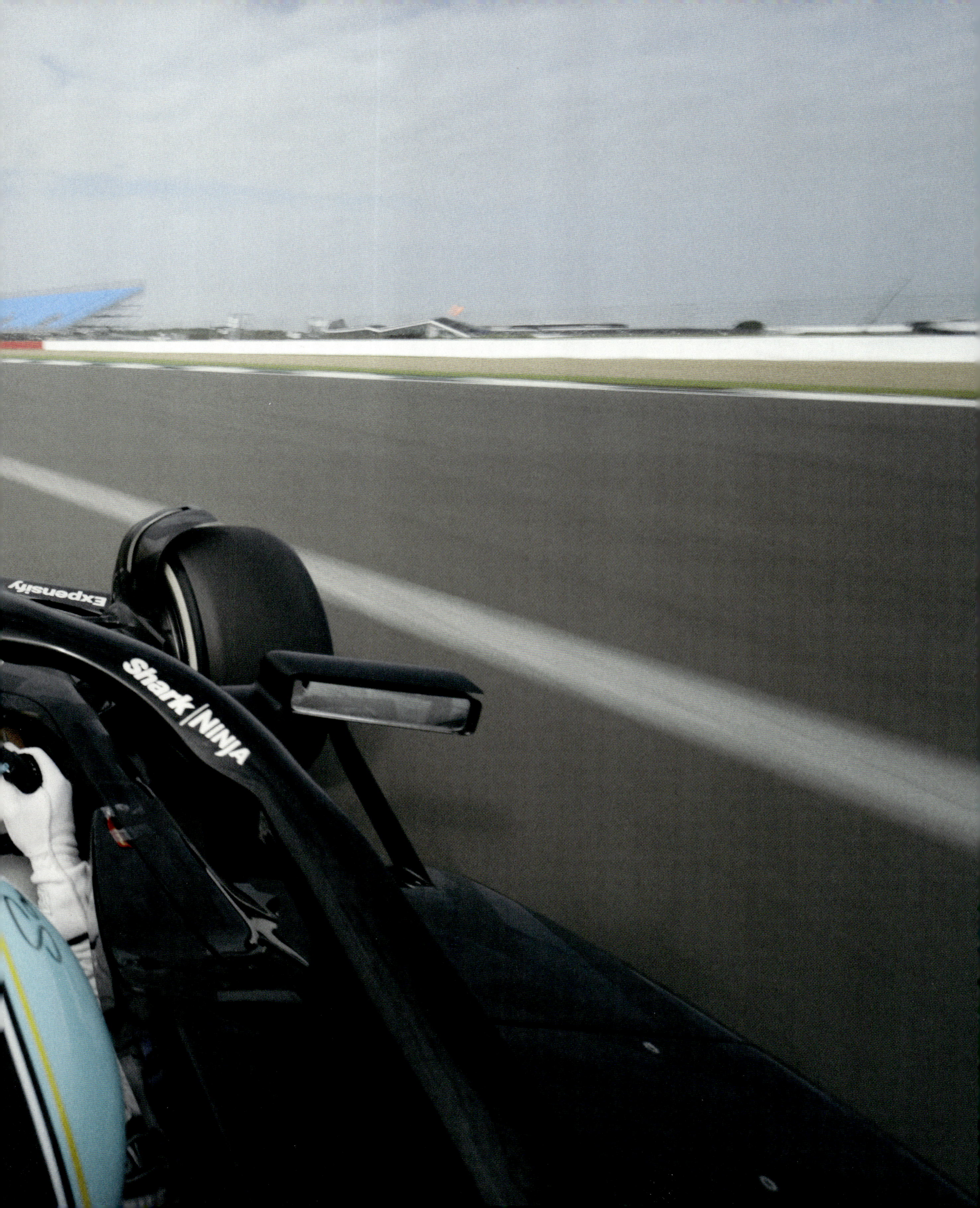
Expensify
Shark
NINJA

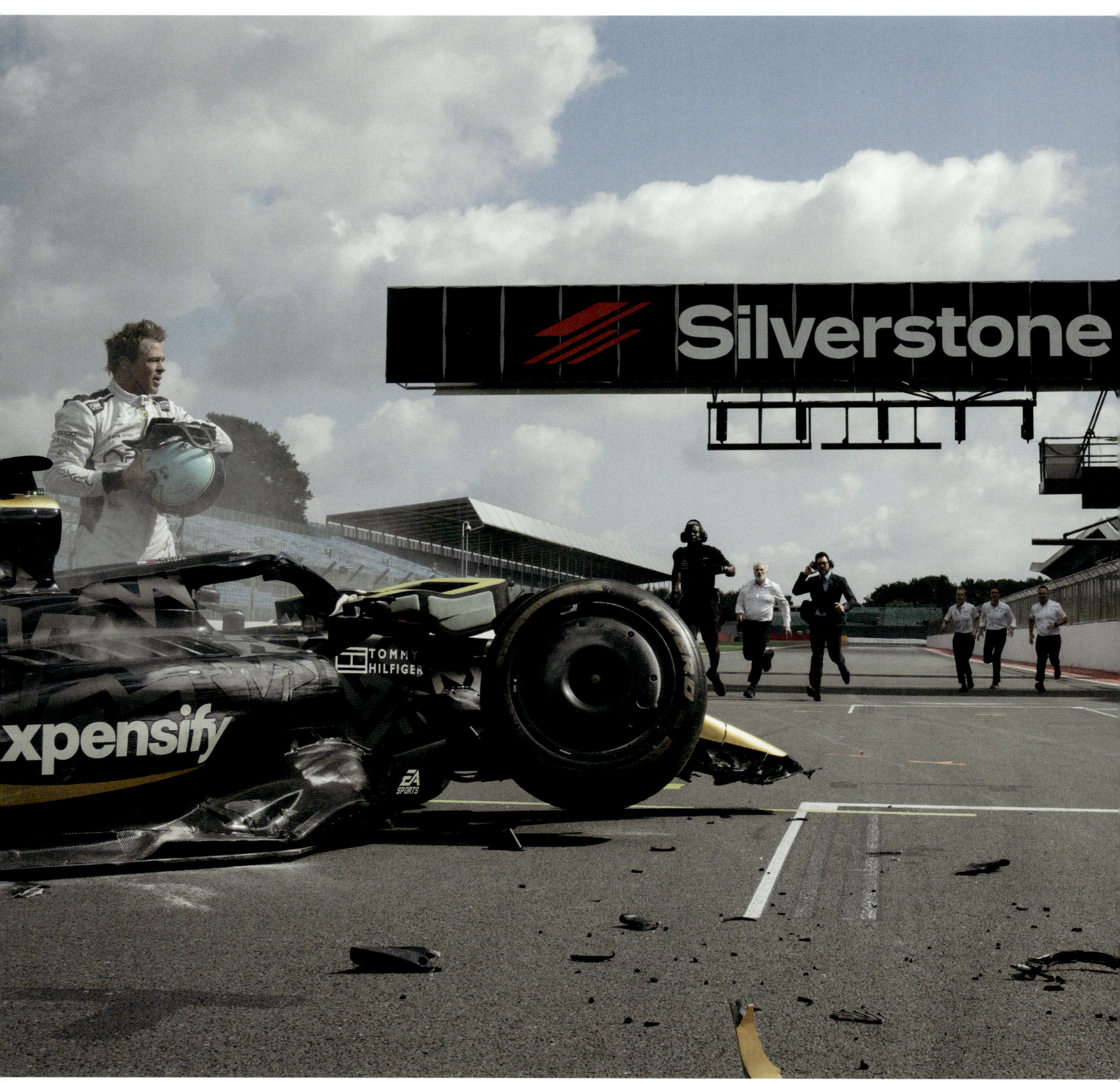

Above: While auditioning for APXGP, Sonny (Brad Pitt) crashes his car at the Silverstone racetrack.

Top Right: Ruben (Javier Bardem) and Kaspar (Kim Bodnia) stare as Sonny (Brad Pitt) arrives at Silverstone.

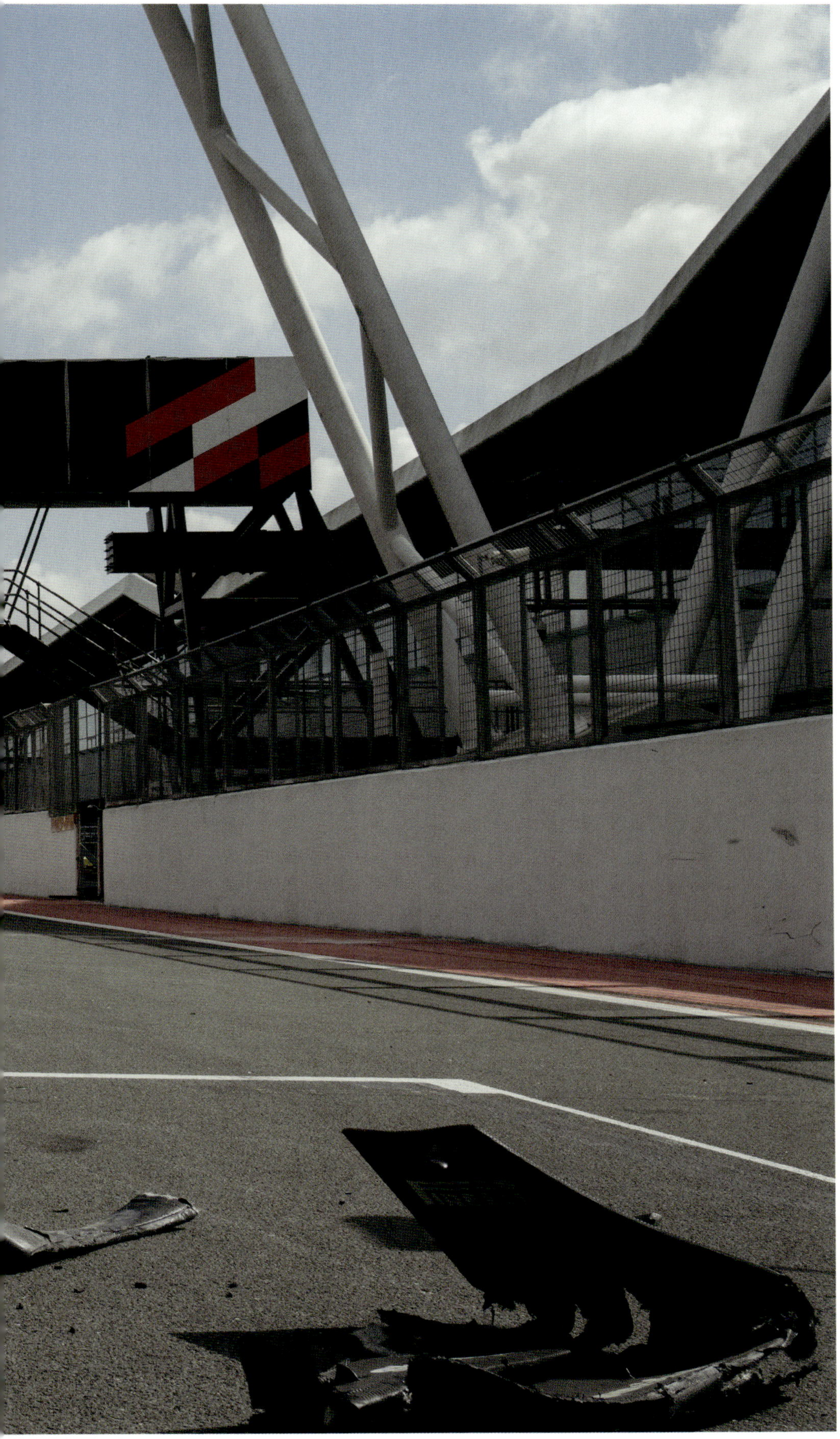

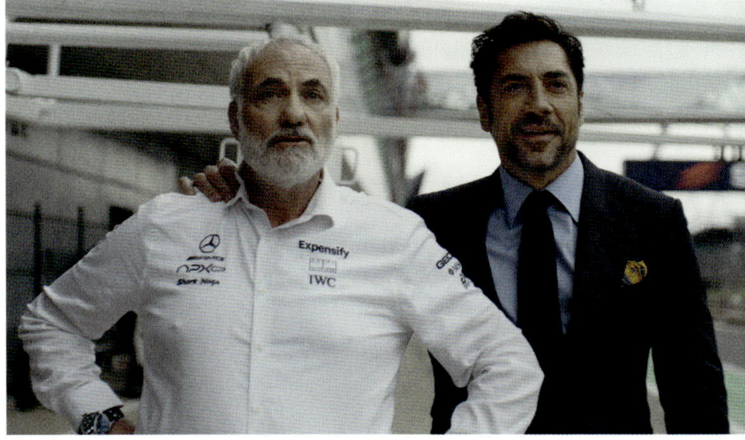

After helping the Chip Hart racing team to victory at Daytona, Sonny (Brad Pitt) travels to the U.K., where APXGP is testing at Silverstone. There, he gets his first taste of driving a Formula One car in more than three decades.

"It was important for us to show that as good a driver as Sonny is in Daytona, this is a different level of expertise," says screenwriter Ehren Kruger of the Silverstone test. "And it was important that the first time he gets in an F1 car, he wrecks it. Because we couldn't tell an audience it is easy to drive in Formula One at the start."

When Sonny arrives in Silverstone to audition for his seat, he meets APXGP team principal Kaspar (Kim Bodnia), technical director Kate (Kerry Condon), race engineers Nickleby (Will Merrick) and Fazio (Joseph Balderrama), chief mechanic Dodge (Abdul Salis), as well as his potential new teammate, Joshua (Damson Idris), who, fearful of losing his race seat, is immediately on the defensive.

"Joshua is very dismissive of the idea that a driver of Sonny's age could even compete in Formula One, much less compete with him," says director Joseph Kosinski. "But when Sonny proves he still has some tricks up his sleeve and makes Joshua look bad, it sets up a great dynamic between these two."

The pair trade a few verbal jabs in the APXGP garage before Sonny, who learns he wasn't Ruben's first choice—he was, in fact, number nine—straps in and takes the car for a spin, saying if he can't post a time within a second of Joshua's fastest lap time, he'll walk away. And despite an early lock-up, Sonny manages to beat Joshua's lap time to secure his drive, but not before smashing the car into the pit lane wall.

SUPPORTING CAST

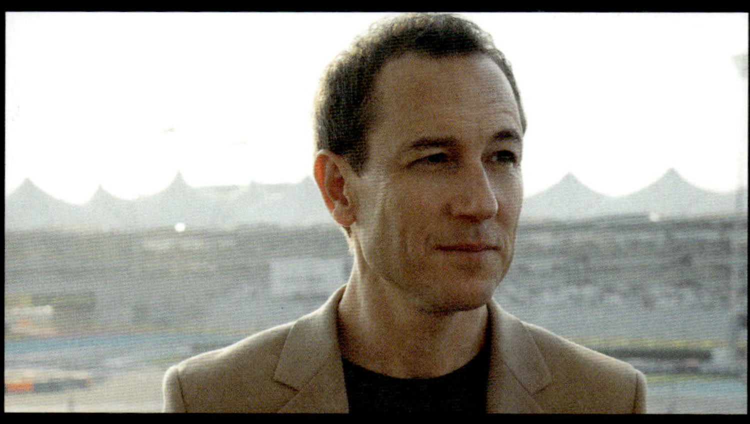

PETER BANNING (TOBIAS MENZIES)

A close associate of Ruben Cervantes and an investor in the ailing APXGP team, Peter Banning is the closest that *F1* has to a bad guy, hoping that neither Sonny nor Joshua win so he can take over the team. "The heart of the Banning story is he isn't quite what he seems," says Menzies, who won a best supporting actor Emmy for playing Prince Philip in seasons three and four of Netflix's *The Crown*. "At the beginning, he appears to be this enthusiastic but naive participant. But as the story goes on, you understand he's playing a long game to try and get the team off Ruben, and he knows a lot more than he's letting on. The character on the page was a little bit different. It was written as an English gent, kind of suited and booted. I felt I'd seen that before, so I pitched the idea of Banning being a tech bro, and we took the character in a different direction to poke some fun at those a bit."

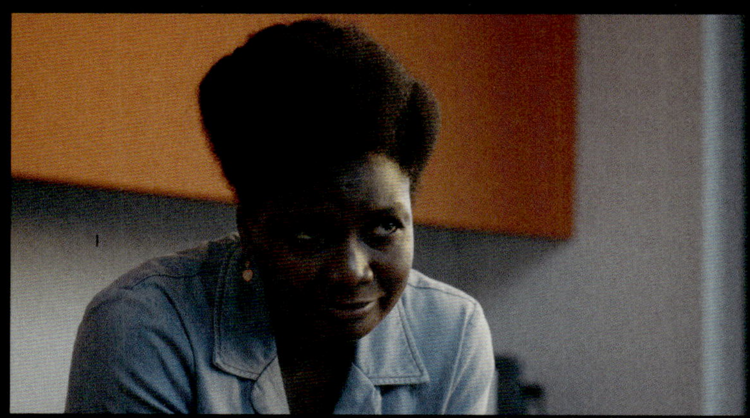

BERNADETTE (SARAH NILES)

The driving force behind Joshua's presence in Formula One, Bernadette is a strong single mother who has supported her son against the odds from day one. "I loved the fact Joshua was going to have a mum as opposed to a dad who's pushing the story," says Niles, who starred as Dr. Sharon Fieldstone in Apple TV+'s *Ted Lasso*. "I've always been fascinated by Lewis Hamilton's journey into F1. His father's from the Caribbean; my family's from the Caribbean. Since Lewis, there have been so many people introduced to this sport who don't come from elitist backgrounds. That's why it's important to see someone like Joshua, a young Black man from London, and the people who support and back him up; it's always family."

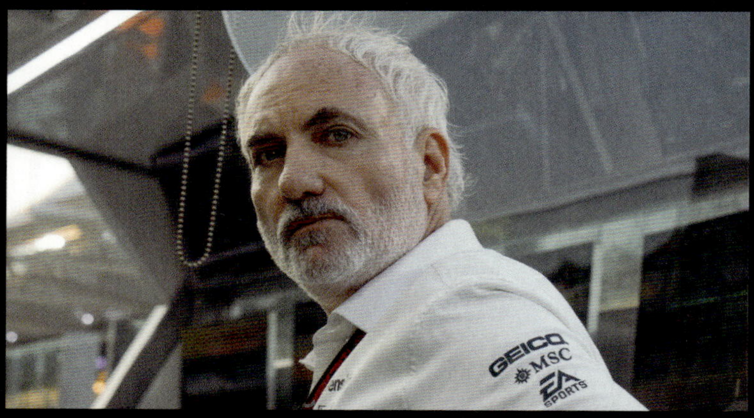

KASPAR SMOLINSKI (KIM BODNIA)

A former Ferrari mechanic during the years Michael Schumacher won five world titles for the Italian team, APXGP team principal Kaspar Smolinski now finds himself at a professional and personal low. "When we meet Kaspar at Silverstone, his situation is quite rough," says Danish actor Bodnia, whose credits include Scandinavian TV series *The Bridge* and the Emmy-winning *Killing Eve*. "My team hasn't won any points, and this is probably my last chance at being team principal too. Second, my wife is tired of being with me. So, I have a lot of work to do as a team principal to make the team feel positive and give them power to do what they must do, as well as try and save my marriage." The arrival of Sonny Hayes doesn't help matters. "If I lose this job, I also lose my wife. So, it's important for me to win to keep my wife. Because it won't just be my job I'm losing, it'll be my whole life."

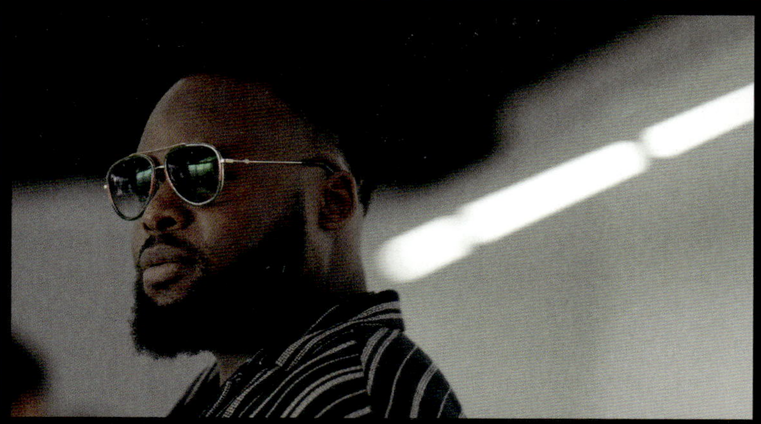

CASH (SAMSON KAYO)

A "vibrant, hardworking grafter" and cousin of Joshua Pearce, Cash is also the rookie driver's manager. "Cash is all about making money," says Samson Kayo. "His name's Cash, so he's all about that dollar. His job is to make sure Joshua does everything he needs to be doing brandwise and capitalize on the many sponsorship opportunities coming his way. But he's also there as family, to keep Joshua's head on his shoulders and watch him shine for the family." Kayo grew up in Peckham, south London, the same as Idris. "We've known each other since we were eighteen, nineteen years old and my first theater audition," the latter recalls. "So, the chemistry between me and him, it's insane. I mean, we're both Nigerians and he's talking Yoruba slang to me in the film. Joe was like, 'What does that mean? Let's keep it.' So, we were able to take our characters' relationship to a different level because of the authentic relationship we have in real life."

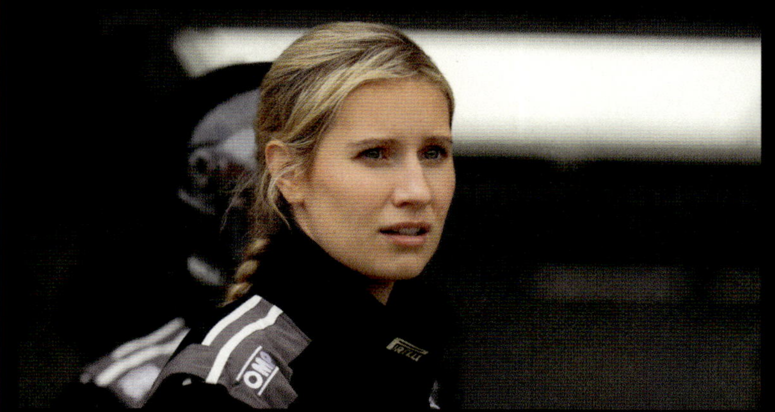

JODIE (CALLIE COOKE)

While it's the drivers who are the face of a Formula One team, every person working for that team, either at the track or back at the factory, makes a valuable contribution to its fortunes. Jodie is the only female mechanic in the APXGP pit stop crew, a tire gunner whose performance can make or break a race. "She's a bag of nerves," says Cooke, who grew up near Silverstone and even waitressed there when she was fifteen. "She's been having terrible race after terrible race, and we meet her after she's made quite a catastrophic mistake at a Grand Prix. Everyone is butting heads in the team, and Jodie is part of that mess. But she goes on such an amazing coming-of-age journey throughout the film."

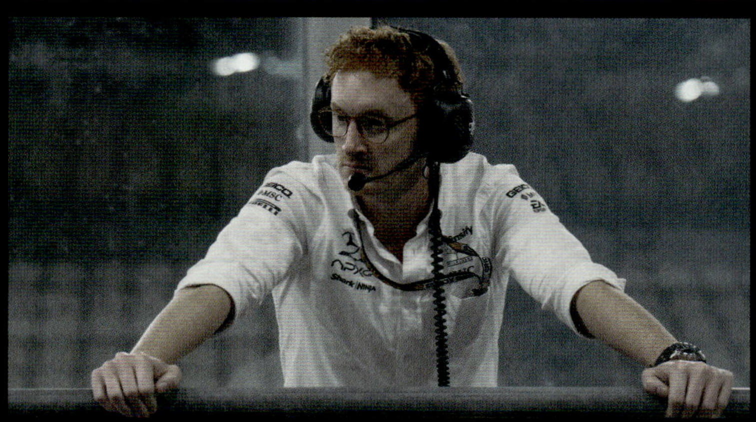

HUGH NICKLEBY (WILL MERRICK)

As Sonny Hayes's race engineer, Hugh Nickleby sits on the APXGP pit wall alongside technical director Kate and team principal Kaspar. "It's a film about a family," says Merrick, who made his on-screen debut in the cult British TV series *Skins*. "They are like families, these teams." When Sonny rocks up at Silverstone to test for APXGP at the behest of team owner Ruben and secures a drive, Nickleby is rather surprised given his age but remains philosophical and professional. "Hugh is like, 'Okay, I guess this is my guy.' But it does take some getting used to because Sonny doesn't really do things by the book. He thinks out-side the box. But then he starts to fill everyone with this enormous belief that it could be our name up there in lights."

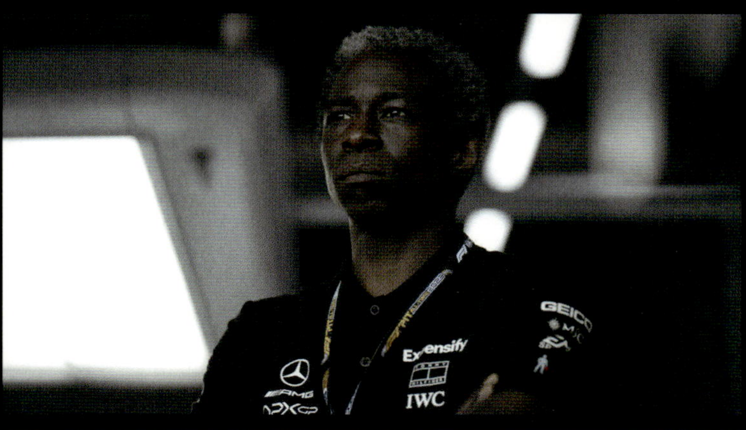

DODGE DOWER (ABDUL SALIS)

As chief mechanic of APXGP, Dodge is responsible for the mechanical well-being of both cars as well as race pit stops. "I've been watching Formula One all my life, so I had a pretty good idea and understanding about what and who Dodge was, and where to place him within the film and within the universe we created," says Salis, who played Eamon Valda in Prime Video's *The Wheel of Time*. "When we first meet Dodge and the team, they're not doing great. They haven't been doing great for a while. But it's not for want of trying. It's not because they're a bumbling bunch of buffoons. It's because of circumstance and bad luck. That's what's put them there. They just need that spark, that something to ignite the season and ignite the team. And that happens with the arrival of Brad Pitt's Sonny Hayes."

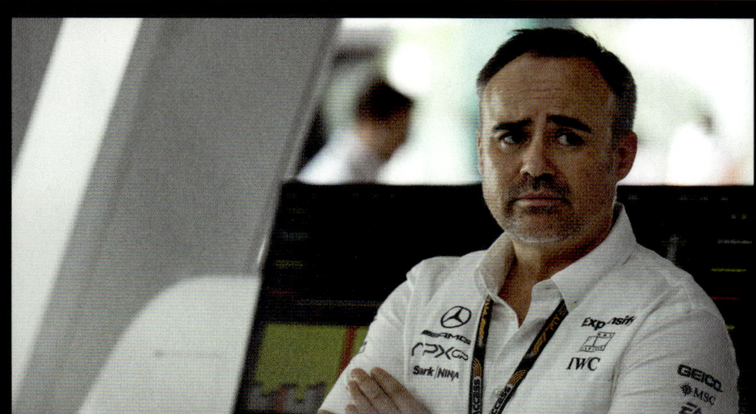

FAZIO (JOSEPH BALDERRAMA)

Joshua's race engineer, Fazio, is played by Mexican British actor Joseph Balderrama, star of the Netflix series *Heartstopper*. "We have the best engineers on the grid, Nickleby and Fazio," says Salis. "They are fantastic. They're like a double act, working for the whole of the team even though they take care of their individual drivers. But what most impressed me is they really do feel and look the real deal."

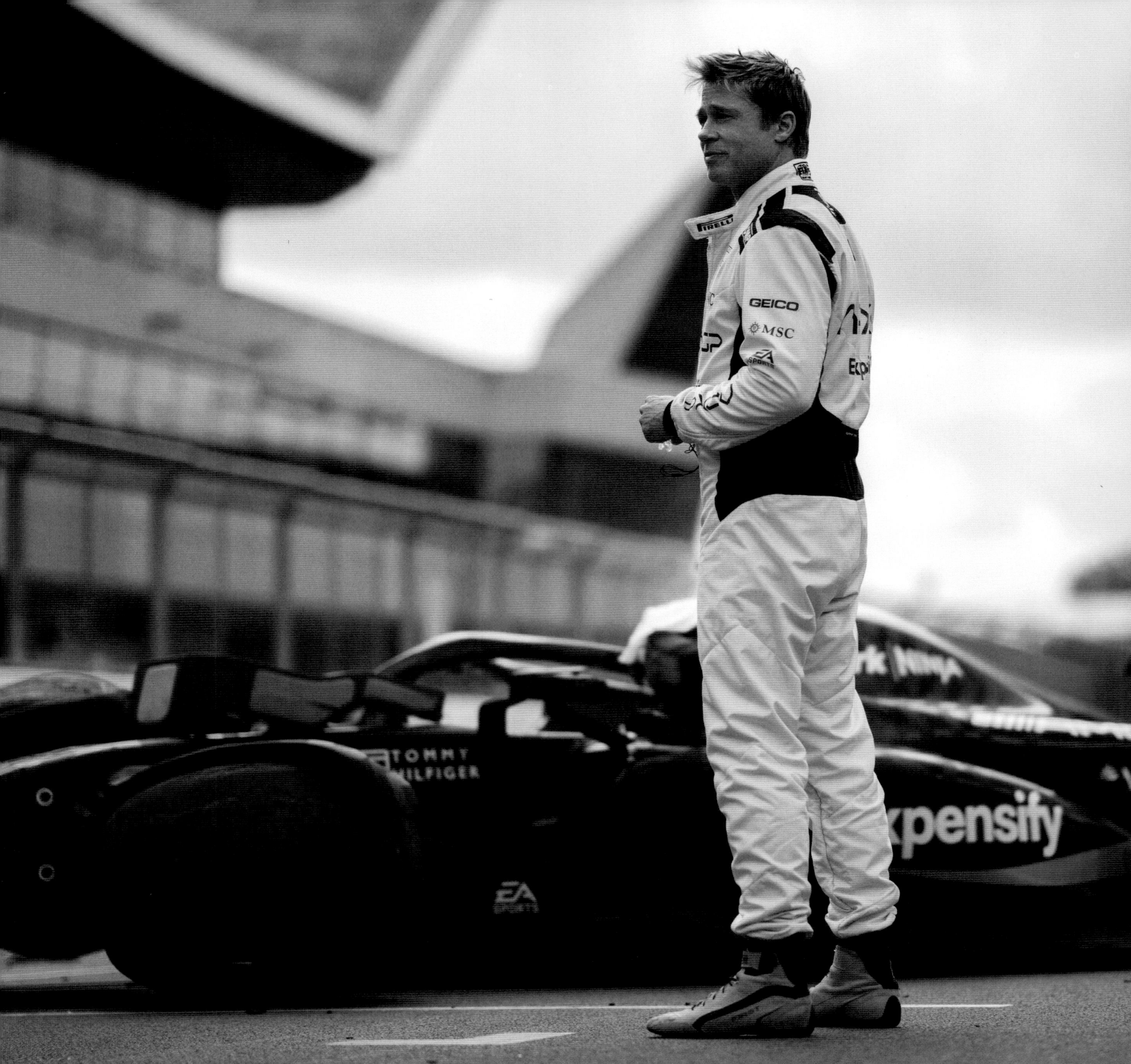

GEICO
MSC
TOMMY
EA

APXGP

SET: SILVERSTONE CIRCUIT | DETAIL: CIRCUIT SCHEMATIC | LOC: SILVERSTONE CIRCUIT, TOWCESTER, NN12 8TN | SCALE: 1:2000 & 1:1000 @A0

WHAT3WORDS (CIRCUIT ENTRANCE) // SLEEPS.FLIPS.DAFFODILS

000
000

N

KEY
GRAVEL
ASPHALT
GRASS
GRANDSTANDS
CURBS/RUMBLE STRIPS
TYRE BARRIERS
BARRIERS

PIT ENTRY
PIT BUILDING
FORMULA 1 PIT LANE
NATIONAL PITS
TRACK DIRECTION

PIT LANE
PIT LANE
FORMULA 1 PIT LANE
SCALE @ 1:1000
SCALE BAR 1:1000
0 20 50 100 200m

SILVERSTONE CIRCUIT
SCALE @ 1:2000
SCALE BAR 1:2000
0 50 100 200 400m

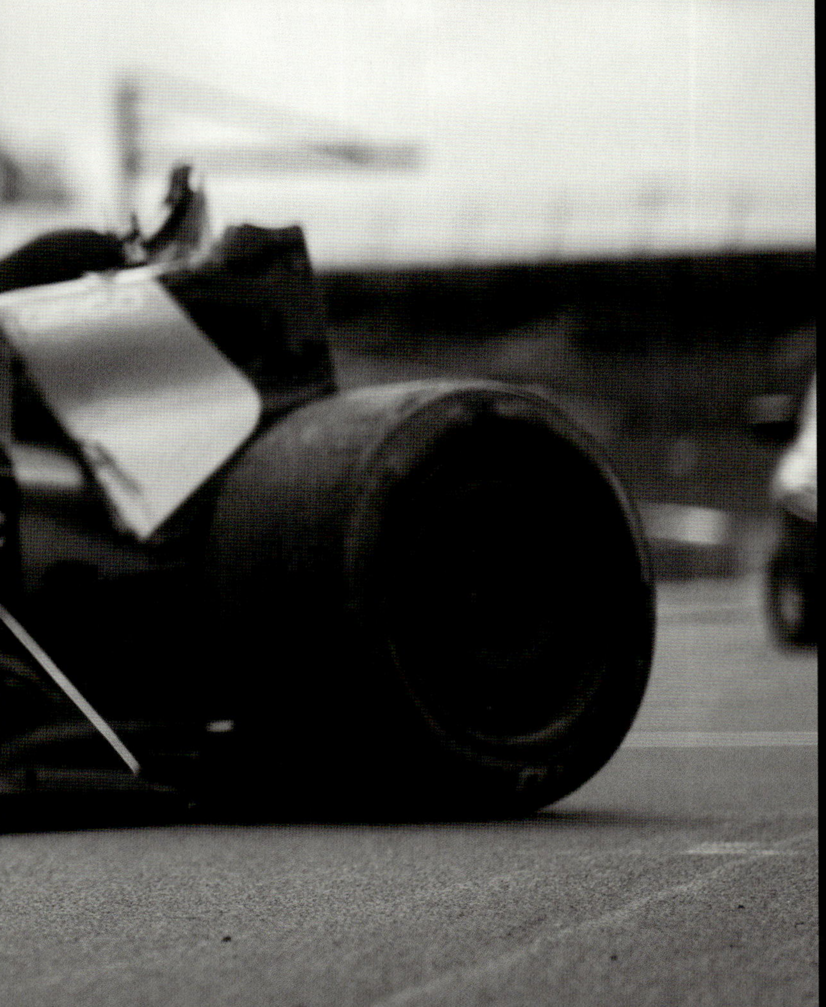

Much like the British Grand Prix sequence that follows, Sonny's Silverstone audition needed to achieve a lot in a short amount of time: explaining to an audience who might not be familiar with Formula One the rules of the world, as well as introduce the core APXGP crew, who are somewhat surprised by his presence. "Sonny needed to shake up the dynamic and be faced with complete skepticism by everyone in the garage," says Kruger. "One of the challenges was that when he got into the car, he needed to do so with the information that he was not Ruben's first choice. He was way down on the list. So, Sonny needed to get in the car with his confidence taken down a peg."

While Pitt was very familiar with Silverstone, having spent a lot of time driving there during training, he was never going to be behind the wheel when Sonny crashes into the wall on the home straight. "Obviously, you're not going to send an actor into the wall at 120 miles per hour," says Kosinski. "But at the same time, I didn't want to do it digitally, since it was our first big crash of the movie. And it was important that it feel as real as possible."

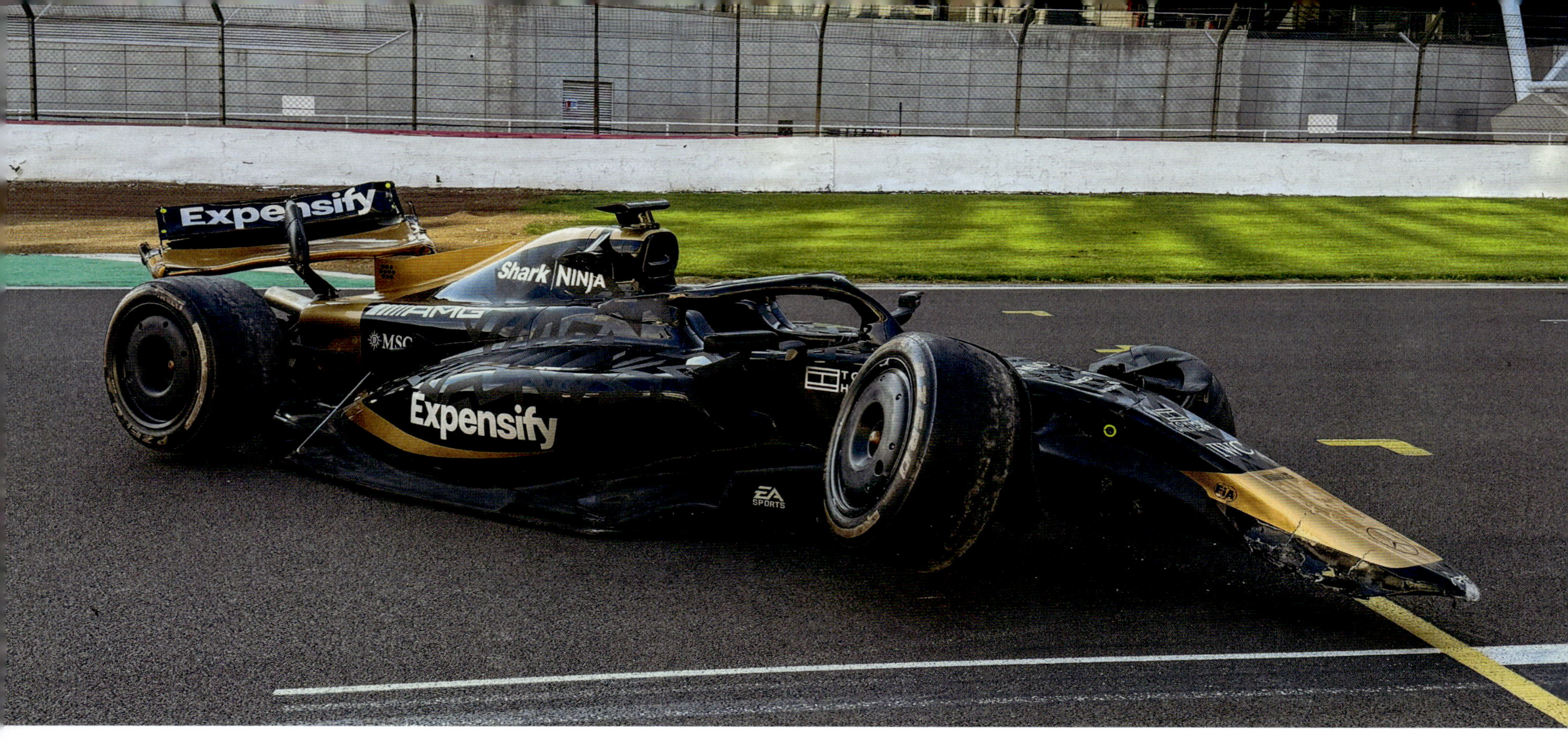

Special effects supervisor Keith Dawson suggested building a full-size car that could be driven remotely and crashed into the wall. "There was a bit of skepticism when we started talking about it, thinking we'd never get it to go fast enough. I'd used it on *Terminator: Dark Fate* and a couple of other shows, but this was the first time we were talking about using it at these speeds," says Dawson, who began with a Smart car, which his team outfitted with a remote-control drive set-up connected via an RF (radio frequency) system to a racing simulator housed inside the back of a Luton van. This prototype was tested at the Rockingham Motor Speedway in Northamptonshire, with Craig Dolby driving, via a camera mounted to the front of the Smart car.

At the same time, Dawson's team worked on a second prototype in the shape of an F1 car, putting a steel frame and remote-control hardware on top of one of Graham Kelly's F2 chassis. This second prototype was tested initially without bodywork—"in case it decided to go rogue"—at Abingdon Racetrack in Oxfordshire, to check it could get to the required speed and stop safely. It was tested again at Silverstone to check the RF connectivity, where Dawson and Dolby did everything apart from crash. "We took it up to speed, around the final bend, and then drove it straight, rather than into the wall," says Dawson.

A replica APXGP body made of fiberglass was placed over the steel frame, complete

A replica APXGP body made of fiberglass was placed over the steel frame, complete with a dummy driver from the waist up, its hands connected to the steering wheel.

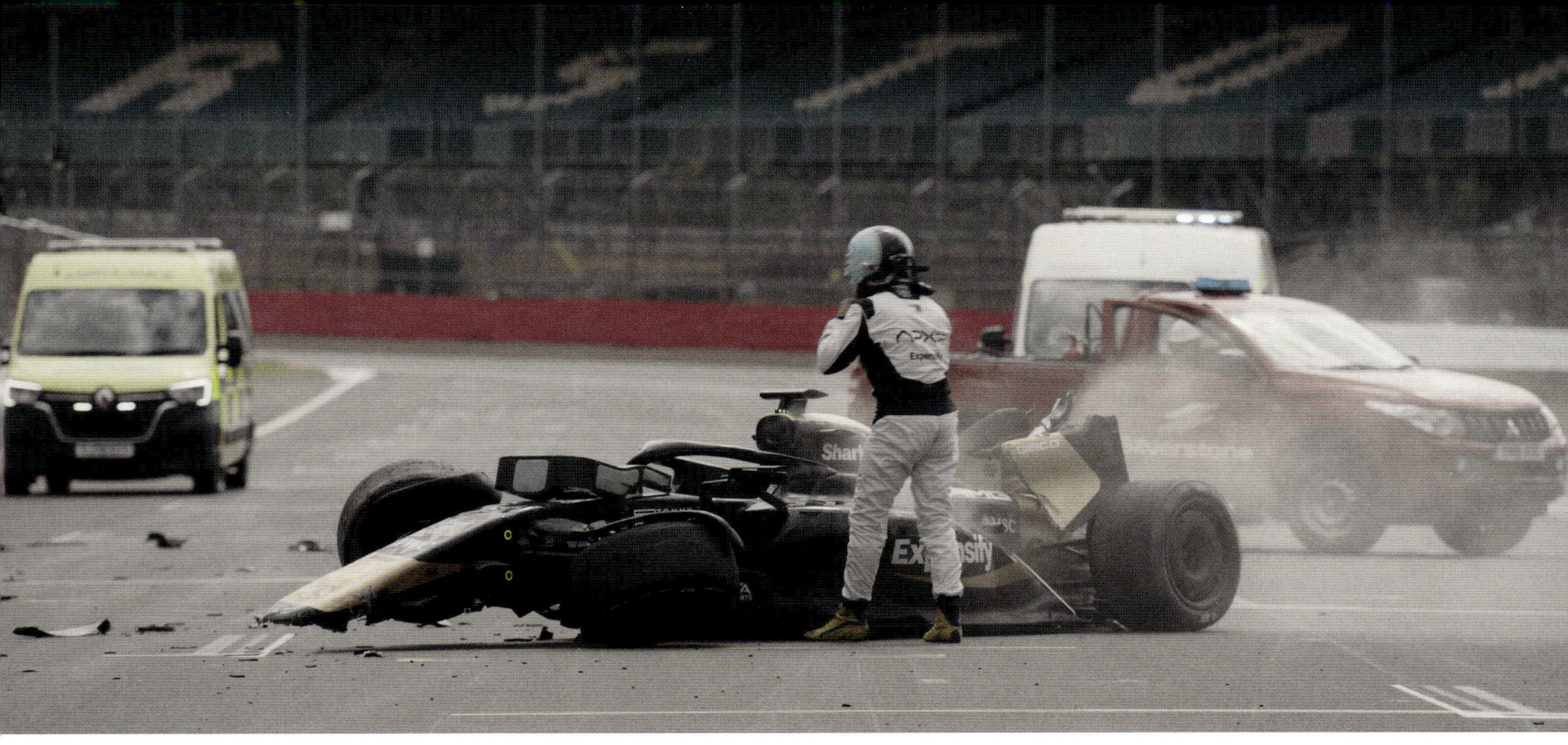

Top Left: To film the crash scene at Silverstone, Keith Dawson built "the world's largest, fastest remote-control car."

Top Right: Sonny (Brad Pitt) stands next to the damaged APXGP car after crashing it during his team audition.

with a dummy driver from the waist up, its hands connected to the steering wheel, which turned when Dolby turned, creating what Kosinski dubbed "the world's largest, fastest remote-control car."

To shoot the stunt, the production returned to Silverstone with two cars. Dolby "drove" the first around the last corner, toward the start/finish straight, but this time veered right on the home straight, crashing into the pit wall. Formula One cars regularly take the last corner at 115-120 miles per hour. The prototype could only reach 80-90 miles per hour, but it was enough, with Kosinski covering the stunt with six cameras, including one on a crane and another on the car directly above "the driver" to film the actual impact.

"We shot it twice," says Dawson. "The first time we didn't quite get the rotation Joe wanted. The second time we were on the money. I think we impacted the wall at about 87-88 miles per hour, which isn't bad. We shot it at 20 frames per second, so we can add a bit more speed in the cut, which gives you a little bit more violence on impact."

"Someone snuck a photo of it, and the headlines the next day were that Brad had crashed the car, and it had caused the whole shoot to be suspended, which was totally untrue," says Kosinski. "But it worked wonderfully and ended up being another great sequence, another plot twist, and a nice bit of drama as well."

As with so many moments in *F1*, the sequence used a combination of stunts, special effects, and visual effects. "We cleaned up the camera rigs on the car. We digitally replaced the front tires, so it looks like Sonny was attempting to get out of the oversteer," says visual effects supervisor Ryan Tudhope. "As shot, the car drove straight into the wall, without turning into the spin a driver would do. We also added Sonny into the car (a digital helmet) and animated him pulling his arms off the wheel, which is something a real driver would be trained to do. But the foundation is the amazing SFX work by Keith and his team in the form of the remote drive car."

Dawson also built an "aftermath buck," a crashed version of the car for when it comes to a stop in the middle of the straight. "The last shot, where the car spins and comes to rest in front of the camera, is primarily digital," says Tudhope. "This was achieved by setting the destroyed car in its final position for Brad to sit in. We pushed the camera in on the car, and once it reached him, he opened his visor. Then, in VFX, we erased the real car and Brad at the beginning of the shot and animated a digital car spinning into that exact place, just as the camera lands there. So, it becomes a transition from a VFX car and digital Brad to the real car and real Brad. We added all the smoke, debris, and other effects as well."

8 HUNGARY TO MONZA

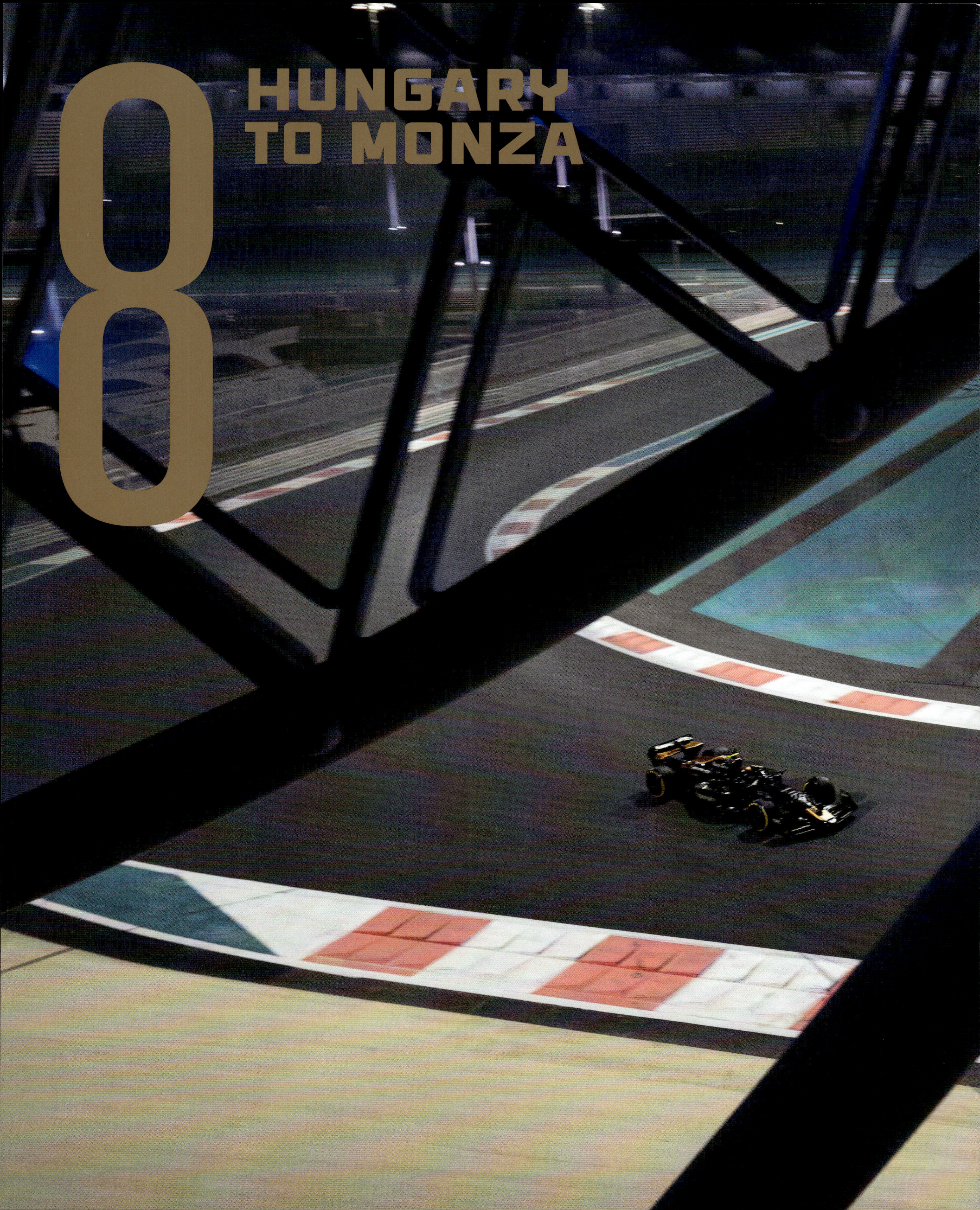

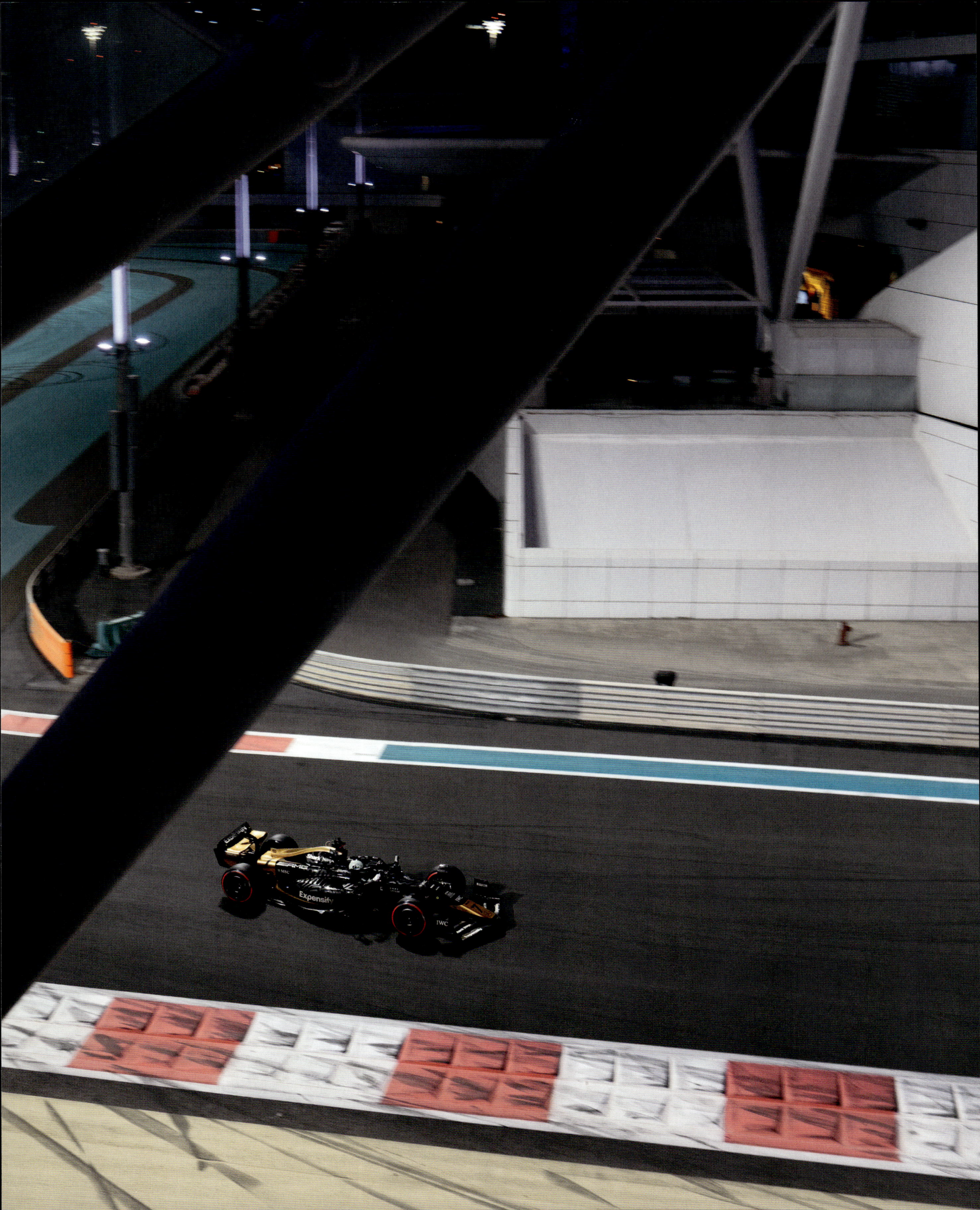
SharkNinja
AMG
MSC
Expensify
IWC

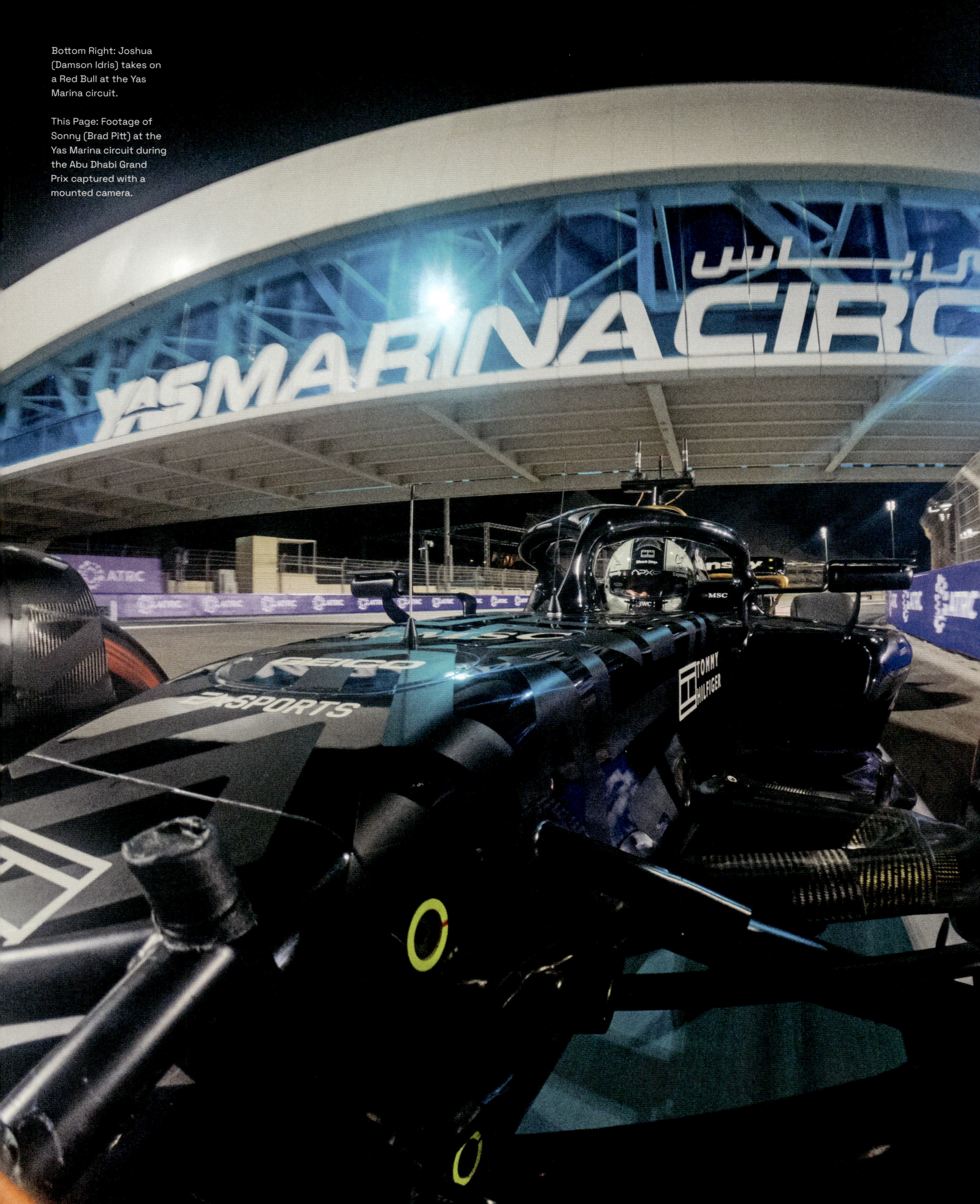

Bottom Right: Joshua (Damson Idris) takes on a Red Bull at the Yas Marina circuit.

This Page: Footage of Sonny (Brad Pitt) at the Yas Marina circuit during the Abu Dhabi Grand Prix captured with a mounted camera.

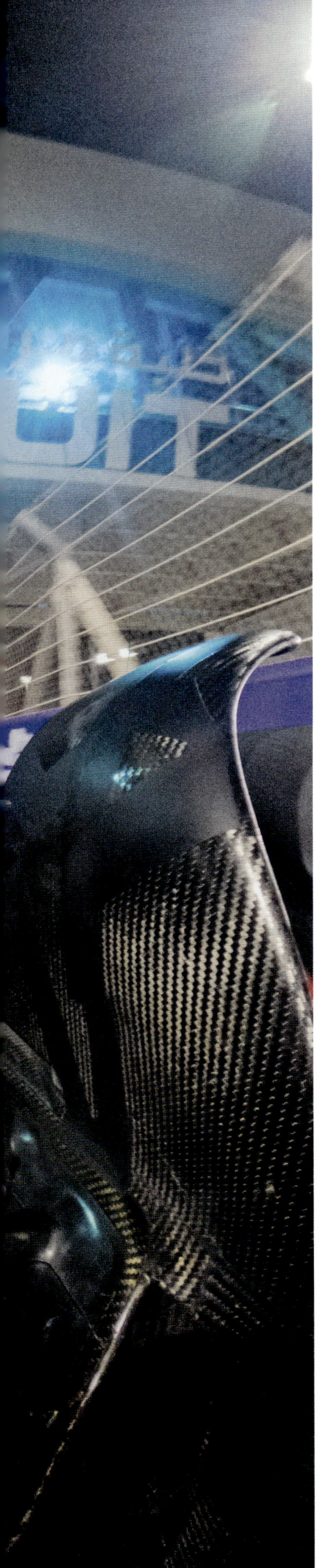

Post-Daytona, the production got itself back on track, prepping to shoot during the 2024 Formula One season that was due to start in Bahrain on March 2, with Brad Pitt and Damson Idris spending a couple of weeks that month at the Yas Marina Circuit in Abu Dhabi reacquainting themselves with driving an F3 car with Luciano Bacheta and Craig Dolby.

At the beginning of April, the four men returned to Yas Marina, where director Joseph Kosinski would spend the next three weeks filming scenes set during the climactic Abu Dhabi Grand Prix that would form a large part of the movie's third act. "Because of the length of the sequence, we knew we were never going to get the amount of time we needed on the track during the Grand Prix," says first assistant director Toby Hefferman. "And after the Grand Prix, there was the Gulf 12 Hours race. So, it made sense to go there when the track was available and shoot as much as we could, knowing we would finish it off in December."

Kosinski shot from Thursday, April 4, to Sunday, April 7, then from Thursday, April 11, to Sunday, April 14, covering a huge amount of action both on and off the track. This included Sonny (Pitt) battling the Red Bull of Checo Pérez as well as clashing with an Alpine and a Haas, with Bacheta and Dolby doubling for the other drivers; Sonny locking his tires; Sonny spinning 360 degrees and recovering, replicating Nigel Mansell's famous 1990 Imola spin and recovery when he was driving for Ferrari; Joshua (Idris) dodging a pinwheeling Alpha Tauri; Joshua, his tires shot to pieces, losing places to a Mercedes and Red Bull; along with pit stops, scenes on the APXGP pit wall and in the garage, and a number of dramatic scenes, among them Sonny saying goodbye to Kate (Kerry Condon).

"One lap could be Brad racing Pérez. Then, once we got that beat, Luch, who's driving with Brad, would then be George Russell for another part of the sequence," recalls Hefferman. "It was a real puzzle, but we figured it out."

With the track to themselves, Pitt, Idris, and the stunt team were under less pressure than during their race weekend hot laps. The downside of the track being empty was a lack of signage and full grandstands. "One of the major needs of visual effects on this film has been filling out those grandstands and also restoring signage to what it was on the actual race day," says visual effects supervisor Ryan Tudhope. "Even on F1 weekend days, our track laps might be in the morning and people aren't at the track yet. And if we shot in the days following, a lot of the signage gets pulled down by fans or is taken down and moved to the next location."

From Abu Dhabi, Kosinski headed to the United States to work with editor Stephen Mirrione, continuing to piece together the movie, before returning to the U.K. in early May to prepare for the upcoming Formula One season and to start filming again on Tuesday, May 21, at Silverstone.

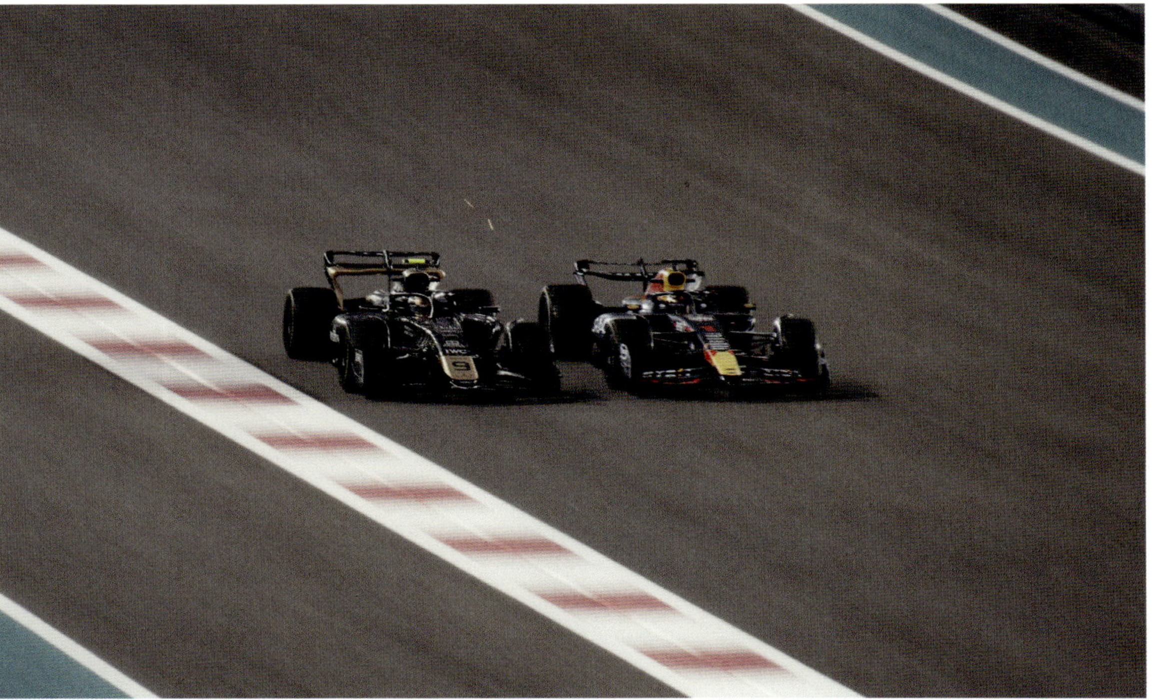

"We had our European tour planned, which was Silverstone, Hungary, Belgium, Monza," says Hefferman. "So, we reverse engineered all the work we needed to do and ended up starting shooting in the middle of May."

The production bought out Silverstone for several weeks, shooting on and off there until mid-June, rebuilding the APXGP garage in advance of the British Grand Prix, filming on the track, in the garage, using the old pit lane for the pit wall at Monza, and the media room for Zandvoort.

Kosinski returned to Silverstone on Wednesday, July 3, once again filming "hot laps" with Pitt, Idris, Bacheta, and Dolby over the course of the race weekend; pickups on the back of the grid with Sonny and Ruben; shots of Sonny getting out of his car and Joshua putting on his balaclava; Hamilton and Verstappen getting ready for the race; as well as more scenes on the pit wall and in the paddock.

Pitt and Idris also filmed a moment that was set post-race at the Hungaroring in the media pen, where drivers speak to journalists during and after qualifying and the race. "We set up our own cameras, had Rachel Brooks from F1 as one of our reporters, and suddenly Brad walks in and everyone's like, 'What the fuck's going on?'" laughs Hefferman. "He came over, did an interview, then he and Alonso did a fist bump, which made it that much more convincing. We did Damson as well."

"Lando [Norris] was pissed off about the race, and I'm walking past, smiling, because, in the world, *I* had a good race," says Idris. "All of that stuff is what's going to make the film fantastic, because you can't fake that."

"It feels like you're dropping your pants in an area you shouldn't be," reflects Pitt. "But we've got to go. I felt bad because Lando had had a bad race. I think he went out early and after a good qualifying. So, he was in there being interviewed and I felt like we were being distracting at one point, and when they said 'action,' I didn't go, because I was like, no, no, there's something sensitive going on there, let's wait. Then we found our little window and did it."

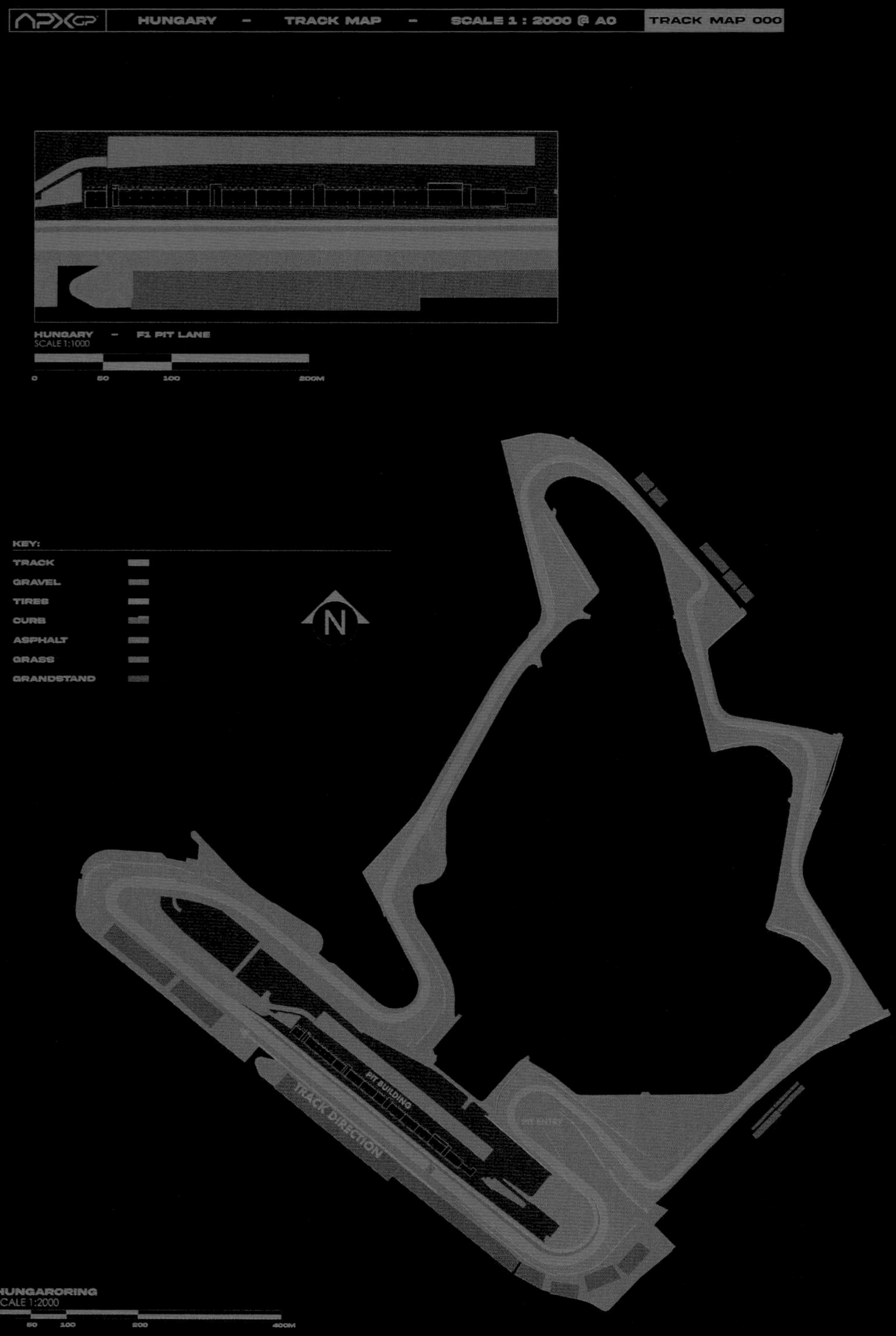

APXGP | HUNGARY – TRACK MAP – SCALE 1 : 2000 @ A0 | TRACK MAP 000

HUNGARY – F1 PIT LANE
SCALE 1:1000

KEY:
TRACK
GRAVEL
TIRES
CURB
ASPHALT
GRASS
GRANDSTAND

N

PIT BUILDING
TRACK DIRECTION

HUNGARORING
SCALE 1:2000

Schematics for Grand Prix tracks in Hungary, Belgium, and Italy.

APXGP | SET: BELGIUM SPA CIRCUIT | DETAIL: CIRCUIT SCHEMATIC | SCALE: 1:2000 & 1:1000 @ A0 | LOC: BELGIUM SPA CIRCUIT, RTE DU CIRCUIT 55, 4970 STAVELOT, BELGIUM

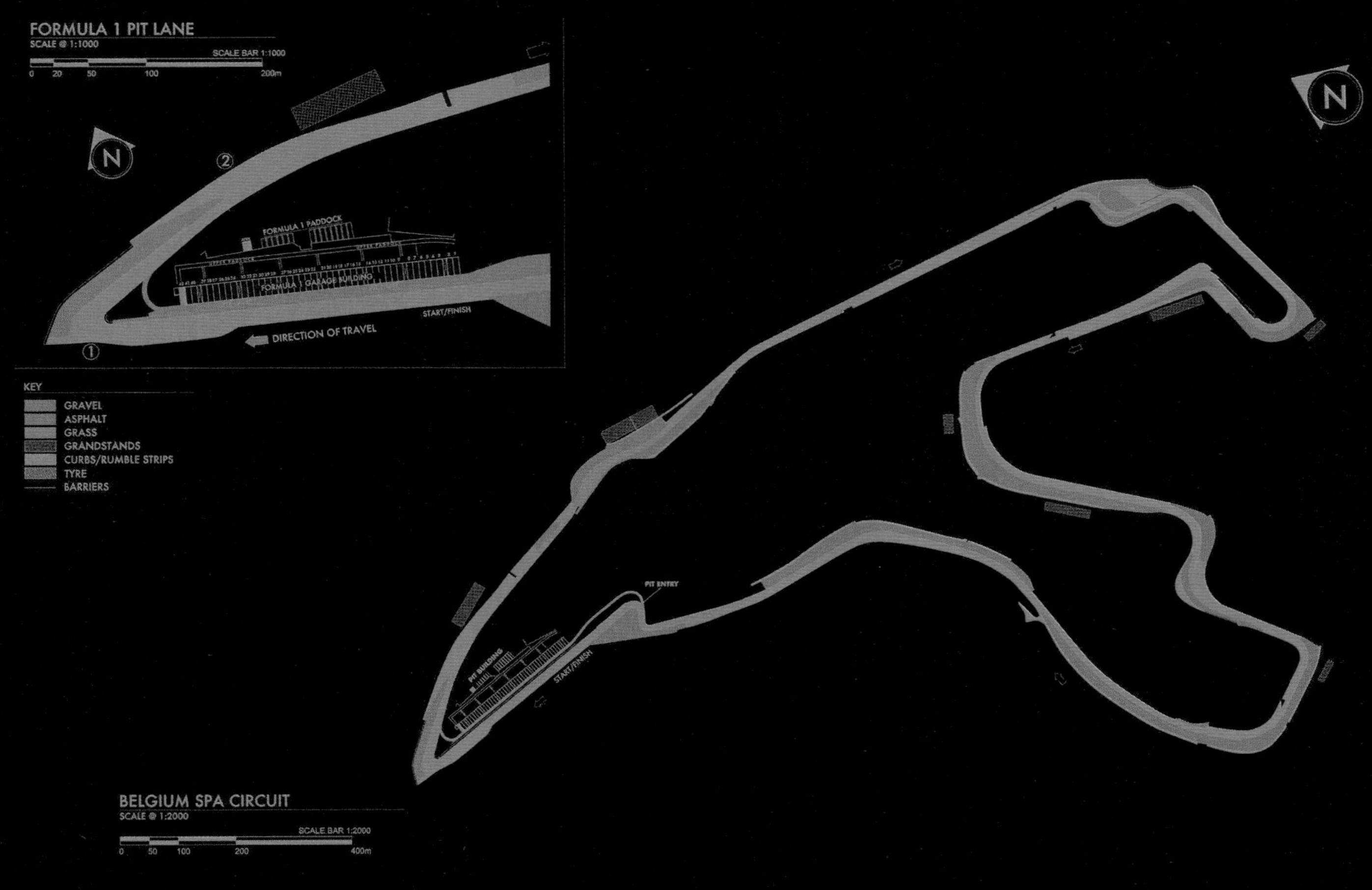

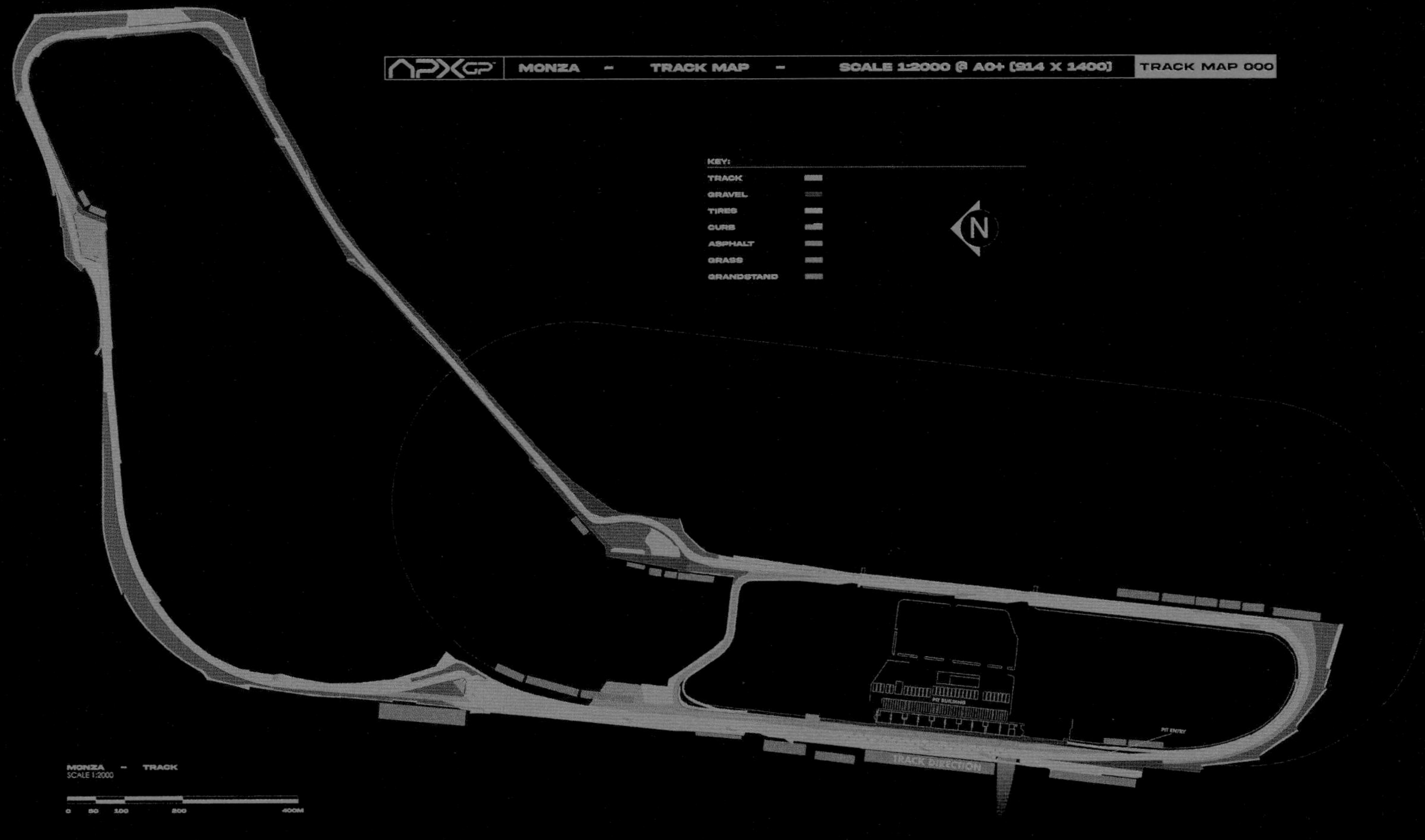

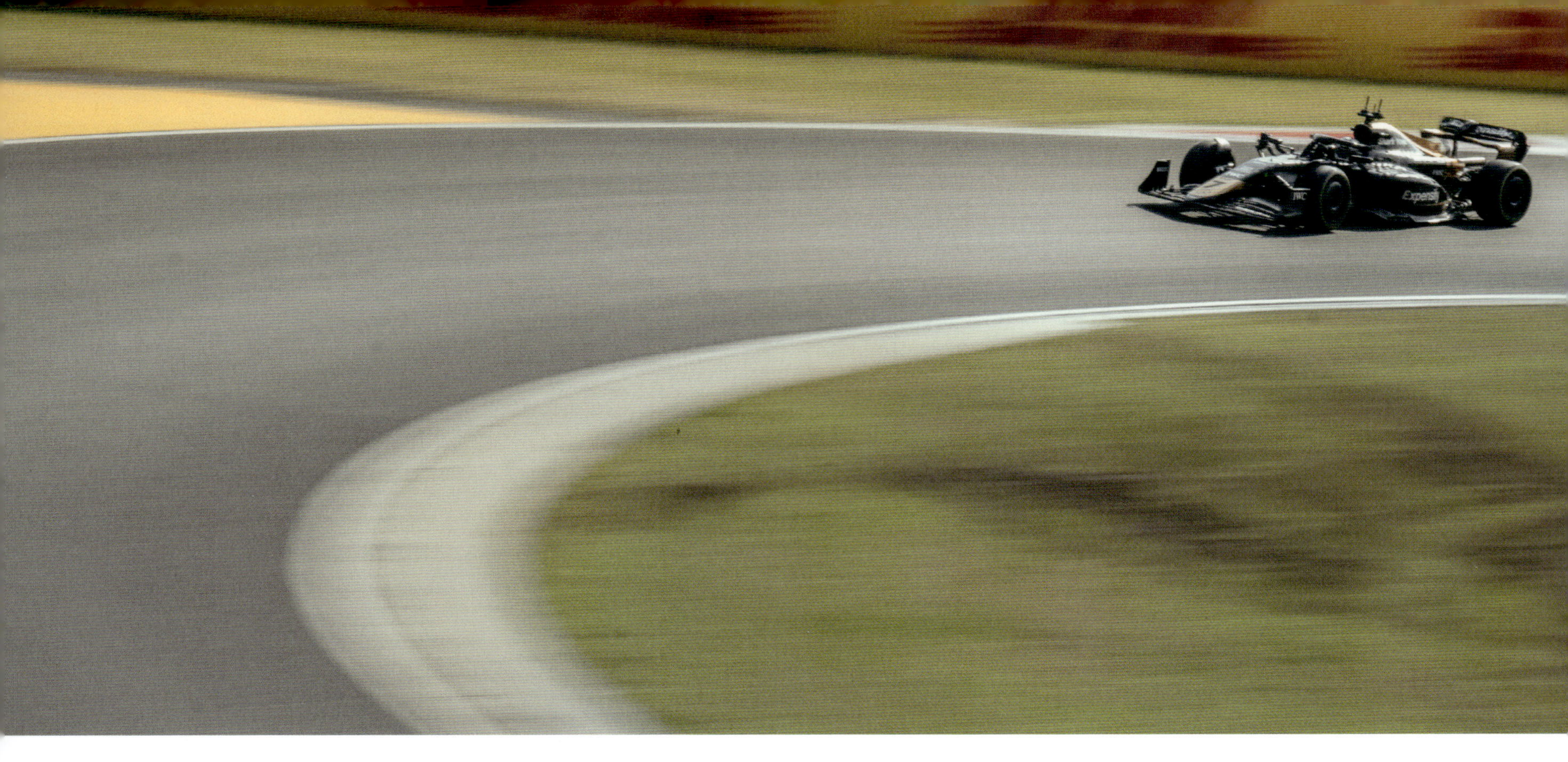

HUNGARIAN GP

The next race was the Hungarian Grand Prix on Sunday, July 21, with Kosinski returning to film scenes on the pit wall as well as "hot laps" on Thursday, Friday, and before and after qualifying on Saturday. "That track is really fun," says Pitt. "It's narrow and scrappy. But when I went out with the crowd, there was something off with my car. It was like the brakes had been glazed over or something, like someone had ridden the brakes, and so I kept locking up. I had one of the worst drives in front of the crowd. I just kept locking up and sliding."

Once again, the FIA allowed the APXGP cars into parc fermé, both post-qualifying and, more important, post-race. Only this time the actors were present, with Sonny and Joshua celebrating the team's first-ever World Championship point alongside the APXGP pit crew, after a series of safety cars, caused by Sonny's "reckless" driving, has gifted Joshua tenth place.

"It was a little bit of déjà vu, because I had been there the year before without the actors," says Kosinski. "So, this time was filming the other half of the scene with them. The energy, the light, the track, the confetti. Everything was exactly the same. The weather was the same. Same time of day. Same time of year. The sun was in the same place. It was a little weird to shoot two halves of a scene exactly a year apart, down to the minute. But it was an important scene for the film, because it's the moment where the team starts to believe

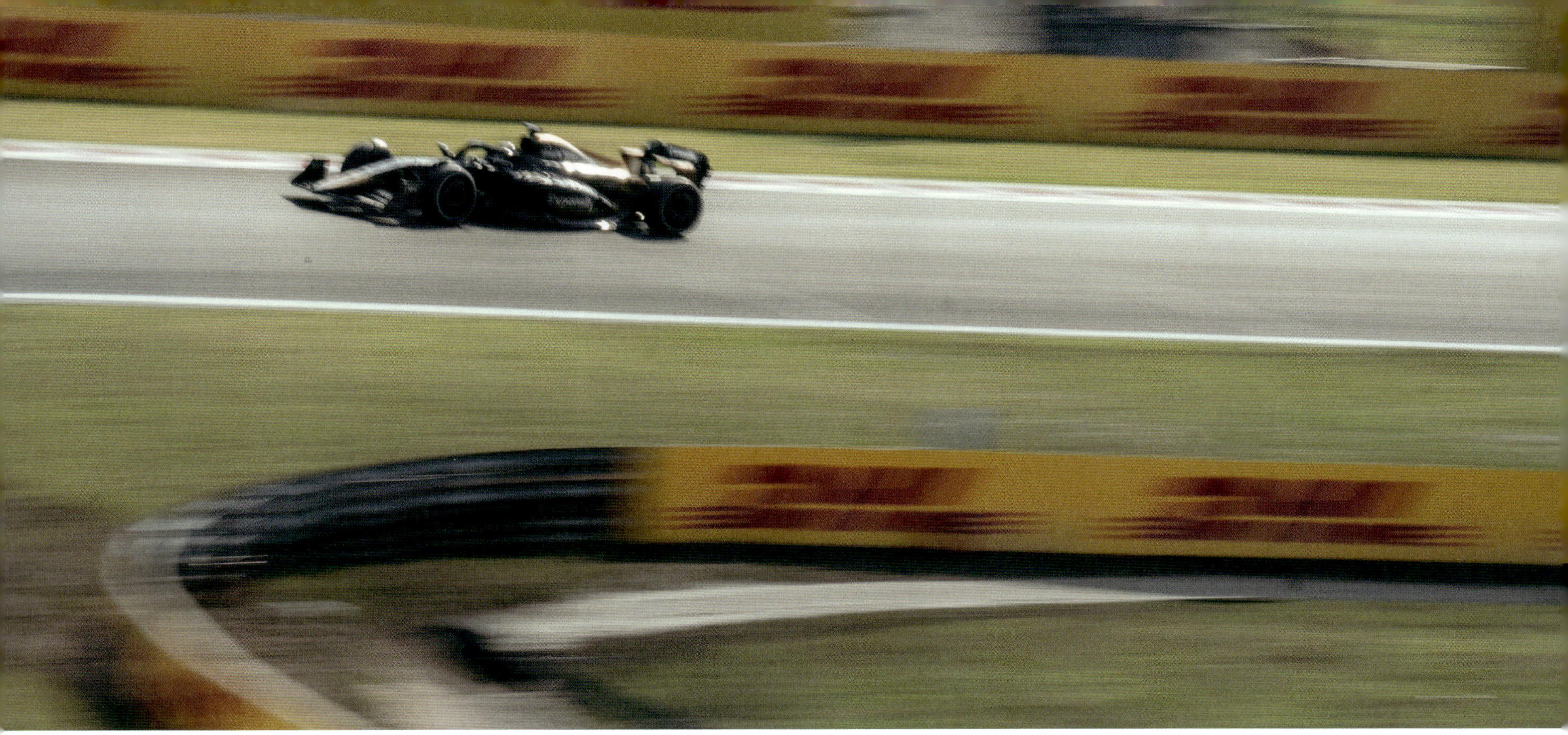

Above: Sonny and Joshua at the Hungaroring.

Below: The APXGP team celebrates the results of the Hungarian Grand Prix.

that this Sonny Hayes guy might know a thing or two."

"I didn't think parc fermé could get any better, but it did," says Hefferman. "We were gathered underneath the podium at the end of the race. So, again, it was epic production value. And the same thing happened. Jo from the FIA was there. The actors went onto the scales. We did it two or three times until we could do it no more. And [it] felt like we were an F1 team."

"It was madness," remembers Pitt. "We have our cars placed in Parc Fermé, and suddenly all the drivers are pulling in, having just finished an almost two-hour race in the heat. And because they're getting out of their cars, we get out of our cars, and we shoot this scene amongst all the pomp and circumstance, in the middle of all the drivers. And we're waiting in line like everyone else to get weighed, and I'd see some of the drivers and lock eyes and give them a little apologetic wave, and then we just carry on."

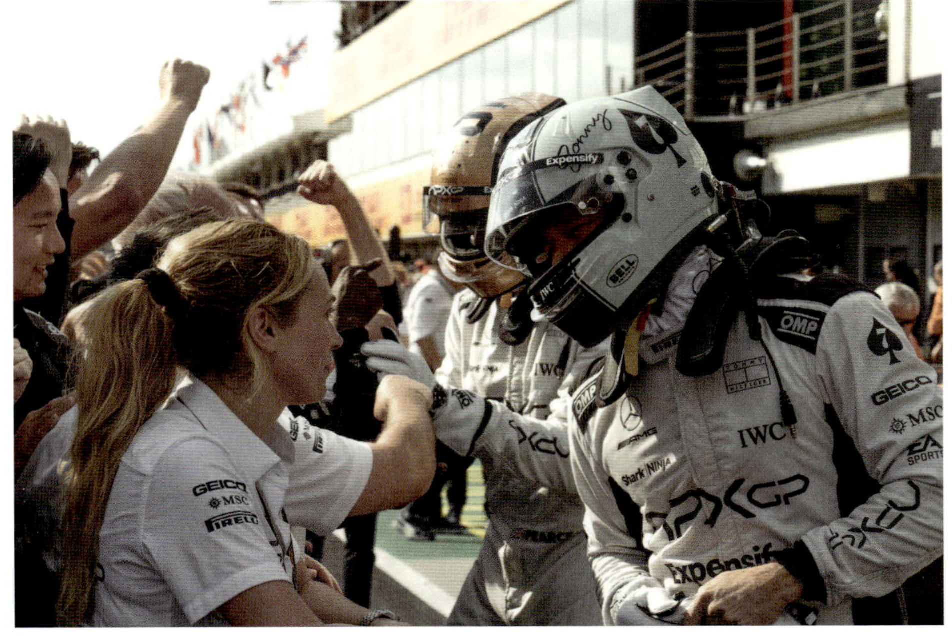

"We pulled up right before the weight scaling, right after the race, and Verstappen pulled up right beside me," recalls Idris. "That was when he and Lewis had tapped at turn one, and he went off, so he was fuming. I made sure not to look at him."

"We rehearsed it without any cars or people days before," says Condon. "But all I remember from Hungary is, 'Don't touch the cars.' They must have told us fifty times. 'If you touch a car, they're disqualified.' I was so nervous. I had this flirty moment with Brad to do. And three takes to do it in. But there's only a certain amount you can do with Brad before people start to recognize him as well. So that's on your mind too. Once people start recognizing him, the jig is up. But it was *incredible*. We were cheering. The confetti went off at the perfect time, for a perfect take. It's so beautiful when things come together."

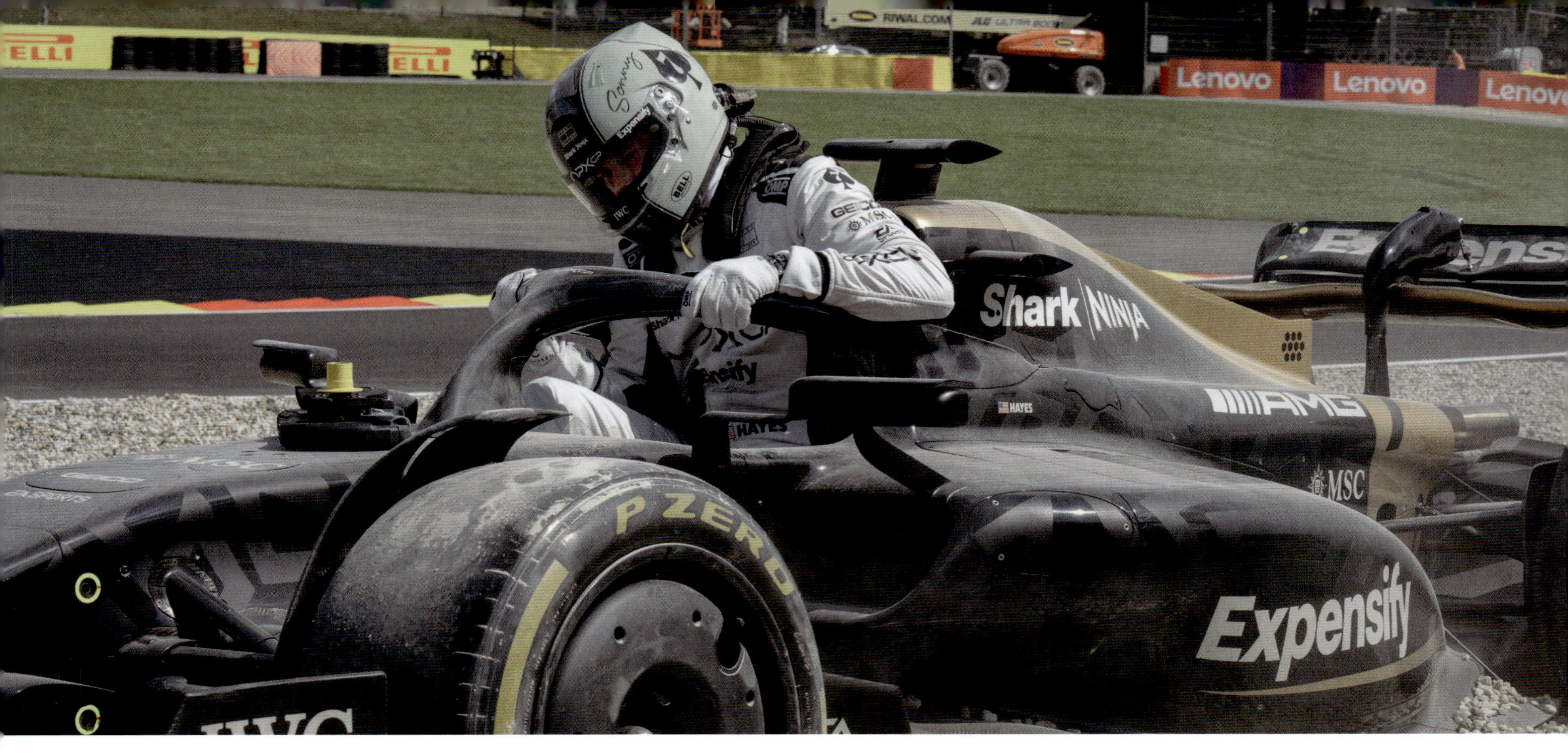

BELGIAN GP

Next up was the Belgian Grand Prix at Spa-Francorchamps, home of Eau Rouge, one of the most thrilling sections of racetrack anywhere in the world, a sweeping uphill stretch of high-speed corners named after the stream running beneath it. The production arrived at Spa on Wednesday, July 24, where Kosinski shot Pitt's Sonny running up Eau Rouge, together with twenty APXGP crew members, as part of his pre-race prep. On Thursday morning, they shot close-ups of Sonny and Joshua in their cars on the grid, having positioned several other cars in and around Sonny and Joshua's APXGPs to look like it was a fuller grid. They also filmed several race starts using their electric APXGP car, a scene in the pit lane with Sonny and Joshua arguing, as well as crowd reaction shots.

But Friday was the big day, with several "hot lap" sessions featuring both actors spread out across the day. "Eau Rouge, like Vegas, was super risky, because it's one of the most dangerous parts of a track in the world, and we had to look at [it] from a risk management point of view," says Hefferman. "And so they were asked not to go so fast, but the drivers argued that if they slowed down, they would lose heat in the tires, which, in turn, would give them less grip and less downforce. And so it's more dangerous going slowly."

"Because there have been so many accidents in the past where people lost their lives at the top of Eau Rouge, they wanted us to

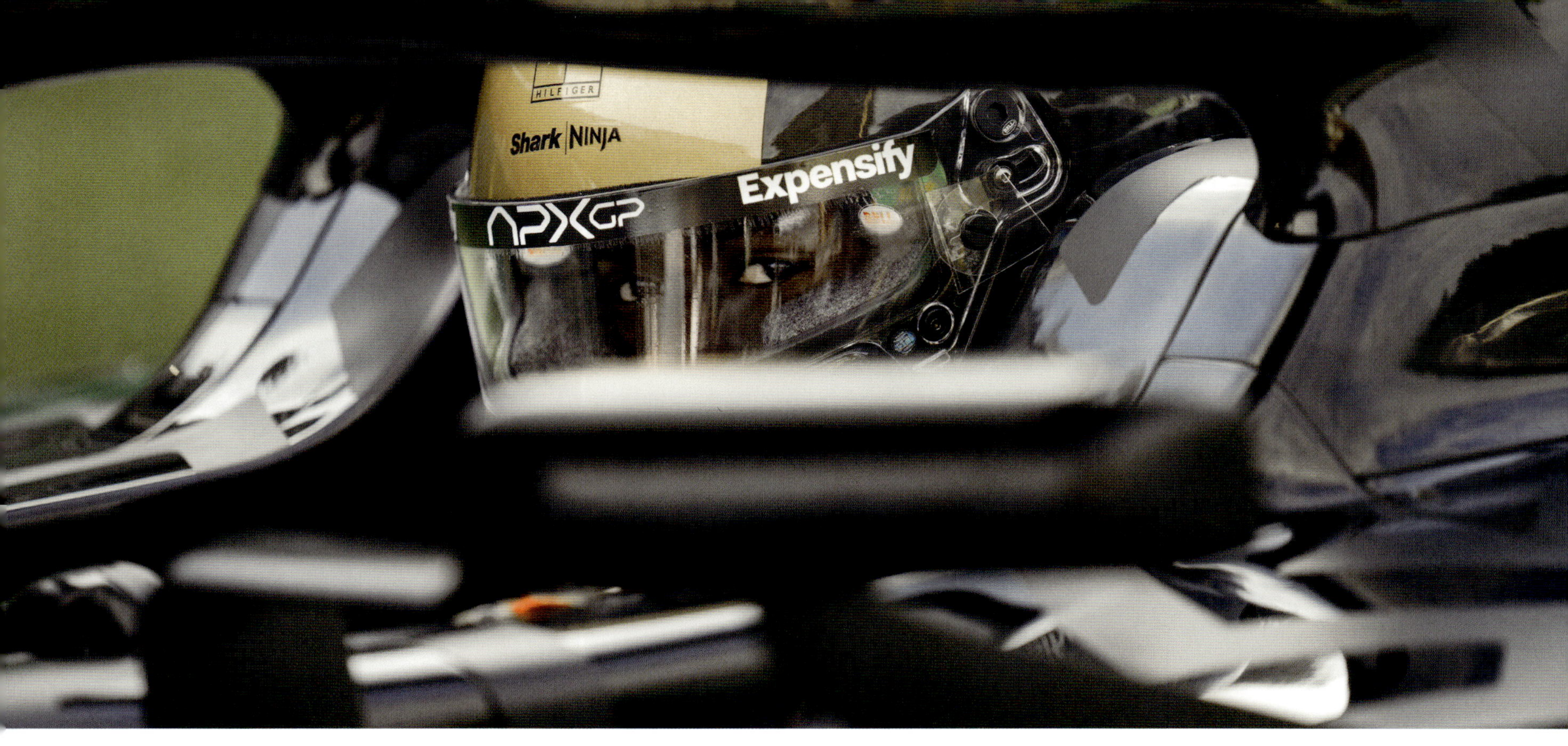

slow down to pit lane speed, which is 60 miles per hour, put on the pit limiter, and go up Eau Rouge at 60. Then, on the back [stretch], slow it down to 60 again. Not only is it dumb as fuck, it's dangerous as hell," says Pitt, who went out with Bacheta as usual, and did as requested. At first. "I would lift going up Eau Rouge...kinda. And I would lift on this back stretch. That was also historically dangerous. But each pass, I'd lift less. Until I knew it was on my last run. I knew this was my last shot at driving this track, and I couldn't help it.

"I mean, Eau Rouge," Pitt continues. "It was one of the first things Lewis described to me. You're coming in at full throttle, you bottom out, and the g-forces are so intense it compresses your spine, it pushes you down into the seat, so all your organs, your brain, everything's being pushed down into the ground. Then you go up this rise, which is an S, and it's like a roller coaster. You're lifting in your seat, so all your organs and your head and your brain are being pushed to the top. Then you come back down, and it's a blind crest."

"The first time he went up Eau Rouge, his face just lit up," remembers Bacheta. "I didn't see it, because I was on track with him, but apparently he had the biggest grin."

"It was the most thrilling experience I've ever had," concurs Pitt. "It's 4.3 miles, huge elevation changes, and on the back there's this big sweeping lift that's the thrill of a lifetime. By my last time out, Luch was having a chuckle because he knows what I'm doing. By the last one out, I was flat. Now, we're not F1 flat, but I'm F2 flat, going up Eau Rouge. And it was just the greatest feeling. The. Greatest. Feeling. I was on such a high for weeks after driving Spa. Spa was the Holy Grail."

In the film, Sonny's "race" comes to a premature end after Joshua steers into his car, sending him into the gravel, another in a long line of Formula One racing incidents caused by squabbling teammates. "The famous one is Senna and Prost, for the World Championship in Suzuka in 1989," says Kosinski. "But that particular collision on that particular corner at Spa, we shot practically. It's a combination of footage from Brands Hatch and Spa." Close-ups of Pitt spinning were filmed using Keith Dawson's 360 Plus rig in the U.K., with an "aftermath buck" doubling for the beached car in Belgium.

Sonny (Brad Pitt) pulls himself out of his car after Joshua (Damson Idris) causes him to crash at the Belgian Grand Prix.

ITALIAN GP

After the highs of Spa, the production headed to Monza, where Kosinski shot Sonny running on a section of the old, banked track along with scenes in the APXGP hospitality suite.

In story terms, Monza was pivotal, as Joshua and Sonny make their way steadily through the pack into point scoring positions when it starts to rain. After Sonny pits for intermediate tires, he accelerates out of the pit lane just ahead of first place Max Verstappen on track, but positionally behind him. He slows down Verstappen to allow Joshua to catch up. As Joshua slingshots past Sonny, the latter urges his rookie teammate to wait for turn one to overtake Verstappen. But Joshua ignores the advice, accelerating past Verstappen a corner too soon. Drifting wide, Joshua hits a diamond curb, which sends his car airborne, into a tree, before bursting into flames. Sonny slams on his brakes, leaps from his stationary car, and rushes toward the inferno, pulling Joshua from the burning wreckage, turning what was looking likely to be the best race in APXGP history into the worst.

Bringing the horrific crash to the screen took the combined talents of the stunt, special effects, and visual effects departments, with the entire sequence filmed by Kosinski.

And while the crash happens at Monza, it was shot at Brands Hatch, where the stunt team drove one of their APXGP cars around a bend at speed, then drifted out wide.

Dawson's special effects team then took over. Using a nitrogen ram, they propelled a fiberglass replica of the APXGP car with a dummy driver in it at around 130 miles per hour along a 30-meter-long monorail, toward a slightly arced, curved pipe ramp. This launched the car into the air like a cannonball, sending it flying 90 meters over a fence and into the treeline.

For onboard spinning shots of Joshua airborne, Dawson created a "rotisserie" rig, mounting the car on a 360 telehandler that could raise, tilt, and spin 360 degrees. This rig was positioned on the same section of track, traveling the same path, in the same weather conditions as the propelled car, only with Idris inside. For shots of the car crashing to earth, Dawson built a pneumatic 45-degree hinged rig, in which Idris could sit, as the car slammed to a stop in the trees.

The next stage was for the car to catch fire. As with all the racing incidents depicted in the film, Joshua's crash took inspiration from real life, in this case Romain Grosjean's horrific crash during the opening lap of the 2020 Bahrain Grand Prix, when his car caught fire after penetrating a metal crash barrier and he sustained second-degree burns in what would prove to be his last race in Formula One. "We looked at Grosjean's crash because it was so intense," says Dawson. "We wanted that kind of chaos, that feeling he's not going to get out. He's knocked out. He comes to. The flames are raging, and he's trapped."

"What was incredible about the Grosjean crash was how long he was in that car, on fire, and was able to emerge relatively okay," says Kosinski. "I know he had burns on his hands and his feet, but the fact he was in there for almost thirty seconds is a testament to the fireproofing and safety in the clothing they wear. Joshua is in that car for a while before he gets out, and we wanted to make sure we were within the realms of reality that you could survive something like that."

To help get Idris in the right mindset, he spoke to Grosjean on the phone about what had happened that fateful day in Bahrain. "He wanted to get the feeling and the idea of what was going through my mind," remembers Grosjean. "If I was scared, what was going on. He wanted to try and replicate it as much as he could."

"He walked me through the horrific moments of that crash, so I could internalize what that would feel like in that moment, when your life is flashing before your eyes, and you have to fight, and you're thinking of everything that you have to lose and everything you're going to leave behind," says Idris.

Top Right: Joshua's (Damson Idris's) car launches into the air after hitting the curb.

Bottom Right: Keith Dawson created a "rotisserie" rig to propel a model of Joshua's (Damson Idris's) car into the air for a scene at the Italian Grand Prix.

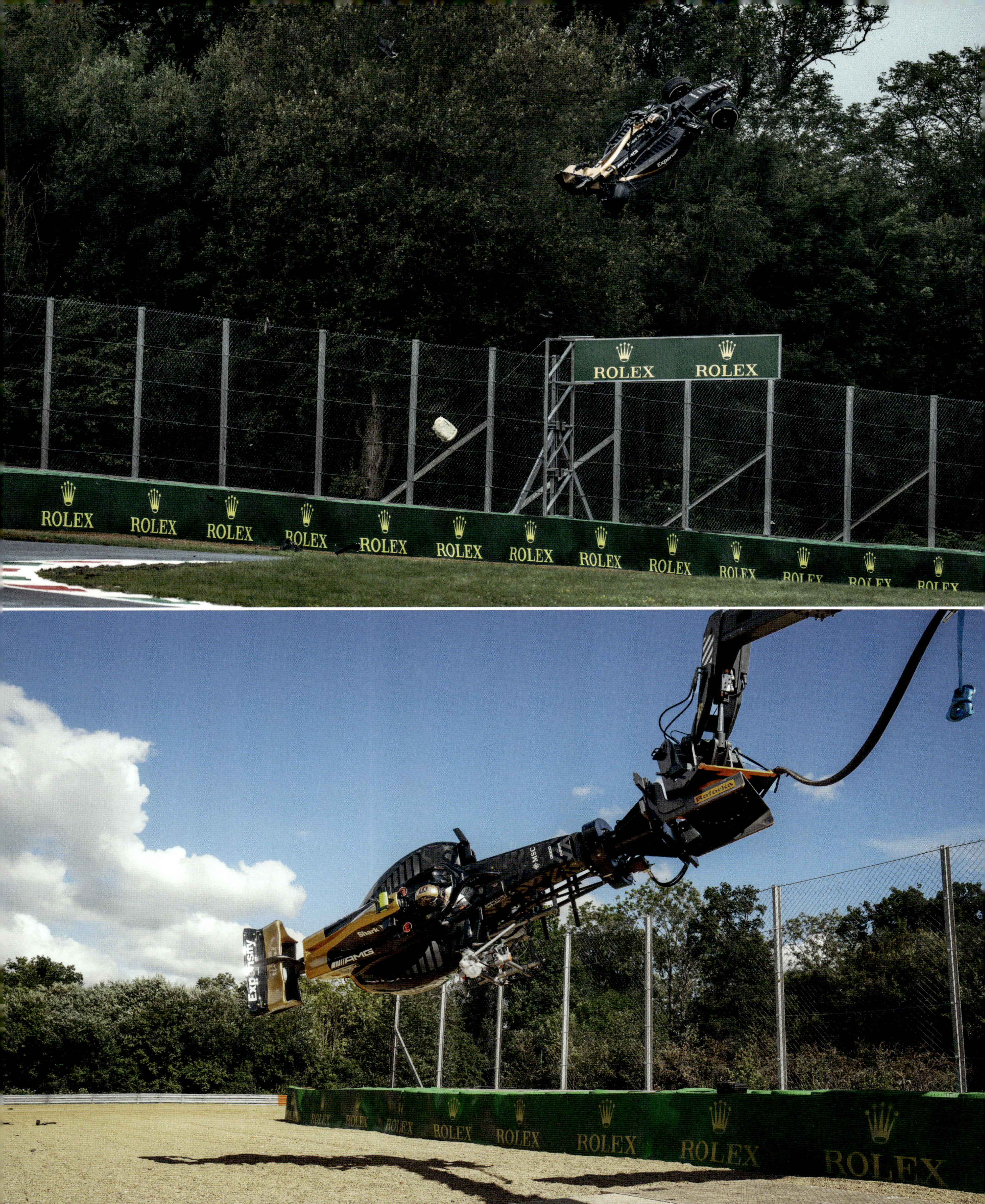
ROLEX
ROLEX
ROLEX
ROLEX
ROLEX
ROLEX
ROLEX
ROLEX
ROLEX
ROLEX
ROLEX
AMG
ROLEX
ROLEX
ROLEX
ROLEX
ROLEX

HOW A MODERN F1 CAR PROTECTS DRIVERS

I guess not panicking, that was a big help. Of course, the safety of the modern cars and the Halo was a big part of it, for sure. And then the desire to live . . . Even though you know you're burning, it's not like you're going to release your hands from there because you need them to extract yourself. So, I guess you remove the pain from the equation, and you just try to jump out."

Romain Grosjean suffered a horror crash in the 2020 Bahrain Grand Prix that saw him trapped in his burning car for around half a minute. But, remarkably, the Frenchman was able to climb out of the fire unaided, with burns to his hands and feet the only injuries after an impact that also registered 67G.

It's one of many amazing examples of drivers surviving huge incidents. But just how does the safety equipment around them offer protection?

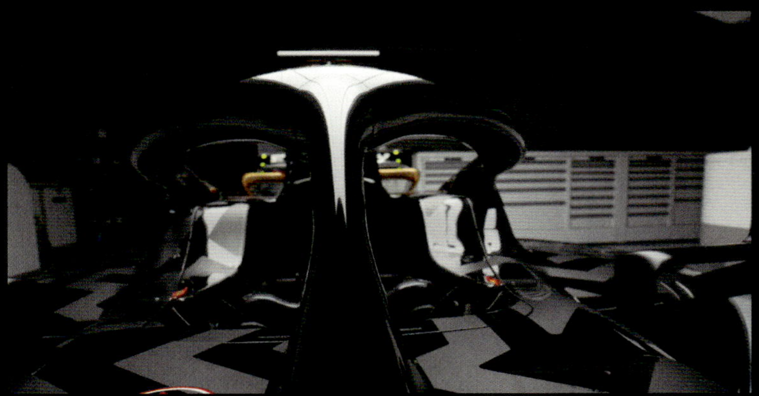

THE HALO

A car has many safety features, but one of the newest is the Halo. This is a cockpit protection device that was introduced in 2018 and can deflect large pieces of debris away from the driver's head. The titanium structure is also strong enough to withstand heavy impacts, including supporting the weight of another car, keeping it clear of the driver in the cockpit.

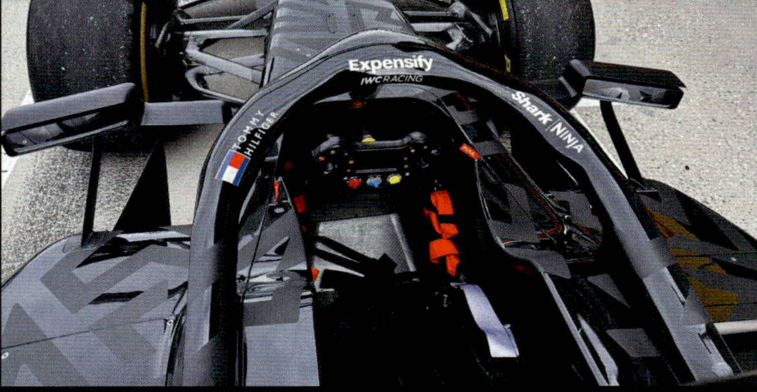

CRASH STRUCTURES

If you strip an F1 car back to its base structure, the area where a driver sits is called the survival cell. This carbon fiber monocoque is subjected to stringent crash testing to show it will not allow items to penetrate the cockpit, protecting the driver inside. Fixed to this are two tubes on each side of the cockpit—known as the side impact structure—that absorb an impact to help decelerate the car. Similar structures are found in the nose and the rear of the car to absorb impacts from those directions, too.

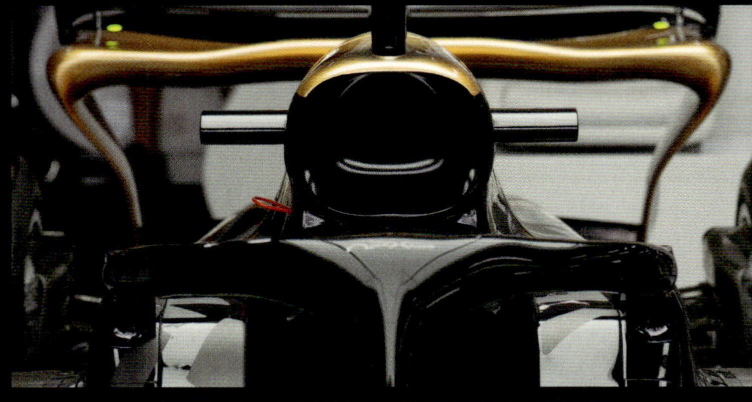

ROLL HOOP

Even prior to the Halo being introduced, but now working in conjunction with it, the roll hoop was a crucial element to protecting a driver's head. The roll hoop structure is just behind the driver and can withstand extremely high vertical loads. This means that in the event of a car flipping upside down, the roll hoop will help keep the driver's head from contacting the ground, or other objects in the environment such as crash barriers.

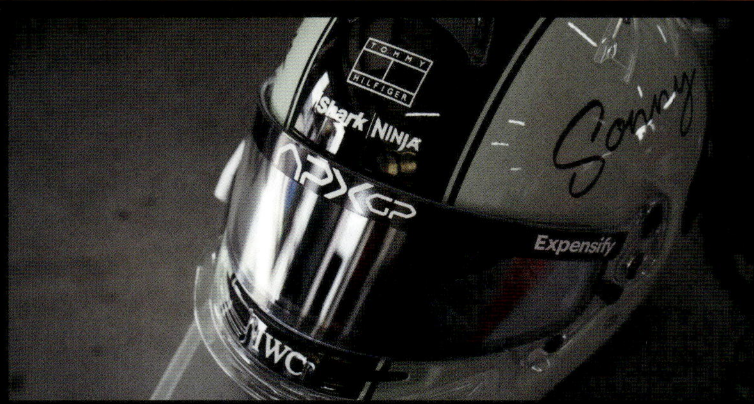

HELMET

Perhaps the most recognizable piece of safety equipment that a driver uses, the helmet serves multiple functions. The protective element is not just from impacts against the side of the cockpit or debris, but also from fire. In the case of Grosjean's crash, the helmet prevented smoke inhalation as well as withstanding the flames. There's a protective strip above the visor to aid with deflecting smaller items, while the visors themselves also help with visibility and can protect against the smallest pieces of debris.

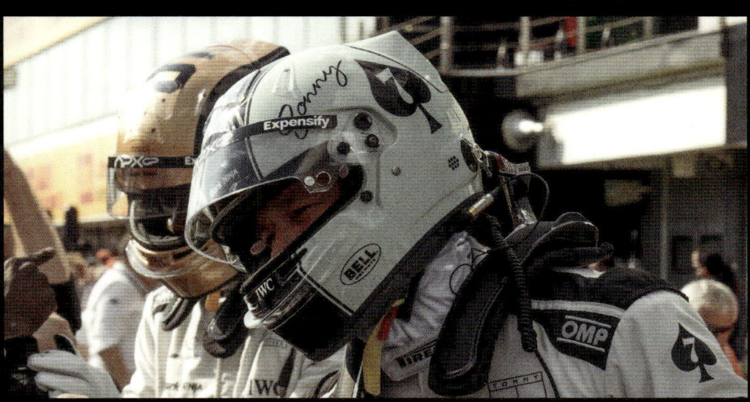

HANS DEVICE

Attached to the helmet is the Head and Neck Support (HANS) device, that has become a vital piece of driver protection since it became mandatory in 2003. The HANS sits over the shoulders of a driver—the seatbelts can then run on top of it—and extends upward behind a driver's neck, from where it is tethered to the helmet. The device prevents the head from decelerating too quickly during an impact, essentially protecting against whiplash and severe neck and head injuries.

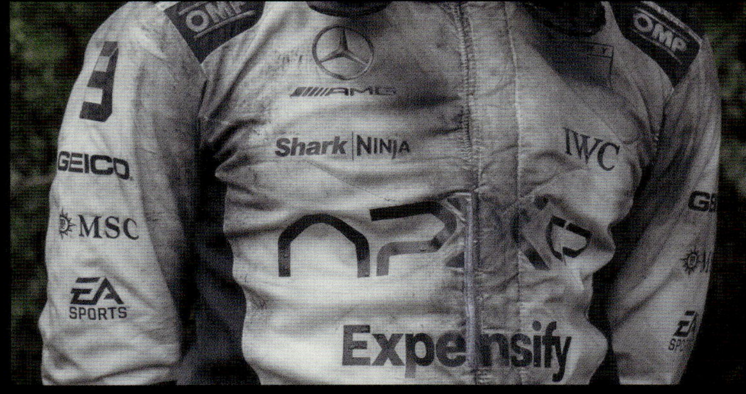

FIREPROOF OVERALLS

Drivers wear race suits in the car to help with heat and fire protection. Made from the flame-resistant fabric Nomex, the race suit has multiple layers that absorb the heat, preventing it from reaching the inner layer of the suit—and therefore the driver—in the event of a fire. The race suit must be able to withstand temperatures of nearly 1000C for at least 12 seconds, although in Grosjean's case it clearly managed to do so for much longer than that.

Other racewear paired with the suit includes a layer of fireproof underwear in the form of a long-sleeved top, long-john-style pants, and socks, all of which are made from a single layer of Nomex and also help with sweat absorption.

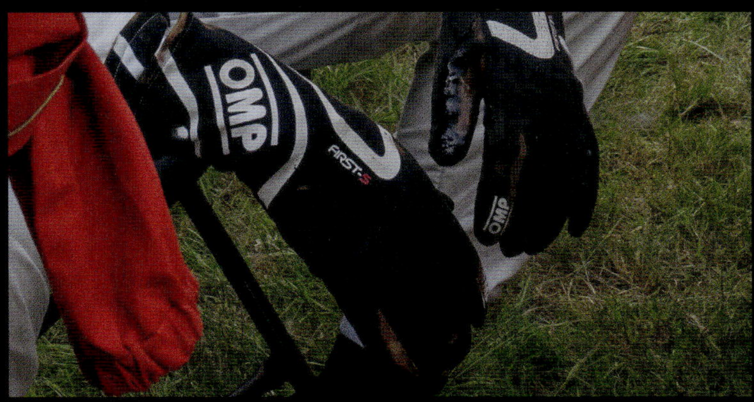

GLOVES

The gloves are particularly important because a driver needs to be able to feel the steering wheel, while still receiving protection from heat and fire. A single layer of Nomex is used that must withstand 800C temperatures for around 10 seconds, up from eight at the time of Grosjean's crash.

Another aspect of the gloves is the fact that they are now biometric. A tiny sensor allows the medical team to monitor a driver's vital signs during a race, so that they can see their pulse oximetry—the amount of oxygen in their blood, alongside their pulse rate—in the event of an accident.

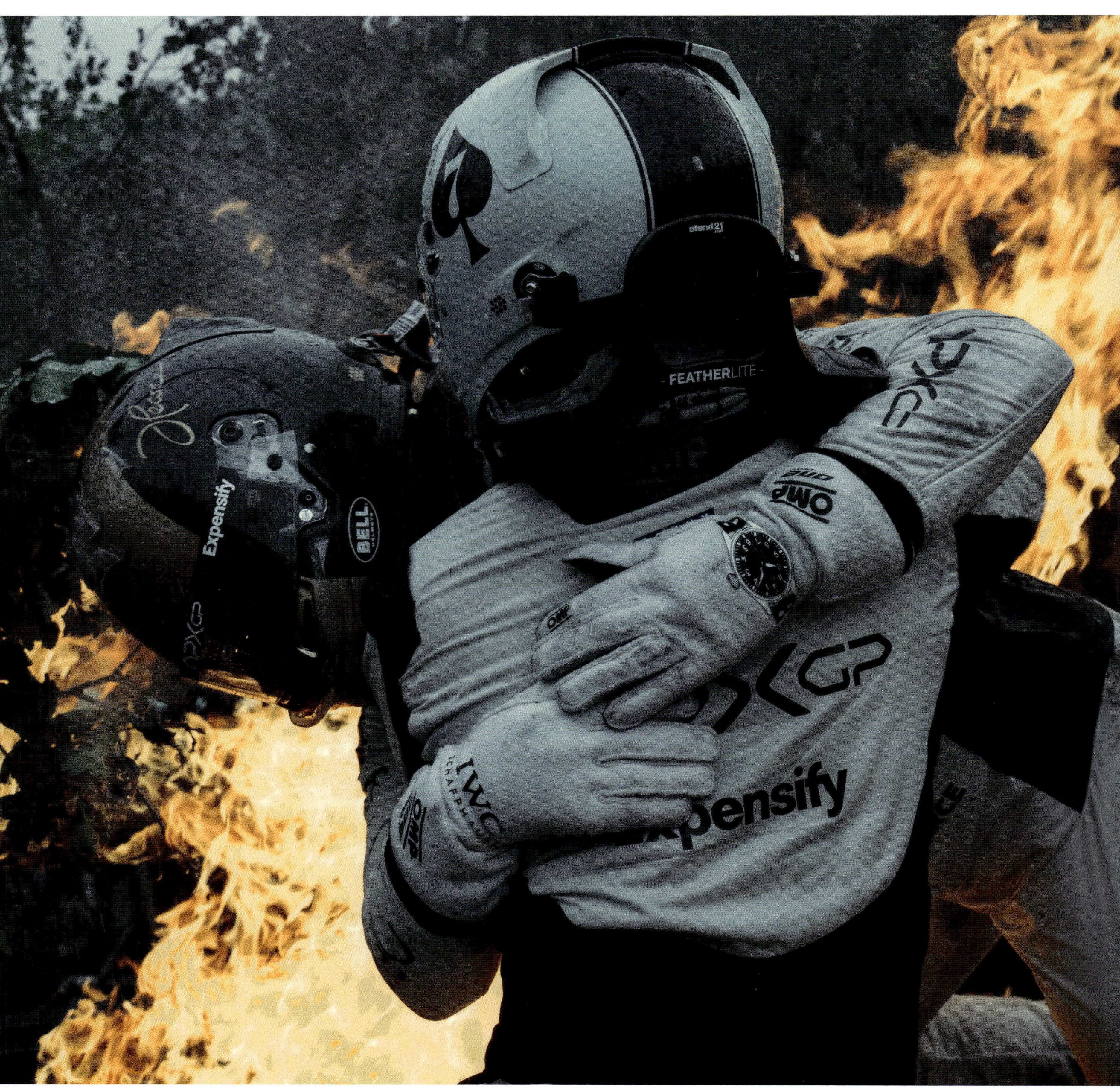

Above: Sonny (Brad Pitt) drags Joshua (Damson Idris) out of the burning wreckage of his car after the crash.

Right: Damson Idris sitting atop his scorched APXGP car.

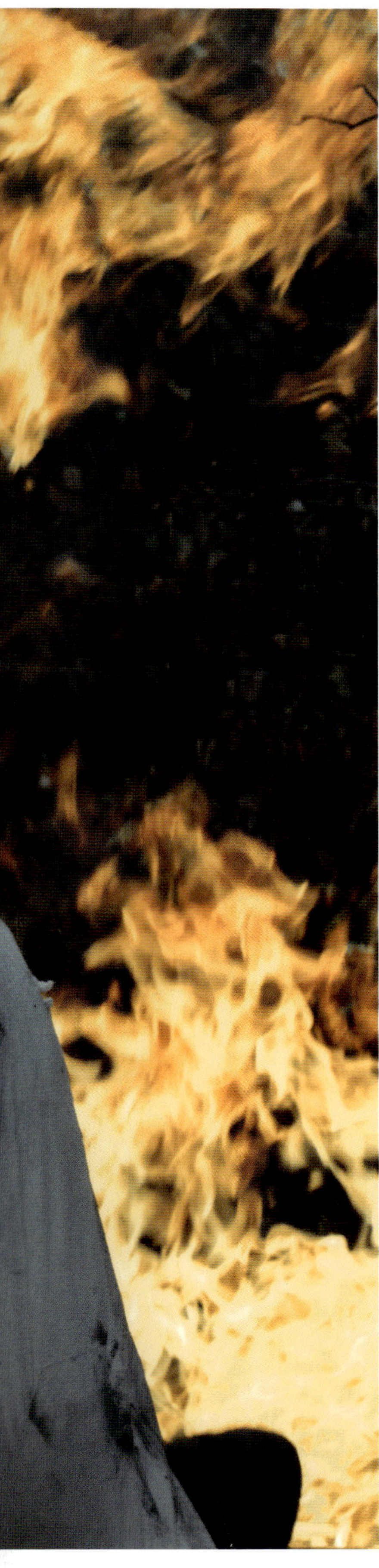

For the burn itself, a fiberglass car was replaced by a steel version built to withstand the heat of the fireball. This was created by a mixture of IPA (isopropanol alcohol)—which gives a cooler burn than petrol—white spirit—which produces orange flame—and cooking oil—which gives off black smoke. A dummy stood in for Idris for the initial explosion. "After that, we switched to flame bars and lower levels of the pumped fuel, which gave you a nice wall of fire in and around the car," says Dawson. "But we sectioned off an area where the driver would be to protect him with silicone shields. I'm not going to lie, it still got hot in there."

It was Pitt who dragged Idris from the fiery wreckage for medium and tighter shots. "This was one of the scenes we rehearsed and rehearsed, so when we shot it, everyone knew exactly what they're doing," continues Dawson. "We shot the burn over two days. Damson was in the car quite a lot. We had a stuntman for when the full burn was going, then brought it down slightly for when we put Damson in the car. It looked fierce, and Brad had to run into that."

"It's amazing how much heat those things put out, even as controlled fires," says Pitt. "But we're so looked after, and we have such a good team, I wasn't ever concerned about it. We were just playing the drama of it all, trying to figure out, how do you get out of this car you're strapped in? How do you get the HANS device off? Where would stewards be? How are you going to get this 200-pound man out?"

Helping round the sequence off was visual effects supervisor Ryan Tudhope. "The crash was largely practical. We had to paint out the rigs and clean it up, but Keith owned all that," he explains. "We did some environment changes because that was Brands Hatch as Monza, so we did some work adding grandstands and cleaning up rain towers."

But Tudhope's main job with Monza was to add rain to a race sequence that, the Brands Hatch stunt aside, was mostly shot in the dry at Silverstone. "There's no way to wet down an entire track. By the time the trucks get around to the other side, it would be drying out. It's also not safe to run those cars on the wet, at the speeds we wanted. So, it became pretty clear we were going to have to do digital wet downs. To help with that, we shot a lot of those scenes right as the sun was behind the horizon, so we didn't have any direct sunlight or shadows, which gave us a better foundation for making it look wet and overcast. We also filmed our actors in one of Keith's rain cars, which was pulled behind another car and had rigs on it to spray water, making it look like they're in the wet. But it was Silverstone behind them, so we made it look like it was Italy."

And with Monza completed, the European section of the *F1* movie tour was over. All that was left to film Formula One–wise were the Mexican, Las Vegas, and Abu Dhabi Grand Prix.

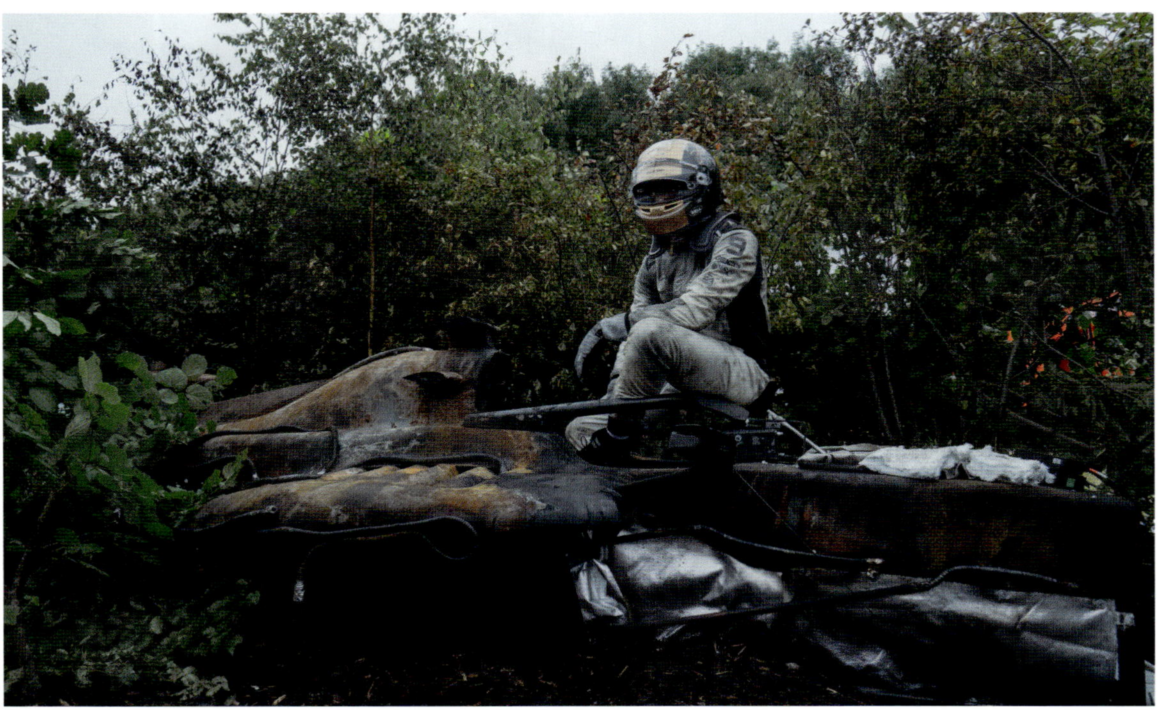

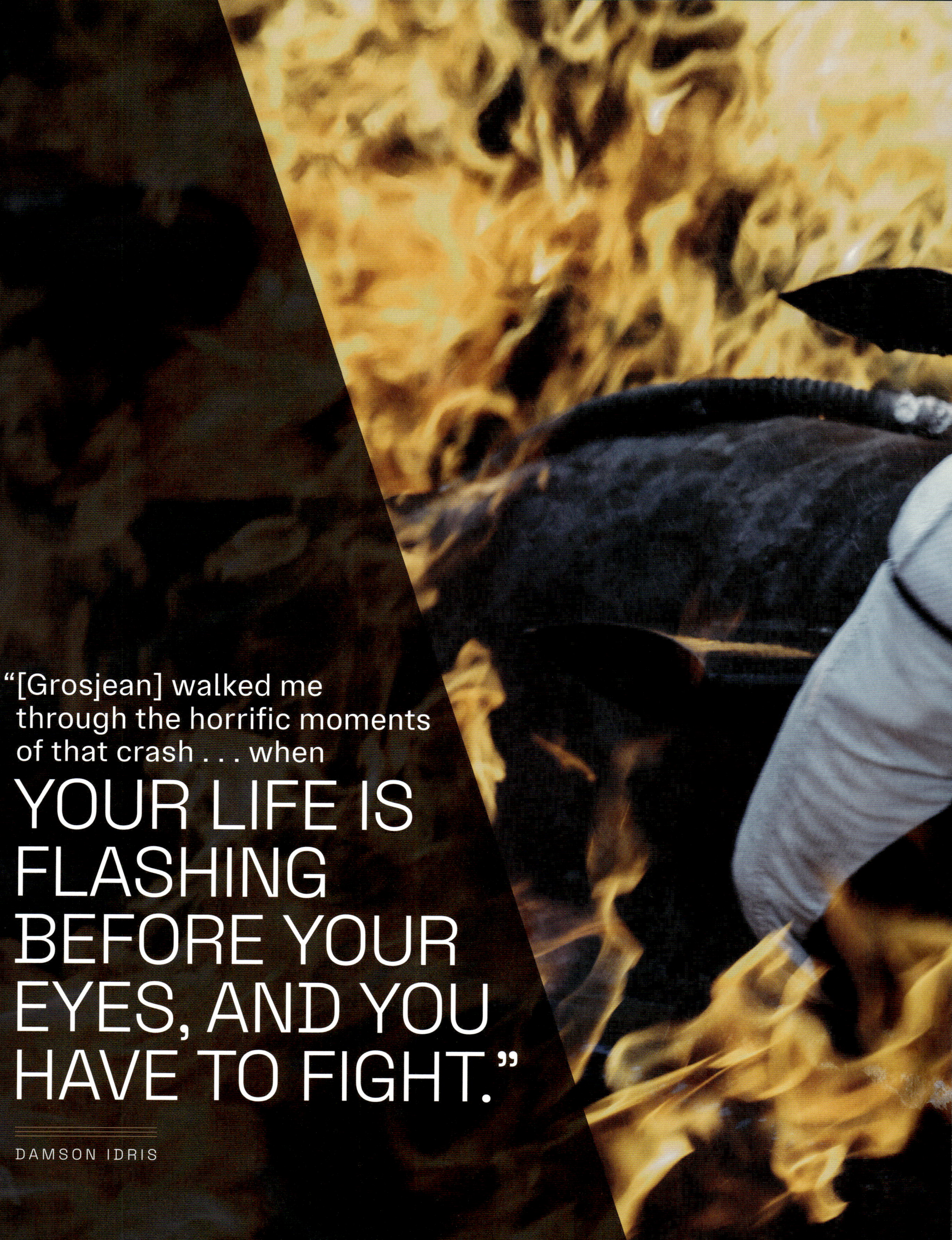

"[Grosjean] walked me through the horrific moments of that crash . . . when

YOUR LIFE IS FLASHING BEFORE YOUR EYES, AND YOU HAVE TO FIGHT."

DAMSON IDRIS

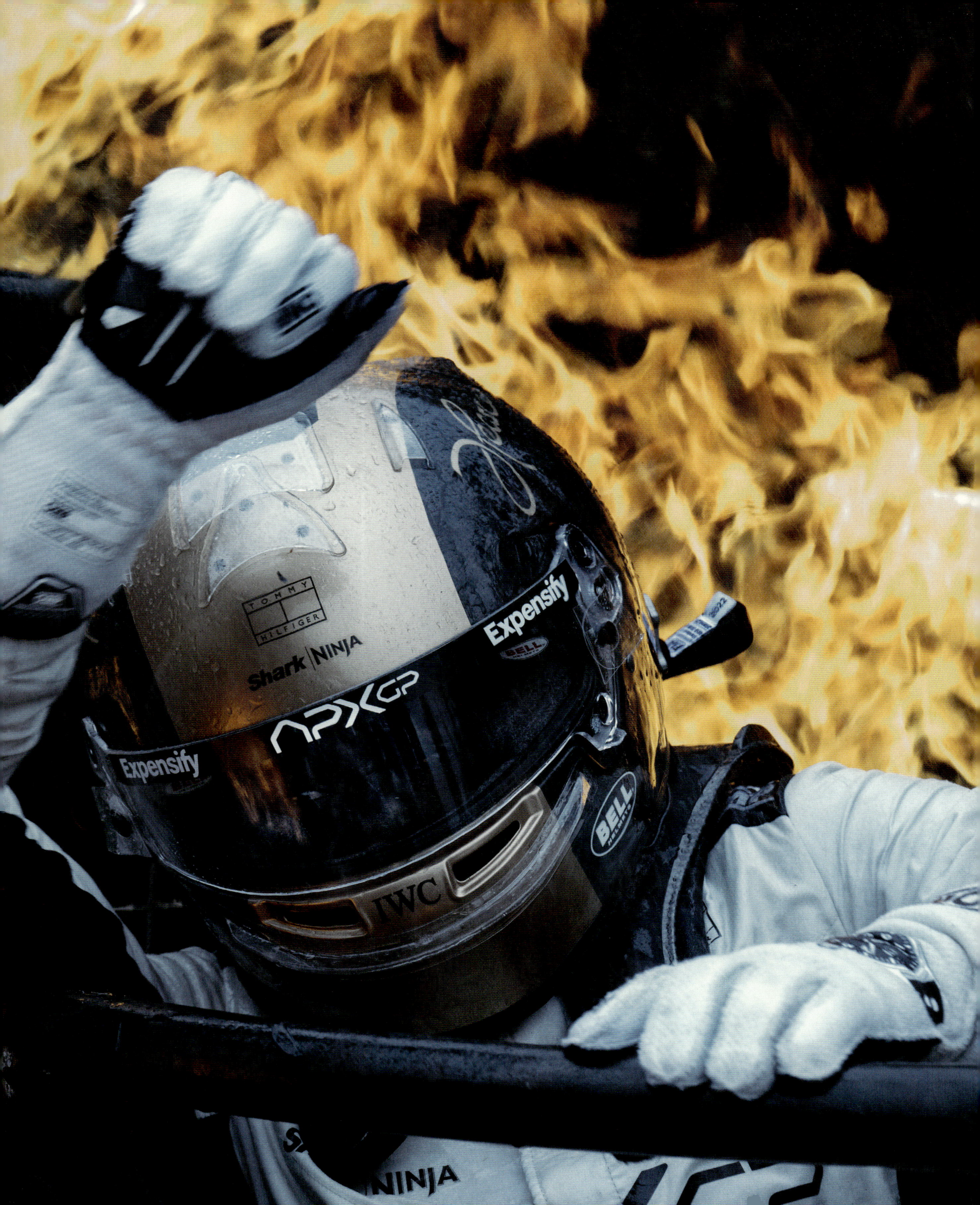
TOMMY HILFIGER
Shark | NINJA
Expensify
APXGP
Expensify
BELL
IWC
NINJA

9 MEXICO CITY TO ABU DHABI

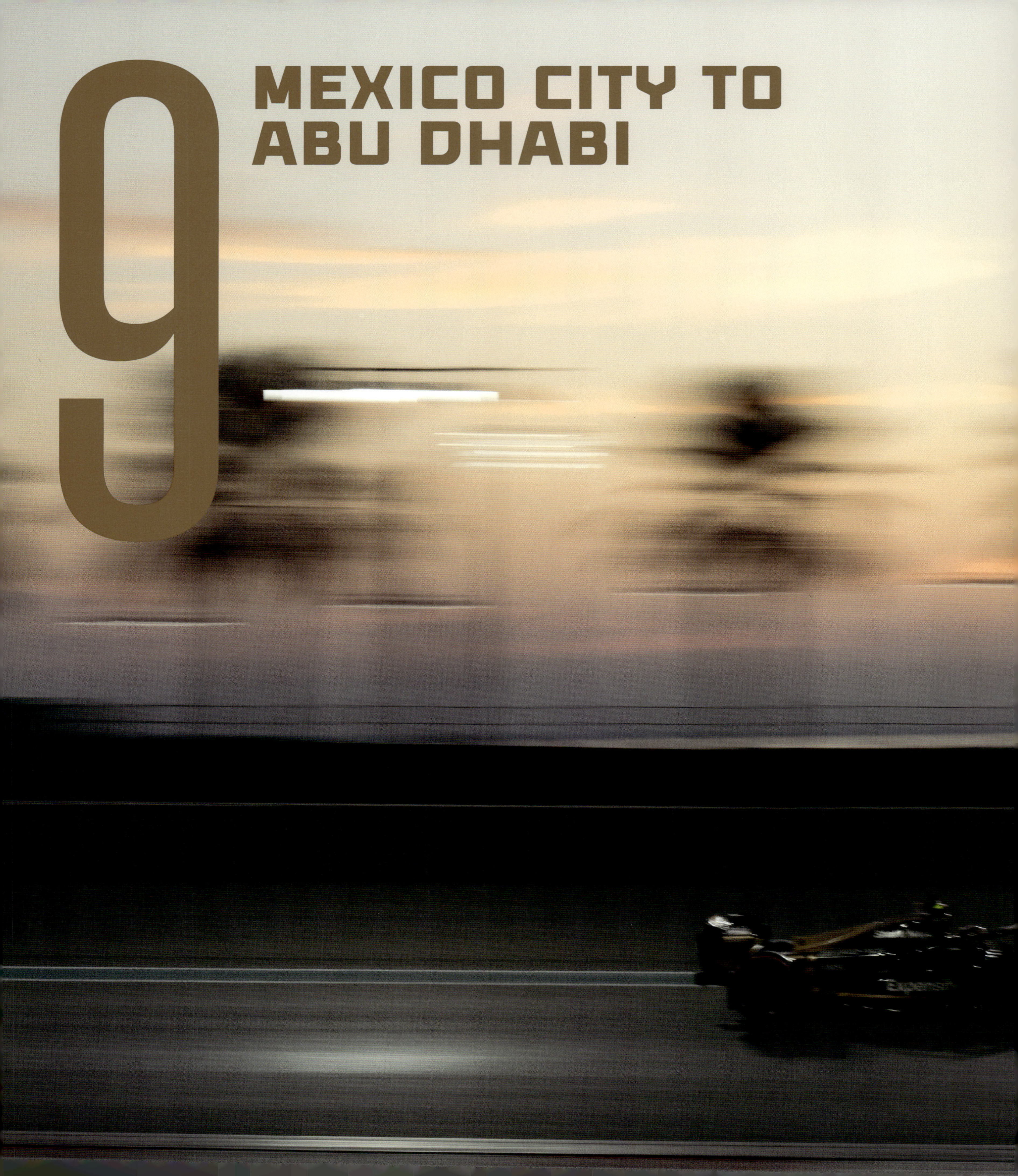

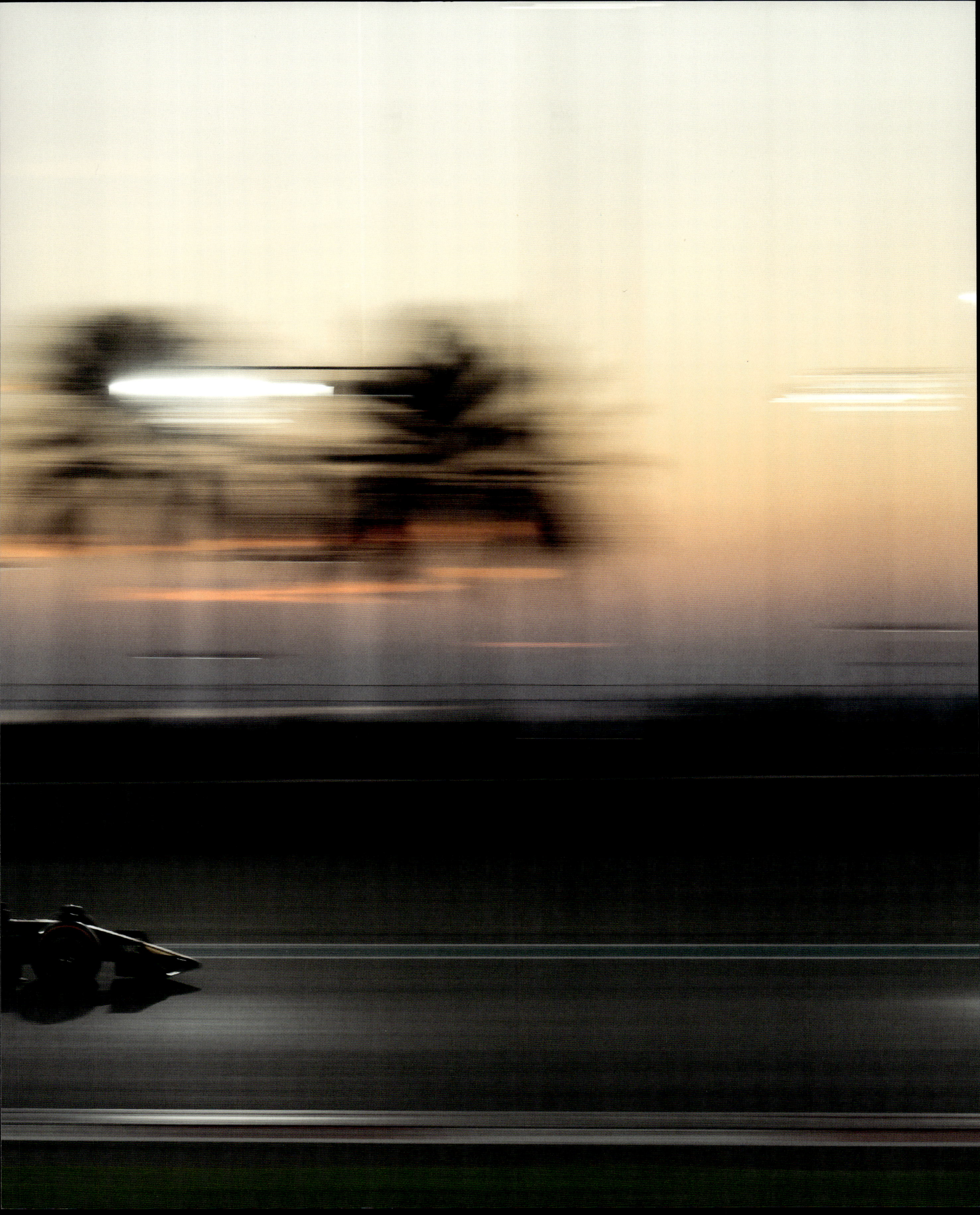

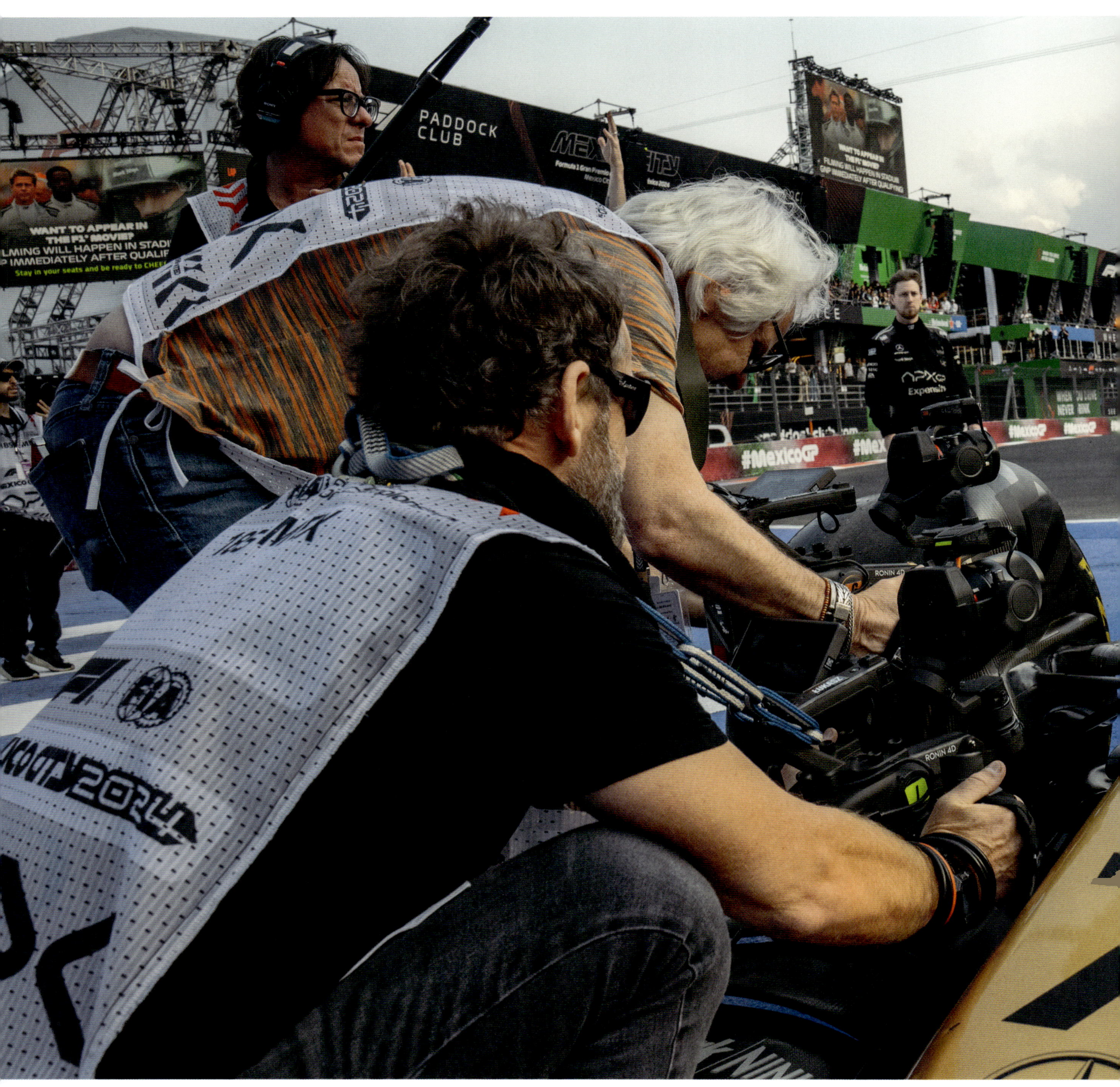

Bottom Right: Toby Hefferman readies the APXGP car for filming at Mexico's Foro Sol stadium.

Above: Cinematographer Claudio Miranda films Sonny Hayes (Brad Pitt) getting into his car.

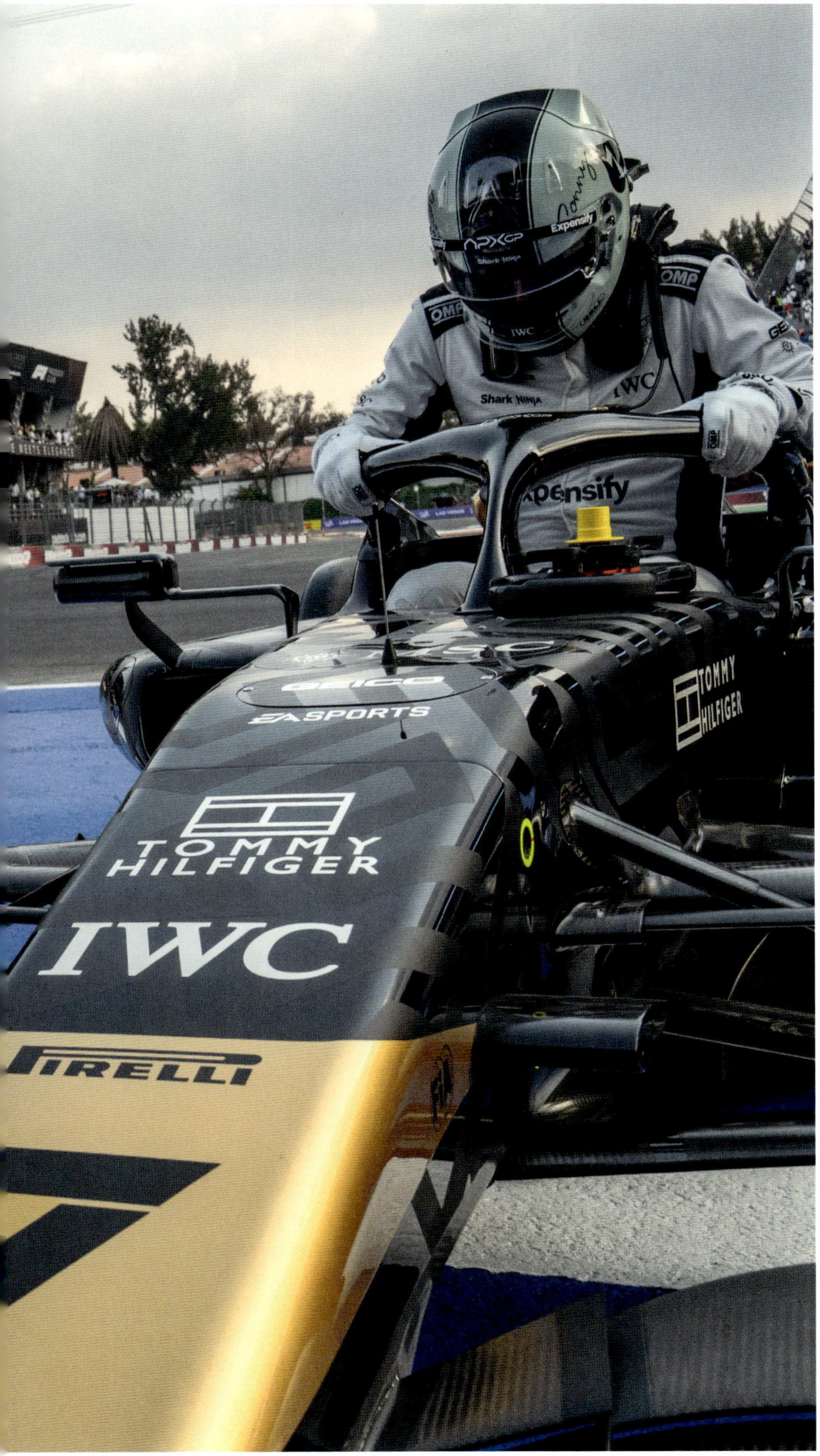

Director Joseph Kosinski arrived in Mexico City in late October ready to shoot scenes at the Mexican Grand Prix, which would form part of the three-race montage along with Zandvoort and Suzuka, both of which were being covered using F1 broadcast footage and a splinter unit shooting background places.

"Although it's a montage, meaning a few shots here and there, Mexico was as logistically challenging as Silverstone," says first assistant director Toby Hefferman. Saturday, October 26, was the biggest shoot day, with scenes in the APXGP hospitality suite as well as in parc fermé after qualifying. "It was the only chance we had, because at the end of the race, there's a whole pitch invasion, which turns it into a carnival. The sensitivity around this was the fact that the three fastest drivers do their interviews straight after qualifying, which was when we needed to film. But what we couldn't do was interrupt the international feed. For us to be shooting while they're doing interviews—especially if [Mexican driver] Checo Pérez was there—would be disrespectful."

Once again, the day was planned out with military-like precision. At 4:05 p.m., Sonny's (Brad Pitt) APXGP car would be moved into position near parc fermé at the Autódromo Hermanos Rodríguez circuit, with Pitt standing by. At 4:10 p.m., Pitt was strapped into his car. At 4:15 p.m., Kosinski started filming, as Pitt got out of the car, exhausted, then removed his balaclava and roared to the crowd. "We had a ten-minute window," reveals Hefferman. "I remember Jonathan Nichols from the broadcast team saying, 'We'll tell you when you can go, because if the interviews are still going on, you can't start. So, you may have ten minutes, but you may have less.' When you load any driver into a car, it's not quick. So, we knew we were going to get a maximum three goes at this."

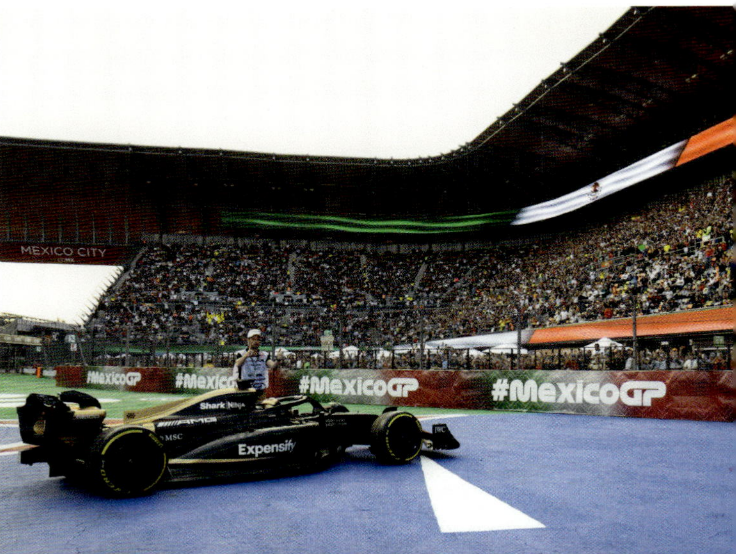

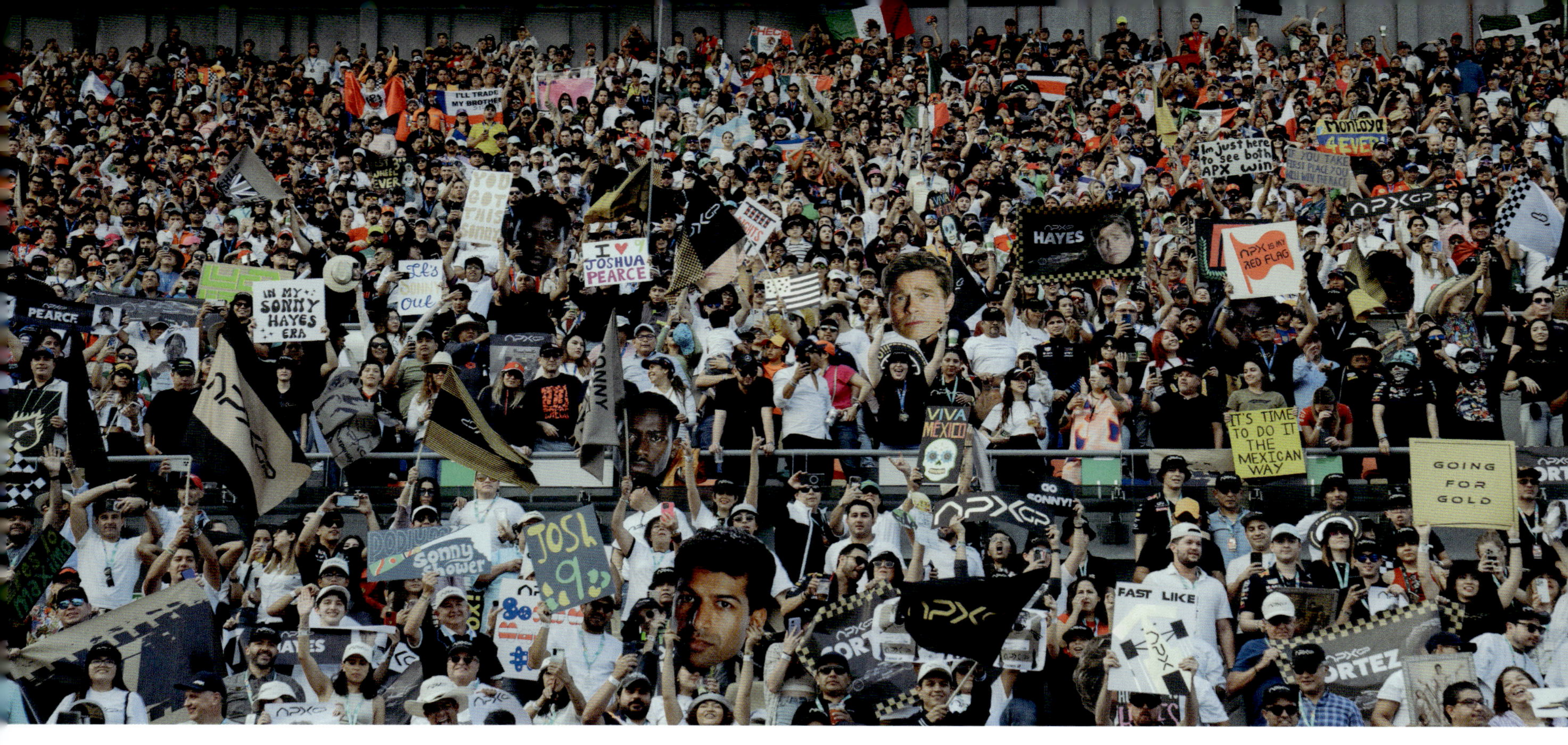

MEXICO CITY GP

At this point in the story, APXGP's fortunes are on the rise, along with the popularity of their drivers. For this race, that meant Sonny and reserve driver Luca Cortez, played by stunt driver Luciano Bacheta. To help sell the illusion, the race's promoters had advertised the fact that filming would be taking place and asked spectators to stay behind, as well as distributed APXGP merchandise—banners, flags, and big cutout heads of Sonny, Joshua (Damson Idris), and Cortez—among the crowd. "It was a coliseum; it was gladiatorial. When Brad got out of the car, everyone went mad. I've never heard anything so deafening in my life. It was incredible," says Hefferman. "We did it three times. Then Brad walked off, grabbed a Mexican flag, did a lap of honor, and the crowd went nuts again."

"The energy there was like nothing else we had seen," says Kosinski. "Everyone told me Mexico was different than most other races, and we found that to be true."

Sunday was race day, with the drivers' parade due to start at noon. Only this time, APXGP's Sonny Hayes and Luca Cortez were going to be taking part, joining the likes of Lewis Hamilton, George Russell, Lando Norris, and Max Verstappen. Pitt would drive Bacheta in a Mercedes SL convertible, the pair joining the parade just after the Foro Sol stadium section.

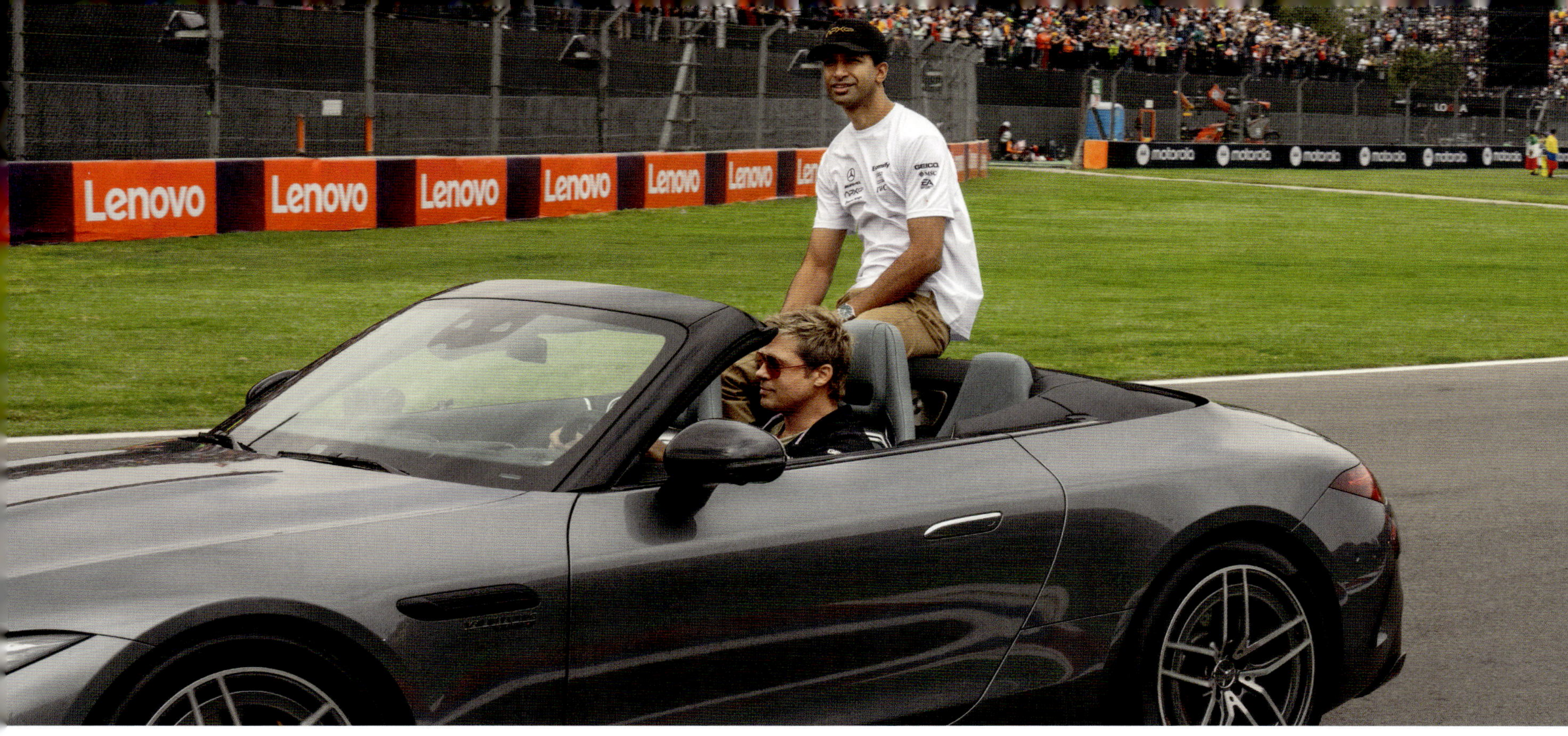

Top Left: At the Mexico City Grand Prix, members of the crowd wave APXGP merchandise and cheer for the team.

Top Right: Sonny (Brad Pitt) drives out with Luca Cortez (Luciano Bacheta) during the drivers' parade on race day at the Mexico City Grand Prix.

Kosinski had two cameras to film the drivers but was also relying on the F1 broadcast team to cover the parade. "Once they got their footage, we asked them to pan to our drivers to get them amongst the others," says Hefferman, who was based in the broadcast team hub (ETC) with Kosinski, in radio contact with Pitt and Bacheta. "When we got the signal from the ETC, we told Brad to go." But there was a mix-up on track with some parked cars, and Pitt didn't pull away as planned.

"We were looking at the cameras, waiting for our car to come into the Foro Sol, but it hadn't arrived," recalls Hefferman, who immediately got back on the radio and told Pitt to ignore the cars and put his foot down. "They got the cue sixty seconds later than they were supposed to," explains Kosinski. "What that meant was the whole drivers' parade had driven away when Luch and Brad pulled onto the track, so Brad drove at 100 miles per hour to catch up. I remember seeing Luch in the backseat, holding onto his hat *and* the car. So, it started in a disastrous fashion, but, luckily, within half a lap, Brad caught up and we got our shots. But we almost missed it."

"I had to bomb. I had to bomb down the track with Luch up on the upper ledge of the convertible like he's a prom queen," laughs Pitt. "I don't know what the crowd thought, because suddenly there was this last-place clown car with someone sitting in the back waving. I don't even think they looked at the driver."

"Apart from Silverstone, the first time around, that was the most surreal moment of the film for me," chuckles Bacheta. "We've got the Ferrari drivers behind us, McLaren ahead of us, and Brad Pitt driving the car, with me, sat on the back, waving at the crowd like I'm the most famous guy in the world."

Alas, the drivers' parade didn't make the final cut, with Kosinski having to trim the Mexican section by forty-five seconds during editing.

After the drivers returned to the paddock, there was still more work to be done, with Kosinski filming Pitt on the grid, as Sonny readies for the race. "We didn't have our car out there this time," says Hefferman. "We walked to where it would be on the grid in the story and shot Brad." They also used the opportunity to film some drivers they had yet to capture. "We were always ticking them off as we went," continues Hefferman. "We'd got [Fernando] Alonso, but hadn't got Lance Stroll, so this was a great chance to have him in the background as Brad was getting prepped."

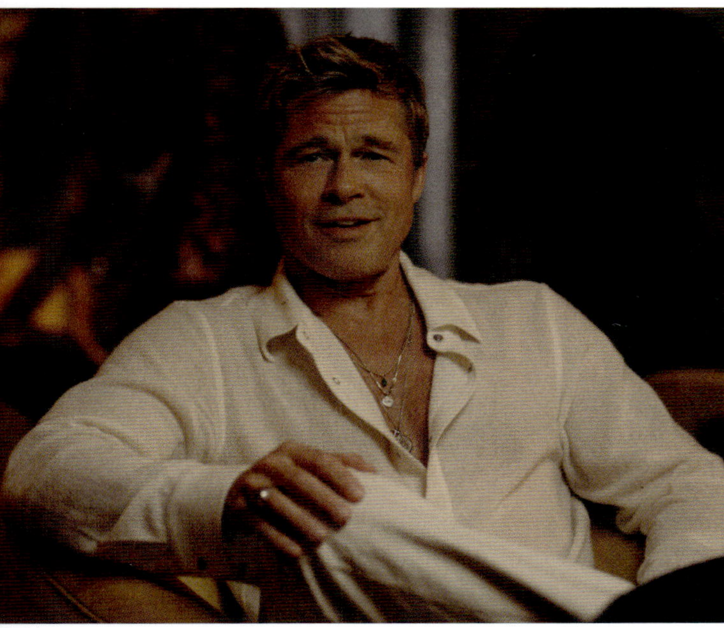

F1 touched down in Las Vegas in mid-November for a week of filming in the buildup to the city's Grand Prix. In story terms, Vegas marks a watershed for APXGP, after their upgraded floor that helps the team score valuable World Championship points is found to be illegal by the FIA. For Sonny and Joshua, too, Vegas sees a thawing of their rivalry, as Kate asks the two drivers to join her for dinner, after which they play poker, with the winner getting to pick who's the number-one driver for the race. Kate's plan is to use the card game as a bonding exercise, with Sonny and Joshua learning that both lost their fathers at age thirteen, a fact that galvanizes them into putting their differences aside and the team first, with Joshua walking away from the table the victor after Sonny throws away his winning hand. This play impresses Kate and proves to be the spark that ignites their relationship.

Sonny (Brad Pitt) and Joshua (Damson Idris) start to understand each other better during a poker game with Kate (Kerry Condon).

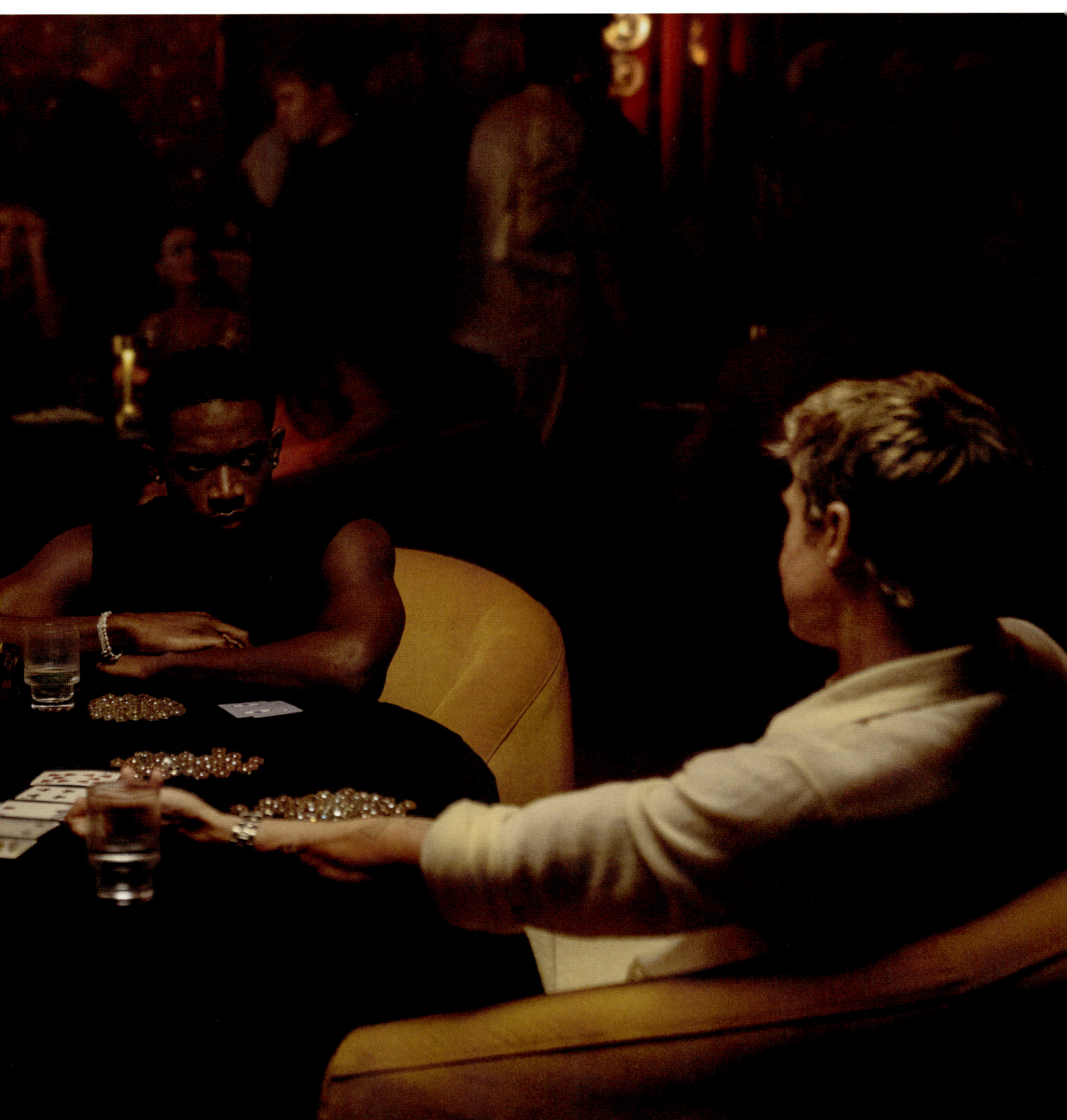

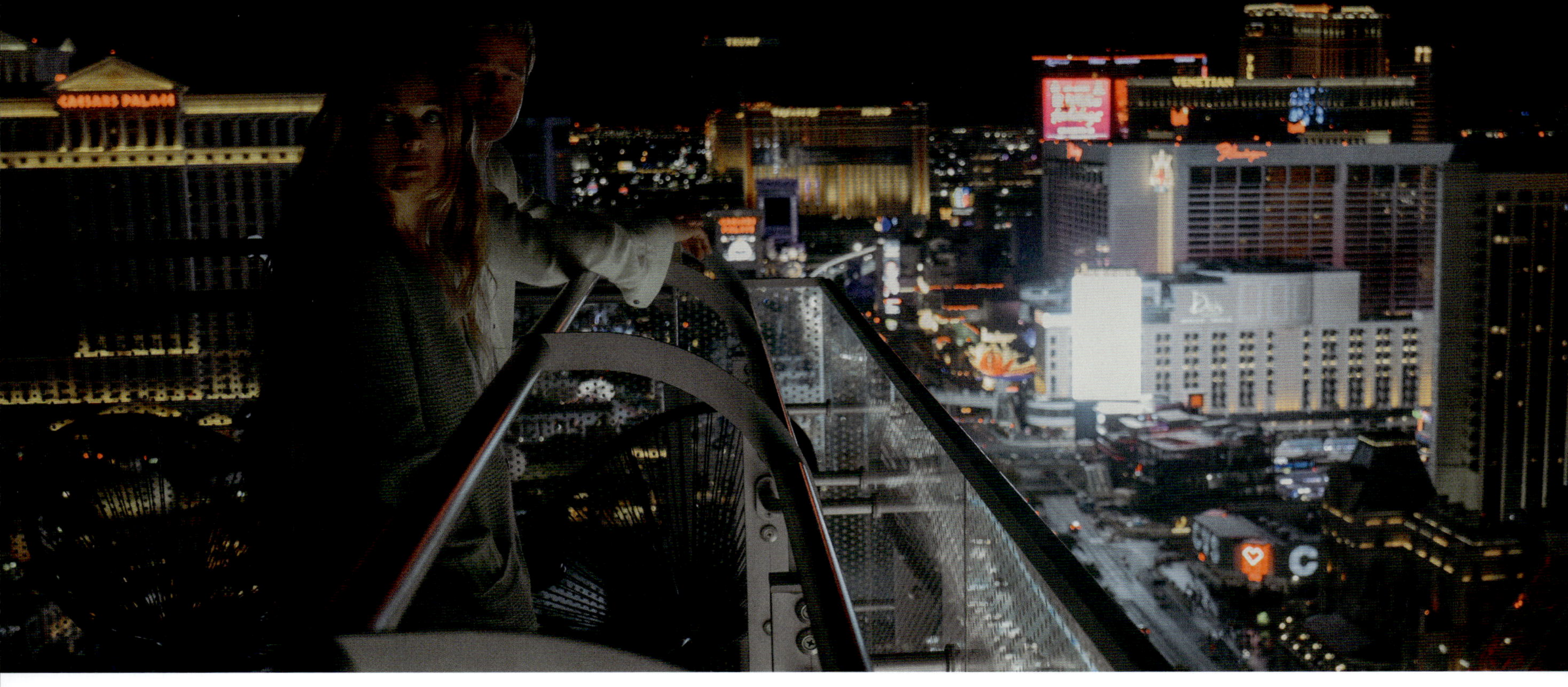

LAS VEGAS GP

Filming kicked off in a Vegas parking garage on the morning of Monday, November 18, for a post-race meeting between Sonny—who has been let go by Ruben on account of his long list of injuries—and the duplicitous Banning, who is conspiring to take over APXGP and wants Sonny to stay on as team principal.

The garage showdown was followed by a scene of Sonny running along the old Vegas strip at sunset as part of his pre-race ritual. "It's not easy putting Brad Pitt in the middle of Las Vegas, running down the street. But we did it, and it was good," recalls Hefferman.

Early Tuesday evening was spent filming a scene on the balcony of the Cosmopolitan of Las Vegas hotel between Sonny and Kate, where Sonny talks about his love of driving, telling Kate it doesn't matter where or when, or even if anyone's watching, what matters is when he's behind the wheel and flying, he feels free.

"It was freezing, and the two of us were in skimpy outfits," reveals Condon. "They put all these heaters on the balcony, and I felt like I was getting third-degree burns from them. I felt like my leg was melting. But Brad was in the middle of a big speech, and I didn't have the heart to stop him. It's an important moment for Brad's character, to reveal a little bit about himself and his motivations for racing."

Sonny's heartfelt moment is interrupted by Ruben, who arrives to let them that know that the FIA has received an anonymous tip that

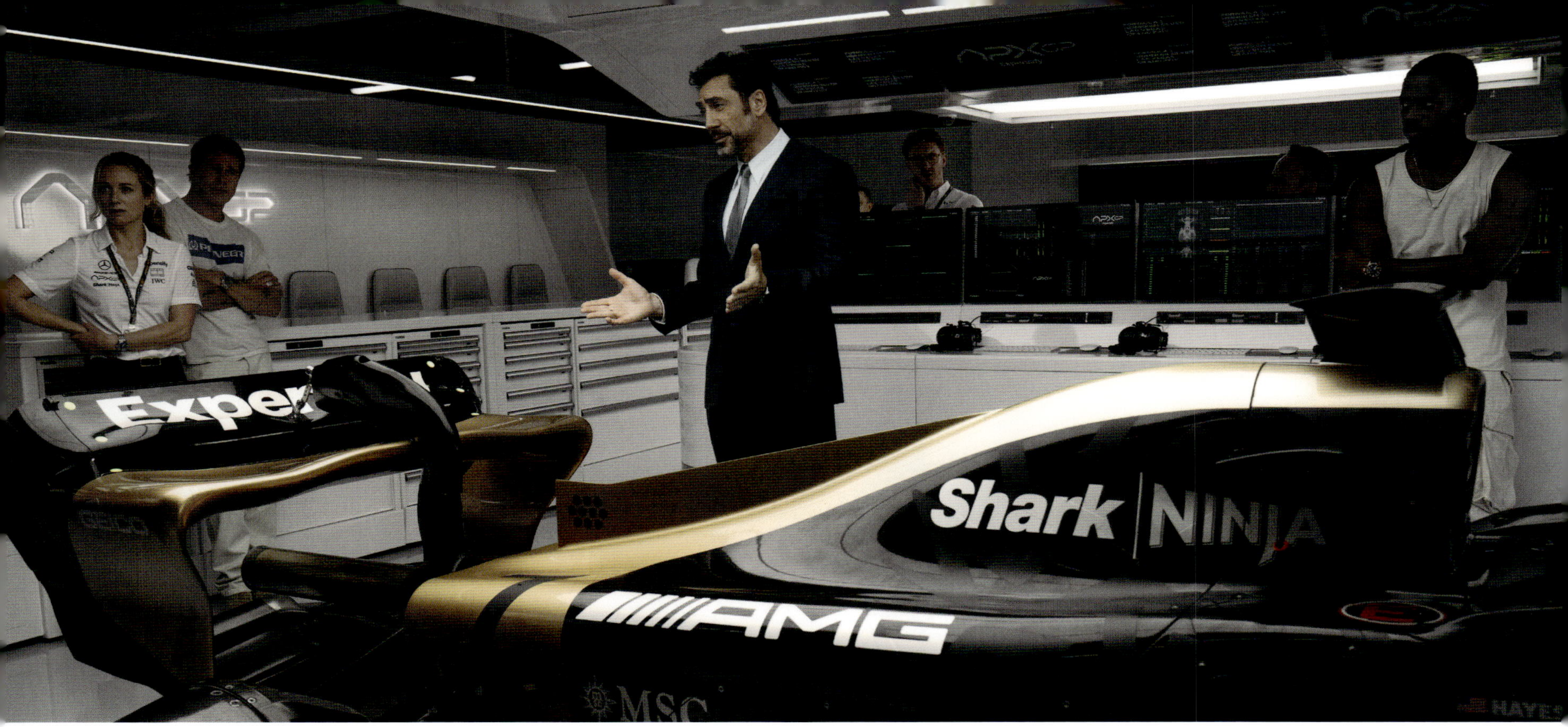

Top Left: Sonny (Brad Pitt) tells Kate (Kerry Condon) about his love of driving while looking out at the Vegas strip.

Top Right: The APXGP team learns that their car's rippled floor design is in violation of Formula One rules.

Below: While in Las Vegas, Banning (Tobias Menzies) tells Sonny (Brad Pitt) that he intends to take over the APXGP team.

their new rippled floor design—built by Kate for "combat"—is in violation of the rules. "They're coming for our car," rages Ruben, a fury that he later redirects toward the examiner from the FIA, who informs them that they must revert to using the old—and less successful—floor design.

"There's nothing better than watching Javier Bardem play rage," laughs Idris. "It's a great moment in the film, because it's the first time that everyone really loses hope of winning. Sonny and Joshua have finally got themselves together, and then—boom—the rug's pulled from underneath them. They go into the Vegas race without their heads. And it leads to a horrible crash for Sonny, which then reveals he has health issues and ultimately pulls him out of the world of racing."

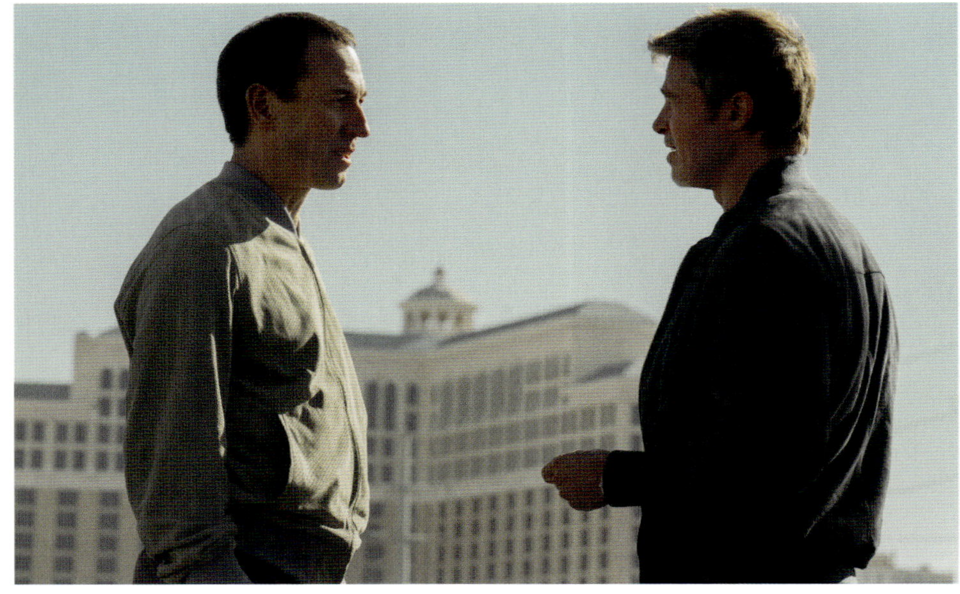

Ruben's tirade, along with the hotel scene between Kate and Sonny, and the poker game with Sonny, Joshua, and Kate, had been shot back in the U.K. in June. "That poker scene took two days," remembers Condon. "That was hard. That was real acting. Because there were no cars distracting me."

"The wonderful Kerry Condon. She's just got this lovely effervescence about her," says Pitt. "In our scenes, she gives off such warmth, and I love an actor who can fill in the blanks between the words. She's got so much going on. She saved my ass in two scenes. She was the engine and kept them alive. I owe her flowers."

Filming wrapped on the Cosmopolitan balcony scene at 1 a.m., then Kosinski and Pitt made their way to the track—which was still being prepared ahead of the race—to join Idris, Bacheta, Dolby, and British racing driver Duncan Tappy for a low-speed sighter lap around the circuit. "We were allowed to get on the track in a regular rental car between 3 a.m. and 4 a.m.," says Hefferman. "We had this hour's window where the drivers took Brad and Damson out on the track as they would drive it. They couldn't go any more than 50 miles per hour, so it wasn't about speed. It was about familiarization. It was the first time they were going to see it with the lights on and understand what they were getting themselves in for."

In reality, Las Vegas was about to host only its second Grand Prix, having joined the Formula One calendar in 2023, with teams racing on a temporary street circuit running 6.2 kilometers (3.85 miles) around the city, incorporating part of the world-famous Las Vegas Strip, with drivers blasting past Caesars Palace, the Bellagio, and the Venetian, and reaching a top speed of in excess of 220 miles per hour.

A street circuit, by its very nature, is unpredictable and trickier to drive, with its narrow confines and concrete walls, making it dangerous for the drivers. "The moment we found we were driving in Vegas, it definitely made you sweat a little, knowing we were going to go there with the cast and get them to drive around a street circuit," remembers Dolby. "On a street circuit, there's no room for error. If you make one little mistake, there's a concrete wall waiting to meet you."

Fortunately, Renee Wilm, CEO of the Las Vegas Grand Prix, F1, and the FIA, agreed to leave the lights on Wednesday night too, to allow the stunt team half an hour, starting at 2:30 a.m., to drive around the circuit in their F2 cars. "None of us had driven it," says Bacheta. "With Abu Dhabi, Austin, Silverstone, and the like, we could tell Brad and Damson exactly what was going to happen because we'd all been there. With Vegas, we hadn't. F1 had only been there once, so knowledge of the place was quite limited. We had very limited track time. We didn't have time to rehearse. We had sighting laps, but our sighting laps were when the track was full of construction workers, so we couldn't go above 30 miles per hour." Moreover, the temperatures that week were warm during the day but very cold at night, which made it harder for the tires to generate friction, meaning less grip. "Aside from it being a street circuit, it was slippery. And it was zero degrees Celsius, so it was freezing *and* tricky. Everything that you'd want in your favor was against us in Vegas."

In the end, only Pitt went out for a series of "hot laps" with the stunt drivers on Thursday

Opposite: Schematic of the Las Vegas track.

Below: The production crew relied on a model map of the Vegas circuit to plan every step of the day's filming.

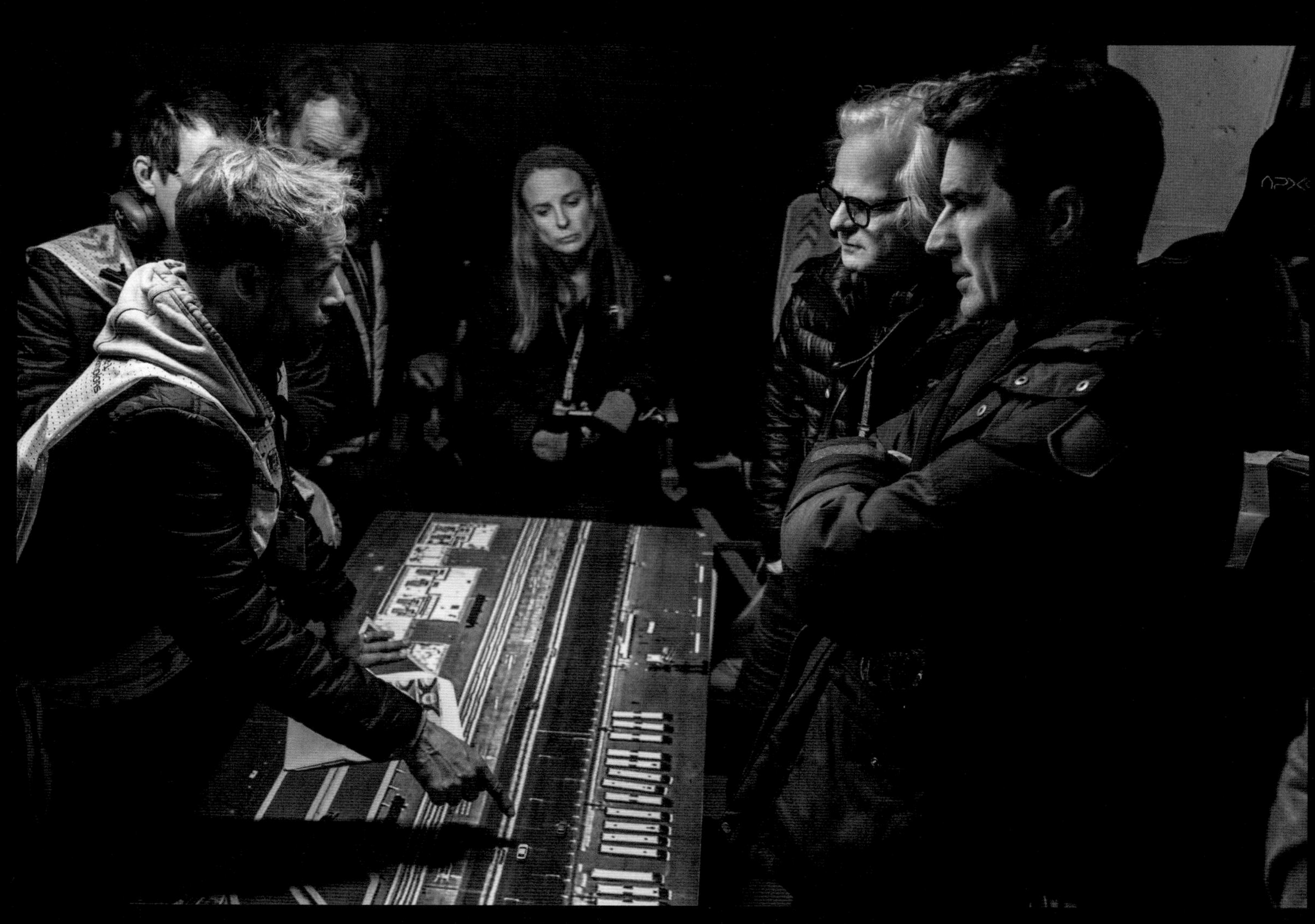

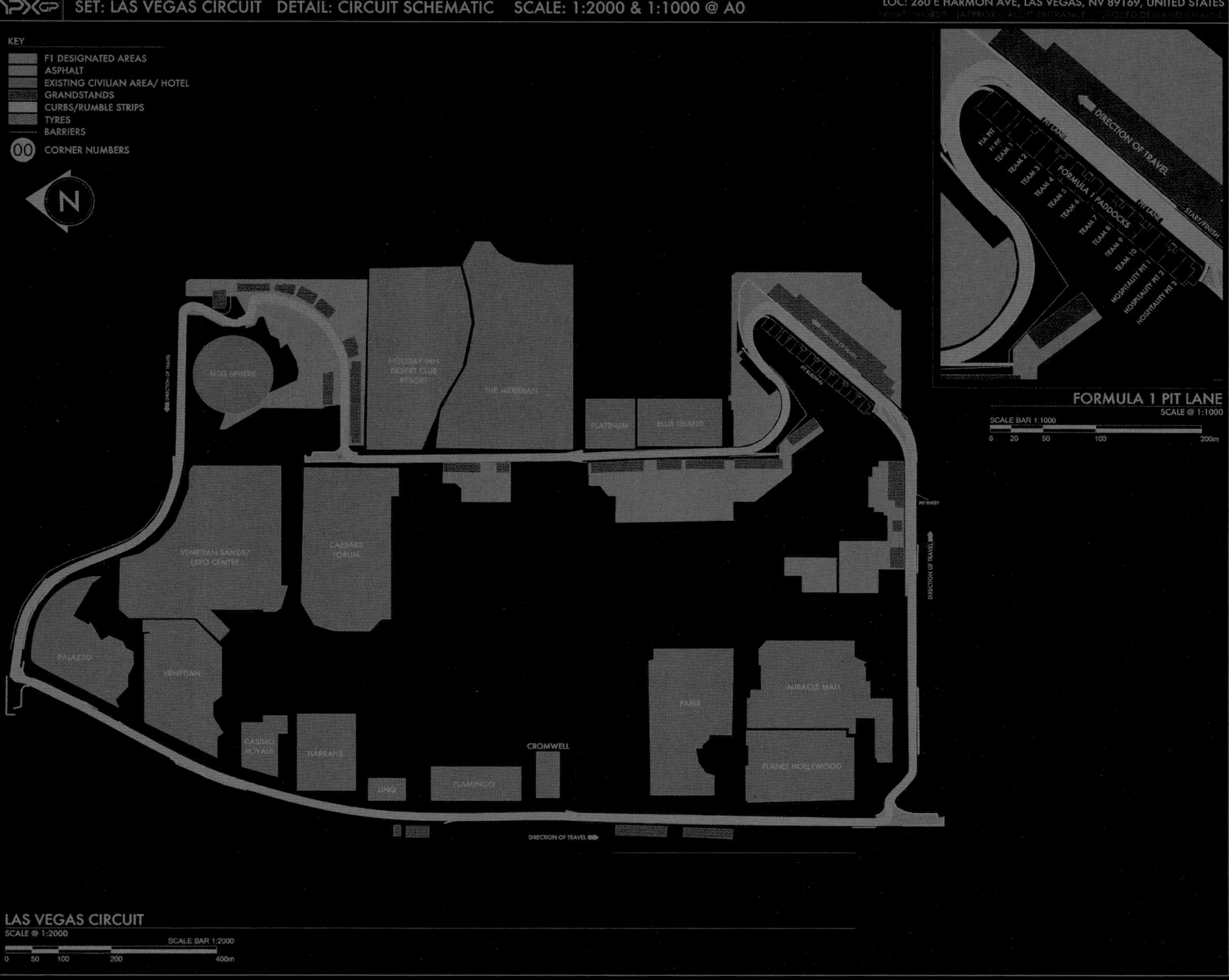

afternoon, for a twenty-minute session, and that evening for ten minutes. "Brad drove incredibly well," Bacheta continues. "The car was moving around for him. It was the least amount of grip he'd ever had in this car and the most critical circuit he had to drive it on. If he made one tiny mistake, he would have been in the wall. Moreover, the risk and insurance guys didn't want cast to drive at all in Vegas, so there was added pressure to not fuck up."

"Vegas was sketchy," Pitt admits. "We didn't get any practice on that track. I'd only seen it on a sim. It was cold. It was damp. And it required a whole other kind of driving style, something we hadn't experienced before. I love how all these tracks have different personalities and different flavors. They're all different beasts that you have to respect and make your peace with. But it was slippery as fuck. It's a strange, scrappy, messy, sketchy kind of experience. Still fun. Going full throttle down the Vegas strip was still a high."

"I watched it once when Brad went out on a 'hot lap' and they were filming it, and I never watched him do a 'hot lap' ever again, because I was nervous," reveals Condon. "I hated it. And that Vegas track reminded me of the danger of it. They're driving on a street I can drive down. At night. It seemed a little bit nuts, to be honest."

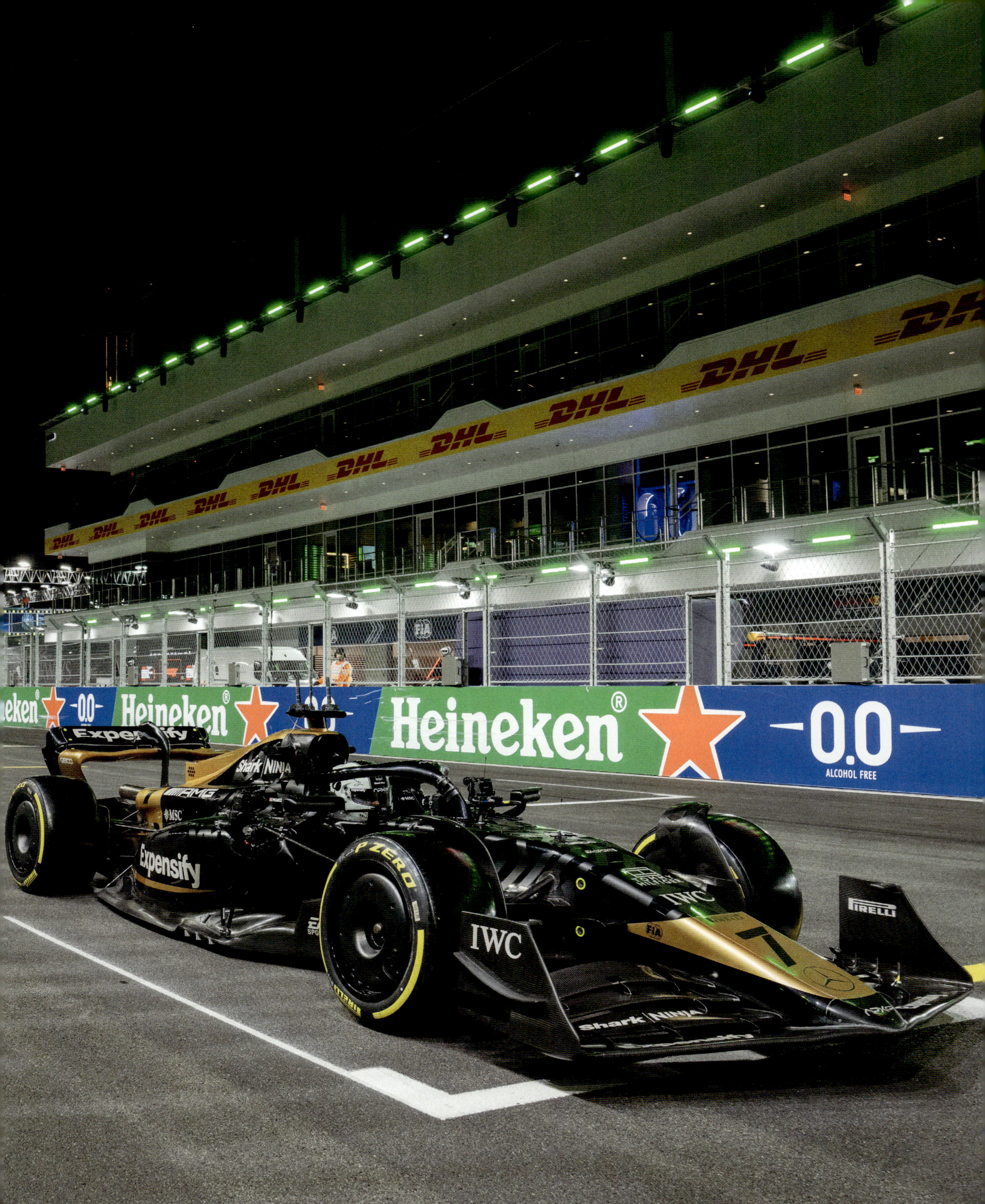
DHL
Heineken
0.0
ALCOHOL FREE
Expensify
IWC
PIRELLI
P ZERO
Shark NINJA

Sonny (Brad Pitt) in place at the starting grid, ready for filming.

Given the tricky conditions, Bacheta decided to take it easy when he went out intially with Pitt, who found his caution a little frustrating. "It was a first feel of the track, and we weren't pushing in any crazy fashion," Pitt recalls. "Anytime you get on a new track, you're starting to become intimate with it, like, where are the bumps? Where are the turning points? Where can you push? Where do you need to be a little cautious? Luch had laid out for me a couple of places that were really sketchy, but it was the one time I got upset with Luch, because he was being more cautious than I was, I guess. And I wanted him to get out of the way so I could drive and bang some curbs."

"Every lap he was coming out of the corners, I could hear, from my car, his wheels spinning on the exit, and I was praying he was keeping it on the track," Bacheta remembers. "I was talking him through it. But he started to have fun with it. He was coming up behind me, trying to overtake, and I was trying to calm him down a bit and tell him not to. But he was having fun with it, which, in hindsight, was really funny, and also shows his racer instinct. At the time, I was really stressed out, because I just wanted it to go well and not crash."

Back in mission control in the APXGP garage, which, in Vegas, was at the far end of the pit lane, Kosinski, Bruckheimer, Hefferman, cinematographer Claudio Miranda, and co. were watching the action unfold on their monitors and also feeling a little stressed. "We'd put Brad on the sim so he could get used to the track, but it only gives you so much," says Hefferman.

But Pitt kept all four wheels on the track and didn't hit the wall during his "hot lap" sessions—unlike his character, who, in the "race," would suffer a spectacular crash in Vegas.

"Brad drove like a pro," says Bruckheimer. "Some of the F1 drivers were slipping and sliding, but Brad pulled it off."

Prior to that, the production still had much to do, starting with scenes at the three-floor OMNIA Nightclub in Caesars Place, with Joshua, Cash, a thousand extras, and Dutch DJ Tiësto on the turntables. "It felt like a real club, a real vibe. Lewis came and had so much fun," says Idris. "It was epic," concurs Hefferman. "Tiësto is such a force of nature. He's also a big Formula One fan. So, it was almost keeping it in the family."

After wrapping at OMNIA, Kosinski, Bruckheimer, Miranda, Hefferman, and co. headed for turn four at the Vegas track where the APXGP cars were housed in a temporary garage during the race weekend, in preparation for Bacheta, Dolby, and Tappy to do their first track laps in a thirty-minute session starting at 2:30 a.m. "No Formula One drivers had been out there yet, so there was no grip," recalls Hefferman. "It was super dusty, because they had been working on the track. They needed their absolute concentration to stay on track. It was super slippery. And it's 2:30 in the morning. Whose brain is really that engaged at that time?"

For Miranda, the Vegas circuit was also tricky, but for other reasons. "They have the track so bright it looks like a *Tron* set. It's like this burned-out, bright light, and the city's kind of dark in comparison," says Miranda, who petitioned for the organizer to dim the lights a fraction, "so that when I exposed the track, Vegas lifts up." Unfortunately, Miranda lost his battle.

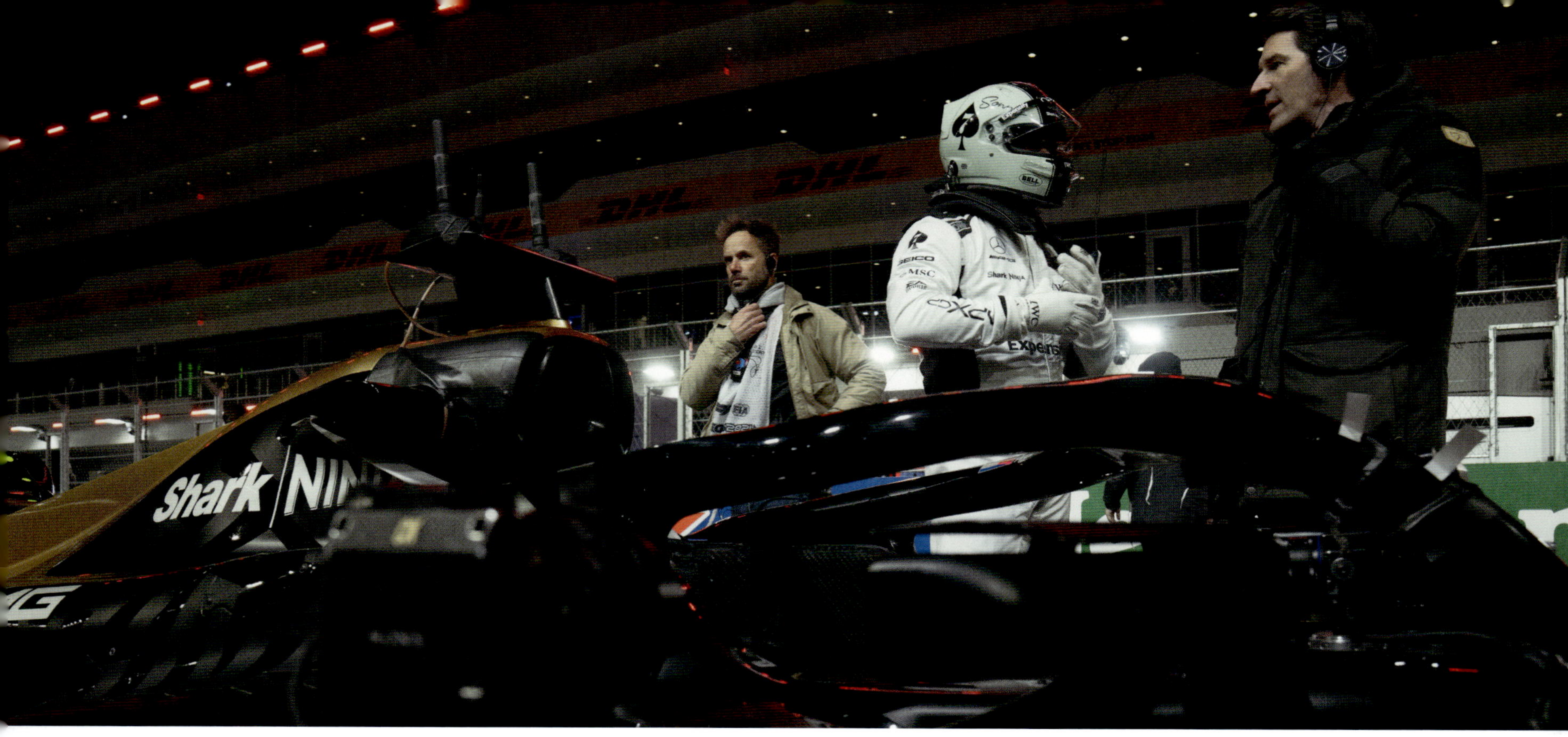

Thursday saw Pitt back out on the track with Bacheta, followed by scenes of Condon, Bodnia, Nickleby, and Fazio on the pit wall, together with a scene just before the lights go out for the start of the race as Sonny, P5 on the grid, realizes he doesn't have a lucky playing card with him—an omen for the horror soon to come. Blindsided by swerving Red Bull, Sonny clips its wheels and is vaulted into the fence, a violent impact that totals his car and sends him to the hospital.

Kosinski also shot scenes on the pit wall, with Condon and the rest of the APXGP crew reacting to the crash. "We had a tiny moment where Lukasz Bielan had to go onto the track to shoot me running to the fence, then they've got to get the hell out of there," recalls Condon. "That was one of those ones where we got two takes, and you've got to get it pretty much the first time. We did it once, and then these vans pulled in behind me, on the pit wall, which kind of fucked up the shot. But we had such a great camera department. He framed it up so he could get rid of the background and just get my face."

For the production, Friday was pretty much a mirror of Thursday, with Bacheta, Dolby, and Tappy putting in more stunt laps and Kosinski filming scenes on the pit wall and in the grand-stand as Hefferman's voice boomed out over the public address system, asking spectators to react to Sonny's "crash" and its aftermath.

Post-qualifying, the production moved out onto the track, where special effects supervisor Keith Dawson positioned a crashed "aftermath buck," the result of Sonny's collision with the wall. "That was one of our old crash cars, and we rebuilt an interior so Brad could get in there," says Dawson. "We had smoke coming out the side pods and from behind him as he gets out. We also did a lot of smoke effects from where he's supposedly come from, so it looks like he's hit the wall, and you've got dust and smoke that's still airborne. We put in a lot of debris from all the crashes we had done over the course of the movie, so it looked like there was a path of destruction leading to his crashed car."

Originally, the production considered doing the Vegas crash for real, using a remote-controlled car like Sonny's crash at Silverstone.

"We started shooting [Sonny's crash sequence] in November 2023 and finished the visual effects shot in early March 2025. . . . That's almost eighteen months from start to finish to do those two shots of the crash."

JOSEPH KOSINSKI

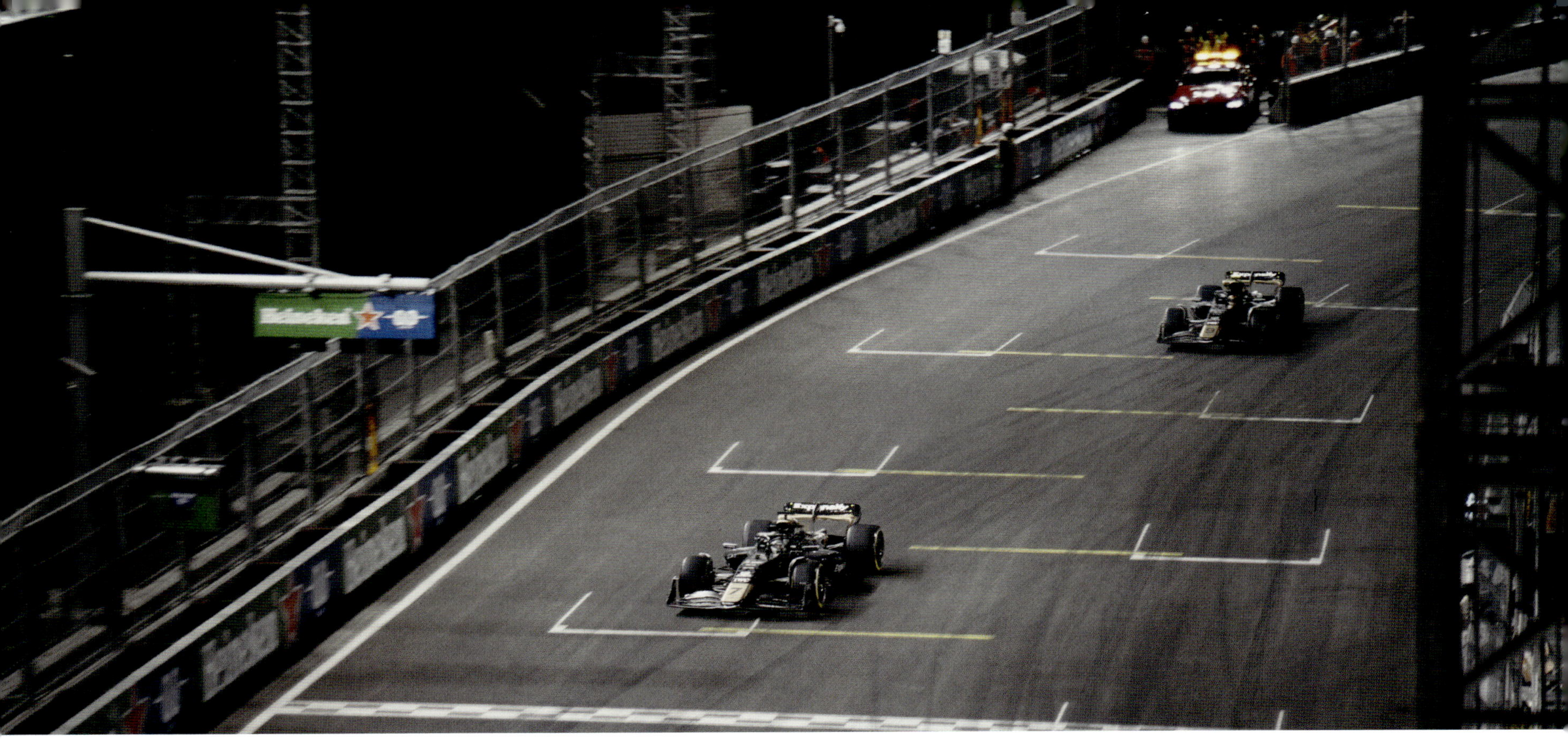

Top Left: Joseph Kosinski and Brad Pitt talk through an upcoming scene in Las Vegas.

Top Right: The two APXGP cars racing at the Las Vegas circuit.

But then Kosinski and visual effects supervisor Ryan Tudhope decided to create the crash digitally—working backward from Dawson's "aftermath buck"—and, once again, basing it on several real-life incidents. "We looked at a lot of reference videos," says Kosinski. "There was a crash in Indy Car, ten or fifteen years ago, where one of the cars went into the fence, and there was a similar one in the Daytona 500. When a car hit a catch fence, it tends to rip all the exterior bodywork off. In both cases, the drivers were fine, which is a testament to how safe these cars are now. But visually, it felt very different to Joshua's crash, which was more of a launch into the air."

There was also another crash, this one involving stunt driver Craig Dolby during filming in Abu Dhabi in April 2024, that also "helped" Tudhope create the shot, providing the visual effects team with real footage they could utilize to provide the basis for the digital version. "We were running the cars at high speed and there was some water on the track or some bumps on the track that upset the car, which happens, and it went into a spin," recalls Kosinski of Dolby's accident. "Again, testament to how these cars were built. No one was hurt. But we did get to see firsthand, with our cameras onboard, what it looks like when a car hits the wall. It was scary to watch it on camera, but luckily Craig was fine, and the car did what it was supposed to do, which was protect him."

In keeping with Kosinski's desire that the racing be as authentic as possible, Tudhope's visual effects team even ran Sonny's Vegas crash by the powers that be at the FIA and F1 to make sure it obeyed the rules of Formula One safety.

"There are a lot of safety considerations in these cars," says Tudhope, "so we wanted to make sure we were not doing anything in the movie that is impossible to happen to the real car and that the sport has taken a lot of effort to avoid happening. For example, all the wheels and tires coming off. That's a real danger, and there's a lot of technology involved in stopping that happening. And we honor that."

Ultimately, Sonny's Vegas crash, much like the Silverstone one, was a fusion of special and visual effects that took many months to complete and involved both practical and digital elements. "We started shooting that sequence in November 2023 and finished the visual effects shot in early March 2025," says Kosinski. "I don't think I've ever spent more time on one shot in any movie I've ever worked on. That's almost eighteen months from start to finish to do those two shots of the crash. Very complex simulations to pull that off, and a testament to Ryan and his team that we were able to create something that looked as photoreal as everything else in the film, because obviously we were not going to do a crash like that for real. It would be too dangerous for everyone involved. To pull that off, using real plates and simulations, was a lot of work, but they did a great job."

ABU DHABI GP

Before George Russell's Mercedes had taken the checkered flag just ahead of teammate Lewis Hamilton at the real Las Vegas Grand Prix, the cast and crew of *F1* had already left the U.S., heading to Abu Dhabi for several weeks of filming. This would take them up to and beyond the Grand Prix on December 8, which marked both the end of the 2024 Formula One season and the end of the movie.

"It's the bulk of the third act," says screenwriter Ehren Kruger of Abu Dhabi. "It's a long race, and a lot needed to happen. It was also the race where we wanted to use the fewest tricks or rule bending. We wanted to depict that this team had come a long way, over nine races; everyone had become more proficient at their job, from the garage to the way these two drivers work as teammates. They're still rivals. They both want to win. But, for the first time, they're operating as a team."

Despite being fired by Ruben in Vegas on account of his medical condition, Sonny rocks up at the Yas Marina circuit for one last shot at Grand Prix glory, joining Joshua on the starting grid with APXGP's very future at stake. With Kate's rippled floor now deemed legal—it was Banning who sent the falsified paperwork to the FIA, which led to its disqualification—Sonny and Joshua are in a bullish mood. Although only a victory will save APXGP. So, when Sonny crashes into a wall with three laps to go, that win looks increasingly unlikely. The accident brings out the red flag, which stops the race, and Sonny must get his car back to the pit lane, without aid, to not be disqualified.

The red flag was a late addition to the script. "We wrote it a few weeks before we shot the Abu Dhabi section," recalls Kruger. "To stop the race at the eleventh hour and have a high-stakes finish was something we hadn't done in any previous race. It would be new, exciting, and perfectly realistic. To make or break your career, your life, or your reputation, all of that, into three laps. And when you're in the car, those three laps would feel like an eternity."

The idea for the red flag belonged to Luciano Bacheta. "Joe was very open to ideas, so the script was always evolving," reveals the stunt driver. "With Abu Dhabi, Joe said, 'Just write something.' So, I sent it over. He said, 'That's great.' Then he sent it to Lewis, who made some changes. Stuff you only really know if you're in Formula One day in, day out. Those specifics Lewis was able to really dial into."

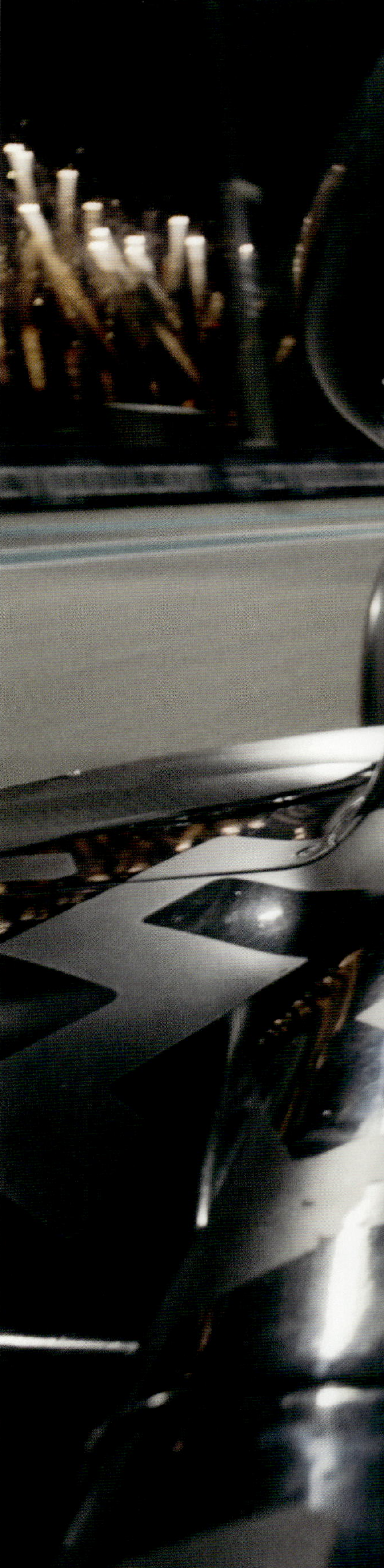

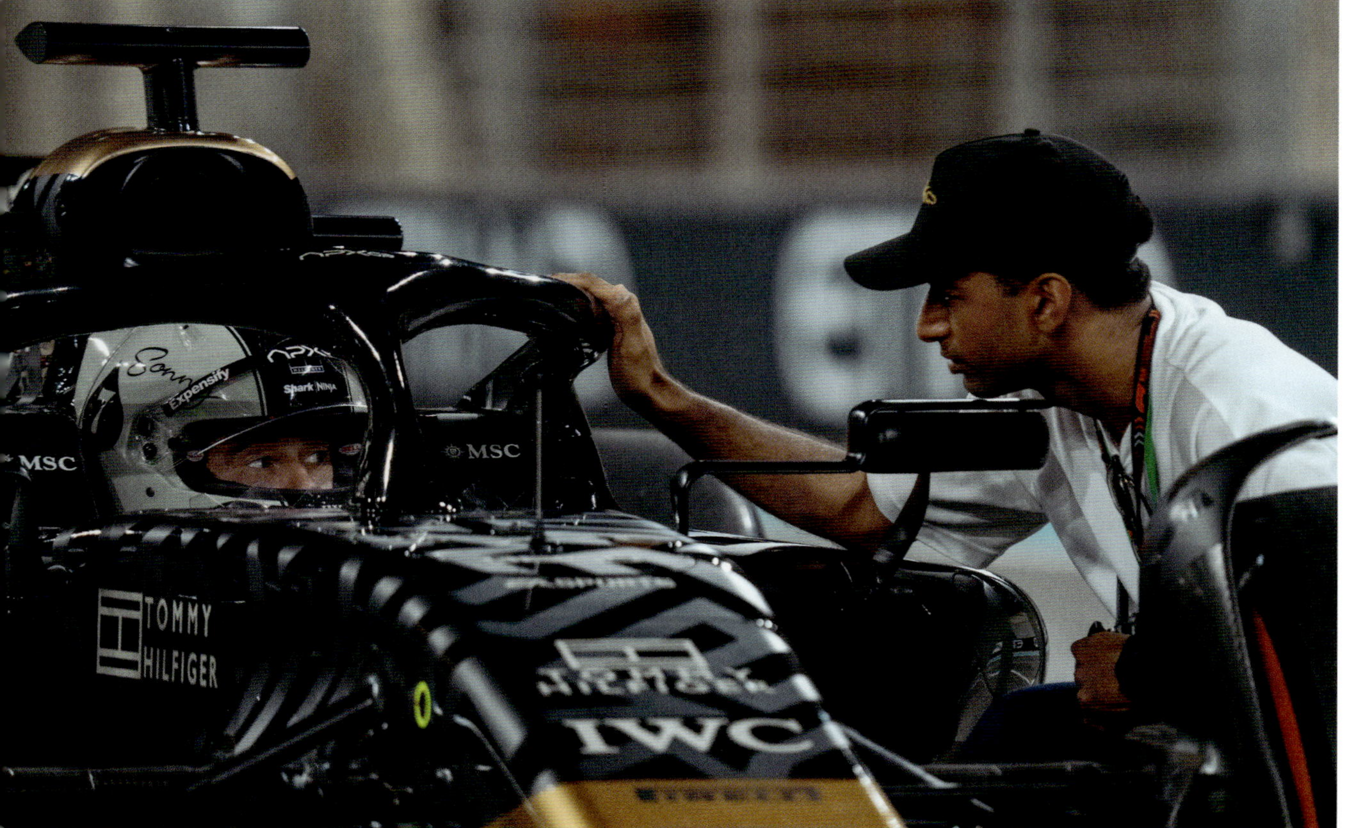

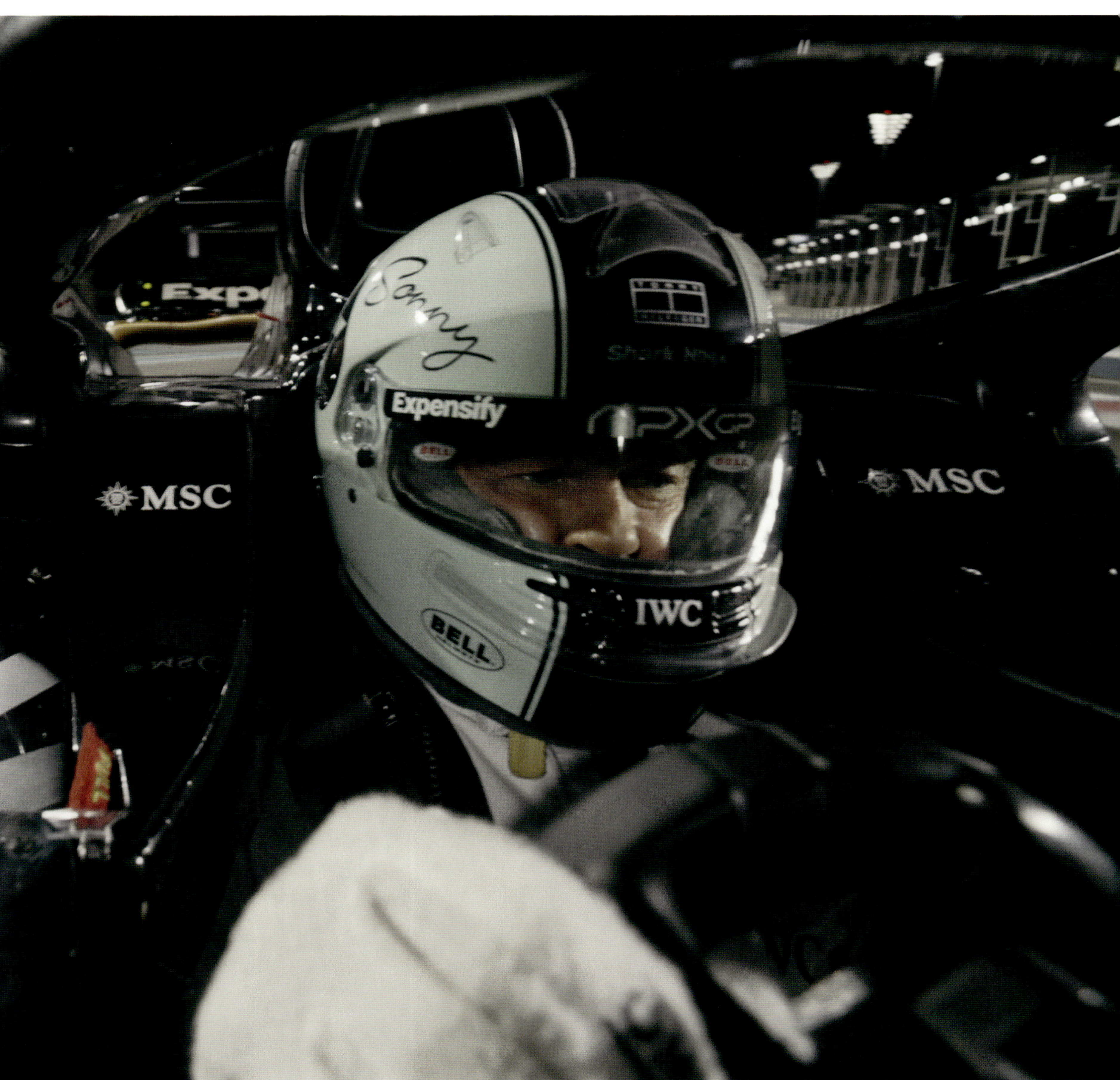

Bottom Left: Luciano Bacheta gives Brad Pitt a pep talk before taking to the track.

Above: Sonny (Brad Pitt) struggles to maintain his APXGP car during the Vegas Grand Prix, moments before his crash.

KEY PERSONNEL ROLES

Formula One teams are made up of hundreds—in some cases, thousands—of employees. The drivers are the most recognizable, but there are several other senior personnel who also receive a slice of the limelight.

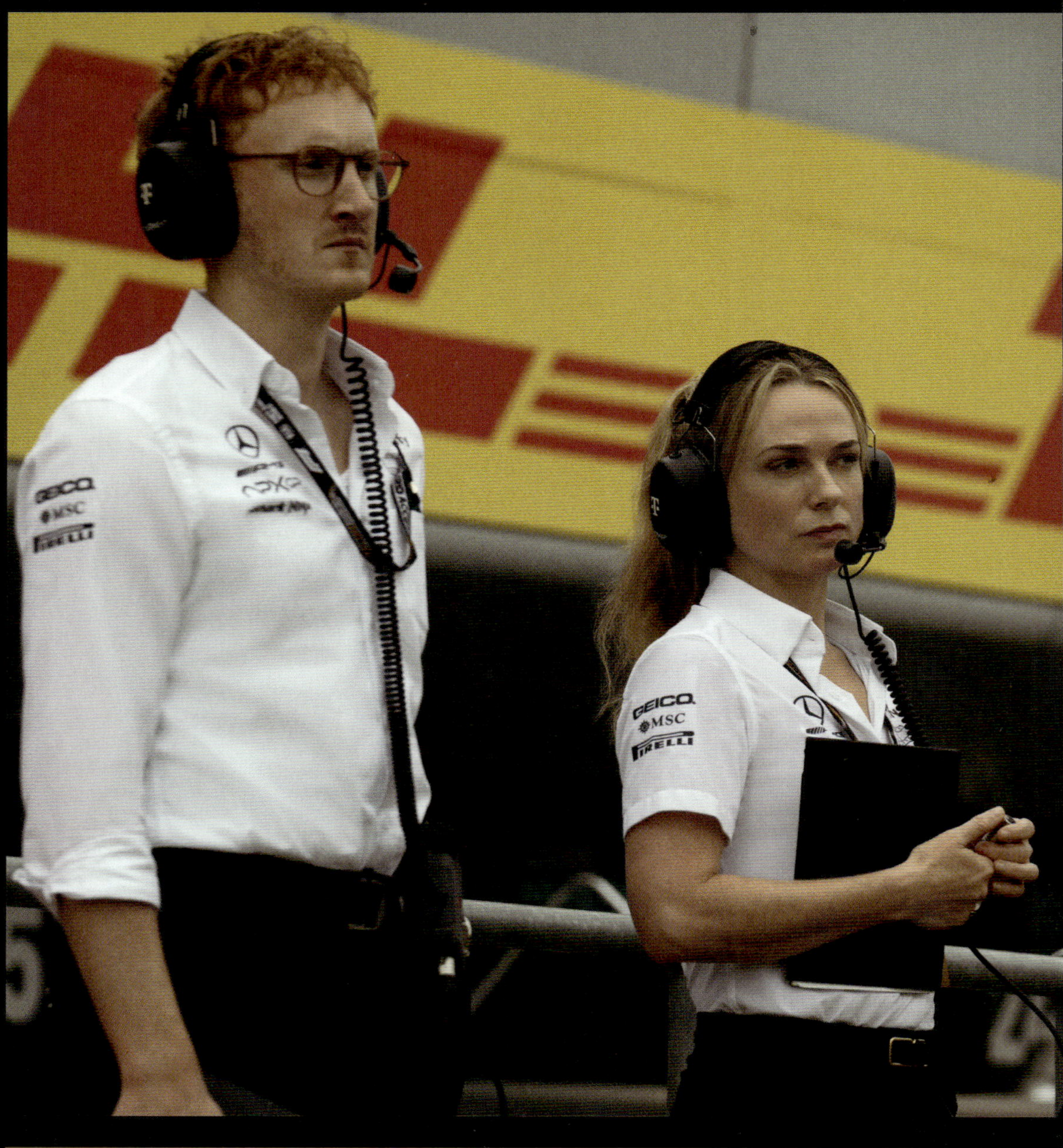

SPORTING DIRECTOR

Teams have many departments, but their main goal is to be as successful as possible on the track. So, everything that relates to race performance falls under the sporting director's remit.

The sporting director will represent the team in discussions about rules and regulations with the FIA—the governing body—and attend all meetings during race weekends that outline how an event is going to be handled.

The sporting director often has the entire race team reporting to them, so any support that is needed, from the drivers to the mechanics, will go through them. This can also include overseeing the pit stop crew and the overall operation of the team during a race.

CHIEF STRATEGIST

The fastest way to finish a race is not always by driving flat out, due to issues such as tire wear and fuel consumption. The chief strategist leads the strategy engineering team to work out how to best approach a race weekend. That starts with the run plans before the first practice session, so the team can gather the data from all the track running. This can also involve understanding new parts that have been put on the car, as well as how it performs with both low and high fuel loads.

The chief strategist will work through all of the information to understand how the car, tires, and drivers are performing in comparison to their rivals. Thousands of race simulations are then run to try to best guess how a race will pan out—factoring in the weather forecast and what other teams will do—to identify the best strategic options.

In each race, the regulations dictate a driver must use at least two different types of slick tire, mandating a pit stop in dry conditions. The timing of this pit stop can be crucial in terms of gaining or losing positions, as can the type of tire.

These strategic options are often outlined as "Plan A," "Plan B," and so on, and while a driver will start on "Plan A," incidents within the race can see other plans adopted as it evolves.

RACE ENGINEER [NICKLEBY]

The race engineer is the link between the driver and the rest of the car's engineering team, known as the car crew. Each driver has their own race engineer, who is on the team radio, talking about strategy and asking the driver for feedback on the car's performance. As the sole direct point of contact for the driver when they are in the car, the race engineer will relay the information the driver needs in a way they can understand while behind the wheel.

TECHNICAL DIRECTOR [KATE]

While the sporting side is looked after by the sporting director, the car development is the responsibility of the technical director. While a big part of the role is factory-based, technical directors are often in attendance at races as well, to see how the car is performing on the track and to hear the feedback the drivers give during a race weekend.

The technical director oversees the entire car design and development, pulling together the different professionals that work on a car, including aerodynamicists and other engineers. They sign off on the upgrade plans for the season and delegate resources among different projects, including the current car and the following year's chassis.

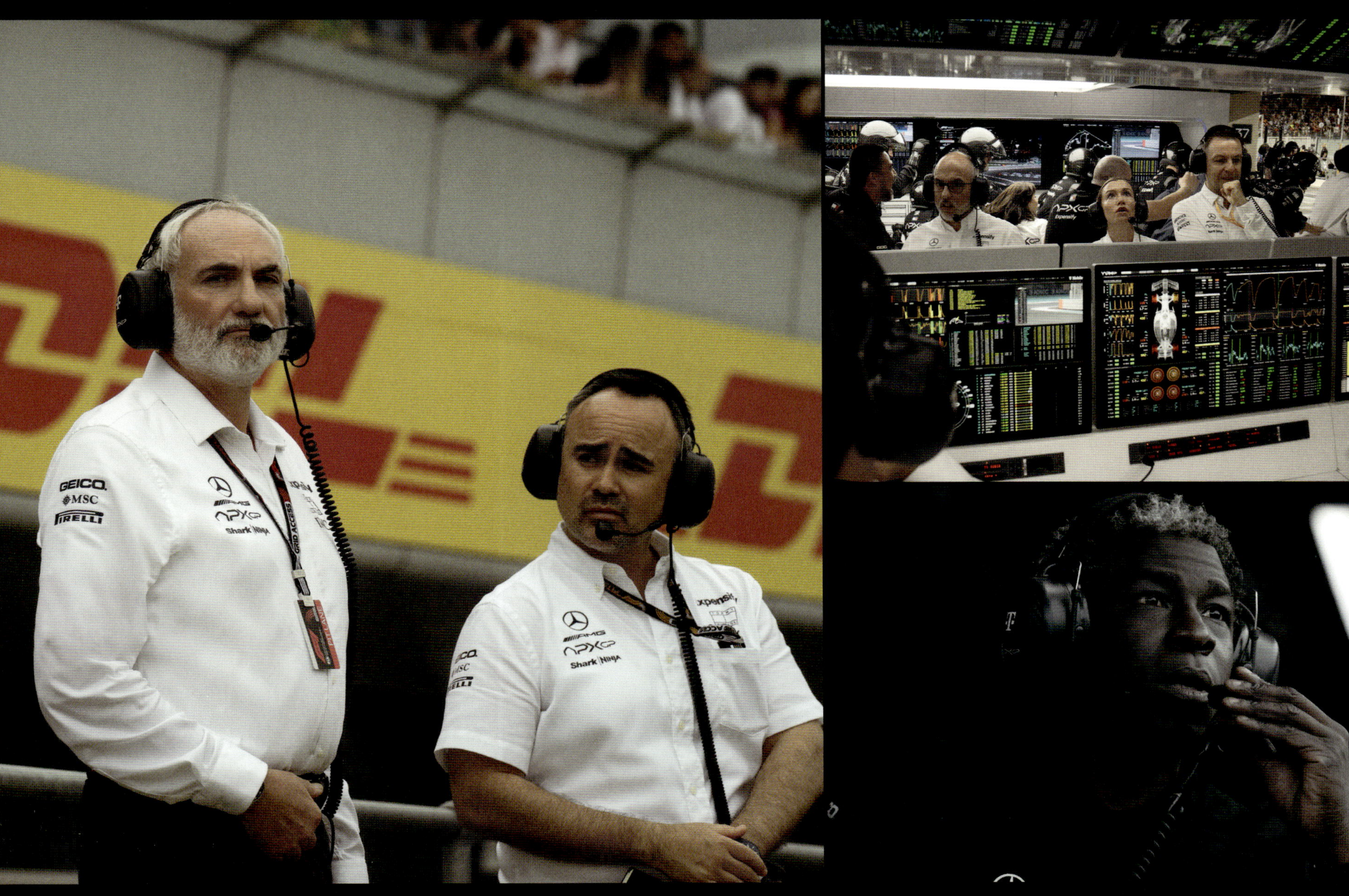

TEAM PRINCIPAL [KASPAR]

The team principal is essentially the boss. On a Formula One team, they are responsible for the overall operation of the company, including driver selection and the hiring and firing of most personnel.

The team principal is who you will see on television speaking to the media, the face of the team who also deals with sponsors and guests. The team principal looks to create a structure that will work best from a managerial point of view, as well as cultivate the culture they want within the team.

A team principal might delegate key responsibilities to other personnel, but any final decisions are often made by them.

RACE ENGINEER [FAZIO]

The race engineer also liaises with the car crew to suggest changes that can improve the car based on the driver's comments, sorting through the data between sessions to devise potential engineering solutions.

CHIEF ENGINEER [DODGE]

A chief engineer has an overview of how both cars are performing on the track and works on solutions in real time. The chief engineer is in contact with the two race engineers (see left) as well as the rest of the trackside engineering team and the factory-based personnel to try to get the best possible performance out of the car.

While drivers have their own likes and dislikes when it comes to car handling, the chief engineer's position across both cars allows them to identify common themes and areas for improvement, as well as suggest set-up options based on what each car is doing. The chief engineer can also look after the car's compliance with technical regulations, communicating with the FIA on such matters if necessary.

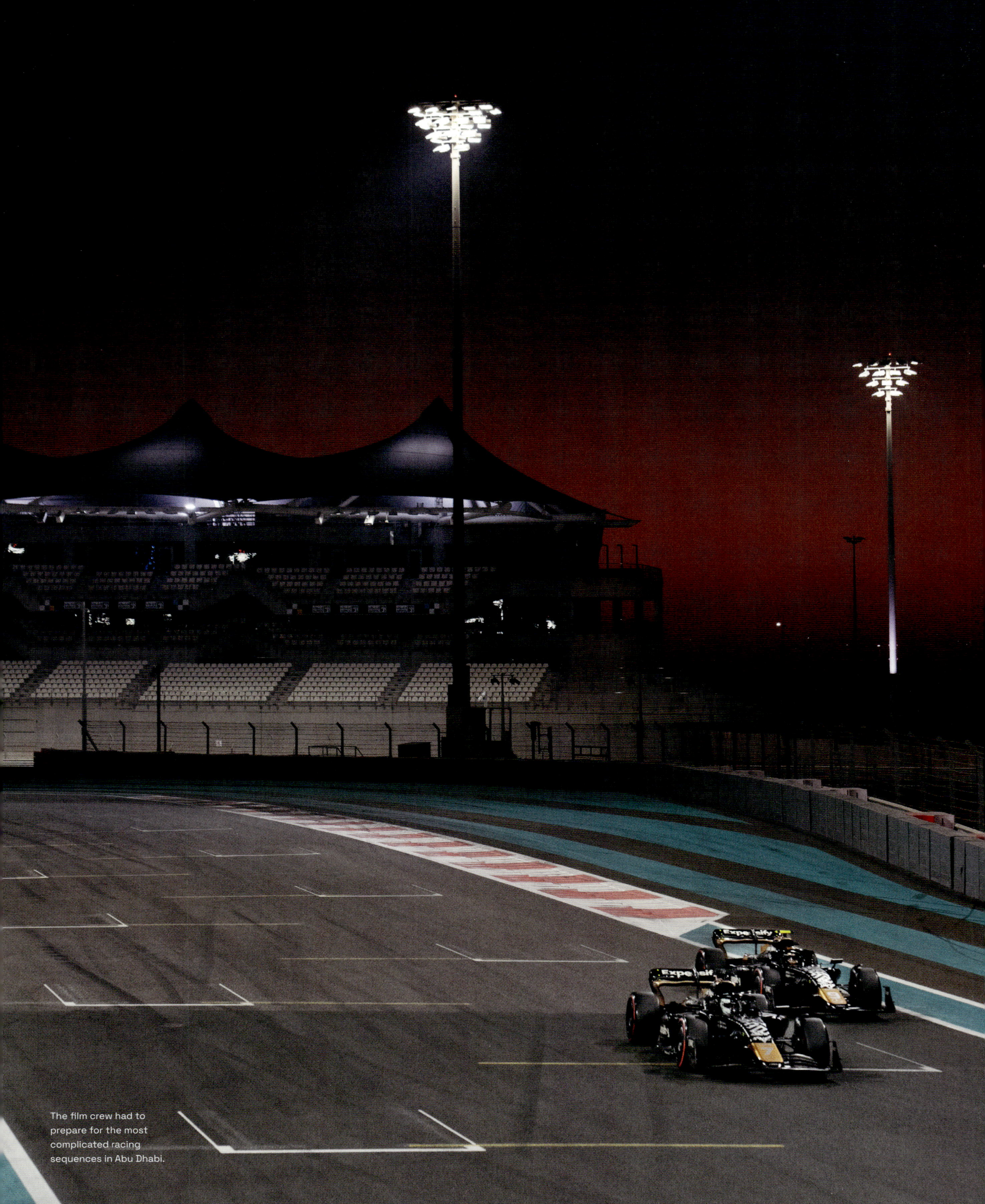

The film crew had to prepare for the most complicated racing sequences in Abu Dhabi.

"It was a scene we wrote to up the drama of the final race," says director Joseph Kosinski. "It was a great idea, and it makes the movie. It makes that final sequence that much better."

Before Kosinski could film that sequence, however, the production had a lot of work to get through. "Abu Dhabi was always going to be really challenging. Abu Dhabi was the biggest thing any of us had done," recalls first assistant director Toby Hefferman. "We had to get all our gear over, air freight the cars, unpack, rebuild them, and prep what we were doing. And we had no backup plan. At Silverstone [in 2023], we had the luxury of that location. With Abu Dhabi, we didn't. We did what we could in April, but we only had limited time after the Grand Prix before the Gulf 12-hour race started. We had limited time to rehearse. And it wasn't just actors. The crew needed to know exactly what they were doing. We couldn't just do a bunch of coverage. Operators, ACs, grips, the crew we have on the grid, they must all know exactly where they're standing, so they're not in the back of the shot. We did a couple of days' prep, and we just went into shooting from Friday, November 29."

At first, Kosinski concentrated on inside the APXGP garage along with driving scenes involving Brad Pitt and Damson Idris. "They had driven in Abu Dhabi in April, but now we have sports signage up, and so we cherry-picked exactly what we needed from them and the stunt drivers," says Hefferman. "We also had to do the Mexican Hospitality Suite because Tobias Menzies wasn't available for Mexico because he was doing a play in London. So, we did wide shots there and close-ups here."

One quirk of the Abu Dhabi Grand Prix is that it starts during the day and goes into the night, meaning the shooting schedule needed to be planned out to the minute, particularly when it came to scenes in the APXGP Wendy House. "It's a full race, so it starts at five and transitions through sunset into blue hour into night. And there's so much parallel action going on," says Hefferman. "You've got the Wendy House, the drivers, hospitality. You've also got inside the garage, where Ruben is, with Bernadette and the mechanics. You've got sunset, blue, and all the rest of it to do there as well. I had to look at the number of sunsets we had and work out what we were going to shoot when, knowing sunset is ten minutes. Blue hour's six minutes."

Adding to the challenge was the enormous amount of dialogue between the pit wall and the drivers, and sound pollution was a problem. The answer was to have the sound department record Pitt and Idris saying their lines with stage directions narrated by F1 reporter Will Buxton, which could then be played back through the pit crew's headsets.

"We did an annotated script just for the Wendy House, so we could do it in chunks," explains Hefferman. "Abu Dhabi was eight parts. Production sound mixer Gareth John and his team created a playlist, so you would press a button to feed in the track. Joe can hear the playback in his cans, the actors have got theirs, and we run it. We've got somebody in the sound department in mission control with the cues, and off we go, because you have to wait for the actor to deliver their line. And you want those natural pauses, so you've got to allow them."

"It was the most complicated race," agrees Kerry Condon. "But it was kind of perfect, because by that point, we'd done so many pit walls. We all felt, you know what, bring it on, we got this. We can handle this one. It's very long. It's very complicated. But we can do it. I had a lot of fun on that pit wall." Occasionally, a little *too* much fun. "We all had to really commit to reactions," Condon continues. "Obviously, we're not really reacting to crashes and stuff, we're reacting to nothing. In those instances, you must really commit, or else don't do it at all. I used to get a note from Joe a lot: not so giddy, less giddy. Because I was so excited."

With the Las Vegas Grand Prix, cinematographer Claudio Miranda had introduced two new camera mounts—2L and 2R—to the APXGP car between the front wheel and the nose. "We knew for Abu Dhabi we wanted to do something special," says Kosinski. "We also had what we called the ripple mount, which we introduced in Vegas, where you could look directly at the upgraded floor on the side. And then we had the flying mount in Abu Dhabi, which was that clean point of view right off the nose of the car, with an 8K camera, so that we were able to do that flying section at the very end where the camera feels like you're floating or banking around the turns rather than being fixed directly to the car. All of those were developed for those last two races."

Alongside the enormous number of script pages that needed to be completed each day, the production also had to rehearse two major sequences that exceeded anything they had achieved before. The first would take place in the pit lane, when the race is red-flagged with three laps to go after Sonny crashes, and would require the input of all the other teams on the grid; the second would take place immediately after the race and would mean filming on the track, during parc fermé, and on the winner's podium. "What we were attempting to do in Abu Dhabi was a whole other level," says Kosinski. "Everything from Brad pulling up in parc fermé to the trophy ceremony, which was the final step."

During the red flag, all the remaining cars line up in the pit lane in order. "How are we going to do that? Because it's not about putting our six cars out there and reskinning cars," Hefferman reflects. "And it's not just a matter of a few bodies around a car. If you've seen a red flag in a pit lane, everyone's out. It's like the start of a race. So, we've got to see if there's a world in which F1 will give us a time we feel is achievable."

"The easiest time to do it would have been right at the beginning of the day, but we needed it dark because it's a night race," says Tim Bampton, who initially suggested doing it on the Tuesday evening following the Grand Prix. "But that was at the end of a triple-header and was always going to be a big, big ask for the teams." After many weeks of discussions between Kosinski, Bruckheimer, F1, the FIA, and all the teams, the filmmakers were given one hour on Thursday evening before the race to shoot the scene.

In the film, when the red flag is shown, Lewis Hamilton is in first, Charles Leclerc is in second, with the APXGP pair of Joshua in third and Sonny in fourth. For Sonny, it's a race against time as the APXGP pit crew have ten minutes to repair his car to race while the marshals clear the track of debris. "We needed a Mercedes in number one and Ferrari in two," says Hefferman. "Then behind us we had to have the other cars. We didn't have to have the other drivers; we could have people dressed as drivers. But we need their personnel and their cars—or a certain number of cars—to get the wide shots, because this is the third act of the movie. This has got to be as big as it can be. This has got to be epic."

"I always laugh, because when I wrote 'The cars come in and do their repairs in the pit lane,' I never considered that the production would have to ask Formula One to put every F1 car in the pit lane so we can shoot it," says Bacheta. "Didn't even cross my mind."

"It's a big sequence," says Hefferman. "It takes place over ten minutes. You've got Brad in the car, you've got all this parallel action, you've got the guys on the pit wall, you've got Joshua doing his thing with his engineer, you've got Kaspar who comes off the Wendy House to fix the car. Then we have to reset and go again. It takes time. And it's not just time. For our pit crew, it was physically exhausting, and they had to do these pit stops, continuously, for an hour. The red flag was an absolute headache."

The production rehearsed in the pit lane on the Sunday, blocking out the scene with Kosinski, Bruckheimer, Miranda, production sound mixer Gareth John, Bampton, and the other heads of department, then spent two hours the day before—this time with the actors, camera department, and teams present—finalizing everyone's responsibilities and positions. Hefferman created a timeline of the red flag, so everyone knew exactly what the scene entailed.

"It was like a stage show," he explains, "so we needed the mechanics to understand it's a thing to construct. Because within those ten minutes, things are constantly happening. The coolers go into the vents. The tires come off and go into warmers. The drivers go for a piss. Everyone has a role within that time. And we only had an hour. So, we timed it where we could do the scene in three to four minutes and reset, because we're not running it for ten minutes. I had to explain to the mechanics, we're shortcutting it. We're pretending. And they were great."

To film the scene, Kosinski and Miranda had four "turkeys" to cover the various elements, together with a camera crane at the very front to capture the entire pit lane in wide shot. They also co-opted two of the F1 broadcast team's cameras "to get as much production value out of it as possible and make it real. We didn't want close-ups. We wanted the biggest shots we could get."

Storyboards showing the red flag being called after Sonny's car is damaged, spilling debris onto the track.

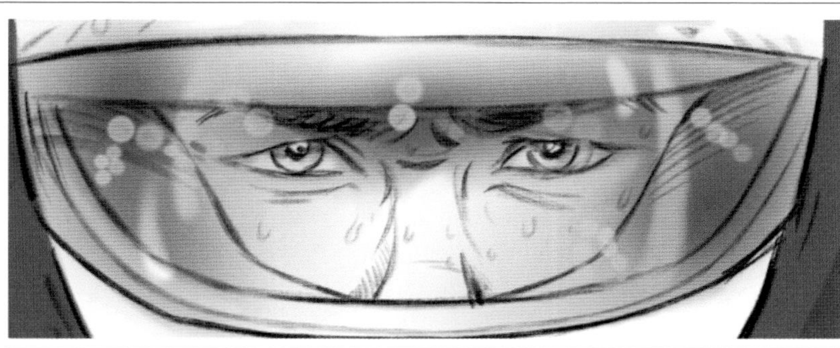

MAIN ABU DHABI RACE 228
IN SONNY'S CAR: Recovering from spin, Sonny's disoriented—

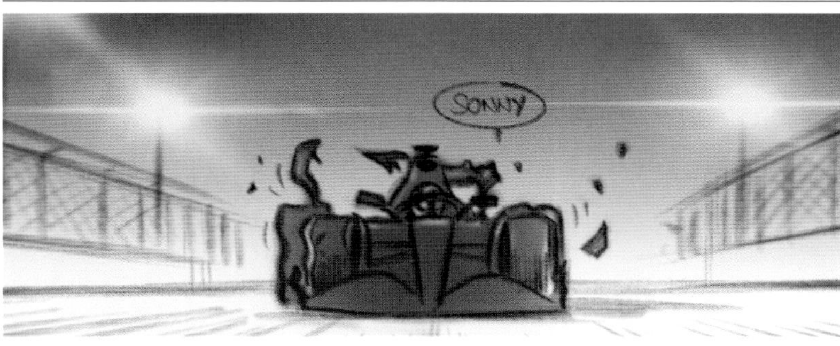

MAIN ABU DHABI RACE 229
A massive collision for Hayes and Perez! Debris all over the track!

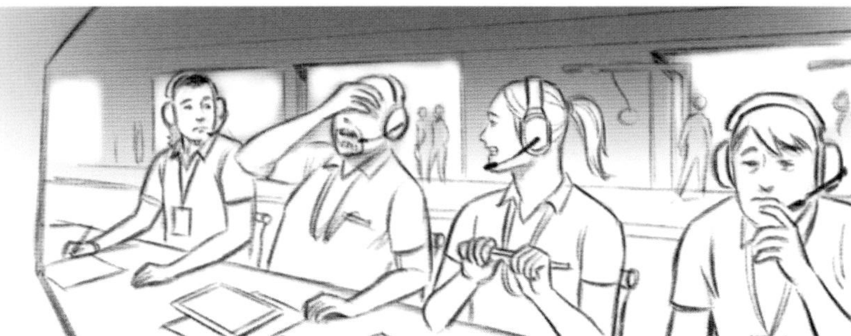

MAIN ABU DHABI RACE 230
Kaspar and team react on pit wall.

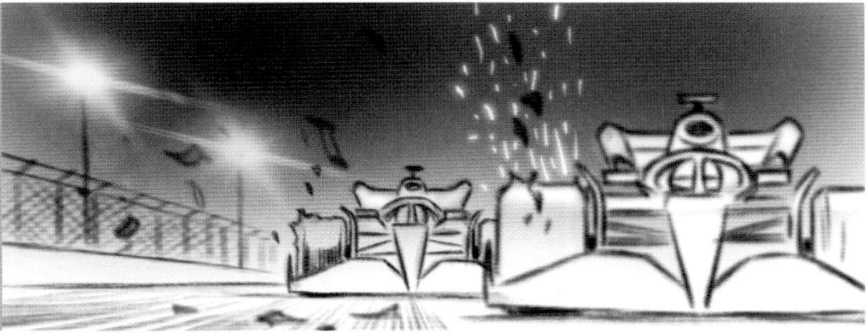

MAIN ABU DHABI RACE 231
He's still moving, but slowly, seeing CARS coming behind him—

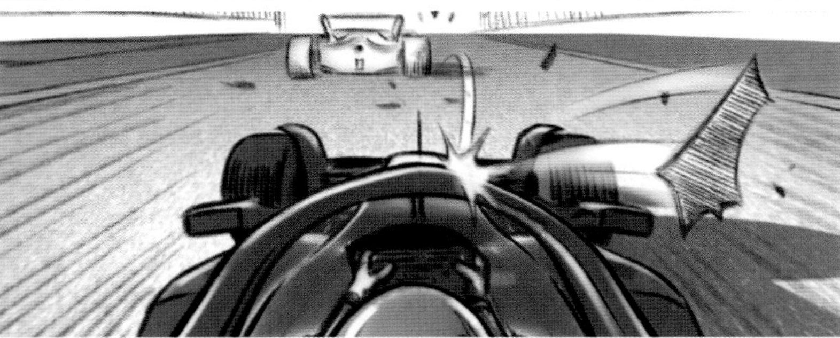

MAIN ABU DHABI RACE 232
TELEPARTNER (V.O.)
Stewards may have no choice but to red-flag this race . . .
ON TRACK: The debris causes an uninvolved car (P6) to get a puncture, another piece of debris flicks up and bounces off a car's Halo narrowly missing the driver.

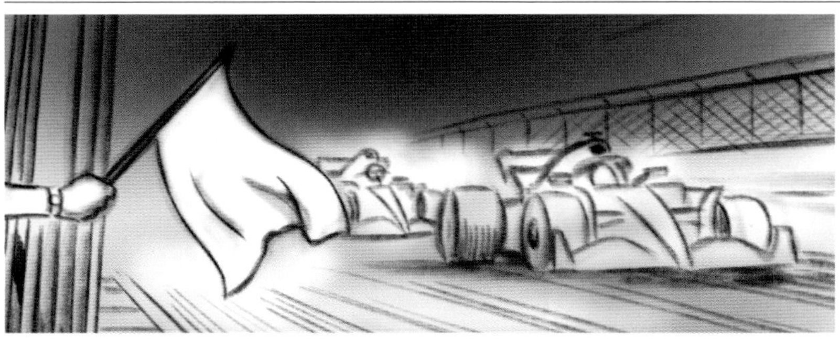

MAIN ABU DHABI RACE 233
RED FLAGS wave.
TELECAST (V.O.)
And there it is! With only three laps to go, the Abu Dhabi Grand Prix has been stopped. Cars will return to the pits, and we'll have a grid restart once the track can be cleared for safe conditions.

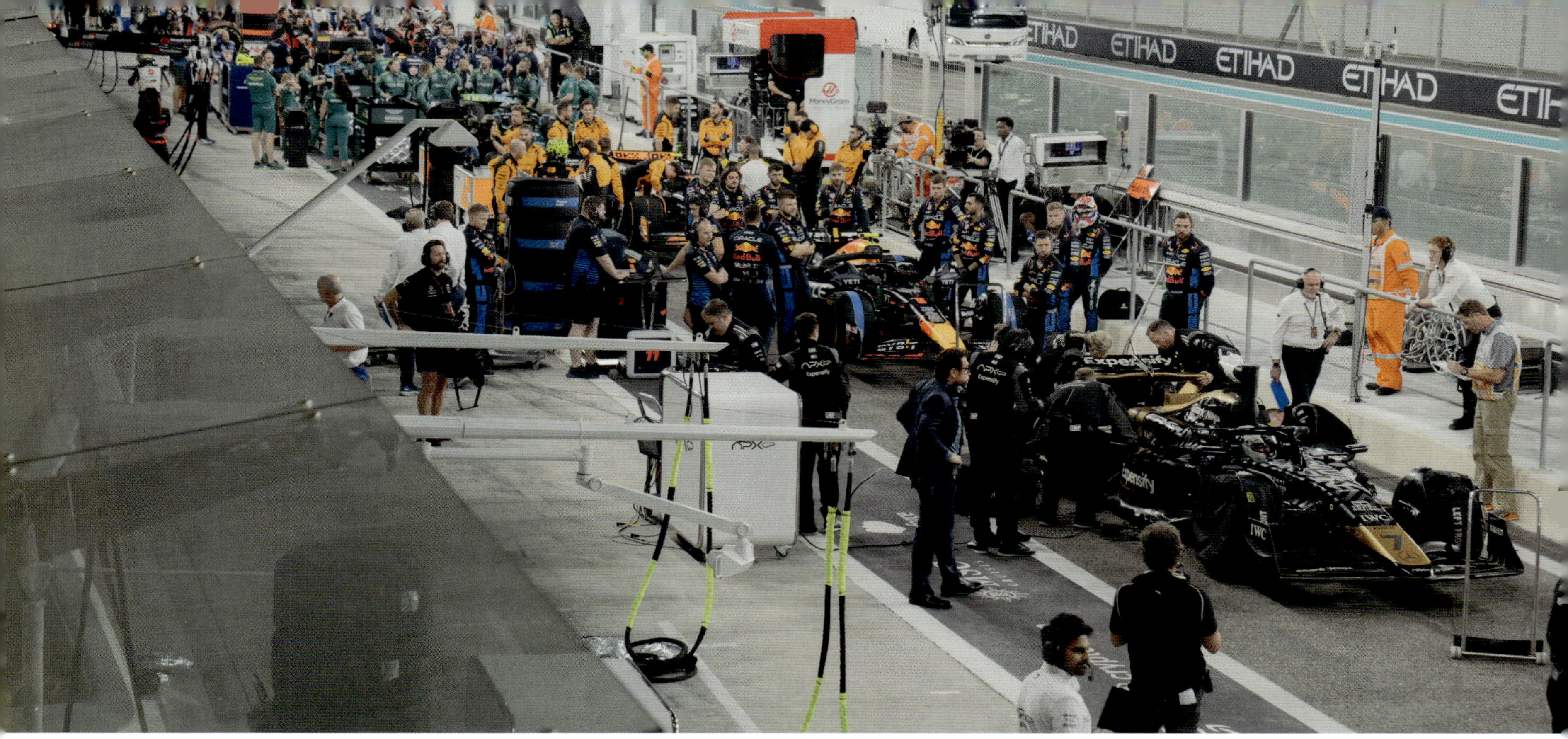

At 7 p.m. on Thursday, December 5, the production went through its last-minute checks, in preparation for 8 p.m., when the teams were due to join them in the pit lane. "I remember James Boughton, our F1 track supervisor, came up to me and said, 'You better have your shit together,'" Hefferman recalls. "I said, 'Why's that? I'm always really prepared.' And he said, 'These guys are a different breed. These aren't the team principals. They're not the drivers. These are the guys who run the garage. They're hardcore.'"

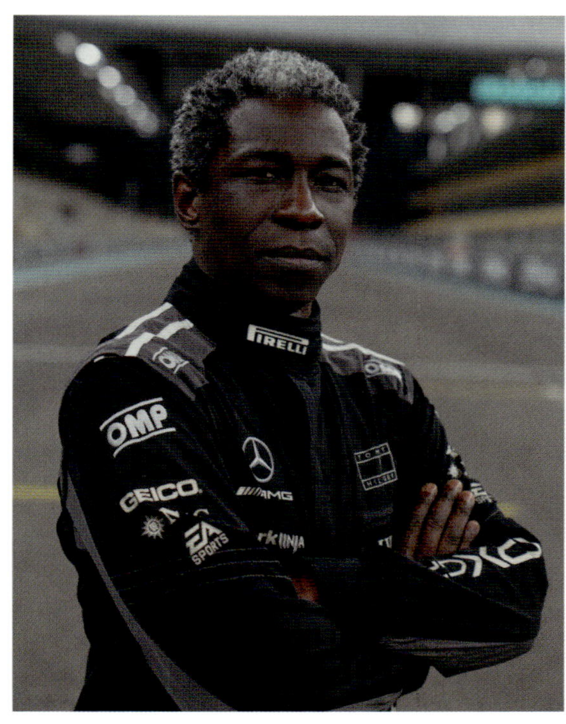

Just before 8 p.m., cast and crew moved into the pit lane, standing near the two APXGP cars, which were parked in third and fourth, directly outside the APXGP garage, waiting for the clock to hit the hour. "We knew the Mercedes and Ferrari were going to skate by us to get into one and two," says Hefferman. "But it was like something from *Braveheart*. Suddenly, from the back of the pit lane, everyone arrived together. It was like we were going to war. And all of us, no matter how experienced, got the chills. This was serious shit. Each car came with an army and their gear. They started positioning and were so quick, so military. I was like, shit just got real here. Brad was in the car, and I said to him, 'You don't want to see what's going on behind. It's like we are just about to go to war.'"

"Can you imagine the production value there?" muses Pitt. "We have these $150 million cars lined up, and all their crews are working like it's an actual red flag. Every team, every car on the grid, in the pit lane. And I'm in the car strapped in the whole time. Even my mirrors were busted, so I couldn't really see, other than what was in front of me, until I get out, and I look back and see the madness of what we just pulled off."

But despite the high-priced spectacle, there was work to be done, several dramatic scenes among all the madness, including Javier Bardem emerging from the APXGP garage and

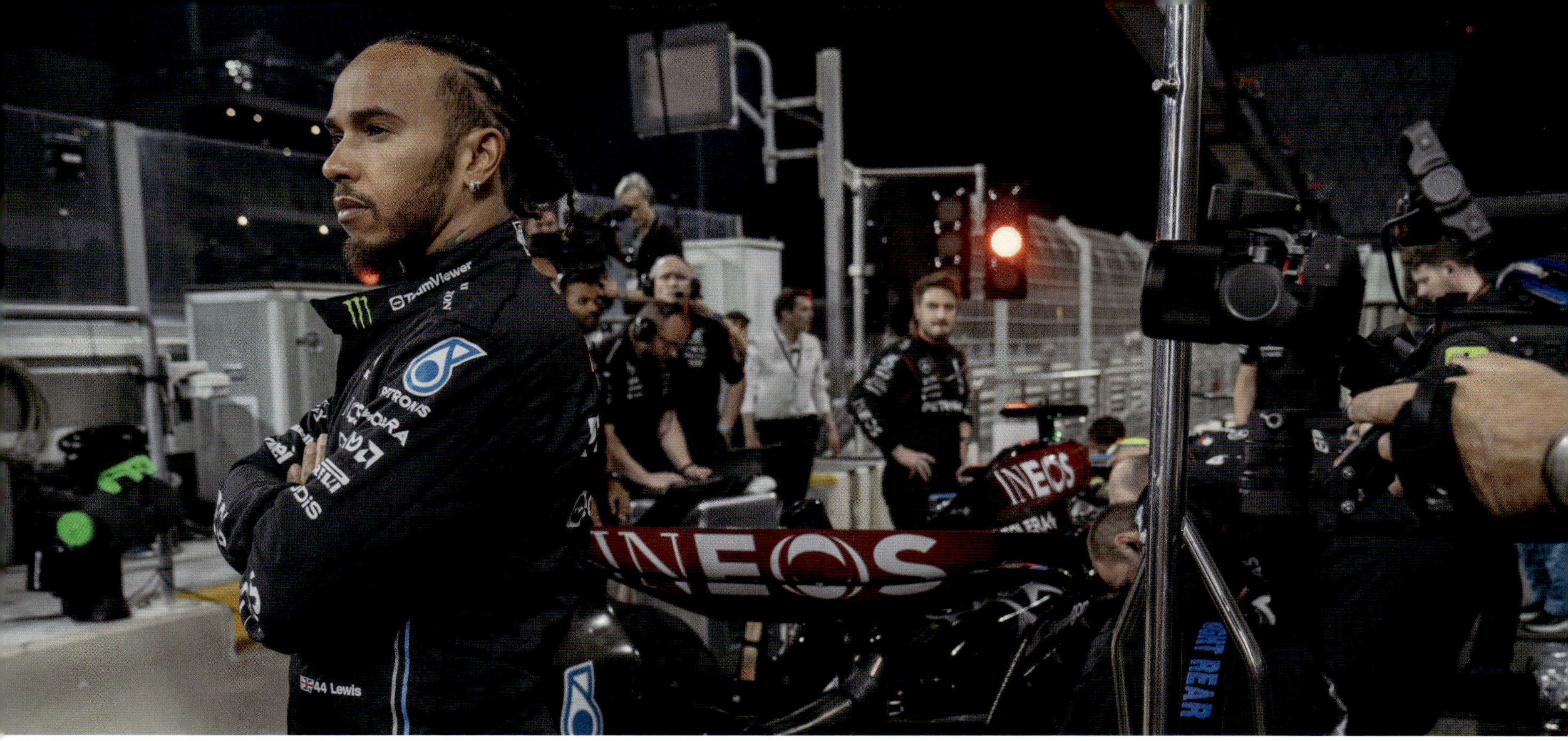

Top Left: All ten teams and their pit crews join the two APXGP cars in the pit lane to film the red flag sequence.

Top Right: Lewis Hamilton wore two crucial hats for the *F1* film: driver for Mercedes-AMG and an executive producer for the movie.

Bottom Left: Abdul Salis, who plays Chief Engineer Dodge, was in the pit lane alongside Graham Kelly's pit crew when filming the red flag scene.

a moment between Joshua/Idris and Lewis Hamilton in the pit lane. "It was a very busy weekend for Lewis, because it was his last race for Mercedes, so he had all these things planned. But I texted him and said, 'We're shooting a red flag race. All the teams are bringing their cars out. Is there a chance you could come and play yourself, because you're in P1. And I thought maybe you can just give Joshua a hard look from P1, because Josh is in P3,'" recalls Kosinski. "Then 8 o'clock rolls round, all the mechanics came out, all the teams show up with their $25 million cars and roll them all into place. I've only got an hour, and there's no sign of Lewis. But I've got to start shooting. So, I do. I run behind my monitor, I'm watching it all happen, then someone says to me, 'Lewis just walked in. And he wants to know what to do.' So, I said, 'Tell him to do what he usually does.' I look, and Lewis is standing next to his car, pulling on his balaclava, slipping his helmet on. He just slid into the scene. Damson gets out, looks at Lewis, and they eyeball each other. It was one of those surreal moments that we were able to capture and put in the movie."

For the last ten minutes of their allotted hour, the filmmakers instructed the teams to do what they'd normally do when a red flag ends and the mechanics remove all the gear from around the cars. "It was like a real red flag," says Bampton. "We had comms on the pit wall and gave the teams a real countdown as per the regulations.

"It was brilliant, just watching the precision of these crew," says Hefferman, who includes the APXGP pit crew in that. "Our pit crew were brilliant in as far as how synchronized they were, and how professional they were. And that's not just Graham Kelly's team. That's Callie Cooke and Abdul Salis. They were actors playing mechanics. But we said to them, 'You're not actors in this scene. Don't get your instructions from Joe. Be mechanics.' Everyone smashed it."

One person who wasn't there that day was Kerry Condon. "Interesting fact, I was in the hospital when we shot that," she sighs. "To this day, the boys wind me up about it. But when we came back to do my coverage later, Brad stayed and did his off-camera stuff for me. And I ended up getting a good close-up, which I don't think I would have gotten on the day."

At 9 p.m., the teams cleared the pit lane, leaving both APXGP cars in position, and Kosinski continued to shoot red flag coverage, picking up close-ups of the drivers and pit crew.

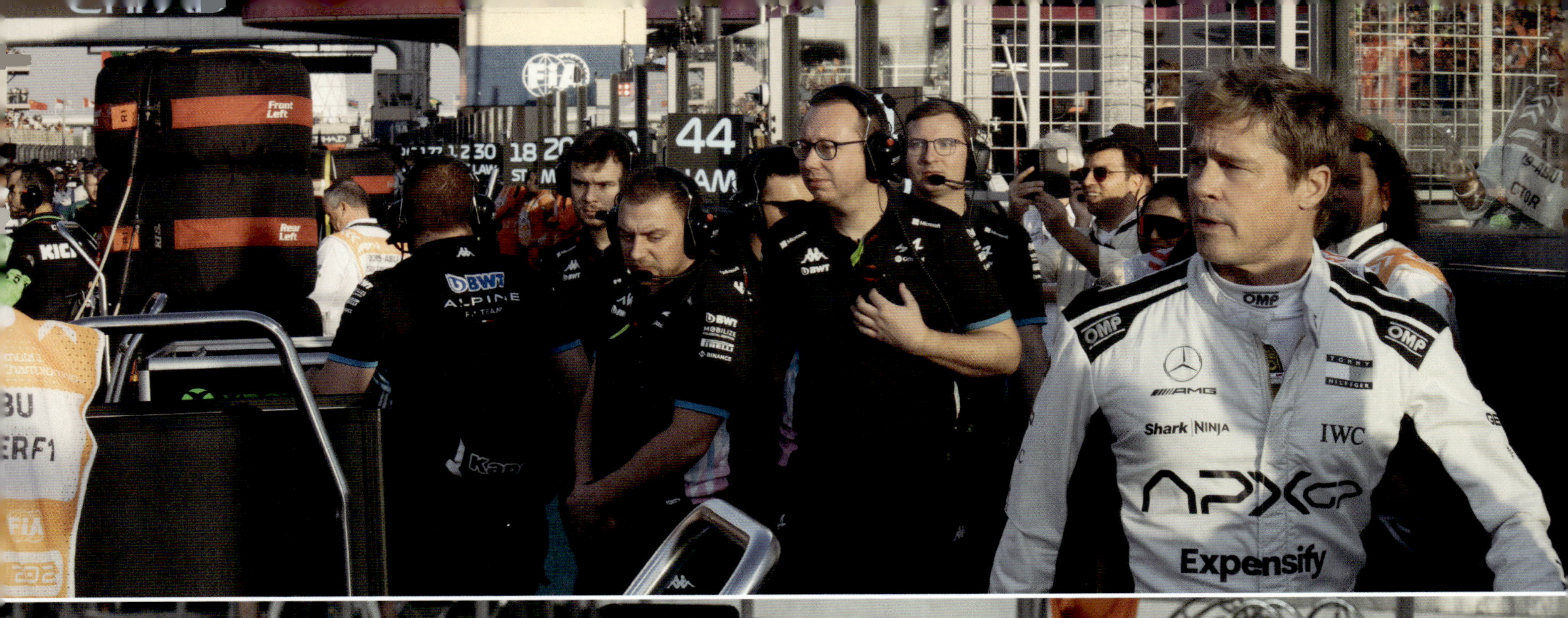
Expensify
IWC
Shark NINJA
AMG
OMP
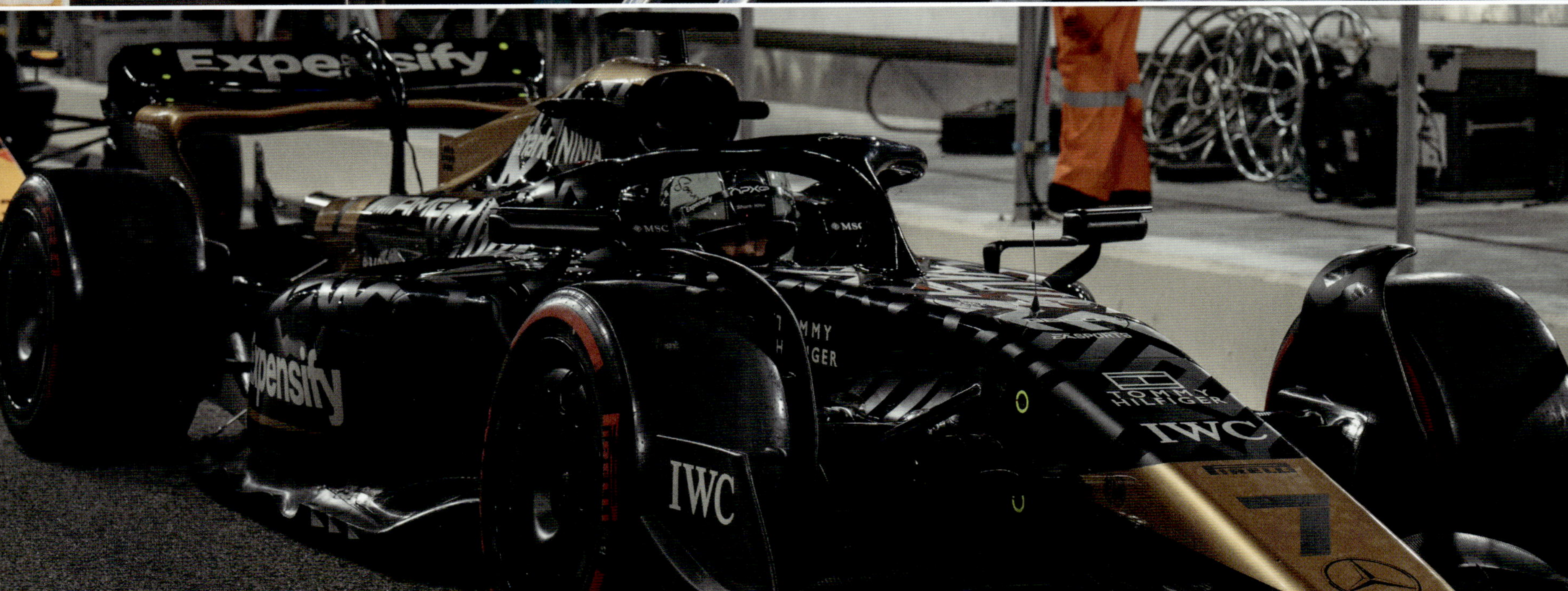
Expensify
IWC
TOMMY HILFIGER
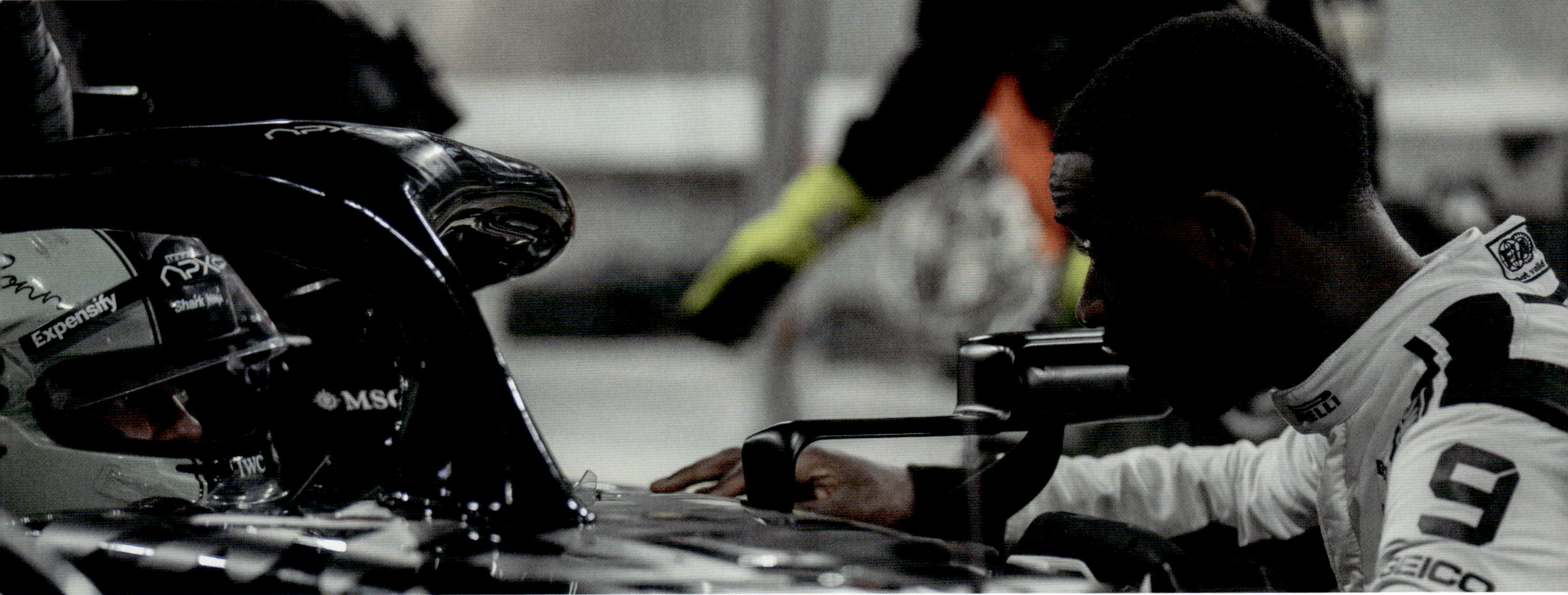
Expensify
MSC

Top: Brad Pitt walks down a busy grid to film the national anthem scene.

Middle: Sonny (Brad Pitt) gets ready to get back on the track for the restart after the red flag is raised.

Bottom: Sonny (Brad Pitt) and Joshua (Damson Idris) strategize together.

Friday was no less busy, with scenes to be shot in the Paddock Club with Banning and in the Sky Sports F1 commentary booth with Martin Brundle and David Croft, along with more red flag pickups, Wendy House work, and track time with the actors. For Pitt, filming in Abu Dhabi was particularly bittersweet as it marked the last time he would get to drive his APXGP car. "Obviously, my thoughts in Abu Dhabi were, *Okay, I'm going to get three more times out on the track. Okay, I'm going to get two more times out of the track. Ah, fuck. This is my last time on the track.* And then I got them to give me an extra run. And they did. Out of sheer sympathy."

"There was a moment when Brad had a genuine slide," recalls Bacheta. "I remember being on track with him, thinking, *Okay, this could go wrong*. But it's in the cut. It's a real moment that Brad had."

Saturday meant qualifying for the race on Sunday, with McLaren and Ferrari neck and neck for the 2024 constructors' championship. For the filmmakers, there were more scenes in the Paddock Club and more track laps with the actors, all in parallel with gearing up for what they had to shoot during Sunday's race.

Immediately after qualifying, with the grandstands still mostly full, the production was given a fifteen-minute window to let off fireworks, while Sonny took the checkered flag. Kosinski returned to Paddock Club to rehearse a specific beat that would be filmed the following day, blocking out the scene with the actors, camera operator, and extras, because he would be elsewhere during the race.

As with Silverstone in 2023, the day of the 2024 Abu Dhabi Grand Prix required military-style preparation to pull off everything the script required. At 3:45 p.m., Kosinski, Hefferman, Bampton, and Pitt waited at the medical center with two turkey head cameras. Meanwhile, up in the Paddock Club, another camera waited to film Banning looking down on Sonny from the APXGP hospitality suite.

At 4 p.m., Pitt moved onto the grid. Ten minutes later, Sonny's APXGP car was positioned on the side of the grid. At 4:26 p.m., Kosinski started to film the scene of Sonny asking for his cellphone to message Banning in the hospitality area. The two men shared a look. Kosinski also filmed a cameo with James Vowles (team principal of Williams Racing). "We had twelve minutes to get everything before we moved off," says Hefferman, "but in shooting terms, it was six to eight minutes to get all that stuff in."

At 4:40 p.m., the APXGP car was removed from the grid. Between 4:38 and 4:42 p.m., Kosinski filmed Sonny walking down the grid, before they arrived at the front for the national anthem, at 4:44 p.m., with Sonny joining Joshua alongside the other drivers, just as they had at Silverstone in 2023. "We had four minutes to walk from the back of the grid to the front to position ourselves," says Hefferman. "Two additional turkey heads joined us. So now we have four. And all are shooting the national anthem."

"It was a fitting end to the shoot," says Kosinski, "because we started at Silverstone with Brad and Damson at the national anthem and that walk down the pit lane. At that point, our first week of shooting, it seemed impossible to pull something like that off, but we did. So even though we had been through it before at Silverstone, I'm even more proud of that shot. Again, we had one go at it. We had the flyover of the Etihad Airlines at the same time, and knowing it was Lewis's final race with Mercedes, and McLaren was vying for the championship with Ferrari, I felt like it was a better version of what we attempted to do at Silverstone the year before."

"It's more spectacular and a really nice bookend, because Josh and Sonny are in such a different place in their relationship at that point," Kosinski continues. "During the first one, they're standing shoulder to shoulder, and neither of them is quite sure how this is going to work, and obviously it doesn't work at all in Silverstone. But in Abu Dhabi, they have that elbows-out fist bump, and you feel there's a bond there that the audience is desperate to [have] happen. I was really happy with how that moment turned out, because four minutes before, I was at the other end of the grid with Brad shooting the scene with Sonny giving Banning the middle finger. We then ran to the front and shot the national anthem. So, in a span of six minutes, we did two important scenes."

"We had the broadcast team shooting for us, everything from cablecam to regular cameras, but it was never generic. Everything was precise. Nothing's ever, *Oh, it would be nice to grab stuff*. It's never that," says Hefferman. "There was always real intent. And that's Joe. He wants to shoot specific stuff that's going to be in the movie."

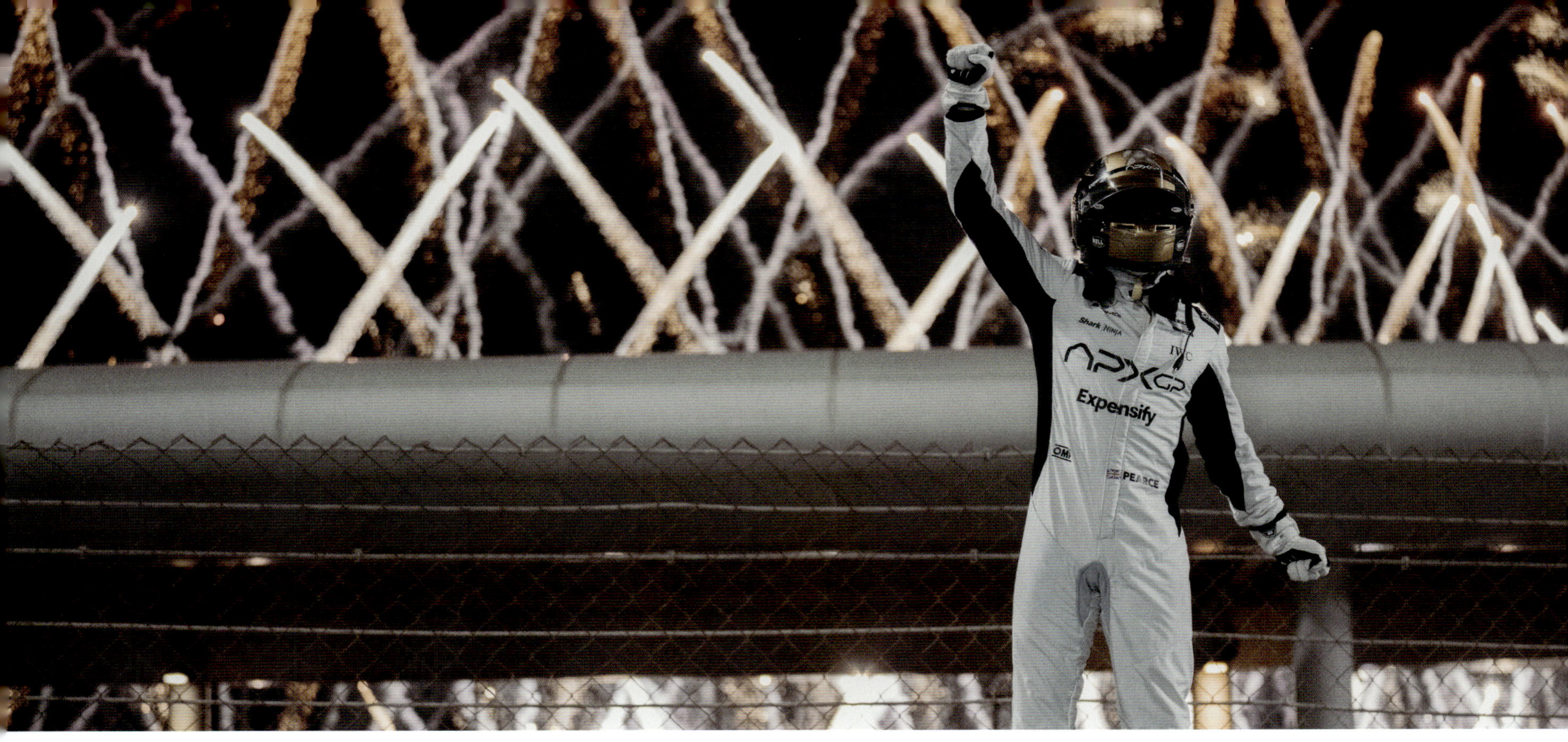

Post national anthem, Pitt and Idris headed off the grid while Kosinski continued to shoot, grabbing shots of Lando Norris, Carlos Sainz, Charles Leclerc, and George Russell as they got ready, with a separate turkey head camera assigned to each driver. As the grid began to clear for the formation lap, Kosinski headed to the APXGP garage to film inside with Ruben and Bernadette while the race was going on, as well as on the pit wall with Condon, Bodnia, et al.

In reality, Norris won ahead of Sainz and Leclerc. But in the film, the winner of the Abu Dhabi Grand Prix is Sonny, who can say, without a shadow of a doubt, that he's the best driver in the world. "That's what I love about Formula One," says Kosinski. "It is the top of the motor racing pyramid. There are only twenty people who get to do that week in and week out. And I don't know if there is a more exclusive sport in the world. So, if you win in Formula One, you can make a good argument that you are the best driver in the world. For Sonny, it's a very redemptive moment for someone who's been chasing that for decades and was never thought to be good enough to achieve it. And to achieve it in a way that is so well earned. It's not by thinking about himself. It comes from thinking about your teammate. Both sacrificed for each other in those final moments, and that's why the team gets the victory, because they approach it from a purely selfless point of view."

To film Sonny's victory at Abu Dhabi, the film crew wanted to piggyback on the real winner's celebrations, on the track, on the pit wall, in parc fermé, and, finally, on the podium. "We started planning in April of 2024," says Bampton, "we went back over the '23 race, and from the moment the checkered flag fell we started timing everything. Where did the APXGP car need to be? At what point would it start moving without interrupting the actual winner's ceremony?"

The first element to be shot was Ruben and Bernadette rushing from the APXGP garage, combined with the celebrations of the pit wall crew as Norris's McLaren took the checkered flag and the fireworks went off around the circuit, with the production asking F1 to extend the fireworks for as long as possible. "Meanwhile, we're running across the pit lane with Javier and the other actors, celebrating," says Hefferman. "We also nabbed a cameo with F1 Racing's Stefano Domenicali."

"That was another one where it felt the pressure wasn't so much on me, more on the camera department and everybody else," Condon recalls. "But we had rehearsed it, and did the bit from them winning, then running down the pit lane. I didn't know if we were going to get so many takes, because they were doing the fireworks. But we got to do that three or four times. Javier is such a playful actor. He brought his kids and was totally going for it. It was a fun moment. But we all knew it was the end of the movie, too. So, there was this sense of just 'go big or go home.' It felt like the perfect way to end it. But kind of bittersweet."

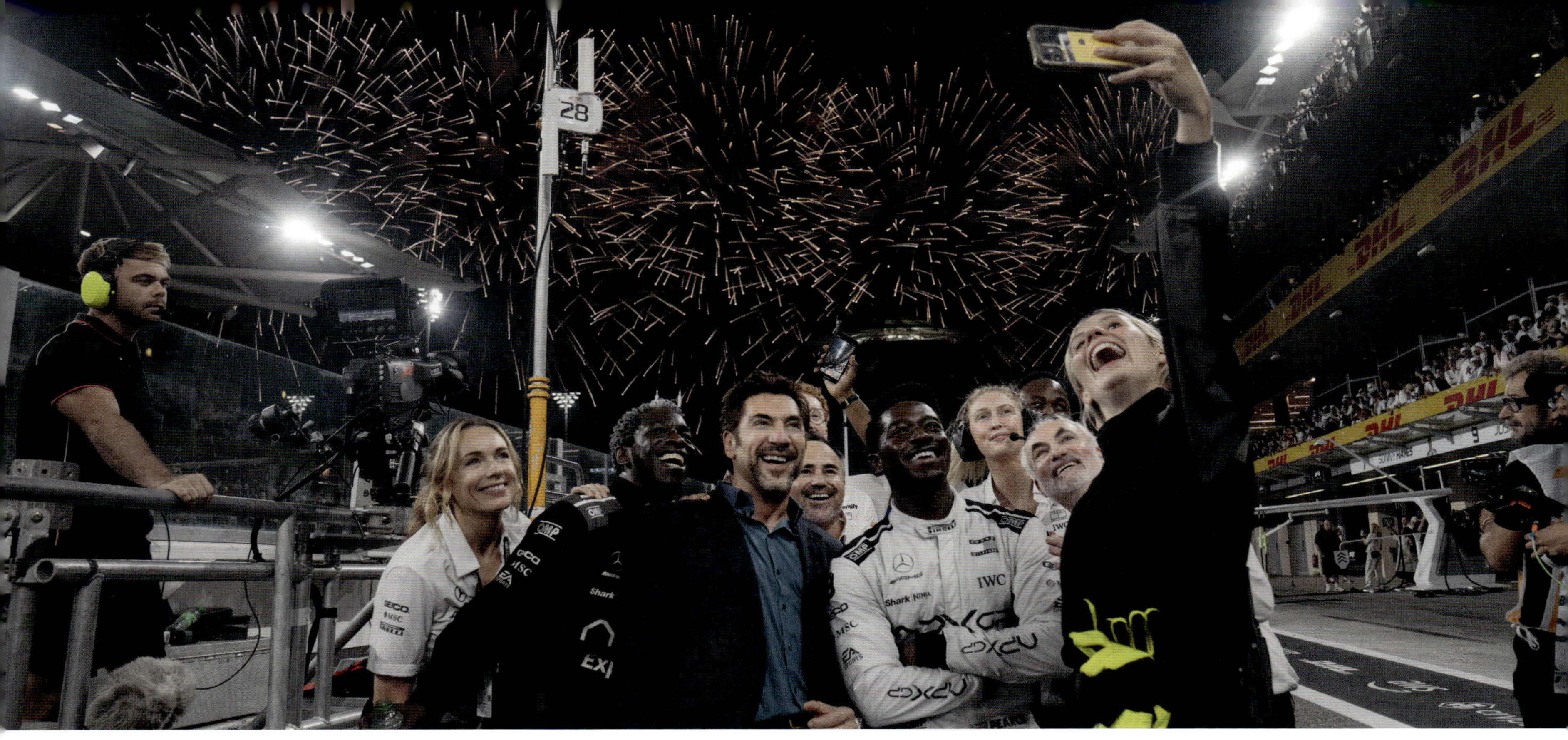

Top Left: Joshua (Damson Idris) celebrates Sonny's victory in Abu Dhabi.

Top Right: The APXGP cast celebrates after filming Sonny's victory scene.

"We go to the fence, and we go crazy. It's impossible to act it badly. Because if I suck in that moment, I'm the worst actor in the world," laughs Javier Bardem. "Because they're giving you everything you need to believe what you're doing. It was an explosion of reality within the fiction. Also knowing it was the end of our shooting. It was emotional. Everybody was feeling the same."

"I was there for the last scene when they win," says Domenicali, "and the guys from the garage, jumping onto the pit wall, it was exactly the real atmosphere that you get from a garage in Formula One when you win. It was perfect."

As the top three got out of their cars to be interviewed post-race, Kosinski, Pitt, Idris, Hefferman, Miranda, Bampton, Ben Munro, and four cameramen snuck onto the track and slowly filed down the lefthand side, across from the main grandstand.

"We were literally tracking the real world by three or four minutes," recalls Bampton. "We didn't want to get in the way of the sport. We had to move the interviews with the top three drivers for the international feed to a different location in the pit lane to allow what we needed to happen on the grid."

As Norris, Sainz, and Leclerc finished their interviews, the APXGP car was wheeled onto the track in front of the "first place" marker board. Pitt was strapped into his seat, only for him to leap out in celebration moments later. "We have a six- to eight-minute period before the real drivers go up on the podium," says Hefferman. But after filming Sonny's "victory," Pitt insisted they do one with Joshua as well, so Idris was strapped into the car and repeated Sonny's celebration. "I wanted to shoot us both in the winner's circle, and put him in the car, because we got a crowd of people, and everyone's got a camera phone, but it didn't seem like anyone fell for it," laments Pitt.

By this stage, Norris, Sainz, and Leclerc had made their way into the cooldown room, ready to head up to the podium.

As the winning APXGP car was moved off the grid, Kosinski dispatched two of his four turkey heads under the podium, to shoot Condon, Bodnia, Niles, and the rest of the APXGP pit crew celebrating alongside the real teams. "Joe had rehearsed them. We'd worked out the shots in advance, but, again, Joe couldn't be there to direct them."

Kosinski was still with Pitt, Idris, and now Bardem, as they waited to enter the cooldown room, as the real podium was taking place above them. Soon as the real ceremony finished, the production was planning to stage its own, this time with Sonny Hayes as the winner, with George Russell and Leclerc on the podium with him.

"The idea was, as soon as they come off the podium, we go on," says Hefferman. "And we'd had a conversation about holding the teams under the podium and the people in the grandstands for as long as we could. So, when we do our podium, we've got as much production value as we can."

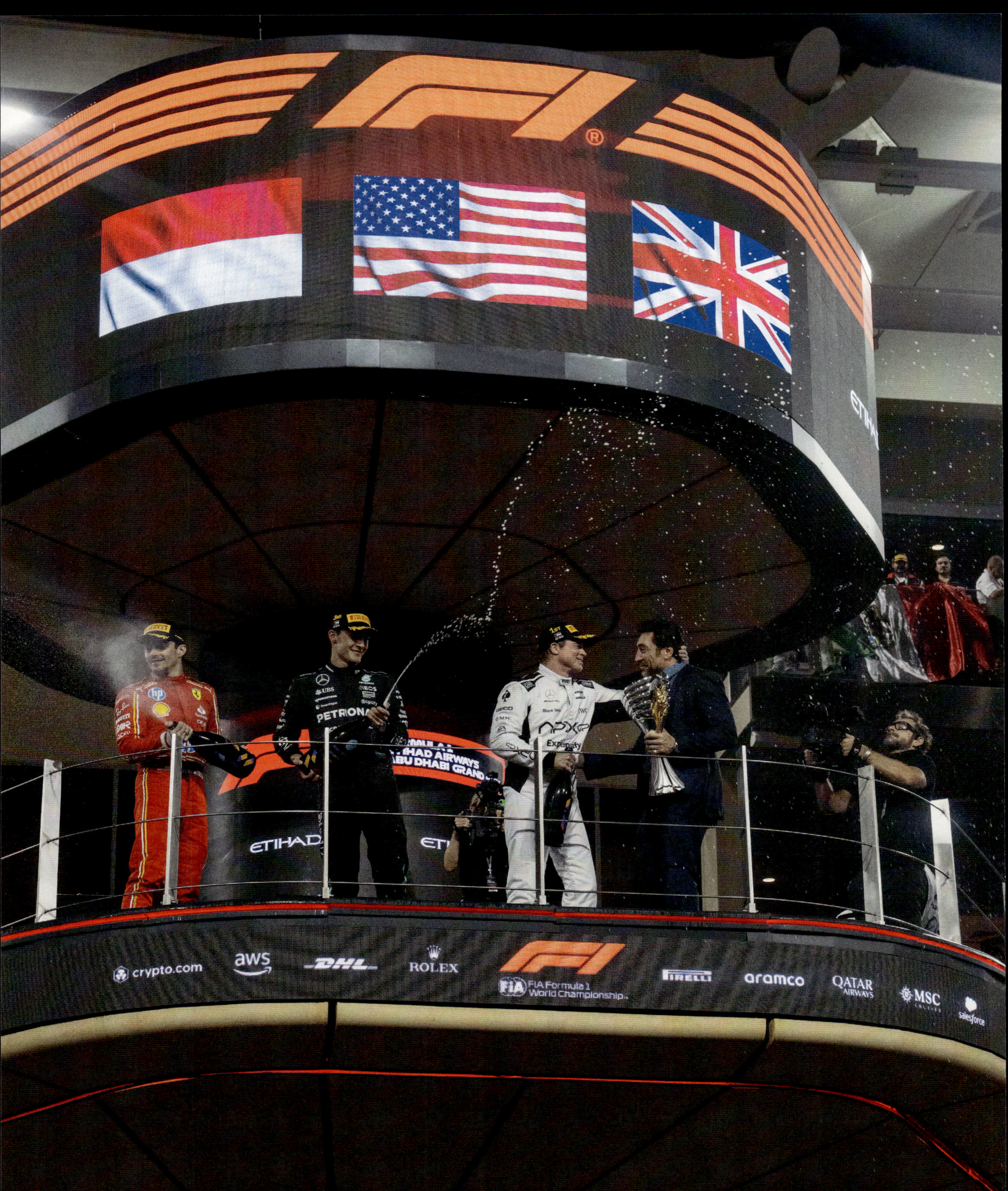
F1
ETIHAD
crypto.com
aws
DHL
ROLEX
FIA Formula 1 World Championship
PIRELLI
aramco
QATAR AIRWAYS
MSC
salesforce

Left: Real-life F1 drivers Charles Leclerc and George Russell pop open the champagne as Sonny (Brad Pitt) and Ruben (Javier Bardem) celebrate the APXGP victory.

At this point, George Russell joins them in the corridor leading to the cooldown room, and they walk to the entrance to the podium, on which the graphics have been replaced with those from the previous season. "We had ten minutes to execute it," says Bampton. "It was fast-paced and frenetic, but it had been prepped and rehearsed."

But Hefferman was starting to worry. "I'm looking out at the grandstands, and I can see people starting to leave. I'm like, 'Fuck, we've got to get on there.' And Tim said, 'No. Wait. I'll tell you when.' Leclerc's doing his thing. He's just finished a race. I looked at Tim, and he was talking to Zak Brown. I looked outside and I saw this microphone with a long lead that we'd requested so I could talk to everyone in the grandstands."

Hefferman decided to take matters into his own hands. "I grabbed the mic, ran out, and said, 'Ladies and gentlemen, welcome to the Abu Dhabi Grand Prix, would you like to be in a Hollywood movie? Please stick around. We're going to be coming out any minute.'"

Moments later, Bampton gave him the thumbs-up. "We brought Charles, George, Javier, and Brad out and did our celebration, which we'd rehearsed," says Hefferman. "George and Charles didn't know what the fuck was going on. Of course we'd primed them, but it was so organic."

"George and Charles kept asking if they could spray Brad," chuckles Kosinski. "They were so excited. I had to tell them, please let me get a couple takes of the scene first because once you spray him, and once he's wet, I can't shoot the beginning half of the scene anymore. I think we got one or two takes where they didn't spray him, but then I realized the clock was ticking, so I said, 'All right, guys, on this one, go for it.' That's the take that's in the movie, where you see George and Charles standing next to Brad and Javier and the crowd is going crazy."

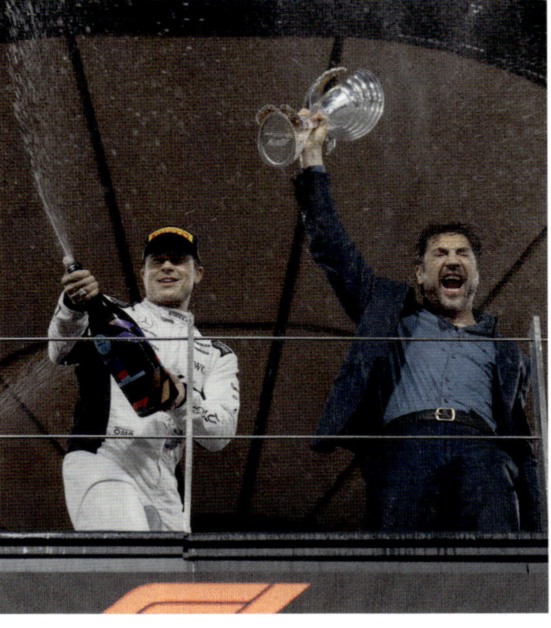

"George was, 'Now? Now can we spray him?' And then I got douched," laughs Pitt. "I think that was payback for thinking we could even stand next to these guys. It was madness. Madness. I felt a bit of a jackass doing it, but you've got to. And knowing that was our last time with everyone, and we pulled everything off without a hitch, it was beautiful."

For Hefferman, however, there was still the practicality of moviemaking to consider. "All I'm thinking about is, *My God, they're getting so wet*. We were never going to be able to reset. But we were freestyling by this stage. We had a ten-minute window with Charles and George, and we went again and again and again. At one point I thought I was going to get removed, but it would have been worth it. We did as much as we could, to the point Javier and Brad were so wet, then we finally let go of George and Charles."

"The whole podium was stressful," reflects producer Jerry Bruckheimer. "To get up there, to get everything we needed, it was a lot to coordinate. The drivers. And big crowds. It had to go perfectly for it to work. And when you see the movie, it's flawless."

"I'm really proud of that scene and how it turned out," says Kosinski. "There was just no way you could stage it, which was what my hope was for this film, that it feels like you're in the moment, like you're up there with them."

"Again, it was a great example of the teams, the FIA, Formula One, and the movie unit working in collaboration to get that away," says Bampton. "George and Charles were naturals."

With the podium celebration finished, Kosinski headed down to film more of Condon, Bodnia, and the rest of the APXGP pit wall celebrating with the real teams under the podium, before shooting a scene between Toto Wolff and Joshua in the pit lane. And when the real teams began to leave, the production had three hundred extras waiting in the wings, ready to move in so they could continue filming. Eventually, the production called it a night, knowing they were coming back on Tuesday for six more days of filming, including close-ups for the red flag and podium scenes, as well as the final bit of driving action.

"As a cast and crew, we had been together for eighteen months. And because we'd been through so many of these types of situations, I think we were finally prepared to pull something this ambitious off," remembers Kosinski. "Like everything live, there are always variables, things that don't go quite like you expect. But the important thing is to just keep shooting. 'Cause even if it's not going the way it was supposed to exactly, you might capture some magic. And that's what we did that day."

Monday was a rest day for the production, while Formula One returned to Yas Marina for a post-season test. Then, on Tuesday evening, Kosinski was back at the circuit to film the red flag race restart with Dolby and Bacheta doubling for Joshua in third and Sonny in fourth, just behind Charles Leclerc's Ferrari in second and Lewis Hamilton's Mercedes in first. In the film, both APXGPs are on new soft tires, with Sonny and Joshua working together to engineer victory. When Hamilton spins off, taking Joshua with him, Sonny is able to claim his and APXGP's first and only victory in Formula One.

With Hamilton set to join Ferrari, he wasn't permitted to take part in the post-season test and had already left Abu Dhabi. And so Russell stood in for him on track for two filmed race starts, along with Leclerc. "Ferrari and Mercedes agreed to put their real drivers and real cars on the track alongside the APXGP cars, which had every producer and insurance-minded person freaking out on our side, because if there was any sort of contact or collision with the F1 cars, it was essentially uninsurable," reveals Kosinski. "It almost didn't happen. But everyone agreed this was a once-in-a-lifetime opportunity. And, honestly, we needed the footage, because if I hadn't got that in camera, I don't think I would have been able to finish the sequence in time."

"Every department had to lean in to make this movie, from the broadcast people to the cameramen to the officials to the drivers to security," says Bruckheimer. "And there was unfettered cooperation from Formula One. It really helped to have Brad, obviously, because he's a huge movie star, representing their sport."

"Stefano was instrumental," says producer Chad Oman. "He has a big vision. He saw the bigger picture of what a big film could do for them and kept fighting for us. It was a herculean task and it took someone with conviction and big balls to do it. But he really had a lot of confidence in us and made it possible. Stefano deserves an incredible amount of credit. So does Tim."

When it came to filming the first start, Russell and Leclerc lined up in the wrong positions on the grid. For the second, the drivers were in the right places and pulled away as planned, but Leclerc locked up into turn one. "Charles had cold tires and almost ran into George in the first corner, which gave us a little extra drama," says Kosinski. "It's in the movie. But that was a close call. It could have been a disaster. But luckily, they just managed not to collide. And we got that lap in camera."

During the first third of each lap, the four cars raced; the rest was treated as a cool-down lap. "They were pushing, and by pushing, I mean *our* cars were pushing," says Kosinski. "Charles and George were driving at 80 percent, because they're in the real deal and we're carrying all that camera equipment. I imagine for Craig and Luch, it was an opportunity of a lifetime to be in proximity to the real deal. For me, it was an amazing way to end."

"I remember walking back down to the Ferrari and Mercedes garages with Joe and Jerry to say thanks to Charles and George," says Tim Bampton. "They both asked, 'Did you get what you needed? Did we do a good job?' Joe and Jerry said, 'That was fantastic, that was incredible.' And both Charles and George were like, 'It was no big deal.' But it was. It was a *really* big deal to get that."

For Pitt, his last time on track in the APXGP car was supposed to be the Abu Dhabi race weekend, but he hadn't enjoyed the experience. "It wasn't my best drive," he admits. But then Pitt was told they needed to shoot some close-ups of him driving for the Vegas race. "That gave me an excuse, three nights later, to get back out on the track, and it was probably the best drive of my life. Throughout the year I was cutting seconds off. Then I got to the point where it was, *Can you get a tenth out of that?* I got up to my level in Abu Dhabi, and I felt so free. It was at night. It was so beautiful. We had the track to ourselves, and I had such a sublime experience, like that drive at Spa that I'll always keep with me. I felt such a sense of peace and awe and wonder and love that I can't quite explain."

Top Right: Brad Pitt takes a lap in the APXGP car at the Yas Marina circuit.

Bottom Right: George Russell and Charles Leclerc line up with the APXGP cars on the grid.

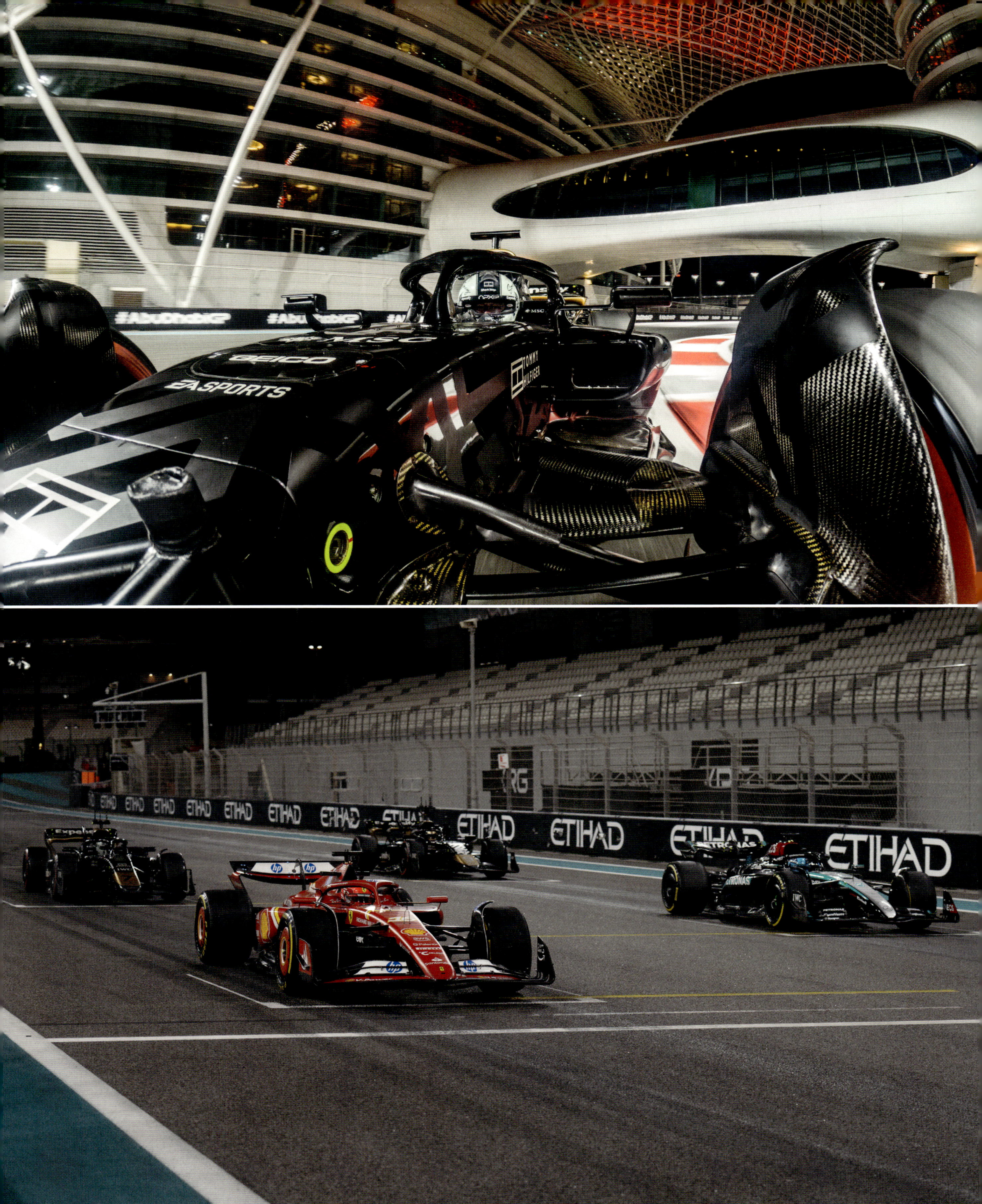

#AbuDhabiGP
GEICO
EASPORTS
TOMMY HILFIGER
ETIHAD

BAJA

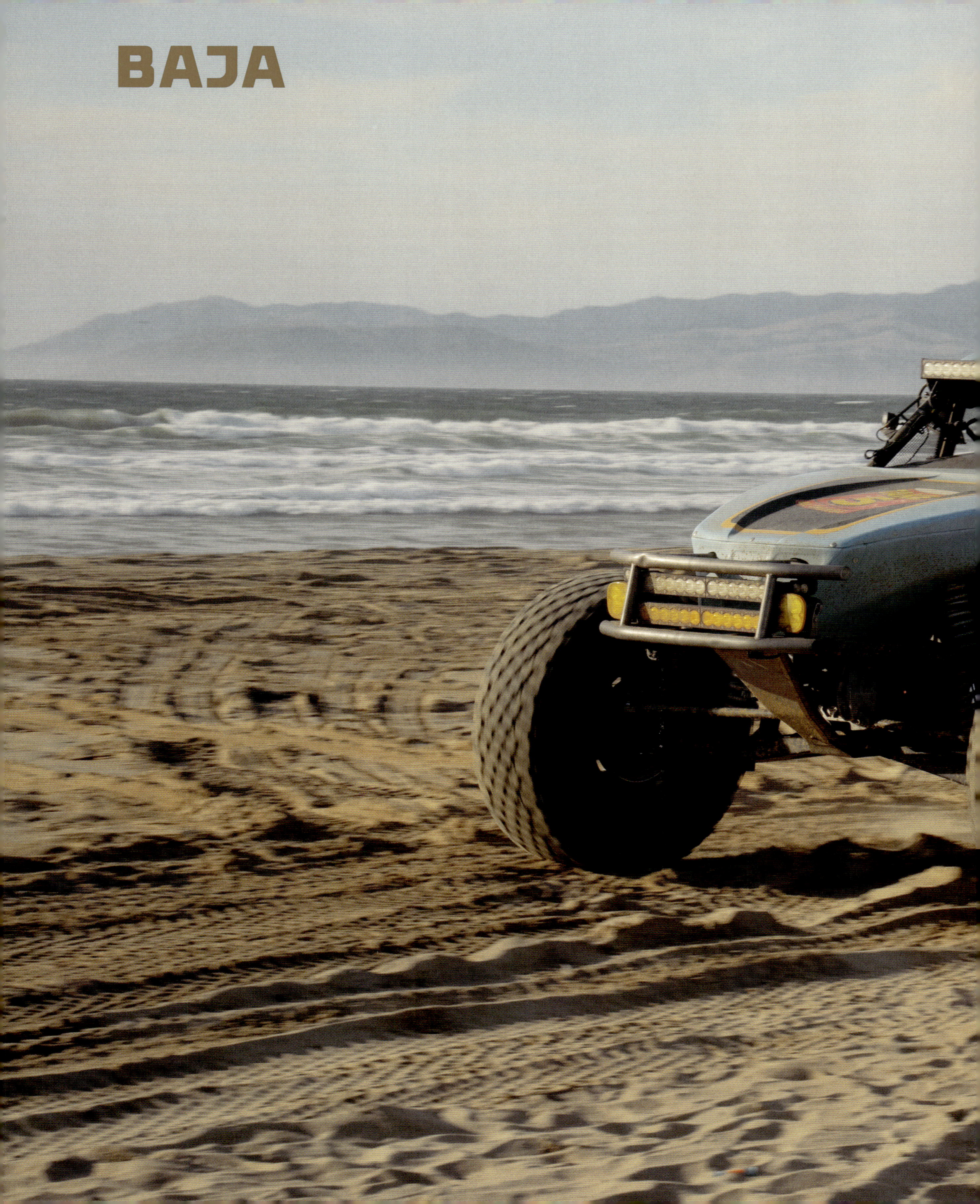

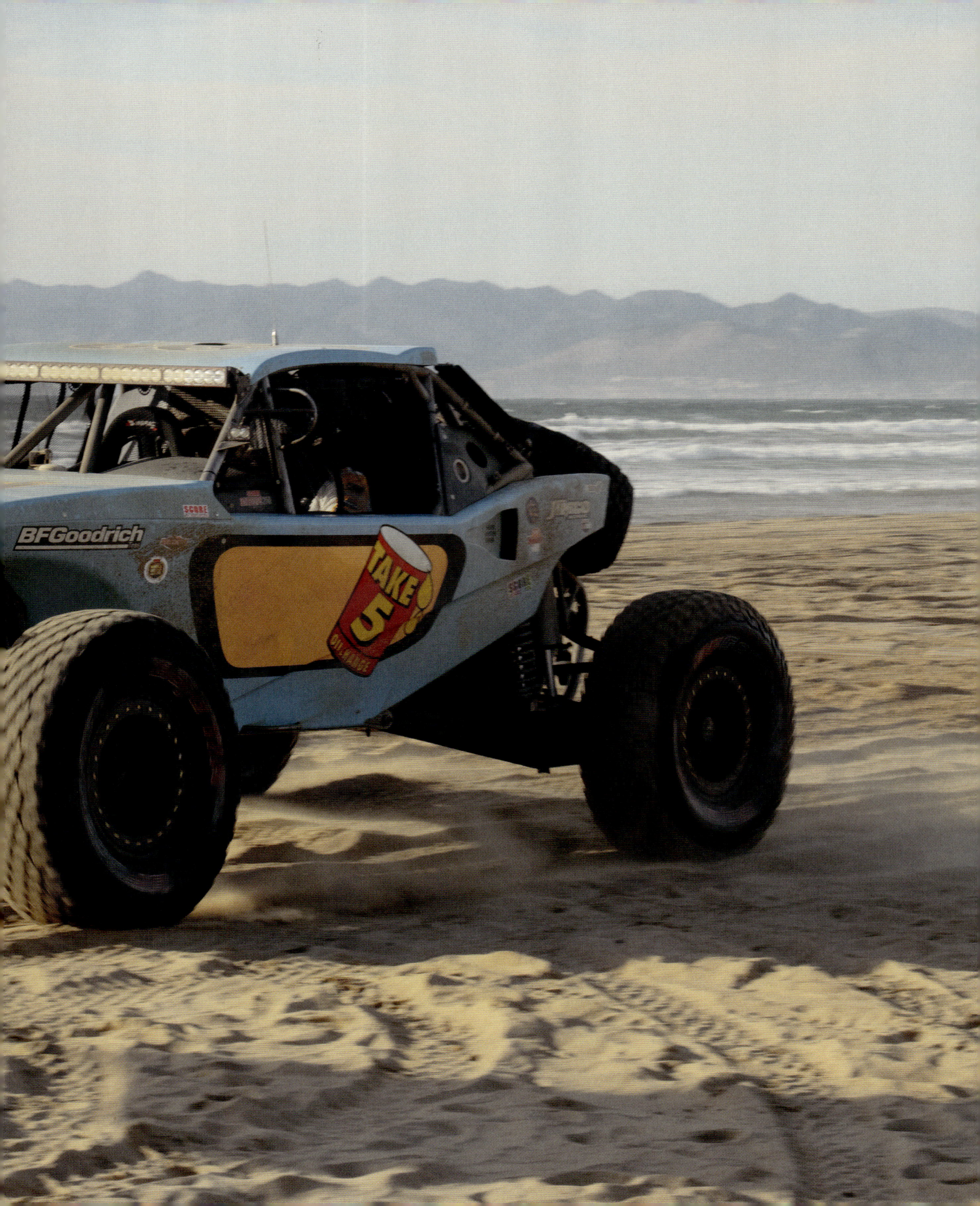
BFGoodrich
TAKE 5
OIL CHANGE

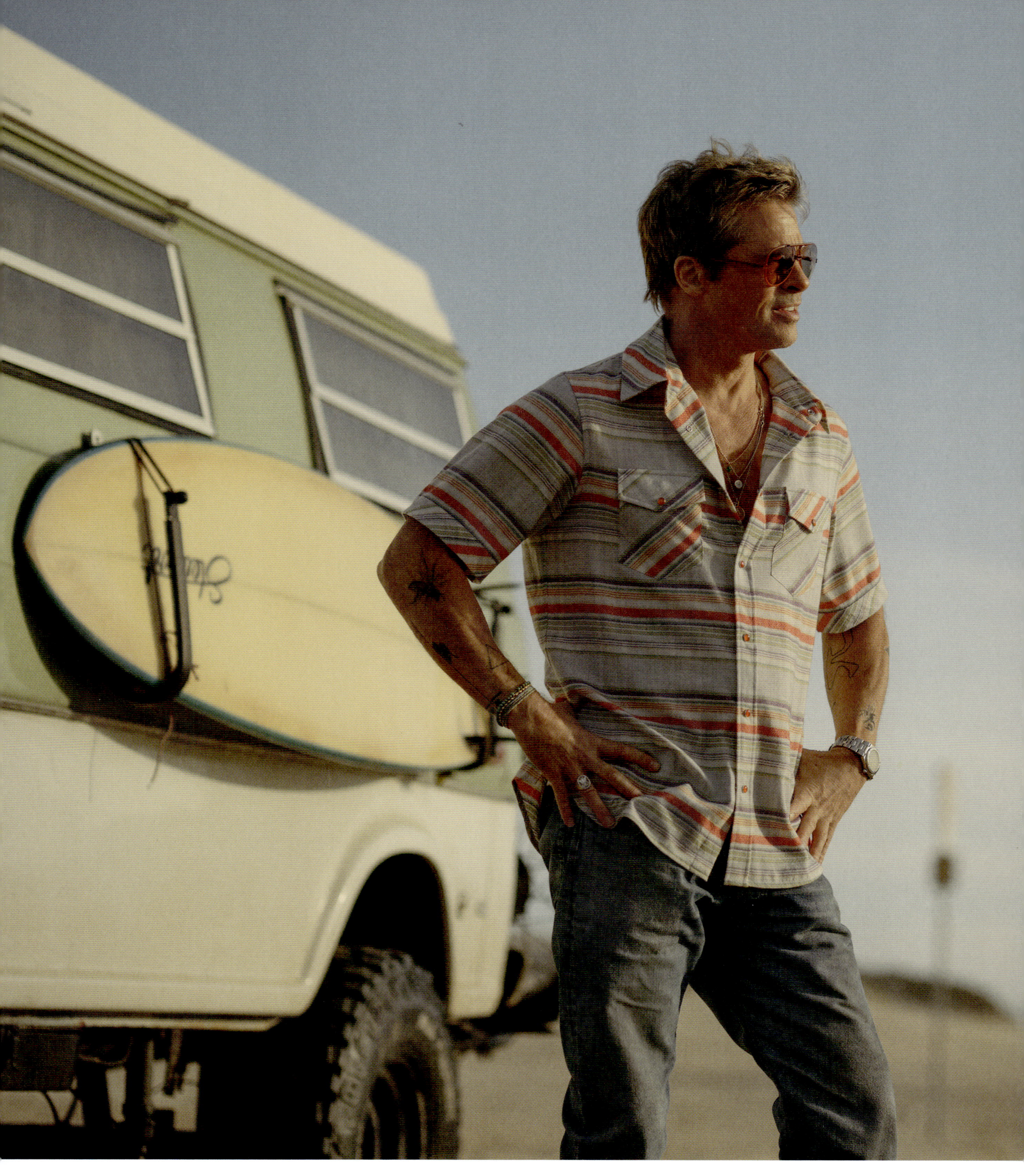

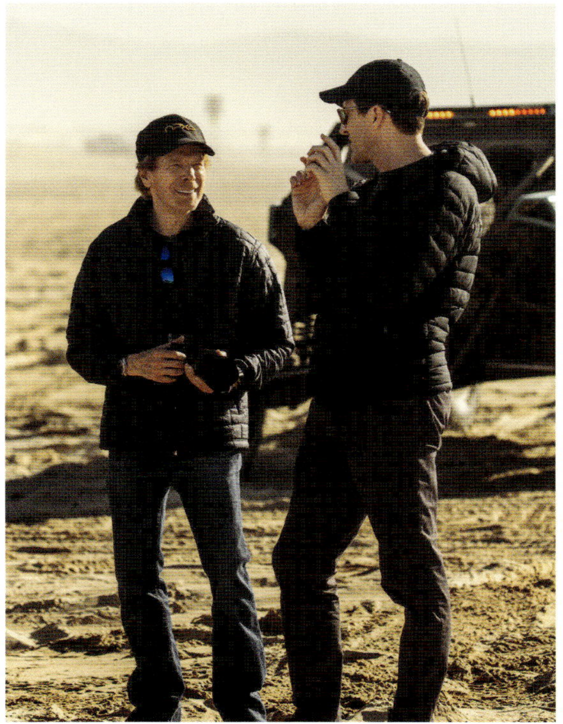

True to form, Sonny leaves Abu Dhabi in search of his latest adventure, heading to Ensenada, Mexico, for a drive in the Baja 1000. And as the credits roll, we see him behind the wheel of a dune buggy. "A class one dune buggy, which is the quote/unquote Formula One of dune buggies," laughs Kosinski. "These things that race at the Baja 1000 have unlimited, crazy horsepower, crazy suspension, very dangerous. So, it's the very tippy top of that type of racing. That's where Sonny Hayes's new challenge is going to be. I liked the idea that Formula One ends up being an incredible side road he takes. But, ultimately, it's yet another stop on this adventurous life he's leading." The production filmed the Baja sequence at Pismo Beach in California in early November 2024. "It was a fun couple of days," says Kosinski, "and a very different vibe than the world of Formula One, which was the whole point."

Left: Sonny (Brad Pitt) arrives in Baja.

Above: Joseph Kosinski and Jerry Bruckheimer behind-the-scenes while filming in Pismo Beach for the Baja scene.

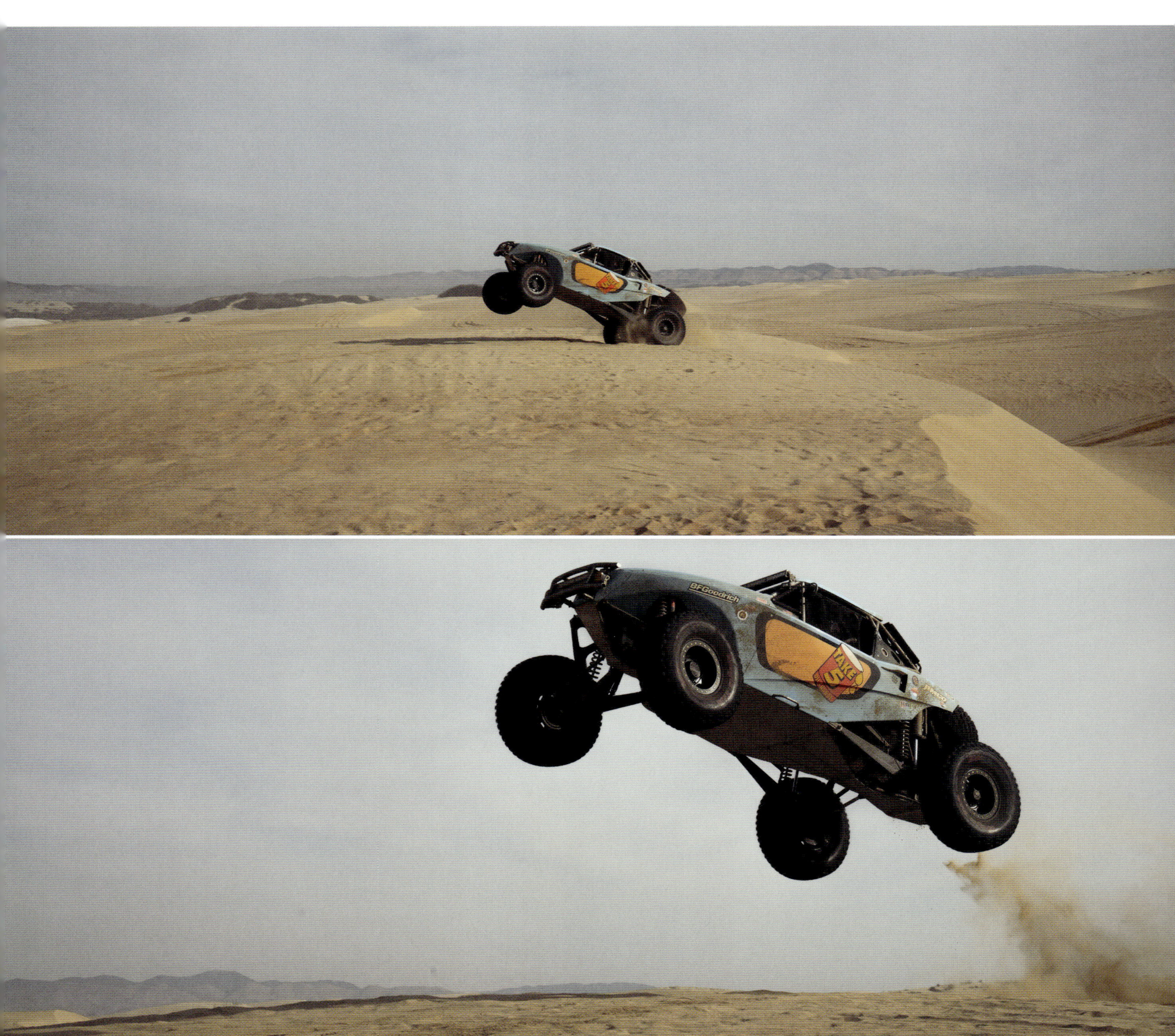

The film crew captures a JIMCO dune buggy catching air while driving laps around Pismo Beach.

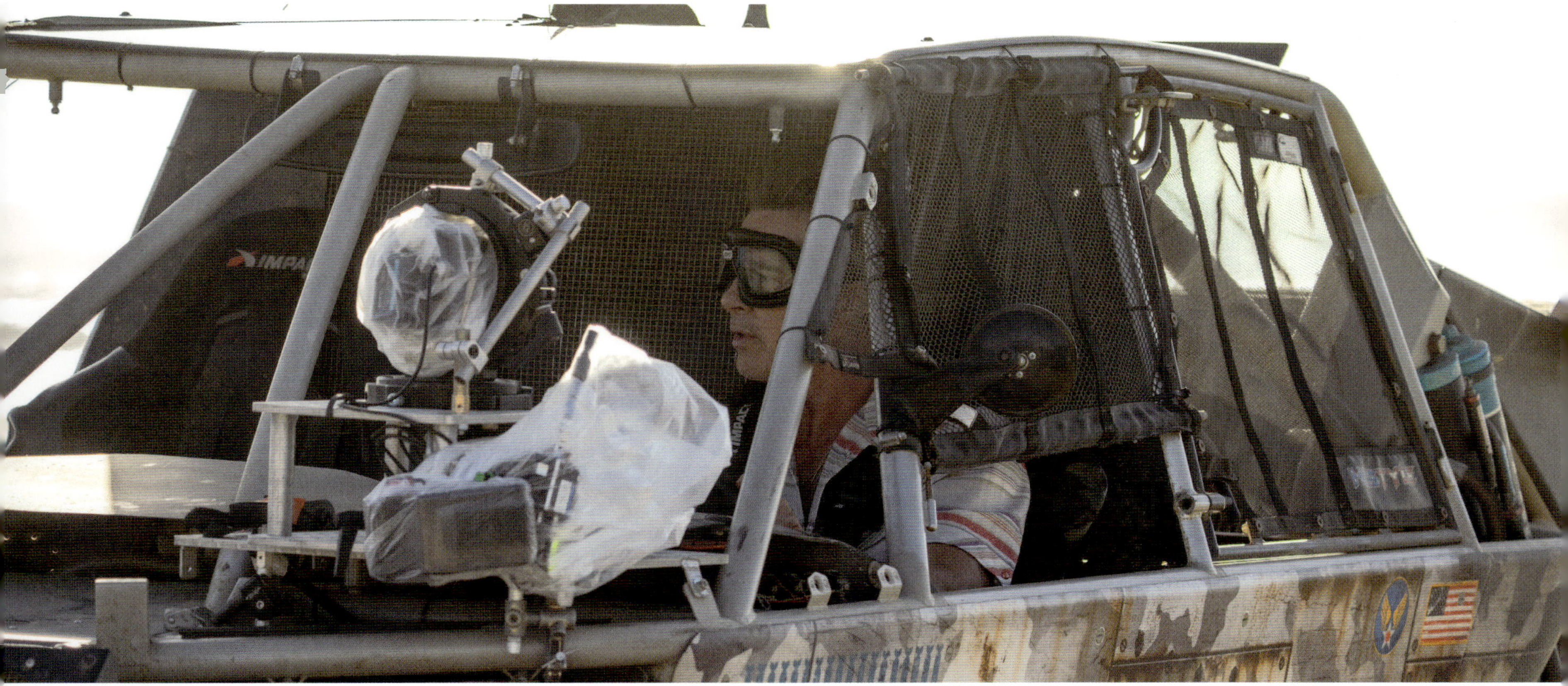

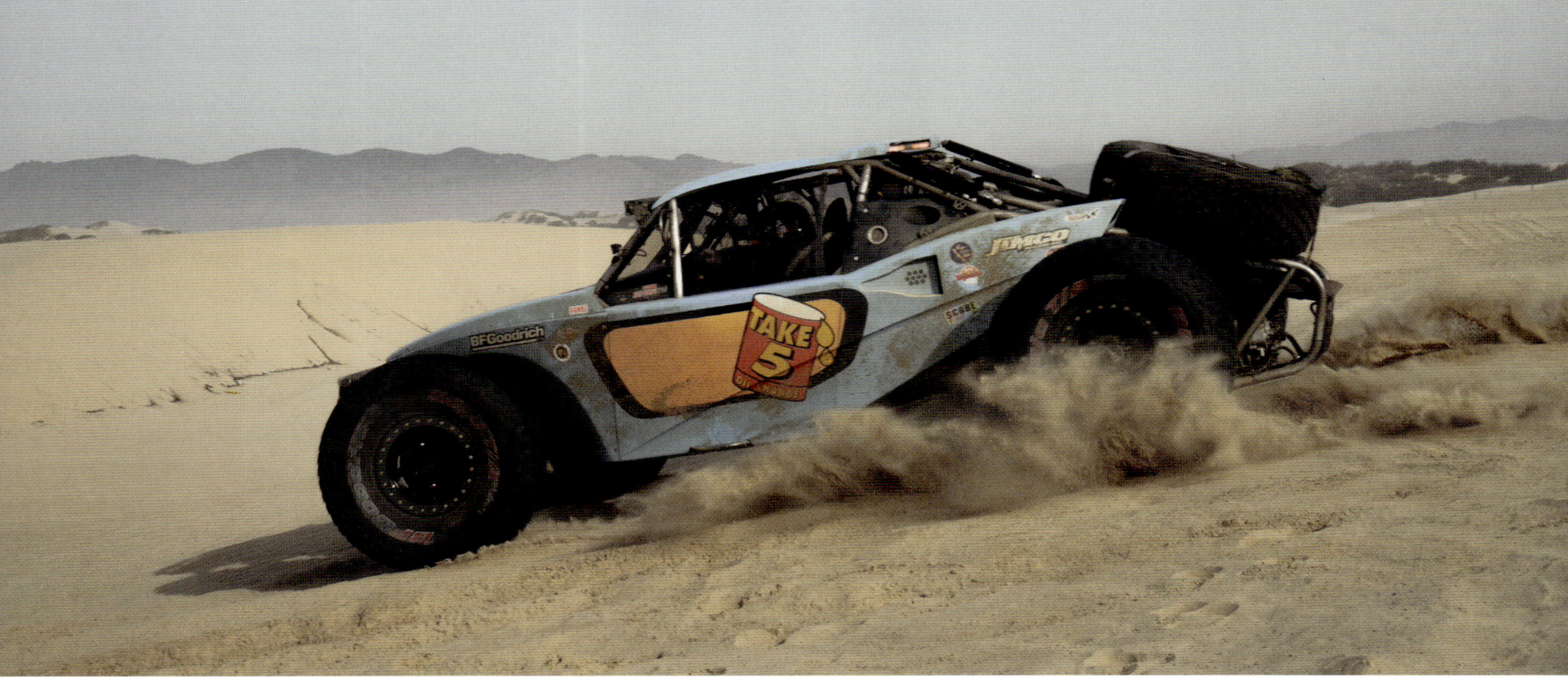
BFGoodrich
TAKE
5

10 AUDIO AND VISUAL DESIGN

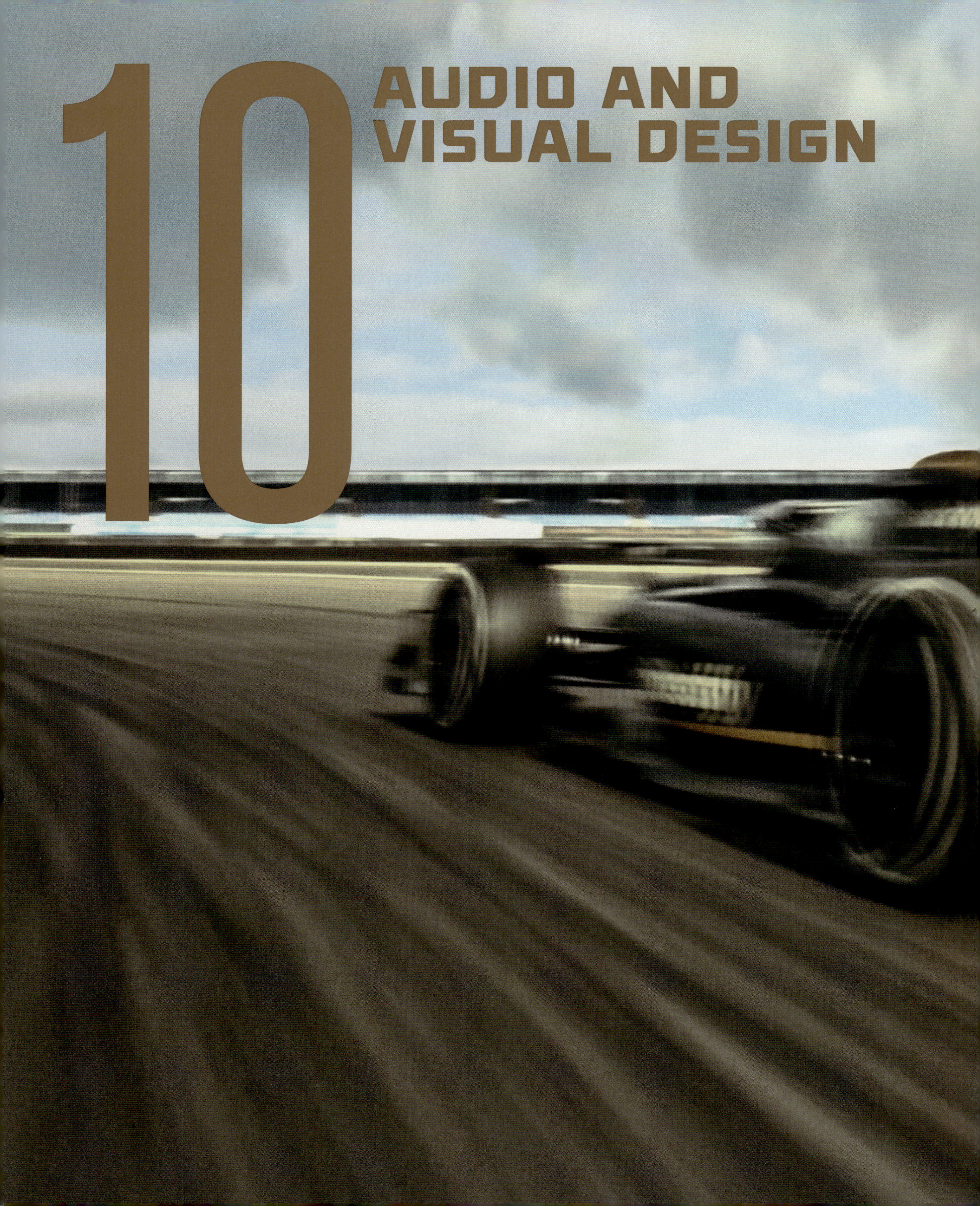

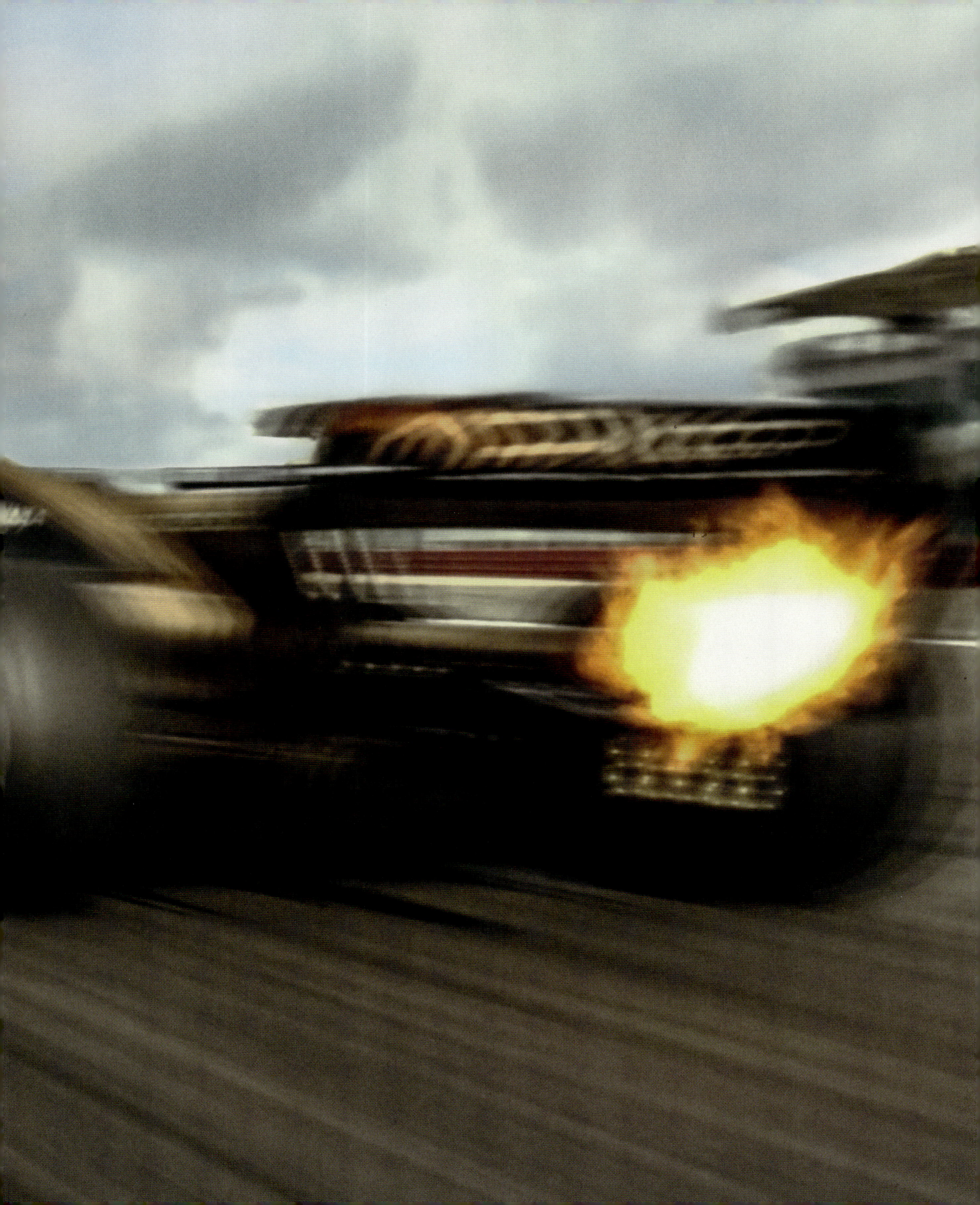

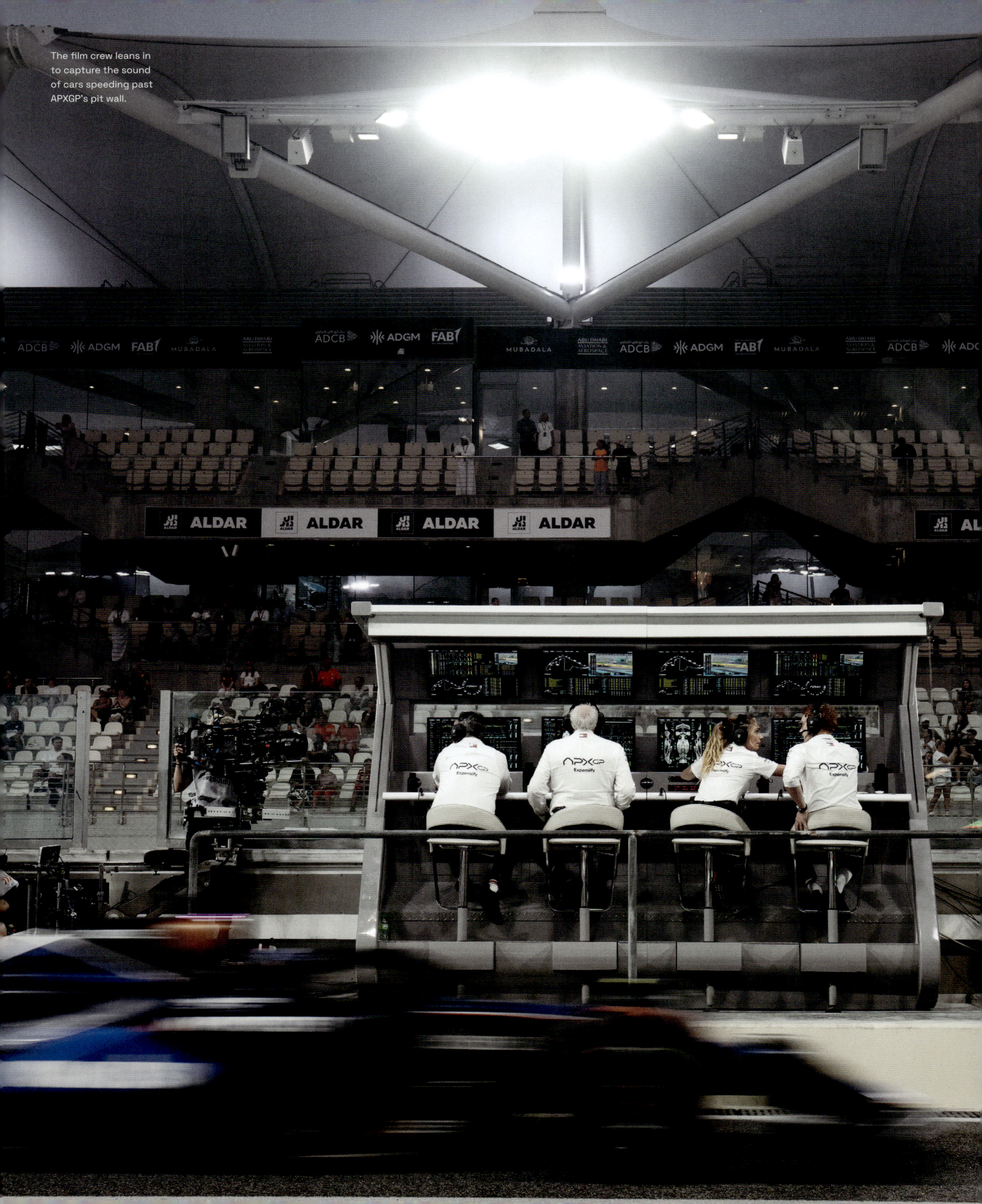

The film crew leans in to capture the sound of cars speeding past APXGP's pit wall.

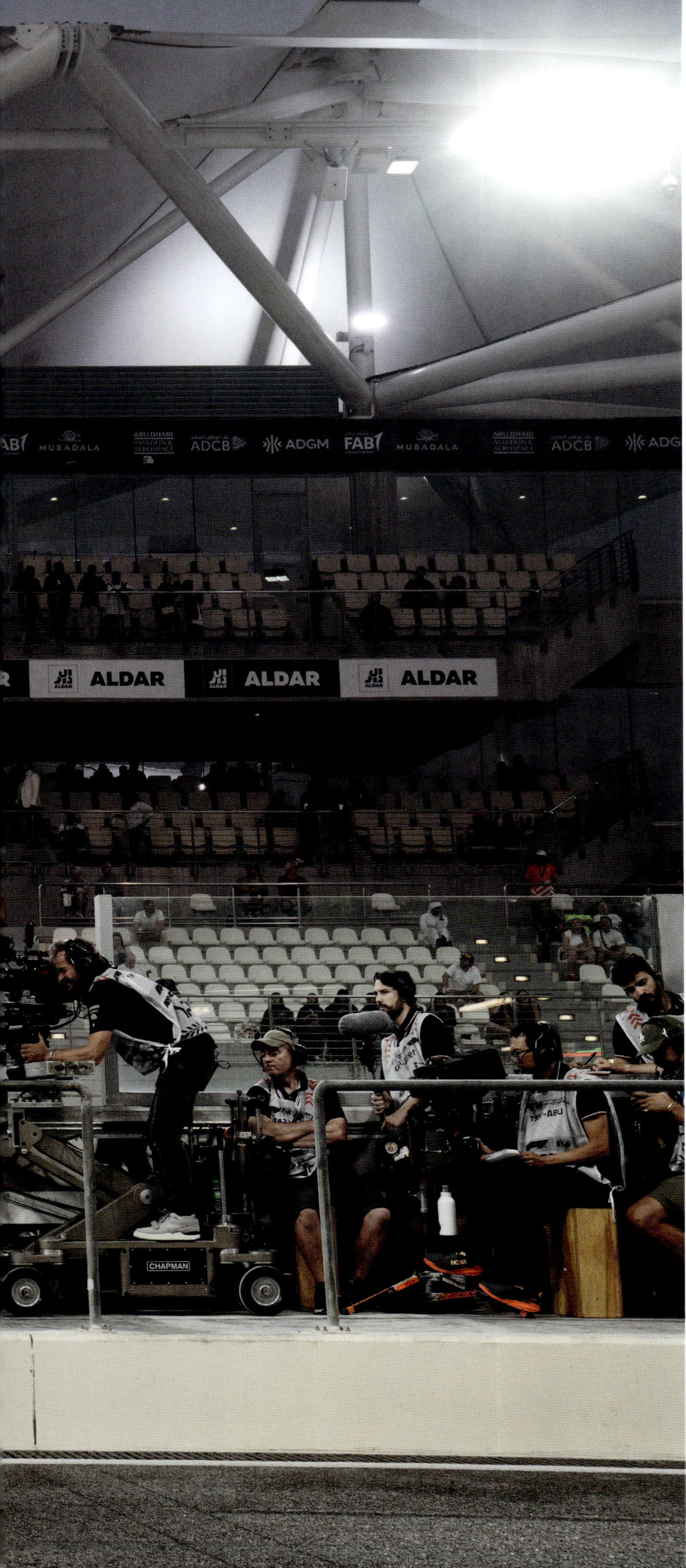

“We wanted you to experience what it’s like to be a Formula One driver in the same way that with *Top Gun: Maverick* we wanted you to experience what it was like to be in a fighter jet,” explains *F1* sound designer Al Nelson, who won an Oscar for *Top Gun*. “We wanted you to feel that speed. We wanted to be authentic. So, our first goal was to get as much authentic sound as we could. With *Top Gun*, I was on aircraft carriers recording jets in parallel to Joe shooting, and early in the process here I said to him, ‘Will we get access to Formula One cars to mike them up?’ Joe said, ‘Doubtful.’ You can’t just borrow a McLaren and take it out on track. The amount of people it requires to operate these cars is huge. The cost is crazy.”

And so, starting with the British Grand Prix in 2023, Nelson visited four race weekends—the other three being Las Vegas in 2024 and Abu Dhabi in 2023 and 2024—as well as two tire tests, recording as much authentic audio as possible of cars on track, in the pit lane, and in the garage. “Some of our most successful recording was at the tire tests. All cars on track with no crowds, PAs, or helicopters,” says Nelson, whose credits include the three Pixar *Cars* films. “From there we were able to use that material for the others as needed.”

Initially, he stuck mostly to the pit wall. “I had hours of cars going by at 200 miles per hour, and they all sounded the same. Even Lewis attested to that. He said on board, it’s a different feeling, but from the outside you can’t tell if it’s a Red Bull or a Ferrari. Going slowly, however, they all have a different personality.”

In addition to his own recordings, Nelson utilized those made by the film’s production sound recordist, Gareth John, as well as audio and video captured by the F1 broadcast team. “At each race, F1 has cameras and around a hundred microphones,” he explains. “Normally, those microphones are mixed for the broadcast. What we did was pick them off before they hit the broadcast, to record each channel discreetly. So, we had over a hundred channels of every turn of every track we shot at. Then we could reach out and say, ‘Can we get the onboard for Pérez at Silverstone? Can we get the onboard for Verstappen at Abu Dhabi?’ I could listen to those recordings. I could hear what the cars were doing and say to myself, ‘Okay, for turn one Monza, I’m going to use turn five at Abu Dhabi and make it sound the same.’ But we had a lot of material to cull through.”

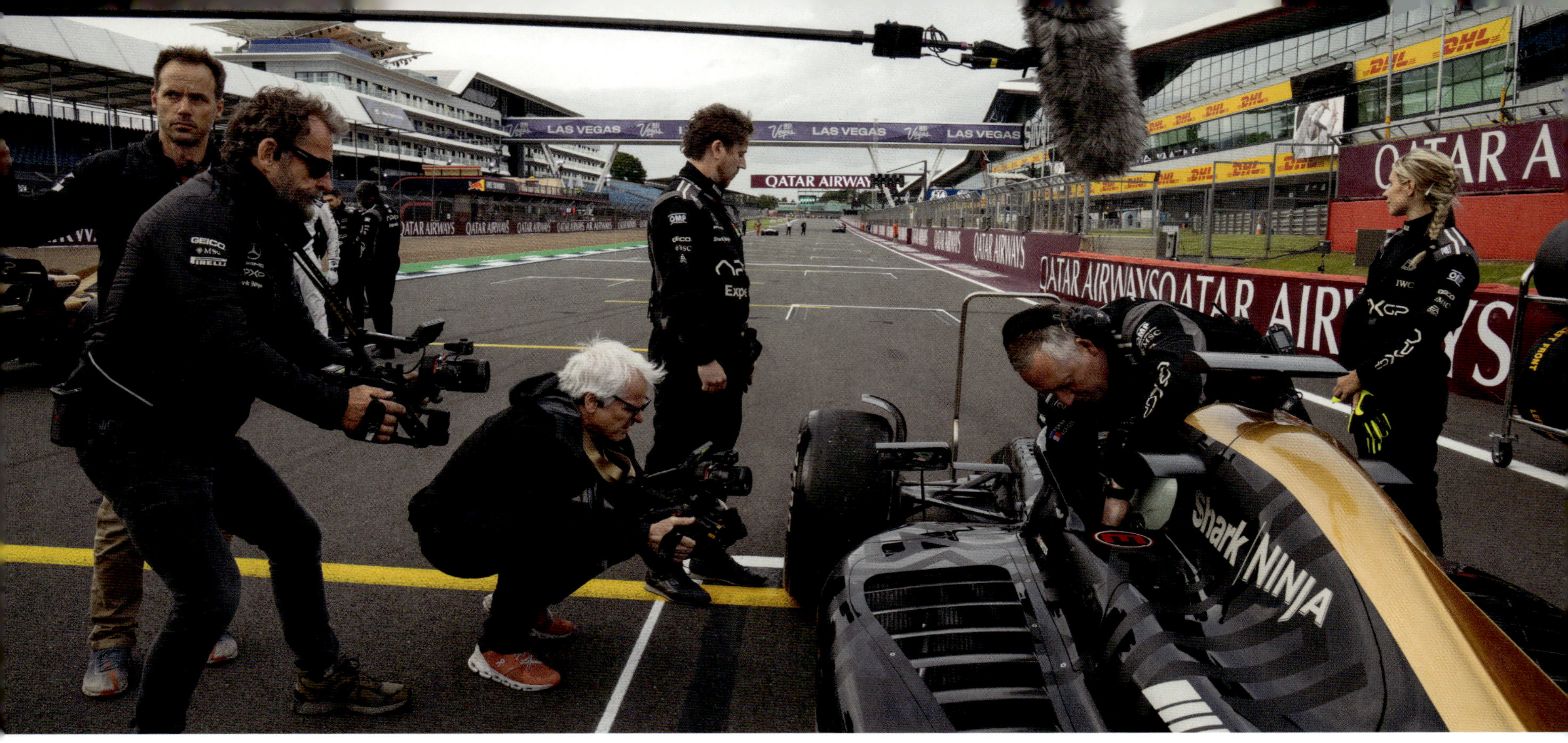

The biggest challenge, however, was creating the sound of the APXGP cars, which were modified F2 cars fitted with F2 engines, so they didn't sound like Formula One cars. But thanks to Mercedes, Nelson was able to put recording rigs on George Russell's car during tire testing in Abu Dhabi. "That was very helpful because we really wanted to define the sound of Sonny and Joshua's cars with new material," says Nelson, who used Russell's Mercedes for the APXGPs. "We could have used material from the F1 broadcast, but it's not as good quality, and we wanted to take it to the next step in the same way Joe was using the latest technology with the cameras."

Nelson suggested placing a Zoom F3 recorder, which weighs around a couple of pounds, on Russell's Mercedes but was turned down. In the end, he opted for a Tentacle Sync TRACK E recorder, which is about the size of a matchbox. "It records mono, so I used two, along with DKA microphones, which are the same kind they use for the F1 broadcast. There are always two microphones on each car, but there was no way for us to pick off those microphones and get it at the quality required."

The Tentacle recorders were placed on the floor of Russell's car with insulated, fire-retardant-covered wires leading to the microphones near the exhaust and gearbox. "As George pulled away, I thought, *Those are going to cook in about five minutes, so I'm going to*

The biggest challenge was creating the sound of the APXGP cars, which were modified F2 cars fitted with F2 engines.

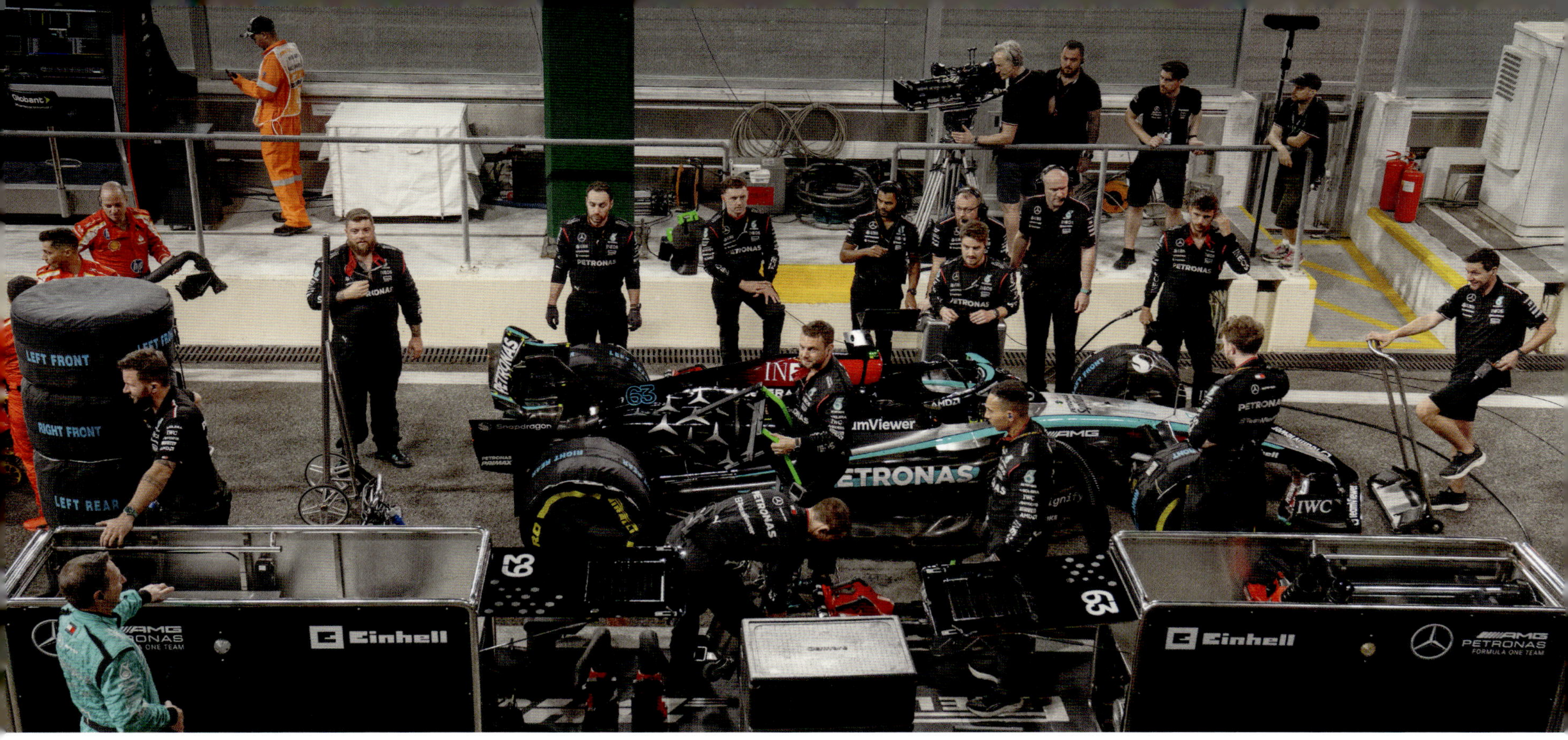

get about five minutes of material, and I hope it's good enough. But when George pulled in after 11 hours' testing, they were still recording. They got a little warped from the heat, but they survived. So, I had some amazing material to work with."

Not that the APXGP cars sound identical to Russell's Mercedes. "We made it as throaty as we could, so the APXGP sounds warmer, fuller, and less mechanical," says Nelson. "It's also about how that translates on the big screen and in Dolby Atmos in the theater. The more mechanical a sound, the less inviting it is to my ears." Moreover, all modern F1 cars have V6 hybrid engines and therefore required a little finessing for the benefit of cinema audiences. "That's when we start to apply our sound design techniques, which isn't to say we've added lion roars," Nelson continues. "These cars are not super punchy. They don't have big petrol pipes putting out that V8 roar. They are very precise and economical. But we portray them as super powerful, full of energy, and full of pop and punch to make it feel like we're moving in a rocket."

To further sell the illusion, Nelson and his team, which included supervising sound editor Gwendolyn Yates Whittle, and re-recording mixers Gary A. Rizzo and Juan Peralta, played with the sound mix, augmenting the engine roar with air and wind. "We used a lot of tire noises, so you feel the road under you, so if you listen to the track and turn off the actual engine of the car, you still feel like you're moving fast," says Nelson. "You feel the wind. You feel the whooshes. You feel the sound of things whipping by. You feel the sound of the tires. You feel the sound of the suspension. When you see those grid planks scraping and causing sparks, you feel the sound of the car bottoming out as you go over the curbs. I spent a lot of time getting curb sounds, making sure that all the personality the car presents, both onboard and from the exterior, is in the film."

Top Left: While the production crew used microphones to capture car sounds, they couldn't be used in the final cut as the APXGP cars had an F2 engine.

Top Right: To capture base audio of the APXGP cars, the production crew fitted F1 driver George Russell's Mercedes with fire-retardant recorders.

As Kosinski and editor Stephen Mirrione started to piece the film together, Nelson was able to "pinpoint exactly what was missing and what I needed," he says. "There's so much material that happens in the pit lane. The car hitting the limiter, the car accelerating out of the pit stop. They do practice pit stops during FP3, usually, so I was able to get the teams doing practice pit stops. And I was able to get in the garage with Lewis and Russell when they started their cars. Each time I would go back and record, I would have new objectives. I would need more approaching the pit lane. I would need extreme downshift as they approach a sharp turn. I would need downshifting and taking the curbs."

Nelson's most successful recording session was at Abu Dhabi in December 2024: "At that point, I'd seen almost all the film. I knew a lot more about what we needed and how to get it and where to go. Don't hang out at the pit wall. Get on the other side of turn one where they're downshifting, then accelerating away, so you can get behind them. We wanted to make sure to emphasize that everywhere you are on a track, you're either downshifting or upshifting or at speed."

As much as Hamilton had called bullshit on anything not realistic in the script, his input in the sound mix was equally invaluable. "Lewis would tell Joe that a sound was wrong on a shot because we'd taken a sound from a different part of the track, and the sound of the engines would be different closer to a wall," reveals screenwriter Ehren Kruger.

Nelson recalls Hamilton watching an early cut of Sonny's Silverstone audition as well as the British Grand Prix sequence. "We spent a day with Lewis, and his knowledge of what the car sounds like in each location is impeccable," Nelson says. "He would say, 'You are correct with sixth gear there, but I usually lift a little.' Or 'I can hear you're using the sound of the car on the straight. But that straight is on the grid, past pit wall, and I can hear the reflection as opposed to when you're out on the straight between five and six, in the open, and there's no reflection.' It was very helpful."

That said, given that neither APXGP driver is as good as seven-time World Champion Hamilton, some leeway was allowed. "Sonny hasn't driven an F1 car in many years, so he's a little rusty, and Joshua's still learning. So, we have some rules we can bend," says Nelson. "But hearing the perspective from a professional racing driver was very helpful. He had a lot of notes. On paper, it's right. In my ear, that's wrong. Then we had another Zoom with him, and he had some great insights."

Hamilton also performed several maneuvers on track especially for Nelson to record. "He said, 'I'm going to do grid starts for you,' and he would pull up. He was usually last, and he'd rev and rev, then he would take off. I got those at Las Vegas and Abu Dhabi."

When it came to capturing Daytona, Nelson had more access to Sonny's Porsche and the other GT cars. "I was there on location when they were shooting. I was able to hang around the garage, and they did allow me to get a small recorder on the Porsche," Nelson says. "Gareth also got recorders on some of the other cars, so we got some good material. There were not just GTs there; there was a variety of cars, LMPs and LMP2s. Having those various colors was helpful. I was able to go all around the track and record a lot of different sounds, and we put this scene together."

"We had it really dialed in, but Joe wanted to make sure the scene was epic, so we identified several places where Sonny was driving insanely and arranged for a recording session at a track in Palm Springs. [Daytona driver and consultant] Pat Long brought out a GT3, and my colleague Scott and I recorded him doing whatever we needed, which were extreme down and upshifts, where he was shifting gears very erratically and very quickly. It was a huge help and made that sequence feel disjointed and energetic, like you're really in the car."

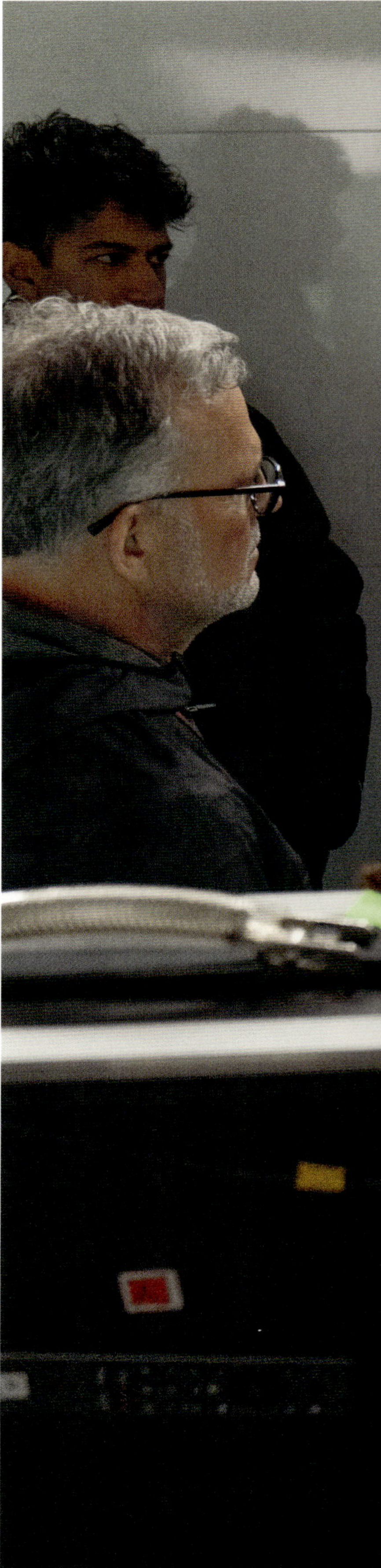

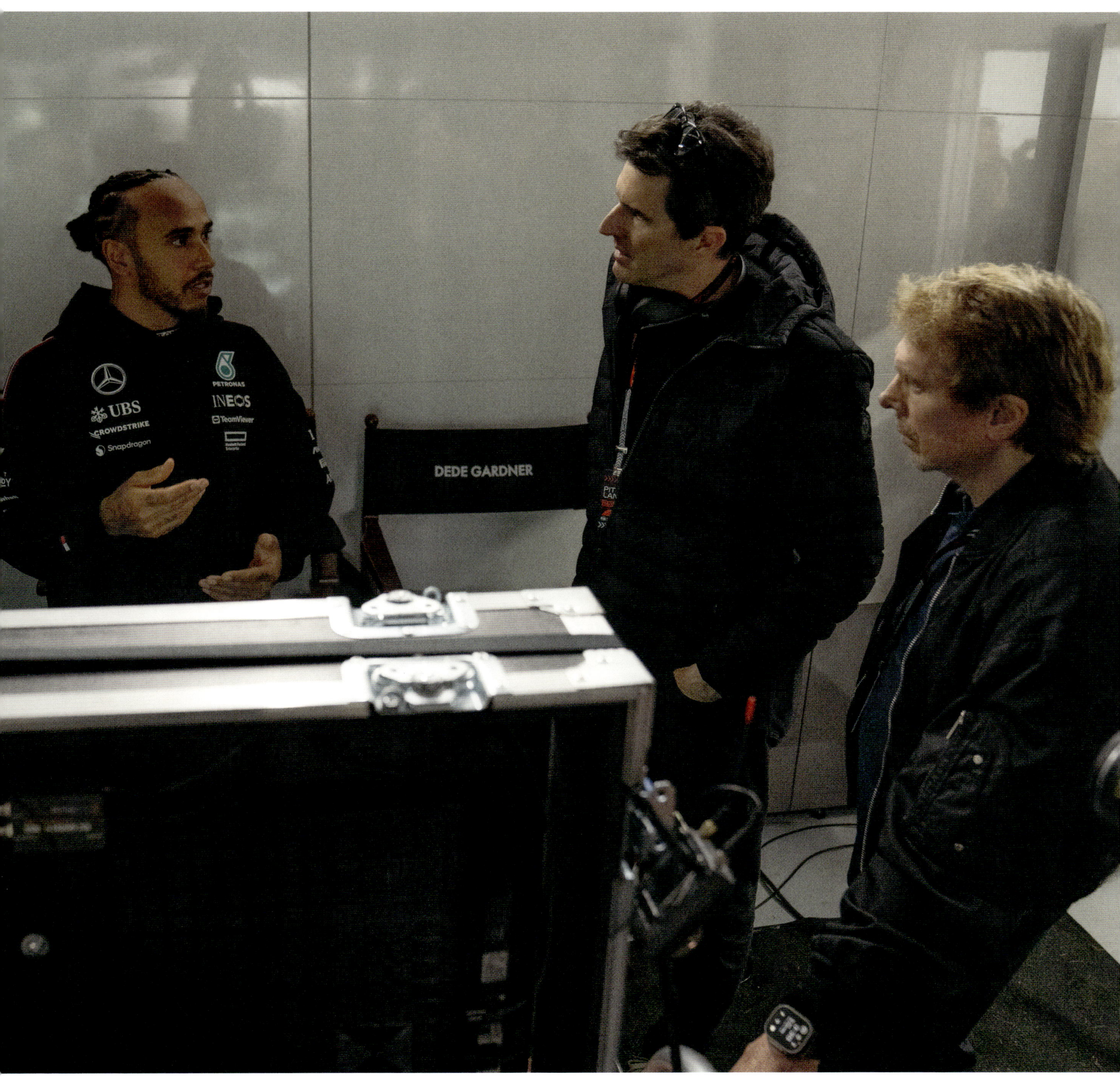

Lewis Hamilton provided crucial feedback on how the APXGP cars should sound to ensure the film had an authentic sound design.

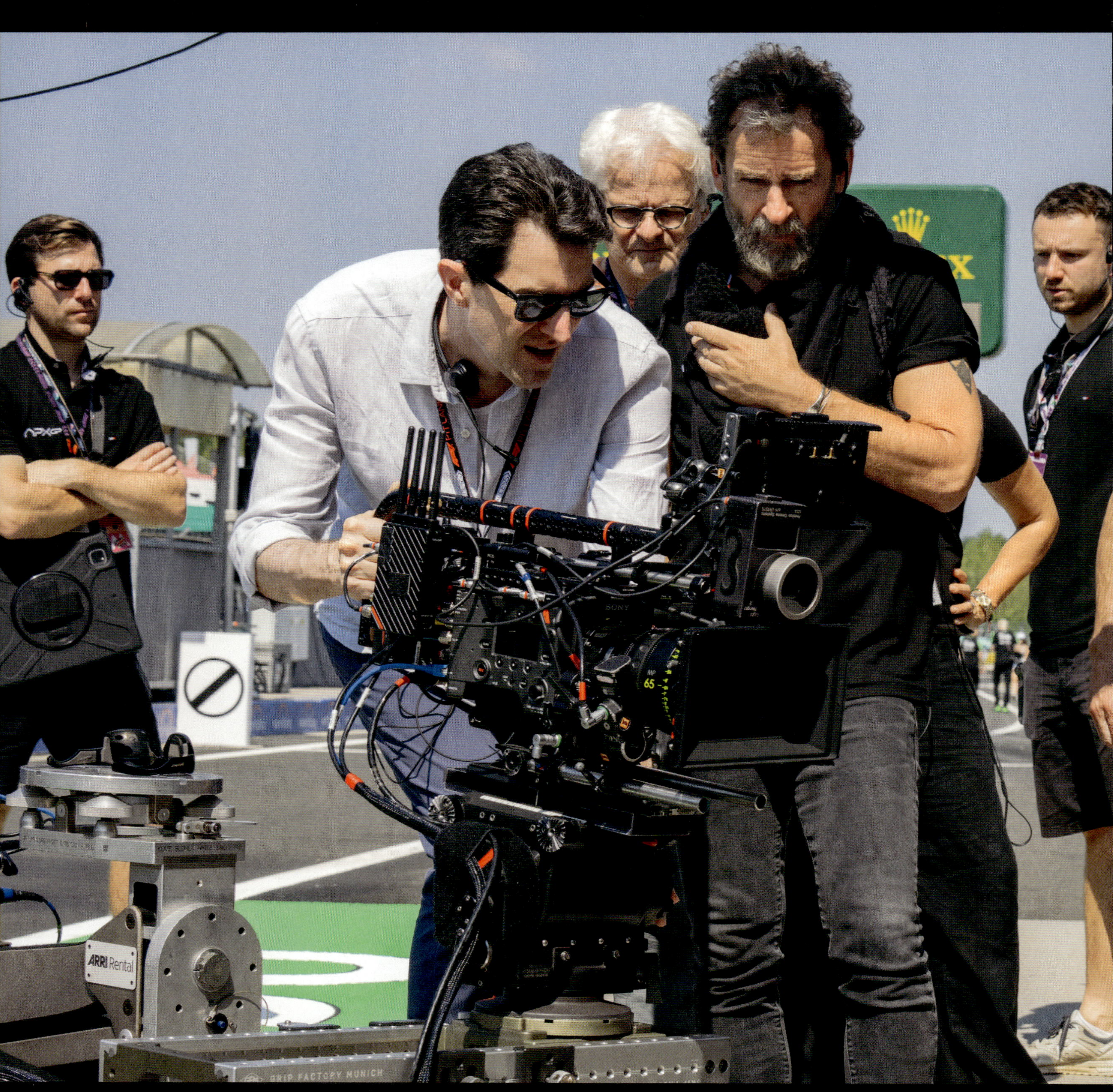

Above: Joseph Kosinski and the
film crew shot real F1 and F2 cars in

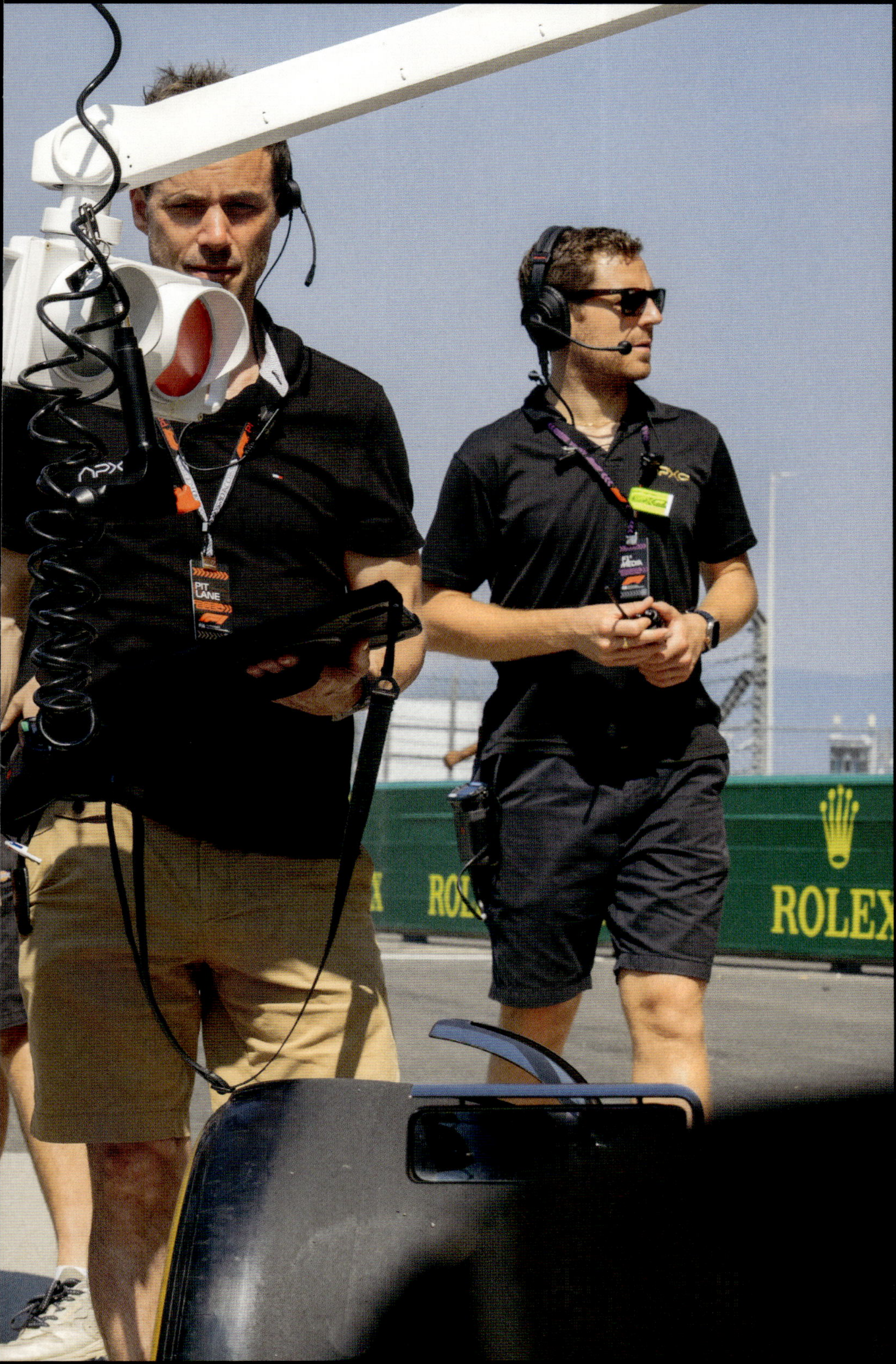

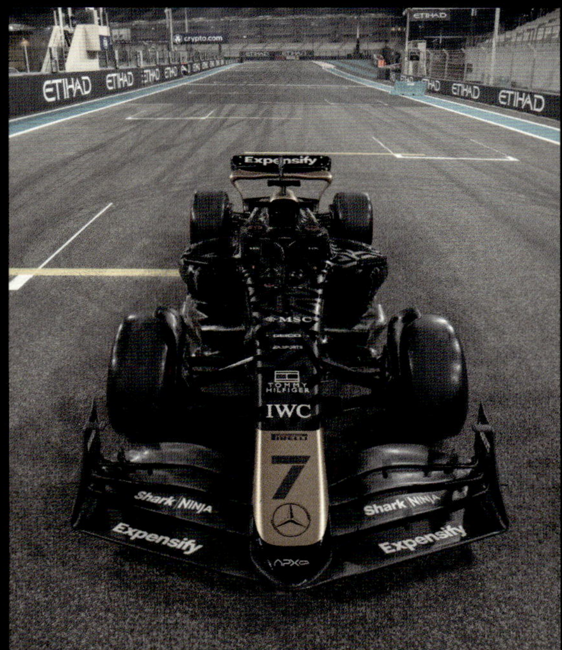

Director Joseph Kosinski and Ryan Tudhope, his visual effects supervisor on *Top Gun: Maverick*, *Spiderhead*, and *F1*, have a simple but effective philosophy when it comes to visual effects: Always start with as much real photography as you possibly can.

"With *Top Gun*, we were shooting real military jets that would get digitally reskinned into a foreign fighter," says Kosinski. "It was the same technique here. Shoot as much real Formula One and Formula Two cars. Get it as much in camera as possible, then reskin to put our car in the race. And because you're starting with real photography and real lighting and pulling focus and there's vibration, it results in something that's indistinguishable from reality."

"Rather than inventing shots out of thin air and letting the visual effects team drive the shot design, what we do is let the on-set crew—the camera operators, Joe, our DP—drive the design," says Tudhope. "Then visual effects take it the rest of the way and add elements we couldn't film, things obviously important for the story. But the fact you have that 'foundational plate,' as we call it, means there are happy accidents as well as the limitations that occur when a real person is trying to capture something going by quickly—be it a fighter jet or a Formula One car."

In the case of *F1*, that "foundational plate" required filming the real APXGP cars during race weekends or separate track day sessions, or else using footage captured by the F1 broadcast team, then turning a Ferrari, Mercedes, Red Bull, or McLaren into an APXGP car, "so it looks like our team is battling real cars on the track."

Both methods would involve reskinning challenges for Tudhope's team. "Because it's a film that happens in the real world, it must be absolutely grounded," says Kosinski, "so our visual effects work had to be seamless and invisible. It's the same scale as *Top Gun*, if not bigger, but the complexity is even higher, just because of what's going on in every frame. It's very distinct, very recognizable, very bespoke Formula One cars, racing next to each other in front of a couple of hundred thousand people. I think we took it to the next level in terms of pulling off that magic trick that makes the movie work and makes you feel like you're there with Sonny and Joshua, alongside all the other drivers."

The film's two primary visual effects vendors—between them they would create around 2,500 visual effects shots—were Framestore, tasked with handling all the F1 races, and Industrial Light & Magic (ILM), which looked after the Daytona opener among other sequences. "My goal was to make the visual effects as invisible as possible, which starts with trying to predict what the team might require down the road, and help solve those issues while we're filming," continues Tudhope, who, early on, realized that visual effects would need to create a virtual version of all the tracks where they would be filming. This meant using LiDAR (Light Detection and Ranging) to make a series of high-resolution 3D maps. "We explored buying that data from someone, then concluded we would have Clear Angle Studios, a U.K.-based company, scan the tracks. Every time we would travel to a different track, Clear Angle would show up. We would film during the days, then, at night, they would go around and scan everything. It took multiple nights to get around these massive tracks, and we walked away with data that's equivalent to what the F1 teams have, if not better, down to millimeter accuracy of track undulations, as well as the stands."

In addition, the production sent an array vehicle, fitted with eight cameras, to film 360-degree imagery of the various circuits, as well as straight up. "We ran that down the race line on F1 weekends, so we were effectively taking twenty-four photographs per second all the way around. What that did was document all the signage and crowds, giving us a reference we could refer to when adding things to our footage."

Then there were the cars themselves. "On films like this, one of the most important things to get right are the assets themselves, meaning how good the cars look when you put them in hundreds of shots. What you don't want is to be dropping a car into a particular lighting situation and it not look real," says Tudhope, who had special effects supervisor Keith Dawson build a full-size turntable, on which he placed one of the APXGP cars, then filmed it spinning slowly. He also shot the car with a Steadicam, moving in close, then away. From the resultant footage, Tudhope created a digital version of the APXGP car, which he would view alongside his footage of the real car. "When you can't tell which one is real and which one is digital, then you know you've got to the point where you need to be for the film."

Right: Previs of the Silverstone audition scene.

Below: The array car was used to film 360-degree imagery of different racing circuits.

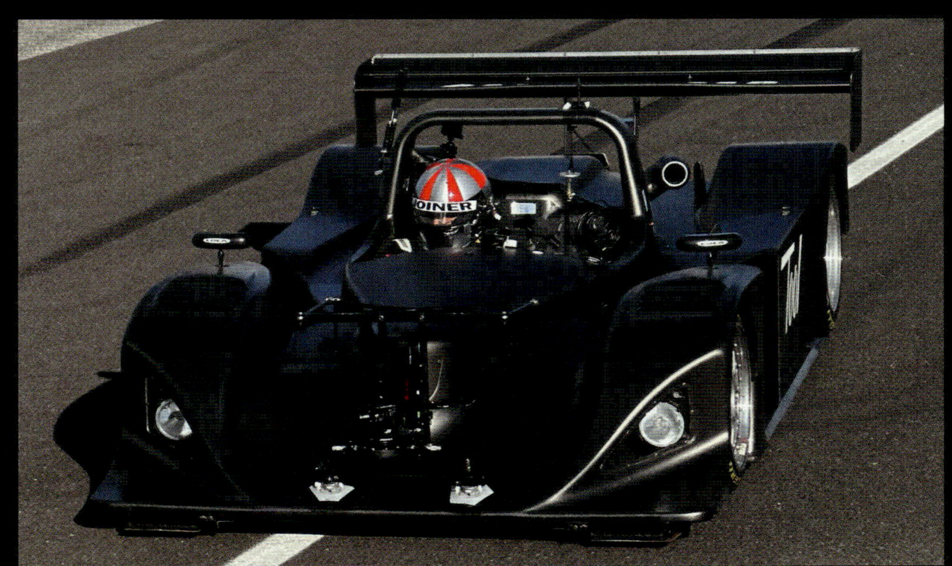

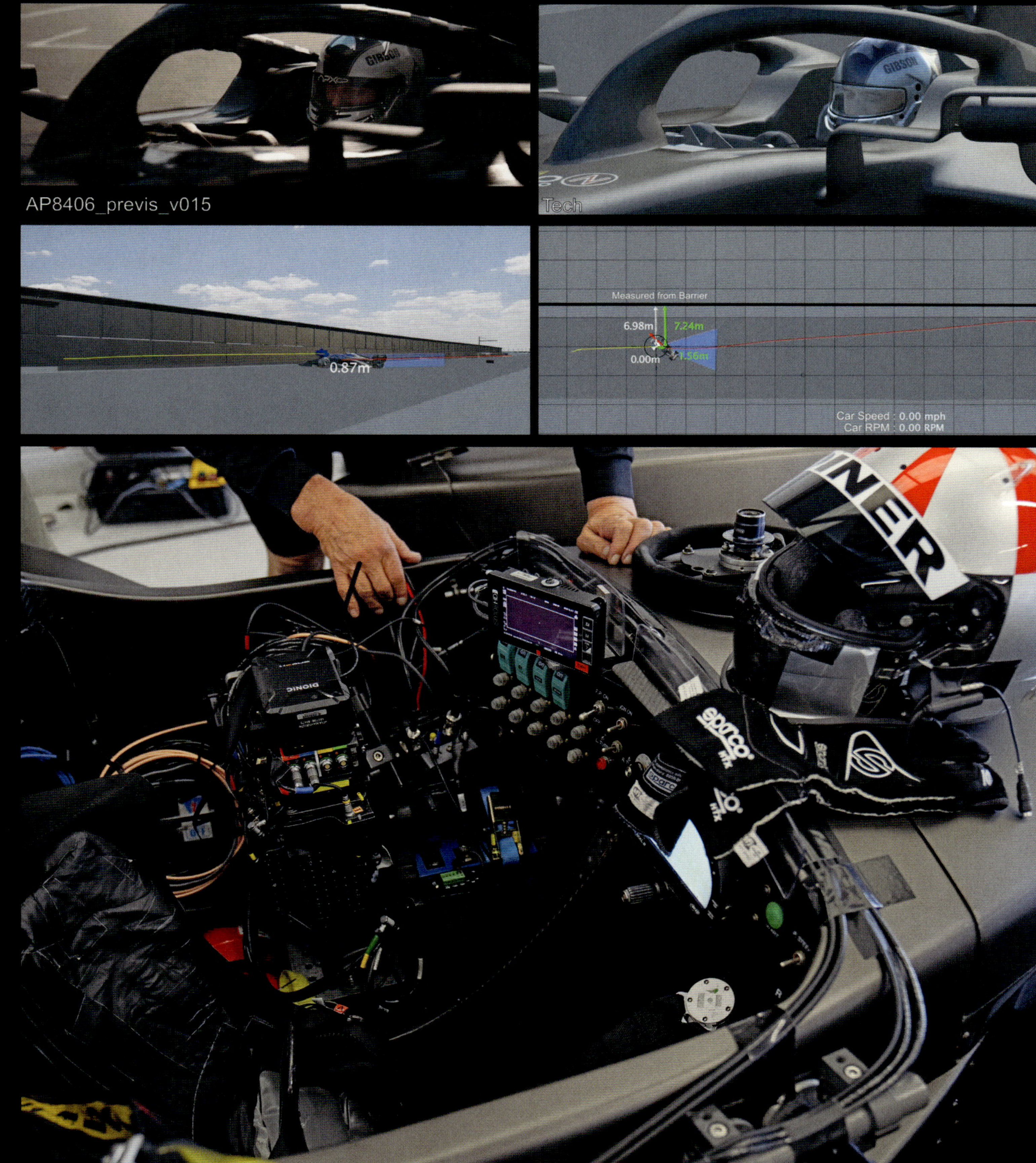
AP8406_previs_v015
Tech
GIBSON
Measured from Barrier
6.98m
7.24m
0.00m
1.56m
0.87m
Car Speed : 0.00 mph
Car RPM : 0.00 RPM
DIONIC
sparco

Unfortunately, it was not possible to repeat the process with the other twenty cars on the Formula One grid. "We knew we couldn't scan their cars but needed to re-create them for the movie, so we treated them like we were the press and photographed them when they were on the grid or coming through the pit lane," says Tudhope. "And then you get into a variety of other things, like capturing the clouds and the sky and the lighting environment through principal photography. Typically, when filming, I'm near Joe, Claudio, and Jerry, keeping an eye on everything we're shooting."

As Kosinski and editor Stephen Mirrione began cutting sequences together, they would turn the footage over to the visual effects team. "This might include a mixture of broadcast and stuff we shot," says Tudhope. "In the case of F1 stuff, Framestore would start animating other cars, putting things together. It's what we call a 'postvis phase.' The goal being to roughly reskin cars and add digital cars in the distance to help the edit. It's rough, it's fast, but it's getting cars in the right spot so Stephen and Joe can watch it and say, 'That's working' or 'Let's tweak this.'"

Once everyone was happy, Tudhope's team started to refine the animation, adding sparks, smoke, or rain, painstakingly matching the real lighting, to seamlessly integrate the effects into the footage. "That process can be upwards of a year. Sometimes it's much faster, a matter of a month or two."

As well as creating digital cars or reskinning existing ones, the visual effects department also created digital versions of all the drivers. "Let's say Brad is battling Verstappen. In real life he would have been battling Craig or one of our other stunt drivers. We look at that footage, put our Verstappen helmet on top of

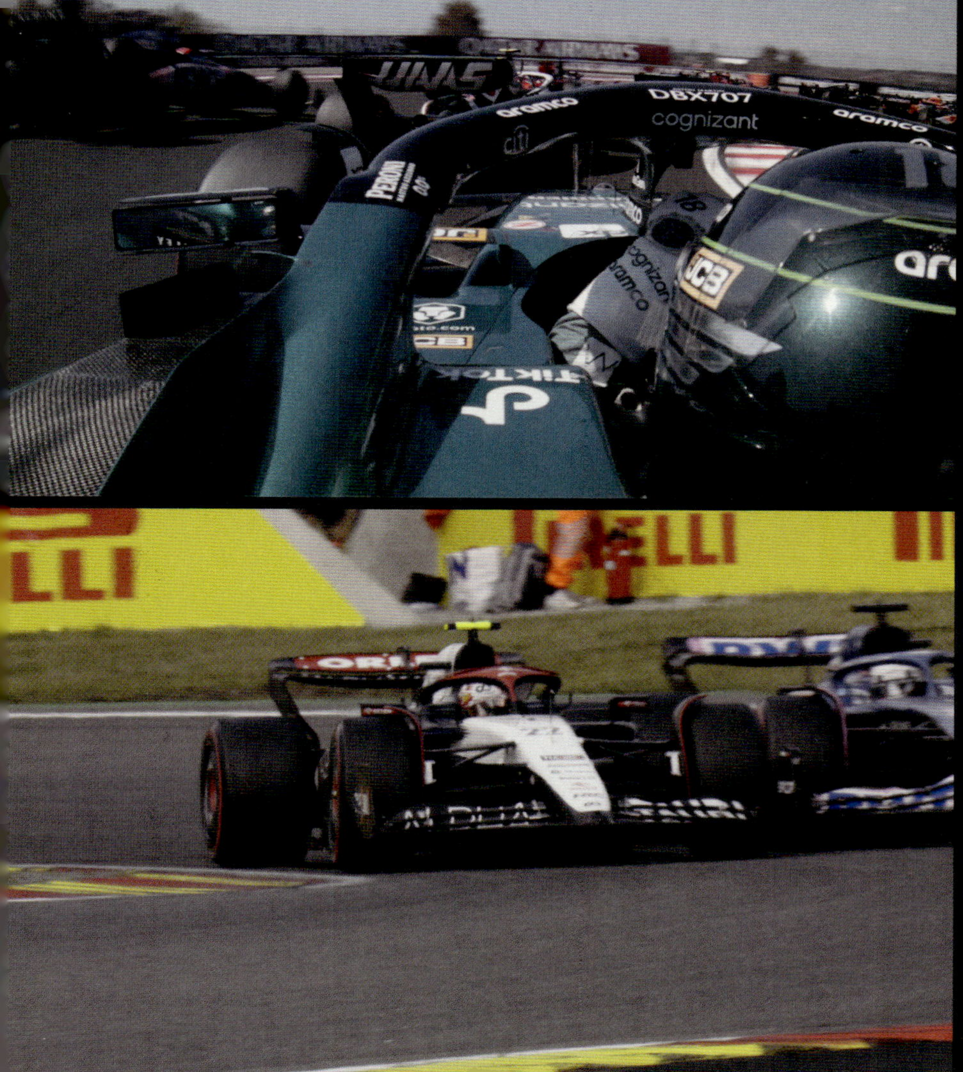

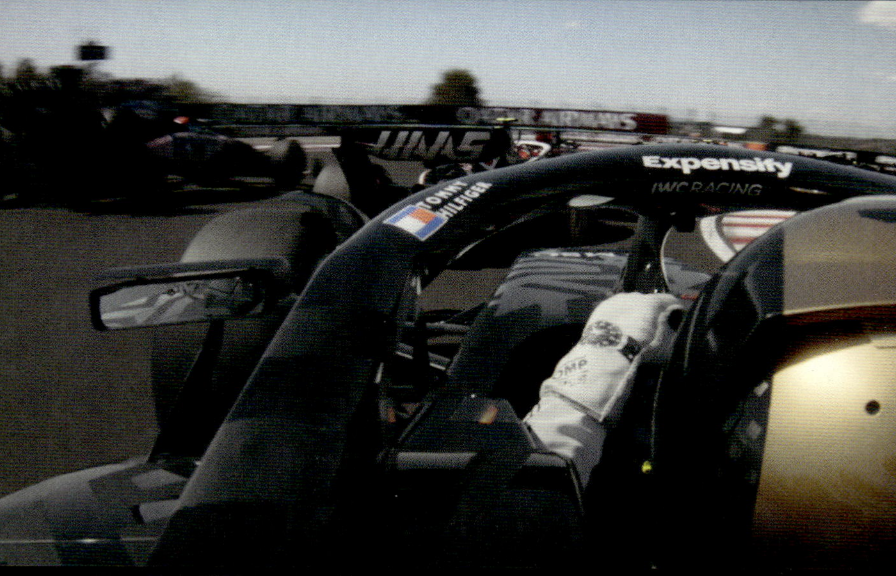

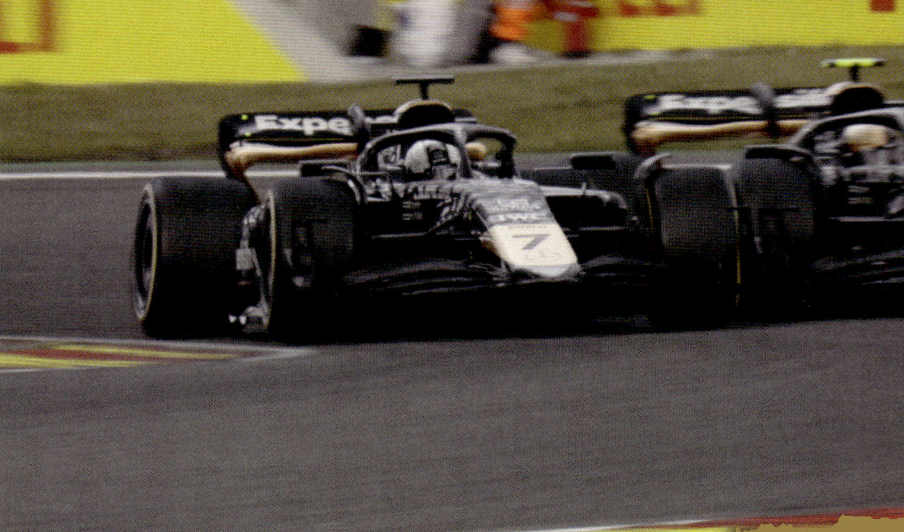

Bottom Left: Other F1 cars were reskinned by the visual effects team to look like the APXGP car.

Bottom Right: The fourth race car built for the film was reskinned to resemble the APXGP car, with other vehicles also digitally added in post-production.

Craig's, and make sure it moves the exact same way Craig did," says Tudhope. "Thankfully, all the F1 drivers have very shiny visors, so you don't really see their faces, which makes it a little easier, whereas our drivers have clear visors, so you see them in our footage. We also have digital versions of our drivers. So, if it's a digital car, it's a digital Brad or digital Damson inside. Although, generally, if you're looking at Brad, it's Brad. Where we used a digital Brad is if we have a piece of broadcast footage and it's a McLaren and we want it to be an APXGP car."

But a huge amount of Tudhope's team's work involved signage and crowds. "Typically, we filmed at racetracks in the days leading up to or following F1 races, sometimes at F1 races too. But for our 'hot laps,' the crowds were not always at full capacity. Even on an F1 weekend, our 'hot lap' might be in the morning, so there were less people in the stands. Or if we shot in the days following a race weekend, a lot of the signage would get pulled down and moved to the next location. So, one of the major visual effect tasks was filling out those grandstands and restoring signage to what it was on the actual race day."

This was even more of an issue as filming took place across two different Formula One seasons—2023 and 2024—with main sponsors changing, impacting the signage at the various tracks. "When we went back to Hungary in 2024, instead of Workday being the sponsor, it was MSC Cruises or something like that," says Tudhope. "So, between Joe, Stephen, and me, we decided what was jarring and what wasn't, and attacked the things we felt we needed to change and let things go we didn't feel were necessary."

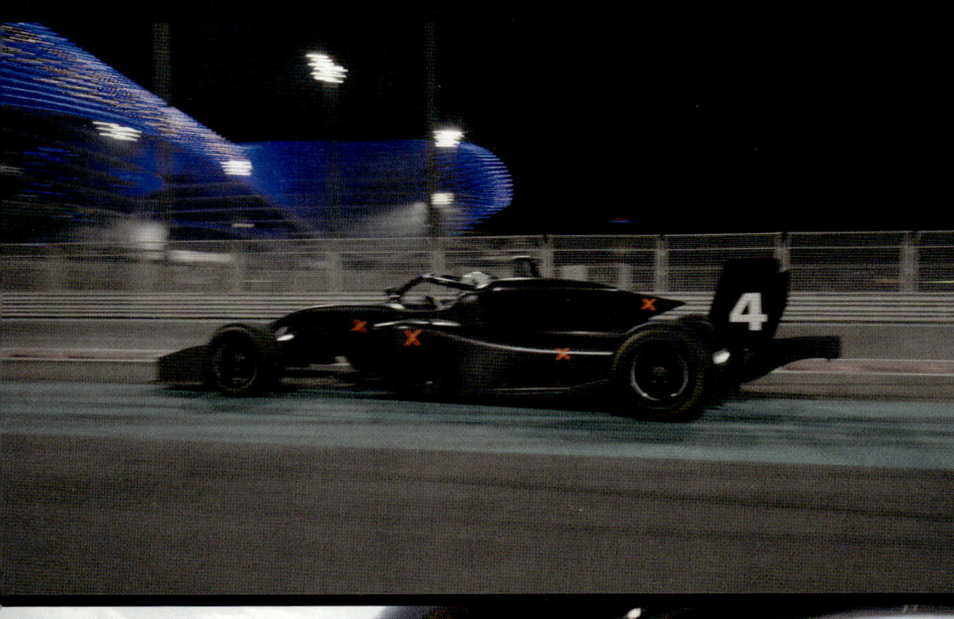

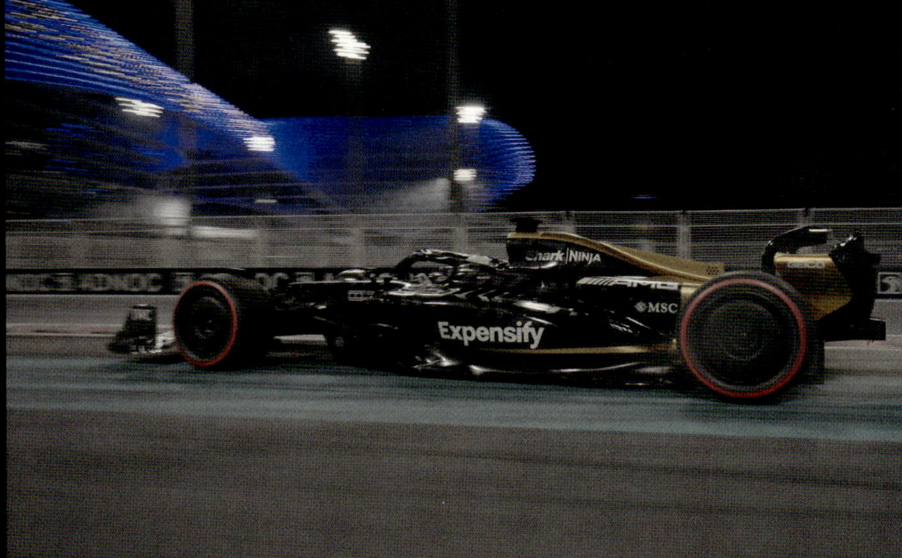

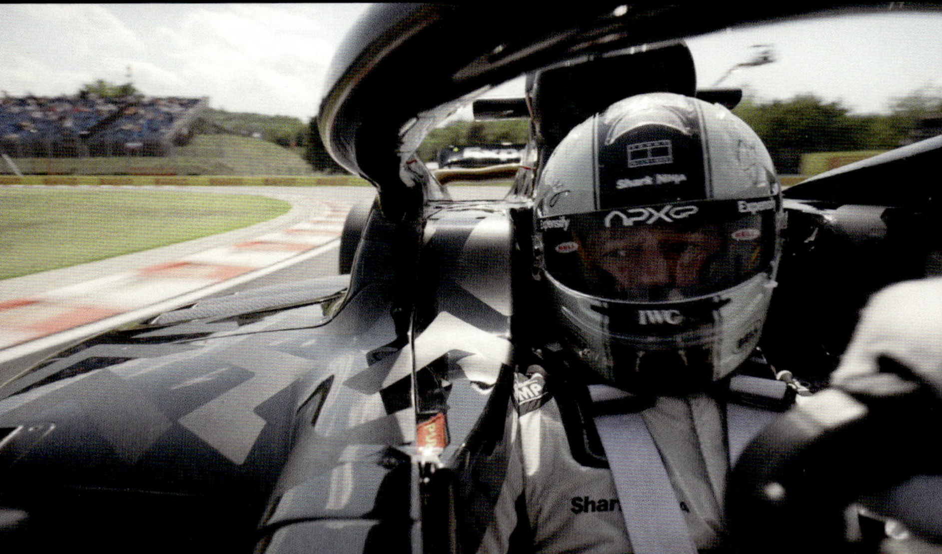

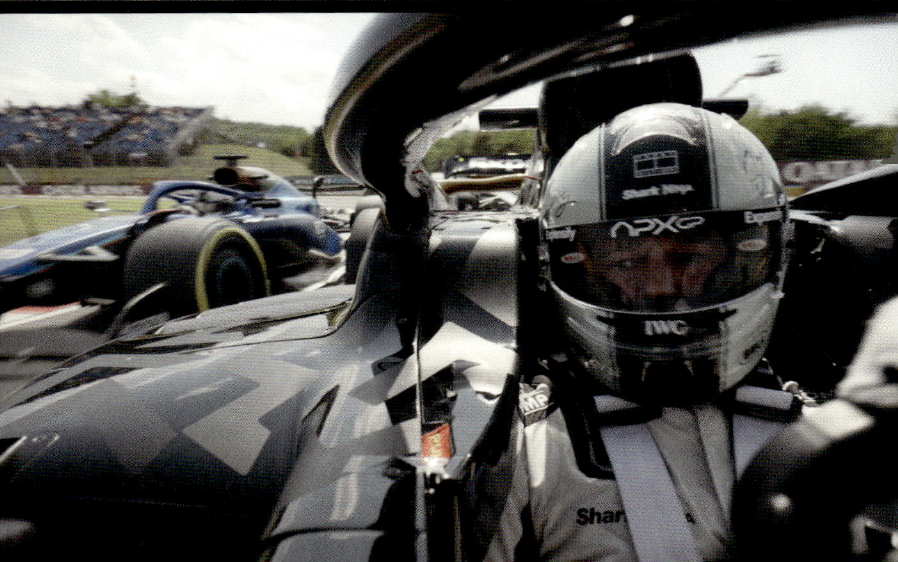

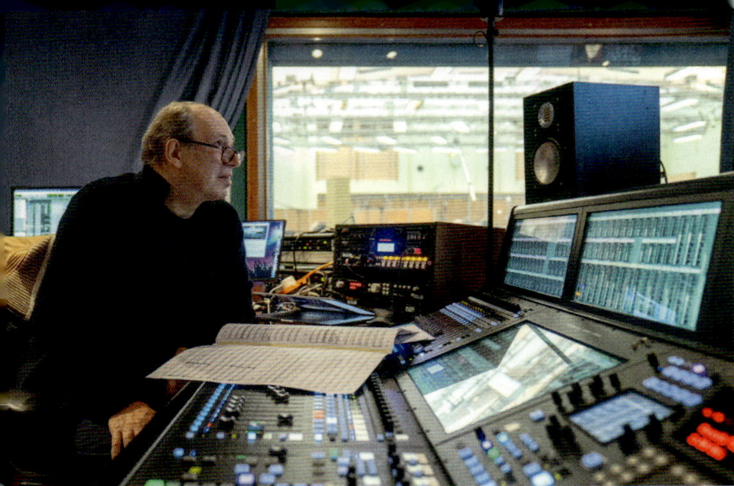

To compose the music for *F1*, director Joseph Kosinski and producer Jerry Bruckheimer turned to Hans Zimmer, the two-time Oscar-winning composer of *Gladiator*, *Inception*, *The Lion King,* and *Dune*. The composer and producer first worked together on 1990's NASCAR movie *Days of Thunder,* and their many collaborations since include four *Pirates of the Caribbean* films, *Black Hawk Down*, *Crimson Tide,* and Kosinski's *Top Gun: Maverick*. "We convinced Joe to use him on *Top Gun* because he had other people in mind," recalls Bruckheimer. "But Joe had such a good experience that for *F1* he said, 'Let's get Hans.'"

"Hans is a legend. And for a reason," says Kosinski. "He creates melodies. He creates themes. Which is what makes his music timeless. I wanted a score that had a central theme to it and Hans brought that. You hear it, starting with the opening titles. Then you hear it throughout, in so many different forms and iterations."

"I come from a car-mad family. I grew up with F1, and this is my third race car movie," reveals Zimmer, who also composed the music for Ron Howard's Formula One film *Rush.* For *F1,* he again partnered with fellow composer Steve Mazzaro, the two having worked together on *Dune*, *Wonder Woman 1984*, *Widows*, *X-Men: Dark Phoenix*, *Dunkirk*, *Interstellar,* and *Man of Steel,* among others.

Before they began, Zimmer spent time with Lewis Hamilton learning what it is like to drive a Formula One car. "He was talking about how much he had to work out because of the g-forces during cornering," remembers Zimmer. "I would sit there with my mouth open because I had never really thought it through, that going at those speeds, then suddenly taking a corner, what that does to your body physically. It's brutal. At the same time, it's dangerous, yet incredibly elegant. That really influenced how I wanted the orchestra to sound. It influenced how the tunes were written. The electronics were very much about the grace and beauty and power of those incredible cars."

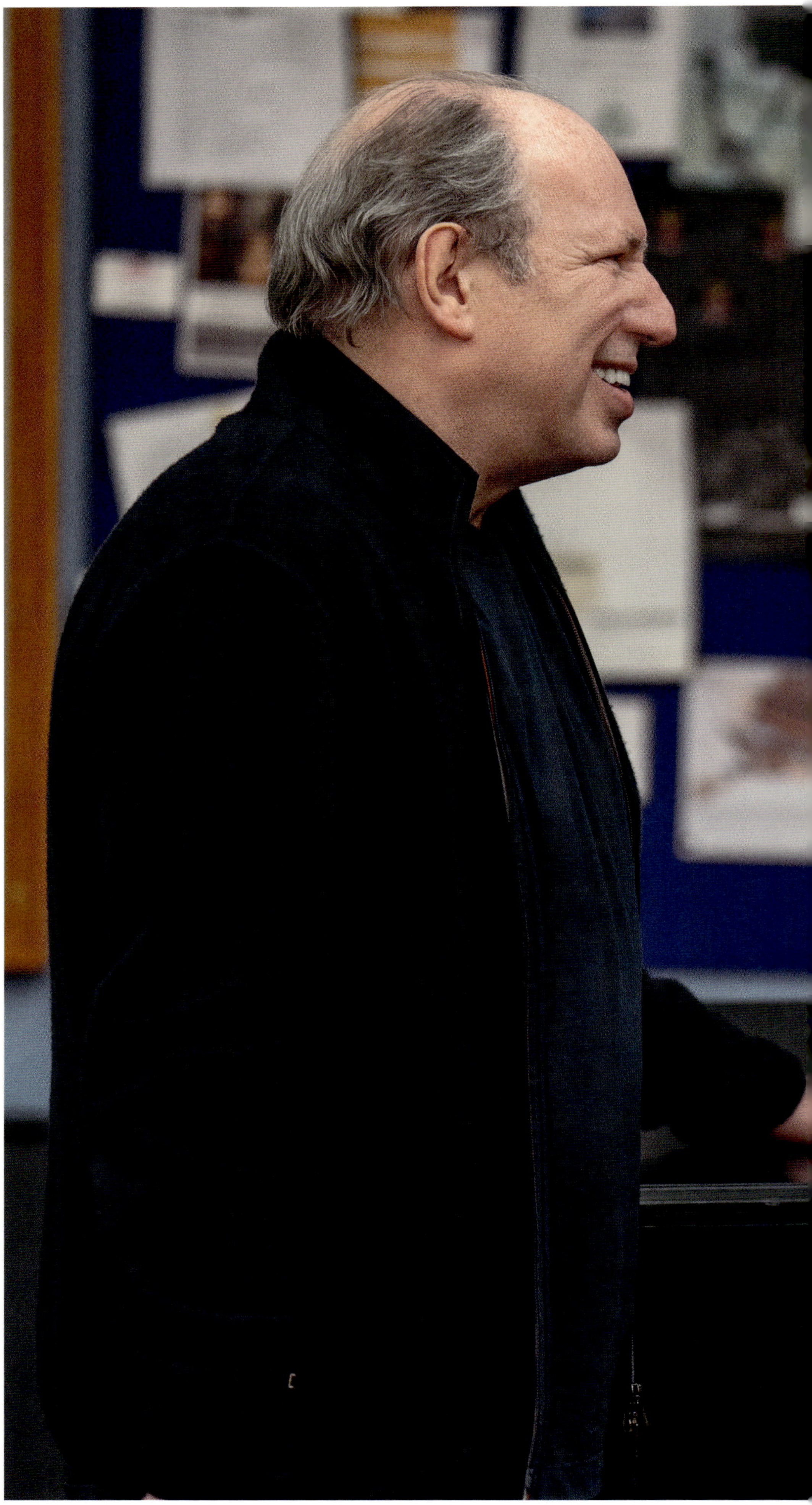

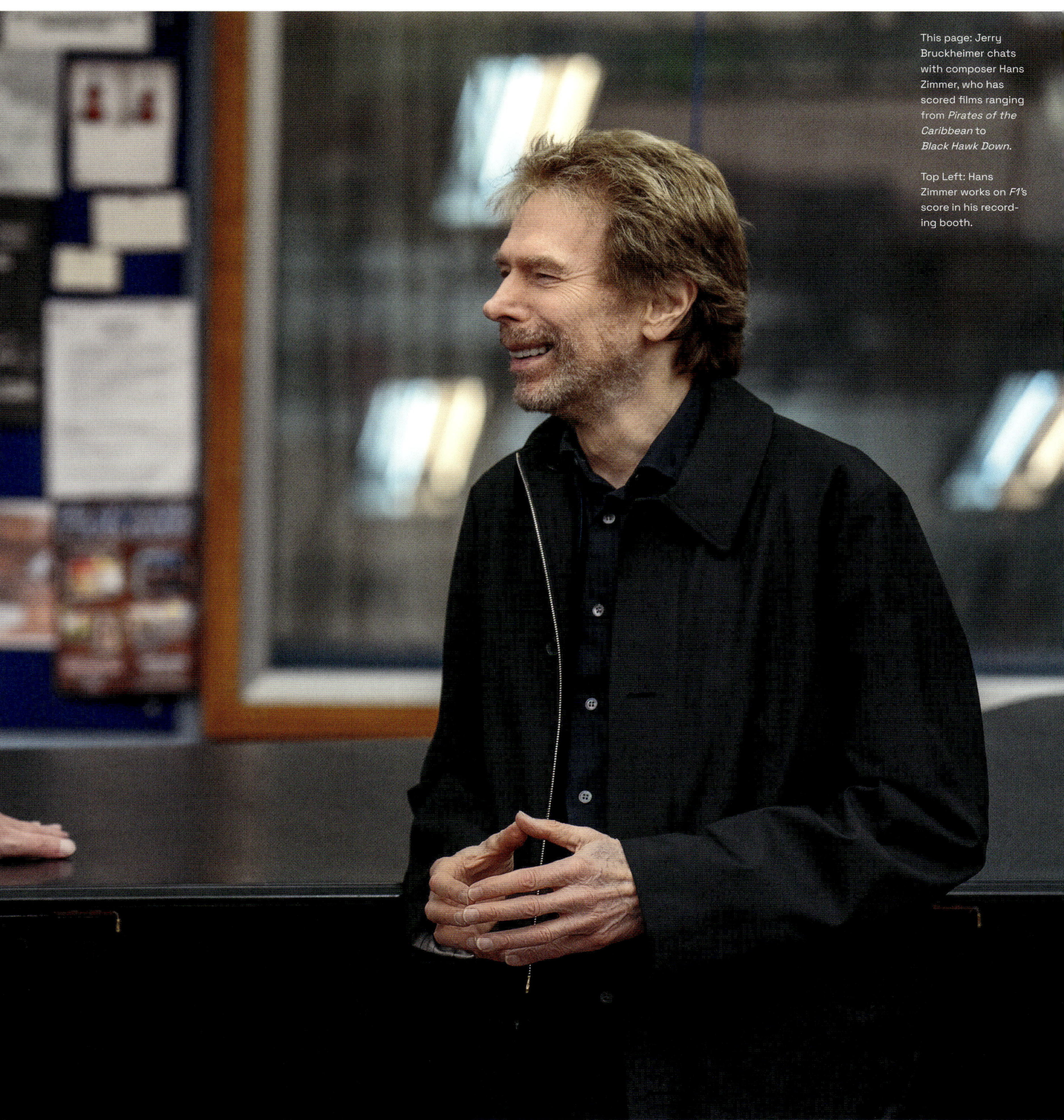

This page: Jerry Bruckheimer chats with composer Hans Zimmer, who has scored films ranging from *Pirates of the Caribbean* to *Black Hawk Down*.

Top Left: Hans Zimmer works on *F1*'s score in his recording booth.

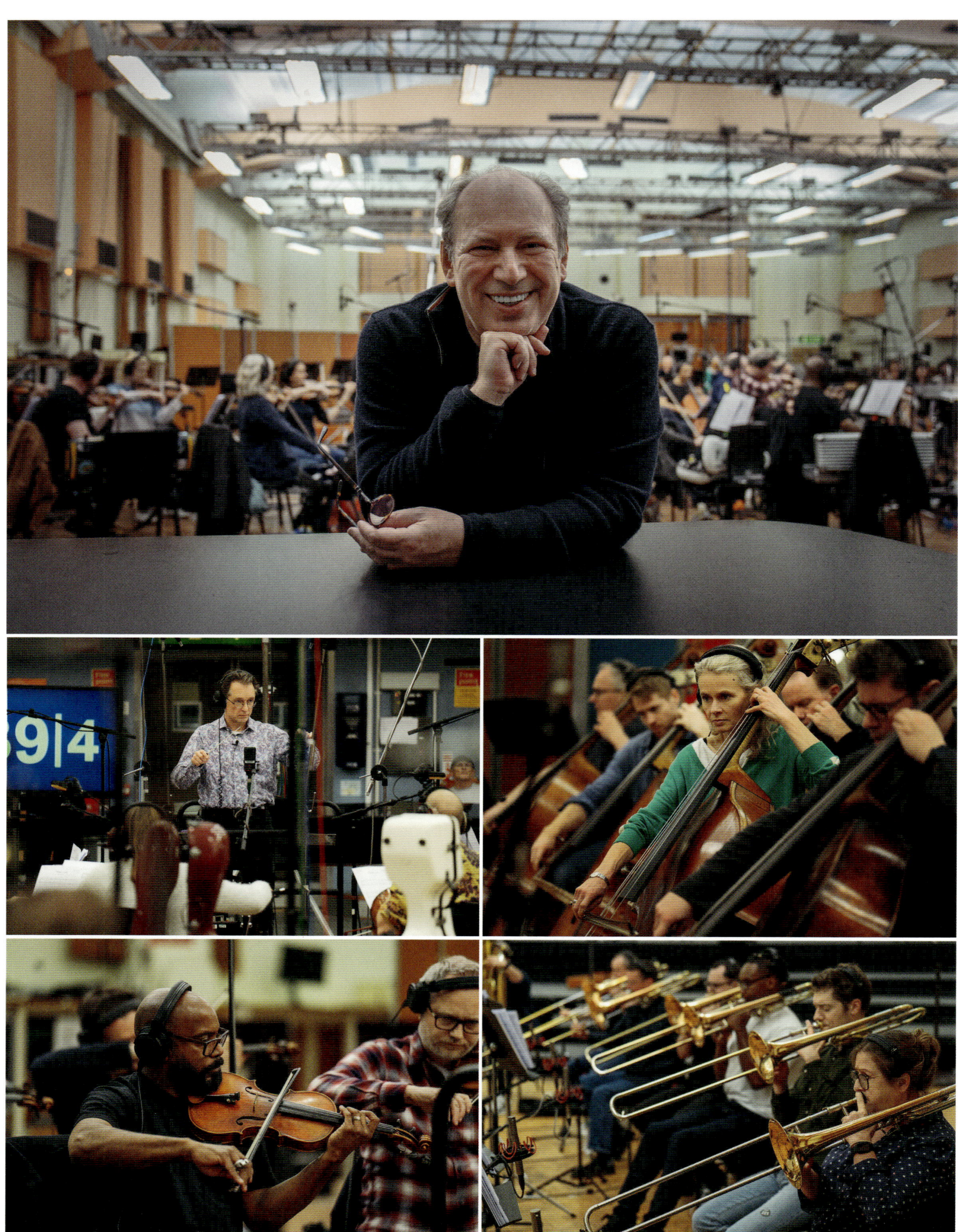
9|4

Hans Zimmer directed a live orchestra to record the music for the film's dramatic scenes, but relied on electronic synthesizers to provide the score for race sequences.

"The machines are beautiful. The drivers are handsome. Plus, the sounds of the cars, it's like music," notes Bruckheimer. "And Hans captured it with his score. There's so much going on for your ears that it's such an impossible task to hit the right tones, the right frequencies to cut through, and yet let the cars be as dynamic as they are. What Hans added to the phenomenal sound quality of the film made it romantic. It's operatic; it's also emotional, and it comes from the gut. You feel the rumble of the cars, and you feel it with Hans and Steve's music, with the horns and the drums and all the things they've added."

"My job is to do what the director can't even imagine. But the movie must become one expression; my colors must fit with the colors Joe uses in his cinematography," explains Zimmer. "I have seen movies ruined by music. Music is a dangerous animal because it influences the way you feel. So, if we are not in sync, it becomes less of a movie. And we work very hard at becoming in sync. I spent forever figuring out the tempo of the music against the picture, because if you went too fast, the picture looked slow. If you went too slow, it was out of sync. And there was a way of finding an overall tempo that seemed to enhance the speed of the film. One of the things, which is I think unusual, is we never slow down; even in dialogue sequences, there is still a pulse of something going on, because these characters are always speeding through life. The music must go on this journey as well. It develops, just like the story develops. It does all these different things."

Zimmer was keen to mix orchestral with electronic for *F1*. "I felt very strongly this should be a hybrid score," he says. "For me, the orchestra was always the human that sits inside the machine, and the electronics the machine itself. One of the great things about electronics is they make things slightly unpredictable. When you have humans playing, you can tell, from note to note, emotionally what's going to happen next. With sequencers and computers and synthesizers, you don't quite know. There's always the element of surprise built in that is very important in a movie like this—that the score surprises you, that you're never quite set on safe ground."

"Hans was excited about the idea of going back to where he started, which was more a synthesizer-based score," says Kosinski. "And because this is a story about the past colliding with the present, he liked the idea of bringing in some of that early synth sound, combining it with the orchestra to create something that would work with the loud and intense sounds of these cars. During the racing sequences, it's more electronic, because that's able to sonically punch through. During the dramatic scenes, it leans more into the orchestral side."

"Joe was very specific about which race was a music race and which race would be a sound design race," continues Zimmer. "The sound of the cars is so powerful, so there's a partnership [with sound design], which is going on all the time. One of the difficulties about this film is that the engines are a very hard sound. So, you need to make things more human. You need more warmth. But this is a film about race cars. And the engine is a character in the film."

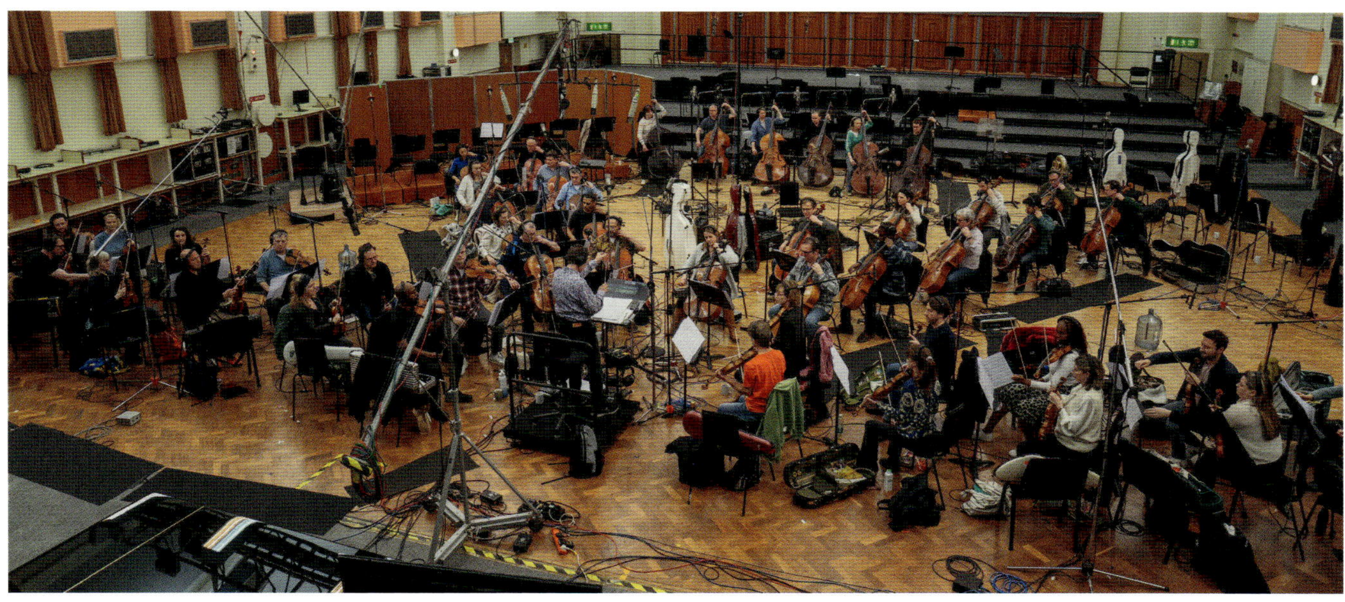

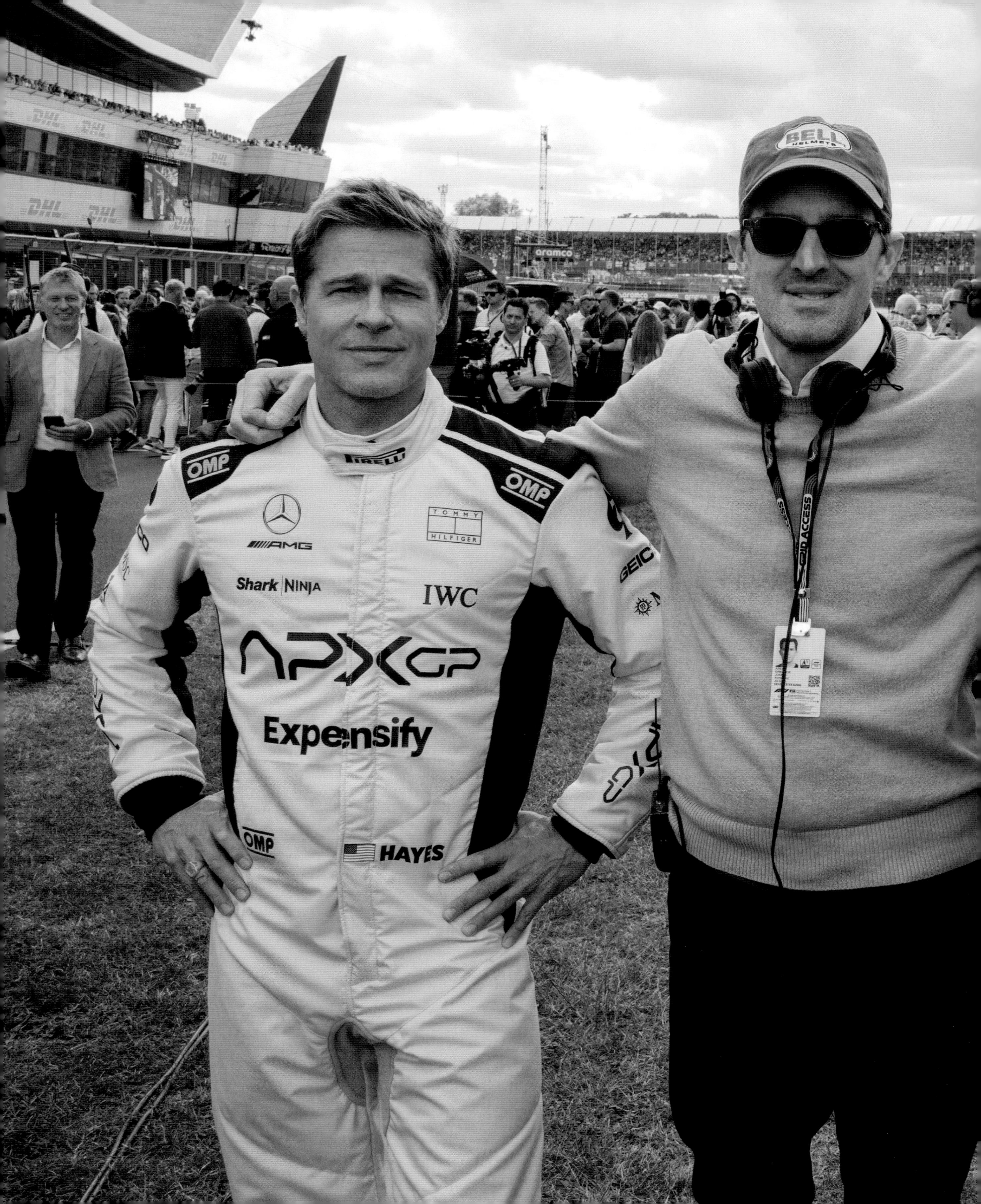
DHL
aramco
BELL HELMETS
OMP
PIRELLI
AMG
TOMMY HILFIGER
Shark NINJA
IWC
APXGP
Expensify
HAYES

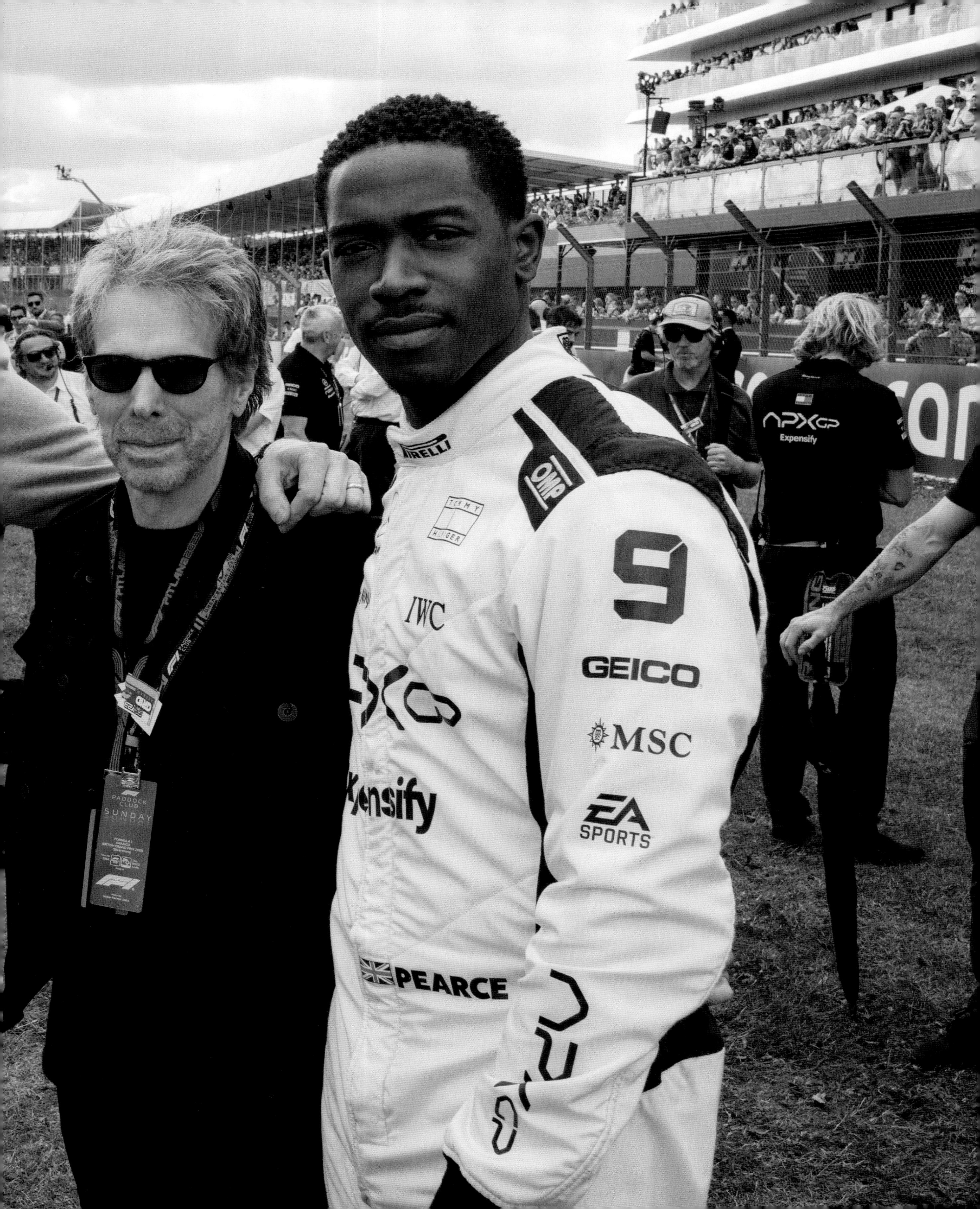
PIRELLI
OMP
9
IWC
GEICO
MSC
EA SPORTS
PEARCE
APXGP
Expensify
PADDOCK CLUB
SUNDAY

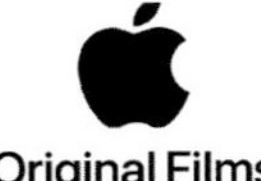

Set Photography: Scott Garfield
Cover and Primary Concept Art: Daniel Simon

Acknowledgments: Jerry Bruckheimer; Joseph Kosinski; Brad Pitt; Damson Idris; Kerry Condon; Javier Bardem; Lucy Bevan; Emily Brockmann; Ryan Tudhope; Hans Zimmer; Julian Day; Stephen Mirrione; Mark Tildesley; Ben Munro; Claudio Miranda; Daniel Lupi; Toby Hefferman; Toto Wolff; Stefano Domenicali; Tim Bampton; Lewis Hamilton; Dede Gardner; Jeremy Kleiner; Chad Oman; Ehren Kruger; Graham Kelly; Gary Powell; Luciano Bacheta; Craig Dolby; Emily Cheung; Al Nelson; Gwendolyn Yates Whittle; Gary A. Rizzo; Juan Peralta; David Leener; Lewis Hamilton; Daniel Simon; Andrew McCarthy; Véronique Melery; Gareth John; Keith Dawson; Steven Morris; Denise Kum

Tim Cook, Eddy Cue, Zack Van Amburg, Jamie Erlicht, and everyone at Apple who have been incredible collaborators.

Additional Imagery Courtesy of:
Charlie Cobb: 122, 123; Keith Dawson: 180; Joseph Kosinski: 88; Ryan Tudhope/Framestore: 289 (top row), 300, 301.

Alamy Stock Photo: Avpics: 98 (1970s); Eduardo Comesaña/Editorial Abril: 30 (1950s, photo of Juan Manuel Fangio); BFA: 11 (posters for *Le Mans* and *Days of Thunder*); BNA Photographic: 30 (1960s, photo of car); Chronicle: 98 (1906), 198 (photo of Luigi Fagioli); DPA Picture Alliance: 30 (1960s, photo of Jochen Rindt); John Gaffen: 99 (1980s); GP Library Limited: 30 (1950s, photo of car), 198 (photo of Luigi Fagioli driving); Independent Photo Agency: 153 (photo of Bernie Collins); Jonathan Little: 98 (1950s); National Motor Museum/Heritage Images: 30 (1906, photo of two seater car); Pbpgalleries: 98 (1960s); Photo 12: 30 (1906, photo of car and crowd); Mark Scheuern: 31 (1980s); Smith Archive: 30 (1950s, photos of Giuseppe Farina and Prince Bira at Silverstone).

Getty Images: Lars Baron: 185 (Lewis Hamilton vs. Max Verstappen, top); Bernard Cahier: 198 (photo of side view of Louis Chiron's car); Paul-Henri Cahier: 182 (Ayrton Senna vs. Alain Prost, bottom left) 183 (James Hunt vs. Niki Lauda, top), 183 (Michael Schumacher vs. Mika Häkkinen, top), 184 (Lewis Hamilton vs. Fernando Alonso, bottom); Michael Cooper/Allsport: 183 (Michael Schumacher vs. Mika Häkkinen, bottom); Jean-Loup Gautreau/AFP: 77 (photo of car crash); Paul Gilham/Getty Images Sports: 184 (Lewis Hamilton vs. Fernando Alonso, top); Grand Prix Photo/Hulton Archive: 183 (James Hunt vs. Niki Lauda, bottom); Alexander Hassenstein/Bongarts: 69 (photo of Fernando Alonso); Andrej Isakovic: 185 (Lewis Hamilton vs. Max Verstappen, bottom); Dan Istitene/Formula 1: 31 (photo of trophy); LMPC: 11 (poster of *Grand Prix*); Clive Mason: 185 (Lewis Hamilton vs. Nico Rosberg, top and bottom); Andreas Rentz/Bongarts: 99 (2000s), 198 (Fernando Alonso); Clive Rose: 184 (Michael Schumacher vs. Fernando Alonso, top and bottom); Pascal Rondeau/Allsport: 182 (Ayrton Senna vs. Alain Prost, top and bottom right); Rainer Schlegelmilch: 99 (2010s); Sergio del Grande/Mondadori Portfolio: 31 (1970s); Sutton Images/Stringer: 77 (photo of Martin Donnelly); SSPL: 198 (photo of Louis Chiron in his car); Michael Tee/LAT Images: 198 (Philippe Étancelin), 199 (Arthur Legat).

Wikipedia Commons: Bundesarchiv, Bild 183-82487-0011 / Kohls, Ulrich / CC-BY-SA 3.0: 199 (Kurt Kuhnke).

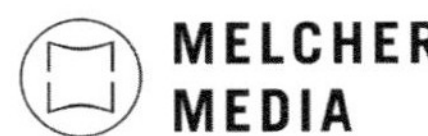

This book was produced and published by Melcher Media.
FOUNDER, CEO: Charles Melcher
VP, COO: Bonnie Eldon
EDITORIAL DIRECTOR: Lauren Nathan
PRODUCTION DIRECTOR: Susan Lynch
EXECUTIVE EDITOR: Christopher Steighner
SENIOR EDITOR: Megan Worman
ASSISTANT EDITOR: Kevin Li
EDITORIAL ASSISTANT: Sonia Menken
EDITORIAL INTERN: Grace Luckett

Melcher Media gratefully acknowledges the following for their contributions: Cheryl Della Pietra, Amélie Cherlin, Suzette Lam, Tanya Ross-Hughes.

Written by Mark Salisbury
F1 Features by Chris Medland

Art Direction and Interior Design by Paul Kepple at Headcase Design.
Headcasedesign.com

Additional Design by Chika Azuma

Printed in Germany
ISBN: 978-1595911506